IFRS in a Global World

Didier Bensadon • Nicolas Praquin
Editors

Essays in Honor of
Professor Jacques Richard

IFRS in a Global World

International and Critical Perspectives on Accounting

Foreword by Stephen A. Zeff

Springer

Editors
Didier Bensadon
University of Paris-Dauphine (DRM),
PSL Research University
Paris
France

Nicolas Praquin
University of Paris-Sud, Paris-Saclay
Sceaux
France

ISBN 978-3-319-28223-7 ISBN 978-3-319-28225-1 (eBook)
DOI 10.1007/978-3-319-28225-1

Library of Congress Control Number: 2016938703

Springer Cham Heidelberg New York Dordrecht London

Printed on acid-free paper

Springer International Publishing AG Switzerland is part of Springer Science+Business Media (www.springer.com)

Foreword

It has not always been self-evident that financial accounting has economic, political, and social consequences. In the days before the advent of national standard setters, and even during the early years of standard setting, financial accounting was widely viewed as an arcane activity of interest only to accountants, to company comptrollers and auditors, and to few others. In many Civil Code countries, financial accounting focused on the 'legal accounts' only and was tailored to the demands of company law and the fiscal statutes and court opinions. Stewardship reigned supreme, and shareholders would receive the accounts required by law. Companies listed on stock exchanges would provide the same information to the investor community, often in an abbreviated format, unless the exchange demanded more expansive disclosure.

As the years passed, investing in the securities markets gradually became more widespread among households, not just an activity undertaken by financial speculators and professional investors who might have access to 'inside' information about company news that had not yet been revealed to the public. Some governments and stock exchanges began to see a need to take steps to make the securities market more of a 'fair game' by overseeing, if not actually trying to regulate, financial reporting to the broader market. By the 1950s, standard-setting bodies, as we now call them, sprouted in several countries, notably the United States, the United Kingdom, Canada, and Japan. The development and issue of accounting principles or standards in the early years of these bodies was a new and uncertain game, and their pronouncements, varying in content from country to country, tended to be more generic than narrowly prescriptive or detailed. Furthermore, in most of the countries, even a failure to follow a generic standard for a material item would not necessarily cause the auditor to give a qualified opinion or a regulator to reprove the company. Financial reporting in those innocent days was a *laissez-faire* activity. The financial press, if there was one in a country, usually ignored financial reporting altogether, believing that no one cared or would understand what was being written anyway. It was easy to believe in those times that financial accounting was wholly devoid of economic consequences.

But then in the 1960s in the United States and Canada, and in the 1970s in the United Kingdom, and not long afterwards in a few other countries, the standard setters, often under government or public pressure, or both, began tightening their standards. Auditors—if only because of a spate of lawsuits against, or public investigations of, some of their brethren—began raising the level of their performance, and regulators or stock exchanges began to take a greater interest in listed companies complying with the standards.[1] At the time of an increasing incidence of cross-border corporate mergers and trading of shares, and the emergence of multinational enterprises, in a much more sharply competitive securities market, companies and their powerful trade associations began standing up to the standard setters and resisting the impositions of restraints on the flexibility which the companies had been enjoying in preparing financial statements. Earnings management began to be more widely practiced, and workers' councils and unions began to realise that lower or more volatile earnings could affect the prospect of wage rises and employment decisions. When an increasing number of top company executives began to be compensated handsomely by bonuses based on accounting profit and by share-based payments, and as 'head-hunters' began to create an active labour market for executives, companies' boards of directors or supervisory boards became even more interested in how accounting standards affecting their company's performance reporting could inhibit their ability to retain, and recruit, corporate talent.

Beginning in the 1970s with the establishment of the International Accounting Standards Committee (IASC) in 1973 and certainly in the early 2000s with the arrival of its successor, the International Accounting Standards Board (IASB) in 2001, financial reporting issues began to capture the attention of company executives, regulatory bodies, and governments, especially in countries that had not previously had national standard-setting bodies. This interest accelerated in the 1980s when the International Organization of Securities Commissions (IOSCO), then based in Montréal and later in Madrid, charged the IASC to tighten its generic standards in order to earn IOSCO's endorsement and therefore the prospect that its regulator members around the world might accord them standing in their respective national environments. IOSCO's endorsement came in May 2000, but it seems to have had little impact on regulator behaviour.

No country's regulator or government required listed companies to comply with the IASC's standards, but the coming of the IASB in 2001 ushered in a new era in worldwide financial reporting. With its approval of the IAS Regulation in 2002, the European Union (EU) required that all listed companies adopt the IASB's standards in their consolidated statements by 2005. It was then that, at the international level, the preoccupations over the multiple impacts of financial reporting—economic, political, and social—ascended to become regional and even worldwide issues. An impact became especially acute when the IASB issued a standard in 2003 which, in

[1] Indeed, the US Securities and Exchange Commission had begun proactively supervising listed company compliance with accepted accounting principles soon after its establishment in 1934.

effect, obliged certain commercial banks (as they saw it) to alter their hedging practices, and a number of major French banks promptly and effectively brought this matter to the country's President for redress. Later, in 2008, the IASB came under intense pressure to issue a standard, without any due process, to enable banks to reclassify their portfolio holdings of debt securities from their fair value in a volatile market to amortised historical cost. The alternative to issuing this standard, it was alleged, was to precipitate a serious financial crisis in the banking sector. Major banks had appealed to the European Commission to insist that the IASB issue such a standard, which it did. The IASB promptly put out the standard but in an air of resignation.

In some countries, especially the United States, and in the experience of the IASB, representatives of preparers have sometimes been severely critical of draft or final standards that, they have alleged, would place companies in a bad light or would work to the detriment of the health of the regional or national economy. If the standard setter seemed not to be sympathetic to their complaints, they often would appeal to legislators or government ministers for a means of stalemating the standard setter.

The World Bank has played a largely unnoticed, but a very influential, role in persuading the accounting profession and governments in developing countries and in countries with emerging economies to move towards the adoption and implementation of the standards issued by the IASB, known as International Financial Reporting Standards (IFRS). With the vital collaboration of the Inter-American Development Bank, the World Bank succeeded in bringing most of the countries in Latin America on board with IFRS. The Banks hoped that, by the use of IFRS instead of their typically defective national accounting codes, companies in those countries would thus have a higher quality of accounting information when making important business decisions.

All of this activity at the international level, together with the increasing battles between preparers and standard setters, put financial accounting 'on the map' for coverage in the daily financial press and every few months in *The Economist*. It became fascinating to academics—not only in accounting but also in political science—that a private-sector standard setter, such as the IASB, could somehow be endowed with public sector authority to set in motion the making of laws or regulations to compel the compliance of listed companies in countries around the world.

All of this has occurred at different times, in different ways, in different countries. Countries have their own accounting, auditing and regulatory cultures and traditions, as well as their own securities market reality, which have collectively influenced the pace and intensity with which the impacts of the standards issued by the IASB have affected their society.

This book is about the economic, political, social, and even environmental consequences of setting accounting standards, with emphasis on those that are alleged to be precipitated by the adoption and implementation of IFRS. The authors also offer their reasoned critiques of the effectiveness of IFRS in promoting genuine global comparability of financial reporting. The editors of this collection have invited authors from 17 countries, so that a great variety of accounting, auditing and regulatory cultures, and educational perspectives is amply on display in their essays.

Among the interesting questions that have been asked, or might well be asked, about the consequences of accounting standards are the following:

- To what extent did IFRS and in particular the use of fair value exacerbate the financial crisis beginning in 2007?
- To what degree has the adoption and implementation of IFRS in the EU, as well outside the EU—in place of the previous multiplicity of national accounting schemes—facilitated a movement of accounting professionals within and into the Union?
- To what extent do accounting standards that require companies explicitly to report on health-care costs or environmental costs provide a stimulus within the companies for greater attention to a rational analysis of the health-care benefits they give to employees and a greater sensitivity to the steps they should take to improve, and not to despoil, the environment?
- To what degree has the use of IFRS facilitated the movement of worldwide capital flows and reduced adopting companies' cost of capital?
- What has been the impact so far of the use of IFRS, and IFRS for SMEs, on the quality of the accounting information and therefore on the resulting more rational business decisions being made by companies in developing countries and emerging economies?
- To what degree does the omission of most internally developed intangibles from the balance sheet affect shareholders' and other investors' perceptions when making judgements about the adequacy of the share price offered in the light of takeover proposals?

A Worrying Issue Relating to the Inordinate Influence of the United States and EU on the IASB

An issue that challenges the IASB has been its inordinate dependence on support from the United States and Europe in the setting of its standards. This role played by the United States has come not only because it has the longest and most respected record of national standard setting but also because its capital market is the world's largest. The role played by Europe, specifically the EU, has come because, with the IAS Regulation in 2002, it provided the IASB with its first major clientele, namely, some 6700 listed companies that were required to adopt IFRS in their consolidated statements—and the Commission has periodically reminded the IASB that it is owed a *quid pro quo* for having instituted this requirement. This unprecedented action by the EU caught the attention of governments and national standard setters elsewhere in the world, starting with Australia, which led to a stream of additional countries adopting, or converging with, IFRS. European influence on the IASB has also been powerful if only because of the proximity of its member states' financial capitals, and especially Brussels, to the IASB in London. In order to compete with this potent influence of the United States and Europe, national standard setters from countries in Asia-Oceania, Latin America, and Africa have organised themselves into regional blocs so as to present their own united fronts to the IASB.[2]

While the main influence from the United States, in line with the mission of the US Securities and Exchange Commission, has been a focus on investor protection, the 12-year convergence programme between the IASB and the US Financial Accounting Standards Board (FASB) has to some degree brought to the IASB's table some effects of the very aggressive lobbying in the United States by special interest groups. A recent example of this lobbying occurred on the leasing project, where 60 members of the US House of Representatives signed a letter in May 2012, which was sent to both the FASB and the IASB, protesting against the alleged negative effects on the US economy of requiring lessees to capitalise long-term non-cancelable leases as assets and corresponding liabilities.[3] The IASB's close link with Europe has also managed to convey to the Board the strongly held views of special interests, notably on accounting for financial instruments.

But this European influence has lately taken a more ominous turn, towards raising the prospect of explicitly factoring the alleged 'economic consequences' of proposed standards into the IASB's deliberations. In a report commissioned by the EU, dated October 2013, written by Philippe Maystadt, 'Should IFRS Standards be More "European"?', the author charged the European Financial Reporting Advisory Group (EFRAG), whose role has been to recommend the technical acceptability of IASB's standards to the European Commission in connection with the latter's endorsement decisions, with explicitly taking into consideration whether the IFRS 'are conducive to the European public good'.[4] This provision about the 'public good' first appeared in the IAS Regulation of 2002, but it had been seldom mentioned in discussions about the IFRS until the appearance of the Maystadt report. In carrying out Maystadt's recommendations, EFRAG has replaced its Supervisory Board with a 17-member Board, composed of representatives from a wide array of European interest groups (including only one user representative but several from the preparer side), which now is to advise the European Commission on the acceptability of IFRS. In the past, EFRAG's Technical Expert Group, composed solely of accounting specialists, conveyed its view

[2] These have been, respectively, the Asian-Oceanian Standard-Setters Group (AOSSG), the Group of Latin American Accounting Standard Setters (GLASS), and the Pan-African Federation of Accountants (PAFA).

[3] See the letter sent to the chairmen of the FASB and the IASB, based on a study that seemed to be less than objective which was conducted by a consulting firm for the US Chamber of Commerce and other bodies that opposed the joint FASB/IASB leases proposal: http://sherman.house.gov/media-center/press-releases/congressman-sherman-and-congressman-campbell-lead-effort-to-stop-new; http://www.centerforcapitalmarkets.com/wp-content/uploads/2010/04/2012-02-08-IASB-FASB-CA-Report-FINAL-v-3-_2_.pdf

[4] For the report, see http://ec.europa.eu/finance/accounting/governance/reform/index_en.htm

of the technical soundness of newly issued IFRS to the Commission. But, following Maystadt, the EFRAG Board's advice will not be confined to technical issues. It is to be concerned also with whether the new standards are 'conducive to the public good'. Already the EFRAG staff have proposed that three of the several criteria which the Board 'may want to consider' in giving this advice are (1) the standard's likely impact on 'preparer behaviour', (2) that the standard does 'not hinder economic development' in the EU, and (3) that it does 'not endanger [the] financial stability' of European institutions.[5] These latter two criteria are as actually stated in the Maystadt report. These three criteria are avowedly responsive to pleadings by special interests, and they could therefore serve to distract the IASB from carrying out the charge stated for it in the IFRS Foundation's Constitution, which is 'to help investors, other participants in the world's capital markets and other users of financial information make economic decisions' (Section 2(a)). These three cited criteria highlighted by the EFRAG staff would have the IASB take the alleged 'economic consequences' for preparers, for economic development, and for financial stability explicitly into account when deciding on its standards, which could introduce bias via a 'political' element into its deliberations and judgement. Moreover, the European public good may be at variance—indeed, significantly at variance—with the public good in, say, Australia, the public good in Canada, or the public good in South Korea—countries with different political and economic systems and different social realities. What would this mean to attempts by the IASB to set 'neutral' standards that comport with the economic reality in the rest of the world?

To be sure, the EFRAG staff, in its report, sought to temper the severity of these contentious new criteria. It said:

11. The recommendation *is not* that IFRS should be assessed as conducive to financial stability or economic development, i.e. there is no request that IFRS be other than neutral.
12. We can derive from the above that, in the absence of evidence to the contrary, IFRS should be considered as conducive to the European public good when they help achieve a high degree of transparency and comparability as is set in the objective of the Regulation. Helping lower the cost of capital is, of itself, supportive of economic development. [emphasis in original]

Yet Maystadt's recommendations expressly call for EFRAG to be attentive to such 'public good' issues as not endangering economic development and financial stability.

It remains to be seen whether, and to what degree, the endorsement recommendations coming from the new EFRAG Board lead to the European Commission more actively taking on 'economic consequences' issues when making its endorsement decisions. The Commission today speaks on behalf of some 8000 listed

[5] For the staff report, see http://www.efrag.org/Front/m835-279/EFRAG-Board-Meeting-21-November-2014.aspx

companies in 28 countries, and its influence on the IASB cannot be lightly dismissed.

Without question, the economic, political, and social consequences of IFRS are a major contemporary issue, and I commend the essays in this volume honoring Jacques Richard to a wide audience.

Rice University, Houston, TX Stephen A. Zeff

Contents

Jacques Richard's Career

Education

1981 Diplôme d'Expertise Comptable
1980 Docteur d'Etat en Sciences de Gestion. Université Paris Sorbonne
1977 Docteur de troisième cycle en Sciences Economiques. Paris Sorbonne
1973 DES De Sciences Economiques (Paris-Sorbonne)
1969 Diplôme d'Etudes Comptables Supérieures (DECS)
1968 DES de Droit Privé (Paris-Sorbonne)
1966 Diplôme de la Chambre de Commerce Franco-Allemande. Paris
1966 Diplôme de l' ESSEC (Paris)
1964 Licencié es lettres
1963 Préparation HEC/ESSEC au Lycée du Parc (Lyon)
1962 Baccalauréat Mention A Prime

Dissertations

1981 *Mémoire d'Expertise Comptable* (*Chartered Accountant Master thesis*): « L'évolution de la comptabilité aux Pays-Bas » (The evolution of accounting in The Netherlands).

1980 *Thèse de Doctorat d'Etat (PHD dissertation)*: « Comptabilité et systèmes économiques » (Accounting and economic systems). Université Paris1 Sorbonne. Director of Research: Marie Lavigne.

1977 *Thèse de troisième cycle en économie d'entreprise et de branches (Preliminary Dissertation in Industrial Economics)*: « Etude comparative des méthodes d'analyse de la gestion des en*tr*eprises industrielles dans quatre pays appartenant à des systèmes économiques et politiques différents: Etats-Unis, France, RDA, URSS » (Comparative study of the management of industrial firms in countries belonging to different economic and political systems: United States, France, USSR, East Germany (DDR). Director of Research: Marie Lavigne.

Distinctions

2013 *Best Award* delivered by the Academy of Accounting Historians.
2012 *Award FNEGE* for *Comptabilité et développement durable*, Economica
1990 *Lauréat de l'Ordre des Experts Comptables*

Main Functions

2014 Emeritus Professor at Paris-Dauphine University
1994–2014 Professor at Paris-Dauphine University
1989–1994 Professor at IUT de Sceaux
1985–1989 Associate Professor Paris-Dauphine University
1972–1985 Assistant Professor at Paris-Dauphine University
1966–1972 Assistant Professor at ESSEC Business School

Main Fields of Research

Accounting and etymology
Accounting and sustainable development
Accounting history
Accounting regulation
Comparison of worldwide accounting systems
Environmental management
Financial management and financial analysis
Governance of firms

Non-Educational Experiences

2014 (since) Member of the French Accounting Regulation Board (*Autorité des Normes Comptables*)

2013 (since) Expert at Cabinet Compta-Durable (Sustainable development chartered accountant)

2013 Mission to the Conseil Economique et Social of Marocco

2000 Expert at the "International Chamber of Commerce" (Affair Procter and Gamble Holding GmbH versus Ssangyong Cement Industrial Co)

1996–1999 Consultant at Tacis Program (Eurotap Viet)

1990–2010 Member of the French Accounting Regulation Board (*Conseil National de la Comptabilite*)

1983 (since) Chartered accountant at Cabinet Secafi Alpha

1978–1983 Chartered accountant at Cabinet Syndex

1969 Management Accountant at IBM France

1967–1968 Chartered accountant trainee at Cabinet Grevoul and Thibault

Administrative and Collective Responsibilities

(Reviews and Associations)

2014 Member of the Editorial Board of the Ukrainian Review the *Independent Auditor* (Kiev)
2014 Member of the Editorial Board of the Russian Review the *Accounting, Account, Analysis and Audit* (Moscow)
1997–2001 Member of the Editorial Board of the French Review *Comptabilité—Contrôle—Audit (Paris)*
1994–2000 Member of the Editorial Advisory Board of the *European Accounting Review*
1980–1985 Founder member and treasurer of AFC (French Association of Accounting Teachers and Researchers)

University

2012–2013 Member of the board of MSO (Economic, Law and Management (Master) department of Paris-Dauphine University)
2008–2013 Member of the board of directors of Paris-Dauphine University
2006–2013 Founder and director (with S. Trinh) of the Master's degree 'Sustainable development' at Paris-Dauphine University
2006–2010 Member of the board of LS0 (Economic, Law and Management (Bachelor) department of Paris-Dauphine University)
1999–2003 President of the commission for the recruitment of Academics at Paris-Dauphine University
1985–1990 Director of the Master's degree in Accounting (MSTCF) Paris-Dauphine University

International Relations

De 1990 à 2012 Cours ou conférences données régulièrement aux Universités de Saint Petersbourg (Russia) et de Münster (Germany) et de façon ponctuelle aux universités de Vienne (Austria), de Moscou (Russia), et de Kyoto (Japan).
A partir de2008 cours réguliers à l'Université de Shanghai (China).
2006–2014 Co-responsable (avec le Professeur H. Fujii) de la convention de coopération Université de Paris Dauphine-Université de Kyoto (Japan).
1993–2013 Co-responsable (avec le professeur A. Sorokin) de la convention de coopération Université de Paris Dauphine-Université de Moscou (MGU) (Russia). Coopération avec le Doyen VP Kolessov.

1992–1993 Co-créateur du Diplôme commun Université Dauphine-Université Goethe de Francfort (Germany). Collaboration avec le Professeur D. Ordelheide.

1989 Professeur invité (un semestre d'hiver) à l'Université du Québec à Montréal (Canada).

1985–2001 Co-responsable (avec le professeur W. Bechtel) de la convention de coopération Université Dauphine-Université Wilhelm de Münster (Germany). Coopération avec le Professeur J Baetge.

1970–1972 Directeur Pédagogique (avec JM Peretti) de L'Institut de Technologie Financière et Comptable (ITFC) d'Alger (Algiers) au titre de la Coopération Technique. Nombreuses formations pour le compte du Ministère des Finances.

Doctoral Guidances

2015 *Alexandre Rambaud*. La valeur d'existence: application en gestion environnementale.

2014 *Térèsa Bicalho*. Les limites de l'analyse du cycle de vie: l'étude du cas des biocarburants à base d'huile de palme au Brésil.

2014 *Miriam Boukari*. Etude de la pertinence des normes IFRS au regard de l'analyse crédits bancaires des entreprises.

2014 *Claudia Orellana*. L'évaluation comptable des réserves et ressources minières des entreprises de l'industrie extractive.

2013 *Yulia Altukhova*. Comptabilité agricole et développement durable: étude comparative de la Russie et de la France.

2013 *Muriel Benkel*. Comparaison du droit comptable allemand et du droit comptable français: une approche systémique (Ph'D co-director Professor M. Hommel).

2013 *Mohamed Chelli*. Trois études sur la mesure de la performance des entreprises en matière de développement durable: pouvoir disciplinaire et légitimation (Ph'D co-director Professor Yves Gendron).

2010 *Emmanuelle Plot-Vicart*. L'information diffusée par l'exploitant sur le risque nucléaire: quelle réponse aux attentes des parties prenantes?

2010 *Clémence Garcia*. Une étude comparée des normes et pratiques de comptabilisation de l'immatériel en France et au Japon.

2008 *Nguyen Phong*. La réforme comptable vietnamienne: causes, nature et conséquences.

2008 *Karine Fabre*. L'influence de l'évolution des modes de financement des entreprises sur le modèle comptable français (1890–1939): les cas de Schneider et de l'Air Liquide.

2007 *Nassiba Bouraoui*. D'une comptabilité d'économie planifiée à une comptabilité d'économie de marché: stratégie de la réforme comptable en Algérie.

2003 *Nicolas Praquin*. Comptabilité et protection des créanciers. Une étude de la fonction technico-sociale de la comptabilité (1807–1942).

2002 *Mériem Bensalah*. Prévision du risque de défaillance: apprentissage par un algorithme génétique.

2001 *Digna Azua*. Vers un modèle comptable latino-américain? Analyse comparative de l'organisation et du contenu des normes comptables adoptées en Argentine, au Brésil et au Chili.

Current Doctoral Guidance

Catherine Bonne. Syndicalisme et gestion environnementale: les positions de la CGT et de la CFDT (1970–2002)

Thiémoko Diakité. Comptabilité en Afrique et IFRS.

Xiao Rui Wang. La comptabilité environnementale agricole en Chine.

Articles in Peer Reviews

English Written Reviews

2015 The 'Triple depreciation Line" instead of the "Triple Bottom Line'. Towards a genuine integrated reporting (with A Rambaud). *Critical Perspectives on Accounting*, 33, 92–116.

2015 The dangerous dynamics of capitalism: from Static to IFRS accounting. *Critical Perspectives on Accounting*, 30, 9–34.

2014 French Accounting History: New Contributions (comment on a book edited by Y Levant and O de la Villarmois). *The Accounting Review*, 89(6), 234–37.

2013 France's New Economic regulations: insights from institutional Legitimacy Theory (with M. Chelli and S. Durocher). *Accounting, Auditing & Accountability Journal*, 27(2), 283–316.

2012 The victory of the Prussian railway 'dynamic' accounting over the public finance and patrimonial accounting models (1838–1884): an early illustration of the appearance of the second stage of capitalist financial accounting and a testimony against the agency and the market for excuses theories. *Accounting Historians Journal*, 39(1), 89–124.

2012 The limits of LCA in Environmental Accounting-a perspective based on the Renewable Energy Directive (with T. Bicalho and C. Buissou). *Sustainability Accounting Management and Policy Journal*, 3(2), 234.

2011 Economic transition and accounting system reform in Viet Nam (in collaboration with Nguyen Cong Phuong). *European Accounting Review*, 20(4), 693–725.

2008 Towards an understanding of the phases of goodwill accounting (with Y. Ding and H. Stolowy). *Accounting Organizations and Society*, 33(7–8), 718–55.

2005 The concept of fair value in French and German accounting regulations from 1673 to 1914 and its consequences for the interpretation of the stages of development of capitalist accounting. *Critical Perspectives on Accounting* 16, 825–50.

2004 The secret past of fair value: lessons from history applied to the French case. *Accounting in Europe,* 1(Sept), 95–107.

1995 The evolution of the Rumanian and Russian charts of accounts after the collapse of the communist system. *The European Accounting Review*, 4(2), 305–322.

1995 Research Forum: European charts of accounts. *The European Accounting Review*, 4(1), 81–124.

1984 Financial and cost accounting: are they compatible? *Issues in Accountability*, 10, 1–26.

1981 Accounting and Economic Systems. *Soviet Accounting Bulletin*, 10(2), 26–41.

Other Non French Written Reviews

2014 Abstract of article on 'The victory of the Prussian railway "dynamic" accounting over the public finance and patrimonial accounting models' (with the help of Y. Altukhova) In *Vestnik Tcheliabinskovo gossudartsvenovo Yniversiteta* N°18(347) p. 94–102.

2010 « Informatsionoe obespetchenie analiza ystoichivobo razvitia » (The informational basis of the analysis of sustainable development) (with V. Shirobokov et Y. Altukhova). In *Ychet, Analiz i Aydit*, Ekonomitheskii Fakultet Universitet Lomonossov Moskva (University Lomonossov of Moscow) Tome 1, p. 16–20.

2009 Учетно-информационное обеспечение устойчивого развития рационального природопользования (Accounting for sustainable development and rational management of natural resources), (with Yulia Altukhova and Vladimir Chirobokov), *Региональная экономика: теория и практика,* № 8 (101), March 2009, p. 24–34.

2009 Типы бухгалтерского учета окружающей среды (The types of environmental accounting), *Международный бухгалтерский учет*, with V. Chirobokov and Y. Altukhova № 4 (124), April 2009, p. 15–25.

2007 Проблемы применения МСФО по учету сельскохозяйственной деятельности в России и Франции (The problems of appliance of international standards to accounting for Russian and French agriculture), (with Vladimir Chirobokov and Yulia Altukhova), In *Международный бухгалтерский учет (International accounting)*, № 9, September 2007, p. 44–48; № 10, October 2007, p. 39–44.

1998 Actual French accounting: theoretical and practical problems. (in collaboration with N. Dediouhina). *Izvestia.*, Business School of Sankt Petersburg. p. 122–127.

1981 La comptabilité des coûts en URSS et en RDA. *L'Expert comptable Suisse* N°1 p. 12.

1980 La comptabilité dans les pays de l'Est. *Jornal de contabilidade* N°41 p. 31–37.

French Written Reviews

2015 Vers une vraie comptabilité environnementale (en collaboration avec H Gbego). *Revue Française de Comptabilité* N°483 Janvier p. 27–30.

2013 Souplesse des comptables et des juristes, subjectivité du concept de profit: les leçonsde l'histoire de la comptabilité de Lous XIV aux IFRS. *Revue Gestion et finances Publiques*, N°6 (Juin), p. 74–91.

2013 La nature n'a pas de prix..mais sa maintenance a un coût. *Revue Projet*, N°332 Février, p. 81–87.

2009 En finir avec les normes IFRS. *Revue Constructif*, numéro spécial IFRS, Nov p. 78–80.

2007 Les incidences comptables du passage des groupes côtés aux IFRS. *CCA*, numéro spécial IFRS (en collaboration avec M. Boukari), 13(3), 155–169.

2004 Fair value le troisième stade du capitalisme comptable? Le cas de la France. *Analyse et Documents économiques (Cahiers du Centre Confédéral d'Etudes Economiques et Sociales de la CGT* (Fev et Juin, p. 75–81 et 43–47).

2003 De la modernité des normes internationales et de la juste valeur en comptabilité. Clind'œil. *Entreprise et histoire*, N°33, p. 127.

1999 Vingt ans de normalisation comptable en Europe: grandeur ou décadence ? *CCA*, Mai, 5(3), 223–232.

1999 Coût historique, valeur de marché..le pluralisme des bilans existe de fait. *Les Cahiers de l'Audit*, N°7, p. 13.

1994 Faut–il abroger le Plan Comptable général ? *Revue Française de Comptabilité*, N° 254, p. 72–75.

1990 Modifier nos méthodes d'analyse financière. *Banque* N°505, p. 483–489.

1990 Les leçons tirées de deux comptabilités du début du XIXème siècles: « Charlton Mills et Fonderies et forges de fer de la Seine ». *Revue de Droit Comptable*, N°90-2, p. 74–85.

1990 L'audit des performances. *Cahiers français de la documentation française*. N°248, p. 40–41.

1988 Principes et spécificités de l'analyse de la rentabilité des groupes d'après les comptes consolidés. *Revue Française de Comptabilité* (Juin) p. 81–91.

1985 Sur la pertinence des principales méthodes de traduction des comptes des entreprises étrangères. *Revue Française de Comptabilité*, N° 163, p. 26–36.

1985 Panorama de l'évolution des théories des organisations et des critères de gestion aux Etats-Unis. *La Pensée*, N°344, p. 65–77.

1985 Le tableau des flux du cycle. Critique et dépassement des modèles actuels. *Banque*, N°456, p. 1123–1127.

1984 Comptabilité pour l'autogestion: l'exemple de la comptabilité Yougoslave. *Cahiers français de la Documentation Française*. (Numéro spécial sur la comptabilité N°210).

1983 Essai sur l'histoire des pratiques comptables internationales. *Revue du Financier*. (Janvier Février), p. 77–89.

1982 La quatrième directive, un texte inutile? Le cas hollandais. *Revue Française de Comptabilité* (Juin), p. 12–15.

1982 L'impact de la quatrième directive sur la législation de 1970 aux Pays—Bas. *Revue Française de Comptabilité*. (Novembre), p. 26–29

1980 Un renouveau de la chaîne des ratios ? *Revue Française de Comptabilité*. (Décembre), p. 18–24.

1980 La comptabilité des coûts en URSS et en RDA. *Revue Française de Comptabilité*. (Janvier, février, mars).

1988 Pour un plan comptable moniste français. *Revue de Droit Comptable*, n°88-1, p. 43–86.

Books in Foreign Langages

2016 (In Chinese): Environmental accounting (with Prof Li Li Uibe Pekin and XR Wang, (In Press).

1999 (In Russian): Accounting theory and accounting practice. Publisher: Finansi i Statistika. Moscow.

1997 (In Russian): Audit and analysis of economic activities. Publisher: Unity. Moscow.

Books in French

2015 *Comptabilité Financière*: *Cas corrigés* (with D. Bensadon). 3e ed. Dunod

2014 *La gestion environnementale*. (with E. Plot). La Découverte (coll Repères).

2014 *Comptabilite Financière*: *normes IFRS versus normes françaises* (with D. Bensadon and C. Collette). 10e ed. Dunod

2012 *Comptabilité et développement durable*. Economica. Paris.

2000 *Analyse financière et gestion des groupes* (with Becom associés and Groupe Alpha). Economica.

1996 *Comptabilité et pratiques comptables*. Editions Dalloz.

1993 *Analyse financière et audit des performances*. Editions La Villeguérin.

1989 *Manuel de consolidation* (with J.C. Lavoyer) Edition La Villeguerin.

1989 *L'audit des performances de l'entreprise*. Edition La Villeguérin.

1988 *Comptabilité et analyse financière des groupes* (with P. Simons et J.M. Bailly) Economica.

1982 *Le nouveau plan comptable* (with Ch. Collette) Editions Dunod. (This book published for 33 years is in its 10th edition in 2014) (cf infra).

1972 *Comptabilité des sociétés et éléments d'analyse financière* (with J.P. Crétal, Y. Enrègle, S. Koskas). Dunod.

Contributions to Collective Books in English

2016 The Triple Depreciation Line (TDL) accounting model and its application to the Human Capital (with A. Rambaud). In *Finance and economy for society: Integrating sustainability*. Edited by C Karyotis and S Alijani. Emerald Press (in press).

2015 'The corporate world and sustainability: eco-efficiency and the Doxic Shareholder Value' (with N. Chabrak). In *Sustainable Markets for Sustainable Business: a global perspective for business and financial markets*, p. 95–114. Edited by G Aras. Gower.

2015 'Sustainable Finance' (with A. Rambaud). In *Routledge Handbook on Social and Sustainable Finance*. Edited by O. Lehner. Routledge.

2013 'The three Main Schools of the French Financial Accounting Doctrine: A historical survey'. In *Accounting and Business Economics* (edited by Y. Biondi and S. Zambon) Publisher: Routledge.

2001 'Group Accounts France'. In *Transnational Accounting*, Second Edition, Edited by D. Ordelheide and KPMG. Part Publisher: Palgrave.

1998 'Eastern Countries'. In International Accounting. Edited by PJ Walton, A Haller and B Raffournier. Publisher: Thompson Business Press.

1996 « De l'histoire du plan comptable français et de sa réforme éventuelle ». In *Accounting in France/La comptabilité en France* p. 305–320. Edited by Y. Lemarchand and R.H. Parker. Garland Publishing.

1996 'The evolution of Accounting Chart models in Europe from 1900 to 1945, some historical elements'. In The Library of International Accounting. Country Studies in International Accounting Europe. Ed P Walton. Publisher: Elger Reference Collection.

1996 'Life of Eugen Schmalenbach' in *International Encyclopaedia of Management* (first edition). Publisher: Routledge.

1995 « Group Accounts France » in *Transnational Accounting* (first edition). Ed D. Ordelheide. Publisher: Macmillan Press.

Contributions to Collective Books in Other Foreign Languages

2012 'No price for nature but a cost for its maintenance (Care accounting instead of the Worldbank's genuine saving accounting)'. *In Contabilitate control, Si Guvernanta, Liber Amicorum in onoarea Profesorului Nicolae Feleaga*. Ed CN Albu, N Albu and Feleaga L. Publisher: Editura Economica. Bucuresti.

2000 'Ost Europa'. In *Unternehmenspublizität im internationalen Wettbewerb*. Editor Axel Haller.Verlag Poeshel Verlag. (Germany).

1998 'Jahresabschlussinformationen für globale Märkte und die aktuelle Krise des französischen Rechnungswesens' In *Festschrift für Professor Jörg Baetge*. IDW Verlag Düsseldorf. (Germany).

1994 Artikel: 'Frankreich'. In *Lexikon des Rechnungswesens*; Editor Busse von Colbe.Verlag Oldenburg (Germany).

Contributions to Collective Books in French

2016 "Refonder l'entreprise, la société anonyme et l'intérêt social par la comptabilité environnementale" in *Le cadre conceptuel de l'IASB : pilier de la représentation de l'entreprise* ? Centre Français de Droit Comparé (dir), Editions Mazars (in press).

2015 « A propos de l'entrepreneur et de sa comptabilité: les visions des économistes français vers 1860–1870 ». In *Mélanges en l'honneur du Professeur R. Teller*. PUP, p. 187–206.

2014 « La théorie économique de Fisher et la comptabilité Américaine (1906–1966) ». In *Comptabilité, Finance et Politique Mélanges en l'honneur du Professeur Christian Hoarau*. (Coordonné par A. Burlaud). Ordre des Experts Comptables, p. 65–81.

2014 « La naissance des principes comptables cibles des IFRS ». In *Normalisation Comptable actualités et enjeux* (eds W. Nahum). L'Académie des Sciences et Techniques Comptables Financières, p. 48–52.

2012 « La Global Reporting Initiative entre responsabilité sociale de l'entreprise et développement durable » (with F. Depoers). In *Comptabilité, Société, Politique. Mélanges du Professeur B. Colasse*. Economica, p. 173–187.

2011 « Le bilan d'une nation selon la banque Mondiale, IFRS et comptabilité environnementale » (with H. Stolowy). In *Comptabilité Contrôle et Société*. Mélanges en l'honneur du professeur A. Burlaud. Foucher, p. 171–181

2009 « Comptabilités environnementales » in B. Colasse (dir.) *Encyclopédie de comptabilité, contrôle de gestion et audit*. Economica, p. 489–501.

2008 « Le financier a raison, le comptable a tort ». In *Petit bréviaire des idées reçues en management*, A. Pezet & S. Sponem (dir.). La Découverte, p. 187–194.

2007 Rhétoriques comptables et financières, in Challe, *Langue française spécialisée en droit*. Economica, p. 41–49.

2005 'Les trois stades du capitalisme comptable français'. In Capron (ed). *Les normes comptables internationales instruments du capitalisme financier*. La Découverte, p. 99–119.

2005 'Simon, Schmalenbach et Schmidt:les trois "S" de la pensée comptable allemande'. in B. Colasse, *Les Grands Auteurs en Comptabilité*, p. 73–90.

2001 Histoire de la valeur dans les réglementations comptables allemande et française de 1673 à 1914. In *Juste Valeur* (J.F. Casta & B. Colasse dir.) pp. 17–45. Mazars/Economica.

2000 Partie « Gestion ». In *Dictionnaire de l'Economie* (sous la direction de P. Bezbakh). Edition Larousse Le Monde.

2000 Article « Plan Comptable ». In *Encyclopédie de la comptabilité* (sous la direction de B. Colasse) Editeur: Economica.

1997 Articles « Etats de synthèse du plan comptable général de 1982 » et « Analyse financière des groupes ». In *Encyclopédie de Gestion* (sous la direction de B. Colasse). Editeur Economica.

1997 Article « Les conceptions de l'actif ». In *Comptabilité Nationale*, développements récents (sous la directions de E. Archambault et N. Boëda). Editeur: Economica.

1997 « Comptabilité dans les pays d'Europe de l'est ». In *Comptabilité internationale* (coordinateurs B. Raffournier, A. Haller et P. Walton). Paris Editeur: Vuibert.

1992 « De l'histoire du Plan Comptable Français et de sa réforme éventuelle ». In *Annales du management* édité pat R Le Duff et J Allouche. Economica, p. 69–82.

1992 « Comptabilité aux Pays Bas (Netherlands) » In *La comptabilité des sociétés dans la CEE* (édité par L. Klee). La Villeguérin Editeur.

1985 Une réplique aux thèses de W.H. Beaver sur la comptabilité d'inflation. In *Recherches en Finance du CEREG* (sous la direction de J. Hamon et B. Jacquillat) Economica.

1982 *La fonction financière et le Plan Comptable général de 1982* (collaboration). Ordre des Experts-Comptables.

Research Reports

2002 La crise et la réforme du système de surveillance et d'audit des comptes allemands: la loi KONTRAG de 1998. Cahier de recherche du CEREG N°2002-03, Université Paris Dauphine.

2002 La crise et la réforme du système d'information allemand:la Loi KAEG de 1998 sur la facilitation de l'ouverture des capitaux. Cahier de Recherche du CEREG N° 2002 02, Université Paris Dauphine.

2002 Comment la comptabilité traditionnelle allemande protège les créanciers et les managers: une étude historique et sociologique. Cahier de recherche N° 2002-01, Université Paris Dauphine.

1993 Les origines du Plan Comptable français de 1947: les influences de la doctrine comptable allemande. Cahier de Recherche du CEREG N°9302, Université Paris Dauphine.

1992 Dix thèses sur la comptabilisation de l'écart d'acquisition du goodwill. Cahier de recherche du CEREG n° 9208, Université Paris Dauphine.

1986 Une réplique aux thèses de Beaver sur la comptabilité d'inflation. Cahier de recherche du CEREG N°4207, Université Paris Dauphine.

1985 Une opposition contestable, celle des rentabilités financière et comptable. Cahier de recherche du CEREG N° 8507. Université Paris Dauphine.

1983 Limperg et la comptabilité d'inflation: naissance et évolution d'une théorie. Cahiers d'étude et de recherche en économie et gestion N°3, p. 79–126.

Conferences in Foreign Universities and Enterprises (with Names of Inviting Professors)

Austria: University of *Vienna* (Professor F. Wirl)
Bolivia: *Santa Cruz's Association of Chartered Accountants* (Prof J. Hermosilla)
Canada: *UQAM* Montreal (Prof R. Labelle and Prof D. Cormier)
Chile: *Valparaiso* and *Conception* (Prof J. Hermosilla and Prof D. Azua)
China: *Shanghai and Shihezi* (Prof Yu)
Germany: *Franfurt am Main* (Prof Ordelheide); *Münster* (Prof J. Baetge et W. Bechtel)
Japan: Université de *Kyoto* (Prof H. Fujii); Université de *Kyushu-Fukuoka* (Prof Ch. Ozu and Prof J. Oshita)
Poland: *University of Lodz* (Prof A. Jaruga and Prof A. Szychta)
Romania: *University of Bucuresti* (Prof N. Feleaga)
Russia: *University MGU of Moscou* (Prof A. Sorokine et Prof A Sheremet); *Uni Archangelsk* (Mission IFG:Institut Français de Gestion); *Uni Kazan* (Prof V.B. Ivachkevitch); *Uni Krasnodar* (Prof. M. Kuter); *Uni Maykop* (Prof M. Kuter et Prof L Marakova); *Enterprise ALMAZ Mirni* (Sibérie) (Mission IFG); *Uni Perm* (Club Delovie Liudi); *Uni Tcheliabinsk* (Prof D. Pletnev); *Uni Voronej* (Prof V. Chirobokov and V. Altukhov); *Uni Saint Petersbourg Finec* (Prof I. Eliseeva, Prof N. Kamordjanova, Prof A. Larionov, Prof N. Deduhina); *Uni Stavropol* (Prof O. Tomarevskaia); *Uni Nalchik* (Prof M. Kuter and Prof R. Vanoevna)
Spain: University *Computense de Madrid* (Prof M. Campos)
Viet-Nam: *Uni Hanoi* (Ministry of Finances); *Uni Danang* (Prof Nguyen Cong Phuong)

Recent Public Manifestations

10/06/2015 Sustainability, finance and accounting: from the today's Fisherian-(Falsified) Hicksian perspective to a traditional accounting approach (with A. Rambaud). Working Paper presented to the ACRN Oxford.

20/5/2015 European Parliament Strasbourg. Participation to the round table « Accounting for the European private sector: reconsidering accounting objectives from economy and finance » avec Y. Biondi, A. Canzani and T. Suzuki. (Colloqium 'Accounting Regulation and Financial Stability').

12/2/2015 Intervention au Conseil Economique, Social et Environnemental du Maroc (Rabat). sur le thème: « L'immatériel, les IFRS, la Banque Mondiale et la Comptabilité en Coût Historique » (avec Prof J.C. Dupuy).

10/2/2015 UNESCO. Intervention en plénière aux « Assises du Vivant » dans la table ronde consacrée à « Entreprendre autrement: articuler performance et résilience » Table ronde avec K. Raskin, C. Allot, M. Dudaillon, C. Fromageot et S. Benard.

30/1/2015 Télévision chaîne BFM Business. Interview (avec H. Bgego).

14/6/2012 Académie de la comptabilité. Interview filmée au siège de l'Ordre des Experts Comptable sur le thème du développement de la comptabilité Environnementale. Académie de la Comptabilité (Journée organisée par W. Nahum ancien Président de l'Ordre des Experts-comptables).

14/5/2012 LVMH. Présentation du livre comptabilité et développement durable devant le groupe comptabilité de l'association Orée.

13/2/2012Université Internationale de Lausanne (UNIL). Conférence donnée à l'occasion de la parution de mon livre Comptabilité et développement durable, à l'invitation de D. Bourg Professeur à l'Unil.

Mai 2011, Chaire Finance et Développement Durable de l'Université Paris Dauphine. Conférence: « Comptabilité, Economie, Finance et Développement Durable ».

11/2/2011 Sokolov reading International conference in Saint Petersbourg in memory of Prof Iaroslav Sokolov. Lecture of 'Meanings and roots of the word accounting: a comparative study of 65 five languages' (In Session 2 directed by J. Mckinney).

17/10/2010 20 ans de la fondation Nicolas Hulot. Table ronde avec F. Quinn Directeur du Développement Durable de L'Oréal, F. Jany-Catrice Maître de Conférences à l'Université de Lille1 et J.M. Jancovici, membre du comité de vieille écologique de la Fondation Nicolas Hulot.

Articles in Large Readership Newspapers

2011 « Des normes comptables au profit des actionnaires ». *L'Expansion* N°759 Janvier, p. 104–107.

2010 « Taxes contre quotas: le débat environnemental est tronqué » in *Le Monde* du 22/3/2010.

2010 « Comment la comptabilité modèle le capitalisme » in *Le Débat* Gallimard N°161 Septembre Octobre. p. 53–64.

2008 « Pour une révolution comptable environnementale ». *Le Monde de l'économie*, 5/2, p. 6.

2005 « Une comptabilité sur mesure pour les actionnaires ». *Le Monde diplomatique* (Nov), p. 26–27.

Biographies

Editors

Didier Bensadon is Associate Professor of Accounting since 2008 at Paris-Dauphine University, Paris, France. Didier received his doctorate in accounting in 2007 from the University of Nantes, France. His published research appears in books and monographs as well as in articles in academic journals in the fields of accounting with an accounting history perspective. He has recently edited, in cooperation with Nicolas Praquin and Béatrice Touchelay, a French dictionary of accounting history (Septentrion, 2015). Didier Bensadon is the author of two books with Jacques Richard: *Comptabilité financière: normes IFRS versus normes françaises*, Dunod, 10th edition, and *Comptabilité financière, Cas corrigés*, Dunod, 3rd edition.

Nicolas Praquin is Professor of Accounting at the University of Paris-Saclay (Université Paris-Sud, Institut Universitaire Technologique de Sceaux) and member of the RITM laboratory of the University of Paris-Sud. He also holds the French Certified Public Accounting diploma. He has recently edited, in cooperation with Didier Bensadon and Béatrice Touchelay, a French dictionary of accounting history. His researches deal with the way in which accounting structures organisations and society as a whole. Accounting has to be understood in its broader sense—that of accountability—as encompassing accounting techniques, management tools that rely on figures, and organisational governance and accounting institutions (the IASB, etc.). These researches borrow from any and all disciplines that focus on the complexity of socio-economic relationships between and within organisations. It draws much from history in particular, but also from anthropology, political sciences, and sociology.

Authors

David Alexander is emeritus professor of international accounting, University of Birmingham, England. He is co-author of several successful textbooks in the area of IFRS reporting, and he has published numerous articles relating to accounting theory, financial reporting, and the practice and politics of accounting regulation, all with particular emphasis on the European and international dimension.

Jaan Alver is Professor of Accounting at Tallinn University of Technology. Professor Alver is a member of the European Accounting Association. His major areas of research include international accounting, financial statement analysis, cost management, accounting history, and accounting education. His academic record includes numerous research articles and academic conference presentations in over 20 countries.

Lehte Alver is professor of accounting at Tallinn University of Technology. She received her PhD degree from the University of Vilnius (Lithuania). She is a member of the European Accounting Association. Her research areas are international accounting and financial reporting, accounting history, and accounting education. She has presented her research at conferences in over 20 countries.

Digna Azúa holds a PhD in management science from Université Paris IX Dauphine. She is Professor at the School of Commerce of Pontificia Universidad Católica de Valparaiso. Professor Azúa is expert on IFRS and she is member of the Accounting Standards Committee of the Institute of Accountants of Chile.

Jörg Baetge Born 1937. Studied business administration at the Universities of Frankfurt/M., Münster and Philadelphia. PhD (Dr. rer. pol.) awarded in 1968 and habilitation in 1972. Full professor for business administration at the Universities of Frankfurt/M. (1972), Vienna (1977) and Münster (1980–2002). Since 2002, Emeritus and head of the Research Team Baetge. Honorary professor of the University of Vienna. Honorary doctorate (Dr. h.c.) awarded by the European Business School, Oestrich-Winkel. More than 500 publications in the fields of auditing, accounting, financial statement analysis, and rating.

Charles Richard Baker is Professor of Accounting at the Willumstad School of Business, Adelphi University, New York. His primary research interests are in the regulation of the public accounting profession, in particular comparative systems of regulation, ethical issues, independence, and legal liability. Professor Baker received his doctorate in accounting from the University of California, Los Angeles (UCLA), and he is a Certified Public Accountant (CPA) in New York State. He has published articles in leading academic journals such as *The Accounting Review*, *Abacus*, *Journal of Accounting and Public Policy*, *European Accounting Review*, *Accounting History*, *Journal of Business Ethics*, *Human Relations*, *Accounting, Auditing and Accountability Journal*, *Critical Perspectives on Accounting*, *International Journal of Accounting*, and *Comptabilité-Contrôle-Audit*.

Yuri Biondi is tenured research fellow of the CNRS (National Agency for Scientific Research), currently acting as research director of the Financial Regulation Research Lab (Labex ReFi) in Paris. He is founding editor of the Journal 'Accounting, Economics and Law: A Convivium' and convener of the SASE research network devoted to 'Accounting Economics and Law'. He was chairman of the Financial Accounting Standards Committee (FASC) of the American Accounting Association (AAA) from August 2011 to August 2013. His publications include Y. Biondi et al., *The Firm as and Entity: Implications for Economics*, Accounting and Law (Routledge, 2007).

Véronique Blum is an Assistant Professor in Grenoble-Alpes University. Over the last 20 years, she has taught Accounting and Corporate Finance to law students, chartered accountants candidates, and MBAs. Her researches, within the Centre d'Etudes et de Recherches Appliquées à la Gestion (CERAG-CNRS UMR 5820), focus on evaluation, complex assets—such as mineral an mining assets or patents, and efficiency issues.

Paul Brown is a lecturer in Accounting at UTS Business School since 2005, specialising in governance, production economics, and accounting for sustainability. Paul's work has been published in top international journals such as *International Journal of Production Economics, International Journal of Production Research*, and *Journal of Contemporary Accounting and Economics.*

Arnoldo Canziani MA degree in Business Economics at Bocconi, assistant professor (1973–1977), and Lecturer (1977–1990) there. At the same time associate professor, Venice University (1978–1987). Promoted full professor (1986), he teaches since then at Brescia University, where he was—among others—Dean of the Faculty of Law (2011–2013). Author of some 170 publications, he was also the Italian representative within the Accounting Advisory Board 1986–1990.

Jean-François Casta is full professor at the University of Paris-Dauphine, France. He began his career in international audit firms and qualified as Chartered Accountant and Registered Statutory Auditor while specialising in assistance programmes to the creation of stock markets in emerging countries. His research focuses on financial accounting and reporting issues encompassing fair value measurement, stock-based compensation scheme, asset valuation, economic impact of non-financial information disclosures, and financial reporting quality. His contributions have been published in *Fuzzy Economic review, Economic Modelling, Management under Uncertainty (Kluwer)*, and *Journal of the Academy of Marketing Sciences*. He recently co-authored a book on financial reporting and valuation issues under IFRS.

Nihel Chabrak has been publishing in international journals. She is the guest editor of Critical Perspectives on Accounting Journal special issues on 'The French Connection' (2005) and 'The Global Financial Crisis' with Yves Gendron (2015). She is serving in Critical Perspectives on Accounting and Accounting Forum editorial boards. She is the co-founder and organiser of the International CSAF Conference in Tunisia (2009) and UAE (2013).

Eve Chiapello is Research Director at EHESS (Ecole des Hautes Etudes en Sciences Sociales, Paris) where she holds a chair about the 'sociology of the transformation of capitalism'. She was previously Professor at the HEC School of Management, Paris. Her present work is about the sociology of management instruments and the financialisation process.

Denis Cormier is an accounting professor and Corporate Reporting Chair at ESG UQAM, Canada. He holds a doctoral degree in applied economics from Université de Mons (Belgium). His research focuses on the following areas: International Accounting, corporate disclosure strategies, corporate governance, business ethics, and social responsibility management and disclosure. His research works have been published through various scientific and professional journals. He is the author of an auditing book, an international accounting book, and one co-authored book on accounting theory.

Edgard Cornacchione is Full Professor (Department of Accounting and Actuarial Sciences, University of Sao Paulo, Brazil). A Brazilian chartered accountant, he holds a PhD in Accounting (USP/BRAZIL) and a PhD in Education (UIUC/USA). Member of the IAAER Council, his research targets capacity building and accounting education, through organisational and talent development, mainly with advanced technologies.

Fernando Dal-Ri Murcia is an Associate Professor in the Department of Accounting and Actuarial Sciences at the University of São Paulo, Brazil. He is an IAAER/Deloitte Scholar in the Emerging Economies Programme. His research interests fall mainly in the field of Financial Reporting and International Accounting.

Salma Damak-Ayadi is an Associate Professor at IHEC Carthage (University of Carthage) in Tunisia. She teaches financial accounting theory and accounting standards. She completed her PhD at the CREFIGE, Paris Dauphine University in France. Her research areas include social and environmental accounting, international accounting standards, and audit. Her research papers have been published in several international journals. She is a researcher affiliated to CREFIGE (University of Paris-Dauphine, France) and a member of LIGUE (University of Manouba, Tunisia).

Himachalam Dasaraju is a Dean, Faculty of Commerce and Management at REVA University. He has published over 100 papers and 12 books and completed 12 projects. He received many accolades and awards. He is a Commonwealth Fellow and Professor Emeritus and Visiting professor at Essex Business School, UK.

Liliana Feleaga is professor at the Bucharest University of Economic Studies and dean of the Faculty of Accounting and Management Information Systems. She was a member in the 'Public sector' working party of the FEE (2004–2005). Her research interests are the application of IFRS in emerging economies, environmental accounting, intellectual capital, and corporate governance.

Niculae Feleagă was professor at the Bucharest University of Economic Studies and visiting professor at the National Institute of Economic and Accounting Techniques, Paris (1997–2000: one semester each year). He was a member in the 'Accounting' working party (1998–2001) and in the 'Corporate Governance' working party of the FEE (2005–2006) and a member in the PAIB Committee of the IFAC (2008–2010).

Pierre Ferracci is a chartered accountant. He holds a Master of Applied Economics (Université de Paris-Dauphine) and a Diploma of Higher Studies of Economic Sciences. He is founder and chairman of ALPHA Group, a leading French consultancy (1150 persons), specialising in social relations and local development. ALPHA Group has a large array of clients: employees' representatives, companies, local governments, and agencies. He is, moreover, chairman of Paris FC football club, which is the second football club in Paris.

Alexander Flügel studied business administration at the Universities of Münster, Aarhus, and Fudan University, Shanghai, and awarded MSc in business administration (major accounting, minor finance) by the University of Münster in 2013. Since 2013, working in the Accounting Policy Department of an international insurance company and doctoral candidate at the Research Team of Professor Baetge.

Hideki Fujii is a professor at Kyoto University's Graduate School of Economics in Japan, where he received his PhD and has been on the faculty since 1990. His research is related to financial accounting and reporting. He is the recipient of many awards, including the Japan Accounting Association outstanding contribution to the accounting literature award for his book in 1998.

Clemence Garcia obtained a PhD from Paris Dauphine University in 2010. She has been teaching international accounting in Tokyo as full-time lecturer at Meiji Gakuin University (2006–2010), is assistant professor at Rikkyo University (2011–2015), and is now an associate professor at Gakushuin University. Her main research interest is accounting for goodwill.

Michael Hommel is tax consultant and chair of 'Business Administration, especially Auditing and Accounting' at the Goethe-University Frankfurt am Main since 2002. His research interests are International Accounting, Group Accounting, Financial Statement Analysis, and Corporate Valuation. He began his career as a financial inspector and financial consultant at the Hessian Tax Authorities.

Przemysław Kabalski is assistant professor at Accounting Department (Faculty of Management), University of Łódz, Poland. Main research interest—various aspects (organisational, cultural, social, psychological, linguistic) of implementing and using International Financial Reporting Standards. Research papers published, among others, in Canada, the USA, and the UK.

Jon Lundesgaard (born 1943) is doctor of economics from the University of Oslo with theoretical work on asymmetric information. In a tenured position 1993–2013, he worked for Hedmark University College (Norway) as associate professor of business and economics. Over years his main interest and published work have been in direction of the foundations for financial reporting regulation.

Michel Magnan is Professor and the Stephen A. Jarislowsky Chair in Corporate Governance at the John Molson School of Business (Concordia University). He is fellow of the Royal Society of Canada and member of Canada's Accounting Standards Board. His interests encompass financial reporting, financial statement analysis, governance, executive compensation, ethics and the environment, and corporate disclosure.

Alois Panzer Studied economics at the University of Munich and London Metropolitan University. Awarded diploma (equivalent to MSc) in economics in 2010. Worked for a large international audit firm in Munich from 2011 to 2012. Since 2012, research assistant and doctoral candidate at the University of Münster (Research Team of Professor Baetge) in the field of accounting/auditing and working for a medium-sized audit firm in Münster.

François Pasqualini is a private law professor at the Paris-Dauphine University, and he is the director of the master of research in business law. His research works are about accounting law since he wrote a thesis about the true and fair view in 1990 edited in 1992. Between 2003 and 2005, he was a member of the Commission IAS/Law of the National account counsel in Paris. His latest works are about the relation between law and accounting following the IFRS rules (Dalloz, 2013) and the jurisprudence of the Justice court of the European Union in accounting law (Kluwer, 2015). François Pasqualini is also administrator of de French center of comparative law and he organises conferences and seminars about the reform of the IASB Conceptual Framework.

Nguyen Cong Phuong is Associate Professor of Accounting at College of Economics, Danang University. He got his master's in Accounting at the University of Quebec at Montreal and PhD in Administration at the University of Paris-Dauphine. He is currently teaching in MSc and PhD programmes. His research has focused on accounting regulation, corporate governance, and earning quality.

Verónica Pizarro holds a PhD in business administration from Universidad Autónoma de Madrid. She is Professor at the Faculty of Economics and Business of the Universidad de Chile. Professor Pizarro is expert on IFRS and she is member of the Accounting Standards Committee of the Institute of Accountants of Chile.

Olivier Ramond is a full professor at the DRM-Finance research centre of the University of Paris-Dauphine, France. His research articles have been published in refereed journals such as *Journal of Business, Finance and Accounting, Journal of Accounting and Public Policy*, and *Journal of the Academy of Marketing Sciences*. Olivier has also taken part in the edition of books on financial reporting and valuation issues under IAS/IFRS.

Viatcheslav Sokolov is a doctor of economics and professor at St. Petersburg State University of Economics. Partner of PricewaterhouseCoopers responsible for accounting consultancy. Author of more than 100 publications on theory and history of Accounting.

Hervé Stolowy is a Professor of accounting at HEC Paris. He has authored and co-authored nine books (including 'Financial Accounting and Reporting—A Global Perspective', Cengage Learning, Andover, UK, 4th edition, 2013, in collaboration with Michel Lebas and Yuan Ding) and published over 65 articles in academic and applied journals. His research and teaching interests span financial and international accounting and focus more specifically on accounts manipulation, intangibles, international accounting harmonisation, and statement of cash flows. He is a past president of the Association Francophone de Comptabilité (AFC), a past co-editor of *Comptabilité—Contrôle—Audit*, the official journal of the AFC, and the past chair of the Standing Scientific Committee of the European Accounting Association (EAA). He is the Editor-elect of the *European Accounting Review*.

Mutyala Subramanyam is an Assistant Professor at REVA University, Bangalore. To his credit, he has 12 articles published in National and International Journals. He is having international collaboration with Prof. Collins Ntim and Prof. Soobaroyen Teerooven of Southampton University, UK.

Anna Szychta dr. hab., associate professor, Head of Accounting Theory Section in the Accounting Department, Faculty of Management, University of Łódź, Poland. Research interests: theory and history of accounting, cost and management accounting. Author and co-author of about 170 publications, including 15 works published abroad. Editor in chief of Polish scientific journal 'Zeszyty Teoretyczne Rachunkowości'.

Xiaorui Wang is a 3rd year PhD student, member of the research team 'Markets, Organisations, Societies and Technologies (MOST)' affiliated to the Paris-Dauphine University, and laureate of the French government's '2014 Eiffel excellence scholarship' programme. Research interests: social and environmental accountability, Corporate Social Responsibility (CSR), accounting for the agriculture sector, accounting history, and discourse analysis in accounting research.

Stephen A. Zeff is Professor of Accounting at Rice University, where he has been since 1978. He was Editor of *The Accounting Review* and President of the American Accounting Association. He has co-authored two books on the history of the IASC and on the first 10 years' history of the IASB.

Julia Zicke is a research and teaching assistant at the Chair of Auditing and Accounting at the Goethe-University of Frankfurt. She studied business administration at the Goethe-University of Frankfurt and graduated in 2009. Zicke received her PhD from the Goethe-University of Frankfurt in 2014. Her research focuses on empirical issues in earnings quality and earnings management in specific.

Introduction

This publication pays homage to Jacques Richard, one of a number of French pioneers who have thoroughly explored the realm of comparative accounting. Indeed, in the interview that he was kind enough to grant us, it was clear that his fascination for this realm began well before international accounting via IFRS had loomed large for both academics and professionals. By retracing the landmark moments in his career, including his time as a student and the influence of his family, especially his father, Jacques Richard provides us with an excellent overview of his professional journey and a broad view of the changes that have taken place in accounting research and French university thinking over the last 40 years. We learn that French research into accounting was practically non-existent in the 1970s and that the teaching side was tedious, even unappealing to students. Since then, the accomplishments in the field, to which Jacques Richard has been a major contributor, have demonstrated the latent issues facing accounting and how research has revealed these issues. But Jacques Richard did not follow a conventional path towards the position of researcher in international accounting. His first loves were geography and languages and then economics and law, rather than accounting, which only caught his interest after he found himself teaching the subject through necessity. And accounting harboured other complexities, as he explains: 'What intrigued me the most were the underlying ideologies. Conceptual differences in accounting helped illustrate economic and socio-political choices'. Here we can discern the preoccupation of such thinkers as Marx and Proudhon, i.e. accounting is a technical infrastructure which organises the economic and social world; the construction of this world also reflects how we think about it. Jacques Richard first explores this notion in 2005 in his article entitled: *Les trois stades comptables du capitalisme français*,[1] which was published in France and abroad, and which received a favourable review in the general press (*Le Monde diplomatique*). Jacques Richard's desire to remove the technical veneer from

[1] Translation: The three stages of accounting doctrine associated with French capitalism.

accounting is evidenced throughout his career. Indeed, he considers his final battleground (Jacques describes himself as a committed researcher) to be environmental accounting, one that he has been associated with for the last decade and which has allowed him to work alongside colleagues from numerous disciplines, such as agronomy, economics, and philosophy, and to be involved in establishing a hitherto unseen multidisciplinary field of research. In his eyes, this desire to make accounting more accessible has not been helped by the decline in professional freedom and professional emulation, both previously valued by academic circles. Nowadays, administrative constraints and demands to publish predominate, causing uniformity and conformity where there should be creativity and ingenuity. Ultimately, this interview confirms that Jacques Richard is certainly a researcher par excellence, but more than that, it confirms his commitment to making the world a better place and his willingness to question his convictions through scientific research. Jacques Richard does not claim to have all the answers, but he makes it possible for us to understand how research into accounting can increase our appreciation of the world around us.

As for the contributors, they had one constraint only: to write a paper on the subject of IFRS accounting. The variety of the contributions, in both the authors' fields of study and geographical origins, pays tribute to the work of Jacques Richard and at the same time demonstrates how IFRS accounting arouses reflection and debate.

The publication is divided into two main parts. The first part focuses more on the theoretical and conceptual side of applying IFRS, whereas the second is devoted to the issues, either practical and theoretical, or national and regional, that emerge when using international accounting standards.

In the first part, each of the contributors tackle major themes that are close to Jacques Richard's heart, and each goes about it in their own inimitable way: the relationship between economics and accounting, accounting as a social construct, fair value, environmental accounting, and the links between law and accounting.

Economics and Accounting By way of introducing this first part, Baker, in *Accounting and economic systems: A tribute to the work of Jacques Richard*, provides us with a rich synopsis of four themes that Jacques Richard elected to work on throughout his career: the Chart of Accounts, accounting typologies (static, dynamic, actuarial), the role of accounting during the transition from communism to capitalism, and a critique of the concept of fair value. Charts of Accounts are multipurpose (training, internal auditing, and auditing by the state), and they help us understand the role attributed to accounting within a socio-economic system. Accounting typologies derive from a historical study of the move from static accounting theory based on price to a dynamic accounting theory based on costs and then to an actuarial theory of accounting based on discounted cash flows. The transition by various former communist countries in Europe from 1997 to 2003 to a capitalist economy was studied by Jacques Richard. And finally, his criticisms of the concept of fair value essentially stem from the systematic abandonment by the

IASB of the principle of prudence and from the absence of any attempt by international accounting to embrace social and environmental issues.

Accounting as a Social Construct Alexander points out that accounting cannot be dissociated from those within the profession and the motivating factors behind their behaviour, while Fujii emphasises the normative tools in accounting that can be assimilated by an institution.

Thus, in *Frère Jacques and IFRS: Sonnez les Matines?*,[2] Alexander highlights the subjectivity that is inextricably bound to the production of normative accounts through the example of the true and fair view. By moving beyond the 'globish'[3] that has become the common parlance of IFRS, he humanises accounting by bringing to the fore how the concepts, and hence the words that encase them, have different meanings for different groups, in terms of linguistics, schools of thought, and social practices.

Fujii, in *An Institutional theory perspective on accounting evolution: rulemakers' belief and empirical evidence*, expresses surprise that accounting standard setters do not consider the evidence available from scientific research in the field of accounting. Despite the fact that numerous articles inform us that users of accounts would prefer net income (versus cash flow and comprehensive income), the current IFRS approach favours the construction of a belief that for accounting to be viable it must be geared towards capital markets.

Fair Value This theme, and, to be more precise, measuring fair value, has often attracted attention. It is the mainstay of a paper by Casta and Ramond, or approached in a more roundabout way by Blum and Chiapello.

In *Financial reporting and fair value: where do we stand?*, Casta and Ramond enter a full debate on the motives behind the gradual and partial replacement of the historical costs method by the fair value method. They put forward the arguments from a range of protagonists who support one or other of the accounting models and point up the importance of a conceptual framework that will define the aims and objectives of accounting. A key question on the role of accounting is then asked: is the function of accounting to screen for risks via concepts such as historical cost (governed by prudence), or to supply information to users, which is as neutral as possible, via the concept of fair value?

As far as the other contributors are concerned, the notion of value becomes part of a much bigger question, making it subject to diverse criticisms concerning the meaning of financialisation on a global scale and how this financialisation is calculated. Each author views this key question on the determination of value from a very different angle, and these relative perspectives may simultaneously connect and disconnect.

---

2 Translation: Brother Jacques and IFRS: ringing the morning bells?

3 An international version of English as used by and between non-native speakers of English.

Therefore, without actually going into the technicalities of IFRS, Chiapello, in *How IFRS contribute to the financialisation of capitalism*, demonstrates that the financialisation of the world economy relies on a set of calculation methods (cash flow, probable risk, model-based value), which may change power relations and wealth distribution. This morphological transformation of capitalism is borne by three pillars, the building blocks of which are supplied by IFRS: the optimisation of real-time decisions, asset valuation, and risk management. Accounting accommodates this ideological transfer from business-as-institution to business-as-merchandise, and it is an approach which is epitomised by market value and by substituting the impairment test for amortisation.

If we now open the Pandora's box of calculation methods, Blum, in *Fair value and discounted cash flows: value creation or sense destruction?*, seeks to understand the pitfalls and diversions of one of these tools, the discounted cash flow method, which is used to calculate fair value. After reminding us that this method was originally devised as a managerial tool to aid decision-making, he shows that it has become a means for investment managers to build financial portfolios. This new application has turned the original purpose of the tool upside down, since discounted cash flow is no longer one of many elements that aid decision-making in the complex yet known universe of internal business management; it is a tool employed by external investors endeavouring to maximise their returns on an investment portfolio in the unknown universe of investment choices. Discounted cash flow has therefore become a sort of oracle, but this prophesising power has no evidence to support it, as the executive merits of NPV (Net Present Value) have never been proven.

In parallel with the latent tensions referred to above, i.e. the macro input from the world economy versus the micro input from individual calculation methods, three of the other contributors offer their views on value via a meso input from companies.

Firstly, the issue surrounding the choice of monetary aggregate in relation to works councils is discussed by Ferracci in *IFRS and the works council in France*. He shows that neglecting the value-added method in favour of the fair value method has negative consequences for employees, who are deprived of the opportunity to gauge organisational performance from the profit and loss account and hence the sustainability of their company. In addition, Ferracci criticises the fact that human capital is not presented as an asset, unlike intangible factors, which are generally presented as assets.

Next, the role of the firm in the City is examined from the perspective of the investor–fair value combination using a contemporary approach. By taking as her starting point the debate between Berle and Means on the one side, and Dodd on the other, in *The IASB and the market "communion"*, Chabrak revisits the following question: to whom are corporations accountable? She first looks at how Berle and Means make a generalised observation from the ruling by the Michigan Supreme Court in 1919 against Ford Motor Company in a case brought by the Dodge brothers (minority shareholders). She shows that this case constituted the basis for investor-driven accounting decisions, ergo the ideological leap towards the market efficiency hypothesis. By embracing this intellectual construct, the IASB has chosen to abandon the stewardship role of accounting, rather turning it into a provider of financial information that helps investors make decisions.

Biondi, in *The accounting representation of the enterprise entity: an historical perspective*, tackles a relatively similar issue, but from an entirely different angle. His methodology is historical and he compares two types of accounting (static and dynamic), depicting them via four typical examples which all focus on the principle of the enterprise entity. Moreover, he reminds us that the accountants of the nineteenth century and the beginning of the twentieth century were keen to formalise accountancy. However, they neglected the issue of economic substance, which could also have been represented in transactions through the use of accountancy. Biondi's historical perspective illustrates that the enterprise is not on an equal footing with the market and should not be tempted to align itself with the market. It also illustrates that fair value has no meaning in accounting. Finally, Biondi indicates that accounting has a role which is much greater than that given to it by the IASB: it is a common language, a managerial tool, a regulatory device, and a means for good corporate governance.

Interlinking Fields By way of rounding off the first part, Brown and Pasqualini surmise that accounting should move into other areas: one which is in the process of becoming: environmental accounting; the other which has very close ties to accounting: law.

In *Calculation of environmentally sustainable residual income (eSRI) from IFRS financial statements: an extension of Richard (2012)*, Brown bases his arguments on the most recent work by Jacques Richard (2012), who decries the purely financial thrust of IFRS—the standards do not encompass the impact of business activity on the environment. In this way, he believes that companies pay out sham dividends, as only financial capital is allowed for, not environmental capital or social capital. Using the principle that accounting reflects macroeconomic choices at a microeconomic level, and by drawing on the work of Hueting (1969), Jacques Richard provides us with a method for calculating sustainable profits: *Comptabilité Adaptée au Renouvellement de l'Environnement*[4] (CARE). Companies would be required to report the costs of replacing or renewing assets in their accounts by recording the impact of these assets on environmental and social capital. Brown, after noting the inherent limitations to this model (these limitations were also identified by Jacques Richard himself), suggests that the way forward would be to enhance the model by borrowing from a concept based on the idea of residual earnings: eSRI. Brown's model offers the possibility of distinguishing between sustainable investments and less sustainable investments.

Pasqualini, in *In search of the purpose of accounting representation*, uses his expert legal eye to reflect on the close ties that exist between IFRS and accounting standards emanating from European directives; he places a particular emphasis on

[4] Translation: Adapted accounting for a renewable environment.

the way that French legislation echoes this international standardisation. His contribution is valuable for several reasons. Firstly, he approaches the problem from a very different angle, that of a legal practitioner, and hence the analysis of international accounting is removed from an ideological stance which often serves to hide the weakness of the arguments. In this case, the author bases his arguments on law. Next his standpoint becomes more nuanced, and he is an innovator, because amazingly, he succeeds in showing that the divergences between IFRS and European accounting standards, especially those in France, mask numerous similarities, and the central theme of the article, the principle of substance over form, has engendered very distinctive solution procedures. This is because the solutions themselves have come from different sets of traditions in accounting and law. Finally, he demonstrates how French law, via its many branches, has already appropriated the changes introduced by the IASB to the conceptual foundations of standardisation. The work of the IASB is not revolutionary; it merely reflects an evolutionary process which is engraved in the history of accounting.

Over and beyond their individual aspects, this kaleidoscope of contributions clearly shows the existence of a close and unbreakable bond between the method chosen to calculate value, the depiction of this value in accounts, and our construction/perception of the social, economic, and financial world. All of the contributors underline the inherent limitations of IFRS and demonstrate that other approaches to accounting are there to be explored. As we must iterate, the authors reveal the fact that accounting is not a neutral set of practices, but rather a set of practices that both reflects changes in the world and takes part in the construction of this world. And it is probably for these reasons that the conceptual framework, the primacy that is given to the investor, the use of the fair value method, and the provision of financial information in accounts to the detriment of a stewardship role are frequently criticised and questioned as to their legitimacy.

The second part of this publication discusses the way in which IFRS have been disseminated in various regions of the world. The value of the contributions can be seen in the methodologies (qualitative and quantitative) and in the variety of countries involved—over 15 in all. It would have been logical to structure this part according to one of the existing typologies available in accounting classification, for example, from the work by Gray (1988), Nair and Franck (1980), Puxty (1987), Nobes (1983, 2003), and Richard (1996), but it did not take long for us to realise that this was not a sensible option because it would have created strong heterogeneities in the organisation of the publication, and in particular, it would have failed to reflect the concerns of each author, in other words, how they have responded to the issues surrounding IFRS. On reading the contributions, the overriding elements quickly assert themselves: the direction and even the tone of each paper are commensurate with the size of the country, its degree of dependence in terms of the world economy, and its political history. With this as our starting point, we have sought out a non-accounting method of classification, opting for groupings that are currently used by international bodies, such as the World Bank, the IMF, and the UN.[5] We have therefore been able to make a distinction between the BRIC(S),[6] more economically developed countries (MEDC), and emerging markets.

This type of classification has allowed us to observe three overriding elements in the examination of the transition from national accounting standards to IFRS:

- The geographical reach of the BRICS has resulted in the presence of a strong internal market and, consequently, a very limited dependence on IFRS accounting. The contributors call our attention to the existence of a disconnect from international standard setters.
- The strong national accounting traditions of MEDCs, along with their social, legal, and institutional embeddedness, have meant that in theory, the transition towards IFRS was likely to be problematic. On this point, the contributors primarily underline the conceptual incompatibilities that have affected the very essence of accounting and the type of information that it purports to convey.
- The emerging markets examined in this publication are ex-communist regimes, apart from Chile and Tunisia. They can be characterised by a more modest geographical reach, a moderate or low per capita income, and/or a recent, rapid, and often radical political transformation. The adoption of IFRS is often described as a requirement for companies to enter the world of finance capitalism.

BRIC: Brazil, Russia, India, China

In *IFRS convergence and the role of accounting education: the Brazilian case*, Cornacchione and Dal-Ri Murcia retrace the historical process which caused Brazil to adopt IFRS and shed light on the essential role of education in disseminating IFRS. The study has criticisms to make, highlighting the strong sense of national loyalty espoused by Brazilian companies. Indeed, the authors show that the financial statements of listed companies having adopted IFRS continue to be influenced by national considerations, and that even though IFRS are compulsory for SMEs, these companies continue to adhere to national standards, as there is nothing in law to sanction non-conformists.

[5] We used the World Bank's per capita income classification (data from 2014). We therefore distinguished between MEDCs, where the annual per capita income exceeds $40,000, and emerging markets, where economies are expanding rapidly, but where per capita income is less than $20,000.

[6] Brazil, Russia, India, China, and South Africa, respectively. The acronym BRIC was first coined by Goldman Sachs investment bank in 2001; South Africa was added later to make BRICS. However, we were unable to include an article on South Africa, so for the purposes of this publication, we revert to the original BRIC as our title.

Sokolov's contribution in *Can IFRS be considered Accounting?* relates to the situation in Russia. He begins by dwelling on the link that exists between IFRS and finance capitalism and then develops the idea that these standards represent more than just a new set of accounting standards, but a new way of understanding the world. They also represent a method for obtaining statistics on companies which can help direct macroeconomic policy. Nevertheless, Sokolov considers that IFRS cannot be completely assimilated into the Russian accounting system because they remain the 'offspring' of financial globalisation and are hence outside the bounds of national sovereignty.

Dasaraju and Subramanyam, in *Convergence of international financial reporting standards: an analysis of issues in developed and developing economies*, question the elected modus operandi for managing the convergence towards IFRS in India. They underline the main obstacles that Indian companies have to negotiate: the differences between IFRS and Indian accounting methods, the inherent weaknesses of the available training in IFRS accounting, and the taxation issues involved in moving from Indian accounting standards to IFRS. The authors also underline the limitations of the fair value method and the collateral risks of subjectivity and instability.

The issues involved in China's process of convergence towards IFRS are studied by Wang in *The role of the government and academics in the IFRS convergence process of Chinese accounting standards*. She shows how IFRS have had an active role in the economic transition of a socialist economy towards a neoliberal model, and how researchers have had a pivotal role in disseminating these standards—they simultaneously provide ongoing support and scientific rigour. As for the Chinese authorities, IFRS are perceived as a means for breaking into world markets. Conversely, even if the author does not challenge this premise, she comes across as being more circumspect about long-term economic, social, and political consequences.

MEDC: More Economically Developed Countries

Cormier and Magnan, in *IFRS in Canada: Game changer or Neutral mutation?*, firstly describe the institutional environment that existed when IFRS were adopted and the consequences on the capital market of this decision to adopt. They examine two factors that highlight the impact of IFRS (before and after) on corporate governance: asymmetric information and the effects on stock market value. The work of the authors on this second factor is entirely original.

In the case of adopting IFRS in France, Stolowy, in *IFRS and France: a marriage of convenience*, demonstrates the extent to which tensions are high and resistance is strong. Although their use is now compulsory in the publication of consolidated accounts, IFRS are ignored in the publication of individual accounts.

In Germany, two sets of contributors bring more clarification to the situation. Hommel and Zicke, in *The influence of IFRS on the German accounting system: the half-hearted reforms of the German accounting law modernization Act*, detail how legislators have taken into consideration the influence of IFRS by updating the country's commercial code. However, the implementation of IFRS in Germany has been a failure because IFRS are too much at odds with the fundamental legal principles of German accounting law. Moreover, the weight of accounting culture and traditions also explains the level of resistance towards IFRS. The second contribution, entitled *German accounting and IFRS: limitations in the convergence potential of German national accounting standards towards international accounting standards*, is by Baetge, Panzer, and Flügel. They highlight the different approaches to the notions of information, stewardship, and capital maintenance as found within German regulations and IFRS. These differences are gauged according to the concept of creditor protection, the role of the tax system, and the principle of prudence. Mirroring the situation in France, the authors advocate that IFRS should be applied to listed companies only.

In *The transition to IFRS in Italy and elsewhere, or from Code Napoleon to the devolution of sovereignty*, Canziani begins with the principle of the true and fair view, and the uncertainty it has created, to explain the changes caused by the application of IFRS in Italian accounting. Although IFRS have led to a more detailed analysis of transactions and allowed Italy to align its own accounting practices with worldwide practices, the author relates the problems faced by certain Italian companies when implementing IFRS.

Garcia analyses the situation in Japan. In *The Japanese "dynamic-conservative" model to the test of global convergence: from the birth of industrial accounting to the competition with the "Actuarial" model*, she recounts the slow development of the Japanese accounting system from the Meiji era to modern times. By employing Jacques Richard's classification from 1996, the author describes the influence of international accounting standardisation on Japan's accounting system as 'dynamic-conservative'. However, the absence of any consensus on such key elements as fair value and comprehensive income highlights the problem of properly dovetailing national standards and their international counterparts.

Lundesgaard's case study on IAS 19, which he sets out in *IAS 19 and employee benefits: some reflections on the Norwegian experience*, shows the impact of pension obligations on financial statements. The author is keen to understand if the integration of defined benefit pension plans in financial statements represents an improvement in the information available in accounts. Regarding the highly subjective nature of applying this standard, Lundesgaard concludes that this information would be preferable in the form of an appendix.

Emerging Markets

Azua and Pizarro, in *Adopting IFRS in Chile: Influences on companies and the capital market,* consider the impact of IFRS implementation on the fair value measurement of non-current assets (tangible and intangible). Based on a study of

80 companies, they observed a 4 % increase in the book value and conclude that IFRS have had a positive effect on the companies' quoted market value. Alver and Alver, in *Development of the Estonian financial reporting and good accounting practice*, emphasise the transformation in the structure of the Estonian economy and the massive institutional changes that have occurred since entry into the EU in 2004. Using a historical analysis, they point to the fact that the country has shown a preference for implementing IFRS rather than European directives. This strategy can be explained by the country's eagerness to participate in the globalised capital market.

In *Implementation of IFRS in Poland: main effects and problems*, Szychta and Kabalski detail the rites of passage towards IFRS since the 1990s. The barriers in Poland have been many: a difficult transition to a market economy, the reorganisation of the state, its institutions and its companies, and the weight of history as evidenced by the continued existence of *Homo Sovieticus* (the Polish accountant).

Feleaga and Feleaga examine the situation in Romania in *Shifting to IFRS: the case of Romania*. They point out that former Soviet bloc countries are obliged to adopt IFRS if they want to augment their legitimacy in capital markets. After interviewing a number of professionals: auditors, preparers of financial statements, academics, and regulators, the authors stress the importance of institutional factors in the implementation of the process. Once again, the pressure emanating from capital markets and international audit firms is demonstrated.

In *IFRS for SMEs and Tunisian Accounting*, Damak-Ayadi shows the advantages for Tunisian companies in adopting IFRS if they wish to penetrate the market more successfully and attract investors. This proclivity for international standards can partly be explained by the fact that the accounting system operated by Tunisian companies is already a compromise, probably imperfect, between the French system and IFRS. Notwithstanding, the author reserves judgement on the wide-scale adoption of IFRS because of the costs of implementation and the loss of sovereignty for Tunisian regulators.

Finally, in *Institutional theory and accounting change: an analysis of accounting regulations in Vietnam*, Phuong examines the consequences of foreign investors putting pressure on accounting regulators to adopt IFRS. The partial convergence of local standards and IFRS can be put down to several factors, which are identical to those factors identified elsewhere in the publication: the role played by history and a communist past, and the institutional environment. This results in standards which are often inappropriate for the local economy.

We have done our utmost to present the different contributions as succinctly as possible. They are each a tribute to Jacques Richard, so all that remains for you, the reader, is to explore in depth the full gamut of regional/national specificities and diversities, which imply that far from being a neutral set of practices, and devoid of issues, accounting is the denouement of a permanent ideological combat taking place within today's fully globalised economy.

The first part has provided us with the opportunity to show a) how internal theoretical concerns in accounting, such as fair value, can be tackled in various ways (sociological, technical, and managerial) and b) how much common ground exists with other overlapping disciplines (economics, law, and sociology). This range of options alone encapsulates the inherent potential of accounting as a human activity.

The second part is especially notable for the way the authors' contributions indicate that the most positive reactions to IFRS have come from smaller countries with a relatively undeveloped capital market, and yet a high dependency on the global economy, and with a history of rapid, if not brutal, political (ex-communist countries) or economic (Chile) transitions. On the other hand, the most resistance has come from those countries boasting a long-standing accounting tradition or a strong capital market/internal market derived from economic development/significant geographical size. We therefore find ourselves facing a paradox: the most willingness to adopt IFRS is shown by countries which probably are least in need of international standards for their respective economies, insofar as the standards were originally designed for multinational companies operating within advanced economies, whereas the most reticence is shown by countries which are already fully signed up members to the finance capitalism club and have been so for almost half a century.[7] This contradiction demonstrates that the adoption of IFRS is not only a technical process but an ideological challenge where political pressure is placed on the most reticent countries.

'War is much too serious a matter to be entrusted to military men', wrote Georges Clémenceau, a French statesman and one of the architects of the victory over the Triple Alliance during the First World War. The analogy with accounting is worth discussing in terms of the papers written for this publication. In response to criticisms on its lack of political legitimacy, the IASB has often declared that it is merely a technical standard setter. Our contributors, like many before them, have shown that the opposite is true. Indeed, the absence of neutrality in the field of accounting, and more so, its productive capacity for changing the world, raises the issue of answerability for those presiding over its destiny. As is the case of academia, although many researchers, including those outside the field of management, are adding to the accounting debate (its institutions, its context, its practices, etc.), it is high time that this debate entered the public domain so that the social, economic, legal, and political issues underpinning the future of this world are also discussed in the light of the international accounting standards that are used nowadays or at least acknowledged on a global scale. In other words, accounting theory cannot be sustained by accountants and accounting scholars alone, but is crying out for thinkers from other disciplines, such as human and social sciences, to help the profession evolve for the benefit of us all—not simply for the benefit of an

[7] There exists a convergence of phenomena which mark the turning point in the migration from industrial economies to financial economies: the end of the gold/dollar convertibility in 1971 and the arrival of floating exchange rates which contributed to the development of capital markets and structured products, the first oil crisis in 1973 which ended the availability of cheap fossil fuels and led to the transformation of industrial organisation, and finally, the creation of the International Accounting Standards Board (IASC) in 1973.

abstract investor. Moreover, accounting is in no position to dance to its own tune, cutting itself off from national, regional, and international authorities, and this despite the fact that it represents the sole means for a company to measure, calculate, divide up, and distribute the value which men and women create, these same men and women who comprise the company. Accounting is more than a set of technical challenges; it is a set of ethical challenges.

We sincerely hope that all of the articles in this publication fully reflect the pioneering work of our colleague, Jacques Richard, and hence nourish the thinking of each reader on the fundamental role that accounting plays in the organisation of economic, social, and political systems.

Paris, France Didier Bensadon
Sceaux, France Nicolas Praquin

References

Nair RD, Frank WG (1980) The impact of disclosure and measurement practices on international accounting classifications. Account Rev 55(3):426–450

Nobes CW (1983) A judgemental international classification of financial reporting practices. J Bus Finance Account 10(1):1–19

Nobes CW (2003) On the myth of "Anglo-Saxon" financial accounting: a comment. Int J Account 38(1):95–104

Puxty AG et al (1987) Modes of regulation in advanced capitalism: locating, accountancy in four countries. Acc Organ Soc 12(3):273–291

Richard J (1996) Comptabilités et pratiques comptables. Dalloz, Paris

Gray SJ (1988) Towards a theory of cultural influence on the development of accounting systems internationally. Abacus 24(1):1–15

Interview of Jacques Richard: The Accounting Geographer

Didier Bensadon and Nicolas Praquin

Abstract This interview of Prof. Jacques Richard gave us the opportunity to better understand who is Jacques and what was his career. Beyond his own career, this interview is also a mean to understand the evolution of the academic field in the last four decades. After he presented his academic background, Jacques addresses his thoughts about different fields: the different experiences of his teaching and the several tracks of his research, the international dimension of accounting, the social utility and participation of the researcher in the public debate, the formatted accounting research.

1 Education: Law, Accountancy, Economics, History, Geography and Languages

1.1 Basic Education

My father taught French and classics (French, Latin and Greek). He encouraged me to learn languages. I did a lot of etymology—in fact I have an unpublished article on the word "accountancy" in 65 languages, as a tribute to my father. My mother was of Russian descent. I have therefore always been very sensitive to the linguistic and international side of life, and developed a passion for Geography, my favorite subject in secondary school.

After secondary school my father advised me to do a preparatory course for graduate school in business at the Lycée du Parc in Lyon (France).

But at ESSEC Business School, I was disappointed—and bored—by the extremely technical approach to everything I learnt. I enrolled in both an

D. Bensadon (✉)
Paris-Dauphine University (DRM-MOST), *PSL Research University*, Paris, France
e-mail: didier.bensadon@dauphine.fr

N. Praquin (✉)
University of Paris-Sud, Paris-Saclay, Sceaux, France
e-mail: nicolas.praquin@u-psud.fr

D. Bensadon, N. Praquin (eds.), *IFRS in a Global World*,
DOI 10.1007/978-3-319-28225-1_1

Economics and a Law degree course, which gave me a more theoretical background. I also completed a degree in French that I had begun before going to ESSEC.

How did you discover accountancy?

At ESSEC we had accountancy lessons in the first year, taught by professionals, and we had to learn the Chart of Accounts numbers[1] by heart. I couldn't understand it. But in the third year we had Gaston Thibault, who became President of the French Order of Chartered Accountants in 1979. In 1963 he published a book on accountancy theory and practice with André Dalsace[2] with French University Press. It was completely different: a more philosophical approach to accountancy. But I was more or less forced to start accountancy teaching: ESSEC needed accounting teachers: I had no choice.

1.2 Teaching

After my degree, in 1966, I was unsure what to do. ESSEC was recruiting its future permanent teaching staff. At that time almost all the teachers were professionals. I was among the people they asked to become a teaching assistant. I agreed to give accountancy lessons and was then appointed head of the assistants.

At the same time, I began studying to become a Chartered Accountant and completed a DES[3] in Economics and one in Law. It was then that I met Prof. Marie Lavigne, an economist specializing in Eastern European countries. Her class on the conflicts between the various political blocks was fascinating.

1.3 The Thesis

I therefore decided to write a thesis, aiming to confront the capitalist world and the Soviet world. I wanted to compare the accounting systems of the United States, Germany and the USSR; I read English and German, so I learnt Russian. It brought me closer to what I initially wanted to study (Geography). I also wanted to do a sort of geography of accounting, just as there is a history of accounting. I did two theses.[4]

---

[1] French accountancy is based on a chart of accounts, with identical root numbers for all French companies. Even today, these numbers must be learnt by heart.

[2] A former pupil at Ecole Polytechnique (a prestigious French engineering school) with a PhD in Law, André Dalsace wrote numerous books on accounting in the inter- and post-war years.

[3] Diplôme d'Etudes Supérieures (a 2-year post-graduate course).

[4] At that time, it was compulsory to write two theses. The first, at the end of the fifth year at university lasted 1 or 2 years. It was followed by a 'State' thesis, which took several years (up to 10 in certain subjects). These PhDs were replaced by a single PhD in 1984.

The first, a post-graduate thesis, on financial analysis of four countries (France, the US, East Germany and Russia); then the second, or State PhD, on the link between accounting and economic systems. It fed my liking for Geography and Politics.

What drew you to accounting?

Mainly the underlying ideologies. The conceptual differences of accounting helped illustrate the economic or socio-political choices.

But at that time, there was only one academic who could direct a thesis in accountancy in the whole of France: Pierre Lassègue, who taught Accounting at University Panthéon-Sorbonne. I met him while doing my DES in Economics. But as I was interested in the political aspects of accountancy, and in Eastern European countries, I did my thesis with his "young colleague" Marie Lavigne; Pierre Lassègue was nevertheless inevitably a member of the examining board. And my defense in 1980 went very badly. The examiners disagreed about the evaluation of certain conclusions of my work. The 'dominant' ones gave me a "merit" which meant that my work was useless and my career jeopardized. Fortunately, that same year, I went to present the paper at the EAA congress in Amsterdam and the audience liked it. Anthony Hopwood, an eminent professor, even suggested I write an article in his journal!

2 Previous Work Experiences

2.1 *Training to Become a Chartered Accountant (1967–1968)*

During your training, what kind of jobs were you given? How did you enjoy it?

I spent the first few years of my internship in a small, very friendly family firm called Grevoult. The firm had two categories; "proper" accountants who had trained at an accounting school[5] and the others, who had been through graduate school.[6] Grevoult did not therefore consider me as an expert and gave me fairly basic tasks. It was interesting and hands-on, though not very stimulating.

[5] For a long time accounting was rejected by French universities. Parallel schools, often linked to practical education with combined work experience, had therefore been established. Lessons were very technical and not very conceptual. The schools were less sought after socially; but they nevertheless allowed students from the less well-off classes to continue their higher education.

[6] These 'grandes écoles' are engineering or business graduate schools requiring 2 years of preparatory classes before taking the entrance examination.

2.2 Teaching at ESSEC (1967–1970) and the Algerian Experience

When I began as assistant at ESSEC, they were initiating an American conception of classes. As teaching models the ESSEC directors had invited people who had come back from the US with the case studies method. This led to some debate: should the *ex cathedra* teaching methods be replaced by case studies? The cases brought new concepts. It was interesting, but problematic. There were for example conflicts between teachers on the notion of opportunity cost seen in the cases. Not all teachers were convinced about how real this cost was. Those with traditional training were opposed to the ideologies instilled by the American case studies. I was not particularly enthusiastic about them. There was an academic conception that I found fairly strange: instead of confronting the theories we hid them in practical exercises that were supposed to be excellent but which heralded the pre-eminence of finance over traditional budget management.

While still under contract with ESSEC, I then left to work as a Peace Corps volunteer in Algeria in 1970.[7] I was a manager at the Ben Aknoun Finance and Accounting Institute, near Algiers. I took the opportunity to learn Arabic and work with the Finance ministry on the reform of the Algerian Accounting Schedule and accountancy teaching. Very enjoyable.

2.3 In-Company Experience: IBM

In 1969, I was in the Budget Department at IBM to finish my accountancy internship.[8] I had specialist but very administrative tasks. The work was very compartmentalized. I did not like this hyper-specialization, nor the kind of lead weight placed on the executives obliging them to stay late in the evening without really doing anything worthwhile. This experience reinforced my desire never to work in a company.

2.4 Encountering the Unions

In the late 1970s, when I was at Paris-Dauphine University, I met "progressive" economists who suggested I work at Syndex, a firm specialized in helping works

[7] This happened after the Algerian war (1954–1962). In spite of the war, independent Algeria soon asked France for cooperation which was formalized by an agreement on technical cooperation in 1966. Military service could take the form of working within this cooperation.

[8] The internship regulations provided the opportunity to spend 1 of the 3 years in a company.

councils with CFDT sympathies.[9] I accepted and stayed there for a year or 2. Then in 1981 I met Pierre Ferracci who worked for Robert Pirolli and who suggested setting up a new firm specializing in helping works councils with CGT leanings.[10] I accepted this new venture, and became a partner chartered accountant in 1983, mainly in charge of the code of ethics and theory of the financial statements, or essentially the method of interpreting company performance from the employees' point of view.[11] I also worked as a chartered accountant on concrete cases for about 3 years; for example I had to explain the accounts and company strategy to union members; I was opposite the financial manager, whose presence was compulsory. This was not easy, particularly as chartered accountants are often criticized by union members, because of their reputation for being over-technical and not linking the technical aspect to the economic and social issues. As I had other academic preoccupations I stopped this work, which was time consuming and stressful, and took on more of a teaching role in the firm. For several years I also gave free lessons to CGT union members. These people were by no means specialists, but were quick to understand and sought to link accounting issues with their companies' economic problems. It was an excellent teaching school. By giving answers and providing real life examples they made me rethink a lot of my ideas.

2.5 Teaching Accounting at Paris-Dauphine University

In the 1970s, while you were assistant lecturer[12] at Paris-Dauphine University, did you include a comparative and conceptual dimension—as you do now—in your accounting lessons? Or did the students expect a more technical approach?

At first I gave comparative references while maintaining a very technical foundation. It was not until I was head of the first year basic accounting courses

---

[9] Companies with at least 50 employees have to set up a works council made up of staff representatives and chaired by the employer. It deals with economic issues as well as social and cultural matters and is funded by the employer, who also pays for a Chartered Accountant to explain the accounts. The Accountant is appointed freely by the works council, not by the employer. For the most part, these committees are managed by elected officials who belong to the major trades-union organizations, principally the CGT, CFDT, CFTC and FO. Each union has its own firm of Chartered Accountants.

[10] The Confédération générale du travail (CGT) is a French employees union created on September 23, 1895 in Limoges. It is seen as one of the main trades-union organizations in works council elections and among staff representatives. For a long time it was linked to the French communist party.

[11] Here the concept of added value and how it is divided between the employees and the shareholders plays a major role, which is not usually the case in traditional financial analysis, particularly in the US.

[12] In the French higher education system between 1960 and 1984, assistant lecturers (maîtres-assistants) were university teachers at undergraduate level, usually while preparing a state PhD.

in about 1990 that I systematically mixed conceptual and theoretical notions, particularly by including a geographical and historical approach, as can be seen in the changes to the basic course book for beginner students.[13] The head of the MA in Accounting and Financial Sciences and Techniques[14] gave me the opportunity to look into financial analysis. At that time we were working on highly technical aspects and also, with people like Henri Bouquin[15] and André Cibert,[16] on trying to understand the conceptual mechanisms. Later on, I returned to financial accounting as I found it resonated more clearly with my political ideas, of comparing the concepts of profit in the different accounting models.

3 Encounter with Research

3.1 My meeting with Anthony Hopwood

At the very first congresses of the European Economic Association (EAA), there were plenary sessions that attracted 100–150 attendees. It was fantastic; we could present an article before the whole audience! In Amsterdam in 1980, after I had a difficult thesis defense, I shakily presented a paper quoting the works of Derek Bailey, a very well known specialist in Soviet accounting. As we were leaving the room, someone came to tell me my article was interesting and he would like it to appear, after a few corrections, in his journal *Accounting, Organizations and Society (AOS)*. At that time, I knew of neither Anthony Hopwood, as it was he, nor his journal. As it implied resuming an arduous task, I did nothing. At that time we had no idea of the importance of publishing in a particular journal. There were no requirements to publish. Later, it became very difficult to publish in this journal.

Was research not essential then?

There was no big pressure to do it; at least, nothing like what there is today. The big move for one's career was the PhD. That's where the pressure was, not on publishing articles. We still published though.

What drove you? Curiosity? A liking for open debate? The desire to prepare the way for new discoveries?

[13] The current title of the tenth edition of this book is *Comptabilité financière: IFRS versus normes françaises* (Richard, Bensadon, Collette). This beginners' book, first published in 1982, took on a conceptual and historical approach circa 1990.

[14] In French: Maîtrise de Sciences et Techniques Comptables (MSTCF), actually called Master de Comptabilité-Contrôle-Audit (CCA).

[15] Henri Bouquin taught management sciences at Paris-Dauphine from 2003 to 2012. He specialized in management control.

[16] André Cibert taught accounting and wrote a number of books after the Second World War.

There was a kind of friendly emulation among French researchers. Several of us said that we had to pull accountancy thinking in France out of its lethargy, by developing academic associations. That was the beginning of the French Accounting Association and the revival in 1979.[17]

3.2 Choosing Research Topics

Why did you elect to take a comparative approach between France, the USA, the USSR, East Germany and West Germany[18]*?*

The first reason was that I spoke German. I then extended my knowledge of the two German accounting systems by comparing them. It made sense to work on the superpower of that time (the US) and compare it with the USSR, the rival superpower. I also intended to add China at the time, but at Paris-Dauphine University, some professors told me it was unnecessary. This was nonsense, but unfortunately I listened to them. As for topics, it's true that my research for the thesis marked my choice of future topics which have always covered the link between accounting and economic and political systems. However I was also interested in the history of accounting because I needed to explain a certain number of historical elements. I observed important historical changes in these accounting systems and therefore sought to interpret them. The main driving question was basically: do the accounting systems change in the same manner in France and elsewhere? The subject is certainly vast, but that's the way my mind works: I find it difficult to concentrate on a subject if I can't see the whole picture. It's obviously an impossible task: without a precise goal, we are merely amateurs; conversely, in a precise framework, you do not get the holistic view and some major aspects are overlooked. I therefore chose holistic themes, while focusing on certain aspects, particularly asset valuation and charts of accounts. For Germany, I was lucky that German accounting culture is set out by legal regulations and full of controversy, especially from 1914 until the fall of the Third Reich. These debates—particularly between partisans of static and dynamic accounting[19]—left their mark and I wanted to delve further into the question asked by taking it to international level, which the Germans, curiously, have not done.

---

[17] Some authors have estimated that it is because of the Chart of Accounts that France had very little accountancy thinking in 1980: this was evidently false. The problem is the lack of university professors teaching accounting, not the fact that they have a Chart of Accounts.

[18] After the Second World War, Germany was divided into two blocks, West and East Germany. They were reunited in 1990 after the fall of the Berlin wall in 1989.

[19] This is the famous German controversy between traditional lawyers who, like Ring, want a liquidation (static) conception of the company and its accounts and those who, like Schmalenbach, prefer a dynamic conception based on the going concern principle.

3.3 The International Dimension of Accounting

Did this question about international accounting come from a lack of interest in what you found in just French accounting?

What probably dictated my research right from the start is this idea of an "accounting geography" and the desire to understand things globally, by which I mean at the global level: France has never been isolated. Add to that a marked interest in everything foreign. By comparing you can see the differences and gain more understanding of a research topic. From the start, before I even wrote my thesis, I reasoned this way. So it is not the International Financial Reporting Standards as such that brought me to international accounting, but rather international accounting and a liking for the comparative approach that brought me to the IFRS.

Did you feel alone in this sort of approach? Did you feel your colleagues supported you?

Of course people supported me, Bernard Colasse[20] for example. But at that time international studies were few and far between and not greatly appreciated. When I was writing my thesis a professor from Paris-Dauphine University told me that the only country worth studying was the USA. Things are changing slowly: only recently a colleague assured me that he saw no point in bringing back the old German debate about static or dynamic accounting systems! It is true that the theses I wrote on comparative accounting were very holistic and clashed with a context more geared towards the English-speaking world. Very few people have worked on Germany, and even fewer have dealt with the 'eastern' countries.

4 Being a Researcher in Social Sciences

4.1 Performance Indicators

When François Mitterrand won the election in 1981 thanks to a Socialist-Communist alliance, there was a huge intellectual effervescence in France including in Economics and Management. Many believed that the time was ripe for a revolution in corporate performance criteria. I frequented the French Communist Party for a short time. I was invited to meetings of its economics section. Although there were some very sectarian people who urged me to leave the party, there were also some brilliant, open-minded people, like Philippe Herzog,[21] and therefore

[20] Bernard Colasse taught management sciences at Université Paris-Dauphine until 2011, specializing in financial accounting.

[21] Philippe Herzog is a former student of the Ecole polytechnique and taught economics in several French universities from 1973 to 2003.

some fascinating debates. The aim was to better understand the import of policies at the national level and within the firm.

At Government level, some proposed taking macro-economic decisions based on the so-called Effects Method invented by an economist called Marc Chervel.[22] This method—nowadays used in project development in Africa—started from the premise that a nation's decision to invest had impacts before and after the event; the idea was to measure the global added value which had been eliminated or created by a decision to invest or disinvest.

At company level, discussions aimed to replace profit by another indicator more representative of the value created by the production team. These influenced my book *L'Audit des performances* in 1989 which contains a chapter on this subject, including the surplus method and other performance indicators that I personally suggested. One source of inspiration for this was the experience in Yugoslavia.

4.2 The Self-Management Experience in Yugoslavia

Shortly after my thesis, I wanted to study what was happening in Yugoslavia where the corporate governance system was based on self-management. I bought an accounting book in Serbo-Croatian while I was there in 1983 and was astonished to discover that costs did not include wages. In a self-management system, there are no employees, and it is fascinating to see how this type of governance works in accounting. The issue was to define the result of the self-managed working unit. Profit appeared to be sales minus raw materials, services, depreciations, taxes and interest: a concept of distributable added value that replaced profit!

Armed with this new geographical experience I endeavored to classify[23] this extraordinary accounting diversity into a category that has featured in my course book since the 1990s (the Richard and Collette, later the Richard, Bensadon and Collette).

4.3 The Researcher's Social Utility and Participation in the Public Debate

So what really interests you is discover new things?

Yes. My current quest, for example, is to redefine the concepts of performance and capital with the prospect of a new type of accounting for sustainable

[22] Marc Chervel is a former student of the Ecole polytechnique, specializing in development economics. He proposed an alternative project management method to that of the World Bank.

[23] This classification has never been published.

development. In fact I am returning to basic questions like what is capital... but that requires much more hindsight and perspective.

And as soon as these new things become commonplace, you lose interest?

Yes. I prefer to look forward. Unlike the positivists, my approach is more normative and futuristic. Pierre-Yves Gomez, Management professor at the EM Lyon Business School, said, "I have decided (I don't know if it was decided or forced) to no longer publish articles in scientific journals, I only write essays." I personally have not given up publishing in scientific journals, but I also believe that it is extremely important to stimulate the sharing of ideas, to continue to question subjective constructions like the concepts of profit and capital, and so on.

I get the impression that what has changed in your view is the difficulty of concentrating on both an object and its environment. You give the impression today that you have sufficiently pondered these questions to have a kind of cross section view.

Only now do I think that I have a manager's and accountant's view of the economic concepts. My approach is part of an overall, interdisciplinary historical process.

There are some other points we would like to address: what you might call the "researcher in society". For example, you published articles in journals for the general public. How did that happen? What is your position today on these issues?

I think my historic outlook on the changes in the phases of "accounting capitalism"[24] aroused considerable public interest. It began about 8 years ago. Managers of the general press knew I was working on this kind of question; perhaps they had read one of my technical articles and thought it would be of interest to a wider public. The first topic was a historical perspective of the major stages in the profit concept. I wrote articles in *Le Monde Diplomatique* (2007), *Le Débat* (2009) and *L'Expansion* (2011). Sustainable development is the second of my research topics to interest the general public. I published two articles (2008 and 2011) on environmental accounting in *Le Monde*.[25] People working in sustainable development have a holistic approach and therefore more or less have to take an interest in accountants. As I published more in this field, I was invited by economists but also by sociologists and engineers on the profit concept in a wider conception of the conservation of all corporate capital. This is all very exciting.

---

[24] See "Les trois stades du capitalisme comptable français". In Capron (ed). Les normes comptables internationales instruments du capitalisme financier (2005); see also "The concept of fair value in French and German accounting regulations from 1673 to 1914 and its consequences for the interpretation of the stages of development of capitalist accounting". CPA, 16, p. 825–50. This French and German vision was extended in 2014 with "The dangerous dynamics of capitalism: from Static to IFRS accounting", Critical Perspectives on Accounting.

[25] "Pour une révolution comptable environnementale", Le Monde de l'économie, 5/2/2008, p. 6. "Taxes contre quotas: le débat environnemental est tronqué" in Le Monde, 22/3/2011.

Do you have the impression that these slightly different environments feed on academic works and invite management researchers to examine new avenues?

Yes, I think so. Some of these people are interested in new types of management and accounting, particularly the agronomists, but also ergonomists and naturalist philosophers. Some are very interested in the works of accountants dealing with environmental management.

Does what they read about accounting change their decision-making methods?

That is more difficult to say as the process is very gradual. It is a small sphere, but the change could become widespread. I'll give another more thought-based example: a group of specialists in biodiversity or conservation (these are ecologists in the field of hard sciences) wants to give a reply in *Nature* to a very famous article by Robert Costanza[26] which had given a value to the whole of biodiversity (based on the premise that if we are to save it we have to give it value). The group wants to answer that this solution is not appropriate. They read my book *Comptabilité et dé veloppement durable* (Accounting and Sustainable Development) and contacted me, explaining that they want to reason from an accounting perspective. That is totally new in my career. The environmental question pushes back borders. It's extremely interesting, especially as, for once in this field, Europe is ahead of the United States.

You think then that the environment, or at least the environmental question, will bring accounting out of its self-sufficiency?

Yes, absolutely. I recently attended a meeting of the Innovation Center of the Bourse de Paris on the accounting professions. This working group is trying to identify the innovative subjects on which any one company is working. I was invited and defended the idea that we need to encourage small firms in the agricultural sector who are sowing the seeds for new accounting or environmental instruments, saying that it was a unique opportunity in this new environmental accounting. Small firms can then be heard above the noise of the Big 4 and their ilk who are imprisoned in the IFRS ideology. Showing an interest in environmental accounting is, I believe, a way of innovating in accounting.

4.4 Management Science Education

How do you see management science teaching now?

At present I think that people who teach and do research in traditional finance have an extremely narrow view of the questions! But the question of the "macroscope" (in the words of Joël de Rosnay[27]) is absolutely fundamental.

---

[26] Costanza R et al. (1997) "The value of the world's ecosystem services and natural capital". Nature, 387, p. 253–259.

[27] Joël de Rosnay is a French scientist, prospectivist, lecturer and author with a PhD in science. An organic chemist, he specializes in the origins of the living world. He is particularly interested in advanced technologies and applications of the theory of systems (systemics).

Fortunately in a number of universities the first 2 years include a general education, but there are some universities, particularly abroad, which plan to restrict this type of class. On the contrary this contextual approach in the first 2 years needs even greater diversity. In any event, the environmental question suffers from a real lack of diffusion. The world is changing fast and I don't think these matters are sufficiently integrated into the university courses.

More precisely, do you think we need more disciplines or more classes in History, Sociology and Philosophy?

Yes. History is essential. During the first 2 years there should be much more emphasis on the history of management in its international dimension. At a meeting of the Société Française de Management,[28] Armand Hatchuel[29] gave a speech saying that he was reviewing the history of management. He said that there was too much emphasis on American texts and theses in history. Take the example of co-management[30]: who talks about that in the French universities? I would love to know. Yet it is essential to teach the existence of alternative models to the dominant ones, which are also criticized in the US.

4.5 Formatted Accounting Research

How do you compare research passed and present?

The research environment is totally different today. The objectives are much more detailed and the methods rationalized. But does all this provide satisfactory results? I find that methodological guidelines are becoming increasingly fragmented, where there should instead be a more horizontal approach. Admittedly, individual theses are problematic as it is difficult to be good at everything, in historical research, research based on quantitative and qualitative techniques, but you can always find help. Personally, I favor pluralistic methodological approaches and am not convinced that extremely specialized journals encourage this—rather the reverse. It is regrettable that researchers are catalogued according to their choice of methodology. That didn't happen in the 1980s. We all had our own favorite method but no one paid much attention. Today, it all seems much more categorized, to such an extent that in certain journals a particular category of methodology will not be published: everything is uniform. There's no mixing. I don't much like it, especially since there is pressure to compartmentalize tasks. I deplore that fewer

[28] The French Management Society (SFM) aims to create a space for discussion and reflection for management teachers and researchers to help shape management sciences, both for production and dissemination of knowledge.

[29] Armand Hatchuel teaches at the Ecole des Mines Paris-Tech and heads the Chair of Theory and Methods of Innovative Design.

[30] A system of governance instituted in Germany after 1945 that includes on the Supervisory Board (which decides on strategies) both employees and shareholders (in equal measure in the most advanced models).

and fewer people do research plus teaching plus administrative work. I am probably not the only one to think so. I don't want to be nostalgic for a period which no doubt had its own faults. But there is less freedom today and I do not think that really encourages innovation.

To echo what you have just said, what is the social utility of researchers in management sciences or accounting?

I think that researchers in management science, especially in environmental management, must try to pass on their message that can be understood by society at large. Therefore—and this goes against the current valuation methods—they must publish essays and papers, not just for the general public, but intellectual. None of that counts today.

Part I
Critical Issues in International Accounting

Accounting and Economic Systems: A Tribute to the Work of Jacques Richard

Charles Richard Baker

Abstract This chapter presents a tribute to the work of Jacques Richard, who has been both a well-known professor at the University Paris Dauphine, and an important scholar regarding the history and development of accounting systems and international financial accounting standards. Professor Richard has also been an inspiring mentor to a generation of accounting students both in France and other countries.

This chapter is organized into four parts. First, there will be a discussion of Professor Richard's work focusing on accounting systems, and in particular his comparative study of the European experience with charts of accounts. In the second section, there will be a discussion of Professor Richard's work describing the development of the French accounting system through three stages from the static to the dynamic to the futuristic. Third, there will be a discussion of Professor Richard's work related to the transition from socialist accounting to capitalist accounting in former communist countries. Fourth, there will be a presentation of Professor Richard's critiques of fair value accounting and International Financial Reporting Standards (IFRS). In each of these areas Professor Richard has demonstrated a high degree of scholarship and a deep interest in the historical development of accounting systems from a comparative international perspective.

1 Accounting and Economic Systems and Charts of Accounts

Professor Richard has devoted a considerable amount of time to investigating relationships between accounting systems and economic systems. Among his first published works, Professor Richard (1975, 1980) studied the accounting and economic systems of four countries, the United States, France, West Germany

C.R. Baker (✉)
Adelphi University, Garden City, NY 11530, USA
e-mail: Baker3@Adelphi.edu

D. Bensadon, N. Praquin (eds.), *IFRS in a Global World*,
DOI 10.1007/978-3-319-28225-1_2

and the Soviet Union. These efforts were followed (Richard 1995a, b) by a study of the European experience with charts of accounts both prior to and after the Second World War.

The motivation for these research efforts may be found in the works of various European accounting scholars who sought to establish a distinctive perspective with respect to their national accounting systems. During the late nineteenth and early twentieth centuries, there were scholars in different European countries who advanced specific approaches to accounting systems for the purpose of persuading the professional and academic accounting communities of the validity of their approaches. Names like Leautey and Guilbaut (1895) in France, and Schmalenbach (1927) in Germany come to mind. Many of these efforts did not become widely known outside their home countries because they addressed a national audience and they were not often translated into the English language.

More recently, comparative studies of accounting systems written in the English language have emerged which focus on differences between Anglo-American accounting systems and those of other countries (see Choi and Mueller 1978; Nobes and Parker 1985). A common theme running through these comparative studies is that accounting systems ought to be directed towards providing useful information. This is the predominant perspective of accounting in the Anglo-American countries, and in particular with respect to providing information that is useful to investors and creditors in making investment and credit decisions. That this view of accounting has not been the predominant one in many continental European countries is not that widely acknowledged by Anglo-American scholars. We might therefore suppose that Professor Richard has been interested in investigating the history of national accounting systems in order to explain the reasons for, and perhaps to justify, the distinctions between Anglo-American accounting systems and continental European accounting systems.

With respect to the topic of charts of accounts, Professor Richard has argued that in order to better understand the development of accounting systems it would be useful to investigate the European experience with charts of accounts (Richard 1995a). While the topic of charts of accounts may not be of great interest nowadays to accounting scholars, it can be noted that there has been a considerable amount of time, money and effort devoted to the development of XBRL which appears to be a type of chart of accounts that is intended to be used on a worldwide basis (XBRL 2013).

Professor Richard began his study of charts of accounts with two articles appearing in the *European Accounting Review* (1995a, b). In these articles he indicates that there are multiple functions for charts of accounts, ranging from the pedagogical, to internal control of business organizations, to providing information to investors and creditors in making investment and credit decisions, to the control of business enterprises by the state.

Professor Richard states that industrial charts of accounts may have been used as early as the thirteenth century in Europe (Richard 1995b; Scherpf 1955). These early examples of charts of accounts were directed more towards the development of theoretical frameworks to explain double-entry bookkeeping rather than to standardize accounting records. Professor Richard points out that the early charts contained insufficient detail to allow them to be employed to manage business enterprises. In fact, he observes that the concept of creating standardized charts of accounts applicable across a range of companies and industries did not emerge before the end of the nineteenth century. He suggests that three primary factors contributed to the development of standardized charts of accounts: (1) the growth of stock markets which required improved ways to compare the performance of business enterprises; (2) a growing concentration among business enterprises and the expansion of industrial groups, providing an impetus for the development of charts of accounts that would be common across companies and industries; (3) an increase in scientific research regarding standardization in general. Professor Richard also notes that, with respect to teaching accounting, textbooks that employed charts of accounts for pedagogical purposes began to be used in several countries, including Germany (Schär 1922) and Belgium (Blairon 1926).

Professor Richard also cites Fredrick Taylor's (1911) publications regarding the scientific management of work as a factor influencing the creation of charts of accounts in Europe during the early years of the twentieth century. The skeptical and even negative reaction of German industrialists and academics to Taylor's publications led to the creation of both private and public bodies to study the scientific organization of work in Germany. Before 1930, a liberal economic ideology had prevailed in Germany, but this ideology disappeared in the face of the Weimar Republic's inability to control the inflationary German economy or to prevent the rise of National Socialism. Professor Richard indicates that the demise of liberal economic ideology led to the influence of a school of thought that was hostile to free enterprise. He cites Rathenau (1917) who argued that the German economy should be based on scientific reasoning and social responsibility; it should be a "conscious" economy able to struggle against the defects of capitalist society (recession, unemployment, etc.). For Rathenau, this new economy should be structured around three fundamental propositions: (1) the reinforcement of industrial concentration; (2) the creation of interlinked professional and corporate associations that could fix production and prices and close inefficient plants; (3) the creation of a standardized accounting information system for companies' cost and prices. There was an anti-liberal bias to these proposals.

Influenced perhaps by the intellectual atmosphere of his time, in 1927, Eugen Schmalenbach, Professor at the University of Cologne, published an accounting chart model which contained four objectives: *First*, was an educational objective, to teach accounting; *Second*, was to suggest a way of organizing business enterprises based on the principle of decentralization; *Third*, was to design an accounting information system enabling rapid decision making; *Fourth*, was to make cost accounting a useful tool for the German nation. Professor Richard (1995b) argues that the anti-Taylorist nature of Schmalenbach's work was clear when he expressed his regret that "the centralizing principles to be found in the Taylor organization process ... are dominating the majority of companies in Germany, as is also the case in the USA" (Schmalenbach 1935, p. 11). Professor Richard indicates that Schmalenbach had a strong distrust of industrial groups and cartels which, using the power of the state, sought to control prices and thereby the economy. Schmalenbach emphasized "the dangers of bureaucratic administration and state control of businesses" (Richard 1995b, p. 101; Schmalenbach 1935, p. 12).

It is therefore somewhat surprising, given Schmalenbach's relatively liberal attitude towards business economics that his chart of accounts subsequently came to have a significant influence not only on the Nazi economy, but also in France, under the Vichy government, and in the USSR, under the communist regime (Richard 1995b, p. 104). Professor Richard's conclusion regarding this apparent contradiction in Schmalenbach's work is that charts of accounts have been used in both centralized economies and capitalist economies, and that there is no necessary relationship between state control of economic activity and the existence of charts of accounts. The success of the Plan Comptable Général in France provides some evidence regarding this conclusion.

2 The Development of the French Accounting System

Professor Richard (2003b) suggests that the French accounting system developed through three distinct stages beginning with the *static* stage, from about 1800 to 1900; to the *dynamic* stage from about 1900 to 2005; and finally to the *futuristic* stage beginning with the adoption of International Financial Reporting Standards (IFRS) in 2005. These stages have been characterized by different accounting logics pertaining to the valuation of assets and the measurement of the accounting result (net profit).

During the *static* stage of the nineteenth century, there were conflicts between capitalist entrepreneurs and bankers and other creditors who provided external financing. French commercial law of the nineteenth century emphasized the rights of creditors in order to limit creditor losses in the event of bankruptcy (Hilaire 1986). The basic assumption underlying the *static* theory (Schmalenbach 1919) was that every human enterprise is mortal and may experience unexpected death at any moment. Consequently, static accounting theory and commercial jurisprudence emphasized the "principle of death" according to which it is necessary to envision the possible failure of the enterprise and then proceed as if the enterprise must be liquidated. This concept of "fictitious liquidation" requires the valuation of assets at market values. The objective is to determine the amount that is necessary to cover liabilities in the case of bankruptcy (Richard 2003b).

The *static* theory has significant implications regarding the valuation of assets, particularly intangible assets, such as organization costs, research and development, advertising, training costs and acquired goodwill, which have no ready market value. This applies as well to specialized machinery that cannot be sold. Furthermore, according to the *static* theory, not only potential losses are taken into account but also unrealized holding gains. This could be the case, for example, for land, buildings, and financial investments. Because of the difficulties associated with the recognition of unrealized holding gains, the *static* theory began to be modified during the course of the nineteenth century in order to prevent the distribution of unrealized holding gains as dividends. In first half of the nineteenth century, most French companies operated under the legal regime of unlimited liability. Some lawyers accepted the idea that unrealized holding gains could be recorded in the accounts and that the profits arising from these unrealized gains could be distributed as dividends because in the event of bankruptcy the unrealized holding gains could be recovered from the private assets of the entrepreneurs. Towards the middle of the nineteenth century, when new commercial laws allowed for the relatively easy formation of limited liability companies, the *static* theory was modified so that unrealized holding gains could no longer be distributed as dividends. In summary, the *static* theory was based on recording assets at fair values while reflecting the corresponding unrealized holding gains in special reserves or eliminating the unrealized gains from the balance sheet (a sort of "lower or cost or market rule") (Richard 2003b).

The *static* stage of French accounting was largely dominated by a doctrine of economic liberalism in which the format of the profit and loss statement was left to the discretion of the business owner, thereby leading to a wide diversity in profit and loss statements. The basic model of the profit and loss statement involved a classification of expenses by function, thereby allowing a distinction between cost of goods sold and administrative expenses (Lemarchand 1993). This concept, which is generally congruent with an integration of financial and management accounting, was also consistent with a microeconomic view of the firm which focused on the net profit available to the capitalist entrepreneur and demonstrating how that profit was produced at different stages of the production cycle.

The transition from the *static* stage to the *dynamic* stage was motivated in part by pressures from shareholders for the distribution of regular and consistent dividends. Regular and consistent dividends were not feasible when assets were measured at fluctuating fair values, or when no values at all were assigned to intangibles. The *dynamic* theory was based on the idea of recording assets at historical costs and reflecting systemic depreciation of fixed assets and amortization of other deferred costs. Schmalenbach (1919) argued in favor of this *dynamic* approach to accounting. The trend towards a *dynamic* approach was re-enforced by the appearance of the tax administration in the French accounting system. The determination of taxable profit according to the tax law involved the deduction of depreciation measured by dividing the purchase cost of the asset by the number of years of use. During the second half of the twentieth century, most French enterprises applied tax rules at the individual account level (as opposed to consolidated accounts), and these enterprises were obligated to record the legally allowable amount of depreciation in the accounts if they wanted to have depreciation recognized by the tax administration. This meant that a systematic depreciation allowance (usually straight line) without reference to market value, was the most popular method used (Richard 2003b).

After the Second World War, the *dynamic* stage of the French accounting system was incorporated into the individual accounts structure of the *Plan Comptable Géné ral*. With respect to various types of intangibles, such as organization costs, research and development, advertising, training and goodwill, these kinds of assets were required to be capitalized and amortized over a relatively short period of time (less than 5 years). In addition, the individual accounts were the only legal basis for the distribution of dividends. Shareholders wanted to have consistent dividend payments which were only achievable through the use of a systematic system of depreciation charges based on historical costs for fixed assets. In addition, individual accounts were the basis for tax determination. Therefore French enterprises, especially those which were not listed on stock exchanges, became comfortable with tax rules that provided for systematic depreciation (Richard 2003b).

After the Second World War, in a context marked by the influence of the communist and Gaullist political movements and the desire to institute production planning and re-distribution of wealth, the first attempts to construct a national system of economic information emerged. In 1947, the *Plan Comptable Général* was created with a dualist structure, pursuant to which accounts for financial accounting were separated from accounts for management accounting. There was also an attempt to promote a standardized classification of expenses by nature. This first attempt in France at a systematic and nationwide set of charts of accounts did not satisfy stakeholders and entrepreneurs, consequently, in 1982, a revised *Plan Comptable Général* gave birth to a new type of classification of expenses by nature permitting the identification of certain macroeconomic data for each enterprise, such as the measurement of value added and its distribution. However, value added was primarily used by trade unions. This type of chart of accounts was designed to permit better transparency regarding the division of wealth among various stakeholders both at the micro-economic and the macro-economic levels. This change was not well accepted and most French companies were reluctant to use the information to publish value added statements (Haller and Stolowy 1995). As a result, following pressures on the French accounting system from the Fourth European Directive and the introduction of IFRS, the French accounting system no longer includes an obligation to show profit and loss statements classified by nature (Richard 2003b). However, the debate regarding the proper way to measure the accounting result (net profit) continues to re-appear among accounting theorists and business economists, and in more recent periods, also in debates surrounding stakeholder theory and corporate social responsibility. Hence, the subject of value added and its distribution is again becoming of central importance.

3 The Transition from Socialist Accounting to Capitalist Accounting

The fall of the communism in the latter decades of the twentieth century provided an opportunity to study the impact of the transition from a communist type of accounting system to a capitalist system (Richard 2003a, p. 332). This transition offered a unique opportunity to identify those "accounting features" required for a capitalist economy that differ from the accounting features in planned and centralized economies. In this regard, Professor Richard (1997, 2000, 2003a) studied the passage from a communist accounting system to a capitalist system in several Eastern European countries. In his theoretical framework, Professor Richard included a number of categories, including: sources of accounting regulation and standards; fundamental objectives of accounting; the users of accounting information; the basic principles of accounting; basic accounting concepts; rules of valuation; structure of accounting institutions; and the existence of external audits of company accounts. He emphasized that even though the accounting transformations were similar from one country to another, numerous differences could be observed with respect to the specific changes in accounting systems, indicating that each country experiences a distinct set of accounting transformations.

Professor Richard's (1997, 2003a) work in studying the transition from communist accounting systems to capitalist accounting systems has influenced other accounting scholars, including for example Chiapello and Ding (2005). Table 1, adapted from Chiapello and Ding (2005) summarizes the accounting changes that

Table 1 Comparison of communist and capitalist systems [adapted from Chiapello and Ding (2005)]

Communism	Capitalism	Effects on accounting
Category I: Definition of the business entity		
Organized so as to produce goods by means of centralized planning of production	Focuses on profits. Invested capital must produce a profit, which is then reinvested in the business in order to generate additional profit in subsequent periods	Definition of the accounting entity Role of accounting in society Concept of capital and the definition of profit
Category II: Role of the market		
There is no market; businesses are coordinated into hierarchical systems Prices are fixed bureaucratically	There is a market and companies operate in competition with one another Prices depend on supply and demand Uncertainty regarding future prices in markets	Importance of recording receipts and expenses Role of accounting in society Conservatism principle
Category III: Capital accumulation and private ownership		
The funds required for economic activity come exclusively from the State	The funds required for economic activity come from private providers of capital	Format and definition of balance sheet assets and liabilities
The concept of profit does not exist Because incomes are determined by the state, the range of incomes is narrower The distribution of wealth is more equal and includes a wide range of social services	The reinvested profit is combined with the initial capital, which belongs to the shareholders The income of individuals is derived from their work or their capital and incomes vary widely	Definition of the company's income and profit Methods used for distribution of profits Accounting treatment of workers' salaries

Table 2 Model of accounting changes in the transition from communist accounting systems to capitalist accounting systems [adapted from Le et al. (2013)]

	Economic changes			
Accounting changes	Gradual separation of the State from the economic sphere	Alternative to centralized planning: market coordination	New conception of the firm	Financing sources: private capital
Sources of accounting regulation	Ministry of Finance	Government appointed standards setter	Standards setter with professional accounting and company representation	Independent standards setter
Objectives of financial reporting	Accounting is used to coordinate the macro economy and facilitate foreign trade	Accounting information becomes the basis for calculation of taxation	Accounting information is used in corporate governance decision making	Accounting information is used to measure the return on equity, economic performance and to help in decision making concerning the resource allocation within companies
Users of accounting information	Indirect control by the State	Information for significant shareholders (i.e. the State and State controlled banks)	Communication between the company and a growing group of stakeholders	Information for Markets and potential shareholders
Entity principle	• Withdrawal of the State from the State owned and run firms governance • Creation of Company law	The company is recognized as a legal, moral and independent person	Firm responsibility towards shareholders' equity begins	• Creation of equity accounts and birth of the notion of "Shareholders' equity"

have taken place in the transition from communist accounting to capitalist accounting in China.

In a more recent study, Le et al. (2013) have also developed a model of accounting changes in the transition from communist accounting systems to capitalist accounting systems in 14 different countries. This work has been influenced by the work of Professor Richard and reflects some of the ways that accounting institutions, principles and standards change in response to the transition from a communist accounting system to a capitalist accounting system (Table 2).

The works of Chiapello and Ding (2005) and Le et al. (2013) underscore the fact that Professor Richard has had a great influence on accounting scholarship over a period of many years.

4 A Critique of Fair Value and IFRS

Within a relatively short period of time, International Financial Reporting Standard (IFRS) have become the accounting "referential" for many countries around the world. In some quarters this has been a cause for celebration, while from others there has been considerable criticism. Even among the supporters of IFRS there has been a lack of recognition of the different ways in which IFRS has been implemented in different countries (Baker et al. 2010). Thus, it seems that there may be a considerable period of "contested" IFRS from several different perspectives.

Professor Richard (2009) argues that prior to the financial crisis of 2008 to 2014 there was a high degree of consensus regarding the importance of moving towards IFRS and the concept of "fair value" measurements. Many former advocates of fair value have become less vocal or have attempted to show that the underlying causes of the crisis did not come from IFRS but rather from the behaviours of irresponsible managers and traders. Other advocates have continued to argue that fair value is useful, but not during a financial crisis in which markets collapse. This is because during such periods, many markets become so illiquid that market values simply disappear. It is this kind of argument that has allowed the IASB and the other standards-setting bodies to justify their reversal regarding the question of measuring trading securities at fair value and to avoid the disclosure of significant drops in share prices (Richard 2009).

Professor Richard has argued that IFRS are obsolete because they do not respond to crisis situations in the contemporary world. He maintains that the reason for this is the emphasis in IFRS on providing information that is useful to investors and creditors in making investment and credit decisions; in other words, a shareholder and creditor orientation. Professor Richard argues that in an era in which environmental degradation poses a serious threat to the survival of the world, environmental and human capital should become the central focus of financial reporting (Richard 2009).

Professor Richard also argues that IFRS are dangerous because they have rejected the principle of prudence. He maintains that the roots of the 2008 financial crisis can be found in a lack of prudence by managers and shareholders who seek short-term profits. By attempting to remove the principle of prudence, the IASB has contributed to the rise of the irresponsibility of financial capitalists. Professor Richard suggests that we should abandon IFRS in favour of environmental accounting. To achieve this goal, it would be necessary to introduce greater democracy within the national and international bodies governing accounting regulation. Currently, it is primarily the representatives of financial capital who control these bodies. To change this state of affairs, representatives of human and environmental capital, with the backing of public opinion, should become more dominant (Richard 2009).

Professor Richard's critique of IFRS and fair value can be found on the website of the University of Paris-Dauphine. As such, it is not a scholarly academic publication like most of the prior work of Professor Richard discussed in this chapter. Instead, it appears to be a sort of manifesto. In this sense, the critique appears to be similar to other critiques that have been expressed by the *Critical Accounting* movement. The *Critical Accounting* movement has emerged as a counter-weight to so-called "mainstream" accounting research in the last 20 years, and as such it provides a useful viewpoint from which to reflect on contemporary accounting issues (Baker 2011). Professor Richard's academic career has been principally devoted to a series of scholarly investigations of the history of accounting systems from a comparative international perspective and his contributions to the accounting literature have been impressive and outstanding. It is therefore interesting to note this somewhat more polemical side of his academic work appearing in the later part of his career, as reflected in the critique of IFRS appearing on the University of Paris Dauphine website (Richard 2009).

In summary, then, we can say that Professor Richard has produced an important body of work which has contributed to the history of the development of accounting systems from a comparative international perspective, and that he has been an inspiring mentor to his students and his colleagues over many years.

References

Baker CR (2011) A genealogical history of positivist and critical accounting research. Account Hist 16(2):1–15

Baker CR, Biondi Y, Zhang Q (2010) Disharmony in international accounting standards setting: the Chinese approach to accounting for business combinations. Crit Perspect Account 21:107–117

Blairon H (1926) Cours complet de comptabilite des industries manufacturieres, 6th edn. La Revue Belge des Sciences Commerciales, Brussels

Chiapello E, Ding Y (2005) Searching for the accounting features of capitalism: an illustration with the economic transition process in China. Groupe HEC, Jouy-en-Josas

Choi F, Mueller G (1978) An introduction to multinational accounting. Prentice Hall, Englewood Cliffs, NJ

Haller A, Stolowy H (1995) Value added in financial accounting: a comparative study between Germany and France. HEC School of Management, Jouy-en-Josas

Hilaire J (1986) Introduction historique au droit commercial. PUF, Paris

Le T, Barbu E, Baker CR (2013) Towards a new framework to explain accounting changes in transitional economies. Proceedings of the 7th accounting history international conference, Seville, Spain, September 2013

Leautey E, Guilbaut A (1895) La sciences des comptes mise a la portee de tous. Librairie comptable et administrative, Paris

Lemarchand Y (1993) Du dépérissement à l'amortissement. Enquête sur l'histoire d'un concept et sa traduction comptable. Ouest Editions, Nantes

Nobes C, Parker R (1985) Comparative international accounting, 2nd edn. Philip Allan, London

Rathenau W (1917) Vom Akienwesen. Fisher Verlag, Frankfurt-am-Main

Richard J (1975) Etude comparative des méthodes d'analyse de la gestion des entreprises industrielles dans quatre pays appartenant à des systèmes économiques et politiques différents: Etats-Unis, France, RDA, URSS. Thèse pour le doctorat de troisième cycle, Université Panthéon–Sorbonne, Paris

Richard J (1980) Comptabilité et systèmes économiques. University Paris I, Paris
Richard J (1995a) The evolution of accounting chart models in Europe from 1900 to 1945: some historical elements. Eur Account Rev 4(1):87–124
Richard J (1995b) The evolution of the Romanian and Russian accounting charts after the collapse of the communist system. Eur Account Rev 4:305–320
Richard J (1997) Les pays de l'Europe de l'Est. In: Vuibert L (ed) Comptabilité internationale. Vuibert, Paris, pp 351–403
Richard J (2000) Comptabilité en Russie. In: Encyclopédie de comptabilité, contrôle de gestion et audit. Economica, Paris, pp 1317–1327
Richard J (2003a) Eastern Europe: from communism to capitalism. In: Walton P, Haller A, Raffounier B (eds) International accounting, 2nd edn. Thompson Learning, London, pp 332–350
Richard J (2003b) Fair value: towards a third stage of the French accounting capitalism? Cahier de recherche no. 2005–09. Université de Paris–Dauphine, Paris
Richard J (2009) The IFRS are both obsolete and dangerous. CREFIGE, University of Paris Dauphine. http://www.crefige.dauphine.fr/recherche/actualite/richard1.htm
Schär JF (1922) Buchhattung und Bilanz, 5th edn. Julius Springer, Berlin
Scherpf P (1955) Der Kontenrahmen. Max Hueber Verlag, Munich
Schmalenbach E (1919) Grundlagen dynamischer Bilanzlehre. Zeitschrift fiir Handelswissenschaftliche Eorschung 13:1–50
Schmalenbach E (1927) Der Kontenrahmen. Glöckner, Leipzig
Schmalenbach E (1935) Der Kontenrahmen (The Standard Chart of Accounts) (4th edition). G. A. Gloeckner, Leipzig
Taylor FW (1911) The principles of scientific management. Harper & Brothers, New York, NY
XBRL (2013) http://www.xbrl.org/

Frère Jacques and IFRS: Sonnez les Matines?

David Alexander

Abstract This paper in honour of Jacques Richard is framed by the well-known nursery rhyme: Frère Jacques. The theme of the paper relates to the notion of socially constructed reality, leading to inter-subjectively constructed 'facts' which are epistemologically objective, within a given community of like-minded thinkers. We consider the implications of that theme for IFRS. Should we, in the words of the nursery rhyme, ring out the bells in celebration? We have argued that IFRS are, and are explicitly declared by the IASB to be, designed for the purposes of only one of a variety of potential different user groups. These user groups have different purposes. They are all decision-makers, and they all require information. But they require different information, consistent with their different decisions. They are different epistemic communities. They have different 'realities'. They therefore have different perceptions of what does and does not constitute a true and fair view or a fair presentation of their reality. IFRS are explicitly focused on the external supplier of finance. Their focus is publicly defined, and they make genuine, if not always successful, attempts to apply it. For smaller family-financed businesses, or bank-financed businesses where the bank manager sits on the Board, or plays golf with the directors, the needs are different. This is even more true as regards prudential regulators. There are a variety of different epistemic communities, with different realities and therefore requiring, in the general case, different data in financial reports, which will require different regulations.

The paper explores the principles behind this thinking, and then in some detail the implications firstly of different users, and secondly of different valuation methods. The conclusion is that the bells of celebration should be small and muffled. To return to the French song, pour notre Frère Jacques on propose les clochettes étouffantes.

D. Alexander (✉)
University of Birmingham, Birmingham, UK
e-mail: d.j.a.alexander@bham.ac.uk

D. Bensadon, N. Praquin (eds.), *IFRS in a Global World*,
DOI 10.1007/978-3-319-28225-1_3

1 Prologue

The original French version of the song, which should be read noting that in song and poetry the mute vowels of spoken French are pronounced in full, is as follows:

Frère Jacques, frère Jacques,
Dormez-vous? Dormez-vous?
Sonnez les matines! Sonnez les matines!
Ding, daing, dong. Ding, daing, dong.

[Are you sleeping, are you sleeping,
Brother John? Brother John?
Morning bells are ringing! Morning bells are ringing!
Ding, dang, dong. Ding, dang, dong.
All English translations from French quotations are by the author].

I interpret the implications of the song as being of enthusiasm and excitement. Joie de vivre, to use a common English expression. I can think of no better evocation of the spirit of Jacques Richard as I have known him over a good many years. This paper seeks to follow this spirit in being wide-ranging and thought-provoking—being willing to follow ideas where-ever they might lead. Breadth of ideas and influences is privileged over depth. The question I shall eventually lead to is a simple one. To what extent is the advent and progress of IFRS a cause for 'enthusiasm and excitement'? To what extent should we ring out the bells in celebration?

2 Theme

Jacques Richard wrote a paper some years ago which explored the translation of the word 'accounting' into 68 languages. He will surely be sympathetic to the problem of what 'accounting' actually is. A common French suggestion, quoting a book title (Garnier 1947) is l'algèbre du droit [the algebra of law]. This is consistent with the French perception of patrimoine [translated, but never understood in the French sense, as patrimony] as a legal rather than an economic concept, embracing legally established rights and obligations. For a 'full-frontal' explanation see Aubry and Rau (1873).

But this is untypical. First of all the concept of patrimoine is restricted to 'Latin' countries (not to all 'code law' countries, it is unknown in Germany, for example). Secondly it is not universally legalistic even where it does exist. Not in Italy. Here is Besta (1909:81)

"ed è erroneo il dirlo, come fanno il Rossi ed il Cerboni, una somma di diritti e di obblighi". [It is an error to regard it as the sum of rights and obligations, as Rossi and Cerboni do.]

Secondly, and much more commonly, accounting is seen as related to economics. Here is a definition I have always liked.

"Accounting is a service activity. Its function is to provide quantitative information, primarily financial in nature, about economic entities that is intended to be useful in making economic decisions, in making resolved choices among alternative courses of action" (AICPA 1970).

Several points in this definition need to be emphasised. It clearly embraces decision usefulness, and it is restricted to 'quantitative information'. But it is not restricted to 'financial' information. It is not restricted to any particular user (decision-maker), and there is no hint of any restriction to, or even a relative importance of, suppliers of finance. It does not, either explicitly or implicitly, exclude stewardship. It is not restricted to external users. It does not seem all that far away from the much more general notion of party A 'giving an account of' their actions to party B. It is consistent with a philosophy of breadth, transparency and openness.

But this leads to a series of crucial questions. Transparency and openness about what? Transparency and openness to whom? For what decisions? In the modern legalistic jargon, financial reporting is trying to give a fair presentation (IFRS) or a true and fair view (EU Directives). We can debate what these terms mean. But the first question is: a true and fair view of what?

I am a firm believer in the proposition that most things of importance to human beings are social constructions. Metal in its natural state exists without any existence of human beings. But metal coins, and indeed the concept of money, are human creations, artefacts for the coins, and mental constructs for the money. No humans, no money. But still metal. Economic phenomena, and therefore accounting phenomena, are examples of institutional reality which is created via social processes. Reality is in principle a personal and individual belief, and my reality is unique to me. But society and what we hopefully call civilisation require cooperation, and this in turn requires that members of a particular 'community' share a common perception of reality. Such agreed reality can become an institutional fact, a 'fact' which is socially constructed. As Alexander and Archer (2003:5) put it "By virtue of collective intentionality, ownership claims, income, and other conceptual objects of accounting can, under appropriate conditions, be institutional facts". Such institutional facts can become epistemologically objective, though they are always ontologically subjective. But they only become epistemologically objective by agreement within the relevant community, and this can only be achieved by social communication. This requires the use of language (here very broadly defined as a semiotic system capable of being recognised by one or more human senses).

In summary, the economic phenomena that financial reporting seeks to represent are inter-subjectively constructed social facts. So we as accountants are trying to give a true and fair view of something which is itself a subjective human construct. So we have the phenomenon, which is a subjective human construct, we have the linguistic communication mechanism, which is a subjective human construct, and we have the receiver of the communication, who is a human being and a subjective thinker by definition. It follows that whether a particular description as interpreted by a particular receiver is 'true and fair' is determined by the existence, or not, of a commonality or coherence of the various subjectivities. It is not a matter of correspondence between communication and phenomenon, which implies objectivity. It is at best a matter of coherence between the various, and in principle variable, subjectivities involved.

Alexander and Archer (2003) distinguish a correspondence theory of truth (CTT) from a coherence theory of truth (CT). With a CTT there is an underlying reality, to which the representation *corresponds* if the representation is true. But with the CT there is no underlying reality; there is only a series of different, and differently perceived, representations, and the most we can aim at is *coherence* between these different representations and perceptions. It is clear from the previous paragraph that I hold strongly to the coherence theory. There *is* no underlying reality independent of the human viewer. Alexander and Archer (2003:6) quote from the FASB's Statement of Accounting Concepts No 2 (FASB 1980) which defines representational faithfulness as 'correspondence or agreement between a measure or description and the phenomenon that it purports to represent'. We can update this by reference to the IASB conceptual framework as of 2014, which contains the identical idea in paragraph QC12: 'Financial reports represent economic phenomena in words and numbers. To be useful, financial information must not only represent relevant phenomena, but it must also faithfully represent the phenomena which it purports to represent'. But this just does not work. A faithful representation is dependent on time, place and circumstance, and its existence is a matter of pragmatism and socially-constructed coherence. Different ways of doing accounting may be equally 'faithful', in their different contexts. There is no 'right or wrong', but there is a need for coherence between the accounting presentation on the one hand, and the context on the other. So for example there needs to be coherence between the letters ASSET and the perception of the underlying phenomenon. Both the arrangement of the letters and the concept itself are subjective social constructs.

Do we, as accountants, really know what we mean by the word 'asset'? The IASB certainly do not. Here is the current conceptual framework definition (Sect. 4.4(a)): 'An asset is a resource controlled by an entity as a result of past events and from which future economic benefits are expected to flow'. A key concept here is the need for 'expectation'. And here is the suggestion in the IASB's July 2013 'Review of the Conceptual Framework for Financial Reporting', paragraph 2.11: An asset should be 'a present economic resource controlled by an entity as a result of past events', where an economic resource is: 'a right, or other source of value, that is capable of producing economic benefits'. The key concept here is the need for the resource to be 'capable of producing'. This is a much lower requirement than an expectation. A positive 'expectation' is proposed to be changed into a mere 'capability'. Here is the current French definition (PCG section 211.1; down-loaded 20/03/14).'Un actif est un élément identifiable du patrimoine ayant une valeur économique positif pour l'entité, c'est-à-dire un élément générant une ressource que l'entité contrôle du fait d'événements passés et dont elle attend des avantages économiques futurs'. [An asset is an identifiable element of 'patrimoine' having a positive economic value to the entity, that is to say an element which generates a resource which is controlled by the entity through past events, and from which future benefits are awaited.] This is obviously influenced by the international thinking. But it is not identical to it. The use of 'attendre', which is more than 'capability' but less than 'expectation', is a particularly interesting nuance.

Firstly, notice that the IASB refers to 'a resource', but the PCG refers to 'an element which generates a resource'. So, to the IASB an asset is directly itself a resource. But to the PCG it is not, itself, a resource. It is an 'element of patrimony' which then generates 'the resource'. Interestingly, the comment letter on this 'review', written directly in English, sent by the French regulator, the ANC, on 14 February 2014 states on page 7: 'In fact, under the current framework there was no doubt for the ANC as to the fact that the asset is the resource (and not the expected flows of economic benefits) in any of the examples provided in paragraph 2.14'. This seems clearly inconsistent with the definition in the PCG. So perhaps the French regulator does not read the French regulations? Secondly, the PCG introduces a further concept, that of 'patrimoine', but does not attempt to define it. We have discussed patrimoine briefly above. The PCG definition of asset refers to 'avantages économiques', and does not contain the word 'juridique'. So has 'patrimoine' as used today in the PCG lost its traditional legalistic (in France) connotations?

The conclusion is surely clear. We as accountants do not know what we mean by 'asset'. How can we possibly claim, and audit the proposition, that any particular representation 'corresponds' to something when we do not know what it is ourselves? The most we can even try to do is to be coherent. Even here, one wonders......

I now illustrate some implications of these arguments (explore variations on my theme) in relation to the implications of different users (variation 1), and to considerations of different valuation methods (variation 2). I conclude, in proper form both musical and academic, with a coda.

3 Variation 1

By way of introduction regarding users, I quote from Baert and Yanno (2009). 'Cependant, tout en levant le voile sur la fiction du patrimoine juridique, l'approche économique de la comptabilité qui est celle des normes IFRS apparaît quelque peu biaisée par l'orientation de celles-ci vers les investisseurs. En effet, il n'existe pas une réalité économique par nature. Comme en physique quantique, les caractéristiques d'un objet variant selon le point de vue, et il y a autant « d'images fidèles » pertinentes de l'entreprise que d'utilisateurs de la comptabilité. Les normes IFRS ne donnent donc à voir qu'une certaine réalité économique, celle propre à satisfaire les besoins d'informations des seuls investisseurs; mais rien ne dit que les autres utilisateurs de ces normes y trouveront leur compte'. [However, while lifting the veil of the legal patrimonial fiction, the IFRS economic approach to accounting appears somewhat biased by its orientation towards investors. Indeed, a single natural economic reality does not exist. As in quantum physics, the characteristics of an object vary depending on the point of view, and there are as many "true and fair views" relevant to an enterprise as there are users of the accounts. The IFRS standards only give one particular economic reality that which satisfies the information needs of individual investors, but nobody can say that the other users of the accounts will find their requirements there.]

I am very supportive of this statement in all its nuances. It embraces the inter-subjectivity between 'object' and 'point of view'. It explicitly recognises the existence of multiple 'true and fair views'. It even refers to the legal connotations of 'patrimoine' as 'a fiction'! Finally, it rightly and properly recognises what IFRS standards are trying to do, and what they are not trying to do. They *are* trying to be useful to investors and suppliers of finance, they are *not* trying to be useful to creditors, banking regulators and a host of other possible users. User groups, in the terminology developed in this paper, are epistemic communities. As we said earlier, institutional facts, realities, socially constructed 'truths', only exist within the community which accepts them—indeed, only by such acceptance are they created in the first place. A coherency between perceived true and fair view and the phenomenon being 'viewed' requires like-minded thinking and like-minded objectives.

The statement by Baert and Yanno that the IASB has a focus on 'investors' is demonstrably correct. In the 2010 version of the Framework the Board now states (para OB 2): "the objective of general purpose financial reporting (GPFR) is to provide financial information about the reporting entity which is useful to existing and potential investors, lenders, and other creditors in making decisions about providing resources to the entity," and continues (para OB 10): "other parties, such as regulators and members of the public other than investors, lenders and other creditors, may also find GPFRs useful. However those reports are not primarily directed to these other groups." This is unequivocal, and much clearer than the earlier 1989 version was, which did rather claim that IFRS (then IAS of course) were useful to everybody. So, explicitly, 'regulators' (banking regulators were surely in mind) are not expected to find IFRS regulations 'useful'.

Much of the French accounting world is suspicious, or actively critical, of the IASB. The view could be taken, of course, that the epistemic community which is French accounting at the national level, in France for French purposes, with French users and decision-makers, within the French economic, legal and finance-raising context, is entitled to be distinctively 'French'. I would agree completely, and this follows from my theoretical exposition. Indeed I would go further. It *should* be distinctly French. To the, in some ways considerable, extent that it is not properly French (and it is not for me to say in detail what that means), the French have only themselves to blame. Here are Baert and Yanno again, referring to the years immediately before and after 2000. 'Il est regrettable que la décision de faire converger le droit comptable français vers les normes IFRS—aussi justifiée qu'elle soit—ait été l'œuvre du seul CNC et que les modalités de cette convergence aient été définies dans le secret de ses délibérations .... l'alignement s'est ainsi fait au « pas de charge », bouleversant en quelques années les pratiques de millions d'entreprises'. [It is regrettable that the decision to converge French accounting law towards IFRS standards—however justified it may be—was the work of the CNC alone, and that the details of this convergence were defined in secret deliberation. . . . . .the transition has been made "at the gallop" changing drastically in a few years the practices of millions of businesses.] Alexander et al. (2011:150), writing in French, give a detailed illustration relating to IAS 37, complete with quotes claiming justification for the wholesale adoption. The claimed justification is that the existence or otherwise of a provision or contingency *must* be equally (un)likely in group accounts as in individual entity accounts, and therefore that identical accounting regulations are required. But this argument is invalid, as it ignores the multiple true and fair view point, and therefore the need for different numbers for different purposes, so clearly seen by Baert and Yanno. The financial *evaluation* of this likelihood may be quite different for investor purposes (the group) as compared with, for example, creditor or dividend calculation purposes (the individual entity). The reference by Alexander and Segura (2010) to 'une balle dans le pied' [a self-inflicted wound, literally shooting oneself in the foot] is surely justified.

But it is not only French writers and regulators who have ignored the 'relevance for specific user needs' point so clearly put by Baert and Yanno. The process of introducing IFRS into the European Union produced three major documents from Brussels, in 1995, 2000 and 2002. The latter two were 'European Commission (2000) Communication from the Commission to the Council and the European Parliament: EU financial reporting strategy: the way forward, COM (2000) 359 final', and 'European Parliament and Council (2002) Regulation (EC) No.1606/2002 of the European Parliament and of the Council of 19 July 2002 on the application of international accounting standards, Official Journal of the European Communities, L 243, pp. 1–4, 11 September 2002, (the IAS Regulation)'.

In the light of later attacks on IFRS in general, and fair value in particular, by banks, banking regulators and others, it is worth drawing attention to footnote 11 of the 2000 Communication, as detailed above: "The Commission proposal does not address supervisory issues and the specific information required by supervisory authorities. The implementation of the proposal should not lead to a lessening of the prudential requirements for regulated entities". In other words, the Commission believes (believed in 2000) that IAS are implicitly unsuitable for, and explicitly are not recommended to be used for, prudential regulation by supervisory authorities. All mention of this qualification had disappeared in the final 2002 'regulation'. As is well known, IFRS were indeed used by the Basel banking regulatory system after 2005, with disastrous results. The banking regulators have relied on IFRS too much, rather than doing their own rational thinking and setting up their own standards. The stupidity—the word is surely justified—of using information explicitly not designed for such purposes, and demonstrably not suitable for such purposes, is entirely the fault of the 'prudential regulators' concerned. The epistemologically objective reality of the banking community, inter-subjectively constructed within that community, is, and is demonstrably, incompatible with the very different epistemologically objective reality of the distinct and separate corporate investment community. The philosophical underpinnings of this paper are supported, and illustrated in operation.

4 Variation 2

An interest very much shared between Jacques and myself concerns income measurement and asset valuation. He has published extensively in the area, in both English and French. The topic is an enormous one, and I make no attempt at anything remotely approaching a comprehensive survey here. I address two issues, the role of fair values, and the role of replacement cost.

The term 'fair value' has been used with many meanings. In particular, on the one hand, it has been used as a 'catch-all' label for current values of more-or-less any kind (including in the past by Jacques), and on the other hand it has been used by regulators for a variety of specific proposals. Here I address purely the concept of fair value as used by IASB. Following certain changes of wording and punctuation in the 1980s, the IASC definition of fair value settled down to that in para 7 of IAS 18 as issued in 1993: "Fair value is the amount for which an asset could be exchanged, or a liability settled, between knowledgeable, willing parties in an arm's length transaction". Whether the IASC thought they knew exactly what this meant at the time is an open question. In its then new quarterly newsletter, Insight, for October 2001 (IASB 2001:14), the newly created IASB stated: "At some stage, the Board will need to address other issues, for example: should fair value be considered to be an entry value (including buying costs), exit value (deducting selling costs) or something in between entry value and exit value?" This quotation obviously suggests that the IASB did not understand the definition they had inherited. An exchange price, by definition, must be the same for both parties in the exchange. So, as then defined, transaction costs of both parties had to be excluded from the evaluations. In practice as required by particular standards, the logic of his argument was sometimes followed and sometimes ignored.

But the definition is now changed. IFRS 13 'Fair Value Measurement' was issued by IASB in 2011, and is now fully operational. This, ignominiously following the coat-tails of a unilateral declaration by the US FASB (issued at a time of supposedly developing 'convergence'!), changed the definition of Fair Value to an explicitly exit (selling price) concept. Fair Value is now (IFRS 13 Appendix A) "The price that would be received to sell an asset or paid to transfer a liability in an orderly transaction between market participants at the measurement date". This definition is automatically inserted into all standards referring to fair value, except, surely bizarrely, IAS 17 and IFRS 2, which retain the old (different and inconsistent) definition. As regards transaction costs, para 25 of IFRS 13 states that "The price... used to measure the fair value of the asset or liability shall not be adjusted for transaction costs". However para 26 states that transaction costs do not include transport costs. So fair value excludes transaction costs, but transport costs are excluded from the exclusion. This applies, for example, to IAS 40, which contains no mention of transaction costs (and investment properties are not transportable), so the IFRS 13 statements apply in full. 'Pure' fair value is to be used for the asset evaluation. But IAS 41 now states that a biological asset shall be measured... at its fair value less costs to sell, where 'fair value' is already net of transport costs to the market. The resulting number is of course lower than 'pure' fair value, so there is a clear inconsistency between the two standards. Both standards invoke fair value, one with option and one without, but they use fair value in different and quite incompatible ways.

Returning to the basic principles as of 2013, fair value is a market-specific selling price concept, usually more-or-less gross of transaction costs. It is in essence an estimate of the cash flow which would result if the asset was sold today. But as such it has two theoretical flaws. The first is that it is not net of transaction costs, so it is an overestimate of expected cash flows. The second, perhaps partly related, is that it is market specific not entity specific. For both these reasons it is not a good estimate of the cash flows that the particular entity would receive if the asset were sold today. Further, of course, it *wasn't* sold today because it is still in the balance sheet. Fair value is not in general an estimate of the present value of the cash flows which will result when it is actually expected to be sold or used at some future time. So is it useful? Does it carry informational value?

My answer would be that it is an opportunity cost concept. It is broadly (ignoring the two flaws mentioned above) an indication of the cash flows *sacrificed* by retaining the asset for its normal business use. The business had the opportunity to dispose of the asset before the balance sheet date, and did not do so. It has therefore lost, given up, and sacrificed, this possible cash flow. This is genuinely useful information. It is relevant to the appraisal of management competence and management decisions; did management act wisely by *not* selling? But is it a good measure of current performance, and therefore by extension a good indicator of future performance? Does it provide, as a measurement and reporting concept, the information that the explicitly declared chosen 'customers' of IASB, the particular epistemic community which they seek to serve, namely 'existing and potential investors, lenders, and other creditors', need for future decision-making, crucially and necessarily linked to expected cash flows? As the Framework states in para OB3, "existing and potential investors, lenders and other creditors need information to help them assess the prospects for future net cash inflows to an entity". Note that 'to an entity' is certainly entity-specific! So fair value is explicitly, as shown here for several reasons, not designed to provide the required information.

A widely supported reaction to this conclusion seems to be that we should therefore stick to 'traditional' historical cost accounting and the good old 'prudence principle'. The letter of comment from the ANC to the IASB, sent on 14 February 2014, in relation to the proposals for revising the Framework states inter alia that: 'we are convinced that:

(i) The principle of prudence, which implies an asymmetry in the accounting of assets and liabilities, should be kept in the framework from which it was removed in 2010;
(ii) The principle of reliability should equally be preserved contrary to the framework finalised in 2010 and to proposals in the DP'.

But Jacques and I have both argued publically that this does not work. Replacement cost thinking is required.

Consider the simplest of examples. An enterprise has a business model to buy and sell one item at a time. Capital is 100. Buy for 20 (historical 'actual/factual' cost). Buying price rises to 40. Sell for 50. Maximise distribution to owners. Replace for 40 and repeat the process to infinity. How much can be distributed? Using historical cost we have revenue of 50 and cost of 20. After the sale is made the difference of 30 is realized, so can safely be distributed. So cash, originally 100, becomes $100 - 20 + 50 - 30 - 40 = 60$. And the business has contracted! The original 100, before purchase of the first unit, remains as 100, before the purchase of the second unit. But the net cash inflow from the first unit, of $50 - 20$, which under historical cost accounting is also the net income of revenues less expenses, of $50 - 20$, needs to be regarded as two elements: the holding gain of 20 $(40 - 20)$ and the operating gain of 10 $(50 - 40)$. The holding gain of 20 needs to be retained ('permanently held') and is not available for distribution. Only 10 can be distributed, and indeed the profit, the improvement in operating capability, is also rationally and economically only 10. This conclusion applies whether the revenues are realized or not. So the prudence principle and historical cost combine to report an economically excessive distributable profit of 30, whereas the rational increase in economic wealth/resources/net assets is only 10. The prudence implied by the 'prudence principle' is completely false. Combined with acceptance of the principle that realised profits are distributable (as in law they are), it leads to entity failure in the long run. The creditors will lose out, from this method of accounting which claims to be designed for their interests!

The ANC letter referenced above actually states on page 10 as follows: 'At a time when the IASB reaffirms that the objective of accounting is to help users in assessing future cash-flows, the role of cash generation and capital maintenance in the determination of profit should not only be maintained in the framework but also reinstated in practice in standard setting'. Quite so! Therefore historical cost must be rejected, as our little example shows. But the new Directive, 2013/34/EU, issued on 26 June 2013 to replace the earlier 4th and 7th Directives, whilst certainly allowing both historical cost and fair value, has attempted to exclude the possibility of replacement cost accounting altogether. This is economic nonsense, as Jacques and I have argued in the past, both separately and in the same room.

5 CODA

The theme of this paper relates to the notion of socially constructed reality, leading to inter-subjectively constructed 'facts' which are epistemologically objective, *within a given community of like-minded thinkers*. Consistently with the overall declared focus of this whole volume, we consider the implications of that theme for IFRS. We have argued that IFRS are, and are explicitly declared by the IASB to be, designed for the purposes of only one of a variety of potential different user groups. These user groups have different purposes. They are all decision-makers, and they all require information. But they require different information, consistent with their different decisions. They are different epistemic communities. They have different 'realities'. They therefore have different perceptions of what does and does not constitute a true and fair view or a fair presentation of their reality. I attempt no exhaustive list. IFRS are explicitly focused on the external supplier of finance. I do not comment here on whether they operate this focus well. I simply comment that their focus is publicly defined, and they make genuine attempts to apply it. For smaller family-financed businesses, or bank-financed businesses where the bank manager sits on the Board, or plays golf with the directors, the needs are different. These are a different epistemic community, with different realities and therefore requiring, in the general case, different data in financial reports, which will require different regulations. If France has a preponderance of one type of community and the U.K. has a different preponderance, different reporting principles and numbers are implied. We could go on at length: taxation, employees, local communities, emerging/developing economies, sustainability, environment. . . . . . The reader can fill in the details. The principle of distinction, of considering the telos involved in the reporting (accounting, in the general sense of giving an account of) process, is constant.

So what about the bells? IFRS are very much with us. Should we all wake up in the morning and 'sonnent les matines'? It is easy to criticise the IASB on efficiency, and on detail. As IASC/IASB they have, to give one example, been engaged in the process of replacing the original leasing standard since, at the latest, 1999. 16 years and still counting! But I stay at the higher level. To paraphrase Voltaire, in an age of global business, if the IASB did not exist, would it be necessary to invent it? My answer is an unequivocal yes. But its usefulness has to be understood and accepted in practical operation. Further, and crucially, its areas of uselessness have to be understood and accepted in practical operation also. We, as a profession and as a discipline, and perhaps especially the politicians and bureau(Euro)crats who interfere in the reporting process for their own ends against the needs and interests of ordinary citizens, have not done very well in this respect in recent years. The variability and subjectivity of the necessary 'realities' needs to be better understood and better respected.

I suggest that the bells of celebration should be small and muffled. To return to the French song with which we began, pour notre Frère Jacques on propose les clochettes étouffantes.

References

AICPA (1970) Accounting Principles Board, Statement No. 4, 'Basic Concepts and Accounting Principles Underlying Financial Statements or Business Enterprises', paragraph 40. American Institute of Certified Public Accountants, New York

Alexander D, Archer S (2003) On economic reality, representational faithfulness and the "true and fair override". Account Bus Res 33(1):3–17

Alexander D, Segura N (2010) France and international accounting standards: une balle dans le pied. EAA Congress, Istanbul, May

Alexander D, Delvaille P, Eglem J-Y (2011) Quelques réflexions sur le traitement de la valeur des actifs immobilisés dans les états financiers. In: Simon C, Hoarau C, Malo JL (eds) Comptabilité, Contrôle et Société; mélanges en l'honneur du Professeur Alain Burlaud. Foucher, France

Aubry C, Rau C (1873) Théorie du Patrimoine, 4th edn. http://droit.wester.ouisse.free.fr/pages/brocantes/aubry_rau_patrimoine.htm

Baert D, Yanno G (2009) Rapport d'Information par la Commission des Finances, de l'Économie Générale et du Plan, No. 1508, presented to the Assemblée Nationale, 10 March

Besta F (1909) La Ragioneria, seconda edizione, Volume I, parte prima Ragioneria generale, Milano, Vallardi

FASB (1980) Statement of Financial Concepts No. 2: Qualitative Characteristics of Accounting Information. Stamford, CT. FASB

Garnier P (1947) La comptabilité, algèbre du droit, méthode d'observation des sciences. Dunod, Paris

IASB (2001) Insight. October. London. IASB

An Institutional Theory Perspective on Accounting Evolution: Rulemakers' Belief and Empirical Evidence

Hideki Fujii

Abstract In recent years, why have we so often observed the setting of accounting rules that are *not* in keeping with, or have even gone against, the empirical evidence shown by archival studies? And, if these accounting rules are not based on *facts* that have been reported in the form of empirical evidence, then what has determined this rulemaking? Through answering these two questions, this paper demonstrates the formation process of accounting rules and the possibilities that exist for them to evolve, chiefly based on Comparative Institutional Analysis. The discussion and analysis show that rulemakers' belief in "protecting the market" has been overriding the facts that stem from the market and playing a key role in standards setting process. The absence or presence of value relevance of accounting information is not the guideline for rulemaking but the result of it. As market participants become more acquainted with a new rule, their understanding of the accounting information supplied under the rule becomes institutionalized, which may explain evolutionary process of institutional change in accounting as a whole.

1 Introduction

The aim of this paper is to demonstrate the formation process of accounting rules and the possibilities that exist for them to evolve. In this paper, accounting rule is considered an *institution* and the discussion is chiefly based on Comparative Institutional Analysis (CIA),[1] a new institutional economics that provides theoretical tool to analyze changing process of institution. In CIA, an institution is something that arises when people strategically interact in domains such as politics,

[1] CIA is a new economics, which is to analyze variety and dynamism of economic systems by regarding them as an aggregate of various institutions. For this purpose, CIA generally uses applied micro economics and Evolutionary Game Theory. See Aoki (2001) for a basic theoretical overview of CIA.

H. Fujii (✉)
Graduate School of Economics, Kyoto University, Kyoto, Japan
e-mail: hujii@econ.kyoto-u.ac.jp

D. Bensadon, N. Praquin (eds.), *IFRS in a Global World*,
DOI 10.1007/978-3-319-28225-1_4

economy, society, and organizations to become a self-enforcing rule that each and everybody accepts as a given (Aoki 2001, 2002). Under CIA, the process of a norm becoming a social rule can be understood as institutionalization.

While mainly using U.S. examples to be investigated because of their decisive influence on other countries including Japan, this paper will refer to the International Accounting Standards Committee (IASC), International Accounting Standards Board (IASB) and Japanese cases (e.g., Accounting Standards Board of Japan) as well where necessary.

The investigation is primarily based on the following two questions. First, in recent years, why have we so often observed the setting of accounting rules that are *not* in keeping with the empirical evidence demonstrated by archival studies?[2] (Research Question 1) Second, if these accounting rules are not based on facts that have been demonstrated in the form of empirical evidence, then what has determined this rulemaking? (Research Question 2) In the following sections, the author will attempt to answer these two questions. It is hoped that this investigation will lead to an analytical explanation of the patterns behind the changes in accounting rules.

In this paper, the term "practice" is used in the broad sense—at the macro level (the level of standard-setting) as well as at the micro level (the level of accounting choice by individual companies). The reason is that the investigation focuses on interaction of economic agents who choose accounting rules at both levels, the process of which results in formation and/or evolution of accounting institution.

2 Identifying the Basic Facts: Situating Archival Studies within Accounting Research

The investigation begins with identifying the basic facts. Table 1 shows the types of papers that have been published in three main accounting journals (*Accounting Review*, *Journal of Accounting Research*, and *Journal of Accounting and Economics*) over the 5-year period 2001–2005. As seen there, 481 articles were published in these journals during this period, of which 344 (71.5 %) were archival studies. In Table 1, (a) value relevance analysis is a study that tests the correlation between accounting information and market indicators (investment return, stock prices, etc.). And, (b) agency cost analysis is a study based on Agency Theory that investigates the causal relationship between accounting information and the behaviors of economic agents minimizing their agency costs. All other types of archival studies are classified as (c) other archival studies.

[2] In this paper, the term "archival study" is used to mean accounting research, the main aim of which is to find out correlation between variables by statistical analysis of archival data. They are also referred to as "empirical study."

Table 1 Archival studies published in the three main accounting journals (2001–2005) ( )%

	Accounting Review		Journal of Accounting Research		Journal of Accounting and Economics	
1. Total published papers	210	(100.0)	159	(100.0)	112	(100.0)
2. Archival studies	145	(69.0)	113	(71.1)	86	(76.8)
(a) Value relevance analysis	77	(36.7)	72	(45.3)	56	(50.0)
(b) Agency cost analysis	57	(27.1)	39	(24.5)	30	(26.8)
(c) Other archival studies	11	(5.2)	2	(1.3)	0	(0.0)
3. Others	65	(31.0)	46	(28.9)	26	(23.2)

Source: Compiled based on papers published in each journal from 2001 to 2005

All of the studies that do not belong under (a) to (c) are classified as others. The main research in this category comprises theoretical studies based on mathematical models (67 studies) and research informed by experimental accounting (56 studies).

Table 1 constitutes merely a broad overview of accounting research over the 5-year period. Besides, it is difficult to classify some of the papers solely into one category, and the results shown in Table 1 are therefore not to be considered perfect. Yet, in spite of such limitations, it can be said that it is undisputable that archival studies have become an important trend in accounting research. This is also consistent with recent developments in accounting research in Japan. Archival studies now constitute such an overwhelming trend that it is not possible to omit their existence when discussing the significance of accounting research. Thus, if the findings by archival studies have almost *never* been reflected in accounting rulemaking, this leads to question the *raison d'être* of accounting research in society.

3 Empirical Evidence and Rulemaking

In recent years—specifically since the Financial Accounting Standards Board (FASB) was established in 1973—we have quite often observed accounting rulemaking that is not in keeping with the empirical evidence demonstrated by archival studies. This section briefly confirms the situation by referring to the following three topics: (1) cash flow vs. accounting profit, (2) comprehensive income vs. net income, and (3) auditor independence. These three have become focal points of discussion and contention in the realm of rulemaking in recent years.

3.1 Cash Flow vs. Accounting Profit

From the late 1980s through to the 1990s, phrases such as "cash is king" (Copeland et al. 1990, p. 73) and "cash is fact, and accounting profit is opinion" (Wei 2002) became popular particularly in the field of business valuation. Accounting profit includes accruals that reflect the manager's intent through their choice of or change in accounting policies. Since cash flow does not include this kind of bias, the basic argument behind these phrases is that cash flow information is more useful than accounting profit for investment decision-making purposes. Many countries in succession, recognizing the importance of these arguments, proceeded to set their own accounting standards related to cash flow statement (Japanese standard was set in 1998), and the cash flow statement evolved globally into the "third financial statement."

Although archival studies in U.S. and other countries including Japan that had investigated the comparative advantages of the usefulness of cash flow vs. accounting profit recognized the incremental information value of cash flow, almost all studies have presented empirical evidence demonstrating the relatively higher value relevance of accounting profit. That is, archival studies have consistently reported that, in terms of value relevance, the "king" is accounting profit rather than cash flow.[3]

3.2 Comprehensive Income vs. Net Income

The traditional concept of accounting profit has also been criticized from the asset and liability view of accounting.[4] The focal point behind this criticism is that net income, which is based on the allocation of cash flow, is prone to distortion by management intent whereas comprehensive income is based on stock valuation and therefore constitutes clear and objective information. Papers arguing for the necessity of adopting this perspective in standard-setting were published in particularly high numbers during the late 1990s through to the early 2000s. The G4+1 (1999) and IASC (2001) were considered representative of this trend. They argued for a rejection of realization as recognition criterion of accounting profit and the prohibition of the recycling (reclassification) of other comprehensive income. In other words, they wanted to see net income excluded from financial performance reporting and comprehensive income presented as the one and only profit there.

[3] The examples of such studies are Dechow (1994), Penman and Sougiannis (1998), Quirin et al. (1999), Francis et al. (2000), Fujii and Yamamoto (2001).

[4] The asset and liability view is a view of accounting which defines income primarily in terms of increase and decrease in assets and liabilities for a period, not in difference between revenues and expenses. It was formally discussed for the first time in FASB (1976) as a foundation that should be chosen for standards setting.

The FASB/IASB Joint Project of Financial Performance Reporting by Business Enterprises that was launched in 2004 followed this argument by proposing introduction of a new financial performance reporting without net income (FASB 2005).

Yet, almost all archival studies in U.S. and other countries including Japan that had investigated the comparative advantages of the value relevance of comprehensive income vs. net income presented empirical evidence demonstrating that comprehensive income did not have more value relevance than net income.[5]

3.3 Auditor Independence

Auditing today operates under a system of dual responsibility whereby responsibilities are clearly delineated into drawing up financial statements (the company's responsibility) and giving an opinion on whether the financial statements are presented fairly (the auditor's responsibility). The main point of this principle is auditor independence. Thus, until now, the Securities and Exchange Commission's (SEC) main role vis-à-vis professional accountants has centered on ensuring compliance with auditor independence requirements.

One of the main factors that the SEC has considered as impeding auditor independence has been an auditor providing audit and non-audit services to the same company. This is because it was thought that the provision of non-audit services, such as consulting or tax services, generates a conflict of interests, which can have a negative impact on auditor independence. From the late 1990s onwards, this view informed the SEC's efforts to gradually expand regulations on non-audit services. The most decisive development came with the Sarbanes-Oxley Act of 2002 (subsequently, "SOX"). Under SOX, an auditor is prohibited from carrying out the nine non-audit services (Sec. 201). Thus, the provision of non-audit services by an auditor, particularly consulting services, was in effect positioned as an illegal activity.

However, the empirical evidence presented by archival studies carried out in U.S. and other countries for the causal relationship between non-audit services and auditor independence have mostly demonstrated no statistically significant relationship between the two. In other words, almost all archival studies have continuously reported that a systematic dependency of the auditor on the client company, problematized by the SEC and parliament, had not been observed.[6]

It should be added that SOX prohibited auditors from auditing the same company for more than 5 years because it had been judged that auditing the same company over the long term generates a cozy relationship between the client

---

[5] The examples of such studies are Cheng et al. (1993), Dhaliwal et al. (1999), O'Hanlon and Rope (1999), Wakabayashi (2014).

[6] The examples of such studies are Simunic (1984), Craswell et al. (2002), DeFond et al. (2002), Ashbaugh et al. (2003), Larcker and Richardson (2004).

company and the auditor, which would have a negative impact on auditor independence (Sec. 203, SOX). However, Myers et al. (2003) actually reported a positive correlation between the auditor's length of service and quality of earnings. Similarly, Ghosh and Moon (2005) reported a positive correlation between the quality of earnings, the quality of auditing, and the auditor's length of service. These archival studies presented empirical evidence that the quality of earnings and of the auditing itself improves with the length of service. These findings show that the aforementioned prohibition set out in Sec. 203 of SOX is not empirically supported.

4 Features of Rulemaking and Basic Patterns

4.1 What Has Determined Rulemaking?

The literature review in the previous section confirmed that accounting rulemaking in recent years has quite often *not* been in keeping with the empirical evidence demonstrated by archival studies. In this sense, it could be said that recent rulemaking has basically not been implemented based on *fact*. In the social sciences, a transcendental, and thus unfalsifiable, factor that does not depend on fact is known as a "belief." If it would be this kind of transcendental factor that has determined rulemaking in recent years, it could only be belief. This would now enable us to answer Research Question 2, set out at the start of this paper.

The beliefs of the rulemakers, particularly those of the FASB and the IASB, stand like a wall in the way of the empirical evidence, preventing the findings by archival studies being applied to rulemaking (see Fig. 1). The only thing that can pass through the wall of belief is empirical evidence that is consistent with the belief. Facts are powerless in the face of belief. Statements by archival researchers, for example, that it wouldn't be possible to design effective policies without in-depth knowledge of the real world (Okabe 1985, p. 18) or that constructive arguments based on evidence from archival studies would lead to the creation of more appropriate disclosure systems (Suda 2004, p. i), have not shown any signs of reaching the ears of the rulemakers, or at least not yet.

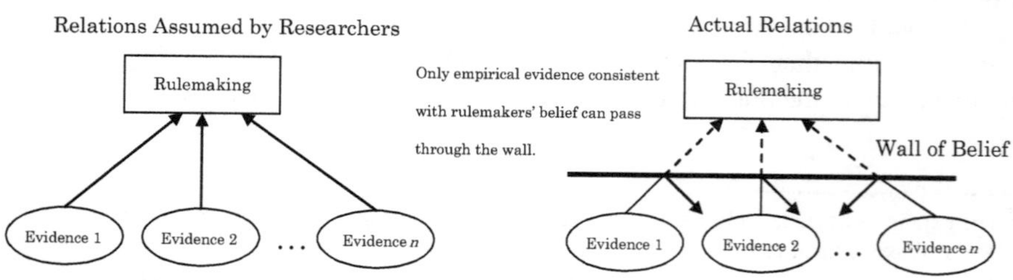

Fig. 1 Relations between empirical evidence and rulemaking

4.2 The Significance of Rulemaking Derived from Belief

In Sect. 3 we saw some typical cases of accounting rulemaking that has not been in keeping with, or even gone against, the empirical evidence reported by archival studies. This observation implies that the accounting rules have not been determined by the facts in market, but the beliefs of those who set them. If so, this raises an incidental question: in such strongly market-oriented U.S. economy, why were these non-market-oriented rules set? If they were determined by beliefs that did not fit with market facts, there must have been some kind of social significance and/or rationality for this to have been maintained almost consistently for more than a quarter of a century.

Yano (2005) provides a useful viewpoint to answer this question. Yano (2005, p. 16) argued that the twentieth century was a time when rules were implemented to protect the market in order to secure the quality of competition and information. Always considering the case of U.S. as a prototype of the scenario, the gist of what Yano (2005) is arguing can be summarized as follows.

During the Industrial Revolutions, discontinuous technological innovation improving product quality led the way, and the quality of competition and information, unable to catch up, fell out of balance with the technology and declined. Since there was the risk that the market itself would collapse if this state of imbalance was not addressed, rules were implemented to prevent such a situation. For example, during the First Industrial Revolution, when industrial capitalism was established in the nineteenth century, in order to avert the risk of the labor market collapsing as a result of the considerable power imbalance between the workforce and capitalist management, a whole range of social welfare rules were established, e.g., the Acts from the mid-19th century, which guaranteed workers' rights. During the Second Industrial Revolution, when financial capitalism was established at the beginning of the twentieth century, in order to avert the risk of a capital market collapse as a result of crashing stock prices, the Securities Acts 1933 and 1934 were enforced with the aim of restoring order and stability to the capital market. During the Third Industrial Revolution, when the new economies emerged from the end of the twentieth century through to the beginning of the twenty-first century, in order to address the negative impact on the market of the risky business practices of the new economies, the associated accounting scandals and loss of public trust in accounting, SOX was enacted with the aim of strengthening corporate ethics and accountability.

Relating these points to the issues under investigation here, it could be said that rulemaking in U.S. was determined by the U.S. belief in "protecting the markets." This then leads to the tentative conclusion that protecting the markets was the U.S. belief, and that, consequently, the essence of the rules to protect the markets was rooted in protecting this U.S. belief. These remarks could now enable us to put forward an answer to Research Question 1.

Watts and Zimmerman, who have discussed the role of theories in accounting regulation, stated as follows: "[t]he dominance of the information objective arose, we suspect, as a public interest justification consistent with and in support of the *raison d'être* of the Securities Acts. The SEC was justified in terms of, and charged with, maintaining the orderly functioning of the capital markets. In particular, the SEC was to protect the public from another stock market crash. That crash was alleged to have been caused in part by inadequate corporate disclosure, although very little evidence exists to support this claim" (Watts and Zimmerman 1979, p. 297).

From a Japanese perspective, the best strategy continues to be maintaining the legitimacy of their presence in global economy by ensuring that domestic rules resemble American ones in an isomorphic way.[7] Strategies such as efforts regarding the international convergence of accounting standards, requiring representatives of listed companies to submit a written oath (implemented from January 2005 onwards on the Tokyo Stock Exchange) and prohibiting auditors from auditing the same company for more than seven accounting periods (Article 24(3) of the revised Certified Public Accountants Act, 2004)[8] are typical cases of this kind of isomorphism that have been seen in recent years. Isomorphism of economic systems and corporate governance, too, will be something that occurs at around the same time. In a nutshell, American experiences are *happened future* for Japan.

5 Mechanisms of Belief Formation

In order to build on the remarks thus far and clarify the formation process of accounting institutions and possibilities for their evolution, there should be another (perhaps more important) issue to be addressed: that is to understand the mechanism behind the formation of the belief. Without addressing this task, the investigation would be nothing more than a superficial analysis of the rule-formation process. This section will expand on the investigation to include a more in-depth study of the mechanism behind the formation of the belief.[9]

The discussion in the previous section would enable us to formulate two types of assertions that fit with the belief. First, accountants should separate accounting procedure from managers' intent as far as possible and faithfully reflect the company's economic reality in the accounting information. Second, all market

[7] Isomorphism is a term used in new institutional sociology to mean "a constraining process that forces one unit in a population to resemble other units that face the same set of environmental conditions" (DiMaggio and Powell 1983, p. 149). Covaleski et al. (1993) applied this perspective to accounting research.

[8] This regulation was later strengthened further through the partial amendment of the Certified Public Accountants Act.

[9] If we try to directly demonstrate the formation process of belief based on the supposition that it emerges from reality, we face the problem of infinite regression. To avoid this problem, the discussion here focuses on the assertions that fit with the belief as a proxy of it.

participants should be mutually independent and have a strong sense of morality. Both constitute clear and simple assertions that are intuitive and easy to understand.

The first assertion could be related to the facts that the comparative advantages of cash flow over accounting profit have been emphasized (Copeland et al. 1990), and that the introduction of full fair value accounting of financial assets and liabilities (JWG 2000) and the prohibition of the recycling of other comprehensive income (G4+1 1999; IASC 2001) have been advocated. The second assertion could be concerned with the realities that under SOX, auditors were prohibited in principle from providing non-audit services (Sec. 201) and from auditing the same company for more than 5 years (Sec. 203), and that the burden of proof was placed on the Chief Executive Officer and Chief Financial Officer regarding the fair presentation of financial statements (Sec. 302 and Sec. 906).

Why, then, do clear and simple assertions such as these, that are not derived from fact or rather are in conflict with fact, fit with belief?

Gaining a scientific understanding of certain questions entails extensive information costs, including the cost of acquiring specialist knowledge: for example, questions such as "What kinds of factors have taken what kind of path to generate an accounting scandal?" and "What kind of cost–benefit relationship is acceptable with regard to accounting regulation?" The average citizen, a different form of existence to the kind of rational market participants tacitly supposed in the previous section, does not have enough incentive to bear those kinds of costs: furthermore, all the average citizen has his "bounded rationality." However, what citizens do know is that some kind of new rule is necessary to prevent a malfunction or collapse of the market.

For such citizens, the aforementioned naïve and intuitive assertions are a lot more likely to be acceptable than scientific assertions, as long as they do not entail obvious contradictions or immediate factual errors. As these naïve and intuitive assertions proceed to permeate society, they come to function as self-enforcing norms for economic agents, even if they are less rational than fact. A. Downs's theory on the "rational ignorance" of citizens is in operation.[10] In such a situation, the fate for the academics who devote themselves to scientific assertions is social isolation.

The discussion in this section implies that the assertions that fit with belief function as an intermediary for the belief to develop into a social rule, and at the same time, the assertion itself gradually transforms into part of the belief through this process.

---

[10] A. Downs coined the term "rational ignorance" to mean that if the cost of acquiring additional information is greater than the benefit it will bring, it is rational—in terms of the economic benefit—for citizens to remain "ignorant." For more detailed discussion in this regard, see Downs (1957).

6 Possibilities for Institutional Evolution in Accounting

6.1 Towards an Institutional Evolution

Based on CIA, the investigation thus far could be taken further to consider that changes in the game situation would be engendering changes to the institution associated with a new equilibrium. This is where the possibilities for institutional evolution in accounting exist. This section will investigate, in more analytical manner, the kind of institutional evolution that can be observed when the game situation changes. The discussion below will be informed by Evolutionary Game Theory (EGT).[11]

6.2 Description of Evolutionary Mechanisms Based on EGT

The discussion starts by describing the mechanisms for institutional evolution based on EGT.[12] Let us say that the game that players in a society are faced with is initially assigned the payoff matrix set out in Table 2. In this game, it is supposed that boundedly rational players will choose one of the two rules, *FV* or *HC*.

It is easy to see that Table 2 corresponds to the "Prisoner's Dilemma." The dominant strategy is *HC*. That is, when the players encounter each other randomly in a game played in accordance with Table 2, all of the players chose *HC*, and this choice becomes the evolutionarily stable strategy. Therefore, based on the historical initial condition of this society, *HC* is institutionalized. An evolutionarily stable strategy is the dominant in a particular society.[13] If a minority group of players who behave in a different way invade a society that has an evolutionarily stable strategy, their low fitness prevents them from producing offspring, and they are unable to grow to become a powerful force.

Let us then say that the strategy conditions change and the payoff matrix changes from Tables 2 to 3. Conditions change in that a player's payoff for choosing *HC* when their opponent chose *FV* falls from 3 to 0. Following such a change, the game

Table 2 Payoff matrix with initial condition

	FV	*HC*
FV	2,2	0,3
HC	3,0	1,1

[11] EGT is highly beneficial here, as it allows us to simplify the mathematical model without sacrificing the reality of the game situation.

[12] The following description of the EGT game situation is informed by Okuno and Takizawa (1996).

[13] See Okuno and Takizawa (1996, pp. 283–286) for a mathematical definition of an evolutionarily stable strategy.

Table 3 Payoff matrix with changed condition

	FV	*HC*
FV	2,2	0,0
HC	0,0	1,1

converges as a pure coordination game with two Nash equilibria of (*FV*,*FV*) and (*HC*,*HC*). However, as mentioned above, the historical initial condition in this society stipulates choosing *HC* as a social rule. Even if the above-mentioned change in the environment occurs, as long as the other players continue to choose *HC*, the best response dynamics for each player remains *HC*, as "inertia" and "myopia" interact in the players' rule choices (Okuno and Takizawa 1996, p. 279).

In the game based on Table 3, the payoff is (2,2) for (*FV*,*FV*) and (1,1) for (*HC*, *HC*). This means that (*FV*,*FV*) Pareto dominates (*HC*,*HC*). Nevertheless, this society continues to choose the Pareto-inferior institution (*HC*,*HC*), as this is stipulated by the historical initial condition. In CIA, this kind of situation is known as "coordination failure," and resolving this failure enables institutions to evolve.

6.3 Application of the Game Situation to Accounting

In this subsection, a more concrete discussion on institutional evolution will be attempted by applying the above game situation to accounting problems.

Let us say that *HC* refers to historical cost accounting and *FV* to fair value accounting. The game situation as per Table 2 is stipulated in the historical initial condition and shows a society where historical cost accounting has taken hold as an institution. This model could broadly apply to the U.S. until the mid-1980s and to Japan until the 1990s. In a society of this nature, the features of historical cost accounting, which are its measurement of "exactness and objectivity" (Werntz 1962, p. 81), "verifiability" (AAA 1966, p. 28), and "hardness" (Ijiri 1975, p. 35), fall in line with the socially expected function of accounting, which is what makes it the dominant strategy. In other words, all other things being equal, historical cost information is more useful than fair value because it has the aforementioned attributes, and it therefore follows that those who choose historical cost will be rewarded with a relatively higher payoff than those who choose fair value. In a society where choosing historical cost has been established as an evolutionarily stable strategy, historical cost choosers reign supreme as overwhelmingly dominant species that literally forbid the reproduction of other species.

But, the game situation in Table 2 suggests that the accounting environment has already become unsettled. That is, a strategy (*FV*,*FV*) exists that offers a payoff of 2, which is greater than the payoff of 1 associated with (*HC*,*HC*). This kind of situation arises when people's expectations of accounting change with the financial-ization and informatization of the economy. However, breaking away from the evolutionarily stable rule of historical cost will have a considerably negative effect on the payoff (including the political cost associated with a non-dominant species being a heretic), and will unilaterally benefit the dominant players, those who chose historical cost. This is why, in a game situation based on Table 2, historical cost will continue to be chosen as a legitimate rule.

Yet with time, the game situation changes from Tables 2 to 3. This change shows that the relative cost of breaking away from historical cost has fallen. The players won't see a unilateral reduction in their payoffs even if they break away from historical cost. This kind of change occurs when the social resistance to breaking away from historical cost decreases with the increasing above-mentioned transit of the economy, and more emphasis is given to the comparability of accounting information in circulation. In such a situation, there will be no payoff unless the players share the comparable information, be it historical cost or fair value.

As a result of this change, the game will converge as a pure coordination game, with the social rule becoming either historical cost or fair value. In such a society, the historical initial condition stipulates choosing historical cost as the traditional rule. Even if the aforementioned environmental change occurs, as long as the other players continue to choose traditional rule, historical cost will remain the best response for all players since "inertia" and "myopia" interact in their choice of rules. Theoretically, resolving this coordination failure will enable the institutional evolution of accounting.

6.4 Conditions for Breaking Away from a Pareto-Inferior State

Let us go back to the discussion in Sect. 6.2 in order to investigate the conditions necessary for breaking away from a Pareto-inferior state and thus resolving the coordination failure.

In Table 3, assume that the proportion of players choosing *FV* is p and that the payoff for choosing *FV* is U_{fv}, and the payoff for choosing *HC* is U_{hc}. This gives the following:

$$U_{fv} = 2p$$
$$U_{hc} = 1 - p$$

It follows therefore that the condition for breaking away from a Pareto-inferior state is:

$$U_{fv} - U_{hc} = 2p - (1 - p) > 0$$

That is, $p > 1/3$

If more than one in three players choose *FV*, this society will resolve its coordination failure and break away from its Pareto-inferior state. As seen from

Table 3, this condition applies when the payoff for (*FV*,*FV*) is double that for (*HC*, *HC*). If the payoff difference increases, for example if the payoff for (*FV*,*FV*) is (3,3) while for (*HC*,*HC*) is (1,1), the necessary condition becomes $p > 1/4$. As the new Nash equilibrium payoff increases in relative terms, the proportion of players making the choice that will promote institutional evolution decreases, that is to say institutional evolution can be realized more easily and in a shorter time.

Conceivable policies to create a situation that would meet the above-mentioned conditions include: (1) cultivating players with new genes who will seek to acquire a higher payoff by choosing *FV*, (2) using government intervention to encourage players to choose *FV* rather than *HC* by implementing policies to increase the difference between payoffs for (*FV*,*FV*) and (*HC*,*HC*), (3) promoting direct contact or exchange with societies where *FV* is the evolutionarily stable strategy.[14] In the field of accounting, any one of these policies would mean taking stronger measures to ensure that disclosing fair value information is the benchmark in accounting practice and rulemaking. The FASB/IASB Joint Project of Financial Performance Reporting by Business Enterprises taken up in Sect. 3.2 could be counted as an example of such policies.[15]

6.5 Noteworthy Points

The investigation in this section includes some points to keep in mind. The author would like to identify the points considered particularly important in understanding the nature of the discussion.

First, in this section, the investigation was carried out under the assumption that while the rulemakers understand the "true" game situation surrounding the choice of rules, the boundedly rational market participants do not, which generates an equilibrium that does not fit with the "true" game situation. Until Sect. 4, it was assumed that the empirical evidence generated by market participants represented basic facts and that the rulemakers were setting rules that did not fit with these facts. If the rulemakers believe that their understanding of the game situation is "true", it is just a problem at the level of belief. Considering this point, the assumptions in the later sections are not different from those prior to Sect. 4. The later sections differ from those prior to Sect. 4 in that the discussion assumes that the game situation that rulemakers believe to be true does indeed correspond to the true one. The assumption was altered in this way because otherwise it would have been impossible to derive the possibilities for institutional evolution from the currently observable

---

[14] (3) applies to the Japanese catch-up model of institutional evolution. See Okuno and Takizawa (1996, pp. 288–293) for the EGT implications of such policies.

[15] Some recent archival studies, albeit in very small numbers, have presented empirical evidence to demonstrate that comprehensive income is more value relevant than net income. See Hirst et al. (2001), Biddle and Choi (2002).

empirical facts and accounting phenomena. If this assumption were to show major signs of collapse, the discussion here would, of course, lose its explanatory power. Such limitations are therefore inherent to the investigation in this section.

Secondly, this section considered the process of institutional evolution in accounting, taking the U.S. belief in protecting the markets as a given. In other words, the topic referred to, historical cost vs. fair value, was positioned as an institutional tool to protect the markets. From the 1920s through to the 1940s, the accounting framework of U.S. underwent a fundamental transition from current (fair) value to historical cost. Therefore, purely based on the relationship between the two accounting frameworks, we could also see the changes that occurred from the 1990s onwards as nothing but an institutional change in the opposite direction. "Evolution" is different to "development." Institutions are always evolving as they come to include new breed of players, but this evolution does not necessarily mean that they are developing towards better one with time. The investigation in this paper is based on this view of history.

7 Conclusion: Implications for Accounting Research

If the formation process of accounting institutions and the possibilities for their evolution are as described in this paper, where does this leave the *raison d'être* of accounting research and archival studies in particular? This question addresses the implications of this paper for accounting research. The author would like to conclude the discussion by giving a tentative answer to this question.

Regardless of whether it is the rulemakers or the market participants who are the more rational party, it is indisputable that archival studies have shown that recent rulemaking has quite often *not* been in keeping with empirical evidence. This means, with the exception of a very small number of cases, e.g., substantial abolition of FAS33 in 1986, the chain of events involving «empirical evidence → rule setting/revision → value relevance improvement» has not existed in reality.

What, then, is the relationship between rulemaking and value relevance of accounting information? In light of the investigation so far, one possible hypothesis would be that a chain exists between the two in the form of «rule setting → market participants learn about the rule → value relevance is generated.» The absence or presence of value relevance is not the guideline for rulemaking but the result of it. Mediation between the two is the market participants learning about the rule. As market participants become more acquainted with a new rule, their understanding of the accounting information supplied under the rule becomes institutionalized. As a result, value relevance is generated for this information, which produces a new systematic relationship between accounting information and market participant behavior.

This is just a tentative interpretation, but focusing on this kind of aspect may suggest that the social *raison d'être* of archival studies lies in sending to the market signals of how strategy distribution has changed in the game, and promoting or hindering changes in the behavioral patterns of market participants by providing them an *ex post* account of how the institutionalization of existing or new rules has progressed or not.

References

AAA, Committee to Prepare a Statement of Basic Accounting Theory (1966) A statement of basic accounting theory. AAA, Evanston, IL

Aoki M (2001) Towards a comparative institutional analysis. MIT Press, Cambridge, MA

Ashbaugh H, LaFond R, Mayhew BW (2003) Do nonaudit services compromise auditor independence? Further evidence. Account Rev 78(3):611–639

Biddle GC, Choi JH (2002) Is comprehensive income irrelevant? SSRN-id316703

Cheng CSA, Cheung JK, Gopalakrishnan V (1993) On the usefulness of operating income, net income and comprehensive income in explaining security returns. Account Bus Res 23(91): 195–203

Copeland T, Koller T, Murrin J (1990) Valuation: measuring and managing the value of companies. Wiley, New York, NY

Covaleski MA, Dirsmith MW, Michelman JE (1993) An institutional theory perspective on the DRG framework, case-mix accounting systems and health-care organizations. Acc Organ Soc 18(1):65–80

Craswell AT, Stokes DJ, Laughton J (2002) Auditor independence and fee dependence. J Account Econ 33(2):253–275

Dechow PM (1994) Accounting earnings and cash flows as measures of firm performance: the role of accounting accruals. J Account Econ 18(1):3–42

DeFond ML, Raghunandan K, Subramanyam KR (2002) Do non-audit service fees impair auditor independence? Evidence from going concern audit opinions. J Account Res 40(4):1247–1274

Dhaliwal DS, Subrananyam KR, Trezevant R (1999) Is comprehensive income superior to net income as a measure of firm performance? J Account Econ 26(1–3):43–67

DiMaggio PJ, Powell WW (1983) The iron cage revisited: institutional isomorphism and collective rationality in organizational fields. Am Sociol Rev 48(2):147–160

Downs A (1957) An economic theory of democracy. Harper and Row, New York, NY

FASB (1976) An analysis of issues related to conceptual framework for financial accounting and reporting: elements of financial statements and their measurement. FASB Discussion Memorandum

FASB (2005) Financial performance reporting by business enterprises. Project Updates. Last Updated: 20 December 2005

Francis J, Olsson P, Oswald DR (2000) Comparing the accuracy and explainability of dividend, free cash flow, and abnormal earnings equity value estimates. J Account Res 38(1):45–70

Fujii H, Yamamoto T (2001) Empirical study on stock-price-explanatory power of Feltham-Ohlson model: case of Japanese firms and stock market. Kyoto Univ Econ Rev 70(1/2):1–11

G4+1 (1999) G4+1 position paper: reporting financial performance. A discussion paper. IASC

Ghosh A, Moon D (2005) Auditor tenure and perceptions of audit quality. Account Rev 80(2): 585–612

Hirst DE, Hopkins PE, Wahlen JM (2001) Fair values, comprehensive income reporting, and bank analysts' risk and valuation judgments. SSRN-id273350

IASC (2001) Report from the IASC Steering Committee on Reporting Financial Performance. Draft statement of principles, reporting recognised income and expense. IASB

Ijiri Y (1975) Theory of accounting measurement. AAA studies in accounting research. No. 10, AAA

JWG (2000) Joint Working Group of Standard-Setters. Financial instruments and similar items. reprinted., The Japanese Institute of Certified Public Accountants

Larcker DF, Richardson SA (2004) Fees paid to audit firms, accrual choices and corporate governance. J Account Res 42(3):625–658

Myers JN, Myers LA, Omer TC (2003) Exploring the term of the auditor-client relationship and the quality earnings: a case for mandatory auditor rotation? Account Rev 78(3):779–799

O'Hanlon JF, Pope PF (1999) The value-relevance of UK dirty surplus accounting flows. Br Account Rev 31(4):459–482

Penman SH, Sougiannis T (1998) A comparison of dividend, cash flow, and earnings approaches to equity valuation. Contemp Account Res 15(3):343–383

Quirin JJ, O'Bryan D, Wilcox WE (1999) The corroborative relation between earnings and cash flows. Quart J Bus Econ 38(2):3–16

Simunic DA (1984) Auditing, consulting, and auditor independence. J Account Res 22(2): 679–702

Watts RL, Zimmerman JL (1979) The demand for and supply of accounting theories: the market for excuses. Account Rev 54(2):273–305

Wei L (2002) This manager isn't rushing to buy. The Wall Street Journal. 28 August, p.D11

Werntz WW (1962) Comments of William W. Werntz. In: Sprouse RT, Moonitz M. A tentative set of broad accounting principles for business enterprises. AICPA, pp 79–82

Materials in Japanese

Aoki M (2002) For the promotion of a major transformation in the system. Nihon Keizai Shimbun (morning edition) on 4 January

Okabe T (1985) Selection of accounting information systems. Chuokeizai Publisher, Tokyo

Okuno M, Takizawa H (1996) Formation and mutual interaction of economic systems: an approach from an evolutionary game perspective. In: Aoki M, Okuno M (eds) Comparative institutional analysis of economic systems. University of Tokyo Press, Tokyo, pp 271–298

Suda K (ed) (2004) Strategies and effects of disclosure. Moriyama Shoten Publisher, Tokyo

Wakabayashi H (2014) Comprehensive income information and stock-price drift. In: Fujii H (ed) Basic concepts of international financial reporting. Chuokeizai Publisher, Tokyo, pp 161–186

Yano M (2005) System reformation in the "Quality Era". Iwanami Shoten Publisher, Tokyo

Financial Reporting and Fair Value: Where Do We Stand?

Jean-François Casta and Olivier Ramond

Abstract Over the past two decades, the accounting standards under which large companies determine and report their performance measures have led to much debate. Indeed, a wide-reaching movement, originally initiated by the U.S. Financial Accounting Standards Board (FASB), and spread at an international level by the International Accounting Standards Board (IASB), aimed to replace historical cost with the market-based concept of fair value. Fair value can potentially be used for measuring a large number of non-financial assets and liabilities (e.g. goodwill, post-retirement scheme values, share-based payments) and can therefore serve as the basis for a new corporate accounting model aiming to provide a more accurate view of the future cash flow estimates' and investment opportunities' uncertainties within financial reports. Based on the extent literature, this article discusses the usefulness of financial information disclosed under the fair value approach. In this respect, the key question—is fair value relevant?—will be analysed in a threefold way: (1) Do fair value-based "accounting numbers" help better estimate the value of a company and the intrinsic risk relating to its activity? (2) How informative are they for financial statements' users? (3) How useful is fair value information for decision-making?

Over the past two decades, through the impetus of Anglo-Saxon standard setters, the fulcrum of the traditional accounting model, namely the accounting standards under which a company's equity and income are measured and reported, have led to much debate. This wide-reaching movement, originally initiated in the United States by the Financial Accounting Standards Board (FASB), and spread at an international level by the International Accounting Standards Board (IASB), aims to replace historical cost—the basis for the measurement of a company's income statement and valuation of its assets and liabilities under most continental European accounting standards—with the notion of fair value. Fair value is currently defined

J.-F. Casta (✉) • O. Ramond (✉)
Dauphine Recherches en Management, University of Paris-Dauphine, CNRS-UMR 7088, Paris, France
e-mail: jean-francois.casta@dauphine.fr; olivier.ramon@dauphine.fr

D. Bensadon, N. Praquin (eds.), *IFRS in a Global World*,
DOI 10.1007/978-3-319-28225-1_5

by the IASB[1] as "The price that would be received to sell an asset or paid to transfer a liability in an orderly transaction between market participants at the measurement date." The concept of fair value is broader and can be applied more generally than that of market value[2]: Indeed, where there is no quoted market price available on an active market, the valuation is determined by the exchange value agreed by two independent parties, by the market price of an item with similar characteristics or by the net present value estimate of future cash flows. Fair value can potentially be used for a large number of non-financial assets and liabilities (e.g. goodwill impairment, post-retirement scheme valuation) and can therefore serve as the basis for a new corporate accounting model which aims to provide a more accurate reflection of the uncertainties affecting future cash flow estimates and investment opportunities in financial reports.

This article discusses the usefulness of financial information based on the measurement of a company's wealth and net income under the fair value approach. In this respect, the key question—is fair value relevant?—can be analysed as follows: (1) Do fair value-based "accounting numbers" help better estimate the value of a company and the intrinsic risk relating to its activity? (2) How informative are they for financial statements' users? (3) How useful is fair value information for decision-making?

In order to address these concerns, we shall first examine the basis and boundaries of the traditional accounting historical cost model. We will then analyse the key determinants of the emergence of the fair value approach, with particular regard to the role attributed to financial statements and the needs of their users. Lastly, we will present a summary of the empirical studies carried out to assess the usefulness of fair value accounting information and will draw out future research avenues.

1 Traditional Accounting Model: Basis, Boundaries and Alternatives

1.1 Corporate Accounting (Re)presentation: A Value-Oriented Framework

The accounting (re)presentation of a company is a contingent structure based on generally accepted principles in a given historical and economic context, which

[1] IFRS 13 (2011), *Fair Value Measurement, Appendix A*. The US SFAS Standard N°107, issued in 1991 and entitled '*Disclosures about Fair Value of Financial Instruments*', provides the following definition that used to prevail under IAS 39 (2005) prior to the introduction of IFRS 13 in 2011: "the fair value is the amount at which an asset (or liability) could be bought (or incurred) or sold (or settled) in a current transaction between willing parties, that is, other than in a forced or liquidation sale".

[2] The market value is the "price that the seller can get (or that the purchaser will accept to pay) . . . on an active market".

together form a model. The legitimacy of this model is based on its capacity to apprehend, evaluate, summarise and monitor over time information relating to transactions that have an impact on the company's wealth and performance. Ideally, this model should enable the definition of a system of measurement for company net income and shareholders' equity that is socially acceptable and also meets the requirements of the wide panel of users of financial statements (employees, managers, suppliers, customers, fund providers, tax authorities etc.).

The standard corporate accounting model is based on an underlying concept of value[3] which, as in economics, can refer to cost, exchange value or value-in-use. The approach selected will determine the structure of the accounting presentation and the criteria used to measure a company's performance—net income—and wealth—net assets.

As shown by Richard (2001), "while valuation at cost price seemed to take precedence in the earlier European regulations, from 1673 to around 1800, realizable value was recommended by jurists and became widely used in accounting regulations in Germany and France during the nineteenth century and even beyond." The current debate surrounding fair value therefore echoes the debate that took place in France and Germany up until the Second World War, between advocates of dynamic accounting (referring to cost) and supporters of static accounting (referring to realizable value in the context of going concern). However, in the United States, banks started to drop references to market price (in favour of historical cost) in 1938, following the Great Depression (Swenson and Buttross 1993). After the Second World War, the historical cost model gained precedence both in Europe and the United States.

1.2 The Mainstream Accounting Model: Value as a Reference to Cost

Today's mainstream accounting model for preparing statutory and consolidated accounts is based primarily on the concept of cost value (i.e. previously accumulated costs), associated with the realisation principle and, depending on national practices, with the prudence principle.[4] Variants of this model differ in the extent to which they recognise the principle of placing (economic) reality over (legal) appearance.

Generally speaking, this model functions like an asymmetrical filter favouring the recognition of potential losses and carrying over gains from the effective completion of a transaction (Basu 1997). It is based on a prudent and non-volatile measurement of net income and equity: since the 1990s, this view has been the

---

[3] For a study of the different notions of value underlying the different accounting models, see Simon (2000).

[4] It is noteworthy that the prudence principle can stand in contradiction with the fair value measurement (see the speech of Hans Hoogervorst, chairman of the IASB, 'The Concept of Prudence: Dead or alive?', 18 September 2012, Brussels, Belgium).

object of much criticism, particularly with regard to the actual relevance of the accounting information reported.[5] Conversely, its proponents[6] attribute a number of qualities to this method, which they feel justify its continuing use and prevalence. For instance, Ijiri (1971, 1975) supports that historical cost is more objective and reliable than alternative methods which are supposedly more relevant, and it is therefore a more effective means of resolving conflicts of interest. In fact, except in periods of inflation, it is a particularly robust model that is highly appreciated by the non-banking business world.[7] The FASB (1984) and the initial International Accounting Standards Committee (IASC)[8] (1989) conceptual frameworks present it as the most frequently used valuation basis.

1.3 Historical Cost Accounting: What Information Do "Accounting Numbers" Provide?

The first empirical studies to assess the usefulness of accounting data for the decision-making process were carried out by Ball and Brown (1968) and Beaver (1968), then taken up by various other researchers in the 1970s and 1980s. This work drew on efficient markets theory and event study methodology, with the aim of highlighting the market's reaction to published accounting information (annual or interim financial statements) in the form of abnormal returns. All of these empirical studies found that the only information content taken into account by the markets is net income. Paradoxically, this work highlighted the extent to which markets anticipate the informational content of accounting data well in advance of its publication in financial statements. The results of these studies thus undermined the assumed usefulness of "accounting numbers" and their relevance in decision-making, leading researchers to suggest they have more than a mere contractual utility (Watts and Zimmerman 1986), and to give precedence to the disciplinary role of accounting, i.e. the accountability.

---

[5] With regard to company valuations, for example, Ohlson (1990) stresses the quasi-systematic bias introduced by the use of *accounting numbers* based on historical cost.

[6] For example, Littleton (1952), Kohler (1963), Ijiri (1971) and, in the context of the current debate surrounding fair value, Ramanna (2013).

[7] Allen and Ramanna (2013) show that FASB members with backgrounds in financial services strongly advocate for the use of fair value reporting during the FASB standard-setting due process.

[8] The IASC was the predecessor of the IASB till 2001.

1.4 Alternative Valuation Methods: A Lot of Proposals But No Obvious Practical Benefits

Researchers put forward a number of alternative valuation conventions in order to restore some relevance and utility to the traditional accounting model chiefly based on the historical cost approach. These accounting models can first be classified on the basis of two types of independent criteria (Boussard 1997), the first relating to the choice of method for the valuation of assets (historical cost versus concept of "value"), the second relating to the unit of monetary measurement (nominal value versus purchasing power). Where there is no inflation, this typology can be further refined by combining the "valuation method" criterion with respect (or relaxation) of the realisation principle, thus highlighting the essential dichotomy in the way results are established (transaction result versus holding result).

The principal models put forward in accounting literature can be separated into three categories, according to the notion of value used as a reference:

- The "current entry values" model, based on the entry value which refers either to the acquisition price or the replacement cost. This model was advocated by Edwards and Bell (1961) in relation to the maintenance of physical capital.
- The "current exit values" model, based on the exit value, which is the price at which an asset can be sold or liquidated. This was put forward by Chambers (1966) and by Sterling (1970).
- The "value-in-use" model, based on the added-value of the asset to the company, and measured by the present value of future cash flows estimate.[9]

In 1984, when it adopted its current conceptual framework, the FASB recognized the following as a basis for valuation[10]: (1) historical cost, (2) current value or replacement value, (3) market value and net market value (excluding any case of forced liquidation) and (4) present value estimates of future cash flows. Method (2) complies with the transaction principle, while models (3) and (4) do not apply this principle strictly.

2 The Emergence of the Fair Value Concept: The Issues at Stake and Leading Factors

Representing a genuine change in direction, fair value emerged as a result of four combined factors to become a central accounting convention under US and international accounting standards.

[9] Difficulties relating to its implementation meant that the authors often considered this method impractical.

[10] In 1989, the IASC conceptual framework recognized the following valuation bases: historical cost, current cost (or replacement value), realizable value and present value.

The first leading factor in this change was the attitude adopted in the new Anglo-Saxon conceptual frameworks—that of the FASB (1984) and then the IASC (1989)—with regard to issues such as the purpose of accounting (assistance with decision-making versus rendering of accounts and controls), the various meanings assigned to the notion of "users" of financial statements (the investor in the generic sense versus many types of users) and, implicitly, certain qualities expected from financial and accounting information[11] (relevance versus accuracy). The objectives attributed to financial statements were clearly biased towards meeting the needs of users—mainly creditors and investors—in terms of forecast data, placing particular emphasis on the usefulness of accounting information for external parties in their economic decision-making. Many researchers support the idea that board members with a background in financial services have been taking over the Boards of the FASB and the IASB and are thus able to make the accounting standards purport that fair value is the correct measurement basis to run a company as it is in the financial industry (Allen and Ramanna 2013).

The second key determinant is the growing use of increasingly complex financial instruments and the high level of market volatility. The widespread use of these instruments has increased levels of risk and aptly highlights the issue of the relevance of accounting information and notably the recognition of financial instruments in financial statements. Derivative products demonstrate this problem particularly well as they initially mobilise modest amounts of capital but generate a significant risk at a later stage. The financial institution bankruptcies observed in the United States at the end of the 1980s underlined the boundaries of the standard accounting model: the historical cost model was unable to provide a timely indicator to the users of financial information of the financial health of banks using derivatives (Barth et al. 1995). For some, the need to prevent systemic crises in the financial sector and to increase the relevance of financial information were behind the emergence of a range of proposals for a fair value method (Cornett et al. 1996).

The third determining factor is the will, of the Securities and Exchange Commission (SEC) in particular, to reduce the discretionary power of directors over earnings management (Levitt 1998; Lewis 2012). The historical cost model gave directors some considerable leeway both to make provisions, and hence integrate uncertainty, and to establish ad hoc results. As provisions are based on a subjective assessment of risk, cost forecasts and non-definitive amortisation of assets, they can be used as a political accounting tool. Conversely, directors can take an opportunistic approach to the concept of transaction results and dispose of assets that conceal unrealised capital gains (while deferring the disposal of assets carrying potential capital losses) in order to generate income, delay the appearance of losses or smooth out results. Consequently, the use of fair value is presented, notably by

[11] The conceptual framework of the FASB identifies the essential qualities of accounting information. *Relevance* is an attribute that enables users of financial statements to make decisions, to confirm or correct previous forecasts and to evaluate the results of past, present or future events. *Accuracy* is a characteristic that means the accounting information can be used with confidence as it is neither partial nor incorrect.

the US market regulator, as a solution for a more reliable valuation of assets and shareholders' equity (Beatty et al. 1996).

The last leading factor is the introduction of finance theory into accounting research since the early 1980s. According to some authors (e.g. Ramanna 2013; Holthausen and Watts 2001), this may have caused to widespread the study of the association of accounting data with market data and gave intellectual rationales to the proponents of fair value.

As a result of the dysfunctions caused by the irregular use of the historical cost model—which has not fulfilled its role as a safeguard—and in order to improve the relevance of information disclosed on certain financial instruments, the standards authorities implemented a programme to break away from the historical cost model—most often used according to the company's intended purpose for holding the assets—and to promote the notion of fair value. The FASB, supported by the SEC and part of the academic world[12] and, on an international level, by the IASC, was decisively involved in this process. However, as noted by Garmilis (2001), "the adoption of standards based on fair value has always caused some conflict, between regulators and standards authorities on the one hand, and companies on the other". In fact, since information requirements have always been badly defined and are often assumed, the promotion of the fair value model is motivated more by the large number of proposals put forward than by any explicit request on the part of users.[13]

3 Fair Value Accounting: Evolution or Revolution?

Having briefly looked at the stages in the accounting standardisation process that led to the emergence of a fair value model, we now discuss the qualities and disadvantages attributed to this measurement model by academics and professionals.

3.1 The Introduction of Fair Value into Accounting Standards

Although the concept of fair value first came into use in the 1950s, it had a limited scope of application and very specific accepted meanings.[14] Actually, the term has

[12] This is particularly the case with the *American Accounting Association* (AAA), see (Cornett et al. 1996).

[13] In view of this, it is necessary to ask, for example: are financial analysts requesting a widespread use of fair value? Do they advocate financial reporting that favours the balance sheet over the income statement? The study conducted among financial analysts by Garmilis (2001) highlights only mild demand for fair value information.

[14] For the origins of the notion of fair value, see Simon (2000).

only been used in its current form since the 1990s. Over this period, fair value began to be used for the disclosure (information on financial instruments in the notes to financial statements), and later for the accounting recognition—i.e. the booking of unrealised profits and losses under earnings—of certain financial instruments and derivatives. It is now becoming more widespread and is being used in a variety of fields, not only as a principle for initial valuation, but also for monitoring the value of assets and liabilities.

Developments in accounting standards in the United States illustrate the increasing popularity of the notion of 'fair value',[15] driven by both the SEC and the FASB, and linked to the growing use of financial instruments. In 1991, SFAS standard 107 (1991)[16] referred to fair value as the valuation basis for disclosure. SFAS 119[17] (1994) similarly referred to fair value as the basis for the disclosure of information on derivatives. With SFAS 115,[18] which institutionalised accounting on the basis of the management perspective in 1993, the notion of fair value became the reference method for reporting certain securities (investment and transaction securities) in the balance sheet and earnings were measured according to the variation in the fair value of these securities. Since then, this valuation method, which takes account of unrealised gains and losses, has underpinned the FASB's strategy to eliminate or limit the effects of discretionary choices in accounting based on intent. Adopted in 1998, despite considerable opposition from banks, SFAS 133 (1998)[19] made fair value accounting of derivative financial instruments—assets and liabilities—in the balance sheet mandatory,[20] both on their initial entry into the accounts and subsequently. SFAS Standards 141 and 142 (2001) extend beyond the scope of financial instruments, stipulating that, in business combinations, all identifiable assets and liabilities should be reported at fair value, and these valuations monitored over time. Similarly, the replacement of the amortisation of certain intangible assets by impairment tests is also based on fair value monitoring.

International accounting standards also evolved during this period. IAS 32 (1995), relating to the disclosure of information on financial instruments, adopted fair value as a valuation basis. However, it was only after 1998, subsequent to a complete review of its standards, that the IASC introduced the notion of fair value into all of its standards, including those relating to business combinations, post-employment retirement scheme, intangible assets, securities portfolios, fixed asset revaluations, etc. Also in 1998, the IASC adopted IAS 39 which, like SFAS

---

[15] For the emergence of the notion of Fair Value in US accounting standards, see Cornett et al. (1996).

[16] SFAS standard 107 (1991), *Disclosures about Fair Value of Financial Instruments.*

[17] SFAS standard 119 (1994), *Disclosure about Derivative Financial Instruments and Fair Value of Financial Instruments.*

[18] SFAS standard 115 (1993), *Accounting for Certain Investments in Debt and Equity Securities.*

[19] SFAS standard 133 (1998), *Accounting for Derivative Instruments and Hedging Activities.*

[20] A more radical proposal, designed to get rid of accounting based on the intention of the management and extend fair value accounting to all financial instruments. Although the FASB was in favour, banks were fervently opposed to it.

133, generalized the use of fair value for the reporting of numerous financial instruments. Highly criticized by credit establishments, the original version of this accounting standard raised a number of problems with regard to its implementation (enhanced volatility of firm performance indicators, pro-cyclical accounting treatment, difficulties encountered during the 2008 financial crisis to identify reliable market data...) although the IASC through this standard aimed to improve the monitoring of risk exposure—through a periodical revision of market values or discounted present values—and to monitor the creation of value more effectively, regardless of the intentions of the parties. However, once again, strong opposition from the professional world during the 2008 subprime crisis deeply undermined this project oriented towards a more 'full fair value' approach.

3.2 *Qualities Attributed to the Fair Value Model*

A number of benefits have been cited to justify the use of fair value in the accounting for financial instruments.[21]

The fair value method is based on the discounting of future financial flows and thus provides information which integrates market trends (Allen and Carletti 2008b). It is therefore perfectly in line with current methods used by investors to compute their cash flow estimates.

Furthermore, the fair value method provides better comparability of financial statements, by giving equivalent values for a financial instrument, regardless of the date on which it was acquired, thus eliminating opportunities for "cherry picking" arising from the improper application of the realisation principle. It also ensures that the measurement of performance is exhaustive: by integrating not only transaction gains and losses but also holding gains and losses, the fair value model provides an entirely faithful representation of the strategy adopted for financial instruments—disposal versus holding. Moreover, it guarantees that the value accounted for is exhaustive, particularly for derivatives where the initial cost is zero.

Ensuring that this approach is consistent with the approach used for operational risk management (interest rate, currency or price) would facilitate the reconciliation of accounting income with economic income. Moreover, the use of fair value would ensure that the information produced is neutral, as it is based on data which is exogenous (market values or, if no active market is involved, model values based on external parameters) and easily accessible (market values).

[21] For the qualities and weaknesses of fair value, see also Cornett et al. (1996), Casta and Colasse (2001).

3.3 Criticisms of the Fair Value Model

Several criticisms[22] have been made against the use of fair value.

Many of these arguments refer to the increased volatility of fair value accounting measures[23] and the consequences thereof. However, in doing so, they in fact raise the more fundamental issue of the actual function of accounting models and the relevance of filtering or, on the contrary, better reflecting the actual volatility of economic activity. Conversely, other criticisms underline the unjustified increase in the volatility of earnings and shareholders' equity as a result of an implicit abandonment of the going concern principle.

The most frequently cited criticism concerns assets not traded on an efficient market,[24] which are consequently valued on the basis of internal models. Detractors stress the lack of objectivity and neutrality in these valuations, and the loss of reliability and comparability due to the use of internal models (Allen and Carletti 2008a).

Other critics argue that the use of the fair value accounting model implies taking a short-term approach to the management of a company.

Lastly, certain detractors of this model stress the prohibitive cost of obtaining information, given the limited usefulness of fair value data for users.

4 Fair Value and Information Usefulness: Empirical Evidence

Despite the increasing popularity of this accounting model, the use of fair value as a general valuation principle poses a number of practical problems and raises major issues. Although the benefits attributed to fair value methods are generally the result of deductive reasoning, assumptions and even affirmations, the criticism often stems from fears rather than actual inadequacies that have been pinpointed in an empirical manner.

The introduction of valuation in financial reporting raises the question of the legitimacy of accounting methods and highlights the need for a theoretical analysis framework. The latter generally refers to the efficiency of capital markets as a working theory.[25] The most widely used methodology involves examining the

[22] For a summary of these criticisms, see Swenson and Buttross (1993), Cornett et al. (1996), Casta and Colasse (2001).

[23] A number of studies have been carried out on the effect of accounting standards on volatility. For a summary, see Ballwieser and Kuhner (1994).

[24] On the conceptual problems of *Fair value* with respect to the existence of active markets, see Barth and Landsman (1995), or Holthausen and Watts (2001).

[25] However, recent studies have questioned the validity of the theory of efficient capital markets, opening up other avenues of research.

effect of an accounting choice—such as fair value—on the market value of a sample of companies, where the price is perceived as an aggregate measure of future cash flow estimates. The theory of informational usefulness associated with an accounting choice is valid if it is possible to establish a significant link between the accounting choice and the change in the price or Market to Book Ratio.

Because a certain amount of time is required before the application of standards can be assessed, the available empirical studies mainly concern either the banking sector and, more often, the effects of the introduction of SFAS 107 or 115 or the goodwill impairment value-relevance over the post-SFAS 142 regime. However, it is already possible to draw certain conclusions in relation to our objectives from this work.

With regard to the information content of "accounting numbers" for the market, empirical studies are not generally able to show that the fair value model is significantly better than the historical cost model.[26] However, some of the work carried out appears to establish a link between fair value and the market price of a company. For example, in discussing the problem of valuing a securities portfolios (Eccher et al. 1996), establish that there is a strong correlation between the fair value of securities and the market value of a company. However, this result cannot be applied to all balance sheet items, such that the fair value of financial instruments, taken on its own, can only account for a small part of the variation in Market to Book Ratio.

With regard to the effect on the market of adopting different accounting regulations (Cornett et al. 1996), show that the events—that is, the different phases in the standardisation process—relating to the introduction of fair value have a negative impact on the value of banks.

Moreover, concerning the problem of volatility, if the earnings of banks are significantly more volatile using fair value than on the basis of historical cost, this amplification does not appear to have any significant effect on stock market returns (Barth et al. 1995). In fact, behind this finding lies a fundamental question concerning the expected properties of the accounting model. Should it be founded on measurements that filter risk—that is, constructed to reduce systemic entropy—or, on the contrary, should it be as neutral as possible in order to pass on information on risks to the users of financial statements?

Lastly, with respect to the usefulness of fair value information according to the method by which it is integrated into financial reporting—that is, whether it is used in accounting recognition or disclosure—(Beatty et al. 1996) show, by studying the reaction of stock market prices to the adoption of SFAS standard 115, that the accounting of unrealised gains and losses is useful solely for regulatory bodies and not for other users. In parallel, researches analysing the impact of fair-value based goodwill impairment over the post-SFAS 142 implementation period find that the

[26] On work carried out on the banking sector, see Barth et al. (1996), Khurana and Kim (2003) and Nelson (1996). With regard to non-financial companies, see Simko (1998).

association between goodwill and future cash flows is stronger (Lee 2011; Li et al. 2011).

Although these empirical studies are still only partial, the results obtained so far have rekindled the debate regarding the usefulness of accounting information based on fair value. As regards its usefulness for decision-making, one interpretation favours the contractual role of "accounting numbers". As Jeanjean (2001) shows, the introduction of the fair value model underlines the highly "disciplinary" role of this method. In fact, as the completion of transactions is no longer determinant in the calculation of income, it is possible to control the activities of managers more effectively and eliminate the opportunistic management of holding gains. Moreover, this model would simultaneously introduce an accounting framework that centred management decisions on the creation of value, and a method of financial reporting that complies with current standards for performance measurement based on shareholder value.

5 Conclusion

The problems surrounding the introduction of fair value into accounting models goes beyond the scope of financial instruments or even the banking sector. Indeed, through the standards relating to business combinations and the depreciation of intangible items, it potentially concerns all companies of a certain size. Moreover, this change in accounting concepts forms the very core of the currently discussed conceptual framework to be implemented by the IASB for the establishment of future IFRS standards. The emergence of this new accounting model will require not only an adjustment of financial disclosures and practices, but also a redefinition of the respective roles of the balance sheet/financial position and the income statement which is currently under debate at the IASB level.[27]

In an effort to re-establish the relevance of accounting information, standard setters are identifying consistent links between "accounting numbers", management indicators and company value. The debate which has arisen over the introduction of fair value has thus shed light on the question of the purpose of financial statements and the usefulness of accounting information. The advantage of this is that it has extended the scope of discussions beyond the purely technical consideration of whether historical cost is a better valuation method than fair value, to look at the effects on the allocation of resources and the underlying economic issues (For whom and for which decisions should this information be produced?).

---

[27] For further details, please refer to the Discussion Paper issued in July 2013 by the IASB and entitled 'A Review of the Conceptual Framework For Financial Reporting', DP/2013/1, 239p.

References

Allen F, Carletti E (2008a) Should financial institutions mark-to-market? Finan Stab Rev 12:1–6

Allen F, Carletti E (2008b) Mark-to-market accounting and liquidity pricing. J Account Econ 45 (2–3):358–378

Allen F, Ramanna K (2013) Towards an understanding of the role of standard setters in standard setting. J Account Econ 55(1):66–90

Ball R, Brown P (1968) An empirical evaluation of accounting income numbers. J Account Res 6:159–177

Ballwieser W, Kuhner C (1994) Accounting standards and economic stability. Gelleschaft für bankwissenschaftliche Forschung e.V., Köln

Barth M, Landsman W (1995) Fundamental issues related to using fair value accounting for financial reporting. Account Horiz 9(4):97–107

Barth M, Landsman W, Wahlen JM (1995) Fair value accounting: effects on banks' earnings volatility, regulatory capital, and value of contractual cash flows. J Bank Financ 19 (3–4):577–605

Barth M, Beaver WH, Landsman W (1996) Value relevance of banks' fair value disclosures under SFAS No. 107. Account Rev 71(4):513–537

Basu S (1997) The conservatism principle and the asymmetric timeliness of earnings. J Account Econ 24:3–37

Beatty A, Chamberlain S, Magliolo J (1996) An empirical analysis of the economic applications of fair value accounting for investment securities. J Account Econ 22:43–77

Beaver WH (1968) The information content of annual earnings announcements. J Account Res 6 (3):67–92

Boussard D (1997) La modélisation comptable en question(s). Economica, Paris

Casta J-F, Colasse B (2001) Juste valeur: enjeux techniques et politiques. Economica, Paris

Chambers RJ (1966) Accounting evaluation and economic behaviour. Prentice-Hall, Englewood Cliffs, NJ

Cornett MM, Rezae Z, Tehranian H (1996) An investigation of capital market reactions to pronouncements on fair value accounting. J Account Econ 22(1–3):119–154

Eccher E, Ramesh K, Thiagarajan R (1996) Fair value disclosures by bank holding companies. J Account Econ 22(1–3):79–117

Edwards EO, Bell PW (1961) The theory and measurement of business income. University of California Press, Berkeley, CA

Garmilis A (2001) Existe-t-il une demande des analystes financiers pour des comptes en *juste valeur* ? Les résultats d'une enquête. In: Casta JF, Colasse B (eds) Juste Valeur : enjeux techniques et politiques. Economica, Paris, pp 271–288

Holthausen RW, Watts RL (2001) The relevance of the value-relevance literature for financial accounting standard setting. J Account Econ 31:3–75

Ijiri Y (1971) A defense for historical cost accounting. In: Sterling RR (ed) Asset valuation and income determination. Scholars Book, Lawrence, KS, pp 1–14

Ijiri Y (1975) The theory of accounting measurement. Studies in Accounting Research. No. 10, American Accounting Association

Jeanjean T (2001) Juste valeur et decision. In: Casta JF, Colasse B (eds) Juste Valeur: enjeux techniques et politiques. Economica, Paris, pp 97–111

Kohler EL (1963) Why not retain historical cost? J Account CXVI(4):35–41

Khurana IK, Kim MS (2003) Relative value relevance of historical cost vs. fair value: evidence from bank holding companies. J Account Econ 22(1):19–42

Lee C (2011) The effect of SFAS 142 on the ability of goodwill to predict future cash flows. J Account Public Policy 30:236–255

Levitt A (1998) The number game. Address to the NYU Centre for Law and Business. 28 September 1998

Lewis CM (2012) Risk modeling at the SEC: the accounting quality model. Address to the Financial Executives International Committee on Finance and Information Technology. 13 December 2012

Li Z, Shroff PK, Venkataraman R, Zhang IX (2011) Causes and consequences of goodwill impairment losses. Rev Acc Stud 16:745–778

Littleton AC (1952) The significance of invested cost. Account Rev 27(2):167–173

Nelson K (1996) Fair value accounting for commercial banks: an empirical analysis of SFAS No. 107. Account Rev 71(2):161–182

Ohlson J (1990) A synthesis of security valuation theory and the role of dividends, cash flow and earnings. Contemp Account Res 6:648–676

Ramanna K (2013) Why fair value is the rule: how a controversial accounting approach gained support. Harv Bus Rev 91(3):99–101

Richard J (2001) Histoire de la valeur dans les réglementations comptables allemande et française de 1673 à 1914. In: Casta JF, Colasse B (eds) Juste Valeur: enjeux techniques et politiques. Economica, Paris, pp 17–45

Simko P (1998) Financial instrument fair values and non-financial firms. J Account Audit Finance 14(3):247–274

Simon C (2000) Valeur et comptabilité. In: Colasse B (ed) Encyclopédie de la Comptabilité, du Contrôle de gestion et de l'Audit. Economica, Paris, pp 1245–1257

Sterling RR (1970) Theory of the measurement of enterprise income. The University Press of Kansas, Lawrence, KS

Swenson D, Buttross T (1993) A return to the past: disclosing market values of financial instruments. J Account January, 71–77

Watts RL, Zimmerman JL (1986) Positive accounting theory. Prentice-Hall International, Englewood Cliffs, NJ

How IFRS Contribute to the Financialization of Capitalism

Eve Chiapello

Abstract The contribution of IFRS to the process of financialization of capitalism can be analysed from several angles. We first propose two meanings that can be assigned to the concept of financialization: first as a process of morphological transformation of capitalism, and second as a gradual colonisation by specific "financialised" techniques and calculation methods. We then show that in many respects IFRS can be regarded as "financialised" standards. Finally we highlight some contributions of IFRS to the morphological transformation of capitalism (that is changes in distribution of wealth and power). As a result, IFRS can be seen as much financialised as financialising standards.

There are many different ways to describe the process of financialization of the economy that has been spreading for some 30 years, and is a major transformation of capitalism: the financial markets' growing influence in economic and financial regulation of investments, the dematerialisation of markets that has made global interoperability possible, the gradual decompartmentalisation of the banking and insurance activities, banking disintermediation, the unfettered inventiveness of financial engineering, the growing importance of financial activities in developed nations' GDP, etc. This article proposes to approach financialization not from these macro-economic angles, but through the transformations of accounting produced by the European Union's adoption of "international" accounting standards for listed companies' consolidated financial statements.

Accounting plays a crucial role in the structuring of capitalism (Chiapello 2005a, 2012). As a knowledge system specific to the economic world, accounting systems are thus central to the operation of the economic system they help to produce, reflecting it through their own constructions, and informing its actors, who rely on this special knowledge to take action. Because it measures the margins generated by the firm's business (including profit), accounting lies at the heart of economic relations between the firm and its many stakeholders (shareholders, customers, suppliers, lenders, employees, managers, public authorities, etc). Many rights to economic benefits are based on calculations made possible by accounting (dividend

E. Chiapello (✉)
Ecole des Hautes Etudes en Sciences Sociales (EHESS), Paris, France
e-mail: eve.chiapello@ehess.fr

D. Bensadon, N. Praquin (eds.), *IFRS in a Global World*,
DOI 10.1007/978-3-319-28225-1_6

distribution, level of interest on debt, additional salary components for employees, taxes, etc). All of Jacques Richard's work can be considered informed by this understanding of the socio-political role of accounting (Colette and Richard 2000), and he himself has frequently called for analysis of accounting changes in relation to changes in the economic system (Richard 1995a, b; Ding et al. 2008). Concerning IFRS, he was one of the first to stress that use of fair value and recognition of unrealized gains in the balance sheet was allowing "impatient shareholders" to take more from companies (Richard 2005a, b).

The theory defended in this article takes these considerations as its starting point and seeks to develop them. The contribution of IFRS to the process of financialization of capitalism can be analyzed from several angles, including the capture by financial actors of growing shares of wealth, and I seek to propose an organized review of the different angles. I begin by further examination of different meanings that can be assigned to the concept of financialization, before looking at how far the IFRS contribute to it.

1 What Approaches to Financialization?

Since the emergence of the notion of financialization (Epstein 2005; Krippner 2005) which was largely carried by heterodox economists seeking to describe the transformations of the capitalist system, many articles have documented the changes observed at macro-economic level. For example, empirical evidence has been provided to show the financial sector's growing influence in the economy (Duménil and Lévy 2001) and the rising proportion of economic income captured by the financial industry (Crotty 2005). These macro-economic studies have been complemented by several sector-specific studies showing the progressively greater importance of financial activities in non-financial firms and business sectors such as the automobile industry (Froud et al. 2002), mass retail (Baud and Durand 2012), the pharmaceuticals industry (Palpacuer et al. 2006), and the food industry (Jones and Nisbet 2011) etc. In view of the declining employment income and rising investment income for some sections of the population, certain regulationist authors have also examined the conditions for introducing a coherent growth regime that would be "driven by finance", with high stock market prices facilitating access to credit that feeds consumption (Boyer 2009).

Most of these macro-economic studies have looked at the consequences of this new capitalism, which leads to recurring financial crises that have a high social cost, tending to divert investment away from the real economy and to feed growing inequalities between workers, and between work and capital. Not only do workers suffer unemployment, but their remuneration is strictly constrained, whereas income from capital is rising. And the best-off workers have both employment income and investment income.

At the micro-economic level, some of the literature on financialization has sought to explain the adoption of financial objectives by non-financial firms by relating it to the growing importance of institutional investors in their capital, and the spread of mechanisms such as stock options, which encourage managers to give priority to increasing the value of equity instruments in their management approach (Gleadle and Cornelius 2008; Ezzamel et al. 2008).

All this research points to a first definition of financialization as a process of morphological transformation of capitalism, entailing the capture of resources by finance in the broadest sense, through expansion of the financial markets, a rise in the number of financial operators (different types of investment funds: pension funds, investment funds, private equity funds, etc.) and finally the development of a service industry associated with financial activities (audit and consulting firms, law firms, assessors, rating agencies, etc.). Certain analysts of capitalism (Duménil and Lévy 2001; Walery 2009) explain that other periods such as the late nineteenth century and early twentieth century also experienced high degrees of financialization, which only ended with the crisis of 1929. But the wave of financialization discussed here, which began to develop in the 1980s and accelerated in the 1990s, has unique features. For a good grasp of this latest wave of financialization, it is important to look at those unique features (Erturk et al. 2008). They include the mass spread of popular savings, reorganisation and professionalization of pension fund management, and other transformations that lead to financial actors gaining more influence. But it should also be noted that this wave is apparently inextricably bound up both ideologically and practically with neoliberal economic theories and the instruments and concepts developed by modern financial theory.[1]

This is why I think it is necessary to adopt a second definition of financialization, built on this very specific theoretical and technical corpus that underpins the process itself. The process of financialization can thus be defined as a gradual colonisation by specific "financialised" techniques and calculation methods. Financialised instruments will be defined as instruments incorporating models and representations specific to finance, the financial economy and financial mathematics. These instruments, which are part of a body of specific knowledge, participate in financialization in the sense that they speak a language that carries the premises, decision-making systems and strong socio-political conventions they spread and reproduce.

Clearly, the two forms of financialization defined above cannot be dissociated. The transformation of the economic system described by the "externalist" meaning of financialization creates growth in the power and wealth of certain groups of actors, which as a result of their increasing importance can more and more easily impose certain instruments, and certain forms of regulation that work to their benefit. Conversely, scientific research and the technical mechanisms arising in the broadest sense from the sphere of influence of the three-layered Chicago school (legal, economic and financial) has been used as ideological justification, scientific backing and practical instrumentation, to establish a different practical organisation of the world and favour the world of finance.

[1] This has in fact become a branch of economics, judging by the frequency with which so called "Nobel Prizes" for Economics are awarded to finance researchers.

Financialization of the economic system is thus very closely linked to financialization of the instruments of calculation, the policies followed and the theories underpinning them.

Looking at accounting, which is known to be crucial in the operation of capitalism, it is clear that adoption of IFRS was a moment of strong financialization of accounting systems for the European continent. The next section highlights the financialised nature of these International Financial Reporting Standards, before an examination of how they contribute more broadly to the financialization of the economic system.

2 IFRS as Financialised Accounting

2.1 What Is a Financialised Calculation?

To define the scope of these standards more precisely, we can start by studying finance textbooks, which are considered to contain the knowledge underpinning the approach and practices of finance professionals at a given point in time. The basic textbook co-written by Nobel prize-winner Robert Merton, a central author in the construction of contemporary financial knowledge (Bodie and Merton 2000), lists three pillars for finance:

- Optimising decisions in time, mainly through assessment of economic choices (essentially investments) based on calculation of current values using actuarial methods.
- Valuation of assets (essentially listed shares and bonds), which requires understanding of the markets and the products traded there, and also knowledge of the techniques and models (such as CAPM) that make these valuations possible. The book also teaches us to differentiate accounting value from stock market value, and adhere to the idea that efficient markets provide the best valuation of assets.
- Risk management, essentially consisting of "transferring" risks through hedging, insurance or diversification. Risk is mainly analysed in terms of probability, with the determination of an expected value associated with a volatility (standard deviation).

This brief summary brings out several features of calculation instruments I shall call "financialised", which can be used to identify various financialised calculative practices:

- A preference for describing economic phenomena in terms of cash flows, receipts and payments (which can then be used to calculate Net Present Value).
- A utilitarian definition of goods based on the services they will provide in the future, principally conceived as future flows of income (or to be translated into flows) which can be discounted to present value.

- Sanctification of market value, considered as the best estimation of the value of goods. The market organises the meeting between all opinions of the future to make prices, which are therefore, in this thought framework, better than every estimated calculation. As the power of veridiction of value is entrusted to the market, all other systems aiming to calculate values are seen as inferior and potentially turned into servants of market value.
- A conception of risks as probabilisable and describable by expectations and standard deviation (the Gaussian distribution), which is introduced into all management and valuation models (Walter 2002). Statistical analysis of risk and the study of volatilities is thus more important than close knowledge (Walter 2010).

Promotion of these forms of calculation relies on the central idea that financial actors, fund managers and investment banks are—thanks to their knowledge—the most capable of allocating available economic resources in an optimal way. Under these theories, these actors' capacity to discern the most profitable investments (through examination of a wide universe of possible investments and application of models of investment choices) and diversify risks (through their portfolio, and through exchanging risks, since these actors are capable of calculating risks, assigning a price to them and trading in them) makes them the most important actors because they are the best able to improve overall economic efficiency.

Financialization of quantifications can be seen in the use of a future-oriented definition of value, the preference for trusting in market price over any other value, the constant concern to assign a value to time and risk, with extensive use of discounting, which requires close attention to cash flows, trust in probability-based statistical analysis for risk assessment and management and finally in the way everything is examined from an investor's viewpoint and analysed in terms of value-producing capital (Chiapello 2015).

This rapid overview enables us to identify what in IFRS is financialised, and can be related to the conceptual framework and the promotion of fair value as a central principle of valuation (Müller 2014).

3 IFRS as Financialised Standards

The conceptual frameworks of both the American and international accounting standard-setters consider that accounting must primarily satisfy investors (Colasse 2009; Zhang and Andrew 2014); the needs of other users of accounting information are considered to be met if investors' needs are met. In the case of the American FASB's conceptual framework, which was developed in the 1970s, this premise could be analysed as a way of solving the controversial question of the purpose of accounting (Young 2006), and a very acceptable way, because the standardisation was initially conceived for the financial markets and the FASB operates in America as a subcontractor of the Securities and Exchange Commission. Since adoption of the IASB's standards was at first only mandatory in Europe for listed companies' consolidated financial statements issued as part of their reporting to investors, the premise could still be considered coherent with the scope of firms obliged to apply IFRS.

However, the meaning of this premise changes when these standards spread beyond listed companies and their financial communication, as can be observed in Europe. EU countries are tending to bring their national accounting standards closer to international standards, or in some cases quite simply adopt international standards for all of their firms. Also, the IASB clearly expresses its hegemonic vocation, as demonstrated in its plan to develop standards for SMEs. Meanwhile, the IFAC (International Federation of Accountants), which is known have long-standing connections with the IASB (Capron 2005), has begun to produce accounting standards for States (IPSAS) based on the principles of the IASB. It is as if it is considered normal for the accounting image of our nations' economic organisations to be constructed in such a way as to give priority to meeting investors' information needs. This aim only holds up because it is deeply rooted in financial theory and the neoliberal economy, which both postulate that investors are the best placed to ensure efficient allocation of the nation's resources and that the public good is thus best served by their capacities for judgement, identifying the most profitable projects and managing risks. If we accept these premises, it is important not only to entrust to them as many decisions concerning us as possible, but also to make every effort to give them the best possible information to form their predictions.

Adopting fair value as the new general principle in accounting for transactions is the logical consequence of this postulate. There is not a single accounting concept it cannot be used to redefine. Even the notion of historical cost has been redefined by fair value. To record any sale or purchase operation or for the first recognition of an asset or liability, whenever a commercial transaction gives rise to deferred payment, the accountant must now discount cash flows to bring the transaction to its present value. To do so, he needs to bring a major assumption into the accounts: the discount rate. The amount of sales revenues differs under IFRS depending on whether the customer pays in a single operation or in ten instalments, and any sales revenue with "significantly deferred" receipts must be recorded at a value below its nominal value in the accounts, with the differential booked in a financial income account. As this very simple example shows, the value of assets under international standards must be calculated by taking into consideration cash flows and assigning value to time, in line with the conventions of finance.

Next, fair value transforms the idea of depreciation, which is now defined as recognition of "consumption of the future economic benefits embodied in the asset". It is no longer straight-line allocation of the asset's original value over a convention-based useful life, and the depreciation schedule, which is supposed to follow the expected pattern of consumption as closely as possible, can be regularly revised. And if a residual value is expected to exist beyond the useful life anticipated by the firm, it can no longer be included in the depreciable amount. So the concept of depreciation is gradually being reworked and moving closer to impairment, which in contrast is gaining ground and legitimacy. For certain types of asset (e.g. goodwill) only impairment is now possible (Ding et al. 2008). Depreciation used to be a technique that brings consideration of time into accounting, particularly the lifetime of an investment, by spreading the initial outlay that is used to calculate a production cost and establishing a reserve to finance other investments. This understanding of the time of an investment generated various theoretical debates about the importance, for example, of basing depreciation on the replacement cost of the investment rather than its historical (to make it easier to re-establish a reserve) or on the possibility of continuing depreciation for a period longer than the initial period, if the asset is still in use, so as not to distort production costs. But those debates are gone too, because there has been a radical change in the way an investment is conceived. The new view of depreciation, together with the concept of impairment, has shifted the focus. An investment is no longer as seen as something used in production, something that wears out, but as something with market value that could potentially be resold. As a result, the decline in value that must be recorded is ideally aligned with the difference between the historical cost and its current price on the market. What matters is assessing the present value of the investment by imagining what could be got for it if the decision was made to sell it, in a portfolio manager-type approach. The point is no longer to ensure continuity of production or assess costs accurately. The accounts are no longer shaped by a producer's concerns, but by a financier's concerns.

However, financial theory postulates a reconciliation between these two outlooks (the producer's and financier's). In the neoclassical economic theory from which financial theory derives, market value (on which the financier's view is based) is supposed to come from utility, which, since the work of Irving Fisher, has itself been operationalised by future uses (in this case, what the investment will be used to make and sell, mainly informed by the producer's view). Provided the market operates perfectly, market value is considered as the best possible estimate of the value in use defined as the future services that will be rendered by the investment. This explains why, when as in many cases no market value is available, firms are obliged to construct models incorporating their forecasts of volumes, useful life, etc. in order to calculate a present value based on anticipated future cash flows, and why this calculation is preferred to using historical cost. If you believe in these neo-classical conceptualisations, you have to accept that economic modelling is the best possible way to calculate the "real" "economic wear and tear" of the investment (i.e. what is consumed over the period of potential income the investment is capable of providing), and that this measure is much better than any other measure supplied by the rudimentary cost-spreading rules of traditional depreciation. If you believe that "market value = value in use = NPV of estimated future cash flows", then the impairment technique is the only appropriate technique. Of course, the current system, which still leaves room for depreciation, even redefined, looks like a compromise between the conservatism principle and the fair value principle (Mennicken and Millo 2013), but there is still a striking shift.

Implementation of the fair value principle has thus brought into accounts made-up models based on a very wide range of assumptions about the future, and introduces an assumption of investments' liquidity: the idea that they could be sold at any moment in order to invest the money more profitably elsewhere.

This assumption of liquidity is in fact impossible to dissociate from financial reasoning, as the systematic use of discounting shows. Application of a discount rate is explained under financial reasoning by the fact that any investment should always be compared with a cash investment as an alternative. Or at least, that is how the earliest users of the method for assessing non-financial investments in the late nineteenth century justified discounting cash flows (Doganova 2014). The underlying idea is that the investor can always, at minimum, choose not to invest and put his money in an interest-bearing account. Therefore, to be acceptable, the investments available to him must offer more than the interest on savings. Discounting thus helps to sustain the fantasy that at any moment in time, the money invested could be recovered and invested with a bank, and that the quality of the investment must be measured by that yardstick. It is based on the assumption that investments are perfectly liquid and interchangeable, which is never in fact the case, since money loses its liquid form as soon as it is invested. The liquidity of markets, as Keynes showed, creates an illusion of liquidity of investments. The actors on the markets may trade shares and be liquid, but the assets in which businesses have invested are not liquid, unless they themselves also invest in financial assets. Financialised calculation techniques have thus incorporated the illusion of liquidity which is specific to the financial markets.

By financialising accounting, these techniques deny the durability of investments made by companies and tend to consider them as merchandise that can be traded. The measures for monitoring assets in the accounts based on cash-generating units are simply a translation of this representation of the firm as a basket of independent merchandise, rather than a singular combination of assets into a working tool.

Finally, for many financial assets, fair value is not only the governing principle for initial recognition in the accounts and calculation of an allowance for as fair value can also be used to revise values upwards. Market value or its best simulation through models as required by the ranking of valuation methods laid down in the regulations (see the three levels of valuation for financial assets in American and international standards[2]) are becoming the only acceptable measures for valuing the firm's assets. It matters little that this value is volatile and depends on the ups and downs of the market, or that it is based on predictions rather than actual facts. It is the information needed by the people whose job it is to choose the most appropriate investments, and who must at all times consider realising their gains or absorbing their losses to go and invest elsewhere.

[2] IFRS 13, released by the IASB in 2011 and endorsed by the EU in December 2012, adopts the three-level valuation logic of the 2006 standard FAS 157. This lays down three ways of determining fair value depending on whether a market price exists (level 1), no market price exists but other observable data can be used in estimation models (level 2), or no observable data exists, in which case valuation is entirely based on modelling (level 3). Regarding derivatives, which played a very important role in the 2008 crisis, it is very unusual for them to have a level 1 valuation.

International accounting standards are thus contributing to a redefinition of the firm and its function. For a country like France where the accounting tradition was far removed from these concepts, the firm described by accounting standards has gone from being an institution-firm that produces merchandise, to a merchandise-firm (Chiapello 2005a, b). The viewpoint from which the accounts are established has changed, from that of the producer of goods and services who are seeking to construct a long-term, profitable economic activity, to that of purchasers of securities on the markets who are interested in making a profit by trading in those securities.

Finally, all these ideas are supported by accounting research that has become a subdiscipline of finance research and is putting the final touches to discrediting accountants' quantification activities whenever they are not based on the financiers' favourite metrics, market price, or if unavailable, financial modelling (Power 2010). This is true of the American research stream that seeks to estimate the "value relevance" of accounts from their level of correlation with market prices, making the "Market to Book Ratio" a fundamental indicator of the value of accounts. Corporate accounts that cannot be used to reach a good estimate of stock market prices has no relevance in this view, because the only real knowledge is provided by market prices. That the "market to book ratio" can be interpreted differently, for example in reverse, as an indicator of the distance between financial markets and the real economy, is an idea that is not even up for debate. Of course, this stream of research has a normative aim and results in company accounts including an ever-increasing number of items carried at fair value, which in the end looks like the simplest way to improve the correlation between the accounting measure and the market measure: making sure they are the same.

IFRS are thus clearly financialised standards. And the penetration by financial conventions into this set of standards can be interpreted as one of the many manifestations of the ideological success of neoliberal ideas, and a result of financial investors' growing influence in our economies as the economy grows increasingly financialised. What I now want to suggest is that this financialization of accounts is not simply a result of financialization, but makes an active contribution to it.

4 The Role of IFRS in the Financialization of Our Economy

The response to this suggestion needs reflection on the role of quantification instruments and their effects on the world. Those effects can be classified according to the various roles of economic quantifications: pragmatic and epistemic. They support action and decision, and they also help us to think, understand and know. This dual function is what makes the conventions on which quantifications are constructed so decisive.[3]

[3] Desrosières (2008) explained that quantifications are both instruments of proof and governance tools, which matches what we call epistemological functions and pragmatic functions. To stress the convention-based nature of quantification work, dependent on systems of political, social and

Accounting is a set of techniques intended to produce knowledge: knowledge about the way the firm operates, its economic health and its issues, its profitability and its risks. Studying the accounting techniques and principles in action indicates what, for the communities concerned, constitutes appropriate knowledge that should be held about the firm and its operations. It designates what is worthy of being explored, scrutinised, examined. The authorities and assemblies that produce today's accounting standards can thus be designated as "epistemological authorities" (Vanel 2008) and the groups of people who make them as forming "epistemological communities" (Haas 1992). Accounting is a practice that both produces knowledge and is founded on knowledge. The sociology of science and techniques has taught us to see calculation centres as decisive spaces of construction of scientific truths (Latour 1987). It is thus possible to see accounting systems as places of construction of economic truth.

What is happening in this assertion cannot be summed up as a simple operation consisting of quantitative description of the economic world. For accounting quantifications and categories contribute to the existence of things and ideas without which they would not exist on the same level as other quantifications and categorisations (Hacking 1999). From this angle, accounting helps to construct reality, to create phenomena by naming them, and this reality then becomes the starting point or stimulant of action.

Quantification systems shape the way we look at phenomena and our understanding of them. They suggest modes of action. These new categories then have an effect on the world they seek to describe, due to the reactivity effects specific to every quantification activity (Espeland and Sauder 2007). IFRS makes it legitimate for a firm to seek to increase the wealth of its shareholders by doing other things as well as selling products and services. Profits can just as well come from the choice of the firm's financing structure, gains on its investments or its cash management. This means non-financial firms are being encouraged to develop financial activities to support their profitability, and this development is, as seen earlier, one of the distinctive features of financial capitalism. Reactivity effects can therefore explain development of financial activities by non-financial firms, which becomes a realistic strategy.

Financialised representations tend to act as if investments made were always liquid, and focus attention on the present value rather than the cost of the investment and the efforts required to draw value from it. They contribute to the short-termism generally associated with financialization. This is a form of performativity of calculative frameworks (MacKenzie et al. 2008), since what is postulated ends up becoming reality. Constantly showing the market value of the firm's assets, even when it has no intention of selling them, ultimately provides an incentive for a certain number of firms to dispose of them and create the liquidity that was initially only postulated.

---

scientific representation, he also explained that quantifying was choosing a convention, then measuring.

The specificity of financial calculative instruments on an epistemic level is that the "truth" they set out often consists of stating wealth (and more broadly, value), and thereby establishing it. The power to create reality through accounting is a power to create wealth, such that the choice of any accounting convention has an impact on distribution of wealth, which itself produces effects. Criticism of the pro-cyclical effects of international standards, which tend to amplify financial market movements—since a rise in stock market prices is reflected in the accounts and in calculation of profit, and a rise in profit in turn feeds rising market prices (Aglietta and Reberioux 2005)—is rooted in this capacity of accounting to state wealth and distribute it in one and the same movement.

This capacity also explains the most persistent criticism of fair value accounting as giving financial actors the opportunity to monopolise gains before they are actually realised, simply on suspicion of favourable expectations (Richard 2005a, b; Capron 2005). Theoretically, this capacity is counterbalanced by the fact that in a crisis period, reversal of expectations should have the opposite effects. This theory was tested during the crisis of 2008 and in fact the fair value principle was suspended as regards recognition of unrealised losses, because of the systemic risk that a sudden drop in all banks' balance sheets would have generated. In this specific case, financialization of accounting appears to have served to direct more value towards the financial actors in a bullish period, without bringing the same actors to pay back in bearish times. The epistemic function of accounting makes it state wealth. And the financialization of accounting has led it to enrich the world of finance simply by changing the conventions used.

Finally, accounting constructions also have political effects. The apparent technical objectivity of calculation obscures the underlying conventions and their distributive consequences. Quantification tends to naturalise the results of the calculation, which seem fair and legitimate, and that legitimacy is strengthened by legal endorsement, because the standards that must be applied are imposed by the law. Accounting thus legitimises social asymmetry and distributions. International accounting standards are the product of a theoretical view of the firm that buries its political nature under technical considerations. They thus participate in legitimisation of its founding ideas, especially the idea that firms should primarily remunerate the providers of capital, and are only secondarily providers of jobs or producers of goods and services. Legitimisation comes partly from the "depoliticisation" of questions, which has been achieved by making them more technical.

5 Conclusion

International accounting standards carry a view of the world and of calculation principles that contribute to the process of financialization of our economies on two levels.

First of all, these accounting standards incorporate postulates and calculation conventions that are rooted in financial theory and promote the viewpoint and interests of financial actors, who are considered by this theory to be the best placed to decide between potential investments for the common good. This financialization of accounting has educational effects, developing understanding of the world and providing incentives for actors to change their practices and their way of acting in response to what the new accounting shows and the interpretation schemas it carries with it. This is one type of effect of financialised accounting, by which agents instructed by its formats direct their action such that firms become financialised (for example by developing financial activities or outsourcing production activities to subcontractors).

A second type of effect is much more prosaic: it concerns accounting's singular ability to state wealth and fairly immediately trigger economic distributions. On this level, the new calculation conventions adopted have had direct effects on economic flows, to the benefit of actors from the world of finance.

IFRS are as much financialised as financialising standards. Of course, due to its language, accounting always has a financialising dimension. It can itself be seen as a vector of a financial view of the firm that has not always been, and is not always, dominant in firms, as shown by several studies presenting differences of opinion between professional groups inside organisations, engineers, researchers or shopkeepers against accountants and financiers (Morales and Pezet 2012; Dent 1991). But I suggest here that there are various ways of performing accounting calculations and making financial concerns exist in firms and in society, and that some very specific conventions embedded in IFRS actively contribute to producing the recent transformation of capitalism named financialization.

References

Aglietta M, Reberioux A (2005) Corporate governance a drift. A critique of shareholder value. Edward Elgar, Cheltenham

Baud C, Durand C (2012) Financialization, globalization and the making of profits by leading retailers. Soc Econ Rev 10:241–266

Bodie Z, Merton RC (2000) Finance. Prentice Hall International, Upper Saddle River, NJ

Boyer R (2009) Feu le régime d'accumulation tiré par la finance: la crise des subprimes en perspective historique. Revue de la régulation 5, Spring. http://regulation.revues.org/7367

Capron M (ed) (2005) Les normes comptables internationales, instruments du capitalisme financier. La Découverte, Paris

Chiapello E (2005a) Les normes comptables comme institution du capitalisme. Une analyse du passage aux IFRS en Europe à partir de 2005. Sociologie du travail 47(3):362–382

Chiapello E (2005b) Transformation des conventions comptables, transformation de la représentation de l'entreprise. In: Capron M (ed) Les normes comptables internationales, instruments du capitalisme financier. La Découverte, Paris, pp 121–150

Chiapello E (2012) La construction comptable de l'économie. In: Nikitin M, Richard C (eds) La comptabilité, la société et le politique. Mélanges en l'honneur du Professeur Bernard Colasse. Economica, Paris, pp 128–135

Chiapello E (2015) Financialisation of valuation. Hum Stud 38:13–35

Colasse B (2009) Cadres comptables conceptuels. In: Colasse B (ed) Encyclopédie de comptabilité, contrôle de gestion et audit. Économica, Paris, pp 103–114

Colette C, Richard J (2000) Comptabilité générale. Les systèmes français et anglo-saxons. Dunod, Paris
Crotty J (2005) The neoliberal paradox: the impact of destructive product market competition and 'modern' financial markets on nonfinancial corporation performance in the neoliberal era. In: Epstein GA (ed) Financialization and the world economy. Edward Elgar, Cheltenham, pp 77–110
Dent J (1991) Accounting and organizational cultures: a field study of the emergence of a new organizational reality. Acc Organ Soc 16(8):705–732
Desrosières A (2008) Pour une sociologie historique de la quantification. L'argument statistique I. Les presses de l'Ecole des Mines, Paris
Ding Y, Richard J, Stolowy H (2008) Towards an understanding of the phases of goodwill accounting in four Western capitalist countries: from stakeholder model to shareholder model. Acc Organ Soc 33(7–8):718–755
Doganova L (2014) Décompter le futur: la formule des flux actualisés et le manager-investisseur. Sociétés Contemporaines 93:67–87. doi:10.3917/soco.093.0067
Duménil G, Lévy D (2001) Costs and benefits of neoliberalism. A class analysis. Rev Int Polit Econ 8(4):578–607
Epstein GA (ed) (2005) Financialization and the world economy. Edward Elgar, Cheltenham
Erturk I, Froud J, Johal S, Leaver A, Williams K (2008) Financialization, coupon pool and conjuncture. In: Erturk I, Froud J, Johal S, Leaver A, Williams K (eds) Financialization at work: key texts and commentary. Routledge, London, pp 1–44
Espeland W, Sauder M (2007) Rankings and reactivity: how public measure recreates social worlds. Am J Sociol 113(1):1–40
Ezzamel M, Willmott H, Worthington F (2008) Manufacturing shareholder value: the role of accounting in organizational transformation. Acc Organ Soc 33(2–3):107–140
Froud J, Haslam C, Johal S, Williams K (2002) Cars after financialization: a case study in financial under-performance, constraints and consequences. Compet Chang 6(1):13–41
Gleadle P, Cornelius N (2008) A case study of financialization and EVA®. Crit Perspect Account 18(8):1219–1238
Jones B, Nisbet P (2011) Shareholder value versus stakeholder values: CSR and financialization in the global food firms. Soc Econ Rev 9:287–314
Haas PM (1992) Introduction: epistemic communities and international policy coordination. Int Organ 46(1):1–35
Hacking I (1999) The social construction of what? Harvard University Press, Cambridge, MA
Krippner G (2005) The financialization of the American economy. Soc Econ Rev 3:173–208
Latour B (1987) Science in action: how to follow scientists and engineers through society. Harvard University Press, Cambridge, MA
Mennicken A, Millo Y (2013) Testing values: financialization, organization and the emergence of impairment rules. Working Paper. London School of Economics and Political Science, London
Morales J, Pezet A (2012) Financialization through hybridization: the subtle power of financial controlling. In: Huault I, Richard C (eds) Finance: the discreet regulator. How financial activities shape and transform the world. Palgrave Macmillan, New York, NY, pp 19–39
Müller J (2014) An accounting revolution? The financialization of standard setting. Crit Perspect Account 25(7):539–557. doi:10.1016/j.cpa.2013.08.006
MacKenzie D, Muniesa F, Siu L (2008) Do economists make markets? On the performativity of economics. Princeton University Press, Princeton, NJ
Palpacuer F, Perez R, Tozanli S, Brabet J (2006) Financiarisation et globalisation des stratégies d'entreprise: le cas des multinationales agroalimentaires en Europe. Finance, Contrôle, Stratégie 3(9):165–189
Power M (2010) Fair value accounting, financial economics and the transformation of reliability. Account Bus Res 40(3):197–210

Richard J (2005a) Les trois stades du capitalisme comptable. In: Capron M (ed) Les nouvelles normes comptables internationales: instruments du capitalisme financier. La Découverte, Paris, pp 89–120

Richard J (2005b) The concept of fair value in French and German accounting regulations from 1673 to 1914 and its consequences for the interpretation of the stages of development of capitalist accounting. Crit Perspect Account 16(6):825–850

Richard J (1995a) The evolution of the Romanian and Russian accounting charts after the collapse of the communist system. Eur Account Rev 4(2):305–322. doi:10.1080/09638189500000018

Richard J (1995b) The evolution of accounting chart models in Europe from 1900 to 1945: some historical elements. Eur Account Rev 4(1):87–124. doi:10.1080/09638189500000004

Vanel G (2008) La normalisation financière internationale face à l'émergence de nouvelles autorités épistémiques américaines. Le cas de la filière des chiffres. Revue de la régulation. 3/4, Autumn. http://regulation.revues.org/4443

Walery S (2009) La crise de la financiarisation post-fordiste, une perspective de longue durée. Working Paper. Forum de la Régulation

Walter C (2002) Le phénomène leptokurtique sur les marchés financiers. Finance 23(2):15–68

Walter C (2010) Le sida de la finance. Cités Philosophie Politique Histoire 41:89–98

Young JJ (2006) Making up users. Acc Organ Soc 31(6):579–600. doi:10.1016/j.aos.2005.12.005

Zhang Y, Andrew J (2014) Financialization and the conceptual framework. Crit Perspect Account 25:17–26. doi:10.1016/j.cpa.2012.11.012

Fair Value and Discounted Cash Flows: Value Creation or Sense Destruction?

Véronique Blum

Abstract The current contribution examines the limits of the Discounted Cash Flow methods, often denounced by Jacques Richard. We defend the idea that beyond the already famous shortfalls that the evaluation methods have demonstrated, those may extend when applied in a very different context, i.e. the one of financial reporting. Indeed the change of set, the loss of unity in capital budgeting decision and risk awareness may increase the potential misuses of the method. Finally, we demonstrate that the concept of infinite life loses consistency in such a framework.

The Discounted Cash Flow (DCF) as a potential measurement for Fair Value has nurtured the contemporary accounting debate, notably involving the international standard setter, and which Jacques Richard participated in by defending the necessity of a critical approach. To Jacques Richard, the current conflict is a sequel of an older one, started at the beginning of the industrial revolution and opposing the tenants of price-values reporting versus the defenders of cost-values reporting. The subtleties are numerous in accounting matters, and the previous sentence encloses at least two of them while in conflicting cases, terminology precision appears to be fundamental. In that unique debate, many definitions co-exist, which may not exactly coincide with economical or financial interpretations though they borrow their concepts. While we review those semantic tensions, we will also underline their implications.

This contribution first confronts the existing perceptions of values, prices and costs, all of them being candidates to measure an object. In a second part, the conditions for a rigorous application of DCF tools for an assessment of fair value are examined. As they are unfortunately rarely checked in real life cases, the second part reminds how much cautiousness must be exercised in results interpretation when applying the rules prescribed by the tools. The use of DCF methods indeed presents a double risk exposure: to the method itself and to the rules derived. As real life is undeniably likely different from a theoretical life, the use of the theoretical tools and the rules derived from theory can hardly be strictly applied and may

V. Blum (✉)
Université Grenoble-Alpes, CERAG – CNRS UMR 5820, Grenoble, France
e-mail: veronique.blum@iut2.upmf-grenoble.fr

D. Bensadon, N. Praquin (eds.), *IFRS in a Global World*,
DOI 10.1007/978-3-319-28225-1_7

require some balanced and prudent adjustments. Arguably, there is in the usage, room for the emergence of inner tensions, which may possibly harm the business. Our third part shows that the strict application of the rules may elude other important business decisions. The key decision factor is graphically represented versus what it hides, in order to bring arguments in favour of a greater awareness. At worst, beyond the technical limits of the methods, the strong focus on shareholder's value creation may hide embedded risks and become sense destructive. It is by this demonstration that we hope to pay a fair tribute to the work of Jacques Richard. In a last part, we seize another key topic to Jacques Richard et al. (2014): the treatment of the Goodwill by the International Standard Accounting Board (IASB). In the DCF framework, we show that the infinite life makes little sense. Globally, the chapter aims at formalizing arguments supported by Jacques Richard by expressing in a financial language.

1 The Circular Referential Triangle of Cost, Prices and Values

This section examines the concepts of cost-values to price-values as opposed in the introduction.

1.1 Cost, Value and Price Definition

A common mistake would be to exclusively understand cost-value as a theoretical managerial production cost while it can also represent the acquisition cost, i.e. the price paid to purchase a good, such as an asset. The cost is then deemed a realized price. Interestingly, cost-values are not necessarily different from a market price, whether the trading occurs over-the-counter (OTC) or via an exchange. Indeed, in a competitive market, the purchase price is a transaction price supposedly reaching equilibrium when supply meets demand. We come back to that notion below. The second pivotal concept is the one of a price-value, defined as an observed one on the market, i.e. a market-price, which therefore may only be observed and may not be realized. In such a case, the price-value describes the price at which a good could be virtually sold if the "owner" decided to do so. When seizing the (confusing) topic, accounting authors have also referred to the opposition between the entry price (realized purchasing price) and the exit price (potential sale value) (Nobes and Alexander 2005; Alexander 2005), in a dichotomy that appeared to be appealing to American and international standard setters. The subprime crisis exemplifies the difference.

In a cost-value economy, a borrower has access to a sum of money relative to the purchase price of the underlying good. If agent A wishes to become the owner of a 200,000 € house, he can only borrow a portion of that money. Likely if prudency applies; the portion size is proportional to the recurrent revenues which agent A perceives or earns. In a price-value economy, the situation starts the same way but is modified when market prices get higher. Let's assume that as an external impact of increased ease in access to property, the housing market experiences a raise in prices. Agent A now virtually owns a 400,000 € worth house. As in most of mortgage contracts, the real property simultaneously plays the role of security for the loan. Then, A's banker holds an optional value of 400,000 € and feels now comfortable with offering the possibility to increase the debt of agent A. The mechanism is very naïve: the house can virtually be sold back at 400,000 €, then it may generate that value, on average, a practice that has been identified as a cognitive mistake in capital budgeting (Savage 2009).

Two remarks follow: (1) the price-value based economies imply the acceptation of a convergence to the mean, (2) if one bets on an infinite price growth, there is less money to borrow in an entry-price economy than in an exit-price economy. In the latter case, when prices decrease, a crisis occurs and the market knows what is deemed a correction.

Likely, the price-value economy will experience bigger corrections than the cost-values economy. The process favouring more substantial money flows able to nurture the distance from the correction price is coined pro-cyclicity. Danjou, currently an IASB member (Richard 2004) once wondered '*if it is not better to avoid rushing to audacious accounting reforms*' in a period of instability of markets, all the more so when '*it is not clear that the shareholders want to read the value of their enterprise in the balance sheet*'. There is undeniably a dynamic interpretation of values in the price economy and a static one in the cost economy while dynamics may be source of volatility. Moreover, there is a widespread doubt about the trust in virtual values expressions, as compared to realized prices. We next discuss the accuracy of market prices as observed.

1.2 The Porosity of Accounting to Finance Reasoning has Favoured the Financialization of the Economy

From a financial point of view, and it should here be reminded that financial evaluation is an applied exercise in microeconomics, the settlement of a transaction signals the meeting of supply and demand. Following very basic economic theory, it is only when the transactions are numerous, in pure and perfect competition that the transaction prices converge to a market equilibrium price. Implied assumptions are numerous, they suppose: a large number of buyers and sellers, no barriers to entry or exit, perfect factor mobility, perfect information, zero transaction costs, profit maximisation, homogeneity of products, absence of externalities and agents' rationality. All those assumptions have been extensively discussed, notably by behavioural finance researchers (Kahneman 2011; Kahneman and Tversky 1979), whom demonstrated in length their little chances to be simultaneously checked, if checked at all.

In our accounting classes, there are huge chances that a transaction described as observable is understood as one that is realized. In other words, to the external observer, the price of the transaction is the main object of observation in an economy driven social system. Demand and supply meet a convergence point, which once the trading is done, becomes the realized price. There is to our knowledge no market for virtual prices able to reach an equilibrium price. More specifically, observed real prices allow the assessment of virtual prices while the reverse doesn't hold. If we replace virtual prices by values, we reach the idea that is generally accepted that a value is based on a price observation (prices allow to formulate values with transformation) but a value does not technically define a price, as the price is the meeting point of different values. Therefore, to most of our accounting students, a price or a cost is realized and past. On the contrary, a value is considered estimated, it is the idea that an economical agent develops to approach a potential price.

In financial evaluation classes, as many manuals and many auditing firms internal process will testify, the price settlement is reached when the values are fine-tuned by the negotiating parts whom alternatively have expressed and adjusted their self-estimated values. An interesting feature is derived from that widely adopted by practitioner's mechanism: the will to come to an agreement and exchange a good or a service has a strong impact on the final settlement price. In the latter paragraph, we are taking a significant distance from the terminology suggested during the industrial revolution: price-values have become values while cost-values are similar to prices. We also support the idea that intentions drive values while prices are testifying of realizations.

From those observations, we can precise the definitions which we will retain for the rest of the paper. Take two negotiating parts X & Y. X is selling the good G; Y wants to buy it. Costs represent the amount of money it takes to "buy" or "build" a good. At the beginning of the negotiation, only X can claim the existence of a cost for the good G. When a transaction is envisaged, a value is assessed and expressed as a desired selling price. Likely, the value for X is estimated on the basis of the cost information X possesses and on the extra-value that is associated to the good, and relying on external information (market price, shortage in G procurement…). On the Y side, another value is estimated as the contribution of the good G to operations may substantially differ from the one of X. The value assessed by Y likely includes most of the information that X integrated while X has little information about the destination of G for Y. The negotiation is undoubtedly an asymmetric game. If, and only if, an agreement is reached, likely after a potentially long bargaining process, a transaction will occur and the agreed value becomes a price. Eventually, the so called price will be different from the two values expected by on one hand the selling side and the other hand, the purchasing side, respectively X and Y. Assuming that value finally meets the condition to become a price, it also becomes a so-called exit-price (realized exit-price) to the seller and an entry price to the buyer. In the latter case, it is a cost. The circularity between costs, prices and values is now obvious. Each protagonist's stance evolves in a triangular space.

We are now turning to an important question: How does Y estimate the potential contribution of the good G to its operations? The asymmetrical part of the negotiation has many chances to be drawn from a business plan, which includes projected cash flows. Once the cash flows are estimated, the DCF methods deemed an appropriate substitute to a price-value (Richard et al. 2014, p. 63) can come into play. The latter analogy has been of great help in finance theory to resolve long lasting puzzles such as the Real Option Valuation since Myers coined it in 1977. It took more than two decades for Copeland and Antikarov (2001) to suggest the MAD (Marketed Asset Disclaimer) approach. In a very short explanation, the trick allows to evaluate a project by focusing on its future cash flows in place of the problematic alternative consisting in looking for a portfolio of similar assets on the financial markets. In this framework, the MAD approach tells a story written from the cash flow lines. Concretely, the MAD approach exactly recommends substituting a regulated market price by an over-the-counter price and considers the potential settlement price as defined between a company and itself. This makes a lot of sense in a financial perspective, in the unique scope of capital budgeting, as it offers to construct a collegial decision on a combination of strategic view, financial business plan and decision criteria relying on the same informational grounds. In such a case, the shortcut generates risks but the people allowing for the forecast bear the risk. There is no transfer of risk, but a conscious acceptation of it.

Once "the trick" is imported to an enlarged accounting information scope, it faces two main issues. Firstly, it is not anymore circumscribed to internal information used to build an internal shared vision and to decide to invest or not. Secondly, there is a shift in the type of decision and its location. Originally, the DCF based decision is a capital budgeting one, likely focused on real assets or a mix of real and financial assets; it is made inside the company, and part of a common to all dependant deciders investment portfolio, moreover sharing a strategy. When applied to financial reporting, it next becomes an investment decision, focused on financial assets, made outside of the company, with deciders being independent shareholders, holding an infinite variety of diversified financial assets portfolio, with potential opposite strategies.

The reasons why the DCF concept has penetrated the accounting area, ignoring those tremendous differences, may still require some investigations. Indeed, beyond the potential tautology, as any technical tool, DCFs require some precautions for not being led astray. A subsequent question could be: does the shareholder understand what story he/she is buying when deciding to invest on numerical story-telling basis?

2 Determinism as a Surrogate to Risk Recognition

It is the approach adopted in this contribution to examine the possible *unfairness* of the DCF methods and to subsequently suggest ways to moderate the conclusions that were held as sacred decision rules in the 1950s/1960s. As potential drivers of misleading, the convergence to the mean and the story-telling embedded in the use of DCF are addressed in this essay, which though critical, doesn't recommend to abandon the DCF methods but praises for an aware use. As it has been often stated: the most beautiful theory can only give what it has. Among those, we identified three shortfalls meeting Jacques Richard's concerns. The first one is linked to the already famous mathematical embedded limits in the DCFs. The second one illustrates how a gap between reality and virtuality can emerge by confronting NPV (Net Present Value) assessment to cash generation process, in a reasoning, which finds resonance with the dividend distribution puzzle. The last shortfalls open a discussion on the significance of an (im)possible infinite life concept.

2.1 The Slow Emergence of a Sophisticated Decision Tool

The DCF method, often deemed a heritage of the work of Irving Fisher and a building block of modern finance, has experienced a fast spread in the second part of the twentieth century, supported by a continuous advertising effort lead by scholars like Stonehill and Nathanson (1968) and their numerous followers, and also by its conceptualization power and the emergence of fast calculators (Bernstein 2008). However, despite the common belief that the method is as modern as modern finance can be, the DCF method doesn't root in neo-classical theory. In the origin there is the Fibonacci's work, undertaken seven centuries before the DCF methods were designated as the most performing capital budgeting criteria. The author, also known as Leonardo Pisano, had conceived the calculation method in his year 1202 Liber Abaci.

A question arises: why didn't the DCF evaluation tools breakthrough during this seven-century period? Is this inertia only a consequence of the inexistence of the necessary calculation tools? Indeed, DCFs became fashionable during a scientific era; they fit perfectly well in the early twentieth century glorifying deterministic models. With the emergence of the prospective school, especially on the European Continent, a shift to a less deterministic era surfaced in the 1950s. Although this chapter doesn't ambition to track a historical veracity, it aims at underlining how DCF may deviate from the business sense. Indeed, the authors are convinced that a late adoption of the DCF may betray its inadequacy with the vision that the deciders carry. The next sections bring arguments to support that conviction.

2.2 *The Power and the Weaknesses of Conceptual Tools*

2.2.1 DCFs Allow the Transposition of Money Amounts on the Time Scale

Modern finance theory as developed with capital markets has long celebrated the use of DCF methods for their ability to capture the time and inflation effects. Indeed, the famous "time is money" once coined by Rockfeller has deeply marked the minds and one can only recognize that a preference for receiving 100 € today likely wins over the idea of receiving 100 € in 1 year. To most of us, this phenomenon is captured in an easy mathematical calculation process which is called "compounding" when one desires to figure out how much 100 € today will be worth in a year (the future value) and "discounting" when one wants to assess the current equivalent of 100 € to be received or paid in a year or more. The method allows a translation of monetary amounts on a time scale under the very restrictive assumptions that (1) there is full certainty about the cost of money, (2) the interest rate, also coined the discounting rate, used in the model is known. Two basic formulas set the foundations of the methodology for all users, including accountants and finance practitioners.

$$\mathrm{VF} = \mathrm{PV}*(1 + \mathrm{i})^{\mathrm{n}}\mathrm{PV} = \mathrm{VF}/(1 + \mathrm{i})^{\mathrm{n}}$$

With PV = present value, FV = future value, i = the discounting rate and n = the number of years

Those equations are used to compound (transform a PV in a FV) or discount (transform a FV in a PV) a single flow. A little more sophisticated formulae can help calculating the PV and FV of series of constant flows; they are useful to operations like the calculation PV of a retirement rent or to estimate the monthly payment which one needs to make to reimburse his/her debt. Another extension conceptualizes the dividend as the basis of a perpetual rent, and derives the share price, coined "the fundamental value", mobilizing the famous Irving Fischer and Gordon-Shapiro models.[1]

2.2.2 The NPV

In a real life project, like the purchase of G here before described, flows are likely not constant neither in value nor in time. To face such issues, it is possible to sum up

[1] The first one considers that the price of a share equates the discounted value of the future dividends, while the second adds the assumption of a constant dividend growth rate. Designed in the 1950s, the formulae fit a very flat non-volatile market. Other variations exist: the Bates and Modlowosky models are examples.

different flows (here below F), one after the other, as expressed at their individual (planned) deadlines. We then refer to a Net Present Value (NPV).

$$NPV = F_0 + F_1 / ((1 + i)^1 + F_2 / (1 + i)^2 + \ldots.. + F_n / (1 + i)^n$$

A NPV therefore calculates the value of a sum of flows, each supposedly generated at the end of different exercises, in order to assess a global value, which represents the accumulation of the flows, but expressed in a current monetary amount. The discounting rate is a key factor in the model as it strongly influences the subsequent rule application. According to the NPV rule, a positive result represents the amount of money created by the project. It is sometimes described as the value destined to shareholders while a better description would be the one of the value created by the project for the company, and source of a potential shareholder wealth increase. On this basis, the NPV rule has been formulated: invest if the NPV is positive and when one needs to choose between several projects, invest in the one generating the highest NPV. Easily understandable are the underlying assumptions, which assume that the cash flows are already known, to the deadline, and are certain, moreover, the rule assumes that there is no doubt about the discounting rate all along the project life. This is typically a deterministic tool. What happens when the real life cash flows don't meet the estimated ones? Or when the interest rates suddenly increase, inevitably raising the discount rate? It doesn't change the project representation, because the NPV is never used as a follow-up tool, managers prefer using management control tools. This process may seem usual to most readers but its implication maybe more dramatic than expected. Indeed, NPV is a one instant decision tool, for a single go–no go choice. Astonishingly, five decades of usage haven't allowed any assessment of the NPV performance as a decision-making tool. Of little help to adapt the decision to a renewed context, a NPV follow-up would a minima permit the recension of mistakes.

2.2.3 The IRR

Another criteria has been derived from the same equation, by solving a null NPV, the discounting rate being unknown and the solution. Obviously, we are solving a polynomial. The criterion, called the Internal Rate of Return is supposed to capture the yearly profitability of a project. However, it also suffers shortfalls, which are widely described in the literature: there may be no or several solutions to a polynomial, the intermediary cash flows are assumed to be reinvested at the IRR rate. Therefore if the IRR was seen as convenient in the early times of DCF methods predominance, for its simplicity—anyone understands quite well an interest rate—the decrease of its use favoured the NPV adoption.

The DCF methods started to diffuse in the 1950s in the US and ever since, their rate of adoption has continuously increased (Blum 2011), as surveys prove, though most of them have been conducted in the USA. Chart 1 shows that consistently with

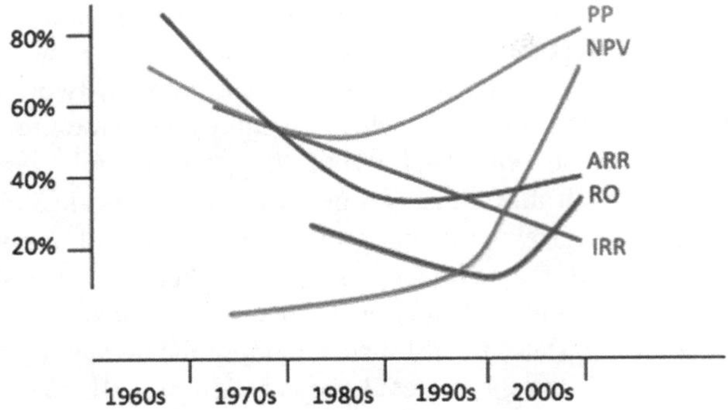

Chart 1 Adoption of methods as primary criteria in capital budgeting decisions. *PP* Payback Period (non DCF), *NPV* Net Present Value, *ARR* Accounting Rate of Return, *RO* Real Options, *IRR* Internal Rate of Return (*Source*: Blum 2011)

scholars' recommendations all along the decades, practitioners have slowly abandoned the Payback Period and the Accounting Rate of Return to prefer the DCF methods. Also observable is an inversion of adoption curves between NPV and the IRR which has lost popularity with time. For the above-mentioned reasons, more recent surveys show that if DCF methods remain popular in the USA, Real Options or Decision tree methods have become primary decision criteria in countries such as France or Germany. The latter are heritage of the prospective theory, which became very popular during the second half of the twentieth century and a sign of decline in the faith in deterministic models.

As the next paragraphs demonstrate, the described limits unfortunately may have some resonance in the real world when the conceptual models are strictly applied.

3 Tensions Between DCF Methods, Accounting and Real Business

3.1 *Net Present Value: Short-Term Money for the Shareholder, Long-Term Trouble for the Business?*

As their adoption rate grew, the DCF methods soon have been blamed responsible for poor decision-making and specifically they have been suspected of underinvestment for the following reasons: the problematic too high interest rates (Hayes and Abernathy 1980), the under values estimated with NPV computation (Dean 1951), the lack of interdependencies in between flows capture (Myers 1977), the poor usage made (Hodder and Riggs 1985).

Another accusation emerged quite early when the short-termism behaviour of the financial markets was first denounced (Hayes and Abernathy 1980), blaming the over attention given to shareholders. Short-termism has been characterized by Laverty (1996) as "*representing decisions and outcomes that pursue a course of action that is best for the short-term but suboptimal over the long run*". The next section offers an illustration of this trade-off.

Take a company having the choice between two mutually exclusive projects: project A and project B, which also have the same lifetime. Both require the same initial investment of 800, but the projects will generate different cash flow sequences (Table 1). A is a novel product: it scales up slowly and experiences a high-speed growth rate after a few years. B slightly improves the existing products and is expected to meet a known market that will slowly disappear. There is obviously an important strategic decision to make.

IRR rule states the following "choose the highest yearly profitability", following it, B should be the selected project. Setting a 10 % discounting rate, the NPV is respectively for A and B: 500 K€ and 344 K€ M. If we apply the NPV rule, A should be chosen. Making the tools more complex (adjusted NPV, adjusted IRR. . .) can solve the conflict in criteria, but one can also think through. NPV is a measure of the value at the end of the project life, it can also be computed at the end of each exercise in order to better capture its generation process. It is what Chart 2 represents. On the x-axis, one can find the end of exercises, on the y-axis, the cumulated discounted cash flows. When the curves cross the x-axis, the discounted Payback Period are readable, which is a bit further away in time than the non-discounted Payback Period.

If the curve describes the NPV generation, it is also worth mentioning that the NPV is the very last dot of each curve. In other words, the NPV rule states that a decision should be made on the observation of a unique single dot, moreover, based on prospective uncertain data.

Concretely, the capital budgeting decision is not made on the observation of the whole life NPV generation, i.e. the entire curve, moreover a deterministic curve, but only on the hypothetical final result. Stating that the decider should select the

Table 1 Cash flows, in thousands € and IRR for projects A and B

Cash flows	0	1	2	3	4	5	6	7	8	NPV (10 %)	IRR
A	−800	80	90	150	200	260	338	473	662	500 €	20 %
B	−800	300	309	263	210	168	134	108	86	344 €	24 %

Chart 2 NPV generation process

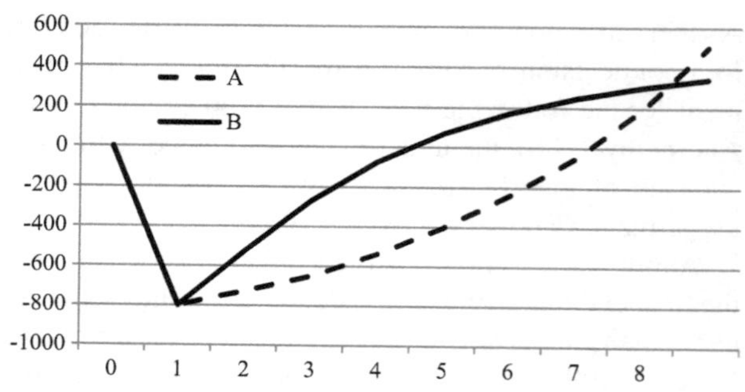

project with the highest NPV is equivalent to measure the distance between the x-axis and the last dot of each curve. The longest positive distance wins. According to scholars, one should focus on the NPV, for the technical limits of IRR. In the above illustration, criteria (NPV & IRR) are conflicting. The best IRR matches the lowest NPV and reversely. Subsequently, project A should be selected.

But why is IRR lower for A? The whole chart provides some beginning of an answer: project A requires more money, the surface of the A curve below the x-axis is twice as big as the one of project B. What does theory tell about this? It stipulates that if a manager can convince funds providers that a project is profitable, then, the funds will literally flow. In other terms, finding cash is no big deal!

How true is that statement? To anyone operating in real life conditions, it is obvious that money doesn't flow just because a project is promising. The focus on NPV also eludes the potential of project B. By insuring a faster payback, it generates supplemental cash faster. This cash can be useful in at least two ways: avoid insolvency if possible on a consolidated/more global level, and invest in other promising projects. Indeed, project B allows the management to seize options.

Our illustration shows that the restriction of a choice to a single value frees the deciders of much information, i.e. the collection of preceding dots and the way they articulate with one another through time. This remark has two implications. The first lies on the little accuracy of the representation of a project by DCFs for the external reader. When reading only the NPV value, the curve cannot be guessed. The deterministic vision that the projections are assuming is not shown. In short, the story is not told. A focus on the final dot also eludes the cash flow needs (or availability) associated to the project. The second and subsequent implication may lie in the increase of informational asymmetry. Indeed, the one observing the last dot will lack contextualisation. Readers of financial reported information will experience this lack. NPVs and to a wider extent DCFs tell a story which may want to be accounted.

3.2 *How to Share a DCF Story?*

To allow DCFs to tell a story, the focus could be enlarged and questioned. Enlargement allows a more comprehensive view and would for example include the whole curve communication. Arguably, this will be a complicated solution. The French standard setter has once praised for the use of sensitivity analysis. We explore and complement this path in the following paragraph.

Sensitivity analysis to financial evaluators, especially when Anglo-Saxon, refers to the study of the NPV changes when an endogenous element varies. For example, one can increase a cost line by 10 % and observe that the impact on the NPV is a decrease of 25 %. This project would be more sensitive to the cost line than one which NPV would only be reduced by 5 %.

Limiting the study to endogenous variables is problematic in the interwoven world we are living in. When examining exogenous factors, Anglo-Saxons usually refer to scenario analysis. This will for example test the impact of a variation in a commodity price. An interesting approach would be to combine the two and observe the NPV variation for a series of significant variables. A tornado diagrams, that exposes the impact of 10 % changes in each variable would provide information in easily understandable way.

But we believe that this is not enough, if forward-looking information is to be communicated, an effort to describe the risk global exposure, and not only the elasticity of the NPVs, would allow a better awareness from the investor. One solution could rely on the provision of a fluctuation range of the NPV. The lower end of NPV would be computed through a ruin test, answering to the following question: what if the project doesn't work at all? At the highest end, the optimistic vision of the manager could be expressed, as long as this highest end is reachable to the company.

Therefore, even though DCFs carry many shortfalls, they may carry information to the shareholders but the standard setters should insure that the reported values don't focus on a hypothetical long-term outcome but are telling the managerial story, the strategy behind the investment. Of course, this recommendation focuses on numerical estimations and does not imply that figures will do better than detailed narratives. The alternative option contributions should be examined apart.

Our third part demonstrated through a very simple example that DCF methods and namely NPV lack the capture of what is the sense of business and the strategic reasons justifying the investment. NPVs tend to hide the true trade-offs. To avoid the pitfall, we suggest that figures provided enlarge their scope to capture a comprehensive representation of a project life, and therefore provide with a reliable transcription of the underlying strategy. On the topic linking strategy and project life, some current accounting practices admit the existence of an infinite/indefinite life. With DCFs, we now survey that idea.

3.3 *Is Infinite Life an Impossible Concept?*

In the last part of this contribution, we show that the infinite life concept as advanced by the international standard setter lied on pillars of sand regarding DCF. The infinite life is widely used in finance models since Irving Fischer who first considered that the price of a financial asset was the current value of the series of upcoming everlasting dividends.

This value is simple to estimate: it is a ratio with the perpetual constant cash flow value for numerator and the discounting rate for denominator. A constantly growing cash flow is also assumable; the denominator then represents the difference between the discounting rate and the growth rate, with the mechanical limit that the first should be bigger than the second.

In the following table, with a simple exercise, we show how neglectable cash flows become after a given date, which depends on the discounting rate (i). To conduct that demonstration, we first compute the Present Value (current value) of a

Table 2 Present values of a perpetual cash flow of 1000 € and corresponding finite horizon of a finite series of 1000 € cash flow

Discounting rates	2 %	3.5 %	5 %	10 %	15 %	20 %	25 %
C/i	50,000	28,571	20,000	10,000	6667	5000	4000
n	−35	−20	−14	−7	−5	−4	−3

Annuity formula: $PV = C/i * (1 - (1 + i)^{-n})$

series of 1000 € worth perpetual flow (C), using the perpetual rent formula (C/i). The results show sensitiveness to the discounting rate assumptions: when we apply a 2 % discounting rate, the present value is 12 times bigger than when discounted at 25 %.

Next, we use the annuity formula to assess the necessary number of years (n) to obtain the same present value but with a finite series of 1000 € constant cash flow (Table 2), rather than an infinite horizon. Technically, the perpetual rent is the asymptotic limit of the PV formula when n is infinite. Therefore, we can observe that the perpetual rent converges with the finite rent formula. The lowest is the interest rate, the most remote is the convergence point. If one can perpetually invest 1000 € every year at 5 %, the current value of the rent is 20,000 €. The current value of a 1000 € per year investment is also 20,000 € if the deadline is 14 years, and with the same 5 % rate. The very simple explanation of that convergence relies on the fact that any flows invested in years 15 or later have absolutely no meaning in terms of "money of today".

There is in that demonstration some useful insight for accounting matters: the above example shows that there is no such thing as an infinite value. Indeed, after a given number of years, which can be easily defined, the future flows don't bring any supplemental value to the current value.

4 Conclusion

The quest for international or worldwide accounting standards have through the past four decades conducted to a renewal in the concepts underpinning the rules or standards to apply. Amongst them, the measurement debate has been vivid, and particularly Fair Value and its three associated levels. Fair Value can be equivalent to a liquid market price, a comparable price or an entity based model value. In the latter case, the value estimation has many chances to mobilize the DCFs. Jacques Richard has through the last years expressed some concerns regarding Fair Value and specifically, DCFs. The current contribution pays tribute to the author in bringing further arguments and illustrations of the tensions that an improper and unaware use of DCF may nurture.

The importation of financial tools to accounting applications is possible, but also full of traps, relative to the technical underlying assumptions and the hidden structure of the calculation. We have shown that the use of NPV concentrates the decision on a single final projected dot rather than the global cash flows. This shortfall appears to be a vital issue for a company seeking funds, as it may mask a short or medium term lack of cash behind a remote expected value. Indeed, DCF rules don't necessarily meet "good business sense" which of course implies a dose of prudence, or at least a measured risk exposure. Likely, this gap between a future value representation and real life conditions where a price is to be paid for mistakes may explain a delayed adoption of the DCF tools during seven centuries. It also justifies its slow abandon in some places of the world, such as France or Germany. This contribution clearly calls for precautions in the DCF interpretation if one wants to avoid to unnecessarily jeopardize the business continuity. DCFs as deterministic methods can be mitigate by sensitivity and scenario analysis, the combination being a simulation analysis. The provision of the range between the best case and the worst case (the failure of the project) likely will help the stakeholders to capture the risks they are taking. The solution is not perfect but much less risky than the focus on a single only potential dot.

Another topic discussed is the infinite life brought forward by the IASB. It appears—in DCF terms—that it crystallizes other tensions. Precisely, the recognition of a possible infinite life assumes that any cash flows, even the most remote ones have an impact on a current value. This, we have shown, is non-sense, even within a low interest rates context.

The scope of the article is too short to move to specific cases, but future arguments could focus on the weight of environmental externalities on the NPV calculation, which as computed today, completely eludes the question through the practice of a narrow focus. Human capital capture is another field of potential practice. The latter suggestions will come back to our of costs, values and prices initial triangle.

Eventually, the main contribution of this essay relies in the demonstration that though the IASB claims the service of a better economical representation, it may sometimes move further away from the real business world than the norms and standards they once intended to better replace.

References

Alexander D (2005) Fair value: concept and IFRS regulation. In: Alexander D et al L'evoluzione del bilancio di esercizio e l'introduzione dei principi contabili internazionali (IASB). Giuffré, Milano

Bernstein P (2008) Des idées capitales. Quadrige, Paris

Blum V (2011) Five decades of capital budgeting surveys for a contextual approach. Accounting Renaissance. IAAER, Venise

Copeland T, Antikarov V (2001) Real options: a practitioner's guide. Texere, New York, NY

Dean J (1951) Capital budgeting. Columbia University Press, New York, NY

Hayes R, Abernathy W (1980) Managing our way to economic decline. Harvard Business Review July–August:67–77

Hodder JE, Riggs HE (1985) Pitfalls in evaluating risky projects. Harv Bus Rev 63(1):128–135

Kahneman D (2011) Thinking, fast and slow. Allen Lane, coll. « AL TPB »

Kahneman D, Tversky A (1979) Prospect theory: an analysis of decision under risk. Econometrica 47(2):263–291

Laverty K (1996) Economic short-termism: the debate, the unresolved issues, and the implications for management practice and research. Acad Manage Rev 21(3):825–860

Myers SC (1977) Determinants of corporate borrowing. J Financ Econ 5:147–175

Nobes C, Alexander D (2005) Financial accounting: an international introduction. Pearson, London

Richard J (2004) The secret past of fair value: lessons applied to the French case. Account Eur 1:95–107

Richard J, Bensadon D, Colette C (2014) Comptabilité financière, IFRS versus normes françaises, 10th edn. Dunod, Paris

Savage S (2009) The flaw of averages: why we underestimate risk in the face of uncertainty. Wiley, Hoboken, NJ

Stonehill A, Nathanson L (1968) Capital budgeting and the multinational corporation. Calif Manag Rev 39–54

IFRS and the Works Council in France

Pierre Ferracci

Abstract This paper is about Financial Reporting for employees and their representatives. They have specific needs that do not meet those of shareholders. The need for employees to be given comprehensive information on the company's situation is not taken into account by the prevalent reporting standards, i.e. IFRS.

In the first part of this paper, we show how IFRS are detrimental to the specific reporting's needs of employees and works councils. In the second part, we present Jacques Richard's contribution to company's financial analysis, to the benefit of all stakeholders.

Now that the IFRS have invaded the field of accounting and financial reporting, we should fall back on ad hoc forms of reporting, to meet the needs of employees and their representatives. We explore some of these ad hoc forms, only to conclude that they have limited scope and few support from the regulatory bodies.

This conclusion is not satisfactory per se. It comes down to the fact that the IFRS have prevailed, even though they clearly do not meet the needs of users. Moreover, there is no certainty that shareholders will take advantage from the instability created by these standards. The fact that since the last financial crisis, the value of many listed companies is now lower than that of their book value, even when inflated by "made in IFRS" pyrotechnics and updates, indicates a level of pretension that cannot withstand economic cycles.

1 Introduction

The French legislative framework recognised at a very early stage (1945) the need for employees to be given comprehensive information on the company's situation. Through a works council, employees can appoint a chartered accountant to *"analyse all the economic, financial or social elements required in order to understand the accounts."*

P. Ferracci (✉)
ALPHA Group, Paris, France
e-mail: france.thomas@groupe-alpha.com

D. Bensadon, N. Praquin (eds.), *IFRS in a Global World*,
DOI 10.1007/978-3-319-28225-1_8

The educational issue is clear but the question of meaning (understanding of the accounts, in the words of the law) requires us to focus on what is really important to employees.

This work is also a kind of dual mediation (facilitated by the works council and the chartered accountant) between the company's management and its employees. Management can ensure that employees have a clear understanding of the company's situation and the challenges it faces, while keeping control of confidentiality issues.

For more than 30 years, our consultancy has helped works councils to understand the strategic, financial and social challenges in their companies. The needs for information of the works council are different from those of the shareholders. Traditionally, the French accounting standards offered the advantage of a wider reporting, in particular through the analysis of the value added. The value added is a key concept for works councils. For them, it is the value added, rather than the net income that represents the real wealth of the company. Correlatively, it is the whole range of stakeholders (and primarily the employees) that has to benefit of this wealth, and not the sole shareholders. Yet the adoption by France of the IFRS proved to be detrimental on this issue because the value added reporting is only optional.

In the first part of this paper, we will show how IFRS are detrimental to the specific reporting's needs of employees and works councils. In the second part, we will present Jacques Richard's contribution to company's financial analysis, to the benefit of all stakeholders.

2 IFRS or How to Answer Unasked Questions

Without harking back to the origins of the IFRS and the history of their adoption in Europe, it is immediately apparent that they have been detrimental overall to the needs of employees and their representatives (works councils and group works councils), depriving them of the tools needed to analyse the issues closest to their hearts (the entity's activity and performance but also its sustainability) and forcing the shareholders' ideology on them as the only acceptable management perspective.

Employees need high standards financial information, but this is often confused with financial communication. There is no limit to the powers of invention and the tricks used in this area. All companies, especially listed ones, tend to invent their own indicators and sometimes they alone know the definition of these indicators. Even traditional indicators (e.g. EBITDA, ROCE and ROE) do not obey a single calculation rule, because they fall within the scope of financial communication rather than accounting standards.

The fact remains that this copious communication is not always properly assimilated. A CEGOS survey[1] of 800 French employees in 2004 found that financial concepts are not always understood by all employees. For instance, only 36 % of staff think they have sufficient knowledge to decode the financial information supplied by the company. To assess this deficit, CEGOS asked employees to define specific financial indicators. The findings are incontrovertible: 89 % of employees do not know what EBITDA means, and 88 % do not know what working capital requirement means.

Financial communication to employees appears to overlook the obvious, namely the need for education and assimilation. Raising the issue of financial communication also means asking the question "Why", both as regards the companies communicating and the employees on the receiving end of this communication.

R.J. Craig and R. Hussy (1982) suggest that any theory of financial information for employees must be based on four principles, individually or in combination:

1. Management is obliged to provide information on the company's financial situation (this is the case in France),
2. Employees need information on the company's financial situation,
3. It is in management's interest to provide financial information to employees if it wants to improve their commitment and their performance,
4. By distributing financial information to employees, management improves its image in terms of social responsibility.

Principles 1, 3 and 4 are part of a logic of supply. Only principle 2 is concerned with the question of employee demand and the needs of employees. The CEGOS survey cited earlier gives greater insight into their preferences.

Of the varied financial information communicated by companies, employees are most aware of the indicators based on the income statement. 58 % believe that turnover is a key indicator on the company's financial situation. Similarly, 47 % think that the operating result is a major indicator. Conversely, only 30 % are interested in the return on capital employed. This ranks below the company's debt level (39 %), which indicates employees' awareness of the sustainability issues facing their company, rather than any interest in the leverage effect in the company.

This high general awareness of the company's turnover is also evident in the way employees identify with this economic indicator. Overall, 42 % of employees feel a connection to the performance of the company's turnover in the context of their work, with 28 % believing that they can even help directly or indirectly to improve turnover.

These results are very similar to our own professional observations. They highlight the specific needs of employees in terms of financial information. Activity, the guarantor of employment, is monitored closely while profitability

[1] CEGOS's Survey realized in 2004 with 800 French employees, representative of a national sample, which covers three big categories of active persons: executives, intermediate occupations and workers.

(measured by flow of income over flow of activity) is of more interest to employees than return (measured by flow of income over flow of capital).

Productivity indicators also appear to be important to employees. These indicators are rarely to be found directly in financial information documents. But the interest shown in physical indicators such as number of customers (44 %) and volume of sales (43 %) supports this hypothesis. More generally, employees appear to prioritise the sustainability of the company around the three strands of Activity—Employment—Profitability, whereas shareholders, in line with the financial asset valuation model, are more interested in the Growth—Return equation.

This leads straight on to the stakeholder issue. Employees have specific information needs that do not coincide with those of the shareholders.

This presents no particular problem if the scope of financial reporting enables each stakeholder to locate the financial information in which he is interested. Until 2005, the French GAAP framework allowed each user to find what he wanted. Classification of expenses and revenues by type (rather than use) meant that value added could be calculated directly. Organising the balance sheet by growing liquidity (assets) and growing debt (liabilities) met the needs of the bankers.

The application in 2005 of IFRS accounting standards changed the rules of the game and introduced a new accounting and financial reporting model. This innovation concerns not only the accounts of listed companies but also unlisted companies and SMEs, since many IFRS provisions were transposed into French law by the Accounting Regulations Committee.

For proof of this, we need to consider the conceptual framework of the IASB (2001).

By stating that *"The Framework applies to the financial statements of all commercial, industrial and business reporting entities, whether in the public or the private sectors"*, the IASB addresses the question of users.

"The users of financial statements include present and potential investors, employees, lenders, suppliers and other trade creditors, customers, governments and their agencies and the public. They use financial statements in order to satisfy some of their different needs for information. The Framework also concludes that *As investors are providers of risk capital to the entity, the provision of financial statements that meet their needs will also meet most of the needs of other users that financial statements can satisfy...The economic decisions that are taken by users of financial statements require an evaluation of the ability of an entity to generate cash and cash equivalents and of the timing and certainty of their generation."*

One cannot but admire the spin used by the IASB, whose attitude towards the other stakeholders is based on the "accessory follows the principal" method.

The points made by the IASB are debatable on several levels.

It adopts the traditional hypothesis that all providers of production factors, except for shareholders, are remunerated at their opportunity cost (usually assumed to be equal to the price of the factor established on a competitive market). In this scenario, the firm's objective is to maximise value for the shareholders, the sole providers of risk capital. Mechanisms must then be found to align the interests of the shareholders with those of management.

The IASB appears to overlook the basic criticisms directed at this theory. It also ignores the broader definitions of value[2] (Charreaux and Desbrières 1998), the importance of taking a long-term view (Jensen 2001) and the diversity of opinions held by shareholders themselves.

More prosaically, Jack Welch, former CEO of General Electric, regarded by the business world as the godfather of shareholder value and by analysts as the supreme champion of financial return on investment, has now backtracked to the point of declaring in the Financial Times (12 March 2009) that shareholder value *"is the dumbest idea in the world"*. Jack Welch sees shareholder value as a result (in the residual sense of the term). Using it as a strategy amounts to predetermining that which first has to be created (income), by mobilising the real levers of value creation (employees, customers, processes).

It would have been helpful if this awareness had come about earlier (before the crisis for instance), but better late than never.

Similarly, the rise in unemployment and the increased insecurity show that, contrary to the assertions of the IASB, shareholders are not the only providers of critical resources. Employees should be included in this category. Specific human capital, i.e. all the skills, knowledge, networks and personal relations specific to a company and which would be useless in a different company, contributes to value creation while creating a risk of specialisation for the employee. R. Topel (1991) believes that around 10–15 % of the total remuneration of employees in large companies rewards specific skills rather than generic ones. By the same token, R. Topel states that employees who lose their job through no fault of their own suffer an average pay cut of 10–15 % when they find new employment.

This raises the problem of valuation of human capital in the accounts. Although everyone agrees that it forms the basis of the information society, the knowledge economy and the network society, it is still never recorded in the assets, for lack of a suitable normative framework. IFRS make the recording of an asset contingent on its effective control and on proof that a net flow of future cash flows is being generated. There is no such sensitivity when it comes to recording company liabilities (pension liabilities and retirement allowances), which have to be recorded irrespective of their maturity dates.

This reluctance is unfortunate given that the IFRS have no problem recognising other categories of intangible assets such as technologies, processes, customer relations and intellectual property. Human capital is not activated on the balance sheet because, according to the IASB, it is inseparable from the entity. Despite evidence to the contrary, we are therefore forced to conclude that what cannot be measured does not count. Accordingly, a company which spends 10 % of its wage bill on training employees has (according to the IFRS) no more assets than a company that only spends 2 % on employee training. Footballers are the lucky

[2] For Charreaux and Desbrières, value added is the difference, on the whole value chain, between the opportunity price for the customer and the opportunity cost for the supplier. This value added is then distributed among the various stakeholders of the company.

exception: they can be entered as assets on the balance sheet. Hence the ongoing debate as to whether they should be classified as stock or fixed assets.

A further aspect creates a problem from the employees' perspective. This is the preference given to fair value, in other words the market value or any comparable value. The accounts then become procyclical, reflecting the adjustment in the prices of assets and liabilities rather than the company's profitability. The need for explaining factors thus comes up against the definition of the very function of the company, with production and distribution of goods and services increasingly being overtaken by financial activity.

Furthermore, fair value favours a patrimonial idea of the entity at the expense of entrepreneurial vision. Under the IFRS, the income statement may be brief (4–5 lines) and classified by type or use at the company's discretion. A great deal of useful information, such as labour cost, is thus often omitted and at best relegated to a note in the appendix.

Under the IFRS, the income statement, the basis for analysis of the entity's performance, is now accorded inferior status. The conceptual framework is based in the first instance on the definition of assets and liabilities. Income becomes the difference between the opening and closing equity (excluding transactions with shareholders). More to the point, it becomes unintelligible: the items record not only the transactions during the financial year (economic performance) but also the impact of changes in value.

3 What Is Really Important to Employees?

With the advent of the IFRS, financial information often boils down to a presentation of the financial situation (via the balance sheet), the company's performance (via the income statement) and the net situation (via the change in equity).

This form of traditional reporting is of course useful to employees. The balance sheet situation is examined closely in order to:

- make sure that the company is sustainable,
- check the level of debt and the constraints it places on operational management and on employees,
- assess the level of funds committed and the quality of the company's investments. Goodwill is generally regarded with scepticism and its depreciation is often associated with bad bets made on behalf of the company and its employees.

Employees also scrutinise the income statement balances, and profitability issues are often considered from the standpoint of the dual challenges of the company's competitiveness and the equitable distribution of the fruits of growth.

Activity (represented by turnover or total operating revenues) is the most direct link that employees have with the accounts, and is both a projection of their labour on to the market and a guarantee of employment.

This interest often spills over into broader indicators. The order book and order intakes anticipate future activity. The analytical details of turnover by business line and/or region fulfil the need of employees and their representatives for identification and benchmarking.

More generally, the pervasiveness of the international standards (which favour presentation of accounts by use rather than type of expenses and earnings) means that reporting of management balances and especially value added is becoming increasingly rare. Value added has progressively disappeared from the financial reporting stage, under pressure from shareholder value reporting.

4 Profit-Sharing as a Specific Method of Financial Reporting for Employees

Financial information has its roots in more than balance sheets or income statements alone. It also comes in formats specifically designed for employees. Employee profit-sharing is an interesting example of this. For instance, French companies with more than 50 employees have, by law, to implement a profit-sharing scheme with a predefined formula.

The statutory formula [1/2 (Profit − 5 % of equity) × Wages/Value added] calculates a disposable portion of earnings (half). It is based on taxable profit, which is meant to be controlled by a powerful third party (the tax authorities), and therefore less susceptible to the problems of accounting conventions or attempts to smooth earnings. The distribution criterion (Wages/value added) is meant to represent the employees' share in wealth creation. The cost of capital is not neglected since a minimum return on equity is specified.

Then there is an example of a variable and deferred remuneration scheme, whose criteria can be amended by labour negotiation in the company. Companies retain the right to sign exceptional profit-sharing agreements, provided that the benefits guaranteed to employees are at least equivalent to those they might have received if the standard formula had been used.

These exceptional agreements account for 21 % of profit-sharing schemes. This percentage is even higher in companies with over 500 employees (DARES, July 2009).

In fact, given the calculation method used and the growing financialisation of companies, profit-sharing only imperfectly reflects the contribution made by employees to the company's wealth creation.

There are too many cases where the employees of a holding, cost centre company or support company receive (or do not receive) a profit share which bears no relation to their actual contribution.

This explains the growing interest shown by companies in group agreements and/or exceptional profit-sharing agreements. Using the statutory formula, these make it possible to amend the calculation method in order to bring it more in line with the realities of the company. Thus, in a company where equity is clearly too high in relation to operating activity requirements, the exceptional formula may yield a 3 % payout instead of the 5 % stipulated in the statutory formula.

Incentive agreements, in some cases combined with profit-sharing agreements using "umbrella" formulas, have the same objective and create a criterion that reconciles economic performance with social performance and links the entrepreneur's risk to the variable and random nature of profit-sharing and incentive plans.

5 Jacques Richard or Financial Analysis for the Benefit of All Stakeholders

Two works illustrate Jacques Richard commitment: his book "L'analyse financière des groupes" (Richard and Becom 2000), written in collaboration with SECAFI's management and in particular, his book "Analyse financière et Audit des performances" (Richard 1993). The first edition of the book dates back to 1989 under a different title (Audit des performances). Jacques Richard surprised everyone with his choice of publisher (la Villeguérin éditions), known for its fiscal and accounting reviews. Jacques Richard opened the eyes of a generation of aspiring chartered accountants to the political challenges inherent in financial analysis rather than simply training them in its technicalities.

The impact of Jacques Richard's book can be measured by a quick glance at the other three books on financial analysis which "dominated the market" at that time. Elie Cohen (1988) provided a serious and austere analysis matrix in which a preference for EBITDA was combined with colourful descriptions of the sedimentary nature of the balance sheet. Gérard Charreaux (1989) sought to popularise value creation and the return on capital criteria. Pierre Vernimmen (1989) broadened the scope of financial analysis to include corporate valuation. His book, updated after his death by Pascal Quiry and Yann Le Fur, has become the standard textbook on market finance (betas, risk premiums, holding discounts and other concepts of very little interest to Jacques Richard).

Jacques Richard's agenda is totally different, the key theme of his book being the social question. The foreword makes this clear straight away: "*It is essential to make a clear distinction between financial return, productivity and efficiency criteria and to include an integrated analysis of all a company's performance factors.*

The decline of the centralised economies (this was 1993) and the development of relations with China indicate that the incidence of dissociation between financial return and efficiency criteria is bound to increase: Western companies performing to extremely high levels of efficiency will be forced to close their doors as they are overtaken by companies that are perhaps less efficient but subject to less "social pressure"... These are not only clashes between economic productivity and performance. These are social models clashes as well!"

This observation could apply almost word for word to the relocations that occurred following the financial crisis of 2008.

6 Value Added and Productivity: Key Concepts for Jacques Richard

Seldom has a work of financial analysis focused as keenly on efficiency and productivity criteria as Jacques Richard's book.

In contrast, Gérard Charreaux (1989) dismisses value added in just a few lines. He sees no need to include it in the scope of a financial return analysis. He even questions the point of analysing the distribution of value added between different beneficiaries, since "*payments made to creditors and personnel are for the most part fixed and priority payments.*" Our activities with works councils alongside Jacques Richard clearly showed how misguided this statement was, since companies frequently treated employees as an adjustment variable. In many cases, the fixed and predetermined items were capital and dividend levels.

If we had to use a synthetic indicator of the employee perspective, it would be value added. It represents the increase in wealth generated by the use of the firm's resources and provides the basis for distribution between shareholders, creditors, employees and the government.

Academic research (Evraert and Riahi-Belkaoui 1998) sees many virtues in value added reporting. The summary of empirical research points to the following benefits from the information contained in value added:

- It creates a good social climate by emphasising the contribution made by employees to the company's results.
- It ensures that greater consideration is given to productivity issues, in conjunction with the bonus system.
- It establishes a direct link with national accounting and with the models and techniques used by economists.
- It provides a better indicator than turnover of the company's size and importance.
- It is a useful tool for labour negotiations, as it better reflects the aspirations and expectations of the stakeholders.
- It is a better measure of the company's performance, far superior to the information provided by net earnings, which compared to value added, depends far more on the company's conventions and accounting choices.
- It can be a better criterion for measuring the efficiency of the management.

From the employees' point of view, value added allows discussion to focus on the Labour factor and its role both in the creation (or capture) of value and in its distribution.

The importance of the value added concept stems from its position at the intersection of three dimensions of analysis.

Value added is an indicator of production organisation choices: the value added ratio (ratio of value added to total product) is one of the main indicators of the level of integration of production, in other words the ratio of in-house activity to sub-contracted activity. The implications for the qualifications of the company's personnel are very different. The choice between producing goods in-house or having them produced outside the company is at the heart of discussions concerning the business lines of the company, which tends to focus on its core business and outsource functions and activities regarded as non-strategic because they do not generate sufficient value.

Value added is a key indicator of the company's profitability and efficiency. It can also be usefully combined with productivity analysis and linked with the investment rates of companies.

Value added is the basis on which earnings are distributed. It measures wealth creation, which enables payouts to be given (or not, in some cases) to the various stakeholders in the company's business. The employees (including temporary staff) who receive wages, the government which taxes the profits, the group and the partners who are entitled to a share in the company's earnings (profit or loss), which can take different forms (dividends, current account interest, retained profits, etc.) and the lenders who charge interest on the loans granted to the company. This is how the respective shares of each stakeholder can be defined.

It is not surprising therefore that Jacques Richard (1993, p. 379) places high importance on value added: *"the proportion of value added that accrues to each group of partners strongly influences their behaviour; at macro-economic level, changes in the distribution of value added are a key factor in explaining a financial crisis... It goes without saying that changes in the production and distribution of value added will have a huge effect on the morale of the troops and their attitude towards the company."*

We applaud Jacques' far-sightedness. One of the reasons for the last financial crisis was the deterioration over a long period of the employees' share in value added. Since the end of the 1980s, shareholders' return expectations have caused corporate debt to rise and led to pressure on wages in order to boost profits, creating a disconnect between wages and productivity and encouraging household debt so as to maintain consumption levels.

While Jacques Richard devotes 13 pages to an analysis of value added, he devotes twice that number to the analysis of productivity. This was a deliberate decision (some might say provocation) on his part.

Demonstrating all his political prowess, Jacques Richard anticipates the objection that it is productivity levels that cause unemployment and a deterioration in working conditions.

He then makes an important distinction between labour intensity and labour productivity. He uses the example of companies A and B whose hours worked, production output and expenses are identical, but where company A's productivity changes owing to an increased work pace and company B's changes because organisation of the work has changed. Company A's working hours cannot therefore be compared with company B's working hours because they entail a higher expenditure of human energy (or factor consumption).

In making this distinction, Jacques Richard proposes that an income statement based on constant work intensity should be inserted between the two conventional income statements. This is an example of the elegance of Jacques Richard's ideas, which unfortunately have been adopted only on a limited scale.

Equally original is his concept of hidden costs (which he calls dysfunction cost). He defines it as the loss of production plus all the incidental costs. However, Jacques Richard is very careful to distinguish between gross dysfunction cost and net dysfunction cost, which is gross cost less the cost savings the entrepreneur makes by not spending the necessary amounts on preventing dysfunctions. In this way he shows how the company can "profit" from allowing the dysfunction to continue (pollution, industrial accidents, etc.).

In his preface to Richard's book (Richard 1993), Bernard Colasse, French Professor of Accounting at Dauphine University in Paris, laments (and we lament with him) the absence of a chapter on the social climate. It would have been interesting to read this chapter years before the explosion of psychosocial risks and the rise in concerns linked to employee health and working conditions.

7 Twenty Years on, the Employee and the Bubble

In the words of Jacques Richard (Capron 2005, p. 116), we have moved on to the 3rd stage of shareholder capitalism, where *"capitalists want to be able to show the results at the beginning of the investment cycle regardless of the rate of sales, using the discounted cash flow method... What proponents of modern fair value want is to be able to distribute potential profit, including through subjective valuation without reference to the market."*

We have closely followed this development, which favours shareholders at the expense of employees. While the proportion of goodwill (increasingly rarely written off in the balance sheet) has exploded, the level of dividend distribution has remained very high in companies, even at the height of the financial crisis of 2008–2009. This fact is even more astonishing when share buyback (another form of dividend distribution) is added to the equation, now the "investment" of choice for the major listed companies.

At the turn of the century, and amid the euphoria of the internet bubble, the antagonism between managers and shareholders seemed to soften. The standard return on equity predetermined the payout expected by shareholders (15 %), stock option plans ensured that the interests of management were aligned with those of the shareholders, and the full effects of debt leverage were felt. The profit expectations decried by Jacques were already at work, as indicated by the development of creative accounting (not to say fraud) and the complicity of auditors. When the recession hit, it became apparent that capitalism (in more and more of a hurry) was anticipating (sometimes crudely and too obviously, as in the case of Enron) a change which was offered to it on a plate when the IFRS were implemented a few years later.

When this change occurred, employees lost out. The ill-considered risk taken for the benefit of companies was ultimately borne by many employees both in their everyday work (pressure on labour intensity) and as the result of major strategic operations (company mergers, restructurings and redundancy plans).

It is interesting to note that after the internet bubble burst and in the wake of the various financial scandals, the debate on governance[3] focused on realigning the interests of managers and shareholders. No thought was given to greater employee participation in the governance of their companies. We had to wait until the National Interprofessional Agreement of 11 January 2013 for any prospect of employee participation on the boards of private companies, although this mechanism is still too weak to make any real difference to the strategic decisions taken by companies.

8 The Issue of Governance for Employees Has Now Gone Beyond the IFRS

The IFRS can be defined as a symbol of shareholders taking back power after the burst of the internet bubble and of management being under control: off-balance sheet items, which management is now being (politely) asked to reintegrate, provisions, which are no longer classified as reserves to the extent they once were,[4] or of the immediate posting in the accounts of changes in the markets.

In any event, this exclusive dialogue (or infernal duo) between shareholders and managers is at the very least having a stifling effect on the other stakeholders, employees to the fore.

Now that the IFRS have invaded the field of accounting and financial reporting, we should fall back on ad hoc forms of reporting, to meet the needs of employees and their representatives. This conclusion is not satisfactory per se. It comes down to the fact that the IFRS have prevailed, even though they clearly do not meet the needs of users. Moreover, there is no certainty that shareholders will take advantage from the instability created by these standards. The fact that since the last financial crisis, the value of many listed companies is now lower than that of their book

[3] Particularly in connection with the Sarbanes-Oxley Act in the United States and its French equivalent, the Financial Security Act (*loi de sécurisation financière*) in 2003.

[4] In this connection, we look back with some nostalgia at our comments in the 1980s when we referred to the "game of allocations to and reversals of provisions" when analysing net income; and the British colleague who told us that in France we always knew exactly how much should be allocated to provisions but never why it was necessary to create provisions.

value, even when inflated by "made in IFRS" pyrotechnics and updates, indicates a level of pretension that cannot withstand economic cycles.

Fortunately, this conclusion leaves the field open for the definition of new reporting frameworks. However, we must not err on the side of optimism. We only need to remember the ups and downs of the NRE[5] Act of 15 May 2001 to know that the road ahead is full of pitfalls. Article 116 of the NRE Law required some seven hundred French listed companies to include in their annual report information on their social and environmental management connected with their activity.

In 2007, The French government launched The "Grenelle Environnement", a conference bringing together the government, local authorities, trade unions, business and voluntary sectors to draw up a plan of action of concrete measures to tackle the environmental issue. As a result, Grenelle II Act, extended the reporting system resulting from Article 116 of the NRE Law on two fronts:

- expansion of the scope of application of the system to unlisted companies whose total balance sheet or turnover and number of employees exceeded thresholds fixed by decree,
- extension of the scope of information required in the management report.

Between the initial version and the implementation decree of 2012, a number of "adjustments" were made, including definition of higher thresholds than those originally specified and deferral of the date on which the obligation comes into force.[6] Meanwhile, the French law on banking and financial regulation adopted in October 2010 clamped down on staff representatives and stakeholders expressing an opinion on the sustainable development section of the annual report issued by limited liability companies to their shareholders.

This example shows the problems inherent in defining a specific reporting scope, which is usually left to the discretion of the companies. Moreover, obligation is not synonymous with quality of information. An analysis conducted by the ALPHA Group Centre "Etudes et Prospective" on the application of the provisions of the NRE Law is enlightening in this respect.[7] The findings of this study are irrefutable. *"We are therefore a long way from the spirit in which this law was intended, a long way from the stated aim of reporting to shareholders, namely improving the competitiveness of companies. While considerable attention is focused on sustainable development because of the potential solutions it offers in terms of resolving the financial and economic crisis, companies do not always use social reporting as a risk and opportunity management tool, but only as an external communication tool. The way in which the tool shapes the content of companies' social*

[5] New economic regulations.

[6] For unlisted companies with fewer than 500 employees or a turnover of less than EUR 100 million, this obligation will not come into effect until financial year ending 31 December 2016.

[7] Read also: Report on 9 years of enforcement of the NRE Law (*New Economic Regulations*) on company reporting. Alpha Group's Centre Etudes & Prospective, April 2012.

responsibility only confirms our fears. Will company communication one day inspire confidence?"

We are still a long way from implementing renewed reporting standards that take into account other needs than those of shareholders. To his credit, Jacques Richard played a significant part in defining a framework to analyse the specific needs of works councils. The intellectual rigour exhibited by Jacques in his financial and accounting writings never stopped him placing them in their broader macroeconomic context. This went hand in hand with a lifelong passion for social issues. The decision to preserve natural capital was an obvious follow-on from the decision to preserve and develop human capital. This explains his focus on sustainable development issues in the latter part of his career (Richard 2012).

References

Capron M (2005) Les normes comptables internationales, instruments du capitalisme financier. La découverte, Paris
Charreaux G (1989) Gestion financière. LITEC, Paris
Charreaux G, Desbrières P (1998) Gouvernance des entreprises: valeur partenariale contre valeur actionnariale. Finance Contrôle Stratégie 1(2):57–88
Cohen E (1988) Analyse financière. Economica, Paris
DARES (2009). La Participation, l'Intéressement et l'Épargne salariale en 2007. Premières Informations Synthèses, no. 31.2
Evraert S, Riahi-Belkaoui A (1998) Usefulness of value added reporting: a review and synthesis of the literature. Manag Financ 24(11):1–15
Hussy R, Craig RJ (1982) Keeping employees informed. Butterworths, Sydney
Jensen MC (2001) Value maximisation, stakeholder theory, and the corporate objective function. Monitor Company. October
Richard J (1993) Analyse financière et audit des performances. La Villeguérin Editions, Paris
Richard J, Becom, Secafi (2000) L'analyse financière des groupes. Economica, Paris
Richard J (2012) Comptabilité et développement durable. Economica, Paris
Topel RC (1991) Specific capital, mobility, and wages: wages rise with job seniority. J Polit Econ 99(1):145–176
Vernimmen P (1989) Finance d'entreprise. Dalloz, Paris

The IASB and the Market "Communion"

Nihel Chabrak

Abstract Since the 1970s, accountants are suspected for having been contributing to the predominance of the market doctrine by setting themselves the objective of ensuring the efficient functioning of financial markets. In this chapter, we set out to analyze how the IASB project accords with this logic. Using the concept of "communion" borrowed to Gurvitch sociology of law (1948/2001), and some shareholder thinking lent to Stout (The shareholder value myth. San Francisco, CA: Berrett-Koehler, 2012) and Blair and Stout (Va Law Rev 85(2):247–328, 1999), we argue that the concept of "investor" used in the IASB conceptual framework depicts its membership to a form of an active spontaneous sociality we call the market "communion". Through its conceptual framework, the IASB contributes to preserving symbols and patterns, such as the Efficient Market Hypothesis [EMH] and the Shareholder Value Maximization [SVM] doctrine. Poised for intellectual collapse, such shared symbols and beliefs form the collective intuitions that enable mediation and communication between the members of the communion to continue adulating the market ideology. The concept of "investor" used in the IASB conceptual framework is socially constructed. It is both constituted by the IASB membership to the market communion, and yet at the same time is the very medium of this constitution.

1 Introduction

The principle of total disclosure for shareholders has been in force in the U.S. since the New Deal has institutionalized the responsibility of managers towards shareholders in order to re-establish confidence in markets after the great depression. The views expressed by Adolf A. Berle in the great debate that opposed him in the 1930s to another law Professor E. Merrick Dodd Jr., on the issue of "to whom are corporations accountable?" is generally believed to have provided the philosophy

N. Chabrak (✉)
United Arab Emirates University [UAEU] – College of Business & Economics, Al Ain, United Arab Emirates
e-mail: nihel.chabrak@uaeu.ac.ae

D. Bensadon, N. Praquin (eds.), *IFRS in a Global World*,
DOI 10.1007/978-3-319-28225-1_9

on which the US securities legislation of 1933–1934 was based (Macintosh 1999). In the *Modern Corporation and Private Property*, Adolf A. Berle and Gardiner Means (1982) advocate for the shareholder primacy: "all powers granted to a corporation or to the management of the corporation . . . [are] at all times exercisable only for the ratable benefit of the shareholders." Alongside, Edwin Merrick Dodd wrote in *Harvard Law Review* "For Whom Are Corporate Managers Trustees?" in *(1932)* to state that the proper purpose of a public company is beyond making money for shareholders. It includes providing secure jobs for employees, quality products for consumers, and contributions to the broader society. He adds: "The business corporation is an economic institution which has a social service as well as a profit-making function" (p. 1148).

Since Adolf A. Berle view, the provision of information to shareholders became part of the doctrine that corporate managers were virtually trustees for the shareholders and that the powers granted in law to them should be exercised entirely for their benefits. The principle of total disclosure came to be seen as part of the fiduciary theory of corporations according to which corporate managers are responsible to act in a manner that would place the interests of the shareholders above everything else except the law (Macintosh 1999).

In the 1960s, according to Williams (2004), accountants have endorsed a new role that is to serve "efficient" and "self-regulated" markets. Since then, new dimensions of accounting were promoted: accounting is the useful information (Mouck 1998; Williams 2002) and the language (Amernic and Craig 2004) of measurement (Tinker 1980) required for the good functioning of financial markets (Williams 2002). This chapter aims to show that this new turn in accounting thought has prevented accountants from any possible adoption of E. Merrick Dodd Jr. stance who considers directors and managers as fiduciaries not for shareholders but for the corporation, which is a separate legal entity that is accountable to society to which it operates. The new accounting paradigm became part of the ideology of the market, where corporations are instruments to maximize the shareholder value and whereby the market is the only perfect mechanism to bring managers to achieve such an objective. According to Mouck (1998), since the 1960s, the leading academic accounting journals have been dominated by research that attempts to estimate the association between changes in security prices and financial reporting and accounting system.

In this chapter, we use an analytical framework lent to Stout (2012) and Blair and Stout (1999). We claim that the IASB has committed itself in supporting the market ideology. The IASB is suspected of being part of a Market "communion", which concept of "communion" is borrowed to Gurvitch sociology of law (1948/2011). The concept of "investor" used in the conceptual framework is portrayed to be an evidence of the indoctrination of the IASB by the market communion beliefs. The IASB stance has suppressed Edwin Merrick Dodd claim about social responsibility of corporations, by consecrating shareholder primacy. In reality, it has even distanced the accounting role from serving Adolphe A. Berle concern of shareholder protection. In fact, the IASB set a new purpose for accounting information that is to support trading on the market.

The chapter is structured as follows: In the second section, we use the concept of "communion" lent to Gurvitch sociology of law (1948/2011) to describe what we call the market communion and its collective intuitions based on the Efficient Market Hypothesis [EMH] and the Shareholder Value Maximization [SVM] doctrine. In the third section, some thoughts on shareholder thinking are borrowed to Stout (2012) and Blair and Stout (1999) to show the fallacy of the SVM doctrine. Then, we analyze the concept of "investor", used in the IASB conceptual framework, to portray its obedience to the market communion tenets. Several concluding comments are presented in the fourth section.

2 The Market Communion

Firstly, the concept of communion lent from Gurvitch sociology of law (1948/2001) is depicted (Sect. 2.1). Secondly, the market communion is portrayed (Sect. 2.2).

2.1 Gurvitch Sociology of Law and the Concept of "Communion"

Gurvitch (1948/2001) defines the sociology of law as that part of the sociology of the human spirit or of the noetic mind, which studies the full social reality of law. The sociology of the human spirit is "the study of cultural patterns, social symbols, and collective spiritual values and ideas in their functional relations with social structures and concrete historical situations of society" (p. 47). To study social reality of law, the sociology of law starts with its tangible and externally observable expression, in effective collective behavior to interpret them according to the internal meanings. The sociology of law considers jural symbolic patterns fixed in advance, such as organized law, procedures, and sanctions as function of other jural symbols and rules which are flexible and spontaneous, which themselves are explained by jural values and ideas and finally by "the collective beliefs and intuitions which aspire to these values and grasp these ideas, and which manifest themselves in spontaneous *normative facts*, sources of the validity, that is to say, of the positivity of all law" (p.61).

Gurvitch (1948/2001) associates kinds of law with forms of sociality that is the ways of being linked to the whole and by the whole, which differ in degree of intensity and actuality of the inter-individual relations of reunion, separation and fusion. To produce law, two conditions are to be satisfied: (1) the capacity to be a normative fact, which means the capacity of the social fact to embody positive values by their very existence, and (2) to be an active form of sociality even without engendering its own organized superstructure. Two forms of sociality exist according to Gurvitch (1948/2001). The first is direct and spontaneous sociality, while the second is an organized and reflected form of sociality. On the one hand, the spontaneous sociality is said to be more mobile and dynamic. It is generally depicted through immediate states of the collective mind and behaviors, which are guided by more or less flexible patterns. On the other hand, the organized sociality is linked with collective behaviors that are guided by patterns crystallized in deliberate schemes, fixed in advance, which impose hierarchized and centralized conduct. Generally, spontaneous sociality underlies organized one even if it does not entirely express itself in the latter.

Within the spontaneous form, Gurvitch distinguishes two types of sociality: a form of sociality by interpenetration, partial fusion or simple interdependence, and another form whereby the members are integrated into a union of "We". When the fusion is weak and integrates only superficial states of individual consciousness, the form of sociality is called *the Masses*. When the fusion is on a deeper level of the consciousness, an essential part of the aspirations of the personality is then integrated in the "We" but without attaining the maximum of integration, and then we speak of *community*. The most intense degree of union and integration of the most inaccessible depths of the selves lead to what is called *communion*. When the fusion integrates the deepest layers of the selves, the pressure of social spontaneity becomes less obvious.

The communion produces a form of super-functional social law of objective integration in the "We". According to Gurvitch, this kind of law is based on confidence, it is autonomous and can never be imposed from without as it can regulate only from within. It is a spontaneous subordinative form of law that has primacy over any other individual law, for it presents the virtual base of every delimitive jural regulation.

2.2 The Market "Communion"

The IASB as a standard setter could be assimilated to an organized reflected sociality. Alongside, the IASB is part of a direct, spontaneous sociality, which has the form of a communion. This grouping is a super-functional form of sociality that is claimed to be serving the market ideology (Chabrak 2014). Per se, the IASB is a functional form of sociality for its rational and reflected schematism, rested on crystallized and fixed aims which can never express the ends and values that are aspired by the super-functional form of sociality of the market advocates. However, the latter needs a plurality of organized forms of sociality (superstructures) such as the IASB as a standard setter, to achieve the totality of its ends and values. Hence, the IASB, as a standard setter, serves an aim that is only an impoverished intellectual image of values synthesized by the "common interest", which is sued by the spontaneous sociality that is the market communion. Before giving evidences on the membership of the IASB to this grouping, we portray how the markets' advocates constitute a communion.

The market advocates constitute a form of a spontaneous sociality as they have a previous union of consciousness, which makes possible mediation by signs, patterns and symbols to dominate them. A communion is primarily a manifestation of a strong cohesion of the collective mind. It is a "We" that constitutes an irreducible whole. It is a whole that is immanent to its parts and the parts are immanent to the whole. Also, the "We" means an interiority and intimacy of the union that is in an awakened state. Because the "We" exists already, mediation by patterns and symbols is possible between the members of the grouping. The Efficient-Market Hypothesis [EMH] and Shareholder Value Maximization [SVM] are among the patterns and symbols produced to serve as collective intuitions in order to make mediation between the market grouping constituents who are aware of their belonging and their role in the communion. Hence, despite EMH was revealed to be incapable of explaining what happened during the financial crisis in a convincing manner, and despite the fact that this model is clearly shown not to work, and to be a flawed ideology (Greenspan 2008), despite that EMH seems to have been discarded as the basis of sound public policy (Soufian et al. 2013), despite all of this, EMH is still used and shared by the market advocates. To our view, EMH is an unquestioned belief that is shared for the only purpose of reinforcing the strong cohesion of the collective mind and the mediation between the market communion members.

According to Soufian et al. (2013), the EMH, which was developed in 1965 by Eugene Fama of the University of Chicago, a university well known for fervent support of free markets, is not a disinterested scientific endeavor as it is strongly influenced by ideological considerations and the need to preserve the core methodological approaches of neo-classical economics. Firstly the authors explain that the choice of the term 'efficient market' is rhetorical as efficiency is considered as one of the highest social values in the West. Secondly, they argue that the ambiguity of the theory itself is intended to give its advocates a considerable scope to survive critics. According to Fama (1965), EMH suggests the stock prices to move randomly. For Mouck (1998), this fact should be interpreted as the result of information arriving randomly and not to be the result of the irrational character of market participants. For Soufian et al. (2013), the concept of randomness used to support the idea that the actual price of a security in an efficient market wander about its intrinsic value, was intentionally not clearly explained by Fama (1965). They contend that this lack of clarity was intended to leave the EMH advocates with the possibility of an opportunistic use of it to avoid unwelcome refutations of their preferred theory (Soufian 2013). Finally, they argue that the purpose of the EMH is to show that market prices are a perfect guide to intrinsic value, which implication is to admit the market to be considered as a hyper-rational being that can outwit any government regulator or speculator and as an infallible guide to human affairs.

For Mouck (1998), regardless of the "Noah and Joseph effects" that refer respectively to the observed instances of large discontinuous jumps in stock prices, periods of tumultuous change and to the apparent tendency toward long-term trends and non-periodic cycles, the EMH was never replaced by a "fractal market hypothesis". Rather, it was generally taught as fact and accounting researchers have never questioned the theoretical basis of their emerging markets-based accounting research. According to Shiller (1984), quoting Henry Fielding, "Fashion is the great governor of this world; it presides not only in matters of dress and amusement, but in law, physic, politics, religion, and all other things of the gravest kind; indeed, the wisest of men would be puzzled to give any better reason why particular forms in all these have been at certain times universally received, and at others universally rejected, than that they were in or out of fashion" (p. 457). For Williams et al. (2006), the dominance of EMH was not accomplished by dint of its superior explanatory power of the world, but by the shrewd (and continuing) use of political power to sustain that preeminence.

Our view is that even though the history of anomalous evidence, EMH remains a vivid fashion for the role it plays in maintaining the cohesion of the market communion. If EMH is still embraced, it is for the reason that at least it still gives a compelling rationale for the market advocates to continue believing that the market should be entrusted the responsibility of controlling the corporate world in order to reorient companies towards serving the supremacy of shareholders' interests as defended by Adolf A. Berle. Such an endeavor was supported by another theory that is also poised for intellectual collapse: the Shareholder Value Maximization [SVM] doctrine, which purpose was to end with the institutional understanding of corporations as separate legal entities with responsibilities towards the whole society. Rather than being social institutions that are accountable towards the community and stakeholders (Davis 2009), as it was defended by E. Merrick Dodd Jr., corporations should be assimilated to legal-economic devices to entrench powers and rights of their shareholders. As a result, it consecrates the market vision of the corporation and the need to rely on the market force of opinion to make the best capital allocation decision.

3 The Shareholder Value Myth: the Trap of the IASB into the Market "Communion"

We borrow some thoughts on shareholder thinking to Stout (2012) and Blair and Stout (1999) to explain the shareholder value myth and its role in sustaining the market communion (Sect. 3.1). Afterwards, we analyze the concept of "investor" used in the IASB conceptual framework to portray its obedience to the market communion tenets (Sect. 3.2).

3.1 *The Fallacy of the Shareholder Value Maximization [SVM] Doctrine*

According to Blair and Stout (1999), mainstream economics consider "public corporations [as] little more than bundles of assets collectively owned by shareholders (principals) who hire directors and officers (agents) to manage those assets on their behalf" (p. 248). To preserve shareholders' interests, agency theory advocates for an outsider model of governance whereby control is shifted from managers to markets through the distribution of available cash flows (Jensen and Meckling 1976). SVM stipulates that free cash flows should be distributed to investors in forms of dividends and buybacks to be allocated on the market. The outsider model of governance by markets is considered to be the best mechanism to make an optimal allocation of capital (Jensen 1986; Jensen and Murphy 1990) and to improve the performance of the economy as a whole, consistently with the neoclassical theory of market economy (Fama and Jensen 1983a, b). Having made investments without a contractually guaranteed return, shareholders are considered by this paradigm as in the position of having a real interest in monitoring managers to ensure an efficient allocation of resources (Lazonick 2011).

Accordingly, SVM is meant to secure the shareholders' interests by entrusting corporate control to markets (Chabrak 2011; Davis 2009). Public corporations are considered to "belong" to shareholders, who will control the corporation through the force of opinion of the market. Hence, public corporations exist for one purpose only; to maximize shareholders' wealth (Stout 2012), and governance is efficient when based on an outsider model. The team production theory adopted by Blair and Stout (1999) takes issue with the prevailing principal-agent model of the public corporation and the shareholder wealth maximization goal that underlies it, which gives legitimacy to market control. The theory rests on a widely accepted observation that shareholders are not the only group that may provide specialized inputs into corporate production. Even, executives, rank-and-file employees, creditors as well as the local community may also make essential contributions and have an interest in an enterprise's success. The public corporation is a team of people who enter into a complex agreement to work together for their mutual gain. They are presumed to having entered into "*pactum subjectionis*" under which they yield control over outputs and key inputs and they participate in a process of internal setting and dispute resolution. That is to say, they have a real interest in governing the corporation and they do it through an internal mediating hierarchy [a board] and not through market mechanisms and agency contracts.

Moreover, both Blair and Stout (1999) and Stout (2012) argue for the fallacy of the assumption whereby the shareholders do own the corporation, on which SVM doctrine is postulated. Blair and Stout (1999) recall a striking aspect of corporate law, which is generally disregarded. Corporate law views a corporation as a legal person. When owners fill articles of incorporation, in the eyes of the law, a new entity that is totally separate from its shareholders is born. The shareholder primacy violates the very existence of this entity, and transforms it into a legal fiction, whereas the corporation is an independent legal entity that owns itself. For Stout (2012), shareholders do not own the corporation; they own only shares of stocks, that is a contract between the shareholder and the corporation; a contract that gives the shareholder very limited rights under limited circumstances (exactly as any other contracts between the corporation and debt-holders and customers).

For Stout (2012), considering the shareholders as the owners of corporations is a fable. She argues that it is a mistake to think that shareholders have the only residual claim on the firm's profits, and that they are "principals" who hire and control directors to act as their "agents" because of a single outdated and widely misunderstood judicial opinion—the Michigan Supreme Court's 1919 decision in Dodge vs. Ford Motor Company case. According to Stout (2012), The Dodge brothers who were minority shareholders in the Ford Motor Company sued Henry Ford for having stopped paying dividends, while he was doing this for years. The Dodge brothers' plan was to use the cash dividends from their shares to start a new business: The Dodge Brothers Company. Well aware of their plans, Henry Ford stopped paying dividends to not giving them the opportunity to create a rival manufacturing company. He allegedly claimed that the company needed to keep its money in order to offer lower prices to consumers and to pay employees higher wages. By siding with the Dodge brothers, the Michigan Supreme Court decision was wrongly considered, as a case about corporate law requiring shareholder primacy. As a matter of fact, it was a case about the duty a controlling majority shareholder owed to minority ones. As a matter of fact, the judge has ordered Henry Ford to pay a small dividend while allowing him to continue with his plans to expand employment and reduce prices. Quoting Freund (1897), Stout (2012) considers a shareholder acting as an owner as a trespasser. Therefore, to assume that the corporation is to be run primarily for the profit of the stockholders is a managerial choice and not a legal requirement.

Knowing the fallacy of the legal requirement, the relevance of the managerial choice by considering that corporations exist only to maximize shareholder value, knowing that corporate directors or executives have no enforceable legal duty towards shareholders, should be questioned. Why business and policy elites did accept that choice as an unquestionable truth? Shareholder value maximization [SVM] is believed to be desirable because it is thought to offer the best solution to limit the directors' discretion, what Jensen and Meckling (1976) called the agency cost problem. According to Davis (2009), if the corporation should be run for shareholder value, it is premised not on the conclusions that shareholders do own the corporation, but on the view that it could be better for all of us if we act as if they do. Nevertheless, Stout (2012) argues that shareholder-oriented firms do not perform better and this stance lacks empirical support. Moreover, when the focus is shifted from the performance of individual firms to the performance of the corporate sector as a whole, it is even proved that shareholder primacy is bad for investors collectively and might be at the origin of the tragedy of the commons. For Stout (2012), because there are two ways to obtain value, either to create it or to take it from others, SVM is considered as a theory of value extraction. The question on the desirability of SVM remains without a clear and convincing answer!

Despite that EMH and SVM are based on wishful thinking and are poised for intellectual collapse (Stout 2012), economists from the school of Chicago strived to enact the reality they envisioned. The market should be entrusted the responsibility of controlling business activities, which purpose should be only to maximize the value for its shareholders. They constructed the socio-technological geometry that is compatible with their model to form a new world that is nothing but a patchwork cobbled together with elements from their narrative. This imaginary world was made actual by an institutional apparatus (Chabrak 2014). The institutional investors, corporate America but also the U.S. Republican government were instrumental in promoting this shift to pave the way for the shareholder era and its ownership ideology, whereby the maximization of social welfare and well-being is tied to shareholdings and trading on the market (Chabrak 2011; Davis 2009). We contend that this institutional apparatus form the market communion, including the IASB which role is to sustain the shared beliefs of the communion.

3.2 *The Social Construct of "Investor" in the IASB Conceptual Framework and Its Affiliation to the Market Communion*

Many authors have already highlighted the affiliation of the IASC/IASB to the Anglo-Saxon accounting model, which major role was set to facilitate governance by markets (Chiapello 2005; Hoarau and Teller 2007; Botzem and Quack 2009). We argue that the way that the concept of "investor" is used in the conceptual framework depicts the obedience of the IASB to the market communion. The IASB reduces the investor to its role as capital allocator. It ignores all other dimensions related to a shareholding decision, such as stewardship and accountability dimensions, which were compulsory to achieve shareholder protection as defended by Adolf A. Berle. Since, accounting information seems to have only one purpose that is to facilitate the role of investors in making capital allocation [buy and sell] decisions on capital markets. The principle of total disclosure that was institutionalized by the New Deal becomes obsolete. Accounting information does not serve any more to affirm the stewardship and accountability of managers to the proprietors of the company. Accountants have set for themselves the unique function to serve only trading function on capital markets. By doing so, they emptied accounting from one of its natural and intrinsic elements, that is its dominant purpose or root metaphor (Ravenscroft and Williams 2009, 2011), a centuries-old shared living law of stewardship and accountability (Murphy et al. 2013). Therefore, the social construct of "investor" is considered to be salient evidence on the IASB affiliation to the market communion.

The IASB Conceptual Framework sets out the concepts that underlie the preparation and presentation of financial statements. It identifies principles for the IASB to use when it develops and revises its IFRS. In 2004, the IASB and the US FASB initiated a joint project to revise their conceptual frameworks. During the development process, Exposure Drafts [ED] were issued by the Board in 2006 and 2008 for discussion. In 2010, the IASB and the FASB issued two chapters of a revised conceptual framework: on the objective of general purpose financial reporting (chapter "1") and on qualitative characteristics of useful financial information (chapter "3". Today, they are part of the IASB's existing conceptual framework. In 2012, the IASB carried out a public consultation on its agenda and further to this consultation it decided to restart its conceptual framework project without being conducted jointly with the FASB. In the Discussion Paper [DP/2013/1] issued in July 2013, the IASB has decided not to fundamentally reconsider the chapters that deal with the objective of financial reporting and the qualitative characteristics of useful financial information (chapters "Interview of Jacques Richard" and "Frère Jacques and IFRS: Sonnez les Matines?").

In chapter 1, the objective of general purpose financial reporting is set to be: "to provide financial information about the reporting entity that is useful to existing and potential investors, lenders and other creditors in making decisions about providing resources to the entity" (IASB 2013, p. 195). Therefore, capital providers can be considered to be the primary user group of financial statements. Also, the IASB explicitly states that reports are not primarily directed to other users such as regulators and members of the public who cannot be considered therefore as primary users. After the global financial crisis, Sir David Tweedie, the IASB chairman from January 2001 until the end of June 2011, has recommended disconnecting prudential requirements from accounting rules. In his testimony to UK House of Commons Select Treasury Committee on November 11th 2008, he stated: "You can actually break the link and still give the banking supervisors what they want and we will not affect the integrity of accounting. It can be done."[1] According to Sir David Tweedie, to ensure that financial institutions are run prudently, prudential authorities should not use accounting information in a crude way as they did and should make appropriate adjustments to accounting information in calculating capital requirements. This stance by the previous chairman of the IASB clearly supports the idea that accounting information is not produced to be used as it is by regulators and other users.

For Murphy et al. (2013), by reducing the primary users of accounting information to capital providers and by excluding users such as customers, regulators, suppliers and the public from such a group, the nature of the interaction between financial reporting and the social accounting project came to be seen as fundamentally altered. Accounting information has no responsibility to users other than investors and creditors. In other words, accountants have totally dismissed Edwin Merrick Dodd's contention on the purpose of a public company. For Dodd (1932), the role of a business corporation is more than making money for shareholders. The

[1] http://www.publications.parliament.uk/pa/cm200809/cmselect/cmtreasy/144/08111101.htm (last accessed on November 08, 2011).

corporation is a legal entity created for public benefit. It is run by professional managers seeking to serve stakeholders and the public interest. The IASB seems dismissing Dodd's view by consecrating a very narrow understanding of the social service of a corporation, the one that is endorsed by Friedman (1970), according to which, the social responsibility of a business is to increase its profits. Such an idea is linked to the SVM doctrine.

According to the IASB (2013), decisions made by capital providers "involve buying, selling or holding equity and debt instruments, and providing or settling loans and other forms of credit" (p. 195). Such decisions depend on returns the capital providers expect. Hence, the type of information they need is what helps them assess the prospects for future net cash inflows to the reporting entity and to estimate its value. The conceptual framework states "information about a reporting entity's past financial performance and how its management discharged its responsibilities is usually helpful in predicting the entity's future returns on its economic resources" (p. 197). Two conclusions can be driven from what precedes.

Even though the IASB admits that all providers of finance are the primary users to whom general-purpose financial reports are directed, it is obvious that the IASB useful information is designed to serve primarily the capital market participants in making buy/sell decisions. This first conclusion is supported by a statement of Hans Hoogervorst, the IASB chairman made in July 2011 where he claimed that investors' interests should be heard more loudly than it is currently the case in the standard setting process, and as a consequence, the IASB has the intention to strengthen its relations with investors, considered to be the 'end users' of financial information, in the next years.[2]

The second conclusion is that not only creditors and lenders come in the second position but also investors in their capacity as shareholders are left behind. In fact, the conceptual framework seems reducing the concept of "investor" to a capital allocator who makes buy and sell decisions. The shareholding side related to investing decisions is neglected. After having made a capital allocation decision, the investor becomes a shareholder and in his quality as a shareholder, he becomes the principal or one of the principals to whom managers are accountable, as defended by Adolf A. Berle. Yet, the IASB conceptual framework states the accounting information to be useful if it helps making an assessment of returns and to value the entity in the purpose of facilitating trading on the market. Therefore, if information about a reporting entity's past financial performance is useful, it is only because it helps predicting the entity's future returns. For Whittington (2008), the needs of stewardship are assumed to be met within the decision-usefulness objective. Our understanding is that this stewardship dimension is incidental because the shareholding side of the investing decision is ignored. The

[2] "The imprecise world of accounting", speech by Hans Hoogervorst, IASB chairman, at the 2012 International Association for Accounting Education & Research (IAAER) conference (Amsterdam, June 2012), can be downloaded from the IASB website on http://www.ifrs.org/Alerts/Conference/Documents/HHoogervorstJune2012theimpreciseworldofaccounting.pdf.

statements related to stewardship were added to the final version just to calm intense debate sparked by the exposure drafts issued in 2006 and 2008. Accounting information is important if it serves the primary objective of [trading] decision usefulness. Any past information or information about the resources of the entity, claims against the entity, and how efficiently and effectively the entity's managers and directors have discharged their responsibilities to use the entity's resources are considered useful as long as they improve the prediction of future cash flows. Therefore, they are useful not because they help shareholders in assessing accountability of managers by evaluating say how many resources they have sacrificed effectively in achieving the primary enterprise goal, but for their enabling capital allocators to make arbitrage and capital allocation decisions.

The IASB has decided to dismiss stewardship objective, which has nothing to do with decision-usefulness objective it professed, which is focused on the prediction of future cash flows. Stewardship is concerned with agency problems that raise both efficient ex-ante contracting, and ex-post monitoring. It is also concerned with matters related to efficiency, effectiveness, and strategic planning and control. Those agency problems are the by-product of the separation between ownership and control. According to Murphy et al. (2013), stewardship and accountability have even more concerns such as maintaining the order, trust, morality, truth and so forth. According to Murphy et al. (2013), the Trueblood Report (AICPA 1971) and The Corporate Report (ASSC 1973) were emblems in the retreating tide of stewardship recognition by accounting policy makers. Then, for Ravenscroft and Williams (2009), the 1978 FASB report was instrumental in institutionalizing information usefulness. Finally, it is the decision of both the IASB and the FASB in 2006 to finally drop stewardship as a primary financial reporting objective.

In chapter "3", the IASB describes the qualitative characteristics of an information to be likely the most useful to the existing and potential investors, lenders and other creditors for making decisions about the reporting entity on the basis of information in its financial report (financial information). To be useful, financial information must be relevant and faithfully represent what it purports to represent. According to Whittington (2008), the focus on the decision-usefulness objective has several implications on the qualitative characteristics of financial information, including the replacement of the concept of reliability by the one of representational faithfulness. According to the IASB (2013), "to be a perfectly faithful representation, a depiction would have three characteristics. It would be *complete, neutral* and *free from error*" (p. 200). While reliability is concerned with the provision of information suitable for monitoring agent's actions, the latter emphasizes the capacity of the information in capturing the substance of an economic event. Another consequence of the predominance of faithful representation characteristic was also to abandon the old principle of "prudence" as long as it is inconsistent with the quality of neutrality that requires the information to be free from bias.

Our understanding is that the IASB is concerned with efficient market imperatives. The idea of the market has nothing to do with the concept of shareholding that has justified the principle of total disclosure, which was promoted by the regulators in the New Deal. Their purpose was to protect shareholders, those orphans and widows who came to be seen as the owners of Corporate America (Berle and Means 1982; Davis 2009). Because of the separation between control and ownership, they have limited authority, ability, or resources to obtain information. The role of accounting is then to provide such an information to enable them controlling corporate managers who were entrusted powers to be exercised entirely for their benefits, further to the views of Adolf A. Berle in the great debate over the corporate purpose.

The role of accounting according to the IASB conceptual framework is of another nature. It enables sustaining the idea that market prices can meet with fundamental prices and therefore, the market is efficient. Hence, the outsider model of governance that relies on the collective force of opinion exerted by markets in order to regulate corporate conduct (Aglietta 2000) becomes legitimate. It is presumed to having permitted an optimal allocation of capital (Jensen 1986; Jensen and Murphy 1990), in order to improve the performance of the economy as a whole, as described by the neoclassical theory of market economy (Fama and Jensen 1983a, b).

4 Concluding Comments

Using the concept of communion lent to Gurvitch sociology of law (1948/2001), and some shareholder thinking borrowed from Stout (2012) and Blair and Stout (1999), the IASB is portrayed to be one of the market communion constituents. Such a communion is primarily a manifestation of a strong cohesion of the collective mind of its members, which affects the type of law they produce. The IASB conceptual framework is subsumed to the market communion tenets and imperatives. It should be analyzed as a kind of law that reinforces the market beliefs to support its hegemony. The IASB conceptual framework designates investors to be the primary users of accounting information. The concept of investor is reduced to its capital allocation role and the objective of accounting information is abridged to decision usefulness. By ignoring the shareholding side in investing decisions, stewardship dimension is considered by the conceptual framework as a sub-function of decision usefulness and a qualitative characteristic such as reliability is dismissed in favor of faithful representation accordingly.

The kind of law produced by the IASB depicts the values and beliefs of the market communion, that is a form of sociality to which the IASB belongs. The conceptual framework and more precisely the concept of investor is portrayed to be socially constructed. It is shaped by the collective intuitions that organize the communion and at the same time it contributes to maintaining them. The HME and SVM constitute the collective intuitions of the market communion. The laws produced by the members of the communion are socially constructed, maintained and adapted through the exercise of their membership. The IASB conceptual framework is both constituted by the IASB belonging to the market communion, and yet at the same time is the very medium of this constitution. Market hegemony is enabled. Its alleged predictive ability is secured. The IASB has enforced the idea that markets are able to incorporate all publicly available information about companies' future prospects into the share price. As the latter is right and smart, financial markets provide privileged access to truth. By endorsing the efficient market and shareholder value maximization doctrines (based on the rightness of market's judgment and the priority to serve the investors interests), the IASB is contributing to sustain the benefits of deregulated financial markets to the economy as a whole. Accounting becomes more and more entrenched as a vehicle for special interests (Murphy et al. 2013). Moonitz (1961) has already raised the danger of defining accounting function in terms of some special interest. According to Chambers (1980), "it is widely held that a given set of financial statements cannot be serviceable to all users, and that the interest of some class of users must therefore be taken as the primary interest to be served" (p. 171). Nonetheless, Ravenscroft and Williams (2009) state that this choice has deep implications by shifting accounting from an autonomous discipline into a sub-discipline of neoclassical economics.

References

Aglietta M (2000) Shareholder value and corporate governance: some tricky questions. Econ Soc 29(1):146–159

Amernic J, Craig R (2004) Reform of accounting education in the post-enron era: moving accounting 'Out of the Shadows'. ABACUS 40(3):342–378

Berle A Jr, Means GC (1982) The modern corporation and private property. WS Hein, New York, NY (Original edition published in 1932 by Macmillan)

Blair M, Stout L (1999) A team production theory of corporate law. Va Law Rev 85(2):247–328

Botzem S, Quack S (2009) (No) Limits to Anglo-American accounting? Reconstructing the history of the International Accounting Standards Committee: a review article. Acc Organ Soc 34(8):988–998

Chabrak N (2011) The shareholder era and the changing nature of the corporation. A Comment on "Managed by the Markets: How Finance Re-Shaped America" by G. Davis (OUP, 2009). Account Econ Law Convivium. 1(2), http://www.bepress.com/ael/vol1/iss2/4/

Chabrak N (2014) The shareholder value myth and the market communion. Law Finan Markets Rev 8(1):27–38. doi:10.5235/17521440.8.1.27

Chambers RJ (1980) The myths and the science of accounting. Account Organ Soc 5(1):167–180

Chiapello E (2005) Les normes comptables comme institution du capitalisme. Une analyse du passage aux normes IFRS en Europe à partir de 2005. Sociologie du travail 47:362–382

Davis FG (2009) Managed by the markets: how finance re-shaped America. Oxford University Press, New York, NY

Dodd EM (1932) For whom are corporate managers trustees? Harv Law Rev 45(7):1145–1163

Fama EF (1965) The behavior of stock-market prices. J Bus 38(1):34–105

Fama EF, Jensen MC (1983a) Agency problems and residual claims. J Law Econ 26(2):327–349

Fama EF, Jensen MC (1983b) Separation of ownership and control. J Law Econ 26(2):301–325

Friedman M (1970) The social responsibility of business is to increase its profits. N Y Times Mag (September 13)

Greenspan A (2008) Testimony to House of Representatives Committee on Government oversight and reform. Oct 23. http://blogs.wsj.com/economics/2008/10/23/greenspan-testimony-on-sources-of-financial-crisis/

Gurvitch G (2001) Sociology of law. Transaction Publishers, New Brunswick, Original edition (1948)

Hoarau C, Teller R (2007) IFRS: les normes comptables du nouvel ordre économique global ? Comptabilité – Contrôle – Audit. December (thematic issue), 3–20

IASB (2013) Discussion Paper DP/2013/1: a review of the conceptual framework for financial reporting. http://www.ifrs.org/Current-Projects/IASB-Projects/Conceptual-Framework/Discussion-Paper-July-2013/Documents/Discussion-Paper-Conceptual-Framework-July-2013.pdf

Jensen MC (1986) Agency costs of free cash flow, corporate finance, and takeovers. Am Econ Rev 76(2):323–329

Jensen MC, Meckling W (1976) Theory of the firm: managerial behavior, agency costs, and ownership structure. J Finan Econ 3(4):305–360

Jensen MC, Murphy KJ (1990) Performance pay and top management incentives. J Polit Econ 98 (2):225–264

Lazonick W (2011) The innovative enterprise and the developmental state: toward an economics of 'organizational success'. Presented at the conference of the Institute for New Economic Thinking, Bretton Woods, NH, April 10. http://www.newdeal20.org/wp-content/uploads/2011/08/lazonick-innovative-enterprise-and-developmental-state-20110403.pdf

Macintosh JCC (1999) The issues, effects and consequences of the Berle-Dodd debate, 1931–1932. Account Organ Soc 24(2):139–153

Moonitz M (1961) The basic postulates of accounting. AICPA, New York, NY

Mouck T (1998) Capital markets research and real world complexity: the emerging challenge of chaos theory. Account Organ Soc 23(2):189–215

Murphy T, O'Connell V, hogartaigh C (2013) Discourses surrounding the evolution of the IASB/FASB conceptual framework: what they reveal about the "living law" of accounting. Account Organ Soc 38(1):72–91

Ravenscroft S, Williams P (2011) Rethinking decision-usefulness. http://elsevier.conference-services.net/resources/247/2182/pdf/CPAC2011_0064_paper.pdf

Ravenscroft S, Williams P (2009) Making imaginary worlds real: the case of expensing employee stock options. Account Organ Soc 34(6–7):770–786

Shiller TR (1984) Stock prices and social dynamics. Brook Pap Econ Act 2:457–510

Soufian M, Forbes W, Hudson R (2013) Adapting financial reality: is a new paradigm emerging? Crit Perspect Account

Stout LA (2012) The shareholder value myth. Berrett-Koehler, San Francisco, CA

Tinker AM (1980) Towards a political economy of accounting: an empirical illustration of the Cambridge controversies. Account Organ Soc 5(1):147–160

Whittington G (2008) Harmonisation or discord? The critical role of the IASB conceptual framework review. J Account Public Policy 27(6):495–502

Williams PF (2002) Accounting and the moral order: justice, accounting and legitimate moral authority. J Account Public Interest 2(1):1–21

Williams PF (2004) You reap what you sow: the ethical discourse of professional accounting. Crit Perspect Account 15(6-7):995–1001

Williams PF, Jenkins JG, Ingraham L (2006) The winnowing away of behavioral accounting research in the US: the process for anointing academic elites. Account Organ Soc 31 (8):783–818

The Accounting Representation of the Enterprise Entity: An Historical Perspective

Yuri Biondi

Abstract Accounting scholars, standards-setters and preparers have been confronted with a new financial reporting paradigm that has displaced the traditional focus on accountability of the enterprise entity to its stakeholders (including shareholders) and on the general interest. This focus was common to both static and dynamic accounting approaches in continental Europe, as well as to both proprietary and entity accounting perspectives in North America. This chapter develops three conceptual and practical lessons driven from a comparative analysis of traditional and modern accounting paradigms: (i) the enterprise entity should be distinguished from its markets of reference; (ii) fair value and discounting do not belong to accounting; and (iii) accounting should not follow the market, but the market pricing process may take advantage from an accounting lighthouse. Illustrative examples are then taken from the international financial reporting standards concerning intangibles, goodwill and financial liabilities. According to this analysis, the market-based view on accounting is flawed and undermines accounting suitable connection with law and economics of the business firm as an enterprise entity.

1 Introduction

Currently as Tenured Research Fellow of the CNRS [Centre National de la Recherche Scientifique—French National Centre for Scientific Research], I have been working on accounting issues for some 20 years. My first meeting with Jacques Richard was during the preparation of my French-Italian doctoral dissertation (2000–2003), when we discovered and shared our common passion for accounting theory in historical perspective. At that time, we were observing the advent of a new historical trend initiated by US and International accounting standard-setting bodies with the aim of imposing a new 'financial reporting para-

Y. Biondi (✉)
Cnrs – ESCP Europe, Paris, France
e-mail: yuri.biondi@gmail.com

D. Bensadon, N. Praquin (eds.), *IFRS in a Global World*,
DOI 10.1007/978-3-319-28225-1_10

digm' that had been theorized as early as the 1970s, above all by researchers in North America. In fact, this new paradigm had been termed an "accounting revolution" in the 1980s (Beaver 1981). This revolution changes the status and role of the firm as an enterprise entity—formerly the locus of accounting—as well as the way in which corporate income is defined and represented. Accordingly, the metrical connection of accounting figures to share market prices has started to dictate the meaning and role of accounting for business and society, while the traditional focus on accountability of the enterprise entity to its stakeholders (including shareholders) was progressively neglected, and the general interest displaced.

Because my background was in mathematical economics [1990–1995] rather than in accounting, I spent about 10 years studying a large number of major authors to carry out my research. In the process, I became familiar with several accounting traditions that we addressed in a collective work in which Jacques Richard has presented the French national tradition (Biondi et al. 2012b).

In the nineteenth century, accounting theorists and practitioners discussed how to classify accounting elements into several account classes. Concerned with "form" and technicalities, they gave little thought to the economic "substance" of accounting. Starting in the late nineteenth century and extending into the first three decades of the twentieth, the proponents of a scientific revolution heralded the emergence of a new accounting paradigm (Richard 1996). This latter paradigm made the firm as an enterprise entity the centrepiece of control and accountability (Biondi 2008a, b, 2010; Biondi et al. 2007). How accounting elements are defined and classified acquires meaning and purpose based upon the scope and purpose of this accountability, which is to define and represent the income to and position of the enterprise entity. Accounting thought of that time can be broken down into four basic models:

In the traditions of Continental Europe, a static model focused on measuring changes in wealth through the enterprise properties in contrast to a dynamic approach that seeks to determine the operating (i.e. productive) results generated by the enterprise as a whole.

In the North American tradition, the distinction is between an ownership perspective concerned with representing the wealth accruing to the proprietor-entrepreneur, and the enterprise entity approach, which well may be related to both the Marginalist Revolution in economics, and the emergence of institutional economics at the time, with its focus on representing the generation of income for the satisfaction of all stakeholders, including shareholders (Biondi 2012).

Although the dynamic approach and the entity approach dominated the twentieth century prior to the advent of the new financial reporting paradigm, all four models placed the enterprise entity at the centre of the accounting system. The main scope and purpose was not to produce information for investors active on financial markets, but to design a control system useful to all stakeholders (including partners and shareholders) with joint interests in a business venture whose ongoing profits and losses they share. Thus, whether preference was given to an ownership and static approach or to an entity and dynamic approach, the enterprise and its accountability invariably remained the primary focus.

In the 1970s, however, a number of regulators and theorists began shifting away from this view of the accounting information and representation required for the enterprise and its income, towards an emphasis on the market, particularly the share market. Their belief was that current market prices at closing dates should be used as the basis for information provided to investors in financial markets. Therefore, they developed an approach that more or less explicitly viewed the enterprise as a portfolio of disparate assets and liabilities, to be evaluated separately at an arbitrary moment in time. The entity was thus redefined as a legal-economic vehicle designed to be employed by investors active in benchmarking financial markets to hold such assets and liabilities (Biondi 2011).

The effect of this view of accounting has been to rule out any concern with the income generated over time by the enterprise entity as a whole. In this financialised approach, the collective, dynamic dimension of the enterprise has lost its central status. Accordingly, regulators started issuing specialised accounting standards for each distinct accounting item. In doing so, they are rejecting more than a century of progress in accounting theory and regulation. It should be stressed that the conceptual frameworks underpinning the work of the US and International standard-setting bodies do not have a "constitutional" character—in other words, they cannot be used in practice, nor can they serve as a reference for application of the standards when preparing financial statements. Each specialised standard has its ad hoc validity; there is no requirement to refer to key foundational concepts. Moreover, their sets of standards contain no clear definition of the enterprise entity, while standards are typically applied on a case-by-case basis, transaction by transaction, and thus independently of each other.

This amounts to a genuine revolution that creates a whole series of problems. This chapter shall attempt to deal with them in historical perspective, drawing three lessons that I will present in a somewhat provocative manner:

The first lesson is that the enterprise should not be equated with the market.
The second lesson is that fair value is not accounting.
The third and final lesson is that accounting should not take its lead from the market; the market should take its lead from accounting.

1) The enterprise should not be equated with the market

If the enterprise were the same thing as the market, the market viewpoint would prevail and market forces would be omnipresent, determining all types of transactions and economic activities. This is simply not the case, however. Strictly speaking, on the one hand, there are share market prices and a financial investment logic that should be part of how the value of a listed company is estimated. This is the task facing investors, at least so-called fundamentalist or long-term investors active in financial markets. On the other hand, the accounting system defines and tracks corporate performance achieved over time, as transactions are completed and the potential becomes actual. This is a logic of control, of accountability; it is also the management logic that any enterprise needs to be able to function over time and to address a wide range of matters spanning industrial organization, finance and economic relations with stakeholders, both investors and non-investors.

Seen in this light, accounting information should complement market information rather than following it (Biondi et al. 2012a). On the one hand, you have the market with its price system, which generates market information through interaction among investors, each having only limited and dispersed knowledge. Just how relevant and trustworthy such market information is will depend on the state of the market and the opportunities for market participants to access firm-specific information. On the other hand, you have an enterprise entity that is fundamentally distinct from the market and that cannot be comprehended without genuine accounting information, which provides the critical firm-specific knowledge that is common knowledge among investors.

In summary, two systems of information, representation and control are required and present, rather than just one (Biondi 2003, 2010): the accounting system and the share price system.

2) Fair value is not accounting

This brings us to the second lesson from history: fair value is not accounting. If you go back and reread the classic accounting scholars, the ones who wrote before the new wave of financial economists inspired by modern financial theory, you observe that they provided a critique of the idea that company accounts should include profit and loss estimates, i.e. a whole series of valuations guessing on transactions that may never be realized (including Savary 1675). Recent authors like Ijiri (2005) have echoed their concerns in a theoretical debate that is far from over today.

Yet fair value requires such estimates. It portrays the enterprise as a collection of disparate resources that are assumed to be liquid, given that they can be measured at their current market value or by using mark-to-model estimates of that value (Biondi et al. 2008; Biondi and Fantacci 2012). Estimates of this kind thus result directly from a view of accounting as an instantaneous valuation system, with markets supposedly providing the most reliable indication of business value.

Needless to say, this approach subjects the enterprise to the market, whereas the corporate performance can only be produced over time, and with the involvement of the whole enterprise (Biondi 2011). In any enterprise, the outcomes of the various processes, activities and segments overlap and offset each other. That, in fact, is part of the rationale for creating complex enterprise groups spanning several industries and several countries (Strasser and Blumberg 2011). This highlights how regrettable it is to disregard the enterprise entity as a whole that generates corporate income over time. The firm as an integrated entity and going concern should indeed be the focus of any accounting model. In the older accounting paradigm, the principle of the firm as an enduring economic entity was universally recognized and upheld in all countries and regulatory contexts (Hoarau 2006). It follows that there was no need to displace this principle to achieve international accounting harmonization. The reasons for this displacement must therefore be sought elsewhere—in the financialization imposed on corporate activity and accountability.

3) Accounting should not take its lead from the market; the market should take its lead from accounting

This brings us to the third lesson from history. Should we accept the new role assigned to accounting or stick to the old one? The traditional accounting paradigm serves to remind us that the firm is an enterprise entity located in space and time, an enterprise entity fundamentally different from the market. This paradigm distinguishes between and matches cost and revenue streams, instead of lumping them together in discount-based present value estimates. Furthermore, the older model does not entail a net loss of information for investors, because it avoids the use of fanciful profit prophecies, and the application of discount rates that introduces further forms of pro-cyclicality, due to the movement of interest rates used as benchmarks. In this way, a genuine accounting logic emerges. Rather than seeking to achieve the impossible estimate of enterprise value (in the form of market or discounted value), this accounting logic focuses on economic and financial flows in a relevant, reliable representation of invested costs and accrued revenues generated over time by the enterprise as a whole. This historical accounting logic, along with the information it provides, can contribute to smooth price formation in the financial market and be useful to investors, financial analysts and other stakeholders concerned with ongoing corporate affairs (Biondi 2003; Biondi and Giannoccolo 2015).

2 Examples from the International Financial Reporting Standards

The cases of intangibles and goodwill, as well as that of financial liabilities, are significant to comparatively assess the distinctive perspectives of accounting under examination. Take the example of the financing of core R&D expenditures. According to the financial logic (fair value), these expenditures do not constitute separable assets that are disposables at and valuables through their current value. Therefore, the underlying intangible resource is not a corporate asset, financially speaking. However, traditional accounting logic does dissent. Useful resources, be they financial or productive, may never be disposed without losing all the synergies resulting from their combination, and the conditional competitive advantage that fosters corporate income generation. Therefore, the underlying intangible resources may be represented as intangible assets by capitalizing and amortizing related expenditures over time (Ijiri 1975; Biondi and Reberioux 2012).

The case of goodwill generated through business combinations is also significant. According to the financial logic (fair value), goodwill is generated by the difference between the transfer consideration and the sum of revaluated net assets. In this way, the transfer consideration is assumed to be the best evidence of the value of the acquired business; accordingly, goodwill becomes an indefinitely durable asset, only submitted to impairment tests for depreciation. However, the accounting logic does dissent. Transfer consideration occurs under peculiar, exceptional circumstances that should be checked against accounting evidence. As a matter of history, goodwill was distrusted (Ding et al. 2008) and quickly written off (or at least amortized over time), while the pooling method of accounting was allowed to treat all cases where no arm's length transaction occurred in the business combination.

In case of financial liabilities, fair value accounting recommends to account for them at current market prices whenever available, or an estimated value mimicking those market prices. The business entity is then supposed to be a portfolio of accounting elements, be they assets or liabilities, which all are marketable at will. This entity is supposed to hold financial liabilities, not owe them to someone else. However, the accounting logic does dissent. As matters of fact and law, the business entity has entered financial transactions which involve explicit or implicit financial obligations that must be fulfilled in near or remote future according to their terms and conditions. These obligations can be formalized in transferable securities such as shares and bonds, but also consist of obligations with employees, suppliers and fiscal authorities. From this perspective, their possible buy-back involves a distinct financial transaction that is unrelated to their recognition as an advance on future cash inflows generated by the enterprise entity. This advance corresponds to a series of future cash outflows that are expected to become due to the holding stakeholder in the future.

3 Reconciliation of Accounting and Finance

Without paying attention to the legal-economic congeries of the business firm and its specific economic environment that is fundamentally different from the market, the financial reporting paradigm bears the huge risk to advertise self-standing declarations of financial value by management, instead of providing trustworthy summaries of corporate performance and position generated over time.

From an historically grounded perspective, at least two points are fundamental to reconcile accounting and finance: a comprehensive view of accounting as an epistemic, organizational, and institutional device; and the recognition of its special role in the dynamics of Share Exchange as common knowledge of reference, available for subjective valuations and decision-making (Sunder 2002).

First of all, the relationship between accounting and the share market should not preclude accounting's role as a mode of organizing, regulating, and representing the activities of enterprise entities through time. The accounting system has performed and should go on performing multiple functions in economy and society: not only the disclosure of accounting information (including for the share market), but also the construction of operational costs and managerial indicators of performance, and the regulation of dividends, business income taxes, prudential ratios and other institutional matters. Here accounting is understood as a common language (and knowledge) of business (epistemic role), a managerial instrument (organizational role), and a fundamental mode of governance and regulation (institutional role). All together, these roles of accounting embed the working of accounting systems at the intersection between socio-economic and financial systems.

Accordingly, accounting may be expanded following to its own accounting logic. At least three suggestions emerge from the traditional view (Biondi 2011). Concerning the assets side, accounting systems may capitalize invested expenditures on R&D as depreciable assets, according to conventions disclosed by, or even shared among firms (Lev and Zarowin 1999). Although accounting cannot estimate intangibles' value (nor the market can), it may report on actual investments that the management has committed to them. Concerning the liabilities side, accounting systems may recognize the cost of shareholders' equity (Anthony 1983), as financial economic theory does with the "time value of money". Shareholders' equity constitutes a special source of financing for the enterprise entity (Schumpeter 1912; including first English translation of neglected pages in Biondi 2008b): it is then a special liability whose accounting cost may be based on the funds that have been actually provided over time. Concerning business income determination, accounting systems may distinguish unrealized capital gains and losses from operational incomes and incurred costs, in order to avoid standardizing "Ponzi-schemes" among different stakeholders over time (Biondi 2013).

4 Concluding Remarks

In the last four decades, an accounting revolution has pretended to develop accounting as a form of financial reporting, including on potential capital gains. However, past accounting traditions had already understood that accounting is not as primarily about communication as control. Accounting is concerned with cash and non-cash resources committed to socio-economic entities. It establishes then norms, rules, and processes to control, organise and regulate these entities and the related resources in situation. To achieve this purpose, past traditions had based accounting upon the representation of the business firm as an enterprise entity (also called 'going concern' in English, 'Betrieb' in German, and 'azienda' in Italian), that is, a becoming collective entity that evolves over historical time and socio-economic space.

By taking the business firm as their central concept, past accounting traditions had avoided another modern mistake that consists in imagining that only 'markets' stand out in economy and society. However, economic and social relationships cannot be limited to a pervasive price system. 'The' market is not the only (or the one best) way to organise and coordinate economy and society. Actually, whenever markets exist, they work in very different way from what some expect and day-dream. It is somewhat astonishing that 'positive' and 'empirical' researches in accounting have been scarcely concerned with the ways in which markets do factually work, preferring to rely on their own alleged assumptions about market working. As a matter of experience, business firms and institutions exist and function together with markets. Embedded in this broader socio-economic context, accounting system cannot be reduced to a price system. The latter relates to the market as the former does to the business firm, both being distinctive modes of economic organisation and coordination.

Leading scholars of past accounting traditions were often outstanding professors in leading universities; they worked in close connection with major companies and regulatory bodies; they educated professional accountants and helped developing the first accounting model that was globally harmonised: the model of historical cost accounting. The financialised model of nowadays accounting, which is emerging since the 1970s, was not the first attempt to harmonise accounting throughout the world. From an historical perspective, historical cost accounting was accepted by and adapted to most accounting traditions and jurisdictions around the world. Actually, these local variants of the past accounting model were surely less important than both options that are still available in international financial reporting standards, and carve-outs that those standards generate as a reaction to international generally imposed accounting rules. The concept of an accounting representation of an enterprise entity situated in time and space and bearing social responsibilities had been shared by most accounting systems throughout the world. Nowadays, some divergences and carve-outs from international accounting standards may actually depend on resistance and confusion generated by the market-based view of the business firm that those standards drive and impose.

This market-based view relates to the new financial reporting paradigm that has driven accounting into a dead end. Just how badly it has failed is highlighted by recent scandals and the shortcomings revealed by the global financial crisis. Nor should anyone forget that emergency intervention by treasuries and central banks were required to save many of the banking and financial institutions, which were the most subject to the new fair value model. We should drive all the relevant implications on the economic consequences of this model from this natural experiment (Bignon et al. 2009).

To get out of this dead end, we need to make a few basic observations and lay the theoretical groundwork for an acknowledgement of the role of accounting as a mode of representing, governing and regulating business activity that provides relevance and reliability for all stakeholders, including shareholders. An enterprise accounting system fulfils a variety of functions in business and society. It provides information to shareholders (including investors in the share market), while also helping to measure production costs and operating results and to regulate dividends, taxes, prudential ratios and the like. Although this is only a statement of fact, it further paves the way toward a redefined purpose or underlying principle of accounting standardization that may still provide investors with firm-specific information. As for such a common source of accounting information on corporate performance achieved over time offers financial analysts and investors a lighthouse for validating their valuations and expectations. Investors may then be constantly reminded that they are investing in an enterprise, and not just in a supposedly liquid financial security (i.e. one that they can sell on the market at any time). The losses triggered by scandals and financial crises offer just this kind of reminder, but only when it is too late.

The time has come to impress upon financial analysts and investors that, by investing in enterprises, they are exposed to the risks and hazards inherent in the activity of those enterprises. It follows that they, too, need a common, shared, reliable source of information that trustworthily represents the performance of each enterprise entity over time in situation. It is only on the basis of this performance that they can form objective, realistic valuations and expectations. Accounting, therefore, should not be responding to the market; the market should rather be responding to genuine accounting information.

Acknowledgments Yuri Biondi is research director and executive committee member of the Financial Regulation Research Lab (Labex ReFi), ESCP Europe, 79 avenue de la Republique, Paris 75011, France (http://www.labex-refi.com/). A previous version of this chapter was read at and included in the proceedings of the 'Second Symposium on Accounting Research' organised by the Autorité des Normes Comptables (ANC), Paris, 16 December 2011. The current version further draws upon our "Accounting and Business Economics: Understanding the Past to Face the Present and Prepare the Future", published as chapter 18 (pages 485–492) in Y. Biondi, S. Zambon et al. (2012), Accounting and Business Economics: Insights From National Traditions, London and New York: Routledge.

References

Anthony RN (1983) Tell it like it was: a conceptual framework for financial accounting. Richard D. Irwin, Homewood, IL

Beaver WH (1981) Financial reporting: an accounting revolution. Prentice Hall, Upper Saddle River, NJ

Bignon V, Biondi Y, Ragot X (2009) An economic analysis of fair value: accounting as a vector of crisis. Cournot Centre for Economic Studies, Prisme, No. 15. http://ssrn.com/abstract=1474228

Biondi Y, Fantacci L (2012) Les banques sont-elles solubles dans le marché? A propos de la comptabilisation de la dette grecque à sa juste valeur. Economies et Sociétés KF 2(3):571–584

Biondi Y, Giannoccolo P (2015) Share price formation, market exuberance and financial stability under alternative accounting regimes. J Econ Interac Coord 9(2):333–362. doi:10.1007/s11403-014-0131-7

Biondi Y, Reberioux A (2012) The governance of intangibles: rethinking financial reporting and the board of directors. Account Forum 36:279–293

Biondi Y (2003) L'actif comptable entre normalisation internationale et enjeux financiers. In: Hoarau Ch (ed) Dossier Normes IAS IFRS. La Revue du Financier, Issue 144 (Décembre)

Biondi Y (2008a) Entité entreprise, monnaie et comptabilité. Jalons pour un itinéraire de théorie économique. Economie Appliquée 61(2):5–42

Biondi Y (2008b) Schumpeter's economic theory and the dynamic accounting view of the firm: neglected pages from the Theory of Economic Development. Econ Soc 37(4):525–547

Biondi Y (2010) L'entité entreprise au croisement de l'économie, du droit et de la comptabilité. Editions Universitaires Européennes, Saarbrücken

Biondi Y (2011) The pure logic of accounting: a critique of the fair value revolution. Account Econ Law Convivium 1(1):2–46. doi:10.2202/2152-2820.1018

Biondi Y (2012) What do shareholders do? Accounting, ownership and the theory of the firm: implications for corporate governance and reporting. Account Econ Law Convivium 2(2). doi: http://dx.doi.org/10.1515/2152-2820.1068

Biondi Y (2013) Hyman Minsky's financial instability hypothesis and the accounting structure of economy. Account Econ Law Convivium 3(3). doi: http://dx.doi.org/10.1515/ael-2013-0045

Biondi Y, Canziani A, Kirat T (2007) The firm as an entity: implications for economics, accounting and law. Routledge, New York, NY

Biondi Y, Chambost I, Klee L (2008) La juste valeur, enfin une évaluation proche de la réalité. In: Pezet A, Sponem S (eds) Petit Bréviaire des idées reçues en management. La Découverte, Paris, pp 210–218, Chapter 21

Biondi Y, Giannoccolo P, Galam S (2012a) What does financial market do? The formation of share market prices under heterogeneous beliefs and common knowledge. Physica A 391 (22):5532–5545. doi:10.1016/j.physa.2012.06.015

Biondi Y, Zambon S et al (2012b) Accounting and business economics: insights from national traditions. Routledge, New York, NY

Ding Y, Richard J, Stolowy H (2008) Towards an understanding of the phases of goodwill accounting in four Western capitalist countries: From stakeholder model to shareholder model. Account Organ Soc 33(7–8):718–755

Hoarau C (2006) Convergence IFRS - US GAAP: Vers une hybridation des modes de normalisation? Revue Sciences de Gestion 54:39–51

Ijiri Y (1975) Theory of accounting measurement. Studies in Accounting Research no. 10. American Accounting Association, Sarasota (FL)

Ijiri Y (2005) U.S. accounting standards and their environment: a dualistic study of their 75 years of transition. J Account Public Policy 24(4):255–279

Lev B, Zarowin P (1999) The boundaries of financial reporting and how to extend them. J Account Res 37(2):353–385

Richard J (1996) Comptabilités et pratiques comptables. Dalloz, Paris

Savary J (1675) Le parfait négociant: ou Instruction générale pour ce qui regarde le commerce des marchandises de France, & des pays étrangers

Schumpeter JA (1912) Theorie der wirtschaftlichen Entwicklung [The theory of economic development], 2nd edn. Duncker & Humblot, Leipzig, 1926

Strasser KA, Blumberg P (2011) Legal form and economic substance of enterprise groups: implications for legal policy. Account Econ Law Convivium 1(1). doi: 10.2202/2152-2820.1000

Sunder S (2002) Knowing what others know: common knowledge, accounting, and capital markets. Accounting Horizons, December

Calculation of Environmentally Sustainable Residual Income (eSRI) from IFRS Financial Statements: An Extension of Richard (2012)

Paul James Brown

Abstract This chapter presents a flexible approach to evaluating the extent to which an organisation has the capacity to be both environmentally and economically sustainable based on financial statements, namely Environmentally Sustainable Residual Income (eSRI). Problematically, despite International Financial Reporting Standards (IFRS) being a key information source for investors and other stakeholders, they give little consideration to natural and social capital in the construction of financial statements. eSRI builds on the approach to financial statement analysis advocated by Penman (Financial statement analysis and security valuation, 5th edn. McGraw-Hill/Irwin, 2012) and others, whereby users make adjustments to financial statements to derive more informative accounts. eSRI is defined as Net Profit less (i) a capital charge to evaluate economic sustainability, and (ii) environmental sustaining costs. Environmental sustaining costs are an estimate of a charge to replace or restore natural capital degraded in earning the income; essentially an opportunity cost generated by the organisation's activities. The calculation provides a representation (albeit with error) of how much environmental capital has been destroyed in the generation of income. A key advantage of eSRI is that it allows users to combine non-financial information disclosures (such as carbon emissions) with financial indicators in a theory informed manner. eSRI will be of interest to stakeholders with an interest in estimating the extent to which an organisation has the potential to be both economically and environmentally sustainable.

1 Introduction

'Human influence has been detected in warming of the atmosphere and the ocean, in changes in the global water cycle, in reductions in snow and ice, in global mean sea level rise, and in changes in some climate extremes (see Figure SPM.6 and Table SPM.1). This evidence for human influence has grown since AR4. It is extremely likely that human

P.J. Brown (✉)
University of Technology Sydney, Accounting Discipline Group, Ultimo NSW 2007, Australia
e-mail: paul.j.brown@uts.edu.au

D. Bensadon, N. Praquin (eds.), *IFRS in a Global World*,
DOI 10.1007/978-3-319-28225-1_11

influence has been the dominant cause of the observed warming since the mid-20th century.' (IPCC 2013, p. 17)

A number of compilations of scientific literature on global and local ecosystem health have indicated that a range of systems have been adversely impacted by human activities, and that unless human activities are constrained within the laws of nature, that widespread ecological degradation will continue with the likely outcome of ecosystem instability and in some cases collapse (see for example IPCC 2013; Stern 2006; Garnaut 2008). Probably the most significant of these are the UN Intergovernmental Panel on Climate Change (IPCC) reports, the most recent of which presents compelling evidence that unless the amount of greenhouse gas (GHG) pollution from industrial activity is not reduced drastically, that the observed changes in climate will intensify to the detriment of global society. Whilst there have been extensive efforts to reduce GHG emissions by a wide range of stakeholders, the persistently high and growing rate of GHG pollution indicates that more work is needed on developing approaches to transform developed and developing societies in such a way that they can exist without destroying such ecosystems upon which human and other life depends (Ibid.).

There have been a range of efforts to develop and implement regimes of accounting to assist organisation actors, stakeholders, policy makers and other groups to manage the sustainability of organisations and economies.[1] While there have been significant advances in the accounting for physical inputs and outputs, such as Triple Bottom Line (TBL) approaches and the Global Reporting Initiative (GRI), a less developed mode of accounting is the calculation of Sustainable Income (SI). The concept is described by Gray (1992) as 'calculations of which additional costs must be borne by the organisation if the organisational activity were not to leave the planet worse off' (p. 419). Although there are examples where attempts have been made to estimate SI, discussion in the literature as to how the SI concept could be operationalized is rare.[2] More recently, Richard (2012) extended this work and developed an approach labelled 'la Comptabilité Adaptée au Renouvellement de l'Environnement (CARE)'.[3] Richard (2012) advocates for a new regime of accounting which addresses notable deficiencies in International Financial Reporting Standards (IFRS). As acknowledged by Richard (2012), the adoption of CARE in the short term is unlikely, as any effort to adopt such a system would be vigorously resisted by financiers. This chapter describes some of the salient theoretical foundations for the CARE model, and develops an approach for

[1] It is beyond the scope of this chapter to debate the meaning of the word sustainability; hence I adopt one of the most common definitions of sustainability from the oft quoted Our Common Future report (Brundtland Commission 1987: 43): 'Sustainable development is development that seeks to meet the needs of the present without compromising the ability of future definitions to meet their own needs'.

[2] For national accounting see Hueting and De Boer (2001) and organisation level see Huizing and Dekker (1992), Bebbington and Gray (2001) and Howes (2002).

[3] La Comptabilité Adaptée au Renouvellement de l'Environnement (CARE) translates as 'accounting adapted to the renewal of the environnement'.

calculating a firm level summary performance indicator based on CARE; namely Environmentally Sustainable Residual Income (eSRI).

eSRI combines key aspect of the CARE model with an approach to financial statement adjustment and analysis popularised by authors such as Penman (2012). The approach allows users to modify IFRS accounts by means of a number of adjustments, in a manner analogous to the estimation of residual income (Penman 2012) and Economic Value Added (EVA™) (Stewart 1991). The approach outlined has some flexibility which allows for different stakeholders to focus on their area of interest, providing that firm specific information relevant to the calculation of eSRI is available. To keep the discussion tractable, I primarily focus on ecological capital and financial capital, whilst acknowledging the role of social capital in the calculus described by Richard.[4]

The chapter is organised as follows. First I discuss the role of accounting in supporting system wide ecological degradation, followed by a discussion of two theoretical approaches to modifying accounting. I then present a method of calculating eSRI, followed by the conclusion.

2 Accounting and System Wide Ecological Degradation

In this section I present a brief background to and a number of criticisms of IFRS and contemporary sustainability reporting practices. In addition two arguments are presented drawing on Richard (2012) which suggest that (i) the way accounting constructs accounts of organisation activity provides a context in which widespread ecologic degradation is supported via a payment of 'fictitious dividends' to financiers, and (ii) that the way accounting is used in the context of cost benefit analysis leads to a dynamic which makes widespread ecological degradation inevitable, termed 'dynamic externality'. These arguments suggest that the socially constructed and institutionalised regimes of accounting are likely a causal actor in the set of dynamic interactions causing global environmental degradation, and hence resistance to and modifications of certain elements of accounting regimes is a legitimate activity for affected stakeholders.

[4] For a recent discussion of employee reporting which addresses key issues in social reporting, see Mäkelä (2013). See Richard (2012) and Rambaud and Richard (2015) for a discussion and analysis of social capital, and how it could be applied in the context of SRI. Richard also locates the development of CARE in the discourse on historical cost versus fair value accounting, a discussion of which is beyond the scope of this chapter.

2.1 *Some Criticisms of International Financial Reporting Standards (IFRS) and Contemporary Sustainability Reporting*

In many jurisdictions, IFRS are the primary standards applied to the production of financial statements, which are a key source of information for shareholders and other organisation stakeholders about organisational activities.[5] Despite IFRS being widely adopted, a range of unintended consequences of IFRS adoption have been identified in the literature (Brüggemann et al. 2013). Most of the studies which investigate IFRS evaluate the relative benefits or costs of IFRS implementation and policies to financiers (Brüggemann et al. 2013). A critical view is that the focus of IFRS has been heavily influenced by supporters of a neoliberal agenda, and that derived accounting numbers act to reinforce the central ideas of that agenda to the detriment of legitimate competing interests.[6] For example, the change in the International Accounting Standards Board's conception of the users of IFRS statements from a list of stakeholders to a narrower focus on 'existing and potential investors, lenders and other creditors' (International Accounting Standards Board 2010, OB2) is supportive of this criticism. Leaving aside the debate as to whom 'ought' to be the users of financial statements, a broad range of stakeholders do rely on financial statements to make investment decisions, and also to hold organisations to account to societal norms.[7]

IFRS gives little consideration to natural and social capital in the construction of financial statements, as the primary focus of IFRS is the preservation of financial capital (Richard 2012). This is problematic as many organisations being accounted for are directly and indirectly implicated in the destruction of natural and social capital though organisational activities (as discussed in more detail below). The lack of transparency in generally accepted financial statements about sustainability issues has driven many organisations to voluntarily disclose such information, which has seen the development and institutionalisation of various ways in which organisations report (or do not report) on such issues. A common strategy is for organisations to present non-financial information alongside the financial information as part of financial reports (loosely characterised as integrated reporting), or in separate sustainability reports.[8]

---

[5] Whilst in this paper I focus on IFRS, the arguments contained herein have application to Generally Accepted Accounting Principles more broadly.

[6] Neoliberalism is generally characterised by 'privatisation of public services; the deregulation of labour and financial markets; the opening of markets to free trade; and the shrinking of governments through tax cuts, austerity measures and reduced regulation' (Harvey 2005, in Zhang and Andrew 2013).

[7] See March (2013) and Murphy et al. (2013) for recent discussions of this topic.

[8] See Rambaud and Richard (2015) for a discussion of this point with respect to the triple bottom line concept.

Gray et al. (1993, in Lamberton 2005) identify three distinct methods of environmental accounting, namely sustainable cost (and full-cost) accounting, natural capital inventory accounting and input-output analysis. According to Gray (1994, p. 33, in Lamberton 2005), sustainable cost is 'the amount of money an organisation would have to spend at an end of an accounting period to place the biosphere back into the position it was at the start of the accounting period'. Sustainable cost accounting includes the concept of SI discussed in the introduction, examples of which are found in Huizing and Dekker (1992), Bebbington and Gray (2001), Howes (2002) and Richard (2012). Lamberton (2005) points out that whilst there are examples of sustainable cost accounting, practical difficulties in estimating sustainable cost remain a challenge. He calls for more fieldwork, case work and transdisiplinary work to address this challenge. There is little evidence of widespread uptake of the sustainable cost approach by organisations (Bebbington et al. 2014; Gray et al. 2014), although there is evidence of its use by policy makers. A prominent example is the estimation and use of social cost of carbon (SCC) by the US government for analysing the impacts of carbon dioxide in a variety of contexts (Interagency Working Group on the Social Cost of Carbon 2010, 2013).[9]

According to Lamberton (2005, p. 9), 'natural capital accounting involved the recording of stocks of natural capital over time, with changes in stock levels used as an indicator of the (declining) quality of the natural environment'. These accounts can be in both financial and non-financial units. Input-output analysis is essentially a form of material accounting as used in engineering and the physical sciences, and provides a detailed account of the physical flows and processes which an organisation is involved in. More recent reviews of the literature present a wider variety of ways in which sustainability reporting has evolved which build off these three methods, and a contemporaneous dramatic increase in the number of organisations which do prepare sustainability reports (see for example Bebbington et al. 2014; Gray et al. 2014).

Whilst there are a range of approaches to sustainability reporting, the approach which at present probably has the widest adoption rates are reports prepared using the Global Reporting Initiative (GRI) standards.[10] The International Integrated Reporting Council has released a consultation draft of a proposed international framework for integrated reporting (see: www.theiirc.org), which has support from a wide range of stakeholders. Whilst there are benefit to organisations for reporting using GRI or similar standards, there at least two key limitations of GRI and various other contemporary ways organisations disclose information about sustainability issues. First, the units of analysis are often different, so information is difficult to compare both within and between companies. For example, if an organisation has increased its water efficiency, they may at the same time have an increase in a different waste output, making it difficult to evaluate the relative environmental performance. Second, the costs, value and price associated with non-financial data

[9] The method used to estimate the SCC is not without criticism. For a discussion see Ackerman and Stanton (2012) and Kopp and Mignone (2012).

[10] See www.globalreporting.org.

is not usually disclosed. Despite the limitations of contemporary sustainability reporting, the disclosure of sustainability related information opens up the opportunity for stakeholders to apply privately obtained estimates of value and costs and apply these to the information.

2.2 *Fictitious Dividends*

Richard (2012) provocatively argues that IFRS has a structural mechanism which allows financiers to benefit from systematically destroying natural capital, via the payment of what he characterises as 'fictitious' dividends. Explicating this concept requires the consideration of how accounting supports financial capital maintenance, in particular the interplay between the depreciation expense and the ability of financiers to receive dividends. The concepts of income and capital maintenance have a long history of debate and disagreement, and so the discussion here is confined to a few key points necessary for the derivation of eSRI.[11] The financial capital maintenance principle is that 'opening capital must be maintained before there can be recognition of such income' (Lee 1985, p. 11). This principle, when applied, allows financiers to separate cash flows taken out of an organisation as being value adding (income), or the withdrawal of capital which was previously invested. The institutionalised mechanism of distributing income to shareholders is via dividends, which can only be paid out of profit. These principles have gained legitimacy and are reflected in various accounting practices and regulatory regimes such as IFRS (see International Accounting Standards Board 2010, paras 4.24 and 4.57–4.65).

A primary mechanism supporting capital maintenance is the depreciation expense. The idea is that the depreciation expense acts as an (imprecise) mechanism to preserve financial capital in an organisation by reducing profit as dividends can only be paid from profit (as contrast to capital withdrawal). The concept of the fictitious dividend is that the increase in wealth recognised in profit for many organisations comes from the degradation of natural resources (which are a windfall gain, having been accumulated over millions of years of ecosystem evolution). That is, the process of accounting legitimates the distribution of wealth which in many cases has been created through the destruction of natural (common) capital (Richard 2012). According to Richard, this dynamic allows financiers and other stakeholders to have an extraordinary life of wealth and excess, which is essentially funded by ecological destruction (destruction of natural capital). In this way, dividends for many organisations are fictitious, in that they do not represent a net gain in total capital, only financial capital. The dynamic is perpetual as once dividends are distributed, they can be reinvested into further destructive investments.

[11] For an informative discussion of the differences between economists and accountants conceptions of income, and some of the controversies, see Lee (1985).

2.3 Limitations of Cost Benefit Analysis for the Preservation of Natural Systems

The problems inherent in accounting structures are not limited to financial statement dynamics (as discussed above). Pearce (1976) presents an analytical model which combines observations about the assimilative capacity of ecosystems to absorb the effects of industrial activity with the central set of characteristics of cost benefit analysis as applied to policy analysis. He defines assimilative capacity as the capacity of an ecosystem to render waste as either inert or recycled back into productive use. In principle, when more waste is injected in an ecosystem than the assimilative capacity, the ecosystem is degraded. He gives an example of cadmium, which is an output of certain productive processes, which the human body can tolerate up to a point. Once certain thresholds are breached a range of effects become evident including renal dysfunction and cardio-vascular problems. Whilst his modelling glosses over a number of practical issues such as the non-linear functions inherent in such a dynamic complex system, the model does provide an explanation for the observed destruction of ecosystems by organisations. His approach treats the level of residual 'assimilative capacity' of the environment as an outcome of organisation level decision-making around the allocation of the scarce resources.

Figure 1 presents one of the key ideas developed Pearce (1976), which is the concept that the application of cost benefit analysis in situations where the costs of maintaining assimilative capacity (an externality) are not borne by those who benefit, then an unstoppable process of ecological degradation will continue up to the point where the surplus 'assimilative capacity' is dissipated. While other authors have discussed the issues related to such externalities at length, Pearce's conception is sufficient to provide a theoretical grounding for the CARE (and eSRI) approach to accounting for sustainable development.

The y-axis in Fig. 1 is the level of waste produced from economic activity (W) and the extent to which an ecosystem can absorb waste (A). X is the physical output of productive goods. The figure has two components, the top half, which is the waste generation function W(X). The starting point of the dynamic process is A_0, which represents the maximum level of assimilative capacity at time 0. Importantly if X is such that $W \leq A$, no externality is present, as the waste from production is assimilated back into the environment. The figure depicts a shift from A_0 to A_2 over successive rounds of cost benefit decisions. The bottom section is the corresponding cost benefit analysis. The line B' represents marginal net profit for organisations (net private benefit). The optimal level of production, where $W = A$, is at point $X_{e,0}$. Although he does not explicitly point this out in his paper, the Pareto optimal level of output for an organisation is X_o (where marginal cost = marginal benefit), which is to the right of the point at which $W = A$. Although the model is a simplification, the conclusion does suggest that in cases where organisational activity (output) confers private benefit to the organisation to the detriment to the assimilative capacity of the environment, the outcome of the

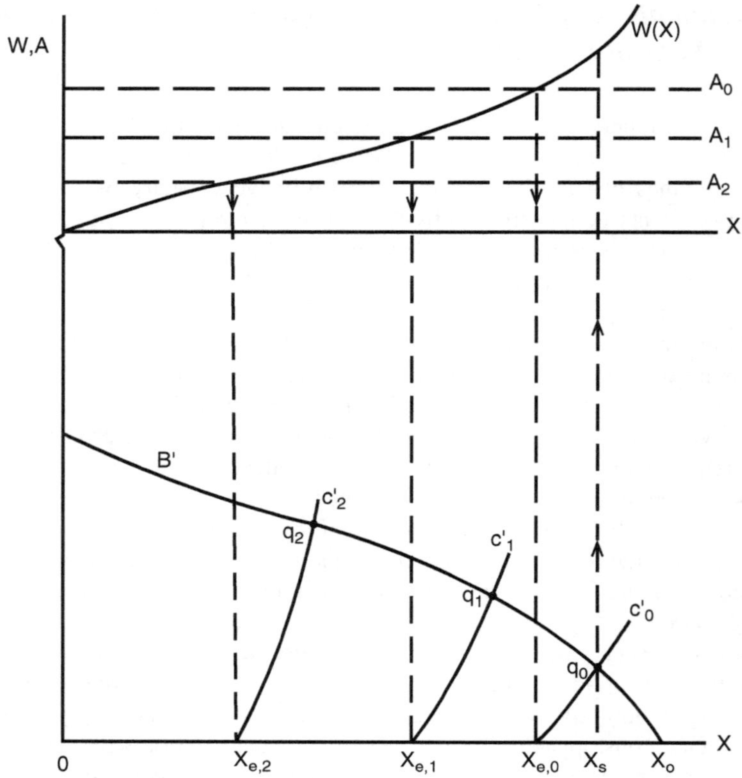

Fig. 1 Perce's dynamic externality. *Source:* Pearce (1976, p 105)

application of cost benefit analysis will inevitably lead organisations to choose that level of activity. Hence, the model illustrates the necessity for regulation.

The curves C'_0 to C'_2 represent the marginal external cost for each of the time periods. Externalities are assumed to occur for a given X once $W(X) > A$ for the given time period. In applying cost benefit analysis from a policy perspective, the Pareto optimal level of production is X_s, where Net private benefit is equal to the net external cost (point q_0). This results in a sub optimal situation, that X_s is greater than $X_{e,0}$ and hence $W(X) > A$. This results in the degradation in assimilative capacity, illustrated by a shift of assimilative capacity from A_0 to A_1. With the shift in assimilative capacity to A_1, the optimal level of production shifts from $X_{e,0}$ to $X_{e,1}$. The dynamic externality problem is manifest in the application of cost benefit in subsequent periods, so where the optimal level of production shifts from q_0 to q_1 to q_2 in a recurring process, until the assimilative capacity of the system is degraded.

Pearce's model illustrates a number of critical ideas:

1. The application of cost benefit analysis to production situations where the resulting waste contributes to 'irreversible' reductions in assimilative capacity will eventually lead economically rational investors (absent regulation) to continue production until the assimilative capacity is dissipated.
2. Production can be sustained where $W(X) \leq A$
3. Firms may avoid regulation where they restrict production to a level where $W(X) \leq A$.

Problematically, whilst Pearce's model illustrates the 'dynamic externality' problem, the model is too abstract to allow for practical application. In particular, a practical problem is how to construct signals of costs and benefits which enable decision makers to know when production is such that $W(X) \leq A$. In principle, such signals would include an approximation for net private benefit to organisations for a given level of production, and information about the level of waste relative to assimilative capacity. In the following section I review two such models which attempt this.

3 Two Theoretical Approaches to Modifying Accounting

3.1 Hueting's Sustainable National Income

The Dutch economist Roefie Hueting built up a body of work which addresses these issues, beginning with the report *Functions of Nature: Should nature be quantified* published in 1969. In 1969 he headed an interdisciplinary team at the Department of Environmental Statistics of the Netherlands Central Bureau of Statistics. His work, being both theoretical and practical, culminated in the development and deployment of a novel method of adjusting Net National Income (NNI) in the Netherlands. His solution was to identify the opportunity costs incurred for restoring any natural capital degraded at the national level (environmental sustaining costs), and to subtract this from national income. He suggested that Environmentally Sustainable National Income (eSNI) could be calculated and used to complement, rather than replace, other national welfare indicators. The eSNI for the Netherlands in 1999 was estimated as 44.1 % of the NNI, indicating that each dollar of NNI contained a 55.9 % environmental subsidy (see Hofkes et al. 2004).

Hueting begins the derivation of eSNI with the concept of environmental functions, which are uses of natural capital which are distinguishable (1993, p 42). Although the natural environment is an endowment, all economic activity draws from it, as do life support systems. Economic activity causes competition between environmental functions (being scarce resources), where the use (loss) of environmental functions are at the 'expense of the use of another (or the same) function by another activity' (Hueting 1993, p 42). Competition between functions brings them into the realm of economics through the concept of opportunity cost, irrespective of whether they are expressed in money or are included in markets (*ibid*, p. 43). Hueting provides the example of deforestation, where the functional benefits of top soil are traded off against deforestation.

Hueting's concept of function encompasses the idea of Ecosystem services which are used by various groups to put a value on natural capital. TEEB (2010) provides a comprehensive list of ecosystem services, which they categorise as Provisioning, Regulating, Cultural, and Habitat or Support services. Hueting identifies a conceptual problem with the approach of valuing natural capital adopted by many economists.[12] He pointed out that a reliable estimation of the monetary value of natural capital requires the estimation of demand and supply curves, which would require a market based mechanism. Complications include the fact that supplies of functions are often free. For example, the use of common atmosphere to dump GHG pollution. Another complication is that it is not possible to represent accurately competing preferences for functions. For example, the preference of future generations to inherit a liveable planet. His solution is to assume that there is a general demand for the preservation of natural capital, in particular life support services such as clean water, air and food production. In this way, users of functions create an opportunity cost of replacing or restating any loss of function they cause. By focusing on environmental functions, in particular life support services, the scope of eSNI is reduced to factors which are well researched, identifiable and amenable to further scientific investigation. Hueting also notes that as technology based solutions are 'dreams' until they are realised, that the application of the precautionary principle demands that the opportunity costs of function degradation be estimated using current technologies and prices (and presumably adjusted as new technologies are realised). The following section draws on the observation that the criticisms raised by Hueting about national income are transferable to IFRS conceptions of income (Richard 2012).

3.2 Richard's CARE Model

Richard (2012) locates accounting as an integral component in macroeconomic dynamics. That is, as many resource allocation decisions are taken at the firm level (albeit informed by broader macro economic factors such as government policy), that macro level sustainability accounting systems require micro level accounting systems.

In essence, the CARE model provides an approach to account for the degradation caused by organisations by matching the cost of environmental function replacement and or renewal against income. In the same way that depreciation is matched against income for the replenishment of degraded financial capital, a

[12] See TEEB (2010) for a summary of different approaches.

portion of income is put aside for the replenishment of the natural capital (NC) and social capital (SC) degraded in earning the income. Richard's (2012) CARE model was outlined in Richard (2008a, b, 2011) and has been extended by Rambaud and Richard (2015) with a focus on the concept of TBL depreciation.

Richard envisions a society where corporations are forced to 'pay their way'. In this society, individual corporate accounts are consolidated to form national accounts. In this society, organisations that cause natural, economic, and social degradation are forced to pay an expense each period, which covers the cost of repairing the degradations. Of course some of these costs are presently borne by organisations via existing regulation. Richard (2012) presents five phases for the calculation of CARE:

Phase 1: Input and output of entity identified and assessed. All natural resources consumed, and all productive and non productive output measured.
Phase 2: Evaluation of environmental impact and natural resource availability.
Phase 3: Restoration and replacement costs estimated.
Phase 4: Income statement is adjusted for TBL depreciation expense.
Phase 5: Renewal fund accounts are adjusted and are treated as Assets (based on historical cost concept), the value of which are also recorded in equity accounts using the categories of NC and SC.[13]

Each particular aspect of NC degradation is assigned to a renewal fund, which is in principle an allocation of cash to pay for the ecological degradation. In essence, Richard is proposing a system of accounting which effectively prevents shareholders from receiving dividends unless they preserve the natural and social capital from which they generate economic profit.

There are at least two main limitations of the CARE model. First, the CARE model requires an assumption that firms have an obligation to preserve natural capital, and hence bear a charge for environmental degradation or its restitution. Whilst there are numerous precedents where firms have had to pay for specific types of natural capital (due to regulatory or market forces), without a complementary regulatory regime, the practical application of CARE is restricted in this respect. Barriers would be high for the adoption of any regime which requires financiers to pay for environmental degradation they cause due to the profit motive of those financiers (Richard 2012). Second, widespread adoption of CARE requires the development and acceptance of standards which support information of a quality and type to calculate CARE.

[13] Accordingly, the accounting equation in CARE is recast as: Owners Equity = Assets—Liabilities—Natural Capital—Social Capital.

4 Environmentally Sustainable Residual Income (eSRI)

In this section I present an approach which builds on CARE which I characterise as eSRI. The approach is similar in principle to the calculation of residual income, where investors (and stakeholders) are able to make adjustments to IFRS Balance Sheets and Income statements, based on private and preferential information, to calculate whether the firms has created economic value. eSRI is an approach which allows for market participants and other stakeholders to apply a modified CARE to IFRS accounts to calculate eSRI. Whilst the approach falls short of the grand vision of CARE, it is a step in that direction.

The residual income approach has achieved a level of acceptance for the evaluation of profit making organisations (despite not being part of accounting standards), perhaps in part due to its ease of calculation using existing information and its usability in a variety of contexts (Stewart 1991; Penman 2012). The standard Residual Income formula can be expressed using the following formula:

$$Residual\ Income_{it} = Net\ Profit_{it} - (r_e \times Book\ Value\ of\ Owners\ Equity_{it})$$

Where: r_e = Cost of capital for equity holders

A relevant point is that the shareholders' required return on capital (r_e) represents an expectation, or intention. Even though an organisation may make profit, if there is negative residual income, from the perspective of financiers the entity is not economically profitable. The required return, in effect, is representative of the opportunity cost of capital for shareholders. By monetising this intention (and expectation), the resulting artefact has symbolic meaning, which enable certain actions and interpretations. For example, residual income is used to screen investments, and valuation models based on it tend to outperform popular alternatives (Ohlson 1995; Bailey et al. 2008). Stern Stewarts EVA™ is probably the most well-known version of Residual Income. The symbolic value of EVA™ has been illustrated in the context of management decisions and control (see for example Stewart 1991).

As described in detail by Penman (2012), adjustments can be made to the accounts by users of financial statements prior to the calculation of residual income. These adjustments are made by analysis and other users of financial statements to correct for any perceived distortions or the preferences of the user. For example, a user may believe that a company has used accelerated depreciation and they would like to know what net income would be under a more realistic depreciation schedule. To do this they would need to estimate the old and new depreciation rate, and for the years they are interested in, make adjustments to the book value of the given asset and adjust the associated depreciation and tax expense (Penman 2012). According to Stewart (1991), accounting adjustments include the capitalising of some research and development expenses, making adjustments to goodwill and inventory accounts, and other adjustments. The flexibility inherent in the way residual income is estimated presents an opportunity to develop a similar approach to evaluate whether a given organisation is able to generate sufficient value to be both economically and ecologically sustainable.

eSRI is the blending of the eSNI, CARE and residual income approaches. It also draws from other similar approaches which have been suggested in the literature (Gray 1992; Huizing and Dekker 1992; Bebbington and Gray 2001; Howes 2002). In essence, eSRI is a measure of whether an investment has the capacity to deliver a return on investment which is sufficient to cover the demands of financiers, as well as the costs of replacement or the cost of restoration of environmental functions. The formula is:

$$\begin{aligned} eSRI_{it} &= Net\ Profit_{it} - (r_e \times Book\ Value\ of\ Owners\ Equity_{it}) \\ &\quad - Environment\ sustaining\ cost_{it} \end{aligned}$$

Where: Environment sustaining cost = The opportunity costs generated by the organisations activities; being an estimate of the cost to replace or restore natural capital degraded in earning the income.

An advantage of eSRI is that it can be estimated using information gleaned from financial and sustainability reports, which can then be combined with private information such as estimates of the cost of replacement and restoration of natural capital degraded. The calculation provides a representation (albeit with error) of how much an appropriate amount would be for a polluter to pay in the generation of income, and hence whether an investment is profitable from an environmentally sustainable perspective.[14] eSRI draws from Pearce's dynamic externality depicted in Fig. 1. An eSRI of 0 in principle represents an investment sitting close to points X_e, where the waste generated is equal to the assimilative capacity of the ecosystem, and where financiers have a net private benefit.

5 Conclusion

There are a number of practical applications of eSRI for organisations and investors. First, investors who are interested in investing in more sustainable organisations will have additional insight to discriminate between more or less sustainable investments. This naturally extends to investments decided within organisations. By calculating the eSRI of different project alternatives, organisations which are interested in operating more sustainably are able to better discriminate between projects. Second, organisations which calculate eSRI are able to evaluate the extent to which their business model is sustainable over the long term, by both observing where they are not sustainable and by being able to benchmark against competitors.

[14] See Almedia and Stearns (1998) for insight into the ethical obligations of organisations responsible for ecological destruction and the tensions between financiers and the communities they affect.

Presumably there would also be an organisational learning outcome from following a process of calculating eSRI in organisations, where organisation participants will be confronted by the lack of data, and also by the magnitude of the 'subsidy' they are receiving from nature and the societies they are operating in.

Policy makers may also benefit from eSRI information, in both helping frame discussions about how best to calculate national accounts, but also to evaluate the sustainability of different sectors. Richard's (2012) suggestion is to consolidate such information from the firm level to the economy level, which would give effect to the model developed by Hueting. In the meantime, calculations of eSRI may complement evaluation of policy agendas, such as by helping policy makers to identify which sectors are theoretically un-sustainable, identifying where support and or regulation may assist organisations to move toward sustainability. Civil society and other organisational stakeholders would find calculations of eSRI practically useful. For example, organisations which cause the greatest burden on society and the environment can be better identified and targeted for influencing efforts. In this way, eSRI provides a tool to resist attempts by organisations which use economic logic to justify ecological degradation of environmental functions, in particular life support services.

The recent policy brief 'Counting all the costs: Recognising the carbon subsidy to polluting energy' by The Climate Institute (Kember et al. 2014) is a case in point. Kember et al. (2014) use a similar approach to eSRI to evaluate the Australian energy sector, with a focus on estimating the total environment sustaining cost caused through GHG emission. Whilst they do not calculate eSRI, they do illustrate the usefulness and flexibility of the approach suggested in this chapter. They use estimates of the SCC from Interagency Working Group on the Social Cost of Carbon (see Interagency Working Group on the Social Cost of Carbon 2013) as a proxy for Environment sustaining cost. They combine the SCC with publically available non-financial data on total GHG emissions for organisations in the Australian energy sector. They find that the environment sustaining costs are between AU$14–39 billion for 2012, and that the combined value of AU$165–500 billion for the years 2015–2030.[15] They conclude that 'the carbon subsidy provided to energy is far greater [than] any of the explicit financial subsidies currently benefitting Australian fossil fuels, let alone any subsidies to Australian renewable energy' (Kember et al. 2014, p. 11). Future policy analysis may go one step further and calculate eSRI at both organisation and sector levels, and evaluate alternative proxies to SCC which are more reflective of environment sustaining cost.

A limitation of this chapter is that I do not discuss how the Environment sustaining cost component of the proposed eSRI formula could be derived in a theoretically defensible way. Whist significant work has been attempted in the

[15] To put the size of subsidy into perspective, the gross value added for electricity supply in AU $22.5 billion (BREE 2013), which contrasts to the Kember et al. (2014) estimate of environment sustaining cost of $7–20 billion per year. This comparison must be interpreted with caution as there is insufficient information in Kember et al. (2014) to accurately match their estimates with gross value added or other measures of performance.

context of Hueting's eSNI (sf. Hueting 1993, 2011; Hueting and De Boer 2001; Van Ierland et al. 2001; Hofkes et al. 2004) and sustainable cost accounting (Huizing and Dekker 1992; Bebbington and Gray 2001; Howes 2002; Richard 2012) more research is need in this respect to enhance the practical usefulness of Richard's (2012) CARE and the eSRI approaches advocated in this chapter.

Acknowledgment I acknowledge the advice and feedback on this chapter from participants of the 2014 CMOS research clinics and Dianne Hiles. All errors and omissions remain the authors.

References

Ackerman F, Stanton EA (2012) Climate risks and carbon prices: revising the social cost of capital. Econ Open-Access Open-Assess E J 6(2012–10):1–25. doi:10.5018/economics-ejournal.ja.2012-10

Almedia P, Stearns LB (1998) Political opportunities and local grassroots environmental movements: the case of minamata. Soc Probl 45(1):37–60

Bailey P, Brown PJ, Potter M, Wells PA (2008) A practical comparison of firm valuation models: cash flow, dividend and income. J Secur Inst Aust 2:22–28

Bebbington J, Gray R (2001) An account of sustainability: failure, success and a reconceptualization. Crit Perspect Account 12:557–587

Bebbington J, Unerman J, O'Dwyer B (2014) Sustainability accounting and accountability. Routledge, New York, NY

BREE (2013) Energy in Australia 2013. Report. Bureau of resources and energy economics. Australian Government, Canberra

Brüggemann U, Hitz J, Sellhorn T (2013) Intended and unintended consequences of mandatory IFRS adoption: a review of extant evidence and suggestions for future research. Eur Account Rev 22(1):1–37

Brundtland Commission (1987) Our common future. Report. World Commission on Environment and Development. Oxford University Press, Oxford

Kember O, Jackson E, Connor J (2014) Counting all the costs: recognising the carbon subsidy to polluting energy. Policy brief. The Climate Institute. http://www.climateinstitute.org.au/articles/publications/counting-all-the-costs.html. Accessed 23 April 2015

Garnaut R (2008) The Garnaut climate change review: final report. Cambridge University Press, Port Melbourne

Gray R (1992) Accounting and environmentalism: an exploration of the challenge of gently accounting for accountability, transparency and sustainability. Acc Organ Soc 17(5):399–425

Gray R (1994) Corporate reporting for sustainable development. Environ Values 3(1):17–45

Gray R, Bebbington KJ, Walters D (1993) Accounting for the environment. Paul Chapman, London

Gray R, Adams CA, Owen D (2014) Accountability, social responsibility and sustainability: accounting for society and the environment. Pearson Education, Harlow

Harvey D (2005) A brief history of neoliberalism. Oxford University Press, Oxford

Hofkes MW, Gerlagh R, Linderhof V (2004) Sustainable national income: a trend analysis for the Netherlands for 1990–2000. Report. Institute for Environmental Studies, Report R-04/02 (June 28). http://ssrn.com/abstract=1009284. Accessed 23 April 2015

Howes R (2002) Environmental cost accounting: an introduction and practical guide. Chartered Institute of Management Accountants, London

Hueting R (1993) Calculating a sustainable national income: a practical solution for a theoretical dilemma. In: Franz A, Stahmer C (eds) Approaches to environmental accounting. Physica, Heidelberg, pp 39–69

Hueting R (2011) Sustainable national income: information for attaining sustainability. Manage Res Rev 34(11):1190–1201

Hueting R, De Boer B (2001) Environmental valuation and sustainable national income according to Hueting. In: Van Ierland EC, Van der Straaten J, Vollebergh HRJ (eds) Economic growth and the valuation of the environment, a debate. Edward Elgar, Cheltenham, pp 17–77

Huizing A, Dekker HC (1992) Helping to pull our planet out of the red: an environmental report of BSO/Origin. Acc Organ Soc 17(5):449–458

International Accounting Standards Board (2010) Conceptual Framework 2010. Issued by the International Accounting Standards Board. ISBN: 978-1-907026-69-0

Interagency Working Group on the Social Cost of Carbon (2013) Fact sheet: social cost of carbon. United States Environmental Protection Agency. http://www.epa.gov/climatechange/Downloads/EPAactivities/scc-fact-sheet.pdf. Accessed 23 April 2015

Interagency Working Group on the Social Cost of Carbon (2010) Appendix 15a. Social cost of carbon for regulatory impact analysis under Executive Order 12866. Final Rule Technical Support Document (TSD): Energy Efficiency Program for Commercial and Industrial Equipment: Small Electric Motors. U.S. Department of Energy. http://go.usa.gov/3fH. Accessed 23 April 2015

IPCC (2013) Summary for policymakers. In: Stocker TF, Qin D, Plattner GK, Tignor M, Allen SK, Boschung J, Nauels A, Xia Y, Bex V, Midgley PM (eds) Climate Change 2013: The Physical Science Basis. Contribution of Working Group I to the Fifth Assessment Report of the Intergovernmental Panel on Climate Change. Cambridge University Press, Cambridge

Kopp RE, Mignone BK (2012) The US government's social cost of carbon estimates after their first two years: pathways for improvement. Econ Open-Access Open-Assess E-J 6 (2012–15):1–41. doi:10.5018/economics-ejournal.ja.2012-15

Lamberton G (2005) Sustainability accounting—a brief history and conceptual framework. Account Forum 29:7–26

Lee TA (1985) Income and value measurement, 3rd edn. Van Nostrand Reinhold, Wokingham

Mäkelä H (2013) On the ideological role of employee reporting. Crit Perspect Account 24(4-5):360–378

March B (2013) Politicizing the expertise of the accounting industry in the realm of corporate social responsibility. Acc Organ Soc 38:149–168

Murphy T, O'Connell V, ÒhÒgartaigh C (2013) Discourses surrounding the evolution of the IASB/FASB conceptual framework: what they reveal about the "living law" of accounting. Acc Organ Soc 38:72–91

Ohlson J (1995) Earnings, Book values, and dividends in equity valuation. Contemp Account Res 11:661–687

Pearce D (1976) The limits of cost-benefit analysis as a guide to environmental policy. Kyklos 29:97–112

Penman S (2012) Financial statement analysis and security valuation, 5th edn. McGraw-Hill/Irwin

Rambaud A, Richard J (2015) The "Triple Depreciation Line" instead of the "Triple Bottom Line": towards a genuine integrated reporting. Crit Perspect Account doi:10.1016/j.cpa.2015.01.012

Richard J (2008a) Pour une révolution comptable environnementale. Le Monde de l'Economie 5(2):6

Richard J (2008b) La comptabilité environnementale: une vraie révolution comptable? In: Richard J, Collette C (eds) Comptabilité Générale. Dunod, Paris

Richard J (2011) Comptabilité, Economie, Finance et Développement durable. Chaire Finance et Développement Durable. May, Université Paris Dauphine

Richard J (2012) Comptabilité et développement durable. Economica, Paris

Stern N (2006) Stern review on the economics of climate change, UK Treasury

Stewart GB III (1991) The quest for value: the EVA™ management guide. HarperCollins Publishers, New York, NY

TEEB (2010) The economics of ecosystems and biodiversity: mainstreaming the economics of nature: a synthesis of the approach, conclusions and recommendations of TEEB. ISBN 978-3-9813410-3-4
Van Ierland EC, Van der Straaten J, Vollebergh HRJ (eds) (2001) Economic growth and the valuation of the environment, a debate. Edward Elgar, Cheltenham
Zhang Y, Andrew J (2013) Financialisation and the conceptual framework. Crit Perspect Account 25(1):17–26

In Search of the Purpose of Accounting Representation

François Pasqualini

Abstract Since 1970, the European Union has developed an accounting model founded in legal and civil bases under the influence of the roman and german culture. Nevertheless, since 2002, she adopted the international accounting rules created by the International Accounting Standards Board to establish the consolidated accounts of the listed holdings. These rules presents a financial culture leading to separate law and accounting. The identification of the object observed by the accounting allows to verify this statement. European law assimilate law subject—limited companies—to the accounting representation object and the IFRS rules proceeds differently because they untie the legal concept and the object represented through a non legal concept: the accounting entity. Both accounting systems are not incompatibles because modern law looks to nuance or push around the greats intellectual constructions allowing to built the relation between law and accounting: legal personality, heritage or limited liability of associates of a company.

Accounting is a language whose purpose is to express a reality or a situation. It corresponds to a certain way of seeing and translating the business using a codified vocabulary. It is a representation of the company, in both numbers and words, since the balance sheet, the profit and loss account, and the notes to the accounts form an indivisible whole. In the contemporary era, accounting nevertheless exceeds this function of representation whose scope is essentially probative and fiscal. It has become an instrument of interaction between the values that it extricates and the environment of the business and constitutes a social construction engendering overall economic effects (Pasqualini 2010: 12). That is why the law cannot be other than interested in it but it is also why its links with the economy are a reality. Moreover, a French author, Pierre Garnier (1947), did not hesitate, already more than 65 years ago, to assert that accounting is not only the algebra of the law, but also a method of observation of the economic sciences. In such a context, the link that the law maintains with accounting can only be ambiguous.

F. Pasqualini (✉)
University Paris-Dauphine – PSL, French Centre for Comparative Law, Paris, France
e-mail: francois.pasqualini@dauphine.fr

D. Bensadon, N. Praquin (eds.), *IFRS in a Global World*,
DOI 10.1007/978-3-319-28225-1_12

The confrontation between European accounting law, based on directives[1] anchored to the base of law, which is fundamentally civil in a Romano-Germanic spirit, and the frame of reference of International Accounting Standards claiming a financial culture, has disrupted the boundaries of accounting. Adopted by the European Union in 2002 for the presentation of the consolidated accounts of listed holdings,[2] the IAS/IFRS standards[3] are at the origin of a true shift in accountancy paradigm as already noted by the IAS-Law council of the French national accounting setter—*Autorité des Normes Comptables*—10 years ago (Progress Report, § 2-1-1, of the IAS-Law Council of the *Autorité des Normes Comptables*). The disruption is such that we can ask ourselves if a breaking point has not been reached today between the law and accounting thus marking the triumph of economics over the law. It is true that, since the identification of the purpose observed by accounting, a profound disagreement would seem to manifest itself between the European directives and international standards. "Where European law operates, in accordance with a legal approach, a connection between the judicial person—broadly speaking, the commercial limited companies—and the purpose of the accounting representation, IFRS standards proceeds in a diametrically opposed manner by disconnecting the legal concept of the object represented through the use of a non-judicial concept, that of an accounting entity, thus allowing a point of view to prevail that may be considered as financial" (Pasqualini and Burbi 2013: 262). However, comparison of the two models reveals neither victor nor vanquished because both have almost as many benefits as disadvantages. Does that mean to say that a rapprochement is possible?

1 Legal Conception of Accounting Representation

According to the legal approach adopted by European law, the accounting information finds its meaning through its dissemination which is justified by the limitation of the liability of the partners in some forms of society, that is to say in limited

[1] Directives 78/660/EEC of the Council of July 25, 1978 on the annual accounts of certain types of companies and 83/349/EEC of the Council of June 13, 1983 on consolidated accounts, repealed in 2013 and replaced by directive 2013/34/EU of June 26, 2013 of the European Parliament and the Council relating to the annual financial statements, the consolidated financial statements and the related reports of certain forms of business, amending Directive 2006/43/EC of the European Parliament and the Council and repealing Directives 78/660/EEC and 83/349/EEC of the Council.

[2] Regulation 1606/2002 of the European Parliament and the Council of 19 July, 2002 on the application of international accounting standards.

[3] The abbreviation IAS refers to the "*International Accounting Standards*". These are the standards published by the *International Accounting Standards Committee* (IASC) between 1973 and 2001 before the change of the governance and statutes intervened in 2001. Since 2002, the standards published by the *International Accounting Standards Board* (IASB), successor to the IASC, are now called IFRS, i.e. "*International Financial Reporting Standards*". Some IAS standards still remain in the international accounting repository beside the more recent IFRS standards without the difference in denomination having any effect on their scope.

companies. The directive of June 26, 2013 explains, as did the directive of July 25, 1978, in its time, that the coordination of the provisions of the national laws of the States of the European Union concerning the structure and content of the annual financial statements, the modes of assessment used as well as the publication of these documents relating to several forms of businesses, is of particular significance from the point of view of the protection of shareholders, partners and third parties because these companies do not offer any guarantee beyond the amount of their net assets (Directive 2013/34/EU, 3rd recital).

In effect, it is easy to understand that the contracting parties of a limited liability company have every interest in being informed about their ability to meet their financial and commercial commitments in order to be able to adapt the conditions of the business relationship with its patrimonial situation. The accepted time limits for payment or the collaterals required will, for example, vary as a function of the accounting image presented by the company. But the need for information does not stop there since third parties, as different as the bankers or the employees as well as the tax or social security authorities, of course, have a legitimate interest in the publication of the accounting information (Pasqualini and Burbi 2013: 261).

The fact that companies are not bound by their commitments other than by their own assets, creditors being without recourse against the partners, explains the preparation of the annual accounts and is a basis of the requirement to publish the information. It is, therefore, clear that the object of the accounting representation is a legal person and that thus there is an identity between the accounting representation and the legal theory.

This approach highlights the principle of legal security through the concerns of the law on credit. That is to say that the reasoning refers to the concept of patrimony and to the principle that "the debtor's assets are a common pledge to his creditors" (*Code civil*, French Civil code, art. 2285-1). And the fact that the directive of June 2013 refers to the amount of the net assets and no longer to the patrimony, as did the text of 1978 (Directive 78/660/EU, 2nd recital), does, without a doubt, not change the conclusion since the concept of net assets is a key to determining, at least in a statistical and minimal way, the valuation of the business in a cautious patrimonial approach, without seeking to anticipate its future profitability.

If the object of the accounting representation is thus characterized and justified, one should again query its utility. The latter is relative since it varies according to the needs of the users. In most countries of continental Europe, the partners and the public authority can show their satisfaction since the remuneration of the parties to the partnership contract and the levies of the administrations are determined from the annual accounts of the company. However, this satisfaction depends on the legal, economic and social context. It would be sufficient for the legislator to decide to separate the calculation of the dividend or the determination of the tax from the accounting result for this utility, which, as is seen, is artificial rather than natural, to be questioned.[4] The same remarks could be made about the employees who participate in the results of their company (*Code du travail*, French Labour Code, art. L. 3321-1 and following), of company officers responsible for proposing any refinancing of the company in the event that the equity has decreased excessively (*Code de commerce*, French commercial code, art. L. 223-42 and L. 225-248), or even of the adjudicator charged with verifying that the available assets have indeed decreased to less than the liabilities due when asked to start collective insolvency proceedings (*Code de commerce*, art. L. 631-1).

That the accounting information relating to the judicial person is useful does not, however, always mean that it is sufficient. From this point of view, the contemporary legislation sometimes, if not often, appeals to independent concepts which exceed the legal person or which are subdivisions. Thus, company law observes an economic and social unit (*Code de commerce*, art. L. 2322-4), the tax law accepts a group concept with the mother-daughter regime or the mechanism of fiscal integration (*CGI*, art. 145 and supra 223 A) as well as a permanently established infra-company unit (*CGI*, art. 259). And the companies law itself is not unaware of the group (*Code de commerce*, art. L. -233v3). That is to say, that the law, from the moment when it sees itself as a specialist, experiences the need to exceed from the top or the bottom the level of the subject of law in such a way as to indicate that it is possible to regard as more relevant for its own sake such and such legal discipline and separate from the prime objective of legal security. In other words, it is possible to conclude *a contrario* from this demonstration that the security sought after be satisfied by an assimilation of the accounting object with the judicial person. This conclusion combines the border between common law and specific law, but must be accepted with caution because it assumes that the company capital and the patrimony effectively play the role of general pledge to creditors, which is not strictly true.

In effect, the assets entered on the assets side of the balance sheet can be subject to the priority rights granted to priority or secured creditors.[5] That is to say that the assets are not a unitary mass of wealth corresponding to different liabilities and that the representation of the legal person's assets is biased by intrinsically legal rather than accounting considerations (Pasqualini and Burbi 2013: 270, no. 30). Certainly, the notes to the accounts are there to complement the balance by giving the readers of the accounts all the necessary additional information (Directive 2013/34/EU, 23rd rectial and articles 16 and following), but these clarifications, as useful as they may be, cannot conceal the fact that the connection between the law and accounting is neither absolute nor free of errors. Should one jettison what was previously

[4] It is, for example, possible to conceive that the dividend is determined from a cash flows statement and that the taxable base be transferred to the level of a group, as is also the case with the mechanism of fiscal integration (*Code Général des Impôts*, French General Tax Code, article 223 A).

[5] The equality of creditors ceases therefore when there are "legitimate reasons for preference": Civil Code, supra article 2285, second proposal.

cherished and reject the link between the letter and the number as the international standards seem to do?

2 Financial Conception of Accounting Representation

"The objective of general purpose financial reporting is to provide financial information about the reporting entity that is useful in making decisions about providing resources to the entity and in assessing whether the management and the governing board of that entity have made efficient and effective use of the resources provided. The reporting entity concept is intended to further this objective" (ED/2010/2, RE2).

This quotation reveals the mode of reasoning of the International Accounting Standards Board which is diametrically opposed to that of the jurists of continental Europe. In effect, the observed object is not subject to an obligation to prepare and disseminate accounting information by reason of its legal form, since it is the usefulness of the information for its recipients that determines the accounting information obligation (Pasqualini and Burbi 2013: 263, no. 10). "A reporting entity is a circumscribed area of economic activities whose financial information has the potential to be useful to existing and potential equity investors, lenders and other creditors who cannot directly obtain the information they need in making decisions about providing resources to the entity and in assessing whether management and the governing board of that entity have made efficient and effective use of the resources provided" (ED/2010/2, RE2).

Thus the accounting entity is defined in a utilitarian manner. It is characterised by the exercise of economic activities, irrespective of their civil or commercial nature, likely to be distinguished in an objective manner not only from the activities carried out by other entities but also by the environment within which the entity evolves, in order that its accounting representation provides meaningful information to users when they are called upon to take decisions regarding the granting of resources and evaluate the management executives' use of resources (ED/2010/2, RE3). Identified in this way, the accounting entity begins to unveil. But it must clarify its boundaries.

"Identifying a reporting entity in a specific situation requires consideration of the boundary of the economic activities that are being conducted, have been conducted or will be conducted. The existence of a legal entity is neither necessary nor sufficient to identify a reporting entity. A reporting entity can include more than one entity or it can be a portion of a single entity" (ED/2010/2, RE4). This assertion leads us back to the distinction between the company accounts and the consolidated accounts. The aforementioned is said to represent the legal individuality responsible for its commitments to its own assets, while the latter represent a set of separate companies as economically linked legal persons. European accountancy law clearly distinguishes between company accounts governed at the origin by the directive of July 25, 1978 and group accounts governed by the directive of June 13, 1983. Both of these now fall under the single directive of June 26, 2013 but this merging of texts has not questioned the separation of the two categories of accounts. On this point, the evolution is more formal than substantial. In effect, the first two directives defined an identical objective—to give a true and fair view (Directive 78/660/EEC, art. 2§3 and Directive 83/349/EEC, art. 16§3)—and prescribed the observance of certain principles of evaluation in order to satisfy this.[6] As for the latter, this endorses the requirement of fidelity (Directive 2013/34/EU, art. 4§3) and resumes the different assessment principles (Directive 2013/34/EU, art. 6) while maintaining the distinction between the two categories of accounts (Directive 2013/34/EU, Chapts. 3, 4 and 6). In other words, there is and always has been a common root and specific rules.

The IFRS standards are not ill-at-ease concerning this differentiation and have shown their preference for the financial information considered to be the most useful, i.e. that provided by the consolidated accounts when a legal entity controls one or more other legal entities. The accounting entity corresponds, therefore, to the group and not to the company, regardless of its place in the organization of the group (holding company, intermediate holding company, subsidiaries), (Pasqualini and Burbi 2013: 263, no. 11).

That having been said, the International Accounting Standards Board does not reject the notion of company accounts in the sense of individual accounts. They are looked upon as supplements to consolidated accounts: "Such 'parent-only' financial statements might provide useful information if they are presented together with consolidated financial statements' (ED/2010/2, RE11). That is to say the international standards follow a logic that is inverted relative to European Accountancy Law for which consolidated accounts complement the company accounts by extending them from the top. The challenge is still the same, since it involves taking into consideration the spatial continuity in which the company is registered (Pasqualini 1992: 73, no. 86 and following) but the methods employed take opposite paths.

This intellectual approach is explained in particular by the cultural origin of the international standards which are strongly impregnated with Americanisms. However, the concept of individual accounts is hardly known in the United States, particularly for an institutional reason. The Companies Law is not within the jurisdiction of the Federal State in contrast to the supervision of financial markets. This results in only the information produced by listed companies being reported to the Federal State and that any obligations of establishing or disseminating company accounts could not be decreed by the Federal States. But they have been reluctant to legislate on the matter.

The reasoning follows the same utilitarian method where it is not a question of a group, i.e. a set of legal subjects, but of a part of a company. "A portion of an entity

[6] Directive 78/660/EEC, supra, article 31, § 1 and directive 83/349 supra, art. 29, § 2, *a)*, specifically referring to the evaluation methods applied to the company accounts of the undertaking that prepares the consolidated accounts.

could qualify as a reporting entity if the economic activities of that portion can be distinguished objectively from the rest of the entity and financial information about that portion of the entity has the potential to be useful in making decisions about providing resources to that portion of the entity. For example, a potential equity investor could be considering a purchase of a branch or division of an entity" (ED/201/2, RE6).

These various remarks might suggest prima facie that the international reference marks a real upheaval in the history of accounting. However, it is not so since the doctrine has developed theories similar to that which is now advocated by the International Accounting Standards Board. "By comparison with the businesses, the accounting entity is equated in an alternative or simultaneous manner to the activity segment (factory, agency, department, division, etc.), to the company itself, fundamental legal component, endowed with the faculties of expression specific to the legal personality, or, finally, to the group, a set of companies related economically and legally. While, in everyday parlance, the entity corresponds to an idea of property, in accounting law it acquires a particular meaning, since it is the symbol of the synthesis. The accounting entity is a unit of observation at the level of which a summary of the characteristics of the object studied can be extracted" (Pasqualini 1994: 46, no. 10). It is, therefore, understood that the revolution is only an evolution and that it very probably has its place in the course of history.

3 Legal Design vs Financial Accounting Representation Design

The judicial person is not to be confused with the accounting entity, even if it is possible, under certain conditions, to accept their similarity. "A single legal entity that conducts economic activities and does not control any other entity is likely to qualify as a reporting entity. Most, if not all, legal entities have the potential to be reporting entities. However, a single legal entity may not qualify as a reporting entity if, for example, its economic activities are commingled with the economic activities of another entity and there is no basis for objectively distinguishing their activities. In some jurisdictions, there may be questions about whether those entities are separate entities under the law" (ED/2010/2, RE5).

According to this design, it appears, at least at first glance, that the financial approach advocated by the International Accounting Standards Board is disconnected from the legal design traditionally preferred by the countries of continental Europe and that a possible point of intersection between the two approaches is only a circumstance of fact, dare we say an accident, as evidenced by the use of the term "likely". This observation leads to a return to the principle of "substance over form", often presented as one of the reference pillars of the IFRS, beside the evaluation method based on the fair value and the concept of control (Pasqualini

2010: 13). In effect, this rule leads to a focus on the substance of each act posted in the accounts, regarded as economic, with respect to its supposedly legal form.

That having been said, one must, for several reasons, be wary of hasty conclusions. In the first place, the principle of "substance over form" has never resulted in ignoring the legal qualification of an act, which has also been noted for a long time (Stempnierwsky 1994: 53 and following). It simply means that in the event of a disagreement between the legal qualification and the economic qualification of a contract, for example, the latter must prevail for the sake of good information. "*In assessing whether an item meets the definition of an asset, liability or equity, attention needs to be given to its underlying substance and economic reality and not merely its legal form*" (IFRS Foundation, Chap. 4, § 4.6). That is why it can be said that the "substance reflects the idea that, regardless of the form of a transaction or a contract, what is important is to describe in accounting the economic reality of the observed act, which is assessed using criteria such as the transfer of risks and benefits or even the control by the entity of the outflow of resources. The search for the substance cannot, of course, completely ignore the law, but it leads to not stopping at its qualifications. It inspires in the accountants a behaviour which consists in not being systematically content with legal solutions and always wondering in order to possibly question them" (Pasqualini and Burbi 2013: 272, no. 34).

Secondly, the European directives do not ignore the rule of substance, even if it was only textually introduced in 2003,[7] since it is inseparable from the accounting objective of true and fair view concept of the company (Pasqualini 1992: 41, no. 49 and following). This conjunction is found from the remainder in the conceptual framework of the International Accounting Standards Board that, in the version published in 2010, deems that "*Substance over form is not considered a separate component of faithful representation since it would be redundant. Faithful representation means that financial information represents the substance of an economic phenomenon rather than merely representing its legal form. Representing a legal form that differs from the economic substance of the underlying economic phenomenon could not result in a faithful representation*" (IFRS Foundation, Ch. 3, BC3.26).

The question that deserves to be asked at this level of the discussion is that of a possible rapprochement of the model of the European directives to that of the international standards setting body thanks to the principle of substance. The very fact of asking questions of this kind allows to relativize the dispute of the legal design and the design of financial accounting representation, this assessment is also confirmed by some liberties taken by the European legislator, particularly with the theory of legal personality, to extend the information requirements beyond the circle of companies whose partners are responsible only to the extent of their

[7] Directive 2003/51/EC of the European Parliament and Council of 18 June, 2003 amending the Directives 78/660/EEC, 83/349/EEC, 86/635/EEC and 91/674/EEC of the Council on annual accounts and consolidated accounts of certain types of companies, banks and other financial institutions and insurance undertakings, art. 1st, § 2. See today: Directive 2013/34/EU supra, article 6, § 1 h).

inputs. Of course, here we will think of the requirement to prepare consolidated accounts (Directive 83/349/EEC, art. 1st, § 1) or again of the extension of the scope of the accounting information to the companies of persons or partnerships in English law.[8] Consolidated accounts have been introduced at a time when, in most European countries, the group was looked upon as an economic individuality, devoid of legal personality, bringing together independent judicial persons, placed under the same control, while some companies without the characteristics of a limited company have, a few years later, been assimilated to corporations from the moment when those of their partners whose liability is undefined are all limited liability companies or joint stock companies (Directive 90/605/EEC, 3rd and 5th recitals). European law has thus started distinguishing between the legal subject and the object of the accounting representation for the obvious as well as natural sake of legal security (Pasqualini and Burbi 2013: 265, no. 15). In addition, it should also be noted that contemporary French law differentiates itself from conventional solutions of company law by asserting the individual responsibility of the partner in certain circumstances.

French legislator, revising once again the law of collective procedures (Ordonance 2014-326, 2014: 5249), has recently created a new case of liability of partners. Henceforth, the opening of a safeguard procedure for the benefit of a company "renders immediately payable the amount of the company capital" (*Code de commerce*, art. L. 624-20). This means that the partners are obliged to support their business as soon as they become aware of financial difficulties, which it is not able to overcome, without being in a state of insolvency (*Code de commerce*, art. L. 620-1).[9] This financial or, more exactly, capitalist responsibility is a response to the under-capitalization of French companies, which is a recurring evil that affects the economy. The problem is certainly not of a legal nature but it is promoted by the conjunction of the tax law and the Companies Law which, together are seen to be permissive. In effect, the general tax Code admits the deductibility of sums advanced by the partners to the account of their business (*CGI*, art. 39-1-3°) while the Commercial Code accommodates a partial release of the amount of the inputs upon subscription (*Code de commerce*, art. L. 223-7 and L. 225-3). The responsibility thus imagined is original in that it is not based on an error, the partner who has not released its inputs is only at fault if he had not responded to calls for funds from the management (*Code civil*, art. 1843-3, §5), but on a risk, that of the lack of company capital.

In addition, the Commercial Chamber of the Supreme Court of Appeal (*Cour de Cassation*), has deemed in a judgment (Feb. 18, 2014, 12-29.752) that the liability of a partner may be retained in respect of a third party co-contractor of the company if it has committed an intentional error of particular seriousness, incompatible with

[8] Directive No. 90/605/EEC of the Council of the November 8, 1990 amending Directives No. 78/660/EEC and No. 83/349/EEC concerning the annual accounts and consolidated accounts respectively, with regard to the scope of their application.

[9] On the notion of cessation of payments, see: *Code de commerce*, article L. 631-1 supra.

the normal exercise of the prerogatives attached to the quality of the partner. By appealing to the subject of a partner the theory of the separable fault and aligning this way the responsibility of the partners with that of the leadership,[10] the jurisprudence "pierced the veil of the legal entity a little more" (Parachkévova 2015: 165, no. 113 h3).

It is clear, therefore, that the contemporary law does not hesitate to qualify, or even to maltreat the large intellectual constructions upon which the relationship between accounting law, the legal personality, the assets or even the limitation of liability of the partners of certain societies had been built. The link between the law and accounting has thus inevitably been changed but it must be acknowledged that it has not so far been broken. As has been said, the group is indeed a judicial person even if it remains devoid of legal personality under French law. Indeed, it is because the group is taken into account that European law has considered it useful to extend the domain of accounting information to partnerships where the partners are limited companies. The substance prevails over the form. The law of collective procedures, for its part, contradicts the theory of patrimony. It is not a cultural revolution, since it is in some way customary. Indeed, the concept of confusion of patrimonies has long since been recognized (*Code de commerce*, art. L. 621-2, §2). Here also, the substance wins against the form. With regard to the commercial judge, he is trying to prevent a partner from being able to escape a personal responsibility by sheltering excessively behind the shield of the legal personality of the company. The partner should not be able to divert the legal personality of the company, that is to say, in a certain way, to abuse it for developing a strategy of avoidance of responsibility. Again, the substance triumphs.

These examples "confirm the non-dogmatic nature of the legal approach and constitute an illustration of the attempts and the difficulties of the law to exceed the inherent boundaries in the use of legal concepts" (Pasqualini and Burbi 2013: 265, no. 15). Would an understanding of accounting based on a substantial analysis and on the idea of synthesis, therefore, not be the basis of a good compromise between the legal design and the financial design of the object of the accounting representation? The answer to this question is neither legal nor economic. It is political because it falls within the agreement of the States of the European Union.

Bibliography

Garnier P (1947) La comptabilité, Algèbre du droit et méthode d'observation des sciences économiques. Dunod, Paris

Parachkévova I (2015) L'associé responsable. Bulletin Joly Sociétés, Avril

Pasqualini F (1992) L'image fidèle en droit comptable. Litec, Paris

[10] In this connection, see for example: *Cour de cassation*, Commercial Division, 20 May, 2003, No. 99-17.092, *Dalloz* 2003, p. 2623, note B. Dondero; *Review of. Companies* 2003, p. 479, note J. -F. Barbieri.

Pasqualini F (1994) Autonomie comptable et qualifications juridiques. In: Nouvelles orientations en droit comptable. Liège: Editions Collection scientifique de la faculté de droit de Liège
Pasqualini F (2010) Regards critiques d'un juriste sur les normes comptables internationales. ACE, Editions Kluwer
Pasqualini F, Burbi D (2013) Droit comptable européen et normes IFRS: une scission entre le droit et le chiffre? Revue des sociétés, Dalloz
Stempnierwsky Y (1994) Le processus menant à la qualification comptable – Approches pratiques et exemples. In: Nouvelles orientations en droit comptable. Liège: Editions Collection scientifique de la faculté de droit de Liège

Eureopean Reglementation

Directive 2003/51/CE (modifying directives 78/660/CEE, 83/349/CEE, 86/635/CEE and 91/674/CEE)
Directive 2006/43/CE
Directive 2013/34/UE
Directive 78/660/CEE (abrogated; see directive 2013/34/UE)
Directive 83/349/CEE (abrogated; see directive 2013/34/UE)
Directive 90/605/CEE (modifying directives 78/660/CEE and 83/349/CEE)
Regulation 1606/2002 of the European Parliament and the Council of 19 July, 2002 on the application of international accounting standards

French Reglementation

Code civil (*civil code*)
Code de commerce (*Commercial code*)
Code du travail (*Labour code*)
Code général des impôts – CGI (General tax code)
Conseil national de la comptabilité, Rapport d'étape de la commission IAS-Droit
Cour de cassation, Chambre commerciale, 18 février 2014, n° 12-29.752, Bulletin Joly Sociétés, juin 2014, p. 382, n° 111z5, note B. Fages
Cour de cassation, Chambre commerciale, 20 mai 2003, n° 99-17.092, Dalloz 2003, p. 2623, note B. Dondero; Revue des. sociétés 2003, p. 479, note J.-F. Barbièri
Ordonnance n° 2014-326, 12 mars 2014, portant réforme de la prévention des difficultés des entreprises et des procédures collectives, JORF n°0062, 14 mars 2014, p. 5249

IASB

Exposure Draft ED/2010/2. Conceptual framework for financial reporting: the reporting entity
IFRS Foundation, The conceptual framework for financial reporting

Part II
National or Regional Implementation of the IFRS: Challenges and Prospects

Brazil. IFRS Convergence and the Role of Accounting Education: The Brazilian Case

Edgard Cornacchione and Fernando Dal-Ri Múrcia

Abstract Our chapter critically analyses the adoption of IFRS in Brazil and argues that accounting education will be an important factor for a broad and complete convergence. The study is divided into five sections. Section 1 presents a short introduction of Brazil and discusses issues such as colonization background, legal system, capital markets and accounting profession. Section 2 reviews the road to accounting convergence in Brazil, focusing on the specificities of the Brazilian process that involved creation of a National Accounting Standard Committee. Section 3 critically analyses the adoption in Brazil of IFRS. We focus on the main issues brought by the change to a principle-based standard and discuss the lack of interpretation consensus among market participants. Due to that, financial statements of Brazilian companies still retain a strong national identity. In Sect. 4, we analyze the competences and capabilities that should be achieved through accounting education that we believe are necessary for a complete and broad convergence in Brazil. Finally, Sect. 5 presents our concluding remarks.

1 Short Introduction to Brazil

A key player in Latin America, and globally, Brazil has been advancing through a myriad of challenges in its history. With its colonization background, largely connected to Portuguese culture and values, Brazil has also a clear influence from other European countries (e.g., Germany, Italy, Spain, France, Netherlands), Japan and some African countries. Monoculture (e.g., gold, coffee, sugar cane) was the major socioeconomic approach during the initial stages of the country. Much more recently, industrial, political and social developments led to a powerful nation, more organized and ready to perform as a global player. A fresh democracy (from 1986) after military dictatorship and a new constitution (from 1988) gave space to two decades of internal reorganization (e.g., political system and inflation). Still,

E. Cornacchione (✉) • F.D.-R. Múrcia
Department of Accounting and Actuarial Sciences, University of Sao Paulo, Brazil
e-mail: edgardbc@usp.br; murcia@usp.br

D. Bensadon, N. Praquin (eds.), *IFRS in a Global World*,
DOI 10.1007/978-3-319-28225-1_13

society (individuals and organizations) has to cope with several challenges based on fast and governmental-led restructuring efforts (Roett 2010).

A wide gap in wealth distribution is still present, even after Brazil experienced a huge increase, overtime, in purchasing power of its minimum wage (about USD 220 per month in 2015). Government-led assistive programs were successful in direct transfer of wealth to families and individuals in deep need (such as *Bolsa Familia* and *Bolsa Escola*, linked to kids and education), such as the universal health care system and the general public pension system (Baer 2008). A complex and large tax system imposes a heavy tax burden on participants of the Brazilian economy, with clear links to support government expenditures.

With one third (200 million people) of Latin America population and about 36 % of its GDP, Brazil could soon overtake UK and France (based on some analysts) in GDP and become the fifth largest economy (GDP) in the world. Brazil has an interesting demographics with over two thirds of its population in the range between 15 and 64, and a total of 6.4 million students enrolled in the Brazilian postsecondary education system (as of 2010, according to IBGE, *Instituto Brasileiro de Geografia e Estatística*, and INEP, *Instituto Nacional de Estudos e Pesquisas Educacionais Anísio Teixeira*): it is noteworthy that as of 2010, more than 41 % of the enrollment was in social sciences, business and law.

Financial infrastructure in Brazil is bold. During the inflation period, Brazilian financial market had to grow stronger to cope with rapid changes in purchasing power. Banking systems and government markets (overnight) became well established even sooner than most developed economies. Telecommunication infrastructure became critical to all this. A continental country such as Brazil could not afford less. Now, financial, credit and capital markets are booming (market capitalization in Brazil picked more than 100 % of GDP in 2007, as reported by the World Bank).

Accounting is a critical profession, mainly if we take a country such as Brazil into this context. With about half million licensed accountants (according to CFC, the Brazilian professional body), 40 % with a bachelor's degree, accounting is very attractive for young students selecting their profession when entering the postsecondary educational system. The country has moved (2010) to full IFRS adoption and the profession is flourishing with the associated dynamics. Accounting education, training and development are all influenced by the new horizons. Organizations of all shapes and sizes, in all industries, call for attention when adjusting their own systems to benefit from a stronger accounting approach to business. It is clear that these numbers in the accounting profession require greater consideration of the organizations dealing with education and professional oversight, to mention only these two.

In order to become a licensed professional, it is mandatory in Brazil: (a) to get a college education in Accounting (typical 4-year bachelor's degree) and (b) pass a professional exam (administered by CFC, *Conselho Federal de Contabilidade*). There is no practical experience (PE) component to this, nor continuing professional education (CPE) requirements. These two requirements (PE and CPE) are only present for those acting as auditors. If we consider the number (about 6 million, as of 2011 by DIEESE, *Departamento Intersindical de Estatística e Estudos Econômicos*) of micro and small sized companies in Brazil (about 99 % of all companies and accounting for about 15 million formal jobs), it is clear the shape of the profession in the country, along with the social relevance in helping this large portion of formal economy to become stronger while coping with Brazilian challenges linked to logistics, tax, bureaucracy, funding options, on top of regular and typical business challenges.

2 The Road to Accounting Convergence in Brazil

Brazilian accounting was initially developed under the influence of European countries, like Portugal and Italy. The first major "revolution" of Brazilian accounting standards came with Corporate Law 6.404 (*Lei das Sociedades por Ações*) enacted in 1976 which strongly followed the accounting model then prevailing in the United States.

The Brazilian Corporate Law 6.404 aligned the Brazilian accounting practices with the international practices, as the American accounting model was considered, at that time (1976), a reference in terms of international accounting. Some examples of this first major accounting revolution brought by the Corporations Act of 1976 were:

- Measurement of property, plant and equipment by their fair value (revaluation option)
- Measurement of investments in subsidiaries by the equity method; and
- Presentation of the Statement of Sources and Uses of Funds.

In this sense, the Corporate Law 6.404 brought some quite complex concepts and accounting requirements already in 1976. Due to that, the Brazilian accounting standards become closely related to the international model.

However, as time passed by, Brazilian accounting standards became heavily influenced by tax authorities. Also, the Corporate Law was not updated in order to follow changes made in US-GAAP or IFRS. This is because further improvements depended on changes in this law; in other words, significant changes to the accounting and reporting framework would require the law to be amended.

The problem with this requirement was that, overall, changes in federal laws in Brazil take a long time. This is because the legislative process can be lengthy and cumbersome, particularly when controversial issues are at stake. Hence, it became difficult to incorporate new accounting concepts reflecting increasingly complex business transactions.

Thus, over the years, the part of the corporate law that dealt with accounting issues became old, outdated and ineffective compared to international practices. For instance, the law did not treat recognition and measurement of derivative financial instruments. Due to that, as time passed by, BR-GAAP became lagged and companies basically used tax rules to recognize and measure economic transactions.

Another issue that brought a challenge to the Brazilian accounting profession during the 1980s and early 1990s was hyperinflation. For instance, the annual inflation rate in 1993 was 2,477 %. At that time, the Brazilian accounting community developed an accounting methodology, called "*Correção Monetária Integral*" to deal with the effects of inflation rather robust, recognized by United Nations as the most advanced model of indexation accounting in world. It is worthwhile mentioning that hyperinflation was successfully controlled in 1994; nowadays, annual inflation rate is around 6 %.

The move towards convergence with IFRS was initiated by the Brazilian Central Bank, reflecting its view of the importance of a single set of international financial reporting standards in use around the world, and the benefits of such standards for the Brazilian economy.

In 2006, the Brazilian Central Bank announced that financial institutions under its supervision should comply with IFRS starting from December 2010 in their consolidated financial statements. In 2007 the Brazilian Exchange Commission and the Brazilian Insurance Supervisor issued similar rulings. These developments were followed by a decision of the Brazilian congress to approve legislation, Law 11.638/07, requiring the progressive convergence of Brazilian GAAP with IFRS for the individual accounts of all listed companies and large for-profit enterprises from 2008.

The Law 11.638/07 established three major platforms for the IFRS convergence process in Brazil. First, it granted the Brazilian Exchange Commission the authority to establish accounting standards for listed companies. Second, it established that the Brazilian Exchange Commission, when determining accounting standards, should ensure that they are in conformity with international accounting standards. Third, it permitted the Exchange Commission to enter into an agreement with an independent entity to seek advice on the accounting standard setting process. This last point was achieved through an agreement between the Exchange Commission and the Brazilian Standard Setter Committee.

For a successful convergence to international financial reporting standards, changes brought by this new accounting model could not lead to income tax impacts, as companies would not fully adopt a new accounting model if they paid more income taxes due to that. In this sense, the Brazilian government passed another act, Law 11.941/09, which became the legal provision that allowed the so-called "tax neutrality" in Brazil. According to this law, all accounting changes brought by international convergence would not have tax effects.

That allowed Brazilian companies to recognize and measure business transactions according to IFRS and subsequently exclude the respective impacts when filling for income tax. In this sense, by the enactment of Law 11.941/09, the two accounting systems, financial accounting and tax accounting, became completed separated.

For some, the enactment of Law 11.941/09 bringing the "tax neutrality" was considered to be the most important step towards convergence. As mentioned earlier, Brazilian financial accounting suffered great influence from the Tax Laws. That influence was considered to be an impediment to the adoption of international standards in Brazil. After all, having high quality accounting standards would be useless, if companies continued to used assumptions and estimates based on the tax legislations.

Another important step towards convergence was the foundation of the Brazilian Accounting Pronouncements Committee (*Comitê de Pronunciamentos Contábeis* – CPC) in 2005. This Committee ("Brazilian FASB") was created by the common efforts and objectives of the following entities: (a) Brazilian Listed Companies Association (*Associação Brasileira das Companhias Abertas – ABRASCA*), (b) National Capital Market Investment Professionals and Analysts Association (*Associação dos Analistas e Profissionais de Investimento do Mercado de Capitais – APIMEC*), (c) São Paulo Stock Exchange (*Bolsa de Valores de São Paulo – BOVESPA*), (d) Accounting Federal Council (*Conselho Federal de Contabilidade – CFC*), (e) Financial and Accounting Research Institute Foundation (*Fundação Instituto de Pesquisas Contábeis, Atuariais e Financeiras – FIPECAFI*), and (f) Brazilian Institute of Independent Auditors (*Instituto dos Auditores Independentes do Brasil – IBRACON*).

The following main needs led to the foundation of the Brazilian Accounting Pronouncements Committee (2005):

- International convergence of accounting standards: reduction of cost for the preparation of financial reports, reduction of risks and cost in the analysis and decision-making process, reduction of capital cost.
- Centralizing the issuing of standards of such nature: in Brazil, several entities were already doing that at the time.
- Representation and democratic process when producing such information: accountants, auditors, users, intermediates, academy members and government.

CPC played a very important role in the Brazilian convergence to international standards. As the country's accounting committee, it was responsible for translating the IFRS to Portuguese, as well as making few adaptations in order to accommodate the Corporate Law No 6.404. CPC was also responsible for submitting the translated/adapted IFRS, called Technical Statements (*Pronunciamentos Técnicos*) to public hearing in order to get the financial community involved. However, few changes were made from the initial translations, as significant differences between the IFRS and the Brazilian Technical Statements would not lead to full convergence of the Brazilian GAAP.

The consolidation of the accounting standard-setting processes into one hand clarified and simplified the body of existing standards. It also helped regulators in their efforts to enhance their enforcement activities. This is because, before the creation of CPC, GAAP in Brazil aroused from a variety of sources, including the Corporations Law and the standards and interpretations issued by up to eight different institutions like the Central Bank, the Federal Accounting Council among others.

The rationale for establishing CPC was twofold: to simplify and consolidate the standard-setting system and unify the body of existing pronouncements into a single set of standards with limited overlaps and no loopholes and to strengthen the institutional setting needed to support the desired improvements in corporate financial reporting and the adoption of IFRS. That was necessary because, in Brazil, the IFRS required the involvement of a national body even though IFRS are issued by an international organization, the IFRS Foundation.

It is important to mention that the IFRS implementation process held by the CPC was performed in two major steps. First, the accounting committee issued 15 Technical Statements to meet the requirements contained in Law 11.638/07, for the year ended in 2008. By that period, partial convergence to IFRS was achieved as companies had to adopt all 15 Technical Statements. For example, companies had to recognize in their financial statements derivative financial instruments, previously treated by Brazilian companies as off-balance sheet items.

Completed this initial cycle, the CPC conducted the issuance of the remaining Technical Statements during the years of 2009 and 2010 in order to achieve the full adoption of IFRS in Brazil. This process ended with the so-called "First Time Adoption of IFRS" by Brazilian public companies, in their consolidated financial statements for the year ended in 2010.

For most of the accounting community, the adoption of IFRS has been considered a "path breaking" event, the biggest change in Brazilian accounting since the enactment of Corporate Law 6.404 in 1976, which, as mentioned earlier, brought the North-American accounting model to Brazil. The IFRS adoption was considered a second "accounting revolution".

3 Some Thoughts on the Implementation of IFRS in Brazil

In this topic we present some thoughts on the implementation of IFRS in Brazil. We argue that although public companies were successful in adopting IFRS, financial statements of Brazilian companies still retain a strong national identity. Also, we state that IFRS are still not applied by small and median size entities. Finally, as the level of judgment increased significantly with the international accounting standards, interpretation and application is not yet a consensus among the accounting community.

3.1 Successful Adoption of IFRS in Brazil But Financial Statements Still Retain a Strong National Identity

We believe that Brazilian public companies were successful in adopting IFRS. The transition to the international standards introduced significant changes in the procedures for the recognition, measurement and disclosure of financial information.

In our view, one of the most positive aspects of the adoption has been the effect on corporate transparency. That is because IFRS require companies to disclose a greater volume of information to their external users, compared to the previous Brazilian GAAP. Because of the wide range of requirements, there was a significant increase in the volume of information disclosed by companies; the financial statements of some companies exceeded 200 pages.

Obviously, for external users who do not have privileged access to information, this increase in the volume of information disclosed can be seen as something positive. The central idea is that more information reduces the uncertainties of users who can make better economic decisions.

However, as we know, quantity does not necessarily mean quality. Rather, in certain cases, the excess of irrelevant information may even confuse the user. For instance, by looking at the financial reports of Brazilian companies is very common to find parts of notes to financial statements that are literally copies of IFRS. In many cases, you have the impression that what you are reading is an accounting standard and not a financial statement. At the same time, some notes to financial statements lack relevant information with respect to certain items, like for instance disclosures regarding impairment of assets (IAS 36). In this sense, although the volume of disclosure has increased, we are quite sure that quality can (and should) be improved.

Although, overall, public companies were able to comply with the new standards, we argue that financial statements of Brazilian companies still retain a strong national identity. Some companies sought to minimize possible changes, whenever IFRS allowed accounting choices (for instance measuring investment property by their fair value), and kept preparing and disclosing financial statements to the market in the same old way.

As we know, accounting practice is influenced by economic and political forces. In this sense, it would be unrealistic to expect financial statements prepared in accordance with IFRS by Brazilian companies not to retain any prior trace from what companies were doing before. After all, the whole process of change, especially when there is completely change of philosophy in the way financial statements are viewed, takes time.

3.2 *IFRS for SMEs: A Long Way to Go*

The IFRS for Small and Median Size Companies was issued in Brazil (and translated into Portuguese) in 2009 with application starting from 2010 to targeted companies. The adoption of this standard has expanded the application of International Financial Reporting Standards to all companies that do not have public responsibility to provide accounts (public accountability).

The result of the approval of the IFRS-SME in 2009 is that the entire Brazilian accounting system is harmonized with the International Standards. Consequently, at least in theory, the accounts of all Brazilian companies should be convergent to the IFRS. This is because: companies with public accountability (listed companies, banks etc.) have to apply the Full-IFRS and companies without public accountability (called “small and median size”) should apply the IFRS-SMEs.

It is worthwhile mentioning that 99 % of organizations in Brazil are small and median companies. Therefore, one can see the importance of this standard to the convergence of BR-GAAP to International Accounting Standards. In other words, convergence would not be completed if it only covered large and public companies.

However, as we know, the standard is just the "law" and companies do not necessarily follow the standards. The authors' own professional experiences have also shown that some of these companies do not even know that this standard already exists, and therefore should be applied. The great majority of small and median size companies only do accounting for tax purposes. There is almost no regulation on these types of companies. There is little or no oversight regarding compliance with this new standard.

Overall, the International Financial Reporting Standards are only applied by Public Companies and some sectors with specific regulation like Electric Energy, Insurance etc. Regarding public companies, the Brazilian Exchange Commission (*Comissão de Valores Mobiliários,* CVM) is empowered to inspect listed corporations and their independent auditors, and to conduct administrative inquiries. It can impose administrative sanctions, which include warnings, fines, restatement orders, and cancellations of registration. CVM has a policy of systematically requiring the restatement of financial statements when the auditor's report mentions a departure from accounting standards.

On the other hand, for SMEs, there is no system to effectively ensure that they adhere to IFRS in their financial statements. The only enforcer of accounting standards for these companies is the Federal Accounting Council system, through the company's accountant. In other words, the company's accountant, as a Council member, is required to follow IFRS.

Also, limited liability (non-public) companies called "*Limitadas*", which are privately owned, are not required to disclose their financial statements to the public. The small "*Limitadas*" are not even required to undergo a statutory audit and or to have any kind of corporate governance control. This hampers confidence in the financial statements of these companies, as there is no independent verification that the information presented by such companies presents an accurate view of their situation.

Therefonre, there is no effective "punishment" for Brazilian companies that do not follow and apply IFRS for SMEs, even though there is an accounting standard requiring them to do it. In our opinion this evidences that enforcement plays a big role in real adoption of IFRS in Brazil. In this sense, regulatory agencies concerned with financial reporting should give more focus to, and strengthen, their enforcement activities regarding the IFRS-SMEs.

3.3 The Level of Judgment Increased with Principle-Based Standards and Interpretation and Application Are Not Consensus Among Market Participants

Due to prior tax influence, many of the assumptions and criteria used by the companies when preparing their financial statements did not reflect the economic reality of the underlying business transactions. A classic example was the amount of depreciation to be charged as an expense each year. Instead of trying to reflect the exact consumption of the fixed asset, companies used the criteria established by the tax authorities. Needless to say, that behavior resulted in misleading financial statements for decision-making purposes.

The adoption of IFRS brought the need to evaluate and judge business transactions in order to reflect economic reality, the so-called "substance over form". That, of course, required more critical thinking skills by accountants and other professionals in Brazil. The change from a rules-based accounting for a principles-based accounting increased the level of judgment required by those responsible for preparing the financial statements.

In this scenario, the inherent complexities brought by some IFRS (for example, accounting for financial instruments: IAS 39, IAS 32 and IFRS 7) combined with the important segregation of accounting for corporate purposes from accounting for income taxes added more subjectivity to the accounting process. In this context, the role of accountants involved in the preparation and dissemination of financial statements became even more important, as the professional now have more responsibility to external users.

On the other hand, the interpretation of IFRS, accounting standards first written in English and from an Anglo-Saxon legal system, sparked many questions. As mentioned earlier, overall, Brazilian law is typically originated from the codified law, rules-based. Concepts like "true and fair view" do seem abstract to most Brazilian accountants. In this sense, it is not uncommon to find practical discussions among accountants, auditors and regulators regarding the interpretation of IFRS in the Brazilian scenario.

Sometimes, views are very different. In a way, it seemed natural as some of the changes brought about by the IFRS requirements have significant impact on accounting numbers that are the basis for a wide range of contracts between economic agents.

In the real estate sector, for example, applying the concept of risks and benefits transferring for the units sold in advance still have divergent views. Some, including auditors, consider that such risks and benefits are only transferred upon delivery of the unit's keys. Others, including companies, argue that the transfer of these risks and benefits occurs gradually over time; consequently they argue that revenue can be recognized using the percentage of completion method.

Another big debate brought by IFRS adoption regards Public Concessions, regulated by IFRIC 12. There is still not a consensus among the market participants regarding which sectors or companies are subject to this standard. In fact, due to specificities of these concession contracts in Brazil, different arguments can be made, as IFRIC 12 is not to be applied by all service concession arrangements.

Overall, the practical application of IFRS still raises questions among companies, accountants and auditors. In our view this suggests the need for ongoing training of all professionals involved in the preparation and dissemination of financial statements.

After all, only quality training will lead to a better understanding on how to effectively implement a complex accounting standardization in Brazil. In this sense, we argue that education will play an important role in the future of IFRS implementation in Brazil. In our view, that will be the key issue that is going to differentiate the full and complete adoption from the "Label Adoption" of IFRS (Carvalho and Salotti 2013).

4 The Importance of Education in Future of Accounting Convergence in Brazil

Assuming this massive transition (at both content and format dimensions) to IFRS, accounting became a different practice and a different area of study. Business and the job-market are different now, particularly in terms of the accounting profession. Brazil faces this same situation. However, it has it uniqueness as we are talking about a country that is facing its own educational development and the economy demands a better workforce. Education and training are no longer interesting add-ons, but now represent critical success factors for society. By changing the change, Accounting Education in Brazil is trying to overcome the natural challenges of the national postsecondary education system, when dealing with a set of changes on its own field. We need to consider the evolving numbers of postsecondary education in Brazil (from 425 thousand enrolled students in 1970 up to 6.4 million in 2010, an expansion of 15 times in four decades, according to official data) and look at accounting changes, on top of that.

Such systemic expansion tends to come with an impact on the existing structure of private and public higher education institutions. Brazil was not any different. Families, organizations, students, faculty members, regulators, education providers among other stakeholders are still learning to adapt. Meanwhile, accounting is changing itself, deeply. And we are not only talking about IFRS.

A massive technological change is catalyzing the transformation of business and education, as we know them. Day after day we witness a new product, a new service, new logistics, new work, affecting the traditional approach to funding, investing, buying, manufacturing, providing, selling, receiving, paying etc. Contracts are unusual, as clients and suppliers behave under a brand new set of approaches. Money is different. Assets and company values tend to operate under new equations. What is accounting? What is this new profession? What is expected of accounting education?

Week after week we see restrictions being removed from the system. For many, this is too complex of an argument to assume yet. Take the language barrier. Both, for education and professional matters, language has been a natural barrier for ages. With technological advances, such as real time spoken language translators (RTSLT), now incorporated into smartphones, education and practice are moving to the next level. Take accounting, IFRS, for instance. The amount of time, energy and other resources that combined we invested to create conditions for practice (e.g., in Brazil all the IFRS translation that took place) and for education (textbooks, cases, exercises, training materials etc.) will cease to be required, in the near future. It is going to be different. Think about the amount of energy spent across the globe to cope with such situations that will no longer be required, and will be instantly available to improve the core of the system.

Similar idea can be considered when we explore the benefits of MOOCs (*Massive Open Online Courses*). Why do we still need thousands of professors around the globe dealing everyday with the same content, topics, cases and goals? Affordances are completely new and we need to collectively take advantage of that in order to improve faster and with more quality, as a profession, as an area of study. In education, we are truly living the dawn of abundance.

In addition to all governmental and regulatory initiatives to drive accounting convergence in Brazil, a relevant part of this success is related to the professionals. Only with well-shaped professionals the change and its institutionalization tend to be smoother. This brings our attention, again, to Accounting Education. The scenario is related to the Accounting Education global situation (see Global Accountancy Education 2012 report, developed with our participation — Karreman 2013).

A clear claim to move from the technical-oriented curriculum, typical in Brazil, to a more humanist and open-minded approach must be made. The IFRS move requires less technical interpretation of rules and more business acumen to cope with the less-structured environment. Many Brazilian universities and colleges have already implemented specific changes, so that they can deal with the new context. But, challenges are big and so is Brazil. When you consider that in Brazil we have over 1,200 undergraduate programs in Accounting, a bit over 3,500 Master's degree holders (in Accounting), and short of 300 Ph.D. holders in Accounting, we can start to see the picture. The change must affect the graduate programs first and it is. In the recent past (up to 2007) there was only one Ph.D. program in Accounting in Brazil (hosted by University of Sao Paulo) and only three Master's programs in Accounting in Brazil (University of Sao Paulo, State University of Rio de Janeiro and Catholic University of Sao Paulo). Thus, most of the faculty members working in the undergraduate system did not have academic credentials for the program, naturally gearing up technical aspects in the curriculum. By the end of 2013, 21 graduate programs (nine PhD granting programs), in Accounting, were accredited by the Brazilian Ministry of Education. ANPCONT (Brazilian Association of Graduate Programs in Accounting) was created to act as a binding organization to help the development of this academic field in Brazil. This amazing expansion is well controlled by the Brazilian accrediting agency (CAPES) and is fully linked to support the advances in our field. But, changing mindset takes time. One thing is the expansion of Brazilian graduate system, another is adjusting the frames of references of those involved with accounting, to a new era.

New institutions with specific models, ventures, strategies, capitals and technology are organized to be part of a new marketplace of inputs, goods, services, and capitals. This marketplace is also populated by individuals, new people, new profiles, bringing different approaches based on gender, generations, dreams, social, cultural and political aspects. This scenario is directly linked to the education system, requiring this new frame of reference. Both, faculty members and students must be aware of such condition, and willing to commit energy to change our profession. It seems to be the case in Brazil, at least at top ranked institutions.

Changing an old mentality is mandatory when we consider accounting convergence. This resonates with a very different set of competencies and is achievable through reinvented accounting education. It is not only about changing your syllabus, textbooks or your cases: if the professor imposes the same old view about the problems, students will end up with an unwanted professional attitude. For instance, we must look at an M&A situation or even a revenue recognition issue, with a different pair of eyes. This is not only linked to IFRS, but to the entire reinvention of business with drastic implications for accounting.

The accounting curriculum is naturally a subject of concern when observing educational objectives and strategies all over the world. In Brazil, it is also the case, with instructional materials and teaching and learning approaches shaped by the existing socioeconomic and cultural set of aspects (i.e., language, business practices, discretionary income, working students/evening classes). The whole textbook industry requires special attention, as the Portuguese language market is way smaller then the English one. For instance, disadvantages (tired students) of evening classes must be outnumbered by its advantages (work experience). Stimulating environmental perception, continuous development, maintaining a global perspective and fostering continuous development are examples of curricular changes that are relevant for accounting convergence. Again, it is not only about the topics, but how to discuss them with students.

Another key element for accounting education is, for sure, critical thinking. In order to make the educational experience more meaningful for both, students and instructors, planning to use precious time to improve critical thinking is as mandatory as challenging. Being able to ask the reason behind an issue and setting the context in a clear fashion is part of such approach.

At University of Sao Paulo, our graduate program offers a research line in accounting education, which offers many opportunities for these discussions to advance. That is the case for experiments with educational interventions such as cases, gaming, simulation, history, critical thinking, neuroaccounting, program evaluation and online learning, with clear implications for accounting education.

As an example of capacity building at the professional level, the research foundation linked to the Department of Accounting and Actuarial Sciences at University of Sao Paulo (FIPECAFI) partnered with the Brazilian Institute of Internal Auditors (IBRACON) to cooperate with the Inter-American Development Bank (IDB) as providers of online education to reach at least one faculty member of each undergraduate program in accounting in Brazil (over 1,200 programs). A significant investment of money, time, structure and ideas to help narrowing the gap related to IFRS and the required education to new accountants in the country. Only an online education model could help achieve this within the time limitations and considering the continental geography of Brazil.

5 Concluding Remarks

The accounting profession is experiencing a period of significant change in Brazil with the adoption of the International Financial Reporting Standards (IFRS) in 2010. However, we can clearly see a strong national identity present in the financial statements of Brazilian companies. This phenomenon has connections with the preparers and the national background, aligned with the discussion present in the global accounting literature.

The departure from the Brazilian rule-based accounting in favor of a principles-based approach represents a major educational challenge for both faculty and students. We argue that the main challenge for the profession, in order to achieve the full (and real) convergence, is adequate accounting training and education. Capacity building for a wide range of major players (from preparers to auditors, researchers, professors, analysts, investors, media, regulators etc.) is mandatory and creative solutions to bring cost-effective quality to this process are welcome.

In this scenario, our chapter critically analyzed the adoption of IFRS in Brazil and argues that accounting education is and will be an important factor for success of IFRS in Brazil. In our view, education will be the key issue that is going to differentiate the full and complete adoption from the "Label Adoption" of IFRS.

In response to this new challenge, some Brazilian universities are revising their accounting curriculum in order to adapt to this new accounting environment. For instance, the University of São Paulo, which is ranked highest among the Brazilian universities in the World Rankings, has signed a cooperation agreement with the University of Illinois at Urbana-Champaign (USA) in order to implement their Project Discovery approach in Brazil. Such curriculum is set to help students develop a more critical view of accounting, which will empower them for this new society and business models.

At the educational level, it is a matter of balancing quantity and quality providers. If we move to the workplace, we are clearly seeing an evolving behavior of the organizations, concerned about accounting in a different fashion, and also the auditing firms, who are reshaping their approach, including selection and training, to cope with the new reality and the new generation of talents.

In addition, we must address the international mindset. As known, Brazil was behaving close to a "closed" economy for many years. However, recently Brazil has emerged and started operating in a true global environment, as a relevant player, with strong potential. In order to keep this move, it cannot refrain from having strong accountants and a strong accounting. Accounting helps the making of a stronger society.

Thus, as we tried to demonstrate, educational abundance, technological shift, accounting convergence, and an altered business model will, altogether, drive a different global profession. Resources are available and the need is assessed. So, the time is for big changes as the country is set for growth, with the help of a strengthened profession, based on overall social, political and financial consolidation.

References

Baer W (2008) The Brazilian economy, 6th edn. Lynne-Rienner, London

Brazil (1976) Corporate Law No. 6.404 of December 15, 1976. http://www.planalto.gov.br/ccivil_03/leis/l6404consol.htm

Brazil (2008) Law No. 11.638 of December 28, 2008. http://www.planalto.gov.br/ccivil_03/_ato2007-2010/2007/lei/l11638.htm

Brazil (2009) Law No. 11.941 of May 27, 2009. http://www.planalto.gov.br/ccivil_03/_ato2007-2010/2009/lei/l11941.htm

Brazilian Accounting Pronouncements Committee (*Comitê de Pronunciamentos Contábeis* – CPC) (2005) The Creation of the Brazilian Accounting Standard Setter http://www.cpc.org.br/CPC

Carvalho LN, Salotti BM (2013) Adoption of IFRS in Brazil and the consequences to accounting education. Iss Account Educ 28(2):235–242

Karreman GH (2013) GAE 2012 – dynamics of global accountancy education. Tilburg University, Tilburg, http://www.accaglobal.com/content/dam/acca/global/PDF-technical/other-PDFs/gae2012-dynamics-of-global-accountancy-education.pdf

Roett R (2010) The new Brazil. Brookings, Washington, DC

Russia. Can IFRS Be Considered Accounting?

Viatcheslav Sokolov

Indeed, there have to be factions among you
1 Corinthians 11–19

Abstract What are the drivers for, and barriers to, IFRS adoption? It is not the fact that people are lazy and conservative that represents the key deterrent for IFRS adoption, but the nature of this system of standards. IFRS should not be treated as a new global guidance to accounting. IFRS represent a new way of thinking, new qualification, and new practice. Russian accountants came to this conclusion largely due to the works of Jacques Richard, a lot of them being translated into Russian and very popular with the readers. The result of IFRS analysis from a traditional accounting standpoint leads to the following conclusion: this system is not an accounting system but a micro statistics one because of data collection and processing methods. IFRS, just like statistics, are aimed at providing information to external users the range of which is unlimited. Accounting is organized by a company itself and is intended primarily for the use by owners and managers. Apart from the information objective it has the objective of control. Irreducibility of IFRS to accounting methods mean that they cannot replace national accounting standards but can only add to it as a new form of statistics.

1 Prologue

I met with Jacques Richard in February 1992 when a Russian translation of his book was prepared for publication in Russia and the publishing house asked me to review the translation. With this task in mind I came to visit him in the university. The professor did not like the idea of the review. "I speak Russian myself." This is how our conversation started. I was impressed by many of Jacques Richard's ideas, they were highly original or, may be, at that time I did not understand French very well as that was my first visit to France. "You, Russians, took Schmalenbach's chart of accounts", and in Russian manuals one could read that this was a Soviet invention

V. Sokolov (✉)
St. Petersburg State Economic University, St. Petersburg, Russia
e-mail: vyacheslav.sokolov@ru.pwc.com

D. Bensadon, N. Praquin (eds.), *IFRS in a Global World*,
DOI 10.1007/978-3-319-28225-1_14

and in very good manuals—that the uniform chart of accounts in the USSR is the implementation of Dumarcher's ideas with whom my teacher, Professor Pomazkov was in active correspondence. Finally I came to the conclusion that Jacques Richard was an active IFRS supporter and did not think much of the French system. How wrong I was! At that time IFRS started their expansion into Russia and Richard's works, many of which had been translated into Russian, helped to correctly interpret IFRS and understand the reasons why the application of IFRS in this country had its restrictions.[1]

2 Introduction

Russia is a country of borrowings: it borrowed the Byzantine religion and Italian accounting system, the best known national dish was invented by a French cook and is called "Bœuf Stroganoff". Russian people usually think that they are right and that they are most advanced. In the sixteenth century under the rule of Ivan III, Moscow was proclaimed the Third Rome—head of Christian civilization. The West was announced to have lost Christianity, in Moscow foreigners lived separately from Russians in a kind of ghetto and chess playing was punished with death penalty. Under Lenin's rule, Moscow became the capital of the Third International and of communism that was proclaimed to be the future for all mankind. Again foreigners lived separately under KGB control, but chess playing received governmental support and the Russians achieved a great deal in it.

But sometimes, for instance under Peter the Great or Boris Yeltsin the Russians suddenly realized that they had considerably fallen behind the civilization and made attempts to import a great number of material and ideal facts. Accounting was no exception. Peter the Great invited German and Dutch accountants who were the first to apply the double entry method.

When I studied in a Soviet University we had a special course on the theory of accounting called "Differences in Accounting under socialism and capitalism", and Accounting under capitalism was proclaimed non-transparent and fraudulent. In our time IFRS are being borrowed as an advanced western accounting system and starting from 1990 announcements about the IFRS transition were made every 5 years. This is because (as Eduard Bernstein taught) "the final goal is nothing while the movement is everything" and the horizon which we are aiming at is removing when approached.

The first attempt to transit to "western Accounting" was to develop a new 1991 chart of accounts with the help of UN experts. After finalizing all necessary agreements the resultant rules had little to do with IFRS and the Government requested to develop accounting rules in accordance with IFRS. But by the end of

[1] My colleagues among Russian accountants especially like to cite Richard's following statement: "IFRS has no future and it follows that in a lot of ways they are outdated" [Richard, 2011: 7].

the 1990s, due to formation of a new legal system in this country, Accounting turned into an "algebra of law" (Pierre Garnier) of which it was free in the Soviet time. Thus Russian Accounting happened to depart even further from IFRS than the Soviet system did. The following decision worthy of Solomon was to narrow the gap between the two accounting systems: consolidated financial statements of issuers were to be prepared under IFRS and non-consolidated financial statements of individual legal entities under Russian rules.

What are the drivers for and barriers to IFRS adoption in Russia and in other countries?

It is not the fact that people are lazy and conservative that represents the key deterrent for IFRS adoption, but the nature of this system of standards. IFRS should not be treated as a new global guidance to Accounting. IFRS represent a new way of thinking, new qualification, and new practice. Russian accountants came to this conclusion largely due to the works of Jacques Richard, a lot of them being translated into Russian and very popular among readers. The following conclusion can be made as a result of IFRS analysis from the traditional accounting standpoint: this system is not an accounting system but macro statistics—by data collection and transfer method. IFRS, just like any statistics, are aimed at providing information to external users the range of which is unlimited. Accounting is organised by a company itself and is intended primarily for the use of owners and managers. Apart from information objectives, it has a control objective. Irreducibility of IFRS to accounting methods does not only mean that they cannot replace national rules, but also makes them unacceptable for Russian practice, though they are useful for purposes of communicating information to global markets.

3 IFRS Specifics from the Perspective of Accounting Tradition

International Financial Reporting Standards (IFRS) should not be treated as a new global guidance to accounting. IFRS represent a new way of thinking, new qualification, and new practice. Jacques Richard has defined IFRS rather concisely as actuarial Accounting (Richard 2005: 110). He demonstrated (Richard 2012: 26), that understanding of Accounting by different national schools can be expressed by a description of the word that names it. The Russian term "buchhalteria" is borrowed from the German language and means book-keeping or literally keeping, maintaining books. It highlights the accountant's role as an important administrator. The foreign word promotes its importance as all official (not ordinary) words in Russian are borrowed words. The German origin vests the word with reliability and presentability as in Russia the Germans were viewed as serious and positive people and even the Second World War did not change this view. At the turn of the XX century the Russian Accounting was under great influence of the French system: Leautey and Guilbault were invited to join the editorial board of the first Russian magazine on Accounting named as a calque of the French "Schetovodstvo" (Comptabilite). But the word "schetovodstvo" lost this game to "buchhalteria" as it was a calque or a translation with a Russian root and Russian roots sound informal to Russians. Assistant accountants started to be called "schetovod". This way Russia demonstrated that for it a book, a register, an entry and a statement of fact are more important than an account, a classification or interpretation of fact. This understanding of Accounting primarily as a system of registration being a basis for control has become traditional for Russia. By the way, the word "schet" ([chiotte] the Russian for account) has a variety of meanings and its accounting meaning is used least of all. The first meaning is mathematical—calculation and numeration, the second is business—invoice, bill and only the third one is compte, account—a classification attribute, accounting entry.

The subject of the traditional Accounting system[2] is an individual fact of business operations, and traditional Accounting is in charge of its registration, the classification of its processing and reviewing. The sequence and methods of these procedures are subject to certain regulations and rules and hence the traditional accounting regulation is known as a rule based accounting system. The Chart of accounts and the respective accounts correlation make the basis for these regulations. As for IFRS, the subject there is the whole financial statements, i.e. a set of certain indicators describing a business and primarily the trends of its operations. IFRS therefore does not govern the accounting process itself, but the results thereof by bringing together accounting data based not on strict regulations telling what should be done but on general rules describing the results of these procedures specifying quality requirements: so-called accounting principle. That is why, IFRS accounting regulations, in the strict sense, IFRS reporting regulations are called principle based regulations.

With a focus on the system of indicators describing a business, IFRS primarily look up to measuring changes in the financial results of the business, i.e. in its equity. That is why, under IFRS, only profit making, i.e. equity increasing assets are included into assets. Any liabilities, even of capital nature, are excluded from equity itself. For example, in a limited liability company, the contributions of founders do not shape equity as they are subject to repayment with the founders being entitled to claim the contribution pay-back at any time. If a company has property, plant and equipment which is not profit-making, then such PPE items are excluded from equity and the list of accounting subjects.

With the focus on measuring equity which is determined as assets less liabilities (which corresponds to the English rather than European tradition under which equity is a component of liabilities and equity, i.e. not a difference but a sum of sources (Richard 2011: 109). IFRS reflect not a range of events of business operations and far less individual events but a certain general financial position of an entity actually proved by average and estimated indicators. Such an approach, however, is typical not to Accounting but to statistics. It is a statistical estimation of

[2] See definition of this term in Richard (2012: 15–16).

business operations that represent "a description of a group of subjects in terms of their certain average qualities forming this group, i.e. in terms of qualities typical to some extend to a number of these individual subjects" (Pyatnitsyn 1976: 156). In statistics, estimation of resources is the identification of all those general features typical to the whole group of resources of a company, or a region, or the whole national economy. In this respect, statistical estimation is always an aggregate estimation. Although estimation of particular items in statistical observation is required, it is based on the concept that estimation of all items may not represent simply the total of individual estimates (Winshtein 1960: 83). Statistical estimations should "describe each business entity in a manner that allows to serve as the basis for the development of a group of economically similar and comparable indicators that can be summed up for the purpose of a summarised description of the whole production" (Rotstein 1932, p. 18). It is obvious, that this objective fully matches IFRS goals which are to provide information acceptable for making business decisions, and a sample list of decisions specified there[3] indicates that IFRS do not represent an accounting system but a microstatistic system, statistics of a financial item (a group of companies); they do not represent accounting regulations, but statistical reports prepared through the processing of accounting data. The accounting subject matter ends up with the statements, while the IFRS subject matter starts with them. Accounting studies the way of observing and recording events, evaluating and classifying them. But IFRS, as they may be interpreted, represent data collection and recognition. In this case, the core of Accounting remains behind the scene, out of interest and sometimes out of understanding of those who use IFRS. That is why, in the future, the word "traditional" may be excluded from "traditional accounting" leaving it simply as "accounting", since Accounting is always traditional, and may be state it just like "Accounting and IFRS".

4 Accounting and IFRS

There is much in common between IFRS and Accounting. According to J.F. Schär, Accounting is also a type of statistics[4]: items subject to observation are facts of business operations. Accounting and Statistics apply such general procedures as observation, grouping, consolidation, and finally preparation of statements. IFRS statements are prepared on the basis of Accounting. This does not make Accounting and IFRS equal. After all, as St. John Chrysostom said, "we have nothing in common with the Devil only, however we have much in common with all other

---

[3] Framework for the preparation and presentation of financial statements.

[4] "Accounting is applied statistics", J.F. Schär wrote, "as it functions as a self-controller of the situation, on the one hand, and on the other hand, reveals" the change in values, their cause and effect (quotation by Ivanov 1915, p. 101).

people".[5] The main challenge in the use of accounting data when preparing IFRS statements, as a result of the current records, lies in the difference between estimates applied. Accounting estimates are individual, while IFRS estimates are aggregated as a rule. For example, impairment is measured for a whole group of assets, e.g. PPE, but not for a separate item the value of which is not decreased in accounting record. Thereby, evaluation and interpretation of events by Accounting and IFRS are different in their nature: Accounting measures individually every event of business operations, while IFRS treat a group of individual events integrated into lines of the financial statements. This group is considered to be a new event. The group is not just a set of components. In addition, it has a whole number of original features.

IFRS express, above all, interests of investors and financial analysts rendering them advisory services. It is no coincidence that IFRS are called "instruments of speculative financial capitalism" (Capron 2005: 17). These users promote the idea of transparency of the statements, and transparency as they understand it, "ignoring the requirements of other type users" (Capron 2005: 16). Transparency is more a category of statistical reporting than of Accounting. In a way, it contradicts the principle of verifiability. In Accounting, verifiability is one of the inherent principles of preparing statements, the condition of fair presentation of the statements. "A verifiable accounting system is that which is subject to regulations" (Colasse 1991: 357). In IFRS, verifiability does not serve as an original (key) concept. The current version of IFRS ignores it. The results here consist of the possibility of reaching a consensus by different users able to estimate the statements in various terms, as well as of eliminating the application of a single criterion for such estimation, i.e. of no detailed regulations available (IASB (2006) Discussion Paper: QC23). To achieve transparency, IFRS suggest using a pure statistical approach. Statistical data itself is treated as a priori true, and if its reliability is open to question, then the trouble is with data collection methods, not with final numbers. Therefore users focus on the principles of arranging the process, rather than the regulated process itself: Accounting based on principles/framework, not regulations, thus more of statistics rather than of accounting nature.

IFRS require the preparation of primarily consolidated financial statements, more precisely consolidated statements, not the stand-alone statements of an entity. IFRS regulate above all consolidation procedures, not the statements preparation itself. Most of IFRS rules cover consolidation matters. Therefore, unlike Accounting, IFRS provide data processing starting from figures and moving towards events. The figures themselves represent aggregated data of a group of companies, of the business of the group and are governed by the law of large numbers. It is assumed that a large number of accidental events, under certain stable conditions, provide results having almost no impact from the accident. In this respect, the effect of certain immaterial indicators or elements of indicators on statements may be ignored.

[5] Quotation Kuraev 1997, p. 28.

The key IFRS rule is materiality. As opposed to Accounting which analyses all facts and their recognition regardless of their estimation, IFRS take into account only those facts that may impact the decision making process. Those companies that have no significant effect on the major group results may not be consolidated or may be consolidated with deviation. With materiality being the key rule, the IFRS main method applied is calculation, while recognition is the main method of Accounting. Calculation in Accounting is limited enough. It is basically used in calculation procedures, inventory valuation, and some other cases. But the role of calculation has been extended by IFRS: almost all balance sheet items are calculated using methods of mathematical statistics. Enough is to say that an IFRS accountant makes the following calculations: a) pension benefit payments using actuarial methods; b) bonus payment liabilities, i.e. discounts, customer incentive programmes, loyal client cards, etc.; c) possible future or contingent liabilities (based on the possibility of the latter, deferred tax liabilities or tax assets); d) PPE impairment, balance sheet items discounting if these items are affected by the modification of purchasing power of a currency unit; e) inflation impact on the balance sheet. The purpose of Accounting is not the calculation but the record of facts targeted to provide users with information and keep the information safe. In Accounting, estimates are of historical nature as they are not calculated but are taken from other sources. "Accounting,—Leitner wrote,—does not estimate itself. It does not produce any estimation by itself but borrows them. It only records them." (Leitner 1923: ss. 47–48).

IFRS developers governed by economists rather than accountants were taken captive by the resource theory. In full concordance with this theory IFRS consistently follow an economic definition of property as a complex of resources,[6] gaining profit regardless of property rights. While control over resources is not the same as control over property or funds. IFRS care about the availability of benefit-bringing property, not about respective ownership rights. Assets under lease may be included into PPE of the company operating them. At the same time, assets owned by the company and actually available may be excluded from the balance sheet if they are not profit-making, i.e. are not treated as resources (like the majority of pre-paid expenses). The resource structure is wider than the structure of items recorded in Accounting. It also includes the company's goodwill, its trademark, client base. Even if resources are owned by another company but are used by the group of companies, they may be included into the group's assets. In 2006, IFRS Interpretations Committee proposed introducing criteria under which, in the consolidated financial statements, recorded expenses for outsourcing would be replaced by the capitalisation of funds of such outsourcing companies where services of such companies are treated not as works under contract but as the acquisition of an entity. Such criteria include the transfer of ownership title for outsourcing

[6] According to the framework of IFRS reporting, assets are defined as follows: "resources controlled by an entity as a result of events of previous periods where the entity expects economic benefit in the future" (IASB (2001) Framework: 49).

company's assets used when rendering services to the customer, and the use of outsourcing to gain benefit from a synergy effect reached out of joined efforts of the two companies and from increased efficiency of the assets used (Stallings and Moussy 2006: 4).

Under IFRS, contingent assets are also included into resources. Before that, such assets were only described in the notes when there was a high probability of getting respective assets in the future, which highlights even more their statistical nature. Resources also include human capital of course. Today many specialists request that the value of human capital be included into the assets of a Company (Wallman 1996; Westphalen 1999; Eccles et al. 2002), some authors recommend describing human capital value in the notes if capitalization in the balance sheet is not allowed (Obert 1996: 25). Human resource capitalisation is possible both through the estimation of expenses for staff training and estimation of benefits by the capitalisation of income per employee or the cost of innovations the employee has made (the latter is of more importance for research or consulting companies) (Tournier 2000: 114). The only difficulty in identifying a new subject of Accounting is not the unavailability of ownership right for staff, but no possibility to maintain total control over them (e.g. preventing them from changing job). It is obvious that this approach is of purely statistical nature. As a rule, statistics reviews resources available in terms of industry, region, and state as a whole regardless of resources ownership. The same approach is used by IFRS where resources operated, i.e. controlled by the group of companies, are consolidated in case the group prepares IFRS financial statements. According to Pierre Garnier, the purpose of Accounting is also to "establish a legal basis for the facts of business operations" (Garnier 1975: 394). Accounting should not ignore issues of ownership and the legal structure of an entity and its transactions. The transition from Accounting of items to the records of resources results in the classification of IFRS accounting subjects in accordance with their use, but not their nature. IFRS stipulate that the functions of one and the same item may modify in the course of its operation according to intentions of administration or owners. For example, if there is a decision to sell PPE items, then such items should be immediately transferred from PPE to current assets. Under IFRS, costs are registered primarily in terms of resources, and expenses are classified by cost components, i.e. by types of resources consumed, while Accounting provides for recording according to the purposes of use and location of costs.

Transition from a legal definition of assets, where assets are described as property, to an economic one, where assets are treated as resources used by a company itself and by controlled entities, results in changes in the concept of liabilities if compared to that of traditional Accounting. Equity of a company and even its share capital are divided into equity capital and raised capital. Equity capital includes only equity financial instruments which are issued provided that the following conditions are fulfilled simultaneously. Firstly, there are no contractual obligations for their repurchase on conditions unfavourable to the issuer. Secondly, these instruments are not options or other derivatives providing the transfer of other equity instruments in the future. For example, preferred stock subject to exchange for common stock will be likely recorded as accounts payable of the issuer as the exchange is usually done on terms favourable to shareholders. Limited liability companies and various partnership associations have no equity at all as their contributions represent a direct ownership share of participants and partners which may take it back. Accordingly, IFRS provide that such companies should show accounts payable to owners instead of equity.

Accounting and IFRS also differ in their approach to the time of events. Accounting provides continuous registration of events of business operations. The registration is done indirectly, based on a system of both external and internal documents. Even direct observation during a stock-count will be recorded (described) in accounting only using a stock-count sheet which unfortunately is not always a result of direct observation. Accounting does not record the facts of business operations—phenomena, but the noumena i.e. accounting events, only those events and only as to their part, where they are subjects of the accountant's reasoning which itself is "not positive and does not represent any knowledge about certain matter, but represents an idea about something in general which takes me away from any form of sensual contemplation" (Kant 1787: 721). The time of recording an event, not the actual time of the event itself, is more important and natural for the Accounting. Accounting records all accounting facts as they arise, i.e. as information on underlying facts becomes available. These facts are facts of business operations. For example, annual leave payments are recorded during the month when they were charged, i.e. the period of preparing a pay order, not in the period an employee has got the right to take an annual leave. Balance sheet is primarily of an accounting nature. It represents a synthesis of balances of open accounts, i.e. it is based on registered facts, not facts in general. This balance sheet is not adjusted neither by additional events such as deferred taxes or events detected after the reported period, nor by calculations such as adjustments for inflation or discounting. Adjustments due to the results of stock-taking do not modify the accounting nature of the balance sheet as stock-taking is not a tool for preparing a balance sheet. It is a tool used to verify accounts, correct errors in time and prevent a significant gap between accounting records and facts of business operation. All errors identified in accounting are corrected at the moment of their identification but not at the moment the errors were made. The latter is impossible as accounting represents time-based registration procedures which do not allow moving backwards. Retrospective correction or rewriting the register book is treated as fraud and forgery. Retrospective adjustments are well described by Orwell. The official duty of the main character of "1984" Winston Smith was to re-write old newspapers in line with the new party policies.

5 IFRS Is Micro-statistics

IFRS are a set of rules for the preparation of statements, a set of data of accounting records. This set may be applied at any time in relation to the balance sheet day. To prepare the statements for a 3-years-ago period is not only a regular thing but a necessity as the statements should have comparative date of the previous periods. When statements are prepared, all events known by that moment are taken into account. They serve as the basis for additional calculations. When errors are identified, the statements are reissued, i.e. are prepared over again with respective corrections, and previous statements are considered to be incorrect and invalid, i.e. as if they had not existed before. It is obvious that here we see a statistical not an accounting approach: the data are disavowed and new tables are prepared to be filled in. In IFRS, as well as in statistics, "the purpose of every figure identified is to make a comparison. That is why statistical processing of expenses should always deliver comparability..." (Schumpeter 1982: 192), that is why each amendment to accounting policy is recorded retrospectively: past periods' data are recalculated, and opening balances are updated. In addition, IFRS allow not only the reissue of past period statements, but require it for the purpose of error correction. We may say that IFRS repeat Orwell's statement who said "Who controls the past controls the future: who controls the present controls the past", while Accounting, following H. Hesse, states that "the past is passed". It is obvious that it is possible to update statistical data and tables, but, in this case, the links with documentary recording and the link of the statements with continuous registration will be broken.

That is why Accounting has deliberately ignored the most important requirement of the statistics which is comparability of items observed and time periods. Temporal comparability of estimates is not reached due to the impossibility of permanent re-estimation (frequency of observation in Accounting is much less than that of statistics. Observation in Accounting may be considered to be continuous in a way) and the use of prices of the previous periods, which does not allow measuring the trends of the volume of items in accordance with accounting data. Comparability of estimates on certain items is also not provided by Accounting due to the dependence of the latter on the value of a currency unit which changes in the course of time. The principle of comparability requires maintaining estimates unchanged for any assets flow both inside and outside a company, for compensation-free transfer as well as for sales. Such an approach is natural for statistics as it estimates the total value of national wealth. The location of its individual elements does not impact the total amount. But, as for Accounting, such accounting procedures defeat the purpose of the balance sheet and accounts, which cease to reflect the results of an entity and start to show past expenses of other entities new owners may not be responsible for.

Probabilistic nature of accounting data is another source of incomparability. An accounting estimate, just like any other estimate, has a certain level of probability. Meanwhile, even a cash estimate cannot have the probability level of 1. Estimates of all other asset items are unlikely to be viewed as a certainty. The accounting treatment of contingencies serves as evidence of the probabilistic nature: highly probable contingent events are recognised on the balance sheet and less probable are disclosed in the explanatory note, while unlikely events are ignored. Reliability of accounting estimates may be improved by way of reducing their accuracy. However, such an improvement of reliability will nullify the value of accounting information and therefore cannot be accepted. Attempts to improve the accuracy of accounting very often just illustrate the well known statements of C. Gauss: "The lack of mathematical education is most obviously revealed in the excessive accuracy of numerical expressions" (Citation for Morgenstern 1986: 96). For elimination of probabilistic incomparability of accounting data O. Morgenstern proposed using expected value of company assets instead of their accounting value. "Comparability of balance sheets of different entities,—he wrote,—can be achieved to the extent that each of them indicates probabilities that it uses. This provision is valid if the above probabilities are not interdependent" (Morgenstern 1986: 76–77). Such average estimates are more and more widely and universally applied in IFRS under the name of "fair value". The fair value has become the IFRS basis just like average amounts are the basis of statistics.

Finally, IFRS and Accounting have different goals. IFRS, just like any statistics, are aimed at providing information to external users the range of which is unlimited. Accounting is organised by a company itself and is intended primarily for the use by owners and managers. Apart from the information objective it has the objective of control. By its mere existence Accounting warns and by identifying errors and fraud it monitors actions of various agents and correspondents of the company, and in this function it also differs from IFRS. It is no mere chance that IFRS do not consider issues related to documentation, appropriateness of this or that transaction, do not regulate the chart of accounts or accounting system; IFRS has abandoned accounting terminology. It is impossible to imagine a double entry accounting without a balance sheet, and IFRS disposed of the term and replaced it with "Statement of financial position". Meanwhile the new Statement itself is a slightly changed but practically traditional form of a balance sheet for England. The saying: "Is there anything of which it may be said, "See, this is new"? It has already been in ancient times before us" (Ekklesiastes, 1–10). The term "statement" (report) is common for statistical terminology that includes various, one may say any kind of reports, while accounting terminology is traditionally more accurate: accounting reports traditionally include (unfortunately not always and not everywhere) not reports but a balance sheet, a profit and loss account, explanatory note. From an accounting perspective, a "new report" is perfectly described by the following words of C. Pobedonostsev: "There are terms that have been wiped out to banality as they have been used on end without a particular thought behind them, as one could hear them everywhere from anyone; and when saying such a term, a fool imagines that he is wise, a barbarian sees himself at the top of the knowledge building. A widely used word may become such a banality that a serious man may be ashamed to use it as he feels that when articulated such a word reflects all idle and vulgar ideas with which it had become associated in the market of trivial words» (Pobedonostsev 1996: 343).

The refusal from terminology means the refusal from science. The rush for an external understandability and the wish to be only the supplier of figures highlight the final transfer of IFRS from the area of accounting to the area of statistics.

6 Conclusion

The history of accounting for many centuries shows its ability to absorb many economic and legal theories while remaining on the whole traditional and recognizable: over the last 500 years the double entry did not change, only the name of the balance sheet changed. Meanwhile the form and content of financial statements, certain methods of their preparation have been changing. In the Middle Ages people had more trust in verbal evidence—hence audit was a verbal process, then paper became the dominant evidence and now it is giving place to electronic information media. Nevertheless the essence of Accounting, i.e. registration of business facts in their economic measurement and their subsequent treatment and control, remains the core of our science. The works of Professor Jacques Richard witness this indisputable fact.

His analysis of national accounting systems (Richard 1999) shows that their diverse nature is rooted in divergent economic systems. But, not only. The very concept of Accounting itself is largely a function of cultural stereotypes, which manifest themselves through language (Richard 2010). The juncture between culture and economic systems in various historical eras has given shape to a variety of different accounting methods and procedures. Economic globalisation, which incidentally has progressed hand in hand with the spread of English, has given rise to the system known as International Financial Reporting Standards (IFRS), frequently referred to as the “Anglo-Saxon” model. But, nevertheless, this latter system arose firmly within the confines of traditional Accounting. IFRS is truly a child of globalisation. It would not be accurate to equate it with a national accounting system. In general, it [IFRS] is not a type of accounting per se, but rather represents a form of micro-statistics—a collection of data on a group of enterprises, primarily a group of transnational enterprises, part of which is based in various ordinary accounting systems, for example Russian or French accounting, etc. An understanding of the correlation between IFRS and accounting is extremely critical both for the purposes of day-to-day accounting practice and for developing its theoretical basis. In practice, an awareness of the differences between IFRS and Accounting can help in overcoming internal resistance, often at the psychological level, among accountants to the introduction of IFRS. The latter point is especially important for my country, where essentially two groups of specialists have taken shape, which not only do not understand each other, but also carry out training in entirely different ways, [while] quality instruction in IFRS is conducted in English. But, their adversarial relationship would disappear if they understood that they are carrying out essentially different functions. In theoretical research, the acknowledgement that IFRS is not a new theory of Accounting, but rather an entirely new discipline would make it possible to expand the scope of research studies, many of which are currently terminated or remain unfunded due to their "unpromising nature".

References

Capron M (ed) (2005) Les normes comptables internationales instruments du capitalisme financier. La Découverte, Paris

Colasse B (1991) Comptabilité générale, 3rd edn. Economica, Paris

Eccles RG, Hertz RH, Keegan M, Phillips DMH (2002) The Value Reporting Revolution: How to speak with capital market in the language of value, not the language of profit. Translated from English, Moscow: Olymp-Business; Экклз Р.Дж., Герц Р.Х. Киган Э. М. Филлипс Д.М.Х. (2002). Революция в корпоративной отчетности: как разговаривать с рынком капитала на языке стоимости, а не прибыли

Garnier P (1975) Comptabilité commerciale. Comptabilité générale, Paris

IASB (2001) Framework for the preparation and presentation of financial statements

IASB (2006) Discussion paper preliminary views on an improved conceptual framework for financial reporting: the objective of financial reporting and qualitative characteristics of decision-useful financial reporting information (Comments to be received by 3 November 2006)

Ivanov S (1915-16) Essays on accounting and business statistics Commercial school and life. № 4, p. 101 Иванов С. Очерки по счетоводно-хозяйственнной статистике «Коммерческая школа и жизнь»

Kant I (1787) Critique of pure reason. Moscow: Mysl, v. 3; Кант И. Критика чистого разума, 1964

Kuraev A (1997) Challenge of oecumenicity. Moscow: Blagovest; Кураев А. Д. (1997) Вызов экуменизма. Благовест

Leitner F (1923) Bilanztechnik und Bilanzkritik II. band des Grundrisses der Buchhaltung und Bilanzkunde-Berlin-Leipzig, 1923

Morgenstern O (1986) About accuracy of economic observations. Translated from English, Moscow: Statistika. Моргенштерн О. О точности экономико-статистических наблюдений

Obert R (1996) Comptabilité approfondie et révision, Corrigés du manuel. Dunod, Paris

Pobedonostsev KP (1996) Illnesses of our time. Works, St Petersburg : Nauka, Победоносцев К.П. Болезни нашего времени

Pyatnitsyn BN (1976) Philosophical issues of probabilistic and statistical methods. Moscow: Nauka. Пятницын Б.Н. Философские проблемы вероятностных и статистических методов

Richard J (2012) Comptabilité et Développement Durable. Economica, Paris

Richard J (1999) Vingt ans de normalisation comptable française en Europe: grandeur ou décadence? Comptabilité-Contrôle-Audit. Tome 5, 223–232

Richard J (2005) Les trois stades du capitalisme comptable français. In: Capron M (ed) Les normes comptables internationales, instruments du capitalisme financier. La Découverte, Paris

Richard J (2010) Origines du mot comptabilité. Journées d'Histoire de la Comptabilité et du Management, France. http://halshs.archives-ouvertes.fr/docs/00/47/05/37/PDF/WPM_798B.pdf

Richard J (2011) Comptabilité financière. Dunod, Paris

Rotstein AI (1932) The basics of statistics of the social industry, Part 1. Moscow: Leningrad. Ротштейн А.И. Основы статистики социалистической промышленности

Schumpeter J (1982) Theory of economic development. Translation from German, Moscow: Progress. Шумпетер И. (1982) Теория экономического развития

Stallings D, Moussy M (2006) Outsourcing contracts: an accidental business combination? PWC IFRS News Marsh

Tournier J-C (2000) La révolution comptable. Du coût historique à la juste valeur. Edition d'Organisation, Paris

Wallman SMH (1996) The future of accounting and financial reporting, Part 2, The Colorized Approach // Accounting Horizons, № 10, 138–148

Westphalen S-A (1999) Reporting on human capital: objectives and trends. Amsterdam, June 9–10

Winshtein AL (1960) National economy and national accumulated funds in Russia before the Revolution. Moscow: Gosstatizdat of CSD (USSR). Вайнштейн А.Л. (1960). Народное хозяйство и народнохозяйственное накопление предреволюционной России

India. Convergence of International Financial Reporting Standards: An Analysis of Issues in Developed and Developing Economies

Himachalam Dasaraju and Mutyala Subramanyam

Abstract The present paper purports to review the existing International Accounting Standards (IAS) and convergence of International Financial Reporting Standards (IFRS) and its associated issues in developed and developing economies. This is intended to stimulate an academic debate on various issues pertaining to the IFRS in promoting good financial reporting standards in international business world. This paper is structured on the convergence mechanism regarding IFRS in the developing economies based on the existing practices. This uses both primary and secondary data for analysing the background and adoptability of IFRS in the developing countries, more so in Indian context. Further it examines the modus operandi and the practical difficulties in the implementation of IFRS. This examines the origin, development, road map, practical issues and emerging challenges in implementing IFRS in developing economies more particularly in India. This also offers some practicable solutions for overcoming major problems in India. This paper contributes much to the existing literature on IFRS in the world economy in general and in the developing economies in particular. As there is very trivial amount of research on the IFRS in India, this may be useful to the researchers, policy-makers, research bodies and corporate sector.

1 Introduction

The waves of economic reforms and globalization of various countries throughout the world have spread across the globe over the decades. There has been a sea saw change in the international trade and business across the countries, which paved the way for the new kind of global business, led to spreading of multinational companies, foreign investments and corporate governance mechanisms. This change necessitated new and comprehensive business information flows to enable foreign

H. Dasaraju (✉) • M. Subramanyam
REVA University, Bangalore, India
e-mail: dhchalam@gmail.com; drmutyala2013@gmail.com

D. Bensadon, N. Praquin (eds.), *IFRS in a Global World*,
DOI 10.1007/978-3-319-28225-1_15

investors and institutions to understand in a better way to spread their wings throughout the length and breadth of the world. The world has witnessed major changes in financial reporting, under which the most obvious is the continuing adoption of IFRS worldwide. The globalization of business made companies to follow consistent worldwide reporting standards. The IFRS fulfils this need with its inherent reliability, comparability and transparent nature of financial statements to facilitate enhanced cross-border business and investments and good corporate governance practices throughout the globe.

The Accounting has been growing and gaining importance leaps and bounds in terms of its structure and nature in global corporate world. Accounting as an efficient tool of financial assessment, is used in both households and corporate business units. The body of knowledge of accounting has expanded widely at an economic and organization level. An important area of research among the academicians and practitioners as well has been the international accounting. Doupnik and Perera (2007) explain international accounting as a functional epistemology and an integration of two concepts of International and accounting. The IFRS are set by the IASB and the process began by issuing International Accounting Standards since 1973. The underlying objective of both IFRS and IASB is to develop a globally acceptable accounting framework. This framework can be applied or converged with the accounting standards, principles, rules of individual country's accounting standard. Extending the framework to converge local accounting standards with IFRS, offers the opportunity to harmonize the accounting and reporting aspects across the world in the changed corporate global environment.

2 Historical Background of IFRS

The IFRS has gained importance and value across the countries in recent years. The origin of IFRS can be traced back to the beginning of 1970s when the International Accounting Standards Committee (IASC) developed a universally acceptable single set of International Standards. The Europe have initiated and introduced IFRS, first of its kind in the world in 1995 and it has spread to most of the developed and developing countries. It has initiated and also has transformed with the formation of International Accounting Standards Committee followed by first financial statements comparability project (1987), European Commission supports use of International Accounting Standards (IAS) by European Multinationals (1995), Norwalk agreement: FASB & IASB agree to remove differences between IFRS and US GAAP (2002), IFRS in effect for European and Australian companies (2005), SEC allows foreign companies to file IFRS without GAAP reconciliation (2007), SEC releases IFRS road map proposal (2008), Canada, Russia, China, India and other countries plan to complete their IFRS transition (2011) and United States adoption of IFRS (2014). All the countries both developed and developing in nature are at it to adopt IFRS to strengthen their accounting information base. Now more than 100 economies have effectively converged in the IFRS.

The International Accounting Standards Board (IASB) has issued a set of financial reporting standards which are recognized under the brand name International Financial Reporting Standards (IFRS). The IFRS is a trade mark of the International Accounting Standards Committee Foundation. Generally it requires more disclosures than most countries' local GAAP requirements. The International Accounting Standards Board (IASB) and its predecessor, the International Accounting Standards Committee, have worked since early 1970s to develop a single set of globally acceptable international standards. The IFRS have gained acceptance and traction in all major regions of the world. Since 2005, the global corporate financial reporting landscape has been transformed in a big way across the countries. Good number of countries and enterprises around the world adopted international financial reporting standards (IFRS) as basis for the preparation of financial statements. All the member States of the European Union have adopted IFRS endorsed in the European Union for the preparation of consolidated financial statements of listed companies in their respective jurisdictions. The benefits of a common set of high-quality financial reporting standards are very significant. Nevertheless, depending on the general economic situation, existing regulatory framework and financial reporting tradition of a given member States, practical implementation of IFRS poses considerable challenges. These practical challenges relate to the coherence of the regulatory framework and the state of preparation of relevant institutions, enforcement and technical capacity (United Nations Conference on Trade and Development (UNCTAD) 2008).

To bridge the gap between accounting standards among countries, the International Accounting Standards Committee (IASC) was founded in 1973 by a group of professional accounting practitioners with an attempt to formulate a uniform and global accounting standards that would aim at reducing the discrepancies in international accounting principles and reporting practices. In this light, the International Accounting Standard (IAS) was proposed which has actively been championing the uniformity and standardization of accounting principles over two decades now (Carlson 1997). Meanwhile, in April 2001, the International Accounting Standards Board (IASB) took over the setting of International Accounting Standards from the International Accounting Standard (IASC). Henceforth, the IASB updated the already existing International Accounting Standard (IAS) and referred to them as the International Financial Reporting Standards (IFRS). This study uses Ghana as a typical case of a developing economy adopted the International Financial Reporting Standards.

In January, 2007, the Minister of Finance and Economic Planning—Ghana formally launched the adoption of IFRS. By December 2007, listed companies, government business enterprises, banks, insurance companies, securities brokers, pension and investment banks and public utilities are expected to prepare their financial statements in accordance with the IFRS. In an address to the participants at the launching, the minister referred to a report on Observance of Standards and Codes (ROSC) on Ghana that the world bank issued in March 2006, and noted that "the adoption of IFRS would address certain weaknesses the ROSC of Ghana has identified" (UN 2007).

Adoption by various countries in the World

Nation	Legal adoption	Effective dates	Estimated number of accounting professionals	Cost per company
Armenia	2008	2011	853 licensed	N/A
Austria	2002	2005–2007	Up to 141,000	0.31 % of Turnover in small companies to 0.05 % of Turnover in large companies
Azerbaijan	2004	2006–2008	Over 200 licensed accountants and over 50 audit firms	N/A
Belarus	2007	2008	Up to 110,000	N/A
Belgium	2002	2005–2007	Up to 156,000	0.31 % of Turnover in small companies to 0.05 % of Turnover in large companies
Bulgaria	2002	2003–2007	Over 680 licensed	0.31 % of Turnover in small companies to 0.05 % of Turnover in large companies
Canada	2006	2011	Up to 627,000	68 % state less than $500,000. 22 % state between $500,000–$5,000,000. 5 % state over $5,000,000, and 5 % unknown
Croatia	2007	2010	Up to 30,000	N/A
Cyprus	1981	1981	Up to 16,000	0.31 % of Turnover in small companies to 0.05 % of Turnover in large companies
Czech Republic	2002	2005–2007	Up to 5200 accountants and 300 audit firms	0.31 % of Turnover in small companies to 0.05 % of Turnover in large companies
Denmark	2002	2005–2007	Up to 141,000	0.31 % of Turnover in small companies to 0.05 % of Turnover in large companies
Estonia	2002	2005–2007	Up to 400 auditors and 50 audit firms	0.31 % of Turnover in small companies to 0.05 % of Turnover in large companies
Finland	2002	2005–2007	Up to 117,000	0.31 % of Turnover in small companies to 0.05 % of Turnover in large companies
France	2002	2005–2007	Up to 745,000	0.31 % of Turnover in small companies to 0.05 % of Turnover in large companies
Georgia	2005	2005–2006	~20,000	N/A
Germany	2002	2005–2007	Up to 402,000	0.31 % of Turnover in small companies to 0.05 % of Turnover in large companies

(continued)

Nation	Legal adoption	Effective dates	Estimated number of accounting professionals	Cost per company
Greece	2002	2005–2007	Up to 83,000	0.31 % of Turnover in small companies to 0.05 % of Turnover in large companies
Hungary	2002	2005–2007	Over 5700 auditors and over 1800 audit firms	0.31 % of Turnover in small companies to 0.05 % of Turnover in large companies
Iceland	2002	2005–2007	Up to 5300	0.31 % of Turnover in small companies to 0.05 % of Turnover in large companies
India	2010	2011–2014	Over 110,000 licensed accountants and over 53,000 audit firms	N/A
Ireland	2002	2005–2007	Up to 24,000	0.31 % of Turnover in small companies to 0.05 % of Turnover in large companies
Italy	2002	2005–2007	Up to 1,060,000	0.31 % of Turnover in small companies to 0.05 % of Turnover in large companies
Japan	2009	2010	Up to 65,000	N/A
Kazakhstan	2002	2004–2006	Up to 1500 licensed	N/A
Kyrgyzstan	2002	2007	Up to 1130 licensed	N/A
Latvia	2002	2005–2007	Over 200 licensed	0.31 % of Turnover in small companies to 0.05 % of Turnover in large companies
Lithuania	2002	2005–2007	Up to 44,000	0.31 % of Turnover in small companies to 0.05 % of Turnover in large companies
Luxembourg	2002	2005–2007	Up to 12,000	0.31 % of Turnover in small companies to 0.05 % of Turnover in large companies
Moldova	2008	2012	Up to 1000	N/A
Netherlands	2002	2005–2007	Up to 407,000	0.31 % of Turnover in small companies to 0.05 % of Turnover in large companies
Norway	2002	2005–2007	Up to 137,000	0.31 % of Turnover in small companies to 0.05 % of Turnover in large companies
Poland	2002	2005–2007	Up to 37,000	0.31 % of Turnover in small companies to 0.05 % of Turnover in large companies
Portugal	2002	2005–2007	Up to 86,000	0.31 % of Turnover in small companies to 0.05 % of Turnover in large companies

(continued)

Nation	Legal adoption	Effective dates	Estimated number of accounting professionals	Cost per company
Romania	2002	2005–2007	Over 2400 auditors and 20,000 accountants	0.31 % of Turnover in small companies to 0.05 % of Turnover in large companies
Russia	2011	2012	3,500,000	5000–140,000 USD
Serbia	2002	2004	Over 30,000	N/A
Slovakia	2002	2005–2007	Up to 64,000	0.31 % of Turnover in small companies to 0.05 % of Turnover in large companies
Slovenia	2002	2005–2007	Over 500 auditors and 40 audit firms	0.31 % of Turnover in small companies to 0.05 % of Turnover in large companies
South Korea	2006	2009—2011	Over 6400 auditors and 10,400 companies that require audits	N/A
Spain	2002	2005–2007	Up to 503,000	0.31 % of Turnover in small companies to 0.05 % of Turnover in large companies
Sweden	2002	2005–2007	Up to 321,000	0.31 % of Turnover in small companies to 0.05 % of Turnover in large companies
Tajikistan	2002	2004–2007	200 licensed	N/A
Turkey	2005	2008	Over 64,000	N/A
Turkmenistan	2010	2011–2014	Over 300 licensed	N/A
United Kingdom	2002	2005–2007	265,000	0.31 % of Turnover in small companies to 0.05 % of Turnover in large companies
United States	2008	2011–2015	1,290,600	0.125 % to 0.13 % of revenue

Source: Researcher Compilation & http://msfz.minfin.gov.ua/en/IfrsOtherCountries/About IFRS in other Countries/Pages/List Countries Using IFRS.aspx

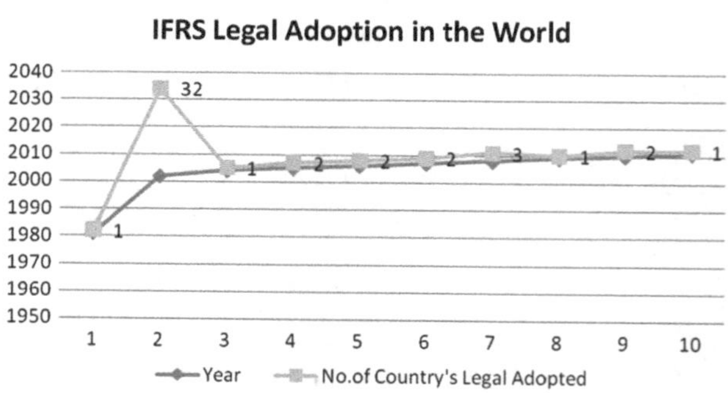

Legal Adoption This is the year when the national government decided that IFRS would be the appropriate method for financial reporting.

Effective Date(s) This is the year or range of years when the nation required that IFRS began being used as the method for financial reporting. This date, in comparison to the adoption date, allows for a comparison between countries that allowed the same timeframe for implementation. Effective dates can be a range in some countries based upon the legal requirements for certain types of entities (banks, public companies, etc.)

Cost Per Company This is the best available data for the costs expected to be incurred by companies that are required to implement IFRS.

Estimated Number of Accounting Professionals This data reflects the number of accounting-related individuals or entities in the labour force of each nation. The purpose of submitting this data is to provide Minimum Financial with an appropriate gauge for identifying other nations with a similar amount of accounting professionals that would require IFRS training and/or that may deal with a national regulator on accounting issues. The methodology to determine these figures was to first use the sum of the explicitly stated number of registered/certified/licensed accounting professionals in Reports on the Observance of Standards and Codes (ROSC) reports. If the nation did not have a World Bank ROSC, the figures were taken directly from national statistics agencies/bureaus or media reports.

2.1 Origin and Rationale for IFRS Convergence

The issue of convergence with the International Financial Reporting Standards (IFRS) has been a subject of increasing academic debate (Chua and Taylor 2008; Irvine 2008; Rodrigues and Craig 2007; Perera and Baydoun 2007; Chand and White 2007; Hernandez et al. 2007; Weetman 2006; Harverty 2006; Lewis and Salter 2006; Jemakowicz and Tomaszewski 2006; Fontes et al. 2005; IFAC 2004; Larson and Street 2004; Street and Larson 2004; Stolowy et al. 2006; Cairns and Nobes 2000). The question of whether all countries should adopt a single global accounting standard seems to be a foregone conclusion. However, the issue that is increasingly debated is the process of convergence.

- Worldwide convergence on international standards for financial reporting will make investment and financial reporting more efficient.
- Investors gain access to more investment opportunities and the cost of capital comes down.
- As more countries use International Financial Reporting Standards (IFRS), so international groups can use them for subsidiary reporting and group reporting.
- The International Accounting Standards Committee, the international standard-setter, came into existence in 1973 as an initiative by the accounting profession to address the emerging needs of cross border business.

- The standard-setter negotiated a role with the international co-ordinator of stock exchange regulators as a supplier of rules for secondary listings.
- The International Accounting Standards Board, the successor body, was created in 2000 at the time when the European Union announced it would adopt IFRS for listed companies.
- IFRS are now mandatory or permitted in more than 100 countries. China, Japan, India, Canada, Brazil, and South Korea are set to adopt IFRS in 2011.

The IFAC (2004) explored the challenges and successes in implementing IFRS and observed that achieving international convergence, however, requires more than theoretical support. It requires reaching consensus as to the international standards that will serve as the foundation for financial reporting and auditing globally, determining how to facilitate the adoption of those standards and ultimately, taking the actions necessary to encourage implementation.

The benefits of a global financial reporting framework are numerous and include:

- Greater comparability of financial information for investors
- Greater willingness on the part of investors to invest across borders;
- Lower cost of capital;
- More efficient allocation of resources; and
- Greater economic growth.

Countries and entities adopt IFRS for various reasons, the most common being 'to eliminate barriers to cross-border investing, to increase the reliability, transparency and comparability of financial reports, to increase market efficiency, and to decrease the cost of capital' (Brown 2011: 272). The reasons for adopting IAS/IFRS in various countries in the world and the expected benefits are often expressed in more general terms, and usually are related to economic development. King et al. (2001) indicate that the main objectives were to move rapidly to a market economy and to attract foreign investment by developing a credible and transparent accounting system that provides users, including managers, with good accounting information for decision making.

Advantages to Developing Nations of Harmonizing on IFRS Include The elimination or reduction of set-up costs in developing national accounting standards; the potential for rapid national improvement in the perceived quality and status of financial reports; increases in market efficiency in (inter)national financial markets through the provision of more understandable, comparable, and reliable financial statements; and a reduction in the cost to firms of preparing financial statements" (Nobes and Parker 2004, 76). The costs that developing countries would have incurred in developing their own accounting standards are averted when they adopt IFRS. However, these costs are shifted from setting up to training local staffs in handling the IFRS which by far would be profitable to these developing countries. Invariably the quality of financial reporting in these developing countries would increase considerably taking into account the source of these standards. It would also boost the international activities of firms in that they can present reliable and comparable financial information. More so, companies in these developing countries can raise capital from international financial markets since their financial reports can be compared to other international companies.

The international accounting harmonization objective is that, "Globalization of capital markets appear to be the driving force behind the proposed changes and while for this reason they may well suit the purposes of the first world nations, their effect on third world countries could be catastrophic" (IASC, 1990 as cited in Chamisa 2000). In this light therefore, developing countries adopt the IFRS with the sole aim of satisfying their accounting and financial reporting requirements but not purposely aiding in harmonizing accounting standards. These developing countries therefore select the standards that would help their course and modify those that would not be extremely beneficial to them. Developing countries pursue international harmonization of these accounting standards as far it does not hamper on the local accounting needs, laws and regulations. If the main objective for proposing the IFRS is to achieve a globalized capital market whiles most developing countries possess weaker or no capital, then surely adopting these standards can be disastrous to some degree.

In addition to the above, the "International Financial Reporting Standards are "carbon copies" of standards originating from the UK and the USA with strong orientations towards maximizing shareholders" wealth rather than the social functions of accounting" (Rahaman et al. 2004). Most developing countries have weak structures in place to develop good accounting system and for that matter the first point of call when it comes to accounting issues is shaping and developing meaningful accounting system rather than adopting already structured standards from the developed countries. More so, the fact that these standards were developed with the economy of these developed countries as a yardstick makes the importance of the adoption of IFRS questionable. The other authors also argue that accounting should not be treated as the object of providing useful information to investors only, but a craft that serves the purpose of divergent interested groups. Since most developing countries would be pursuing different socio-economic development policies, the usefulness of standards developed with significant influence from the advanced industrialized nations remains contestable" (Mir and Rahaman 2005). The bearing of IFRS on the economic growth of developing countries which have adopted them is conflicting considering the precious studies conducted. For instance, Wooley (1998) studied the bearing that the adoption of IAS has on the economic growth of some Asian countries and came to the conclusion that the average economic growth rate of developing countries when grouped by their approach to adoption or non-adoption of IASs was not significantly different which underscores the point that the adopters were not better off nor worse off as compared to the non-adopters. However, a similar study conducted in Africa observed a higher level of economic growth for countries that adopted with some form of modification of some of the standards to suit the local environmental factors.

2.2 IFRS in Developing Economies

Internationalization of economic trade and globalization of businesses is on the ascendency. Consequently, financial statements prepared according to a nation's local accounting system may hardly meet the needs of investors, business partners, financiers and decision-makers who are conversant with international standards. Meanwhile, developing and emerging markets are the target of the world's leading industries that are operating in the saturated western countries. To better undertake their activities in developing countries; they must adopt international accounting standards that suit needs (Zeghal and Mhedhbi 2006). Additionally, hence foreign investment is major boost to the economies of developing countries and investor may demand vivid and comprehensible financial information - underscoring the reason why developing countries must adopt International Accounting Standards (Zeghal and Mhedhbi 2006).

2.3 Challenges Involved in Adoption of IFRS

A financial reporting system supported by strong governance, high-quality standards and a sound regulatory framework is a key to economic development. Indeed, high-quality standards of financial reporting, auditing and ethics form the foundations of the trust that investors place in financial information and therefore play an integral role in contributing to a country's economic growth and financial stability. As the forces of globalization prompt more and more countries to open their doors to foreign investment and as businesses expand across borders, both the public and private sectors are increasingly recognizing the benefits of having a commonly understood financial reporting framework, supported by strong globally accepted standards. However, before these benefits can be fully realized, there must be greater convergence with a single set of globally accepted high-quality standards. International convergence is a goal that is embraced in the mission of the International Federation of Accountants (IFAC) and shared by IFAC members, international standard-setters and many national standard setters.

When IFRS are adopted in a given jurisdiction, they become part of existing laws and regulations. However, the provisions of relevant national laws and regulations might not be amended in due course of time to recognize the introduction of IFRS. In some cases, the IFRS requirements contradict applicable provisions in national laws and regulations. The institutions needed for ensuring a smooth transition to a global set of financial reporting standards are not in force. The enforcement of such global standards at the national level poses practical challenges due to absence of adequately resourced enforcement institutions and lack of adequate coordination mechanisms among relevant institutions. Many member States, particularly developing countries and countries with economies in transition, lack a critical mass of competent accountants and auditors capable of applying highly sophisticated and voluminous global standards such as IFRS. In general, training materials on IFRS are scarce, particularly in languages other than English. Furthermore, proper application of certain measurement requirements in IFRS requires input from competent professionals in other areas such as actuary, property valuation and others. Lack of technical capacity poses a significant barrier to the successful implementation of IFRS.

3 IFRS Convergence in India

Convergence with IFRS has gained momentum in recent years all over the World. 110+ countries including European Union, Australia, China, New Zealand, and Russia currently require or permit the use of IFRS. Apart from India, countries like Japan, Sri Lanka, Canada and Korea have also committed to adopt IFRS from 2011. United States of America has announced its intention to adopt IFRS from 2014 and it also permits foreign private filers in the U.S. Stock Exchanges to file IFRS complied Financial Statement, without requiring the presentation of reconciliation statement.

In this scenario of globalisation, India cannot insulate itself from the developments taking place worldwide. In India, so far as the Institute of Chartered Accountants of India (ICAI) is concerned, its aim has always been to comply with the IFRS to the extent possible with the objective to formulate sound financial reporting standards. The ICAI, being a member of the International Federation of Accountants (IFAC), considers the IFRS and tries to integrate them, to the extent possible, in the light of the laws, customs, practices and business environment prevailing in India. The Preface to the Statements of Accounting Standards, issued by the ICAI, categorically recognises the same. Now, as the world globalizes, it has become imperative for India also to make a formal strategy for convergence with IFRS with the objective to harmonize with globally accepted accounting standards. In India, Accounting standards are formulated by council of Institute of Chartered Accounts of India (ICAI). In 2007 India has decided to converge with IFRS in 2007. The ICAI started the process of developing a complete set of accounting standard that are "converged with" IFRS-which will be known as Indian AS. There is a difference between adoption and convergence to IFRS. Adoption means using IFRS as issued by IASB. Convergence means that the Indian Accounting standard board and IASB would continue working together to develop high quality, compatible accounting standard over time.

3.1 Need for Convergence with IFRS in India

In the present era of globalisation and liberalisation, the World has become an economic village. The globalisation of the business world and the attendant structures and the regulations, which support it, as well as the development of e-commerce make it imperative to have a single globally accepted financial reporting system. A number of multi-national companies are establishing their businesses in various countries with emerging economies and vice versa. The entities in emerging economies are increasingly accessing the global markets to fulfil their capital needs by getting their securities listed on the stock exchanges outside their country. Capital markets are, thus, becoming integrated consistent with this World-wide trend. More and more Indian companies are also being listed on overseas stock exchanges. Sound financial reporting structure is imperative for economic well-being and effective functioning of capital markets.

The use of different accounting frameworks in different countries, which require inconsistent treatment and presentation of the same underlying economic transactions, creates confusion for users of financial statements. This confusion leads to inefficiency in capital markets across the world. Therefore, increasing complexity of business transactions and globalisation of capital markets call for a single set of high quality accounting standards. High standards of financial reporting underpin the trust investors place in financial and non financial information. Thus, the case for a single set of globally accepted accounting standards has prompted many countries to pursue convergence of national accounting standards with IFRS. Amongst others, countries of the European Union, Australia, New Zealand and Russia have already adopted IFRS for listed enterprises. China has decided to adopt IFRS from 2008 and Canada from 2011. Insofar as US are concerned, Financial Accounting Standards Board (FASB) of USA and IASB are also working towards convergence of the US GAAPs and the IFRS. The Securities & Exchange Commission (SEC) has mooted a proposal to permit filing of IFRS-compliant financial statements without requiring presentation of a reconciliation statement between US GAAPs and IFRS in near future.

3.2 Road Map for Adoption of IFRS by Indian Corporate

Based on the recommendations of the Core Group set up to facilitate IFRS convergence in India, the Ministry of Corporate Affairs (MCA) has announced the approach and timelines for achieving convergence with IFRS. ICAI is under the process of issuing IFRS equivalent Accounting Standards. For companies with exposure in European markets through equity or debt, such transparency is essential to raise capital cheap and hence, the proactive approach. The Indian accounting standards body, the Institute of Chartered Accountants of India (ICAI), has set a time line of 2011 for compulsory switchover to the new standard. There will be two separate sets of Accounting Standards under Section 211(3C) of the Companies Act, 1956. The first set would comprise the Indian Accounting Standards, which are converged with the IFRS (IFRS converged standards) and which shall be applicable to the specified class of companies in a phased manner. The second set would comprise the existing Indian Accounting Standards (existing accounting standards) and would be applicable to other companies, including Small and Medium Companies (SMC). The Announcement states that a separate roadmap for banking and insurance companies will be prepared and submitted to the government for consideration after consultation with the concerned regulators by 28 February 2010. The Announcement lays down a phased approach to convergence. This is similar to the proposed approach of other countries such as Japan and the United States. Convergence with IFRS is planned in three phases as set out below:

Phase 1 Companies covered in this phase will prepare an opening balance sheet in accordance with IFRS converged standards as of 1 April 2011 and will follow the IFRS converged standards from this date. The following companies will be covered in Phase 1:

Companies included in the Nifty 50 of National Stock Exchange; Companies included in the Sensex 30 of Bombay Stock Exchange; Companies which have shares or other securities listed on stock exchanges outside India; and Companies (whether listed or not) which have a net worth in excess of Rs. 1000 crores.

Phase 2 Companies covered in this phase will prepare an opening balance sheet in accordance with IFRS converged standards as of 1 April, 2013 and will follow the IFRS converged standards from this date. All companies (whether listed or not) with a net worth in excess of Rs. 500 crore but less than Rs. 1000 crore will be covered in Phase2;

Phase 3 Companies covered in this phase will prepare an opening balance sheet in accordance with IFRS converged standards as of 1 April, 2014 and will follow the IFRS converged standards from this date. All listed companies with a net worth less than of Rs. 500 crore will be covered in Phase 3 (ICAI 2007).

3.3 Major Challenges in the Process of Adoption of IFRS in India

IFRS is a set of international accounting and reporting standards which will help to harmonize company financial information, improve the transparency of accounting, and ensure that investors receive more accurate and consistent reports. Despite several benefits as may be looked out by the different people, there will be several challenges that will be faced on the way of IFRS convergence.

Difference in GAAP and IFRS Adoption of IFRS means that the entire set of financial statements will be required to go through a severe change. There are ample of differences. It is the challenge to generate awareness of IFRS and to identify its impact among the users of financial statements.

Training and Education Lack of training amenities and academic courses on IFRS will also pose challenge in India. There is a need to be educated on IFRS and its application.

Legal and Regulatory Considerations Presently the reporting requirements are governed by various regulators in India and their provisions override other laws. IFRS does not recognize such overriding laws. The regulatory and legal requirements in India will act as a challenge unless the same laws have addressed by respective regulatory.

Taxation Aspect IFRS convergence would affect the majority of the items in the financial statements and consequently the tax liabilities would also experience a change. Thus the taxation laws should address the dealing with tax liabilities arising on convergence from Indian GAAP to IFRS.

Measurement Using Fair Value Fair value approach is used by IFRS as a measurement base for valuing the majority of the items of financial statements. The application of fair value accounting can bring a lot of volatility and subjectivity to the financial statements. It also involves a lot of hard work in finding the fair value and expert's valuation have to be used.

Reporting Systems Companies would have to make sure that the existing business reporting model is amended to go well with the reporting requirements of IFRS. The information systems should be planned to capture new requirements related to fixed assets, segment disclosures, related party transactions, etc.

Measures that should be taken by companies to address the challenges:

1) The companies should follow the recommendations given by Accounting Standard board for changes required in rules and regulations of various regulatory bodies.
2) The companies should use the interpretations of accounting standards issued by ICAI, with a view to resolve various complicated interpretational issues arising in the implementation of new accounting standards.
3) Companies should take benefit of the guidance notes, background materials on newly issued accounting standards issued by ICAI.
4) For the purpose of supporting its members, the ICAI council has created an expert advisory committee to answer queries from its members. Companies can ask to the experts for resolving the critical issues.

It is worth mentioning that, harmonizing of IFRS by developing nations would mean the adoption of a set of accounting standards unsuited or irreconcilable to national needs. At firm and national levels, this may result in standards overload as firms strive to comply with IFRS that exceed their business requirements in complexity and the ability of local accounting staff to implement or comply with them (Perera 1989). Increasing harmonization and complexity in accounting standards tends to facilitate expansion of large international accounting firms at the expense of local firms in both developing and developed countries.

The worldwide convergence on International Standards for financial reporting will make investments and financial reporting more efficient and effective. No exception to India in this regard, as it is one of the fast developing countries with an effective integration of financial markets with other countries. India has decided to adopt IFRS with effect from 1st April 2011 on a phased manner based on the criteria of net worth. The phase II and III are effective from 1st April 2013 and 1st April 2014 respectively. In the process of convergence with IFRS, all the countries are facing some problems of adoptability, despite benefits derived from adoption of IFRS. These issues should be sorted out and improvements should be made continuously for reaching for excellence in IFRS. This will go a long way in reshaping the entire accounting system in emerging economies in general and in India in particular.

References

Brown P (2011) International Financial Reporting Standards: What Are the Benefits? Account Bus Res 41(3):269–85

Cairns D, Nobes C (2000) The convergence handbook: a comparison between international accounting standards and UK financial reporting requirements. The Institute of Chartered Accountants of England and Wales, London, December, p 108

Carlson P (1997) Advancing the harmonization of international accounting standards: exploring an alternative path. Int J Account 32(3):357–378

Chamisa E (2000) The relevance of and observance of the IASC standards in developing countries and the particular case of Zimbabwe. Int J Account 35(2):267–286

Chand P, White M (2007) A critique of the influence of globalisation and convergence of accounting standards in Fiji. Crit Perspect Account 18:605–622

Chua WF, Taylor SL (2008) The rise and rise of IFRS: an examination of IFRS diffusion. J Account Public Policy 27(6):462–473

Doupnik TS, Perera MHB (2007) International accounting, 1st edn. McGraw-Hill, Boston, ISBN-13: 978-0-07-250775-1, ISBN-10: 0-07-250775-6

Fontes A, Rodrigues LL, Craig R (2005) Measuring convergence of national accounting standards with international financial reporting standards. Account Forum 29:415–436

Harverty JL (2006) Are IFRS and US GAAP converging? Some evidence from People's Republic of China companies listed on the New York Stock Exchange. J Int Account Audit Tax 15:48–71

Hernandez SM, Manzano MP, Hazera A, Quirvan C (2007) Latin American banking institutions trading on the New York Stock Exchange-convergence-divergence of Latin American accounting standards and US GAAP. Adv Int Account 20:225–251

ICAI (2007) Concept paper on convergence with IFRSs in India

IFAC (2004) Challenges and Successes in Implementing International Standards: Achieving Convergence to IFRSs and ISAs. International Federation of Accountants. September

Irvine H (2008) The global institutionalisation of financial reporting: the case of the United Arab Emirates. Accountant 32:125–142

Jemakowicz EK, Tomaszewski SG (2006) Implementing IFRS from the perspectives of EU publicly traded companies. J Int Account Audit Tax 15:170–196

King N, Beattie A, Cristescu AM, Weetman P (2001) Developing accounting and audit in a transition economy: the Romanian experience. Eur Account Rev 10:149–71

Larson RK, Street DL (2004) Convergence with IFRS in an expanding Europe: progress and obstacles identified by large accounting firms' survey. J Int Account Audit Tax 13:89–119

Lewis PA, Salter SB (2006) Europe and America. Together or apart. An empirical test of differences in actual reported results. Adv Int Account 19:221–242

Mir MZ, Rahaman AS (2005) The adoption of international accounting standards in Bangladesh – an exploration of rationale and process. Account Audit Account J 18(6):816–841. doi:10.1108/09513570510627720

Nobes C, Parker R (2004) Comparative international accounting. Prentice Hall, Englewood Cliffs, NJ

Perera MHB (1989) Towards a framework to analyze the impact of culture on accounting. Int J Account 24:42–56

Perera H, Baydoun N (2007) Convergence with international financial reporting standards: the case of Indonesia. Adv Int Account 20:201–224

Rahaman et al (2004) The adoption of international accounting standards in Bangladesh—an exploration of rationale and process. Emerald

Rodrigues LL, Craig R (2007) Assessing international accounting harmonization using Hegelian dialetic, isomorphism and Foucault. Crit Perspect Account 18:739–757

Stolowy H, Haller A, Klockhaus V (2006) Accounting for brands in France and Germany compared with IAS 38 (Intangible Assets). An illustration of the difficulty of international harmonization. Int J Account 36:147–167

Street DL, Larson RK (2004) Large accounting firm's survey shows emergence of two standard systems in the European Union. Adv Int Account 17:1–29

UN (2007) International accounting and reporting issues. United Nations Review

United Nations Conference on Trade and Development (UNCTAD), 2008

Weetman P (2006) Discovering the "international" in accounting and finance. Br Account Rev 38:351–370

Wooley R (1998) International accounting standards and economic growth, an empirical investigation of their relationship in Asia. Working paper series. School of accounting and Law, RMIT, Australia

Zeghal D, Mhedhbi K (2006) An analysis of the factors affecting the adoption of international accounting standards by developing countries. Published by University of Illinois

China. The Role of the Government and Academics in the IFRS Convergence Process of Chinese Accounting Standards

Xiaorui Wang

Abstract Regarding China's convergence with the International Financial Reporting Standards (IFRS), contrary to concerns on the resistance associated with the socialist nature of the country and its economy, the process seems to be relatively smooth compared to other current and former socialist countries. In this paper, we seek to conduct a "Critical Discourse Analysis" (CDA) on government discourses and academic publications related to the evolution of China's national accounting standards within the context of the Chinese economy and that of the globalisation. The findings indicate that the Chinese domestic accounting researchers appear to be closely attached to the government, who plays a leading role in this event, and that the efficient convergence with the IFRS is largely because of Chinese authority's strong willingness to promote a neoliberal ideology through this process, in the hope of speeding up China's financial and economic integration into the global market.

1 Introduction

Having been officially recognised as "substantially converged"[1] with the International Financial Reporting Standards (IFRS),[2] China's national accounting system went through a long journey to this stage and is still in the process of self-adaptation. However, contrary to concerns about the resistance related to the "socialist" nature of the country and its economy, China's international

[1] As indicated on the IFRS Foundation website and also confirmed in Ministry of Finance (MOF) (2010), the mission was accomplished on 2005.

[2] For simplicity, we refer to both International Accounting Standards (IAS) and the IFRS as IFRS in this article.

X. Wang (✉)
DRM-MOST, Dauphine Doctoral School, Paris-Dauphine University, PSL Research University, 75775 Paris Cedex 16, France
e-mail: ray.wangxr@gmail.com

D. Bensadon, N. Praquin (eds.), *IFRS in a Global World*,
DOI 10.1007/978-3-319-28225-1_16

convergence process seems to be relatively smooth compared to other current and former socialist countries.

The aim of this study is not to present a complete retrospection and forecast of China's accounting development. Instead, by analysing relevant discourses, we look at the evolution of China's accounting standards in the context of China's spectacular economic growth and that of the globalisation. This focus on the national and international contexts is mainly because, firstly, accounting is widely viewed as a powerful mechanism of economic and social management (Catchpowle et al. 2004), and therefore greatly influences, and is also influenced by a country's economic changes. And secondly, as claimed by Hopwood (1989), "accounting has never been a purely national phenomenon". (p. 1) In our case, the international standards that China seeks to converge with are initiated by the Anglo-Saxon countries and then adapted by the others, including China, according to their local conditions.

Through a series of discourse analysis applied to relevant discourses delivered by the 'key players', especially the Chinese government and accounting academics in the event of China's international accounting standard convergence, we seek to know how the institutional factors of a country could sway the adoption of the international standards, and what is the underpinning ideology that have forged the attitudes of these institutions towards this event, as well as towards a "social change" (Fairclough 1992) in a broader sense.

The remainder of this paper is organised as follows. After a brief presentation of the methodology, the analysis is conducted based on the three-layer structure of the discourse process. The two following sectors present the discourses of the international and national government bodies and those of the academics. Then the stands taken in these discourses and the roles played by these institutions in this event are investigated. What is followed is an analysis of the ideological underpinnings of the above mentioned institutions in a broader economic and social context. And finally the discussion is concluded with a brief summary.

2 Methodology

In this paper, we employ the methodology inspired by Foucault and Bourdieu's ideologies (*cf.* Foucault 1969, 1970; Bourdieu and Thompson 2001) related to language and power, namely the "Critical Discourse Analysis" (CDA). The three-layer conception of discourse is illustrated in the following figure (Fig. 1).

As shown above, this paper sets out from the *text* layer of discourse, which is the verbal elements of policy documents and academic publications (see below), and further extends to their *context*, or "the social practice" Fairclough (1992) of the discourse. The choice of examining the "ideological sub-category of practice" (Leitch and Palmer 2010, p. 1203) in particular, is mainly based on the premise that in China, a socialist country under the de facto state capitalism (Wooldridge 2012), dominant beliefs do exist, in an explicit or implicit way, and they greatly influence critical decisions regarding the society.

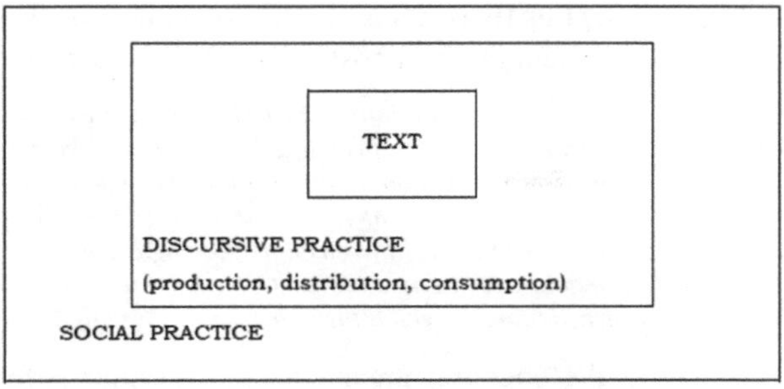

Fig. 1 The conception of discourse (*Source:*, Fairclough 1992, p. 73)

In this study, we mainly focus on discourses delivered by two key players, namely the authorities and the academics, in the hope of revealing the actual roles played by them in the event of China's accounting standards' international convergence and the underpinning ideology. The sources of data mainly consist of the official websites of the international and national institutions, such as that of the International Accounting Standards Board (IASB)[3] and that of the Ministry of Finance (MOF)[4] of the People's Republic of China, the databases of ScienceDirect and the China Knowledge Resource Infrastructure (CNKI),[5] as well as international and national leading news outlets.

3 The Official Tone: Forging Ahead Toward Convergence

China started to make efforts on converging with international accounting standards in the late 1970s, when the state was up to revert to political and economic normality and the accounting system was accordingly to be reformed in order to inform various economic activity practitioners, instead of being perceived as book-keeping instrument to ensure the achievement of central plans (Phuong and Richard 2011; Qu et al. 1999).

Currently, the IFRS-converged Chinese accounting system includes the Accounting Standards for Business Enterprises (ASBE, became effective from 1 January 2007), which is composed of Basic Standard, 38 specific standards and application guidance, as well as the Accounting Law of the PRC and other relevant laws and regulations. As repeatedly praised by the Chairmen of the IASB, China's efforts on the convergence have been remarkable (Hoogervorst 2011; Tweedie

[3] http://www.ifrs.org/, website of the IFRS Foundation and the IASB.

[4] http://www.mof.gov.cn/, and notably the website of its subordinate Accounting Regulatory Department (ARD): http://kjs.mof.gov.cn/.

[5] http://www.cnki.net/. As described on its "Introduction" page, the CNKI is "the most comprehensive gateway of knowledge of China" that endowed with a "monopolist status" (Zhao and Qiu 2005). This database is mostly used to acquire academic papers of domestic researchers in this study.

2006), and the positive effects of it seem unquestionable, both in terms of attracting foreign investment and of boosting international trade:

> *"The benefits of these accounting reforms for China are clear.* [6] *The new Chinese standards that incorporate accounting principles familiar to investors worldwide will encourage investor confidence in China's capital markets and financial reporting and will be an additional spur for investment from both domestic and foreign sources of capital. For Chinese companies that are increasingly playing a global role, the acceptance of the new standards should also reduce the cost of complying with the accounting regimes of the different jurisdictions in which they operate." (Tweedie* 2006*)*

Echoing the encouragement and the promising future pictured by the IASB chairmen, the positive tone is set unanimously by the MOF and other government institutions such as the Chinese Institute of Certified Public Accountants (CICPA),[7] the Chinese National Audit Office, the Chinese Securities Regulatory Commission and the China Banking Regulatory Commission in regard to further steps of the "continuous convergence" (MOF 2010), for example, in an interview regarding the publication of *Chinese Accounting Reform: Towards a principles-based global regime* issued by the Institute of Chartered Accountants of Scotland in 2010, Liu Yuting, (former) Director General of Accounting Regulatory Department (ARD) of the MOF comments that

> *"The enthusiasm of the MOF and related regulators as well as their shared efforts ensured the successful establishment and implementation of the new Chinese Accounting Standards (CAS) which converge with IFRS."*

Moreover, the necessity of China's accounting reform, as well as the "benefits" that Chinese economy has acquired from this convergence are confirmed, typically[8] by Yang Min, incumbent Director General of ARD, as by other high-ranking Chinese officials (see more in Zhang 2012, p. 144–146):

> *"Along with the reform and opening up of the Chinese mainland, the economy of the mainland has become increasingly market-oriented. Accounting information, as the common business language, has to accommodate the evolving market economy. . . . In 2001, the mainland China joined the WTO, and in 2003 the central authority made the formal proposition of establishing a complete socialist market economic system. These events have propelled the mainland market economy toward an era of rapid development, which demands high-quality accounting information. . . . Nearly 20 years' evolution of Chinese*

---

[6] Underlined by the author, same as for all the other underlined parts in the verbatim in italics below.

[7] The CICPA is characterised by features of a government institution rather than a pure accounting professional association, according to the definition on its official website: an organisation under the guidance of the MOF and the State Council. (Available at http://www.cicpa.org.cn/, last consulted on 12/2/2014)

[8] This discourse is judged as "typical" for the reason that the speech has been quoted in leading financial and economic news outlet repeatedly.

accounting standards demonstrates that the formulation and betterment of accounting standards have to be in accordance with the development of market economy."[9]
– *Yang Min* (2011)

"Within the first five years after the new CAS were implemented, we observe that these standards have played a very important role in standardising corporate accounting practice, improving the quality of accounting information, promoting capital markets regulation and safeguarding the public interest. They have laid a good foundation for China's financial innovation and sustainable economic development."[10]
– *Yang Min* (2012)

Indeed, being perceived as the "good foundation" for China's financial "innovation", the IFRS-converged CAS are presented as tools of "standardisation" and "quality control", which are largely endowed with neutrality and which could fit in any form of "market economy" regardless of national boundaries.

4 Academic Views: Forging Ahead Without Hesitation?

As to the academic world, the views are predictably much more rigorous and more problematique-focused, in that most of them refer to economic and/or accounting theories to back up their opinions, and that they address specific research questions, such as the use of Fair-Value Accounting (FVA) and earning management within the framework of IFRS.

Since the academic literature on international accounting convergence is rather abundant, here the reviewing of these discourses is divided in two groups: firstly the publications on international academic journals, then those on domestic ones. This dichotomy is largely in accordance with the official discourses reviewed in the previous section and could be justified by the disparities between the two groups of literature in the following investigation. The choice of reviewing international and national academic journals on accounting in this study is to a great extent because of the fact that the periodical issuing of the journals and the comparatively short length of each article included in every issue allow us to better grasp the dynamics of the academic world regarding the accounting convergence, as well as to have a more extensive review of opinions expressed by a large number of scholars. Based on propositions of Peng (2009), Reinstein and Calderon (2006) and Zhang (2012), two journals, namely "The International Journal of Accounting" (TIJA) and "Accounting Research" (AR), are chosen as the representatives of each group mentioned above, by virtue of importance: according Peng (2009), TIJA is among the top-ranking journals on accounting and has accepted the largest number

[9] Full speech (Chinese version) available at Chinese academic journal *Finance and Accounting*, 2011 (8), one of China's top journals in the domain of accounting. The text quoted here, as well as the other texts below that are originally written in Chinese, is translated by the author.

[10] Full speech (Chinese version) available at http://kjs.mof.gov.cn/, last consulted on 12/2/2014.

of articles involving China; and Zhang (2012) qualified AR as "the most influential among the Chinese accounting community" (p. 154), notably by referring to the ranking of Chinese Academic Degrees Committee of the State Council.

When typing the keyword "convergence" in the ScienceDirect search engine for TIJA, 109 results were found, among which 48 involve the case of China. Though a large number of them being supportive of the international convergence, alternative voices are also expressed extensively regarding this event, typical[11] examples being the discussions of Chen et al. (2014a, b) and Dong (2014) on foreign direct investment; as well as the discussions conducted by both Chinese and foreign researchers (Ding et al. 2005a, b; Hilmy 1999; Papadaki 2005) on cultural and historical factors that may have caused the differences between national accounting standards and the IFRS, as well as the legitimacy of these differences. Among them, the particularity of the Chinese version of the international accounting standards is recognised, for example, by Hilmy (1999) as follows:

> *"[The] recent accounting reform ... allows a limited number of Westernized accounting standards, mostly adapted to accommodate traditional Chinese values. Accounting forms an indispensable component of an overall economic policy."*

Other researchers have shown their reticence notably concerning the use of FVA, the most contestable issue and literally the essence of the IFRS (Cairns 2006), for example, as claimed by (Mısırlıoğlu et al. 2013),

> *"In terms of the most challenging standards, the largest obstacles were presented in relation to FVA in the absence of benchmarks, asset impairment as a somewhat foreign concept, and the classification of financial instruments where management information systems typically do not comply with IFRS requirements."*

As to the equivalent investigation conducted on AR, when typing the keyword "convergence" in Chinese in the CNKI search engine for AR, 66 results were found, all of which are in favour of the CAS and IFRS convergence. Typical examples are:

In general, the accounting scholars believe that

> *"Accounting is the universal language of the entire business world. Therefore its global convergence is an irresistible trend." (Ge* 2006*)*

As to the case of China, they judge that

> *"The new CAS system is a result of combining efforts from both the domestic accounting experiences and the development of the IFRS themselves. These efforts have been widely recognised by the international community. ... Except for some minor differences, it has substantially converged with the IFRS ..." (Liu* 2007*)*

Faced with these "minor differences", they tend to set off to seek

> *"... countermeasures that allow the CAS to converge with the IFRS while safeguarding our national interests, since the essence of the international accounting standards convergence is a contest of interest... .. .." (Feng* 2003*)*

[11] The following discourses are judged as "typical" based on the number of times the articles have been cited.

And concerning the use of FVA, the only opposition that was found in this study is formulated as:

> *"Based on the empirical evidence from the A and B shares [of the Shanghai and Shenzhen stock market], ... we conclude that in the current circumstances where the internal and external regulation mechanisms are neither complete nor effective, which allow the listed companies to have too much liberty for accounting options. This may lead to a decline in information quality, a good example being the abuse of FVA in some cases of the new CAS implementation." (Wang* 2005*)*

Yet the author doesn't provide any concrete example of the "FVA abusing" firms and emphasises at the end that what is needed to be done is to "actively create conditions for the gradual implementation of the IFRS". Moreover, the concerns are further swept off notably by Liu and Zhang (2006),

> *"The new CAS have raised concerns of some people. However, we find that the appropriate use of fair value will prevent profit from being manipulated, debt being restructured, and profit being adjusted through impairment of assets."*

Further, it is even foreseeable that the FVA

> *"is likely to [replace historical cost accounting and] become the measurement basis of assets and liabilities in the 21st century, thanks to its high degree of relevance.." (Lu* 2006*)*

5 Convergence of CAS and IFRS as Constructed Realities

By looking at the discourses presented in the two previous sections, the tone set by the international and Chinese officials is unanimous and extremely supportive of the convergence. Beside the necessity and the benefits articulated in the discourses of both the IASB and the MOF, the Chinese authority also focuses in their discourses on another point, namely the "development of market economy" in China. The event of accounting standards convergence is constructed by the policy-makers as the way one must follow in order to reform China's economy to a more market-oriented one that would gain better recognition of international institutions as well as that of the other economies, and therefore to find a better place in the global market. This neoliberal ideology could be seen as the guidance for all the discourses delivered by the Chinese government and the domestic academics regarding this event.

As to the academics, we find that the views (of both Chinese and foreign researchers) seem to be more diverse in TIJA and less so in AR. One thing noticeable in the investigation of TIJA is that, among the authors of the 48 articles that involve China, when looking at the institutions that the authors are attached to, most of them are research institutions or universities in western countries. It seems that researchers who conduct China-related accounting researches overseas tend to observe and rethink this issue with more critical perspectives, and are more willing to express these opinions. What could be deducted from this finding is that, compared to domestic Chinese researchers, the oversea researchers maintain a rather distant relationship with the Chinese authority because of the geological distance and the language used in their publication. And this might have reduced, or even avoided the influence of dominant ideology that would otherwise exert on their researches.

Through the analysis of AR, we find that though the content of the discourses are characterised with more depth and expertise, the spirit is highly coherent with that of the government ones. It is worth noticing that, as one more keyword "MOF" is added in the category of "institution of the author(s)" in order to search within the 66 results of "convergence", 16 articles were found under these criteria, equivalent of a quarter of the total number. In other words, a quarter of the articles that support the convergence are published under the names of MOF officials. The fact that Chinese government officials also publish in academic journals and that their articles are among the most cited ones may appear strange, yet as noted by Ding and Graham (2007), "academics in China often also hold positions in government" (p. 564) and "it is traditional in China for academics supporting government positions" (p. 571).

What could be a good explanation for this double identity and the highly consistent tone is, as called by Bell and Li (2012), the "meritocratic system" employed in China's leader-picking process:

> *"... So how should leaders be chosen at the central level? Ideally, the process should be meritocratic ... Today, universities are the main recruitment grounds for new members. Students need to score in the top percentile of national examinations to be admitted to an elite university that grooms future leaders. Then they compete fiercely to be admitted into the party. Only high-performing students who have undergone thorough character checks are admitted. ... Once they are part of the political system, further evaluations are required to move up the chain of command. They must perform well at lower levels of government and pass character tests. Then there are more position-specific exams that test for specialised skills."*

For the purpose of better understanding the text, we would like to clarify that "the party" here refers to the Communist Party of China (CPC) and the "character checks" here mainly refer to a review of the person's political affiliation, ideological and moral character. According to the scenario describe above, as being "fiercely competing to be admitted into the party", the (potential) government cadres need not only to show their research competence, but also to continuously demonstrate their commitment to values advocated by the CPC in the "character checks/tests". Moreover, the periodic evaluation of their progress in "specialised skills" often requires them to publish in academic journals, and to pursue "on-the-position postgraduate degrees"[12] in universities, Party Schools[13] or research

[12] A convenient solution for people (especially for government officials) to obtain graduate degrees while maintaining their current positions at work. See for instance Lee (1991) and for more explanations.

[13] According to the official website of the Party School of the Central Committee of the CPC, a party school is "the highest institution of learning charged with the task of training senior and middle-ranking leading cadres of the Party and fostering Marxist theoretical cadres. As an

institutes directly attached to government bodies,[14] all of which suggest a reintegration in, as well as a strong influence to the academic world. Even though it is questionable whether these cadres really have the time and energy to fulfil both duties of working and conducting researches, this system does largely guarantee the direct transmission of the government ideologies to the academics.

6 The IFRS Convergence in the Chinese Context

After reviewing the stands taken by the authorities and the academics, especially those in mainland China, we still have one more question that we attempt to answer: how do ideological underpinnings work in the event of the CAS convergence with the IFRS, and more generally, in the event of a social change?

At this point, we share and develop the view of Zhang (2012), who observes that the Chinese government's rationale for the convergence mirrors the theories that have driven the establishment of international accounting standards in contemporary western societies, and that by presenting the new CAS as an important 'technology', the Chinese government intends to facilitate the establishment of this particular socio-economic infrastructure, which would allow China further integrate into the global financialisation process. This rather neutral perception of accounting fits perfectly in the dominant ideology, namely (the former) President Hu Jintao's "Scientific Outlook on Development". The penetration of this thinking is clearly demonstrated in the 2011 Annual summary of ARD, entitled *Fully implemented the twelfth five-year plan and further promoted the reform and development of accounting under the guidance of the Scientific Development concept.*[15]

Further, as believed by many Chinese domestic academics, the convergence could fit in the theoretical framework of "institutional change", where essentially two types of change are identified: the *induced* and the *imposed* institutional change. According to Lin (1989),

> *"whereas induced institutional change refers to the voluntary change by a group of individuals in response to profitable opportunities arising from institutional disequilibria, imposed change refers to change that is introduced by government fiat."*

---

important organ directly under the Central Committee of the CPC, it is an important bastion for studying and publicizing Marxism, Mao Zedong Thought and the System of Theories of Socialism with Chinese Characteristics and a furnace for tempering the Party spirit. It is also a research institute of philosophy and other social sciences of the CPC." Information available at http://www.ccps.gov.cn/, last consulted on 16/2/2014.

[14] The most appropriate example to be mentioned here is the Institute of Fiscal Science of the MOF. The above cited article Wang (2005) is one of the institute's research publications in the AR journal.

[15] Available at http://kjs.mof.gov.cn/zaixianfuwu/wszt/, last consulted on 26/2/2014.

By recognising accounting standards as an "institution" and therefore the international convergence of standards as "institutional change", Qu et al. (1999) and Li (2007) explored the motivation and economic consequences of this change as well as the costs linked to it. According to them, the recent IFRS convergence in China could be classified as imposed institutional change, where the driving forces mainly come from the Chinese central authority, who intends to accelerate China's further integration into the global market. Indeed, the accounting standard setting could also be seen as a politicalised process, of which the current status is the result of power balancing among "interest groups" of the society. As to the case of China, it seems that this game has been played at its simplified version, where the main participants only involves the international and national regulatory institutions, whilst the domestic accounting professional community, namely the academics and accounting practitioners don't seem to stand as independent think-tanks, nor have manifest power on this matter.

Being labelled as a "government-led economy" and a "state capitalist" country (Wooldridge 2012), China demonstrates its capacity and readiness to perform concerted efforts and an effective organisation of different groups of members in the society so as to accomplish large scale social changes, if only the central authority had made the decision. In our case, the efficient IFRS convergence has again proved this capacity of the Chinese authority within the national scope. Nevertheless, what currently seems absent is the voice of the Chinese authority and academics at international level – since the IFRS themselves are actually evolving, critical perspectives and amendment proposals, rather than feedbacks of full compliance, are much needed as the IFRS being implemented in different countries.[16]

Overall, the IFRS convergence in the Chinese context seems to echo Fairclough's (1992) theory in regard with the ideological dimension of social changes, where discourses are perceived "in terms of processes of hegemony" and if any, "changes in hegemony" (Blommaert 2005, p. 30). Judgemental as this word might sound, a certain 'imposed' social change could not be judged without evidence provided by independent parties, or in absence of which, less biased participants in this event. Consequently, we consulted the report of Lee et al. (2013) prepared for the Association of Chartered Certified Accountants (ACCA), as well as the reports of the "big four" firms such as KPMG (2011) and PwC (2013), and found that in general, their analyses confirms the value relevance of the accounting earnings presented in the financial reports of the Chinese firms under the IFRS converged CAS. However, there is no concrete evidence proving the benefit from IFRS convergence to Chinese economy as a whole.

[16] A good example of this is the amendment to IAS 16 and IAS 41, originally proposed by the Malaysian Accounting Standards Board, in relation to the biological assets.

7 Conclusion

As firmly stated in the "Roadmap for Continuing Convergence of Chinese Accounting Standards for Business Enterprises with the IFRS" (MOF 2010), "international convergence of accounting standards is *the* inevitable choice of a state to achieve economic development and to adapt to economic globalisation". Through a three-layer analysis of CDA, we find that the Chinese authority is 'enthusiast' about the convergence, and that on the way towards the complete convergence, the Chinese domestic academics have been extremely supportive, thanks to their close relations, even the 'fusion' with government bodies. The efficient convergence process with the IFRS conducted, or in other words, 'imposed' by the Chinese authority is largely because of its strong willingness to promote a neoliberal ideology through this process, and to speed up China's financial and economic integration into the global market. Putting aside the question of whether this process is an *induced* or *imposed* one, the effects of this convergence on Chinese economy and society, as well as other political implications of it are still unclear and therefore require further study in future.

8 Appendix: List of Abbreviations and Acronyms

ACCA	Association of Chartered Certified Accountants
AR	Accounting Research (journal)
ARD	Accounting Regulatory Department
ASBE	Accounting Standards for Business Enterprises
CAS	Chinese Accounting Standards
CDA	Critical discourse analysis
CICPA	Chinese Institute of Certified Public Accountants
CNKI	China Knowledge Resource Infrastructure
CPC	Communist Party of China
FVA	Fair-value accounting
IASB	International Accounting Standards Board
IFRS	International Financial Reporting Standards
MOF	Ministry of Finance
PRC	People's Republic of China
TIJA	The International Journal of Accounting (journal)

References

Bell D, Li E (2012) In defence of how China picks its leaders. Financial Times

Blommaert J (2005) Discourse: key topics in sociolinguistics. Cambridge University Press, Cambridge

Bourdieu P, Thompson JB (2001) Language and symbolic power (Seuil)

Cairns D (2006) The use of fair value in IFRS. Account Eur 3(1):5–22

Catchpowle L, Cooper C, Wright A (2004) Capitalism, states and accounting. Crit Perspect Account 15(8):1037–1058

Chen CJP, Ding Y, Xu B (2014a) Convergence of accounting standards and foreign direct investment. Int J Account 49(1):53–86

Chen CJP, Ding Y, Xu B (2014b) Response to discussant "convergence of accounting standards and foreign direct investment". Int J Account 49(1):97–100

Ding S, Graham C (2007) Accounting and the reduction of state-owned stock in China. Crit Perspect Account 18(5):559–580

Ding Y, Jeanjean T, Stolowy H (2005a) Why do national GAAP differ from IAS? The role of culture. Int J Account 40(4):325–350

Ding Y, Jeanjean T, Stolowy H (2005b) Reply to discussion of "Why do national GAAP differ from IAS? The role of culture". Int J Account 40(4):359–362

Dong M (2014) Discussion of "Convergence of accounting standards and foreign direct investment". Int J Account 49(1):87–96

Fairclough N (1992) Discourse and social change. Polity Press, Cambridge

Feng Q (2003) The imbalances of interests and countermeasures in the internationalisation of accounting standards. Account Res 2:8–12

Foucault M (1969) The archaeology of knowledge. Gallimard, Paris

Foucault M (1970) The order of discourse (Inaugural lecture at the Collège de France)

Ge J (2006) The standards that combine innovation and convergence – comments on the new "Chinese Accounting Standards – basic guidelines". Account Res 3

Hilmy J (1999) Communists among us in a market economy: accountancy in the People's Republic of China. Int J Account 34(4)

Hoogervorst H (2011) Speech by Hans Hoogervorst in Beijing: China and IFRS – an opportunity for leadership in global financial reporting. Beijing

Hopwood AG (ed) (1989) International pressures for accounting change. Prentice Hall

KPMG (2011) An Overview of New PRC GAAP: Differences between old and new PRC GAAP and its convergence with IFRS. http://www.kpmg.com/CN/en/IssuesAndInsights/ArticlesPublications/Documents/New-PRC-GAAP-201109.pdf

Lee HY (1991) From revolutionary cadres to party technocrats in socialist China. University of California Press, Berkeley, CA

Lee E, Walker M, Zeng C (2013) Does IFRS convergence affect financial reporting quality in China? Certified Accountants Educational Trust, London

Leitch S, Palmer I (2010) Analysing texts in context: current practices and new protocols for Critical Discourse Analysis in organization studies. J Manag Stud 47(6):1194–1212

Lin JY (1989) An economic theory of institutional change: induced and imposed change. Cato J 9 (1)

Liu Y (2007) Chinese accounting system: structure, convergence and equivalence. Account Res 3:2–8

Liu Q, Zhang Z (2006) Reflections on the newly issued accounting standards. Account Res 3

Li X (2007) A research on the social costs related to the accounting institutional change since the reform and opening-up. Master's dissertation on Political Economy. Shandong University

Lu X (2006) The international application of fair value accounting. Account Res 4

Ministry of Finance (MOF) of P.R. China (2010) Roadmap for continuing convergence of Chinese accounting standards for business enterprises with international financial reporting standards

Mısırlıoğlu İU, Tucker J, Yükseltürk O (2013) Does mandatory adoption of IFRS guarantee compliance? Int J Account 48(3):327–363

Papadaki A (2005) Discussion of "Why do national GAAP differ from IAS? The role of culture". Int J Account 40(4):351–358

Peng S (2009) Acceptance of China research in western accounting journals (1978–2007). China J Account Res 2(1)

Phuong NC, Richard J (2011) Economic transition and accounting system reform in Vietnam. Eur Account Rev 20(4)

PwC (2013) IFRS adoption by country. http://www.pwc.com/en_US/us/issues/ifrs-reporting/publications/assets/pwc-ifrs-by-country-apr-2013.pdf

Qu X, Chen C, Yang J (1999) Research on accounting standards: references and reflexions. Xiamen University Press, Xiamen

Reinstein A, Calderon TG (2006) Examining accounting departments' rankings of the quality of accounting journals. Crit Perspect Account 17:457–490

Tweedie D (2006) China affirms commitment to converge with IFRSs – full text of Sir David Tweedie's statement at the ceremony of the CAS announcement. Beijing

Wang J (2005) The process of internationalisation of accounting standards in China and its effect – Empirical evidence from the A and B shares of Shanghai and Shenzhen stock market. Account Res 6

Wooldridge A (2012) The Economist: State Capitalism (Penguin Specials): The Visible Hand (The Economist)

Yang M (2011) Promote international convergence of accounting standards for cooperation and common development – Speech of Yang Min on accounting topics for the 7th Cross-Strait Forum. Xiamen

Yang M (2012) China's experience in the development and the international convergence of accounting standards. São Paulo

Zhang Y (2012) Fair value accounting as an instrument of Neoliberalism in China. Ph.D. dissertation on Accounting. School of Accounting & Finance, University of Wollongong

Zhao R, Qiu J (2005) An investigation of the development of CNKI. Inform Sci 23(4)

Canada. IFRS in Canada: Game Changer or Neutral Mutation?

Denis Cormier and Michel Magnan

Abstract With the advent of International Financial Reporting Standards (IFRS), 2011 was certainly critical for Canadian financial markets on several dimensions. On one hand, Canada's Accounting Standards Board decision to adopt IFRS for publicly accountable enterprises ended more than 20 years of formal or informal convergence toward U.S. Generally Accepted Accounting Principles (GAAP). On the other hand, for auditors, corporate executives, regulators, analysts and investors, the release of IFRS-based financial statements modified in a fundamental way the informational landscape underlying Canadian financial markets.

In light of these events, this chapter aims to achieve two objectives. First, we will present and discuss the institutional context that led Canada's accounting standard-setter and regulators to adopt IFRS. Second, we will analyze the implementation of IFRS in 2011 as well as its potential implications for key financial markets' players. Our analysis will be performed through a corporate governance perspective. Ultimately, the chapter's goal is to assess if Canada's transition to IFRS was indeed a game changer for financial markets or if, alternatively, it represented a neutral mutation in the country's institutional landscape with scant market implications.

1 Overview

With the advent of International Financial Reporting Standards (IFRS), 2011 was certainly critical for Canadian financial markets on several dimensions. On one hand, Canada's Accounting Standards Board decision to adopt IFRS for publicly

Michel Magnan is a member of Canada's Accounting Standards Board. However, the views expressed in this text are strictly personal and should not be construed in any way to represent the Accounting Standards Board's viewpoint or to have been approved by the Accounting Standards Board. The Accounting Standard Board's position on any issue is only made through due process.

D. Cormier, Dr Sc Econ, FCPA Auditor, FCGA (✉)
Chair in Financial and Organizational Information, ESG-UQAM, Montréal, QC, Canada
e-mail: cormier.denis@uqam.ca

M. Magnan, PhD, FRSC, FCPA, FCA, ASC, C Dir
Stephen A. Jarislowsky Chair in Corporate Governance, John Molson School of Business, Concordia University, Montréal, QC, Canada
e-mail: michel.magnan@concordia.ca

D. Bensadon, N. Praquin (eds.), *IFRS in a Global World*,
DOI 10.1007/978-3-319-28225-1_17

accountable enterprises ended more than 20 years of formal or informal convergence toward U.S. Generally Accepted Accounting Principles (GAAP). On the other hand, for auditors, corporate executives, regulators, analysts and investors, the release of IFRS-based financial statements modified in a fundamental way the informational landscape underlying Canadian financial markets.

In light of these events, this chapter aims to achieve two objectives. First, we will present and discuss the institutional context that led Canada's accounting standard-setter and regulators to adopt IFRS. Second, we will analyze the implementation of IFRS in 2011 as well as its potential implications for key financial markets' players. Our analysis will be performed through a corporate governance perspective. Ultimately, the chapter's goal is to assess if Canada's transition to IFRS was indeed a game changer for financial markets or if, alternatively, it represented a neutral mutation in the country's institutional landscape with scant market implications.

2 The Road Toward IFRS[1]

Starting in the mid-90s, Canada's Accounting Standards Board (ASB) adopted a two-track strategy which relied on (1) harmonizing with US GAAP and (2) supporting global convergence in accounting standards. This strategy resulted largely from the recommendations of a task force established by the Canadian Institute of Chartered Accountants in 1996 to review accounting standard-setting activities in Canada. In practice, such a strategy implied the mimetic adaptation of U.S. GAAP. In other words, the ASB essentially followed developments at the Financial Accounting Standards Board (FASB), the U.S. standard-setter, and at the Securities and Exchange Commission (SEC), the main U.S. market regulator and the FASB's oversight body.

However, in 2004, the ASB began a process to develop a 5-year strategic plan for the period 2006-2011. Canada's accounting standard-setters knew that they had reached a turning point and that their strategy of mimetic adaptation of U.S. GAAP was reaching the end of its useful life. First, in the past decade or so, IFRS had become a much more appealing alternative. The governance reform that led the former International Accounting Standards Committee (IASC) to form the IASB, the decision by the European Union to mandate the use of IFRS for publicly-listed entities by 2005 and the "rapprochement" between the IASB and its U.S. counterpart, the FASB, all raised the visibility and credibility of the IASB as a standard-setter as well as its worldwide reach. Second, the strategy of following U.S. developments in standard-setting and then adapting them for the Canadian market implied that new standards (1) were not as timely as they could have been, (2) were often missing critical pieces of useful guidance which had been cut in the

[1] Some of the information and facts contained in that section are drawn from Adoption of International Financial Reporting Standards—Background Information and Basis for Conclusion, CPA Canada Handbook, Part 1.

adaptation process and (3) were imposed upon Canadian stakeholders without them, of the ASB for that matter, having taken part in the decision leading to their initial adoption. Third, Canadian firms represent the largest contingent of cross-listings on U.S. stock exchanges from any country, with several hundred firms raising significant financing in the U.S. As the convergence between Canadian and U.S. standards was being enhanced, several Canadian firms debated if it was worthwhile to maintain two sets of financial statements (Canadian GAAP and U.S. GAAP) that more or less conveyed the same information, especially if one set was deemed to be a pale or inferior copy (i.e., Canadian GAAP) of the other (i.e., U.S. GAAP). Fourth, the reach of Canadian GAAP had always been far and wide, with publicly-listed entities, privately-held entities, not-for-profit entities, charities and pension funds all being subjected to apply the same standards (with some limited exceptions in the cases of privately-held and not-for-profit/charity entities). However, the scope and span of the underlying U.S. GAAP implied that Canadian GAAP was being torn apart at the core: for most entities, they were too far-reaching, complex and costly while for a small number of influential publicly traded entities, they were deemed a second-best alternative to U.S. GAAP. For this last group, the attractiveness of U.S. GAAP was becoming irresistible, and some opted to report exclusively under U.S. GAAP.

While pursuing the current strategy was still feasible, it carried the risk to make Canada a bit player in the world or standard-setting. On one hand, not being a IFRS country, Canada and its standard-setter, the ASB, carried less and less weight in international circles as natural allies such as the United Kingdom, New Zealand and Australia moved toward IFRS. On the other hand, following the enactment of the Sarbanes-Oxley Act in 2002, the FASB had essentially became an arm of the U.S. Government: in that context, it would be highly unlikely that as a foreign stakeholder, even a follower of U.S. GAAP, Canada would ever "sit at the table" in terms of standard setting. Thus, either way, by choosing to remain independent, the ASB was compromising its chances to retain and gain influence in the future direction of accounting standard-setting. The facts that the FASB and the IASB had started to work together on several projects and that the SEC had publicly expressed interest in convergence between U.S. GAAP and IFRS reinforced these fears.

Following a consultation process, the ASB reached the key conclusion that having one set of standards for all reporting entities was no longer an appropriate strategy as user needs, expertise, financial capabilities, control systems and governance mechanisms were so different across reporting entities. The ASB thus proposed a multi-faceted standard-setting strategy articulated around three key constituencies: publicly-accountable entities (e.g., firms listed on a stock market or registered with securities regulators), private enterprises and not-for-profit organizations. Relying on a single conceptual framework, each constituency would be provided with a distinct set of financial reporting standards. The strategy received strong support from stakeholders.

While made-in-Canada standards seem logical for private enterprises and not-for-profit entities, the main issue on the table was the choice of accounting standards for publicly accountable entities: made-in-Canada, US GAAP or IFRS? In deciding on this issue, the ASB took into account the views expressed by respondents to its 2004 consultation process. In contrast to the United States, Canada's stock market houses a much larger proportion of small or emerging firms. Consistently, most firms that relied exclusively on domestic financial markets saw no need to abandon domestic standards. Moreover, many respondents, irrespective of their relation to financial statements (i.e., preparers, auditors and users) strongly disliked US GAAP as being too costly and complex to apply. There were also concerns that the infrastructure necessary to support the use of US GAAP did not exist outside Canada's largest cities.

Overall, most of the advice provided to the ASB was to jettison separate Canadian GAAP for publicly accountable entities for the following reasons. First, it was perceived that there were very few unique Canadian circumstances, thus making a separate set of Canadian GAAP for publicly accountable enterprises unnecessary. Second, by staying aside, the continuation of a separate Canadian GAAP hindered the evolution of a single, global set of accounting standards and was inappropriate in an era of globalization of economic activity, especially when Canada's capital markets represent less than three percent of the global capital market. Third, for Canadian firms seeking capital outside the country, retaining made-in-Canada GAAP was a hindrance as both U.S. GAAP and IFRS were considered to be appropriate bases to provide investors with useful information. Finally, moving toward either U.S. GAAP or IFRS would eliminate or reduce any friction when seeking capital outside (i.e., no need to reconcile Canadian GAAP statements with other standards). More generally, it was felt that a mimetic adaptation of foreign accounting standards (either U.S. GAAP or IFRS) was a waste of valuable time and expertise, which would be rather spent on other endeavours.

Once the made-in-Canada option had been eliminated, the question that still remained outstanding was: U.S. GAAP or IFRS? For Canada, the adoption of U.S. GAAP was a tantalizing option considering the close economic and financial links between the two countries, the extensive guidance available for the implementation of U.S. GAAP, the general similarity of Canadian and US GAAP as well as the fact that many Canadian firms had already adopted U.S. GAAP because of their status as a SEC registrant. Hence, there was already much expertise in Canada regarding U.S. GAAP. In contrast, economic and financial links with other IFRS-adopting countries were much more tenuous and knowledge about IFRS within Canada was fairly limited.

However, IFRS still had much appeal for several reasons. First, IFRS were definitely emerging as the global convergence accounting standard, with their adoption gaining ground around the world. Moreover, the IASB was working hard to raise the quality of its legacy standards. The fear was that Canada would be left behind if it did not follow suit. Second, and perhaps most importantly, the IASB and FASB had started to work together on several projects, suggesting that global convergence in accounting standards was on its way: the active involvement of U.S. citizens, especially leading scholar Mary Barth, on the IASB added to the credibility of the IFRS gaining traction as a global standard. Finally, by opting for

IFRS, Canada had the chance to influence the future course of action of the IASB: such was not the case if it had opted for U.S. GAAP. At the end, the decision was made to opt for IFRS for publicly accountable entities, effective in 2011.

The following section now provides an analysis of the financial markets' impact of IFRS adoption in Canada post-2011. More specifically, we strive to answer the question as to whether or not IFRS meet their stated goals with respect to financial statements such as improving their relevance, quality, and comparability is of interest. In other words, beyond IFRS adoption, do their implementation and the enforcement of such implementation through corporate governance bring benefits to Canadian market participants? Toward that end, considering corporate governance, we analyze if IFRS-based earnings bring incremental information benefits to investors compared with made-in-Canada Generally Accepted Accounting Principles (GAAP) used prior to 2011.

3 IFRS, Governance and Information Asymmetry: An Empirical Investigation

3.1 Governance and Information Asymmetry

The adoption and implementation of IFRS can be viewed as being a regime change in terms of governance as financial reporting standards represent a core component of a country's institutional environment. This raises two questions. First, does corporate governance matter in decreasing information asymmetry between managers and investors? Second, are IFRS effective as the IASB claims to mitigate the information asymmetry between managers and investors? Both issues are intertwined because of the overlap between IFRS and corporate governance. We first review prior evidence with respect to the interface between corporate governance and information asymmetry.

In principle, enhanced corporate governance should lead to greater transparency, which enhances stock market liquidity, and reduces transactions costs for a firm's stock (Diamond and Verrecchia 1991). Several approaches coexist for the purpose of assessing a firm's information asymmetry. Kanagaretnam et al. (2007) document that changes in bid–ask spreads at the time of earnings announcements are negatively related to board independence, board activity, and the percentage stock holdings of directors and officers. Their results are consistent with the view that firms with higher levels of corporate governance have lower information asymmetry around quarterly earnings announcements.

A few studies document an association between corporate governance and stock returns or firm value (e.g. Gompers et al. 2003; Beiner et al. 2006).

Focusing on European firms, Vander Bauwhede and Willekens (2008) argue that firms disclose corporate governance information to reduce information asymmetry and agency costs stemming from the separation between ownership and control, thus improving investor confidence in financial reporting. Using ratings on corporate governance disclosure issued by an independent rating agency, the authors show that the level of disclosure is lower for firms with higher ownership concentration and higher for companies from common-law countries. In the Canadian context, Cormier et al. (2010) show that some formal monitoring attributes (board and audit committee size) reduce information asymmetry.

3.2 IFRS and Information Asymmetry

Overall, prior evidence suggests that for a country categorized by strong investor protection and high-quality financial reporting and enforcement, IFRS adoption improves the value relevance of financial reporting for stock market participants. Considering that Canada is a country with a strong enforcement, we do expect IFRS adoption to translate into a positive outcome for investors.

There is some evidence that a switch from domestic standards to IFRS has a modest positive impact on market liquidity and the cost of equity capital, most likely resulting from the reduction in information asymmetry between investors and managers following the implementation of IFRS (Daske et al. 2008; Bruggermann et al. 2009). However, firms that voluntarily adopt IFRS ahead of the mandated year of adoption experience a stronger improvement in the liquidity of their stock and in their cost of capital than firms that only adopt IFRS at the required date. Therefore, it is unlikely that IFRS adoption in itself drives the improvement in the information set that is available to investors: other regulatory or institutional changes probably take precedence. In this vein, Byard et al. (2011), based on a European sample, find that analysts' absolute forecast errors and forecast dispersion decrease relative to a control sample only for those mandatory IFRS adopters domiciled in countries with both strong enforcement regimes and domestic accounting standards that differ significantly from IFRS.

Landsman et al. (2012) investigate whether the information content of earnings announcements increases after mandatory IFRS adoption, based on observations from 27 countries from 2000 to 2007 (16 countries' adoption of IFRS and 11 countries' remaining adoption of domestic accounting standards). Abnormal return volatility and abnormal trading volume are used as proxies for the information content of earnings announcements. The authors find that the information content increased in IFRS-adopting countries, but this happens only when they use abnormal return volatility (not abnormal trading volume) as a proxy for information content. Moreover, they find that increases in abnormal return volatility are concentrated in code law countries.

Hence, overall, the evidence with respect to IFRS impact on financial reporting relevance is rather mixed, and potentially conditional on the strictness of legal enforcement. In a context of strict legal enforcement such as Canada, we posit that both corporate governance and IFRS should improve market liquidity and reduce information asymmetry.

Hence, the following hypothesis:

H1 There is a substitution effect between corporate governance and the advent of IFRS on their impact on information asymmetry.

3.3 Corporate Governance, IFRS and Value Relevance of Earnings

In the context of Australia, a country categorized by strong investor protection laws and active enforcement, and using a longitudinal study that covers pre-IFRS and post-IFRS periods during 1990 to 2008, Chalmers et al.'s (2011) find an increase in the value relevance of earnings post IFRS. Their study suggests that the impact of IFRS-based financial information on financial markets may be driven by a country's institutions regarding investor protection and enforcement, both dimensions underlying high quality financial reporting. Moreover, the use of IFRS information allows firms to improve their coverage by foreign financial analysts as well as the accuracy of their forecasts, especially in countries with high investor protection (Byard et al. 2011). Hence, an increase in relevance for stock markets is observed for firms highly followed by analysts.

Hence, overall, the evidence with respect to IFRS impact on financial reporting relevance is potentially conditional on the strictness of legal enforcement.

Concerning governance, Chang and Sun (2009) argue that the passage of Sarbanes-Oxley Act (SOX) marks the beginning of firms' mandatory disclosure of the audit committee composition and other corporate governance information. They posit that SOX improves the effectiveness of an independent audit committee and other corporate governance functions in monitoring the earnings quality of cross-listed foreign firms. They measure the earnings quality by the sample firms' earnings informativeness (i.e. earnings response coefficient) and earnings management. Their findings show significant positive associations between earnings informativeness and audit committee independence as well as board independence in the post-SOX period. In contrast to the post-SOX results, they do not find a significant association between earnings informativeness and audit committee independence in the pre-SOX period. Furthermore, their results show a positive (negative) association between earnings informativeness (earnings management) and an aggregate corporate governance score, which is a measure of overall corporate governance functions.

Verriest et al. (2011) find that European firms with strong corporate governance mechanisms engage in higher financial reporting quality around the moment of first-time IFRS adoption. Further, the authors notice that firms with more independent boards, more active boards and especially firms with more effective audit committees disclose substantially more information about the impact of IFRS on their financial statements. They also find that strong governance firms disclose more extensively on specific IFRS disclosure standards. Finally, their results suggest that strong governance firms use the timing adoption flexibility in a conservative fashion while weak governance firms tend to use this option in an opportunistic fashion.

Given the importance of corporate governance on the impact of IFRS on the value relevance of earnings, we test the following hypothesis:

H2 Corporate governance enhances the value relevance of earnings to a larger extent under IFRS.

3.4 Method

The sample is based on Canadian firms comprising the S&P/TSX index of the Toronto stock exchange for years 2009 (Canadian GAAP) and 2011 (IFRS). The index comprises 233 firms. From this sample, there are missing data for 13firms (data not available for both years). From the sample of 220 firms, 36 firms use the same set of GAAP for 2009 and 2011 (so-called no-change firms): 17 firms are complying with US-GAAP and 19 firms have a year-end after April 30 or IFRS adoption is postponed for different reasons (e.g. regulated industries). For firms with year-end after April, the data in Compustat database are for 2008 and 2010, i.e. prior to IFRS adoption. This gives a sample of 184 firms. We have missing data for governance (4 firms for Governance Board Games, 32 for ISS Governance score), for forecast dispersion (18 firms), and 3 firms for stock price (see Table 1 for details).

For 2010, Canadian firms must report earnings and balance sheet reconciliations between Canadian GAAP and IFRS. However, financial statement numbers are still presented in Canadian GAAP. We decided not to include year 2010 to avoid confusion and to focus on clear Canadian GAAP and IFRS years. Financial data was collected from Compustat and Stock Guide. Governance scores come from Board Games ranking (The Globe & Mail) and from ISS Governance Quick score. Sample firms operate in the following industries: Financial; Real Estate; Materials;

Table 1 Sample description: Firm-year observations

	Board Games	ISS Governance score	Board Games	ISS Governance score	Board Games	ISS Governance score
	BAS	*BAS*	*FORDIS*	*FORDIS*	*PRICE*	*PRICE*
Sample	368	368	368	368	368	368
GOV	(8)	(64)	(8)	(64)	(8)	(64)
FORDIS			(36)	(36)		
PRICE					(6)	(6)
Final sample	360	304	324	268	354	298

Energy; Industrials; Consumer discretionary; Consumer staple; Utilities; Telecommunications; Information technology; and Health care.

3.5 Empirical Models

We develop the following two empirical models:

Corporate governance and IFRS: Incidence on information asymmetry

$$BAS = LnVOLUME + LnVOLATILITY + GOV + GOV{*}YIFRS + YIFRS \tag{1a}$$

$$FORDIS = BETA + ANFOL + NEGEPS + GOV + GOV{*}YIFRS + YIFRS \tag{1b}$$

Corporate governance and IFRS: Incidence on stock market valuation

The valuation model is inspired by the work of Feltham and Ohlson (1995) and Amir and Lev (1996). Such a model maps a firm's book value and earnings into its stock market valuation.

$$PRICE = EQPS + EQPS{*}YIFRS + EPS + EPS{*}YIFRS + EPS{*}GOV + EPS{*}GOV{*}YIFRS + GOV{*}YIFRS + GOV + YIFRS \tag{2}$$

Where: *LnVOLUME:* Natural log of trading volume; *LnVOLATILITY:* Natural log of share price volatility; *BETA: Systematic risk (beta); ANFOL:* Number of analysts following a firm; *BAS*: Bid ask spread; *GOV*: Governance score; *YIFRS*: Year for financial reporting under IFRS; *EQPS*: Equity per share; *EPS*: Earnings per share.

Complete definitions for the various variables are provided in Appendix.

3.6 Descriptive Statistics

Table 2 provides some descriptive statistics about sample firms' financial variables under Canadian GAAP versus IFRS. We document a decrease in information asymmetry following the adoption of IFRS in Canada. Hence, we observe a decrease in bid ask spread, in forecast dispersion, in share price volatility. We also observe an increase in liquidity as characterized by a higher level of trading activity. Finally, analyst following has increased from Canadian GAAP period to post IFRS.

Table 3 reports on the governance scores. For Board Games, the mean total score is 63.22. Board composition (19.06) and Shareholder rights (20.63) present the

Table 2 Descriptive statistics

	Canadian GAAP (2009)		IFRS (2011)	
	Mean	Median	Mean	Median
EPS	1.10	0.57	1.49	1.02
EQPS	14.401	10.428	11.961	9.855
FORDIS	0.010	0.026	0.008	0.011
BAS (%)	0.686	0.444	0.386	0.258
VOLUME (annual in millions)	31.5	11.6	35.0	14.1
VOLATILITY	68.787	63.786	35.231	31.860
BETA	1.917	1.141	1.661	1.194
ANFOL	6.769	6.0	8.144	8.0
NEGEPS	0.274	0	0.179	0

EQPS Equity per share, *EPS* Earnings per share, *FORDIS* Forecast dispersion scaled by lag price, *BAS* Bid ask spread, *VOLUME* Trading volume, *Volatility* Share price volatility, *ANFOL* Number of analysts following a firm, *Beta Systematic risk*, *NEGEPS* Negative EPS (1/0), *GOV* Governance score

Table 3 Governance score by components 2009/2011

	Mean	Std. Dev.	Min.	Max
Board Games				
Board composition	19.059	5.094	1	29
Compensation	15.485	5.969	2	28
Shareholder rights	20.634	5.959	2	31
Disclosure	8.173	5.086	1	12
Total	63.217	16.082	27	96
ISS Governance score				
Board structure	5.526	5.090	1	10
Compensation	5.335	2.783	1	10
Shareholder rights	4.973	2.821	1	10
Audit	1.178	1.260	1	10
Total	5.431	2.790	1	10
Adjusted Total*	5.461			

*10 – Total +1

highest mean scores. Considering the maximum scores allowed within each component, we get a mean relative score of 0.66 for Board composition (19.06/29), 0.55 for Compensation (15.49/28), 0.67 for Shareholders rights (20.63/31) and 0.68 for Disclosure (8.17/12). For ISS Governance Score, board structure (5.53), compensation (5.34) and shareholder rights (4.97) show quite similar scores.

3.6.1 Multivariate Results

We estimate regressions using OLS with robust estimators since the Breusch-Pagan/Cook-Weisberg tests show the presence of heteroscedasticity. Moreover, multicollinearity is not an issue in any regressions since the highest variance of inflation factor is 4.0. Finally, we exclude from regressions all observations with standardized residuals exceeding two.

Table 4 reports on the relation between corporate governance, the adoption of IFRS and information asymmetry. Based on prior literature, *LnVOLUME* and *LnVOLATILITY* are used as control variables in bid ask spread regressions and *BETA*, *ANFOL* and *NEGEPS* in forecast dispersion regressions. All coefficients except for *ANFOL* are significant and in the predicted direction.

Results suggest that corporate governance is associated with less information asymmetry in the market place as measured by bid ask spread and forecast dispersion. As expected, results show a negative relationship between *GOV* and *BAS* and a positive relationship between *GOV* and *FORDIS*. Also as expected, the advent of IFRS reduces the impact of corporate governance on information asymmetry, suggesting a partial substitution effect (*GOV*IFRS* is positive and significant in all regressions). This is consistent with hypothesis 1. The substitution effect is not complete since the joint tests of the sum of coefficients *GOV* and *GOV*YIFRS* are different from zero in three regressions out of four.

Table 5 reports on the value relevance of earnings considering corporate governance and the adoption of IFRS. First, results show that earnings are value relevant only for firms with good governance (Board Games: *EPS*GOV* = 0.063; $p < 0.01$; ISS Quick Score: *EPS*GOV* = 0.399; $p < 0.01$). Second, it appears that migrating from Canadian GAAP to IFRS enhances the value relevance of earnings, but only for firms with good governance (Board Games: *EPS*GOV*YIFRS* = 0.050;

Table 4 OLS Regressions—Robust estimators: relevance of governance for information asymmetry

	BAS		*FORDIS*	
	Board Games	ISS Quick Score	Board Games	ISS Quick Score
LnVOLUME	−0.068***	−0.065***	–	–
LnVOLATILITY	0.195***	0.211***	–	–
BETA	–	–	0.005***	0.006***
ANFOL	–	–	−0.001	−0.001
NEGEPS	–	–	0.005**	0.008**
GOV	−0.010***	−0.039***	−0.032***	−0.149***
*GOV*YIFRS*	0.007***	0.027***	0.028***	0.075**
YIFRS	−0.526***	−0.251***	−0.024***	−0.010**
Joint test (F test) *GOV* + *GOV*YIFRS* = 0	17.11(0.00)	5.54(0.02)	0.34(0.56)	2.98(0.08)
R-Square	34.3 %	27.4 %	39.2 %	42.7 %
F-Statistic	21.1(0.00)	11.4(0.00)	5.8(0.00)	3.9(0.00)
N	360	304	324	268

BAS Bid ask spread, *FORDIS* Forecast dispersion scaled by lag Price, *LnVOLUME* Natural log of trading volume, *LnVolatility* Natural log of share price volatility, *Beta Systematic risk, ANFOL* Number of analysts following a firm, *NEGEPS* Negative EPS (1/0), *GOV* Governance score, *YIFRS* Year for financial reporting under IFRS

Table 5 OLS Regressions – Robust estimators: relevance of earnings for stock price valuation

	Board Games	ISS Quick Score
EQPS	0.826***	0.924***
*EQPS*YIFRS*	−0.202*	−2.149
EPS	−1.466	0.228
*EPS*YIFRS*	−2.833	1.691
*EPS*GOV*	**0.063*****	**0.399*****
*EPS*GOV*YIFRS*	**0.050****	**0.871****
GOV	0.084*	0.168
*GOV*YIFRS*	−0.024	−2.298*
YIFRS	0.216	34.163*
Joint test (F test) *EPS*GOV-EPS*GOV*YIFRS* = 0	0.05(0.82)	0.49(0.48)
R-Square	88.8 %	53.9 %
F-Statistic	297.6(0.00)	106.6(0.00)
N	354	298

EQPS Equity per share, *EPS* Earnings per share, *GOV* Governance score, *YIFRS* Year for financial reporting under IFRS
*$p < 0.10$; **$p < 0.05$; ***$p < 0.01$

$p < 0.05$; ISS Quick Score: *EPS*GOV*YIFRS* = 0.871; $p < 0.05$). Consistent with hypothesis 2, corporate governance enhances the value relevance of earnings in a larger extent under IFRS.

This research highlights the importance to consider corporate governance when evaluating the impact of IFRS adoption for stock market participants.

3.6.2 Recap

In this section, we analyze how the advent of IFRS affects the role of corporate governance on information asymmetry between managers and investors and the value relevance of earnings. We bring some evidence that migrating from Canadian GAAP to IFRS provides investors with more relevant information by reducing the information gap between managers and investors. First, the advent of IFRS coincides with an increase in analyst following and trading volume, a reduction in bid-ask spread, and analyst forecast dispersion. Second, IFRS enhance the value relevance of earnings. Third, results suggest that corporate governance is associated with less information asymmetry on the market place as measured by bid ask spread and forecast dispersion. Fourth, the advent of IFRS reduces the impact of corporate governance on information asymmetry. A partial substitution effect is observed. Fifth, results show that earnings are value relevant only for firms with good governance. Finally, it appears that migrating from Canadian GAAP to IFRS enhances the value relevance of earnings, but only for firms with good governance.

4 Conclusion

This chapter presented the process taken by the Canadian Accounting Standards which ultimately led to Canada adopting IFRS for all publicly accountable entities, starting January 1st, 2011. Then, in line with the ASB's objective underlying its decision to adopt IFRS, we investigate the impact of IFRS adoption of Canadian financial markets, in terms of information asymmetry between managers and investors and value relevance for investors, Our analysis is performed through a corporate governance perspective as IFRS adoption is expected to change Canada's institutional regime, a key aspect of corporate governance.

Our discussion of the process leading to IFRS adoption highlights the challenges faced by a standard-setter, both domestic and global. Some aspects of Canada's business and organizational landscape led the ASB to adopt a three-track standard setting strategy for publicly accountable entities, private enterprises and not-for-profit organizations, thus reflecting the unique needs of each constituency. The choice of IFRS for publicly accountable entities reflected a rational assessment of domestic business realities, user needs and Canada's strategic aims on the global standard-setting scene. The transition went relatively smoothly and our empirical results suggest modest yet tangible informational benefits from the adoption of IFRS. However, it appears that a firm's governance does affect how an institutional change such as IFRS adoption influences corporate practices. Moreover, there is some substitution effect between governance and IFRS in influencing information asymmetry. Hence, our research highlights the importance to consider corporate governance when assessing the impact of IFRS adoption for stock market participants. As far as we know, this is the first study to investigate the value relevance of earnings integrating the quality of corporate governance.

Our study contributes to accounting and corporate governance literatures in at least two ways. We contribute to the literature on IFRS by studying the impact of corporate governance on information asymmetry prior versus under IFRS. Second, we contribute to the literature on the stock market valuation effects of mandatory IFRS adoption by investigating the value relevance of earnings integrating the quality of corporate governance.

Our analysis does lead us to reflect upon the challenge of an IFRS-adopting country when faced with some IASB decisions that are not to its liking or potentially detrimental to the interests of some domestic stakeholders. A potential course of action could be to suspend application of a particular standard or modify it. However, for many Canadian firms that are cross-listed in the U.S., such a departure from strict application of IFRS as adopted by the IASB would preclude them from taking advantage of the exemption to reconcile their earnings with U.S. GAAP earnings. Any advantage to be derived from such a strategy would therefore be compromised by additional reporting and control costs. Another alternative is to carve out particular sectors of the economy that are deemed to be prejudiced by IFRS. However, while appealing in the short run, such a strategy implies that there is an alternative local set of standards that is readily available to supplant IFRS for publicly accountable entities: sustaining such a set of standards would be a costly endeavour. As the number of IFRS adopting countries grows, and the number of global stakeholders increases, instances where some Canadian stakeholders' interests and IASB's perspective are bound to happen and even to increase in number. This issue is also a challenge for the IASB as it seeks to retain its credibility and its appeal. The final outcome is still uncertain but it is likely that compromise, arguments and extensive listening are going to be taking place.

Definition of Variables

GOV. Vafeas (2000) finds that earnings are more informative for companies with more effective boards while Dey (2005) reports that earnings credibility increases with board quality. These findings suggest that higher corporate governance quality should be associated with less information asymmetry and improve analyst forecast accuracy. A negative (positive) association is expected between *GOV* and BAS (*FORDIS*). Two governance scores are used. The first one is based on Board Games (The Globe and Mail's annual report on corporate governance),[2] which includes four components: 1) board composition; 2) shareholding and compensation; 3) shareholder rights; and 4) disclosure. The grid is based on a total of 100 marks (Board composition; 31 marks; Shareholding and compensation: 26 marks; Shareholder rights: 31 marks; Disclosure: 12 marks). The second score is based on ISS Governance Quick score. The grid is based on a total of 10 marks, 1 meaning an excellent and 10 meaning a weak score. The score is based on board structure, compensation, shareholder rights, and the audit. To facilitate interpretations, we change the score so that an excellent score is 10 instead of 1 (10 − total score +1).

LnVOLUME and *LnVOLATILITY*. Prior research document that trading volume and share price volatility are fundamental determinants of bid ask spreads. An inverse relationship between spreads and trading activity is expected (Demsetz 1968). Price volatility is also a determinant of bid ask spreads and as such incorporated in information asymmetry models of the spread (e.g. Copeland and Galai 1983; Aitken and Frino 1996). Hence, we expect a negative (positive) relationship between BAS and *LnVOLUME* (*LnVOLATILITY*). The logarithmic transformation of these two variables is used to reduce the skewness and potential heteroscedasticity problems (Aitken and Frino 1996).

BETA. Patton and Verardo (2010) observe that the increase in systematic risk is greater for earnings announcements with larger positive or negative surprises, and with greater analyst forecast dispersion. We expect a positive association between *BETA* and *FORDIS*.

[2] The Globe and Mail is Canada's leading financial newspaper in terms of reach and readership. Its governance survey has been widely used in prior research (e.g., Klein et al. 2005).

ANFOL. Analyst forecasts precision is likely to improve, as more information about a company is processed and disclosed by analysts (Alford and Berger 1999). Hope (2003a) documents a negative relationship between analyst following and forecast error. Thus, a negative association is expected between *ANFOL* and *FORDIS*.

NEGEPS. Hope (2003a) documents that negative earnings are associated with more forecast error, suggesting that earnings is more difficult to predict for companies that experience losses. Consistent with Hope (2003a, b), an indicative variable for negative earnings is used. We anticipate a positive relationship between this binary variable and *FORDIS*.

References

Aitken M, Frino A (1996) Asymmetry in stock returns following block trades on the Australian stock exchange: a note. Abacus 32:54–61

Alford AW, Berger PG (1999) A simultaneous equations analysis of forecast accuracy, analyst following, and trading volume. J Account Audit Finan 14(3):219–40

Amir E, Lev M (1996) Value-relevance of non-financial information: the wireless communication industry. J Account Econ 22(1–3):3–30

Bruggermann U, Daske H, Homberg C, Pope PF (2009) How do individual investors react to global IFRS adoption? http://ssrn.com/abstract=1437542

Cormier D, Ledoux MJ, Magnan M, Aerts A (2010) Corporate governance and information asymmetry between managers and investors. Corp Gov 10(5):574–589

Beiner S, Drobetz W, Schmid M, Zimmerman H (2006) An integrated framework of corporate governance and firm valuation – evidence from Switzerland. Eur Finan Manag 12:249–283

Byard D, Li Y, Yu Y (2011) The effect of mandated IFRS adoption on analyst' forecast error. J Account Res 49(1):69–96

Chalmers K, Clinch G, Godfrey J (2011) Changes in value relevance of accounting information upon IFRS adoption: evidence from Australia. Aust J Manag 36(2):151–173

Chang J-C, Sun H-L (2009) Crossed-listed foreign firms' earnings informativeness, earnings management and disclosures of corporate governance information under SOX. Int J Account 44(1):1–32

Copeland TE, Galai D (1983) Information effects on the bid-ask spread. J Finan 38:1457–1469

Daske H, Hail L, Leuz C, Verdi R (2008) Mandatory IFRS reporting around the world: early evidence on the economic consequences. J Account Res 46(5):1085–1143

Demsetz H (1968) Why regulate utilities. J Law Econ 11(1):55–56

Dey A (2005) Corporate governance and financial reporting credibility. PhD, Illinois, North Western University

Diamond D, Verrecchia R (1991) Disclosure, liquidity, and the cost of capital. J Finan (September) 46(4):1325–1360

Feltham G, Ohlson J (1995) Valuation and clean surplus accounting for operating and financial activities. Contemp Account Res 11(2):689–731

Gompers A, Ishii JL, Metrick A (2003) Corporate governance and equity prices. Q J Econ 118 (1):107–55

Hope OK (2003a) Disclosure practices, enforcement of accounting standards and analysts' forecasts accuracy: an international study. J Account Res 41(2):235–272

Hope OK (2003b) Analyst following and the influence of disclosure components, IPOs and ownership concentration. Asia-Pacific J Account Econ 10(2):117–141

Kanagaretnam K, Lobo GL, Whalen D (2007) Does good corporate governance reduce information asymmetry around quarterly earnings announcements? J Account Public Policy 26 (4):497–522

Klein P, Shapiro D, Young J (2005) Corporate governance, family ownership and firm value: the Canadian evidence. Corp Gov Int Rev 13(6):769–784

Landsman WR, Maydew EL, Thornock JR (2012) The information content of annual earnings announcements and mandatory adoption of IFRS. J Account Econ 53(1–2):34–54

Patton AJ, Verardo M (2010) Does Beta Move with News? Firm-Specific Information Flows and Learning about Profitability. Working paper. Duke University

Vafeas N (2000) Board structure and the informativeness of earnings. J Account Public Policy 19 (2):139–160

Vander Bauwhede H, Willekens M (2008) Disclosure on Corporate Governance in the European Union. Corp Gov Int Rev 16(2):101–115

Verriest A, Gaeremynck A, Thornton D (2011) The Impact of Corporate Governance on IFRS Adoption Choices (November 6, 2011). Available at SSRN: http://ssrn.com/abstract=1266698 or doi:10.2139/ssrn.1266698

France. IFRS and France: A Marriage of Convenience

Hervé Stolowy

Abstract This contribution aims to provide a chronological examination of the relationship between France and IFRS/IAS, which appears to have been (and still be) very turbulent. We shall seek to describe this relationship through several themes: what was France's position before the early 2000s and the arrival of EU regulation 1606/2002? What happened after that regulation was adopted? What role did accounting standardization play, especially France's Accounting Standards Authority (ANC) which was set up in 2010? What stance did French academics take in the debates over the role of the IASB?

1 Introduction

French accounting has had for a long time the reputation of being State-influenced and not oriented towards international issues. French accounting, at least for individual (stand-alone) financial statements, follows the guidance of the General Accounting Plan (*Plan Comptable Général*), which provides definitions and rules in the following areas: (1) terminology; (2) methods for valuing assets and liabilities and measuring operating results; (3) the functioning of the chart of accounts and the presentation of financial statements; and (4) recommended cost accounting systems (HSD Group 1988). The example of the French "plan" has been significant internationally, especially within the European Community and served as a model for other member states that have instituted national accounting codes such as Spain, Belgium, and Greece. It has also influenced the accounting practices of a number of African countries with colonial or cultural links with France, which have instituted national accounting codes (Standish 1990).

As mentioned by Groupe Calan Ramolino (1997), the General Accounting Plan was first issued in 1947, mainly to ensure comparability between nationalized industries. In 1957, the first version of the "*plan*" was modified (a) to suit the reporting needs of different types of industries and (b) became compulsory for

H. Stolowy (✉)
HEC Paris, Jouy-en-Josas, France
e-mail: stolowy@hec.fr

D. Bensadon, N. Praquin (eds.), *IFRS in a Global World*,
DOI 10.1007/978-3-319-28225-1_18

financial reporting, for tax purposes and for facilitation the establishment of national statistics. The same year, the French Government created the "*Conseil National de la Comptabilité*" (CNC), the organization responsible for the definition of accounting policies and practices. The CNC's mission, from its inception, includes the formulation of recommendations, interpretations or clarifications about or beyond the 1957 "*Plan comptable général*", that impose additional reporting requirements so as to keep it current and relevant.

Following the introduction of both the Fourth and Seventh [European Union] Directives, the 1980s were a period of substantial change for French accounting (Scheid and Walton 1995). The provisions of the Fourth EC Directive were included in the 1982 version of the "*Plan comptable*", especially the concept of "true and fair view". Since 1983, the general accounting principles have been incorporated in the *Code de Commerce*, the formal body of French commercial and business law, giving it more power. As a consequence, accounting law and practices in France comply with both the EC Fourth Directive (European Economic Community 1978) and the Seventh Directive (European Economic Community 1983). However, because of the great influence of tax law on French accounting principles and practices, the financial statements for both reporting and tax purposes are identical; thus conservatism and prudence remain of prime importance in French individual (stand-alone) financial statements.

On July 19, 2002 the European Union adopted Regulation 1606/2002 (European Union 2002) stipulating (art. 4) that for each financial year starting on or after 1 January 2005, "companies governed by the law of a Member State shall prepare their consolidated accounts in conformity with the international accounting standards (. . .) if, at their balance sheet date, their securities are admitted to trading on a regulated market of any Member State".

France's situation in respect of this regulation seemed clear: the consolidated financial statements of listed French groups had to comply with IFRS/IAS[1] from 2005.[2] But with almost 20 years hindsight,[3] the relationship between France and IFRS/IAS in fact appears to have been (and still be) very turbulent.

---

[1] On April 2001, the IASB approved that "all standards and interpretations issued under previous constitutions continue to be applicable unless and until they are amended or withdrawn". These previous standards adopted by the IASC are named "International Accounting Standards" (IAS). The IASB also announced in April 2001 that the IASC Foundation trustees had agreed that accounting standards issued by the IASB would be designated "International Financial Reporting Standards" (IFRS). To reduce the possibility of confusion for the reader, following Stolowy et al. (2013, p. 165) we use the term "IFRS/IAS" to mean all international accounting standards. We thus make no distinction between IFRS in the strict sense (i.e., standards adopted by the IASB after 2001) and IAS (i.e., standards adopted by the IASC before 2001, some of which have since been revised, amended, or otherwise reformatted by the IASB).

[2] For a presentation of IFRS/IAS in French, see Raffournier (2010) and Obert (2013); for an English presentation see Picker et al. (2012).

[3] Referring to the first discussions on the application of international accounting standards in France.

This contribution in honor of our colleague Jacques Richard aims to provide a chronological examination of the period since the 1990s, when the question of French groups adopting international standards began to become acutely relevant.

Several expressions come to mind in considering the relationship between France and international accounting standards: Do they make good bedfellows? Or are they in a marriage of convenience or a forced marriage?

We shall seek to describe the current relationship status through several themes: what was France's position before the early 2000s and the arrival of regulation 1606/2002? What happened after that regulation was adopted? What role did accounting standardization play, especially France's Accounting Standards Authority (*Autorité des NormesComptables*—ANC) which was set up in 2010? What stance did French academics take in the debates over the role of the IASB?

2 The Failure of the Law of April 6, 1998

On April 6, 1998, the French parliament adopted an important "Law reforming accounting regulation". This law addressed two major issues: (1) the reform of the French standard-setting process, and (2) the possibility for French companies to use international standards. One of its objectives was to promote French companies' international development by allowing them to use international standards for the presentation of their consolidated financial statements (Stolowy 2002).

Before this new law, when a French company wanted to issue consolidated financial statements under a set of international or foreign (in practice, American) standards not compatible with French standards, it was obligated to issue two sets of accounts.[4] The *Commission des Operations de Bourse* (COB)[5] also noted[6] that since no set of international standards had been adopted at the national level, French companies must prepare their accounts and financial statements published in France in accordance with French regulations. However, the COB added that as in many cases French accounting rules are not very different from international or American standards,[7] it did not object to companies stating that their accounts or financial statements, prepared in accordance with French standards, also complied with international or American standards.

As Stolowy (2002, p. 186) reminds us, the objective of article 6 of the Law of April 6, 1998 reforming accounting regulation was to allow French listed-companies to avoid having to publish two sets of accounts. This article was a

[4] COB, in its "Annual report", 1995, p. 105.

[5] Now renamed AMF (*Autorité des Marchés Financiers*): the French equivalent to the US Securities and Exchange Commission (SEC).

[6] COB, in its "Bulletin", No. 321, February 1998, p. 3.

[7] This assertion by the COB is a simplification to say the least. It is perhaps explained by the COB's aim to help French firms by making their financial reporting work easier.

response to the request made by France-based international groups raising funds on international financial markets to be allowed to have to prepare a singleset of consolidated financial statements under standards used on the major stock markets (as issuing two sets of accounts is an expensive process which interferes with communication policy and does not benefit investors).

These France-based international groups were supposed to be exempted from following French standards if they applied international standards approved by the newly created[8] French Accounting Regulation Committee (*Comité de la ré glementation comptable*—CRC). The intended beneficiaries of the new consolidation regime were French listed international groups whose shares were trading on foreign capital markets, and such groups seeking to be listed on foreign stock exchanges.

The law stated that listed French groups were exempt from applying French standards in preparing and publishing their consolidated financial statements if they used international standards, subject to the conditions specified by the CRC: the standards used had to be set by the IASC, translated into French and approved by (endorsed as) a CRC rule. At the very end of the discussion of the law's text, the French National Assembly introduced a requirement that international standards could be applied only if they were compatible with European regulations.

France's new law had been adopted with the best of intentions, but as is often the case, in practice it faced some major difficulties. We have identified two main types of difficulties: (a) compliance of international standards with European regulations, (b) time necessary to implement the law.

2.1 Compliance with European Regulations

An "inventory" of divergences between the international standards and European regulations was drawn upby the European Commission and identified several differences. Some countries, like Germany, believed that certain international standards were incompatible with certain European regulations (Stolowy 2002, p. 190).

2.2 Practical Implementations

The adoption of international standards by a CRC rule was problematic, since the CRC had to wait until the end of the revision process at the IASC level, and this delayed the law's entry into force. Looking back, the importance of this obstacle is even more evident than at the time. In 1998, France could reasonably expect the

[8] Formed by the same law of April 6, 1998.

IASC's revision of the standards to be completed in1999 or perhaps 2000, but today we know that the process took a lot longer, and, indeed, this fact supports the argument by certain critics of the IASC (which has since become the IASB) that the standardization lacked stability.

On this concept of stability, Chand and Cummings (2008) note that the IASB sought to provide a "stable platform" of high-quality standards that would enable a smooth transition by individual countries from national standards to IFRS. By March 31, 2004 the IASB had established such a stable platform of new and revised standards, applicable from 2005. Chand and Cummings review the major changes made by the IASB to its stable platform of standards since 2004, and illustrate how politics and lobbying influence the standard-setting process.

3 Intervention by President Chirac (and the French Banks) in 2003

France never actually applied its law of April 6, 1998, for the reasons stated earlier but also because the European Commission published a "Communication" (European Commission 2000) on June 13, 2000 stating that it would present a formal proposal "requiring all listed EU companies to prepare their consolidated accounts in accordance with one single set of accounting standards, namely International Accounting Standards (IAS)". On February 13, 2001, the European Commission published a proposed regulation, which was adopted in July 2002 as Regulation 1606/2002 referred to earlier.

It is conceivable that the Communication of 2000 showed France that all the provisions of its law of April 6, 1998 were becoming irrelevant. Also, as mentioned earlier some of them were difficult to apply in practice. However, it is impossible to maintain that the Communication of 2000 took France (and other European countries) by surprise, since as early as 1995 the European Commission had released a Communication (European Commission 1995) presenting a very thorough diagnosis of the difficulties of European accounting harmonization, and among various solutions recommending convergence towards the IASC and IAS.

On July 4, 2003, Jacques Chirac, then President of the French Republic, sent a letter to the President of the European Commission Romani Prodi to warn him that "certain accounting standards currently being adopted in the European Union could lead to increased "financialization" of our economy and business management methods that would place too much emphasis on the short term". He added that the European Union should "... have more influence on the elaboration of standards by IASB". For the first time, a top-ranking politician was directly taking part in the accounting debate and bringing it out of the accounting circles to which it had been confined.

As Colasse (2012, p. 4) states, President Chirac's letter in fact concerned primarily standards 32 and 39 covering the definition, measurement and recognition of financial instruments (see also Colasse 2004).

This direct intervention by the French President probably resulted from action taken by the French banks,[9] which in September 2002 published a document entitled "Loss of confidence in the financial markets and International Accounting Standards"[10] stating that the banks were concerned that, "in their current state, the (. . .) IAS/(. . .)IFRS approved by the IAS Board present serious deficiencies that run counter to [the] goals which have led the European Union to impose the use of these standards by large quoted companies from 2005 [onwards]".

In any case, it is very possible that Jacques Chirac's letter explains why on July 16, 2003 the European Accounting Regulatory Committee, which consists of representatives of European Union member states, decided to adopt all standards prepared by the International Accounting Standards Board (IASB) except for standards 32 and 39 (our own emphasis).

4 Adoption of IFRS/IAS in France in 2005

The European Union keeps a table showing the implementation of IFRS/IAS in each member state. The most recent published update dates, to our knowledge, from February 2, 2012.[11] This table is fairly complex because, apart from the straightforward case of listed companies' consolidated financial statements, Regulation 1606/2002 covers other cases for which the question of an obligation or ban regarding use of IFRS/IAS may arise.

The current situation in France for each of these cases is summarized below.

4.1 Listed Companies

4.1.1 Consolidated Financial Statements

Member states have no choice in this case, which is the main situation in which international standards must apply. In fact this case is not even included in the European Union's table.

[9] Insurance companies were also against the international standards on financial instruments.

[10] http://www.fbf.fr/fr/files/87JBNH/Memo_FBF_revision_projet_normes_IAS_2002_EN.pdf (Last retrieved: December 21, 2015).

[11] http://ec.europa.eu/internal_market/accounting/docs/ias/ias-use-of-options_en.pdf (Last retrieved: December 21, 2015).

4.1.2 Annual Financial Statements

For "annual" (i.e., individual or stand-alone) financial statements, Regulation 1606/2002 offers member states two options:

- they may permit IAS in the annual financial statements for listed companies
- they may require IAS in the annual financial statements for listed companies.

France has not taken up either of these options, and therefore listed companies must use French standards for their annual stand-alone financial statements.

4.2 Other Companies

4.2.1 Consolidated Financial Statements

For "other" (i.e., non-listed) groups, Regulation 1606/2002 offers member states two options:

- they may permit IAS in the consolidated financial statements for other companies
- they may require IAS in the consolidated financial statements for other companies.

France has taken up the first option, and consequently non-listed French groups are allowed to present their consolidated financial statements in compliance with IFRS/IAS. As the two options are mutually exclusive, France has not chosen to oblige non-listed groups to apply international standards.

4.2.2 Annual Financial Statements

For "other" (i.e., non-listed) firms and their annual financial statements, Regulation 1606/2002 again offers member states two options:

- they may permit IAS in the annual financial statements for other companies
- they may require IAS in the annual financial statements for other companies.

France has not taken up either of these options, and therefore non-listed companies must continue to use French standards for their annual financial statements.

4.3 Analysis of the French Situation

The table below summarizes the current situation in France as regards application of IFRS/IAS (Table 1).

Table 1 Implementation of IFRS/IAS in France

	Consolidated financial statements	Annual (individual or stand-alone) financial statements
Listed companies	IFRS/IAS required	IFRS/IAS prohibited
Other (non-listed) companies	IFRS/IAS permitted	IFRS/IAS prohibited

The information in the above table is drawn from the French Finance Ministry's ministerial order (2004/1382) issued on December 20, 2004, which allows companies to apply IAS in the preparation of their consolidated financial statements from 2005 onwards. This order was ratified by French law of December 17, 2007.

As Dandon and Didelot (2006) observe, at this point in time the French standard-setter had realized the difficulty of having, in the long term, several different coexisting sets of standards, a problem essentially concerning annual financial statements, but also, to a lesser extent consolidated financial statements. This led to a process of convergence of France's General Accounting Plan (*Plan comptable général—PCG*) towards IFRS/IAS, which began in 1999 when the PCG was rewritten (Regulation CRC 99-03). Several French laws and regulations governing annual financial statements were amended. For example, Regulation CRC 00-06 regarding liabilities is in fact a transposition of IAS 37 "Provisions, Contingent Liabilities and Contingent Assets".

The position adopted by France for annual financial statements was largely explained (a) by the great importance of tax rules in France, and (b) by the fact the convergence process as it applied to individual company accounts was a long way off completion, even though it had begun more than 10 years before. This process has encountered several difficulties, the main one being the role of taxation. For IFRS/IAS, accounting and taxation are disconnected, but in France article 38 *quater* of appendix III of the national Tax Code lays down the principle of a connection between accounting and taxation: "firms must respect the definitions laid down in the General Accounting Plan, provided they are not incompatible with the rules applicable for the tax basis. (. . .) As a result of this connection, accounting options continue to exist after the convergence process in order to avoid losing the benefit of tax advantages" (Dandon and Didelot 2006, p. 29).[12]

According to the press release presenting the governmental order of December 20, 2004, the modernization of the General Accounting Plan (PCG) was to "take place at a steady pace, in consultation with professionals and respecting an objective of tax neutrality" (Roy 2005, p. 33).

This situation has led Didelot and Moris (2013) to wonder whether the PCG's partial convergence towards IFRS is not, in itself, a source of interpretation problems. They illustrate this idea through a technical point: the accounting and tax treatment of advances paid on orders for fixed assets in foreign currencies.

The situation in France raises other problems as well.

[12] All translations of documents for which no existing translation is available are our own.

The EU table of implementation of IFRS/IAS referred to above shows that the situations vary widely between different member states. Several countries (e.g., Denmark, Italy, Netherlands, United Kingdom, etc.), allow the use of IFRS/IAS in the annual financial statements of non-listed companies (which make up a large proportion of these countries' economic fabric).[13] Clearly, France has taken a different approach from several European countries.

Finally, France's position can only create difficulties for listed French groups whose French entities (subsidiaries, affiliates) must establish their annual financial statements under French accounting standards, although the consolidated financial statements must comply with IFRS/IAS.

5 Intervention by the ANC

The ANC (*Autorité des normes comptables*)[14] was created by order 2009-79 of January 22, 2009 and has been in operation since January 1, 2010. It has since its inception been under the chairmanship of Jerome Haas, a high-ranking civil servant who was deputy manager of the French Treasury immediately prior to this appointment.[15] Through its chairman and its official documents, the ANC has expressed reservations about IFRS/IAS and the IASB several times since 2010.

In its strategic plan for the years 2010 and 2011,[16] the ANC declared that it had two key priorities from the start: accounting standards for SMEs, and international accounting standards. On this last topic, the strategic plan stated that one objective was to "ensure that international accounting standards give a view that is economically, and not just financially, relevant".

The ANC plan continued with explicit criticisms of the IASB: "The ANC identifies two major issues:

- Conceptually, the international standard setter identifies the investor as the privileged user of the accounts, supposedly interested in finding in such accounts the instantaneous value of the company (sic). However, in France and in most of Europe the accounts are a central part of the legal organization, in which they provide a unique set of reliable numbers, established with a middle-term perspective, to numerous stakeholders, among them: the company itself for its management, its shareholders, creditors, employees as well as the tax authorities.

[13] This possibility applies to all companies in some countries and certain companies in others.

[14] The ANC website (http://www.anc.gouv.fr/cms/accueil/for-the-english-readers.html), which has several documents in English, does not give an official translation of the organisation's own name: its English home page is headed "The French accounting standards setter: The Autorité des normes comptables (ANC)". In the rest of this paper we use the acronym ANC.

[15] Chairman Haas passed away on May 8, 2014, aged 51. A new Chairman, Patrick de Cambourg, coming from the accounting profession, has been appointed on March 3, 2015.

[16] Source: http://www.anc.gouv.fr/cms/accueil/plans-strategiques-et-rapports.html// (Last retrieved: December 21, 2015).

– In terms of governance, the IASB does not ensure a satisfactory representation of all such stakeholders".

In 2012, in other words at some distance from the strategic plan drawn up in 2010, ANC Chairman Jerome Haas made reference in a speech at the 51st National Congress of Forensic Accountants[17] on September 21, 2012 to "the conditions for convergence between the European accounting model and IFRS".[18] More specifically, he reminded his audience that application of IFRS was restricted to the consolidated financial statements of listed firms.

He then raised the question of the coexistence of two systems (French standards and IFRS/IAS), providing an unambiguous answer: "Yes, we are letting the two systems continue because they have their logic and their necessity (. . .). Yes, we are trying to reconcile them. In the French standards we have tried to import certain good ideas from the international standards, particularly the gaps and the blanks that have been filled-in by the international standards, for example because we had no accounting standards to cover financial markets and financial questions.

"Can we go much further? Many experiments in many countries have tried to use international standards in individual company accounts, i.e., for legal purposes. It's a catastrophe. Italy is on the brink of disaster (. . .) The United Kingdom tried, and it only took them two months before they realized it was a bad idea and backtracked."

In his annual report for 2012,[19] Chairman Haas continued to criticize the IASB: "Rather than the uncertainties of the production process [for] international standards, what is worrying is its general orientation. (. . .) The standards are becoming increasingly complex and abstract, and practitioners are increasingly using instruments other than the accounts to express and understand corporate performance. IFRS in our opinion contribute to a loss of reference points, and thus amplify the globalization effect. Loss of reference points in time: IFRS focus actors on the short term, whereas the economy needs to return to a long-term frame in order to come out of the financial bubble. Loss of reference points in space: the international development of IFRS is chaotic, and their "flexible choice" application is a source of risks".

"What is being questioned is not the IFRS themselves, but their recent development and the return to a certain conceptual radicalization. A change of direction is wanted—but criticisms are not being heard by the IASB. Yet the more out-of-step the standards, the less they will be adopted and correctly applied in the rest of the world—which takes us further from the world standard project called for by the G20, to which the ANC is intensely contributing."

But Chairman Haas continued, on a more optimistic note: "In a certain number of cases, the ANC is quite rightly proud of the real progress achieved by the IASB

---

[17] « *Congrès national des Experts-comptables de justice* ».

[18] Source: http://www.anc.gouv.fr/cms/accueil/publications.html (Last retrieved: December 21, 2015).

[19] Source: http://www.anc.gouv.fr/cms/accueil/plans-strategiques-et-rapports.html (Last retrieved: December 21, 2015).

and in its relations with the IASB. Simplification of the Notes to the financial statements, recording of CO^2 quotas, rules for writing-off bank loans, recognition of the central importance of the business model, creation of a body for consultation with the national standard-setters, finalization of the rules for assessing the impact of standards on the economy: these projects are not advancing fast enough to produce the desired practical results, but there is a shared growing awareness and outlook".

Which should be considered more important, the ANC's harsh criticism of the IASB or its Chairman's optimistic note in acknowledging that there is growing awareness of the current difficulties of the international standard harmonization process? Only the future will tell.

6 The Debate Enters the Academic World

While it is not common in France to see academics take clear stances on the question of international accounting standardization, several relatively controversial articles, giving rise to an occasionally intense debate, have been published recently in the French Accounting Association (AFC)'s journal *Comptabilité-Contrôle-Audit*.

Burlaud and Colasse (2010)[20] launched the debate by considering that "in the absence of political legitimacy, international accounting standardization is founded on procedural and substantial legitimacies, which have been challenged by the current financial crisis". Their paper represents a critique of this "constructed legitimacy". In particular, it attempts to demonstrate that whilst due process is admittedly a transparent procedure, it is one in which only players with major financial and intellectual resources can participate. It also highlights the weakness of the theoretical foundation underpinning the IASB's conceptual framework, in particular agency theory and the efficient market hypothesis. This critical study of the foundations of the legitimacy of the IASC/IASB explains the extent of recent political intervention in a field that had previously been neglected.

Burlaud and Colasse's article attracted strongly critical responses, which were also published in *Comptabilité-Contrôle-Audit*. Danjou and Walton (2011)[21] showed that the IASB had the support of the leaders of the world's major economies (G20), as well as the European Commission and European Parliament. The European Commission's policy is to pursue wider adoption of the IASB's standards. Danjou and Walton went on to suggest that politics had never been absent

[20] This article was later published in an English translation (Burlaud and Colasse 2011a), with permission from the journal *Comptabilité – Contrôle – Audit*.

[21] This article was later published in an English translation (Danjou and Walton 2012), with permission from the journal *Comptabilité – Contrôle – Audit*.

from standard-setting, and noted that a number of the positions taken by Burlaud and Colasse were not supported by the mainstream literature.

Gélard and Pigé (2011) believed that Burlaud and Colasse (2010) had expressed very strong views calling into question the legitimacy of the IASB in three areas: political, process and substance. After discussing the arguments, they concluded that while the IASB is not a perfect organization, and could probably be improved by enhancing its accountability to every category of stakeholders, it nonetheless has real legitimacy in the three areas discussed (political, process and substance).

Burlaud and Colasse (2011b) then responded to the comments made by Danjou and Walton (2011) and Gélard and Pigé (2011). From a methodological standpoint, they questioned the other authors' positivist positions and criticized them for terminological approximations. From a conceptual standpoint, they specified the meaning they assign to the notion of legitimacy and thoroughly re-examined and confirmed their view of the IASC-IASB's conceptual framework. In conclusion, referring to Suchman (1995), they interpreted the comments of Danjou and Walton (2011) and Gélard and Pigé (2011) as part and parcel of an academic strategy to defend and restore the IASB's legitimacy.

Later, Colasse (2011a) argued that the international accounting standardization crisis is not a purely technical crisis linked to poor application of the fair value criterion, but an intellectual crisis related to the conceptual framework and its underlying epistemology. This framework, which is the source of international standards, is itself a contributor to market instability, and to an even greater extent, corporate instability. Focusing solely on the information needs of investors, it conveys a representation and stock market management of the company that negates and destabilizes it as an economic and social entity. The international standard-setter finds itself facing a real intellectual crisis that calls for a complete re-think of its conceptual framework through reference to a more all-round view of the company.

Raffournier (2011) reacted to this article by taking issue with (and criticizing) its three main ideas:

- International accounting standardization is in crisis;
- This crisis results from the IASB's conceptual framework, which focuses on investors' information needs;
- The solution will need renewed political involvement in accounting standardization.

Colasse (2011b) closed this debate (but not for good!) by responding to the criticisms expressed by Raffournier (2011).

This series of articles and the ensuing comments, then responses to comments, shows how lively the academic debate is, and it is undeniably positive that it took place "in public".

7 Discussion and Conclusion

As this paper has sought to show, France and the IASC/IASB have had a stormy relationship. There are several explanations for this. Critics of France are prompt (generally off the record) to blame the independence, not to say arrogance, of the French character in all situations concerning international discussions. For example, they are quick to point out France's cultural exception, which is often mentioned.

Raffournier (2007) offers a more rational explanation why negative reactions to the EU's decision to make application of IFRS mandatory for all listed companies were more virulent in France than in other European countries. He attributes this hostility to the profound change of accounting philosophy the adoption of IFRS would mean for the French, and the difficulty for some actors in the accounting standardization process (particularly the Minister for Economy and Finance) of giving up their prerogatives in these areas.

One IASB member, Philippe Danjou, has publicly defended the international standards, publishing a response to ten frequent criticisms about IFRS that are particularly often heard in continental Europe.[22]

But it must be said for France (and perhaps against the IASB) that there is arguably some truth to the criticism that the IASB has, may be, "bitten off more than it can chew". In practice, is the IASB being overambitious trying to cover all types of companies, of all sizes, all corporate forms and trading statuses? Why, for example, start the project for Small and Medium Entities (SMEs) when it would appear obvious that stakeholder in such entities cannot have the same financial information needs as stakeholders in large entities, and that SMEs do not have the same financial and organizational resources for adopting IFRS/IAS? Is it not an illusion to think we can reconcile accounting rules that are tailor-made for investors with rules designed for calculating taxes or reporting on small entities' business activities?

Acknowledgments The author thanks Ann Gallon for her much appreciated editorial help. He also acknowledges insightful comments from Michel Lebas.

References

Burlaud A, Colasse B (2010) Normalisation comptable internationale : Le retour du politique ? Comptabilité-Contrôle-Audit 16(3): 153–176

[22] For the original article in French, see: http://business.lesechos.fr/directions-financieres/comptabilite-et-gestion/normes-comptables/10-idees-fausses-sur-les-ifrs-4686.php# (Last retrieved: December 21, 2015). For the English translation, see: http://www.iasplus.com/en/news/2013/02/danjou-misperceptions-paper (Last retrieved: December 21, 2015).

Burlaud A, Colasse B (2011a) International accounting standardisation: is politics back? Accounting in Europe 8(1): 23–47
Burlaud A, Colasse B (2011b) Réponse aux commentaires sur « normalisation comptable internationale : Le retour du politique ? ». Comptabilité-Contrôle-Audit 17(3): 115–128
Chand P, Cummings L (2008) The political and unstable nature of the IASB's 'stable platform': post-convergence Australian experience. Austalian Accounting Review 18(3): 175–184
Colasse B (2004) Harmonisation comptable internationale : La résistible ascension de l'IASC-IASB. Gérer et Comprendre 75: 30–41
Colasse B (2011a) La crise de la normalisation comptable internationale, une crise intellectuelle. Comptabilité-Contrôle-Audit 17(1): 157–164
Colasse B (2011b) Réponse à la discussion de « la crise de la normalisation comptable internationale, une crise intellectuelle. ». Comptabilité-Contrôle-Audit 17(1): 171–174
Colasse B (2012) Les fondements de la comptabilité, 2nd edn. La Découverte, Paris
Dandon O, Didelot L (2006) La convergence du plan comptable général avec le référentiel IFRS. Revue française de comptabilité 384(January): 29–33
Danjou P, Walton P (2011) La légitimité du normalisateur comptable international IASB : Commentaires sur « normalisation comptable internationale : Le retour du politique ? ». Comptabilité-Contrôle-Audit 17(3): 101–114
Danjou P, Walton P (2012) The legitimacy of the IASB. Accounting in Europe 9(1): 1–15
Didelot L, Moris K (2013) La convergence partielle du PCG vers les IFRS ne pose-t-elle pas des difficultés d'interprétation ? Revue française de comptabilité 464(April): 25–29
European Union (2002) Regulation (EC) No 1606/2002 of the European parliament and of the council of 19 July 2002 on the application of international accounting standards. Official J Eur Commun: L.243/1–L.243/4
European Commission (1995) Communication from the commission—accounting harmonisation : a new strategy vis-a-vis international harmonisation. COM 95 (508)
European Commission (2000) Communication from the commission to the council and the European parliament—EU financial reporting strategy : the way forward. COM(2000) 359 final
European Economic Community (1978) 4th directive on the annual accounts of certain types of companies no 78/660/eec. Official J Eur Commun: 11–31
European Economic Community (1983) 7th directive on the consolidated accounts of certain types of companies no 83/349/eec. Official Journal of the European Communities: 11–31
Gélard G, Pigé B (2011) Normalisation comptable internationale et légitimité - commentaires sur « normalisation comptable internationale : Le retour du politique ? ». Comptabilité-Contrôle-Audit 17(3): 87–995
HSD Group (1988) Doint business in France. HSD Arthur Young International
Obert R (2013) Pratique des normes IFRS, 5th edn. Dunod, Paris
Picker R, Leo K, Loftus J, Wise V, Clark K, Alfredson K (2012) Applying international financial reporting standards, 3rd edn. Wiley, Australia
Raffournier B (2007) Les oppositions françaises à l'adoption des IFRS: Examen critique et tentative d'explication. Comptabilité-Contrôle-Audit 13(Supplement): 21–41
Raffournier B (2010) Les normes comptables internationales (IFRS), 4th edn. Economica, Paris
Raffournier B (2011) Discussion de « la crise de la normalisation comptable internationale, une crise intellectuelle ». Comptabilité-Contrôle-Audit 17(1): 165–170
Groupe Calan Ramolino (1997) France. In: Nexia International (ed) International handbook of financial reporting, 2nd edn. ITP, London, pp 99–108
Roy T (2005) La convergence PCG/IAS : Jusqu'où ? Revue française de comptabilité 378 (June): 32–33
Scheid J-C, Walton P (1995) France. In: Alexander D, Archer S (eds) European accounting guide, 2nd edn. Miller, pp 167–199
Standish PEM (1990) Origins of the plan comptable général: a study in cultural intrusion and reaction. Accounting and Business Research 20(80): 337–351

Stolowy H (2002) Change in international accounting harmonisation: the French viewpoint. In: Zambon S (ed) Informazione societaria e nuovi processi di armonizzazione internazionale—alle soglie del cambiamento. il Mulino, Bologna, pp 185–192
Stolowy H, Lebas M, Ding Y (2013) Financial accounting and reporting: a global perspective, 4th edn. Cengage Learning, Andover, England
Suchman MC (1995) Managing legitimacy: strategic and institutional approaches. Acadmy Management Review 20(3): 571–610

Germany. German Accounting and IFRS: Limitations in the Convergence Potential of German National Accounting Standards Towards International Accounting Standards

Jörg Baetge, Alois Panzer, and Alexander Flügel

Abstract Although several reforms of the German statutory accounting system in the last decades led to a moderate but ongoing harmonization with international accounting standards, there still remain significant—hence deliberate—differences between the two accounting systems. These differences mainly result from fundamental disparities in the underlying purposes and principles of accounting according to the German Commercial Code vs. IFRS. The article provides an overview of the current status of internationalization of German statutory accounting as well as the application and importance of German statutory accounting and of IFRS in Germany. Second, it aims to show the main obstacles for a further internationalization of German accounting standards by comparing the main purposes of the German and the IFRS accounting systems and by explaining some central characteristic principles of the German accounting system, which either do not exist or have a substantially different interpretation in the IFRS.

1 Introduction

Despite the prevailing relevance of national statutory accounting according to the German Commercial Code [Handelsgesetzbuch (HGB)][1] and the Generally Accepted Accounting Principles [Grundsätze ordnungsmäßiger Buchführung (GoB)], the German accounting system was not unaffected by the global internationalization and harmonization tendencies in the field of accounting during the last decades. Since the 1980s, several significant harmonization reforms of the German accounting system resulted mainly from the implementation of the Fourth, Seventh and Eighth Directives of the European Union. However, there still remained

[1] Hereafter referred to by the acronym GCC.

J. Baetge (✉) • A. Panzer • A. Flügel
Westfälische Wilhelms-Universität Münster, Münster, Germany
e-mail: joerg.baetge@wiwi.uni-muenster.de

D. Bensadon, N. Praquin (eds.), *IFRS in a Global World*,
DOI 10.1007/978-3-319-28225-1_19

significant differences between the national accounting systems of EU member states due to the existence of numerous accounting options for member states and different national interpretations of the regulations in the directives. These differences mainly result from fundamental disparities in the underlying aims, purposes and principles of the different national accounting systems, which in turn result from substantial disparities in cultural features of societies and their legal systems and traditions. Therefore, the degree of harmonization in a manner consistent with principles of national sovereignty is limited.

As a consequence, in November 1995 the EU Commission voted for a fundamental change in its strategy towards an internationalization of the accounting systems of EU member states. The new strategy comprised an intensified cooperation with the IASC and aimed at fostering the development of international accounting standards, which are generally in line with the existing EU Directives on accounting matters (Alvarez et al. 2014: note 125). Consequently, in 2002 the EU proclaimed a crucial step towards harmonization of accounting in Europe by announcing the Regulation (EC) No. 1606/2002, which generally required the mandatory application of IFRS as adopted by the EU for consolidated financial statements of public companies that are listed in any EU member state for financial years as of January 1, 2005 (EU 2002). As there was generally broad consensus among accounting standard-setting bodies, regulators and preparers of financial statements that "full IFRS" are not specifically designed to meet the needs and capabilities of non-capital market oriented small and medium-sized entities (SMEs), on 8th of July 2009 the IASB published a comprised standard with substantially reduced complexity in comparison to the full IFRS and with some more concerns about the reliability of the SME financial statements, the so called "IFRS for SMEs" (IASC Foundation 2009a: IFRS for SMEs BC.47, 2009b: 2–3). Under the IASB's definition, all non-capital market oriented companies are considered SMEs and therefore are generally within the scope of application of this standard (Ballwieser 2013: 13).

As shown in more detail in Sect. 3, the application of IFRS in Germany is actually limited to consolidated financial statements of the round about one thousand capital market oriented companies as defined in the Regulation (EC) No. 1606/2002 plus a restricted small number of non-capital market oriented companies, who voluntarily prepare their financial statements in accordance with IFRS. The prevailing dominance of German statutory accounting according to the GCC for the almost three million German enterprises is mainly caused by significant differences between the underlying purposes and principles of the two accounting systems. This article first gives a short overview of the current status of internationalization of German statutory accounting and the actual role and importance of IFRS in Germany. Second, it aims to show the main obstacles for a further internationalization by comparing the purposes of both accounting systems and by explaining some central accounting principles of the GCC, which either do not exist or have a substantially different meaning or interpretation in the IFRS.

2 Moderate Internationalization of the German Accounting System Through BilMoG

In May 2009, the most important reform of the GCC within the last 20 years became effective, the so called "Bilanzrechtsmodernisierungsgesetz (BilMoG)", which can be roughly translated as "Commercial Code Modernization Act". Stipulated by the proceeding international adoption of the IFRS, the German legislator intended to modernize statutory German accounting law through an improvement of the quality of the Commercial Code and a moderate alignment with IFRS. The proclaimed objective of this reform was to develop German accounting standards towards a "permanent and equivalent but more cost-effective and less complex alternative to IFRS", especially for non-capital market oriented companies (Bundesrat 2008: 69; Bundestag 2008: 34; 2009: 1). In addition, BilMoG should also strengthen the informative value and the reliability of GCC financial statements (Bundesrat 2008: 69; Bundestag 2009: 1; Solmecke 2009: 44–46). However, the legislator did not intend to change the well-established general principles of the GCC (Bundesrat 2008: 69–71; Bundestag 2009: 1). Overall, BilMoG achieved its objective to moderately align German accounting standards towards international accounting standards by removing antiquated recognition, valuation and disclosure options and by partially or completely aligning some accounting rules with IFRS rules, however, only to the extent permitted by the generally accepted accounting principles of the GCC (Bundestag 2009: 33–34; Böcking and Dutzi 2010: 798–799).[2] Specifically, there was no alignment at all concerning the mark-to-model fair value concept in the IFRS. Overall, there still remain significant accounting differences between GCC and IFRS. BilMoG on the one hand led to a moderate alignment with IFRS, but on the other hand officially gave the GCC the character of an equivalent alternative to IFRS, especially to the IFRS for SMEs. Consequently, there is currently no ambition for any further convergence, neither by the German legislator nor by preparers of financial statements in Germany.

[2] In a detailed study by Solmecke about the impacts of BilMoG on the system of German accounting principles as founded by Leffson and further developed by Baetge/Kirsch/Thiele, the author came to the conclusion that the existing GoB system as a whole was largely unaffected by the significant changes brought about by BilMoG and that it was even strengthened by the reform, as it overall led to a more consequent implementation of the GoB system in the GCC. See: Solmecke 2009: 263–264.

3 The Current Role of the IFRS in the German Accounting Practice

To further competition in European capital markets, the IAS Regulation 2002/1606/EG required all capital market oriented European parent companies to prepare consolidated financial statements in accordance with IFRS as endorsed by the European Commission for all financial reporting periods beginning on or after 1st of January 2005.[3] The regulation provided the option, that each member state may permit or require the application of IFRS also for separate financial statements of all kinds of companies and for consolidated financial statements of non-publicly traded companies. In Germany, this regulation was implemented and transformed into German law by the Bilanzrechtsreformgesetz (BilReG) in 2004. With the BilReG, the German legislator chose to permit non-publicly traded companies to present their consolidated financial statements voluntarily in accordance with IFRS as endorsed by the EU instead of GCC. Regarding the use of IFRS in separate financial statements, the German legislator decided to allow the preparation of supplementary separate financial statements in accordance with IFRS only for disclosure purposes. Moreover, the German legislator did not adopt the IFRS for SMEs, as they are still considered too complex and not appropriate to fulfill the purposes of financial statements as intended by the German legislator.[4] Furthermore, with the adoption of BilMoG the German legislator explicitly clarified that in the foreseeable future there will be no alternative to the preparation of separate financial statements according to GCC, particularly due to their comparably lower level of complexity as well as their central importance for tax-assessment and the calculation of payouts (Baetge et al. 2012: 155–156).

In Germany, small and medium sized companies, which are often family-owned, account for the vast majority of all business enterprises. These companies are typically financed via bank loans, while capital markets only play a minor role in their financing activities. In 2012, less than 1000 out of more than three million registered German entities were deemed to be capital market oriented and, therefore, are subject to mandatory IFRS accounting regarding their consolidated financial statements (Küting et al. 2013: 53–54). However, even the capital market

[3] The effective date for mandatory IFRS consolidated financial statements could be postponed to the 1st of January 2007 for European parent companies that solely issued debt instruments, that were only impending for securities trading in the EU on 1st of January 2005, that were publicly listed in the USA and therefore reporting under US-GAAP, or that were parent to only one debt issuing subsidiary.

[4] With the Directive 2013/34/EU of June 26, 2013, aimed at replacing and modernizing the existing EU Accounting Directives in order to further simplify accounting and disclosure requirements for SMEs, the EU stopped pursuing a mandatory adoption of IFRS for SMEs. This is justified by the findings of an Impact Assessment, which concluded that the IFRS for SMEs is still more complex than most existing national accounting regulations for SMEs and therefore a mandatory application of this standard would not serve the objectives of simplification and reduction of administrative burden for SMEs. See: EU 2011: 7.

orientation of bigger German companies tends to be less pronounced than in comparable economies (Ballwieser 2013: 6–8). In a representative study conducted by Küting and Lam (2012) regarding the actual exertion of the option for non-capital market oriented companies to prepare and disclose consolidated financial statements according to IFRS, in a random sample for the reporting period 2010 only 108 entities (5.74 %) out of 1883 parent entities exercised the option to replace GCC consolidated financial statements with IFRS consolidated financial statements (Küting and Lam 2012: 1041–1049; Küting et al. 2013: 57–58). These findings illustrate the continuing importance of the GCC, whereas the role of IFRS in the German accounting practice is largely limited to consolidated financial statements of a short list of global players.

4 Comparison of the Accounting Purposes of the German Commercial Code and the IFRS

4.1 Purposes of Financial Statements According to the German Commercial Code

With financial statements according to GCC a pluralistic system of purposes is pursued. These equally important purposes are documentation, stewardship and capital maintenance (Baetge et al. 2012: 93–104). The purpose of **documentation** stems from the codified duty to maintain comprehensible and complete records of all business transactions over the reporting period. Orderly kept records are a prerequisite for the other accounting purposes and constitute legal evidence and unfold a preemptive effect against fraud. The purpose of documentation is the main purpose of bookkeeping and constitutes a prerequisite to ensure the fulfillment of the purposes of stewardship and capital maintenance (Leffson 1987: 45–47). It requires that all business transactions of the reporting period are recorded completely and in a clear and comprehensible manner. The second purpose, **stewardship**, requires that financial statements provide information about the disposition of entrusted capital in a way that enables the users of those financial statements to gain detailed insights into the business activities and to draw their own conclusions about the assets under management and the results achieved from their disposal. Nevertheless, GCC financial reports do not only service third-party information needs, but also provide a basis for management to self-asses past investment decisions as well as to project future capital allocation decisions (Leffson 1987: 63–64).

The third accounting purpose, **capital maintenance**, refers to the determination of a profit for the period, which could be withdrawn by shareholders without reducing the nominal amount of equity capital (Leffson 1987: 92). Capital maintenance is a central purpose of financial statements prepared under GCC as the profit of the period determined under the provisions of the GCC regularly forms the basis for the calculation of payouts to shareholders as well as for the determination of taxable income. The purpose of capital maintenance serves the guiding idea of creditor protection in the GCC. The central aim of this purpose is to preserve the nominal liable equity capital. Capital maintenance urges company owners not to reduce liable equity as long as a positive net income is earned. This concept of capital maintenance via information is relevant for all types of legal entities and is achieved by disclosing the amount of distributable net income (Moxter 2003: 3–4). The specific legal provisions covering capital maintenance via information deal primarily with the valuation of assets and the determination of the annual result under the principles as shown in Sect. 5 (AKEU 1995: 95). In contrast, capital maintenance via regulation refers to idiosyncratic provisions contained in German Company Law and Commercial Code, which are only relevant for limited liability companies (in the legal form of "GmbH" or "AG"). These provisions establish maximum and minimum thresholds for profit distribution (Solmecke 2009: 31–32). Maximum profit distribution is generally restricted by a statutory minimum amount of earnings that have to be retained before any profit can be distributed. Minimum profit distribution aims to protect minority shareholders by granting shareholders certain veto rights with respect to management's proposal on the allocation of unappropriated profits (Baetge et al. 2012: 100–101). By integrating the purpose of capital maintenance into statutory accounting rules, the German legislator intended to safeguard the long-term existence of companies as well as to protect creditors' interests (AKEU 1995: 95–97).

The taxable income of German entities is determined via separate tax statements prepared according to German tax law. However, the calculation of taxable income is closely linked to commercial statements because of the codified principle that accounting treatments under GCC—subject to certain exceptions and adjustments—shall generally be adopted for tax accounts. Therefore, tax accounts of German companies are indirectly governed by the GCC-purpose of capital maintenance and resulting accounting principles, which are shown in detail in Sect. 5 (AKEU 1995: 97–98).

4.2 *Purpose of Financial Statements According to IFRS*

The general purpose of financial statements prepared according to IFRS is defined in chapter 1 of the IASB's Conceptual Framework for Financial Reporting (2010), (Wiedmann and Schwedler 2007: 693–694). According to this definition, the main purpose is to "[. . .] provide financial information about the reporting entity that is useful to existing and potential investors, lenders and other creditors in making decisions about providing resources to the entity" (IASB 2010: CF.OB2), which is commonly referred to as **"decision usefulness"** (Baetge et al. 2012: 142). Therefore, existing and potential investors, lenders and creditors are regarded as the primary users of IFRS financial statements, as they generally cannot require reporting entities to provide information directly to them but must rely on financial statements for most of the financial information they need (IASB 2010: CF.OB5) while the IASB views the interests of regulators and the general public as ancillary (IASB 2010: CF.OB9). The primary users base their capital allocation decisions on expected risk-adjusted returns and therefore are interested in information that enables them to estimate timing and amount of future cash flows from and to the entity (IASB 2010: CF.OB3 and OB10). The role of **stewardship** as a second accounting purpose of IFRS was controversially discussed during the Conceptual Framework project. Stewardship, which is alternatively referred to as accountability, is concerned with easing the principal-agency conflict between resource-providing owners and resource-administrating managers by giving information about management's performance (Wiedmann and Schwedler 2007: 704–706). While stewardship refers to retrospective information as a basis for performance assessment, the provision of decision useful information mainly serves as a basis for prospective estimates for future investment decisions (Küting et al. 2013: 13). The IASB decided not to explicitly state the term *stewardship* as an objective of IFRS financial statements in the revised Conceptual Framework of 2010. Instead, the term's meaning is only concretized in the Basis for Conclusions, noting that, in most cases, information designed for resource allocation decisions would also be useful for assessing management performance (IASB 2010: CF.BC1.24–1.28). This decision indicates that the IASB considers stewardship—if at all—as only a minor objective of IFRS accounting (Küting et al. 2013: 13; Pellens et al. 2001: 121).

4.3 Similarities and Differences

As documentation is a prerequisite for accounting in general, both accounting systems serve the purpose of documentation, despite the IASB omitting its explicit codification. However, the GCC is designed to follow pluralistic purposes in order to balance the divergent interests of all financial statement users, be it capital maintenance as a main interest of creditors or employees in conjunction with the determination of a taxable income for the tax authorities, or stewardship as a key need of owners (Baetge et al. 2012: 102–104). In contrast the IFRS rather focus on the single objective of providing decision useful information to investors, lenders and other creditors, identified as primary users. Thus, IFRS financial statements are prepared without the notion of capital maintenance and without any influence on national tax accounts. Furthermore, the IFRS concept of decision useful information is strictly investor oriented and forward-looking, whereas financial information provided in compliance with the GCC-purpose of stewardship rather have retrospective character (Busse von Colbe 2010: 559–560; Küting et al. 2013: 7). The focus on decision usefulness explains the distinct characteristics of IFRS: market-orientation, early revenue realization, and fair value as an important measurement concept (Küting et al. 2013: 12–13). In contrast, financial statements under GCC are governed by the dominating aim of creditor protection, which is manifested in certain codified principles of the GCC regarding the determination of a prudent—

hence objective—profit. The following chapter provides an overview over those principles and explains if and to what extent those principles are also implemented in the IFRS.

5 Accounting Differences Resulting from Differences in Selected Accounting Principles

5.1 Meaning and Functions of the German Generally Accepted Accounting Principles

The Generally Accepted Accounting Principles ("Grundsätze ordnungsmäßiger Buchführung" or "GoB") are general principles, that must be complied with in order to fulfill the purposes of financial statements prepared under GCC (Leffson 1987: 35). The GoB are needed to implement and complement general legal principles in case of missing suitable codified legal rules. There is no general definition of the term GoB in the GCC. Therefore, the term "Grundsätze ordnungsmäßiger Buchführung" or "GoB" is an undetermined legal notion, which has to be interpreted and construed. In case of missing specific rules, the GCC explicitly refers to the legally undefined GoB. However, through explicit references in paragraphs §§ 238 (1), 243 (1), 264 (2) and 297 (2) HGB these principles receive the rank of binding legal norms (Leffson 1987: 22; Solmecke 2009: 13). The GoB can be subdivided in formal principles, which govern the formal regularity of accounting and financial statements (documentation principles), and material principles, which refer to the correctness of the accounting figures (recognition, measurement and disclosure principles). Furthermore, they can be categorized in codified principles, which are explicitly mentioned in the GCC, and uncodified principles (Baetge et al. 2012: 105–107)[5]. In summary, the GoB constitute an adequate set of principles that help to concretize and supplement the legal provisions of the GCC.

As a detailed explanation of the whole GoB system of the GCC would go far beyond the scope of this article, we subsequently focus our paper on the explanation of three distinctive GoB which govern the determination of profits under GCC. These principles either have a very different meaning or are not existent at all in the IFRS and thus lead to decisive differences in recognition and measurement rules between the GCC and IFRS.

---

[5] Relating to the classification of GoB to different classes of norms see: Baetge and Zülch 1984: note 4–10.

5.2 *Realization Principle*

5.2.1 The Realization Principle of the German Commercial Code

The realization principle, alongside with the matching principle, constitutes one of the two definition principles for annual result (profit or loss) in the GCC. The definition principles for annual result mainly serve the purpose of stewardship of financial statements prepared under GCC (Baetge et al. 2012: 133). According to the realization principle, which is codified in § 252 (1) no. 4 HGB, revenues may only be recognized in the current financial period as long as they effectively have been realized up to the balance sheet date. The main purpose of this principle is on the one hand to avoid the disclosure and distribution of profits that are not yet realized and on the other hand to assure that no profit effects arise from procurement transactions (Baetge et al. 2012: 131). According to the GCC, procurement transactions generally have to be recorded as an exchange of assets with no effect on income and therefore assets have to be valued at purchase or production cost at the time of acquisition. As long as there is no "leap" to the sales market, assets have to be measured at no more than cost. Positive profit contributions result at the time of delivery of the sold goods or services in the amount of the difference between sales price and costs (expenditures). These profit contributions, however, may not be recognized until the decisive economic control over the transferred good or service and the risk of destruction or deterioration associated with that good or service are being passed over to the purchaser (Leffson 1987: 265–272; Baetge et al. 2002: note 189–190). On the one hand, due to the strict bonding of the realization date to the delivery of the asset associated with a transfer of economic power and risk, the realization principle serves the purpose of a prudent determination of income and therefore the purpose of capital maintenance. On the other hand, it also serves the purpose of stewardship, because it helps to objectify asset values and to prevent from subjective influences. In a strict interpretation of the purpose of capital maintenance the latest possible stage of the purchasing process, which is generally the date of payment receipt, should determine the realization date. However, this would conflict with the purpose of stewardship, as by the time of contract conclusion a fundamental part of the whole purchasing process is already accomplished. Therefore, the realization of revenues according to this principle can be considered as a compromise between the purpose of capital maintenance and the purpose of stewardship (Leffson 1987: 467–468; Baetge and Kirsch 2002: note 86; Baetge et al. 2002: note 141–142).

5.2.2 Meaning and Interpretation of the Realization Principle in the IFRS

In the IFRS, the realization principle is not explicitly specified as a separate accounting principle but rather constitutes a sub-category of the principle of accrual basis, which is codified in the Conceptual Framework (CF.OB17) and in IAS 1.27 (Baetge and Zülch 1984: note 216–217). The realization principle in the context of IFRS has a much broader scope than in the GCC. Thus, not only realized revenues are recognized but generally also revenues, which can be considered as realizable with a certain probability (Coenenberg et al. 2009: 6). Furthermore, in contrast to the GCC rules the IFRS allow to a large extent the determination of the fair value of assets and liabilities by present value calculation, which is generally characterized by a significant degree of uncertainty regarding future cash flows.

5.2.3 Resulting Accounting Differences

According to § 253 (1) sentence 1 HGB, at initial recognition all assets have to be measured at their purchase or production costs. Likewise, in most cases purchase and production costs also constitute the applicable value of assets at initial recognition under IFRS. Despite some minor differences regarding the determination of production costs, conceptually initial measurement with purchase or production costs is similar in both accounting systems. However, there is a significant difference with regard to subsequent measurement of assets. As a consequence of the strict interpretation of the realization principle in the GCC, amortized purchase and production costs generally constitute the maximum value in subsequent measurement of assets, which may not be exceeded until the assets take the "leap" to the sales market as described in Sect. 5.2.1 above. Subsequent appreciations after initial recognition may only be disclosed if the associated profit contributions are objectified by real market transactions. In comparison, in the IFRS system the fair value also constitutes an important measurement concept. For example, when the revaluation method for subsequent measurement of property, plant and equipment or of intangible assets is being applied, asset values can exceed the threshold of amortized cost, leading to a disclosure of unrealized gains (Küting et al. 2013: 85). However, for most of all asset types these fair value changes above amortized cost are recognized in the other comprehensive income, so that users of IFRS financial statements can at least differentiate between realized and not yet realized gains.

However, for certain asset classes positive profit contributions through sole fair value changes are recognized directly in profit or loss. For example, after initial recognition IAS 40 allows to choose a full fair value model for the subsequent measurement of investment property.[6] In this case, all changes in fair value are being treated as gains and losses and are reported in the income statement as profit or loss of the period (IAS 40.35), which stands in sharp contrast to the distinctive realization principle as codified and interpreted in the GCC system.

It can be summarized that the IFRS in general favor a more transparent presentation of current values of investment property in order to serve the purpose of

[6] However, even if the cost model is chosen, IAS 40.79(e) requires the disclosure of the fair value of investment property in the notes.

providing decision useful information to investors and other creditors, whereas the strict realization principle in the GCC limits the maximum value of those assets—like of all other property, plant and equipment—to the amortized purchase or production costs. Generally, the different meaning of the realization principle in the IFRS leads to a more future-oriented but less objective profit determination compared to GCC rules.

5.3 Imparity Principle

5.3.1 The Imparity Principle of the German Commercial Code

The imparity principle can be classified, alongside with the principle of prudence, as one of the two principles of capital maintenance in the GCC. These principles consider economic events which lead to negative profit contributions that are already incurred but not yet materialized at the balance sheet date (Baetge et al. 2012: 137). The imparity principle, which is also codified in § 252 (1) no. 4 HGB, requires that all foreseeable risks and losses that are incurred up to the balance sheet date must be recognized in the current period. Therefore, unrealized prospective negative profit contributions have to be anticipated in the period in which they are economically incurred. The main idea behind the imparity principle is that anticipated negative profit contributions should be secured from distribution to investors in order to be able to absorb those negative profit contributions when they actually materialize in future periods (Baetge et al. 2012: 137). The name of this principle is derived from the unequal treatment of foreseeable but yet unrealized gains and losses (Winkeljohann and Büssow 2012: note 34). Though the disparate treatment of positive and negative profit contributions with regard to the realization date serves the purpose of capital maintenance, it conflicts with the purpose of stewardship because it constrains the determination of a comparable annual profit. The anticipation of negative profit contributions of subsequent years in the financial statements of the current year does not lead to a presentation of income according to the accrual basis of accounting. Instead, a lower—but hence distributable—income is disclosed (Baetge and Hendler 2000: 21). Therefore, in order not to fully conflict with the purpose of stewardship, the imparity principle has to be limited to cases where an anticipation of risks and losses is compulsory, that is, when the risks already have emerged up to the balance sheet date (Baetge et al. 2012: 137–138). In order for risks to be considered as having already been emerged up to the balance sheet date, they have to be associated with a clearly definable and already initiated transaction (Baetge and Knüppe 1986: 397). Furthermore, at least one of the causes leading to the adverse event after the balance sheet date has to be already occurred before the balance sheet date (Leffson 1987: 394–395). However, the imparity principle permits accountability with regard to future risks (Leffson 1987: 105). The imparity principle is supplemented and concretized in the GCC by the provisions in § 253 (3) and (4) HGB, which determine different depreciation rules regarding loss anticipation for current and non-current assets. A further concretization of this capital maintenance principle lies in the possibility to recognize provisions for contingent losses from pending transactions pursuant to § 249 (1) HGB (Baetge et al. 2012: 139).

5.3.2 Meaning and Interpretation of the Imparity Principle in the IFRS

In contrast to the GCC, there is no imparity principle codified in the IFRS or in the Conceptual Framework. Pursuant to the main objective of IFRS to provide decision useful information to existing and potential users, generally all sufficiently concretized gains and losses have to be considered in the financial statements—even if they are not yet realized. However, there exist a number of provisions in different standards which—similar to the imparity principle in the GCC—implicitly lead to an unequal treatment of foreseeable but yet unrealized positive and negative profit contributions in the financial statements prepared under IFRS (Ballwieser 2008: note 75; Coenenberg et al. 2009: 65). These provisions, however, are characterized by a varying degree of stringency regarding the unequal treatment of gains and losses (Winnefeld 2006: note 220). Furthermore, this unequal treatment is restricted only to some individual regulations and therefore cannot be considered as having the same importance as the codified imparity principle in the GCC.

5.3.3 Resulting Accounting Differences

A major difference due to the differing meaning of the imparity principle in GCC and IFRS exists in the accounting treatment of derivatives.[7] The GCC does not include any specific provisions regarding accounting for derivatives. Therefore, the general recognition, valuation and disclosure rules as well as the GoB have to be resorted to. As far as derivative financial instruments fulfill the general recognition criteria of assets in the GCC, they have to be initially valued at purchase costs according to § 255 (1) HGB. Those purchase costs generally comprise the premiums paid for the derivative instrument. According to the realization principle explained above, positive value changes above purchase costs may not be recognized until the derivative instruments are either sold or—in case of options—exercised.[8] In contrast, the imparity principle requires that negative profit

[7] The following description refers to stand-alone derivatives and not to derivatives that are designated in effective hedge relationships, because in case of hedge accounting the imparity principle is not applicable to the single derivative instrument as hedged item or hedging instrument but to the hedge itself.

[8] There is an exception for derivative instruments, which are designated to the trading portfolio of credit institutions. According to § 340e (1) HGB, all financial instruments designated to the trading portfolio of banks have to be measured at fair value through profit or loss. See: Brüggemann 2010: 127.

contributions mandatorily have to be anticipated, as soon as they are foreseeable. In case of options which are capitalized with their option premium, negative changes of value first have to be recognized by adjustments to the carrying amounts by conducting extraordinary depreciations according to § 253 (3) and (4) HGB. In all other cases, for example when accounting for futures or forwards, derivatives have the character of so-called pending transactions, which may not be recognized in the balance sheet until they are closed out or exercised. Even in such cases, foreseeable negative profit contributions from those derivatives have to be recognized by setting up a provision for contingent losses on pending transactions according to § 249 (1) sentence 1 HGB. This unequal treatment, where positive value changes may not be recognized in the current period and foreseeable negative profit contributions have to be realized immediately in the current period leads to a strictly prudent disclosure of profits, which is a consequence of the purpose of capital maintenance in the GCC.

In contrast, according to IAS 39.9 all derivatives are recorded in IFRS financial statements on the balance sheet at fair value, with any positive or negative changes in value being equally and immediately reported in profit or loss. Due to the lack of the purpose of capital maintenance in the IFRS there is no need and no cause for a prudent or conservative disparate treatment of foreseeable gains and losses.

5.4 *Principle of Prudence*

5.4.1 The Principle of Prudence of the German Commercial Code

The principle of prudence, which is also codified in § 252 (1) no. 4 HGB, demands that assets and liabilities have to be valued prudently. There is no further concretization of this principle in the GCC. The conceptual classification of this principle in the GoB system is controversially discussed in the literature. Most of the authors interpret the principle of prudence as being a superior principle, with the realization and imparity principles being just two specifications of this superior principle (Moxter 1986: 37–39; Adler et al. 2001: § 252, note 60–63 and 73; Selchert 2002: note 85; Winkeljohann and Büssow 2012: note 29). However, this interpretation is problematic because according to the realization principle—as explained in Sect. 5.2 above—not the most prudent realization date but with the “leap” to the sales market a compromise between the two purposes of financial statements, capital maintenance and stewardship, is chosen (Leffson 1987: 467–468; Baetge and Kirsch 2002: note 86). Therefore, the principle of prudence has to be considered as an equally-ranked principle with the other GoB (Baetge and Zülch 1984: note 94). The principle of prudence does not demand to build up hidden reserves by arbitrarily undervaluing assets and overvaluing liabilities, as this would conflict with the purpose of stewardship and prepare the ground for subsequent accounting policy measures in the form of a silent dissolution of hidden reserves. The principle of prudence is therefore restricted to uncertain future events in cases where, despite legal norms and other GoB, certain valuation discretions remain (Leffson 1987: 466–467). Valuation discretions are limited both upwards and downwards by the most and least favorable value, which have to be determined without any arbitrariness. The principle of prudence has the function to help determining a single value lying within a range of possible values. This value has to be compliant with the purpose of capital maintenance as well as the purpose of stewardship. According to our interpretation, in case of a continuous range of possible values, the most probable value should be chosen, and in case of a symmetric distribution of possible values—e.g. normally distributed values—the arithmetic mean should be chosen (Baetge 1968: 141–166; and based on him: Leffson 1987: 465–492). In order to fully account for the principle of prudence, an idea would be to simultaneously create a special provision (so called "bandwidth-provision") in the amount of the difference of the mean value and the most pessimistic value in order to make resulting hidden reserves transparent. However, the creation of such a provision is not allowed under GCC rules. Therefore, in cases of uncertain expectations a more pessimistic value has to be chosen (Adler et al. 2001: § 252, note 68; Selchert 2002: note 87), whereas unrealistic values or outliers may not be considered (Ballwieser 2008: note 57; Baetge et al. 2002: note 144).

5.4.2 Meaning and Interpretation of the Principle of Prudence in the IFRS

The principle of prudence in the GCC mainly serves the purpose of capital maintenance and thus the aim of creditor protection, which has much greater significance in the German accounting system than in the IFRS. Consequently, by releasing the new Conceptual Framework in 2010 the IASB decided to eliminate the previously codified principle of prudence from its Framework. According to the view of the IASB, the principle of prudence or conservatism is inconsistent with the requirement of neutrality of information, which constitutes an essential characteristic of faithfully presented information (CF.BC.3.27-28). Furthermore, the previously codified principle of prudence in IFRS did not have the character of a fundamental principle as in GCC but rather was interpreted as a provision to exercise sufficient diligence in the exercise of judgments needed in making estimates under conditions of uncertainty (Winkeljohann and Büssow 2012: note 84). However, in some standards there are still tendencies towards a prudent determination of profit contributions (Wawrzinek 2013: note 94). For example, IAS 2.9 requires that inventories have to be valued at the lower of cost and net realizable value. A further example is the revaluation model for intangible assets is only applicable if the fair value can be determined by reference to an active market for the intangible asset (IAS 38.81). However, those provisions do not have the same importance and are by far not as prevalent as the principle of prudence in the GCC. The avoidance of the codification of a principle of prudence in the IFRS is a consequence of the fact that creditor protection—in contrast to the GCC—does not represent a primary goal of financial statements prepared under IFRS.

5.4.3 Resulting Accounting Differences

The absence of a principle of prudence in the IFRS leads to significant differences between GCC and IFRS with regard to the measurement of provisions when there is a bandwidth of possible values. According to § 253 (1) sentence 2 HGB, provisions have to be measured at the amount required on settlement date, determined "with reasonable commercial assessment". The term settlement value implies that provisions have to be measured on a forward-looking basis, so that future price increases have to be considered. The expression "in accordance with reasonable commercial assessment" claims that only intersubjectively verifiable assumptions about future developments may be regarded in the determination of the adequate amount of the provision (Baetge et al. 2002: 425). This also constrains the creation of undue hidden reserves by deliberately overstating future expenses (Baetge et al. 2012: 426). However, when a whole range of possible settlement values exists, the principle of prudence according to § 252 (1) no. 4 HGB is applicable in determining the adequate amount. Generally, it seems commercially reasonable to choose the most probable value. However, the strict interpretation of the principle of prudence in the GCC requires that at least in case of a symmetrical distribution of possible values the most probable value has to be supplemented by a prudence-component. As de lege lata a separate bandwidth-provision is not allowed according to § 249 (2) HGB, in the literature there is consensus to take a more pessimistic value within the previously identified bandwidth instead (Baetge et al. 2002: note 144; Kozikowski and Schubert 2012: note 155). This pessimistic value, however, has to be plausible and objectively justifiable (Selchert 2002: note 88).

In the IFRS, IAS 37.36 requires that the amount recognized as a provision should be the "best estimate" of the expenditure required to settle the present obligation at the end of the reporting period. When the provision being measured involves not only a single obligation but a large population of items (e.g. provision for warranty claims), IAS 37.39 requires the use of expected values as a best estimate. In case of a single obligation, the individual most likely outcome is considered the best estimate (IAS 37.40). Therefore, the use of expected values or most probable values for measuring provisions in the IFRS implicitly assumes risk neutrality (Baetge et al. 2002: note 78). This decisive difference compared to GCC tends to result in less conservative provisioning in financial statements prepared under IFRS.

6 Summary and Outlook

Although the Bilanzrechtsmodernisierungsgesetz (BilMoG) led to a moderate and partial alignment of GCC accounting rules with IFRS rules, there still remain some significant—hence deliberate—differences. These differences mainly result from the different purposes of financial statements in the two accounting systems. GCC financial statements have to serve three equally ranked purposes (documentation, stewardship, capital maintenance), whereas IFRS financial statements are solely intended to fulfill the purpose of providing decision useful information. The characteristic purpose of capital maintenance of GCC financial statements leads to a much greater role of the concept of creditor protection compared to IFRS. This guiding concept is manifested in a row of characteristic principles regarding the determination of a prudent but comparable and objective profit, which in turn are codified in numerous valuation and measurement provisions in the GCC. Moreover, the purpose of capital maintenance also forms the basis of the close link between GCC financial statements and tax accounts by permitting only the realization of sufficiently objectified profits. In Sect. 5 we explained the three most important principles of the GCC regarding the prudent determination of annual profits and showed how these principles lead to considerably different accounting treatments compared to IFRS rules.

In our opinion, there is a strong need to a further development of the IFRS towards a high quality, reliable, understandable, auditable, enforceable and globally accepted accounting system. However, we also agree with the German legislator that a mandatory application of IFRS should continue to be restricted to capital market oriented companies, who regularly make use of international capital markets and are intensely engaged in cross-border activities, whereas German SMEs should continue to prepare their financial statements in accordance with the GCC. Despite the efforts of the IASB to promote the application of IFRS for SMEs for small and medium-sized and non-capital market oriented companies, GCC financial statements will not be replaced by IFRS financial statements in the foreseeable future, because the latter cannot fulfill the purposes the German legislator has assigned to financial statements in general. The principles underlying the GCC evolved and have proven suitable over a long period of time. They can be traced back to the world's first accounting regulations, in particular, the French Ordinance (1673) and the comments on it by Jacques Savary in his famous book *Le Parfait Négociant* (1675) and, building on that, the Napoleonic Code of Commerce (1807).[9] Those regulations, in turn, laid the foundation of the ADHGB (Allgemeines Deutsches Handeslgesetzbuch) of 1861, the predecessor of today's GCC.

References

Bibliography of Manuals and Commentaries on Accounting

Adler H, Düring W, Schmalz K (2001) Rechnungslegung und Prüfung der Unternehmen. Schäffer-Poeschel, Stuttgart

[9] For a detailed description of the historical development of the European accounting theory see: Richard 2005: 826–843.

Alvarez M, Kleekämper H, Kuhlewind A-M (2014) Ziele, Organisation, Entwicklung und Bedeutung des IASB. In: Baetge J, Wollmert P, Kirsch H-J, Oser P, Bischof S (eds). Rechnungslegung nach IFRS. Schäffer-Poeschel, Stuttgart

Baetge J, Kirsch H-J (2002) Grundsätze ordnungsmäßiger Buchführung. In: Küting K, Weber C-P (eds) Handbuch der Rechnungslegung Einzelabschluss—Kommentar zur Bilanzierung und Prüfung. Schäffer-Poeschel, Stuttgart

Baetge J, Ziesemer S, Schmidt M (2002) § 252 HGB—Allgemeine Bewertungsgrundsätze. In: Baetge J, Kirsch H-J, Thiele S (eds) Bilanzrecht. Stollfuß, Bonn

Baetge J, Zülch H (1984) Bedeutung und Ermittlung der Grundsätze ordnungsmäßiger Buchführung. In: Wysocki K, Schulze-Osterloh J, Hennrichs J (eds) Handbuch des Jahresabschlusses in Einzeldarstellungen. Dr. Otto Schmidt, Köln

Ballwieser W (2008) § 252 HGB. In: Schmidt K (ed) Münchener Kommentar zum Handelsgesetzbuch. C.H. Beck, München

Kozikowski M, Schubert W (2012) § 253 HGB. In: Ellrott H, Förschle G, Kozikowski M, Winkeljohann N (eds) Beck'scher Bilanzkommentar. C.H. Beck, München

Selchert FW (2002) § 252 HGB. In: Küting K, Weber C-P (eds) Handbuch der Rechnungslegung Einzelabschluss—Kommentar zur Bilanzierung und Prüfung. Schäffer-Poeschel, Stuttgart

Wawrzinek W (2013) § 2. In: Bohl W, Riese J, Schlüter J (eds) Beck'sches IFRS-Handbuch. C.H. Beck, München

Winkeljohann N, Büssow T (2012) § 252 HGB—Allgemeine Bewertungsgrundsätze. In: Ellrott H, Förschle G, Kozikowski M, Winkeljohann N (eds) Beck'scher Bilanzkommentar. C.H. Beck, München

Winnefeld R (2006) Bilanz-Handbuch. Handels- und Bilanzsteuerrecht, Rechtsformspezifisches Bilanzrecht, Bilanzielle Sonderfragen, Sonderbilanzen, IAS/US-GAAP. C.H. Beck, München

Bibliography of Essays and Monographs

AKEU (Arbeitskreis Externe Unternehmensrechnung der Schmalenbach-Gesellschaft für Betriebswirtschaft e.V. (1995) German accounting principles: an institutionalized framework. Account Horizons 9(3):92–99

Baetge J (1968) Möglichkeiten der Objektivierung des Jahreserfolges. Schriftenreihe des Instituts für Revisionswesen der Westfälischen Wilhelms-Universität Münster, Münster

Baetge J, Hendler M (2000) Verlustvorsorgen und Bilanzkonzeption. In: Bertl R, Egger A, Gassner W, Lang M (eds) Verlustvorsorgen im Bilanzsteuerrecht. Linde, Wien, pp 13–31

Baetge J, Knüppe W (1986) Vorhersehbare Risiken und Verluste. In: Leffson U, Rückle D, Großfeld B (eds) Handwörterbuch unbestimmter Rechtsbegriffe im Bilanzrecht des HGB. Dr. Otto Schmidt, Köln

Baetge J, Kirsch H-J, Thiele S (2012) Bilanzen. IDW, Düsseldorf

Ballwieser W (2013) IFRS-Rechnungslegung. Vahlen, München

Böcking H-J, Dutzi A (2010) Verbesserung der Qualität der deutschen Rechnungslegung durch das Bilanzrechtsmodernisierungsgesetz (BilMoG)? In: Baumhoff H, Drücker R, Köhler S (eds) Besteuerung, Rechnungslegung und Prüfung der Unternehmen—Festschrift für Prof. Dr. Norbert Krawitz. Wiesbaden, Gabler, pp 783–803

Brüggemann P (2010) Finanzinstrumente des Handelsbestands in HGB-Abschlüssen von Kreditinstituten. IDW, Düsseldorf

Busse von Colbe W (2010) Konzernabschluss nach HGB und IFRS: Anmerkungen zu Unterschieden und Gemeinsamkeiten. In: Baumhoff H, Drücker R, Köhler S (eds) Besteuerung, Rechnungslegung und Prüfung der Unternehmen—Festschrift für Prof. Dr. Norbert Krawitz. Wiesbaden, Gabler, pp 555–571

Coenenberg AG, Haller A, Schultze W (2009) Jahresabschluss und Jahresabschlussanalyse. Schäffer-Poeschel, Stuttgart
Küting K, Lam S (2012) Umstellung der Rechnungslegung von HGB auf IFRS—(k)eine echte Option für den Mittelstand? GmbHR 113(19):1041–1049
Küting K, Pfitzer N, Weber C-P (2013) IFRS oder HGB? Schäffer-Poeschel, Stuttgart
Leffson U (1987) Die Grundsätze ordnungsmäßiger Buchführung. IDW, Düsseldorf
Moxter A (1986) Bilanzlehre—Bd. II—Einführung in das neue Bilanzrecht. Gabler, Wiesbaden
Moxter A (2003) Grundsätze ordnungsgemäßer Rechnungslegung. IDW, Düsseldorf
Pellens B, Fülbier RU, Gassen J, Sellhorn T (2001) Internationale Rechnungslegung. Schäffer-Poeschel, Stuttgart
Richard J (2005) The concept of fair value in French and German accounting regulations from 1673 to 1914 and its consequences for the interpretation of the stages of development of capitalist accounting. Crit Perspect Account 16(6):825–850
Solmecke H (2009) Auswirkungen des Bilanzrechtsmodernisierungsgesetzes (BilMoG) auf die handels rechtlichen Grundsätze ordnungsmäßiger Buchführung. IDW, Düsseldorf
Wiedmann H, Schwedler K (2007) Die Rahmenkonzepte von IASB und FASB: Konzeption, Vergleich und Entwicklungstendenzen. In: Baetge J, Kirsch H-J, Thiele S (eds) Rechnungslegung und Wirtschaftsprüfung—Festschrift zum 70. Geburtstag von Jörg Baetge. IDW, Düsseldorf, pp 679–716

Bibliography of European and German Legislative Materials

Bundesrat (2008) Entwurf eines Gesetzes zur Modernisierung des Bilanzrechts (Bilanzrechtsmodernisierungsgesetz—BilMoG)—Stellungnahme des Bundesrates (BR-Drucksache 344/08)
Bundestag (2008) Entwurf eines Gesetzes zur Modernisierung des Bilanzrechts (Bilanzrechtsmodernisierungsgesetz—BilMoG)—Gesetzentwurf der Bundesregierung (BT-Drucksache 16/10067)
Bundestag (2009) Entwurf eines Gesetzes zur Modernisierung des Bilanzrechts (Bilanzrechtsmodernisierungsgesetz—BilMoG)—Beschlussempfehlung und Bericht des Rechtsausschusses (BT-Drucksache 16/12407)
EU (2002) Regulation (EC) No. 1606/2002 of the European Parliament and of the Council of 19 July 2002 on the application of international accounting standards
EU (2011) Proposal 2011/0308 (COD) for a directive of the European Parliament and of the Council on the annual financial statements, consolidated financial statements and related reports of certain types of undertakings from 25.10.2011
EU (2013) Directive 2013/34/EU of the European Parliament and of the Council of 26 June 2013 on the annual financial statements, consolidated financial statements and related reports of certain types of undertakings, amending Directive 2006/43/EC of the European Parliament and of the Council and repealing Council Directives 78/660/EEC and 83/349/EE

Bibliography of Materials from the IASB

IASB (2010) The Conceptual Framework for Financial Reporting 2010. IASB, London
IASC Foundation (2009a) International Financial Reporting Standard (IFRS) for small and medium-sized entities (SMEs) from 09.07.2009. IASC Foundation, London
IASC Foundation (2009b) Project summary: International Financial Reporting Standard for small and medium-sized entities (SMEs)—June 2009. IASC Foundation, London

Germany. The Influence of IFRS on the German Accounting System: The Half-Hearted Reforms of the German Accounting Law Modernization Act

Michael Hommel and Julia Zicke

Abstract At a first glance the IFRS can be described as an accounting system which favors the asset-liability perspective, using a fair value measurement model. This view conflicts with the German cost-orientated tradition. Nevertheless, in the last years there had been some changes in the accounting system in Germany. One of the most important changes is the German Accounting Law Modernization Act which was enacted in 2009.

This article takes the chance to have a closer look into the German accounting rules in force and to analyze whether they changed essentially—and if so in which way the changes were influenced by the international accounting standards. Thus, the authors analyze similarities and differences in the revenue recognition, the recognition of assets and liabilities in IFRS and the German principles of proper bookkeeping and whether a movement of the principles of proper bookkeeping towards the IFRS took place.

1 Introduction

JACQUES RICHARD is one of the most famous accounting scientists in the research field of accounting history and normative accounting. In numerous outstanding articles he sharply analyzes the fundamentals of accounting systems in different countries and systemizes and discusses the contribution of leading accountant theorists and their importance then and now (Richard 2004, 2005; Ding et al. 2008). His own contribution in this research field cannot be overestimated.

Annual financial statements are somewhat like the 'dating advert' of the enterprise and often the only information about the financial standing of the entity the external third parties possess. Hence, to make solid decisions it is crucial for them to understand the contents of the financial statements, how they inform, and what they

M. Hommel (✉) • J. Zicke
Goethe-University, Frankfurt, Germany
e-mail: mh@mhommel.de; zicke@wiwi.uni-frankfurt.de

D. Bensadon, N. Praquin (eds.), *IFRS in a Global World*,
DOI 10.1007/978-3-319-28225-1_20

hide. This applies even more in the light of the special characteristics of national accounting systems which are strongly different due to the historical background and are coined by social, environmental, and socio-ecological factors.

However, in the leading international accounting journals there are few papers dealing with this topic in a greater depth. It was 1995, when *JACQUES RICHARD* criticized that "apart from a few notable articles, the total number of publications devoted to the various chart of accountants used in Europe is relatively low; moreover, studies of the comparative aspect are almost non-existent" (Richard 1995). His criticism continues to be essential even today. Furthermore, this research area is recently even more important since IFRS increasingly gain worldwide influence on individual accounts.

Keeping in mind the European accounting history, the rise of IFRS is remarkable. In July 1978, the Fourth Council Directive was passed by the Council of the European Communities to coordinate the presentation and content of annual accounts of companies with limited liability (Introduction of the Fourth Council Directive). However, the coordination power of the Directive is limited since 62 paragraphs contain at least 76 explicit Member State options (Clayton et al. 1979)—and numerous implicit options resulting from ambiguous rules. Obviously, the majority of the Member States of the EU were not willing to assimilate foreign accounting rules in traditional national law (Haller 2002).

Nearly in the same time period (in 1973), the IASC was founded as a private registered association with the self-imposed goal to harmonize accounting standards worldwide. Regarding the perceptible reservations of most European countries to accept these accounting rules, there had been limited prospects that the IASC would succeed (see also Rost 1991). This problem was aggravated by the fact that in the case of the Fourth Council Directive each of the European nations could actively participate in the decision making process, whereas their influence on the development of IFRS is restricted. However, things turned out very differently. The IFRS developed into the most important accounting standard systems worldwide and since 2005 European listed companies are obliged to prepare their consolidated financial statement in conformity with IFRS.

However, IFRS strongly differ from the German Commercial Code (*Handelsgesetzbuch*—HGB). On the one hand, the IFRS are developed by a group of private individuals whose members are often directly affected by the standards. The important requirement in the standard setting process is the broad acceptance or consensus. Thus, a new standard is consistent and fits into the accounting system only when it is widely supported by the accountants and analysts (Schulte 2010). Already the term 'generally accepted accounting principles' captures this target in its name. In addition, the need to negotiate potential accounting solutions to solve a concrete accounting problem in a way that the new rules or principles are backed by the majority often leads to individual (case-by-case) compromises and tentatively to a rules-based approach with vague contents, which are open to interpretation.

On the other hand, HGB and specifically the principles of proper bookkeeping (*Grundsätze ordnungsmäßiger Buchführung*—GoB) are evolved by the German legislature which is equipped with authoritative support to control the information the entity has to provide and to protect the addressees of financial reports (Moxter 2003). Due to the fact that the entities are not directly involved in the standard setting process and with the previous understanding of the standard setting body to develop accounting rules in the interest of third-parties which are worthy of protection, there is no substantial need that the rules are generally accepted. Thus, the fundament for a principles-based approach is created and as a result GoB "should not be regarded as synonymous with generally accepted accounting practice" (Ballwieser 2010: 67). Furthermore, the accounting law must be practically applicable in a way that judges are able to decide certainly whether a violation of law has been committed or not (Sachs 2011). This calls for objectified and typecasted accounting rules which are consistent; i.e., so that the accountants can predict the legal consequences of their acting.

Last but not least, the objectives of the annual statements of IFRS and HGB seem to be very different. Recently it appears that the IASB prefers an asset-liability approach as benchmark for new standards with fair value as the dominant measurement method (Wüstemann and Wüstemann 2010). In contrast, HGB is much more orientated on the revenue-expense-approach and the cost principle.

The German parliament recognized the increasing influence of IFRS and that their accounting rules are different from HGB. In 2009 the German Accounting Law Modernization Act (*Bilanzrechtsmodernisierungsgesetz*—BilMoG) became effective. Its aim was to modernize the German accounting rules. Specifically, the German legislator pointed out that the intention of the new law is to change the national accounting law of the German Commercial Code into a set of rules that is on a par with the international accounting standards, but much more cost-effective and simpler to manage in practice (RegE BilMoG 2008).

Therefore, it is particularly important to have a closer look at the German accounting rules and to examine to which extent the German legislator adopted IFRS by BilMoG. Thereby, the paper gives some contribution to the understanding of the German accounting system.

2 The Financial Framework in Germany

2.1 The Source of HGB and the Authoritative Principle

The main area of application of IFRS is the consolidated statement, which has to be prepared by parent companies. Besides them, every merchant has to provide an individual financial statement according to HGB and in line with the principles of proper bookkeeping (section 238 (1) HGB in conjunction with section 1 (1) HGB). In addition, all of these firms have to prepare a single annual tax statement (section 140 and 141 Fiscal Code of Germany (*Abgabenordnung*—AO)). It has to be prepared in accordance with the German Income Tax Act (*Einkommensteuergesetz*—EStG) to determine the annual tax payment.

In Germany, the authoritative principle bridges the gap between the annual commercial statement and the annual tax statement. Specifically, section 5 (1) sentence 1 EStG requires that in the tax balance sheet those assets and liabilities should be recognized which have to be reported in accordance with the principles of proper bookkeeping as defined in commercial law.

The authoritative principle is based on a long historical tradition. Specifically, it was introduced for reasons of simplification (Alsheimer 1974). When the authoritative principle was incorporated into law the marginal tax rate was quite low (range from 0.6 % up to 4 %), so the costs of preparing annual financial statements for tax purposes outweighed the benefits (Weber-Grellet 1996). However, today the individuals have to face a significantly increased tax rate. Hence, simplification can no longer justify the continuance of the authoritative principle. Therefore, its justification has to be grounded on the (nearly) identical objectives of the commercial statement and the tax statement.

2.2 The Objective of the Principles of Proper Bookkeeping

In Germany, the essential GoB are laid down in sections 243–263 HGB and supplemented by few principles which are not legally codified but generally accepted as unwritten law (e.g., principle of off-balance sheet accounting of pending transactions). Together they form a gapless but flexible accounting system (*GoB-System*) and apply to all merchants "irrespective of such considerations as the legal form or size of an enterprise, or what industry it is in, or whether its shares are listed" or not (Ballwieser 2010: 66). However, it is obvious that these short advices (21 brief sections and few accounting principles) are vague and open to interpretation. They need to be clarified and supplemented by not codified purposive principles.

However, there is no explicit objective in the German Commercial Code which can be used as a basis for deduction or interpretation (Moxter 2003). Thus, the hermeneutical method is employed representing a simultaneous and interdependent definition of the deduction basis and its underlying principles (Moxter 1987).

The main underlying principles are laid down in section 252 HGB. Particularly, these are the realization principle (*Realisationsprinzip*), the recognition-of-loss principle (*Imparitätsprinzip*), and several principles of objectification (*Objektivierungsprinzipien*); e.g., reporting-date principle (*Stichtagsprinzip*), principle of separate valuation, i.e., no offsetting (*Einzelbewertungsprinzip*), and principle of consistency (*Stetigkeitsprinzip*). Keeping them in mind the hermeneutical interpretation leads to the conclusion that the aim of the German accounting system is the prudent and reliable determination of realized income or the distributable profit (*Ausschüttungsbemessung*) (Beisse 1990). No other objective harmonizes with these principles without violating at least one of them.

Within the GoB the realization principle is the cornerstone of the allocation of payments made and received (Moxter 1984b). It demands that revenues should be matched with expenses that incur to earn those revenues and obliges the entity to anticipate future cash inflows and outflows in the balance sheet if they result from past performance. In addition, it requires to neutralize payments received or made by offsetting the entry in the balance sheet to transfer them to future periods if related turnover is expected after the balance sheet date (i.e., matching principle).

Only the recognition-of-loss principle contravenes the realization principle and requires the recognition of expected but not yet realized losses (Moxter 1984a). The compliance with the recognition-of-loss principle is crucial because the income earned under the realization principle does not contain expected losses which are not yet realized but affect the distributable income as well.

In contrast, the true and fair view principle is not designed as GoB (Beisse 1990). The German Commercial Code acknowledges that it is impossible to inform simultaneously about the distributable income driven by the prudence principle and the unbiased performance of the entity driven by the true and fair view principle (Moxter 2000). Hence, the task to provide true and fair view is placed in a special separate section of the German Commercial Code which solely affects corporations (section 264 (2) HGB). They have to supplement their annual statement with additional notes (*Anhang*) (section 264 (1) HGB) to extend the information given by the balance sheet and the income statement towards a true and fair view. Therefore, the objective of the income statement and the balance sheet can be seen across all legal forms in the presentation of the distributable income, whereas the insight on the true and fair view of the company is provided in notes (*Abkopplungsthese*; Moxter 1986).

Furthermore, payout determination as the main objective of German commercial balance sheet and income statement harmonizes with the objective of the annual tax statement. Due to equality before the law (Article 3 German Basic Law (*Grundgesetz*—GG)) and protection of property (Article 14 GG) the tax authority is only empowered to charge taxes which are based on the entity's economic performance and therefore to tax the annual surplus which is finally earned and open for distribution (Tipke and Lang 2002). Hence, the tax authority can be seen as a minority shareholder sharing the same earned income and the GoB can be interpreted in tax and commercial accounts in identical way (Döllerer 1971; Moxter 2000).

2.3 The Interpretation of GoB with Jurisdictional Support

The Federal Constitutional Court (*Bundesverfassungsgericht*—BverfG) delegates the development and interpretation of the principles of proper bookkeeping to the courts of last resort (BverfG, May 12, 2009, 2 BvL 1/00, BverfGE 123). Therefore, the original competence to interpret the commercial law basically lies with the Federal Supreme Court (*Bundesgerichtshof*—BGH). However, only few of its decisions deal with GoB. In contrast, there are numerous judgments of the Federal Fiscal Court concerning principles of proper bookkeeping. They trace back to 1918

(*Reichsfinanzhof* 1918–1945; *Oberster Finanzgerichtshof* 1945–1950; since 1950 *Bundesfinanzhof*—BFH). Therefore, the Federal Fiscal Court plays a major role in the development and interpretation of GoB. The court has "– in literally thousands of court rulings—established a system of sound accounting principles and detailed standards regarding the recognition and measurement of assets and liabilities" (Leuz und Wüstemann 2004: 457). Even though the commercial law is the source for leading accounting principles for commercial and tax accounts, the interpretation of those principles for both accounts arises from the tax side.

In the following, we have to differentiate between the rules of HGB and GoB. Not all GoB are codified in HGB. They can result from unwritten law (e.g., customary law) or the interpretations of the courts of last resort. And not all rules of HGB represent GoB because they may be driven by the balance sheet policy of the legislator (Moxter 2003).

2.4 Changes Through the German Accounting Law Modernization Act

Due to the ongoing internationalization of the capital markets the German legislator felt constrained to strengthen the information function of the German financial statements to be competitive with international standards. Therefore, several accounting rules were developed or renewed during the modernization of the German Commercial Code in 2009. However, the legislator underlined that the primary goal of financial statements is still the determination of distributable income and kept the *GoB-system* unchanged (RegE BilMoG 2008).

During the development of the German Accounting Law Modernization Act it was argued that the authoritative principle is no longer up-to-date because the close relationship between the entity's commercial and tax accounts leads to biased predestination by interpreting the rules (Arbeitskreis 'Externe Unternehmensrechnung' 2003). If the management has to decide between two alterative interpretations of rules or principles, it will choose an interpretation which minimizes its tax payments resulting in conservative accounting in the commercial accounts as well. Nevertheless, BilMoG kept the authoritative principle basically untouched. Only slight changes were made to clarify the purpose of the principle. For example, the reverse authoritative principle, which was not in line with GoB, was eliminated to strengthen the provision of information of commercial statements and to align HGB with IFRS.

3 Recognition and Measurement Criteria According to HGB and IFRS

3.1 Revenue Recognition

The realization principle (section 252 (1) no. 4 sentence 1 HGB) states that only realized gains might be recognized in income statement. It is supplemented by the recognition-of-loss principle which requires that expected losses from pending contracts are recognized in profit or loss (Moxter 1984a).

In terms of revenue recognition, the realization principle ties the recognition of revenue to the turnover of sales of goods or rendering of services (Moxter 2003). In the management theory there are a lot of sound approaches to measure the performance process. However, they often lead to different pattern of income realization and allow discretionary power which is too ambiguous to pave the way for justiciable reporting. Hence to ensure the principle of objectification and transparency, this crucial point in time is not primarily defined in an economic way but rather from a legal point of view.

In the civil law the transfer of price risk (*Preisgefahrenübergang*) describes a crucial point in the performance process which leads to significant reduction of risk. Often, when the price risk changes from the seller to the buyer, an important part of risk changes between the contracting parties because from that time on the buyer is obliged to fulfill his obligation even if the promised good is destroyed or deteriorated by accident (section 362 German Civil Code (*Bürgerliches Gesetzbuch*—BGB)) (BFH, November 29, 1973, IV R 181/71, BStBl II 1974 202). However, if the price risk has been transferred but significant economic risks remain, which are out of the firm's control and suitable to threaten the payment of the receivable later on, the revenue must be postponed until the corresponding future payment is virtually certain (BFH, February 25, 1986, VIII R134/80, BStBl II 1986 788).

In contrast, IFRS 15 obliges an entity to recognize revenues when it satisfies its performance obligation in a way that the customers obtains control of the promised good or service (IFRS 15.31). That means that the customer is able to direct the use of and obtain substantially all of the remaining benefits from the asset (IFRS 15.33). Control can change over time or at a point in time. While this is not the place for a deeper analyses of the new standard, there are strong indicators that revenue is recognized over time under circumstances which are close to IAS 11, where the revenue of construction contracts have to be recognized under the percentage of completion method (IAS 11.22), irrespective whether the price risk has changed to the costumer or not. If the customer has not obtained control over time, the performance is fulfilled at a point in time. IFRS 15 gives some guidelines to the entity, to operationalize this moment where the change of price risk is only one criteria among others and therefore of small importance (IFRS 15.38).

Contrary to IFRS 15, in GoB the control approach plays a minor role and serves primarily as an expression of the substance over form principle to attribute the economic ownership of an object to the entity without answering the question whether the entity as a legal owner of this object has fulfilled its contractual obligation in the sense of the realization principle or not (section 39 (2) no. 1 sentence 1 AO).

In addition, the percentage of completion method is not employed in HGB. The German Accounting Law Modernization Act in 2009 offered an opportunity for a radical change and its adoption. However, this method would lead to unrealized earnings and contradict the realization principle. After weighing the pros and cons of the alternatives, the legislator confirms the prudent revenue recognition for construction contracts and requires the recognition only in case of approval of the complete construction asset or an independent part of the construction asset (RegE BilMoG 2008).

3.2 Recognition and Measurement of Assets

The realization principle and the recognition-of-loss principle determine the point in time when assets and liabilities should be recognized (Ballwieser 2008). However, focusing solely on the realization principle would result in recognition of accruals in which financial burdens and benefits are possible or probable but cannot be approved in a justifiable way (Schmalenbach 1962). To be in line with the principle of objectification they should be more concrete. The task is fulfilled by the asset and a liability criteria (Moxter 2007).

In contrast, in its most recent pronouncements the IASB increasingly favors the asset-liability approach (Wüstemann and Wüstemann 2010). It follows an inventory guideline where the balance sheet is prepared by counting, measuring, weighing, and calculating the items existing at the balance sheet date without worrying about the revenue process of the entity. Gains or losses are the result of value changes in assets and liabilities and not of the exchange of goods or services (Pferdehirt 2007). Thus, the realization principle plays only a minor role, if any at all.

The German Commercial Code contains no definition and recognition criteria of an asset. The interpretation is primarily done by the Federal Fiscal Court. The definition of assets in HGB is similar to the definition in IFRS. However, internally generated intangibles are special cases. It is often difficult to answer the question with sufficient clarity whether and when they meet the asset criteria. Hence, according to the objective to determine distributable profits, the old version of section 248 (2) HGB strictly typed the recognition of intangibles. It stated that non-current intangible assets, which have not been acquired for valuable consideration, were not allowed to be recognized as assets in the balance sheet.

In addition, it is very difficult to judge whether a goodwill acquired in a business combination exists or whether the calculated residual payment is just the result of an unfavorable deal. Further, the subsequent measurement of this kind of asset grants an enormous scope for discretion. Thus, the old version of section 255 (4) HGB contained solely an option to capitalize the acquired goodwill.

Regarding the measurement of assets in HGB, the cost principle is employed. It derives from anticipation or translation of payments ruled by the realization principle. In subsequent periods, measurement of assets has to reflect the pattern in which the future economic benefits are consumed by the entity without being concerned about their fair value (Moxter 2003). For acquired goodwill the old version of section 255 (4) sentence 2 HGB required to recognize in each subsequent financial year at least one quarter of the capitalized goodwill as amortization expense. Alternatively, the legislator allowed an amortization over the useful life of goodwill (old version of section 255 (4) sentence 3 HGB), but in this case asked for additional rationale in notes (section 285 no. 13 HGB). As a result, by setting stringent disclosure requirements, the legislator tries to ensure the objective of prudent profit calculation.

For the purpose of improving the information content of German financial statements, BilMoG requires the recognition of acquired goodwill (section 246 (1) sentence 4 HGB; the recognition option in the old version of section 255 (4) HGB was deleted) and introduces a recognition option for internally generated intangible assets (section 248 (2) sentence 1 HGB). However, the legislator seems to have general doubts about the value of the recognized internally generated items because he implements a payout block in section 268 (8) HGB to ensure that the corresponding increase in income is not free for distribution.

Further, in section 248 (2) sentence 2 HGB the German legislator prohibits, by using nearly the same words as IAS 38.63, the capitalization of internally generated brands, mastheads, publishing titles, customer lists, and assets similar in substance. Additionally, section 255 (2a) HGB allows solely the capitalization of development costs of internally generated intangible assets and requires the capitalization from the time they first meet the asset criteria (Bundestag-Rechtsausschuss 2009).

Regarding the measurement of assets, the government considered to weaken the realization principle during the ordinary legislature proceedings of BilMoG. The government argued that fair value measurement is common practice and identified practical needs as well as requirements for that reform. Hence, the first government draft obliged fair value measurement of financial assets held for trading for all entities (RegE BilMoG 2008). The plan was dropped due to the impact of the financial crises. At the end, the legislator restricts this requirement to financial institutions only—and thus ironically to the companies which were blamed to be responsible for the extent of the crises by misusing the fair value method.

According to the new rule, the financial entity is neither obliged to objectify the fair value nor to demonstrate the existence of an active market for the asset. Thus, both the realization principle and the principle of objectification are violated. However, to stay partly in line with the prudence principle the financial institution is required to measure financial assets at fair value less an appropriate deduction for risk (section 340e (3) sentence 1 HGB). Furthermore, realizable but not yet realized gains from fair value measurement are restricted for distribution (section 268 (8) HGB).

Therefore, the purpose of the German Accounting Law Modernization Act to align HGB with IFRS is only partly fulfilled. Regarding the definition and recognition criteria it should be noted that the entities are only allowed but not required to capitalize internally generated intangible assets. In addition, the legislator avoided defining the criteria of internally generated intangible assets. He discussed the adoption of the requirements of IAS 38.57 in detail but rejected it after all (RefE BilMoG 2007). Considering the valuation of assets, it is remarkable that the legislator retained the measurement at cost as the dominant measurement method. Fair value accounting is restricted to assets which are held for trading of financial institutions. Concerning the acquired goodwill, the legislator maintains its scheduled amortization over economic life time. However, in cases where the amortization period exceeds five years the entity has to give additional rationale in notes (section 285 no. 13 HGB). Therefore, the legislator sustained the stringent disclosure requirements.

Although the changes made by BilMoG were marginal, they tangle the GoB-system. Capitalization of internally generated intangibles can be seen formally as in line with the matching principle. However, up to date no recognition criteria exist to limit managerial judgment. Thus, the new approach weakens the prudence principle and the principles of objectification and jeopardizes the primary goal of the German accounting system. Concerning changes in measurement regulation, the new rule for financial institution measuring financial assets held for trading at fair value leads to an unsystematic sectoral rule without conceptual reasoning. Moreover, it contradicts the realization principle and weakens the conceptual clarity and consistency of HGB. However, emplacing the new rule in a special part of the German commercial law, which concerns only financial institutions, the legislator clarifies that this advice is not an element of GoB because they are independent of the entity's legal form.

Consequently, although the German government began the German Accounting Law Modernization Act with the ambitious objective to reduce the differences between HGB and IFRS, at the end of the reform there are only minor modifications to highlight. The initial target of the project obviously failed. HGB and IFRS continue to be incomparable. Even more, the half-hearted reforms interfere with the compelling nature of HGB.

3.3 Recognition and Measurement of Liabilities

By and large the definition and recognition criteria of liabilities in HGB are similar to those in IFRS. However, according to the prudence principle the probability criterion in HGB is interpreted in a qualitative way. The entity shall demonstrate that there are good and sound reasons for which it has to fulfill the liability in future (Eibelshäuser 1987). But there is no need that the probability is greater than 50 % because this restriction would contradict the prudence principle which is satisfied when the degree of probability is lower, but in line with reasonable business judgment.

Moreover, the old version of section 249 (1) sentence 2 HGB requires the recognition of provisions for deferred maintenance which will be fulfilled within three months after the balance sheet date and provisions for removal of waste residues which will be fulfilled within the next fiscal year. Additionally, firms had a recognition option for provisions for deferred maintenance if the obligation will be fulfilled not before three months after the balance sheet date but at least within the next fiscal year (old version of section 249 (1) sentence 3 HGB) and for provisions for expenses in the sense of Article 20 (2) Fourth Council Directive, which can be viewed as purely internal liabilities because there is no obligation toward third parties (old version of section 249 (2) HGB).

Most of these exceptions are long-term impacts of the accounting practice. Hence, the legislator anchored these provisions in the law to ensure that they can be recognized. However, there is no obligation toward third parties. Thus, their consideration is a clear breach of GoB.

In opposition to IFRS where provisions are measured at best estimate (IAS 37.36), in HGB provisions were generally measured at their most likely outcome considering the prudence principle. Further, due to the realization principle the old version of HGB did not allow to discount non-interest-bearing provisions and therefore to recognize unrealized interest income. The consideration of future events that may affect the fulfillment amount of the liability at the balance sheet date is contentious because there is a trade-off between the realization principle and the prudence principle on the one hand and the reporting-date principle on the other hand. The first two principles demand an anticipation of total future outflow of resources and the anticipation of expected price and wage increases. However, the old version of the commercial law favored the reporting-date principle to support an objectified reporting.

To come in line with IFRS, the German legislator deleted the recognition options for provisions for internal obligations and for provisions for deferred maintenance costs that will be fulfilled not before three months after the balance sheet date but at least within the next fiscal year. In addition, the legislative changed the measurement of provisions. According to the new ruling, future events shall be considered in the measurement of provisions if the entity has sufficient objective evidence that they will influence the amount to settle the obligation (RegE BilMoG 2008) and long term provisions with a remaining term of more than one year need to be discounted using market interest rates for liabilities with corresponding maturities, averaged out over a period of seven years which are released by the German Central Bank (section 253 (2) sentence 1 HGB).

The reform of the liabilities is stuck half-way. The recognition criteria of provisions in IFRS and HGB still differ in main points. Whereas the IFRS interpret the probably criteria in a quantitative way (i.e., more likely than not), HGB interprets it qualitatively (i.e., good and sound reasons). In addition, contrary to IFRS the German Commercial Code permits furthermore the recognition of provisions for amounts for internal costs such as provisions for deferred maintenance costs which are going to be settled within three months up to the balance sheet date and provisions for removal of waste which will be fulfilled within the next fiscal year (section 249 (1) sentence 2 no. 1 HGB).

Only at first glance do the measurement criteria of provisions of IFRS and HGB seem to be identical. In fact, in HGB the determination of the discount rate of provisions is objectified and typecasted whereas in IFRS its assessment lies in the responsibility of the management. In addition, the anticipation of expected price changes is a novelty in German accounting and the degree of prudence implemented by its estimation is open for interpretation. Due to the prudence principle in HGB the premium for future wage and price increases should be higher than in IFRS. However, the principle of objectification which is more pronounced in HGB than in IFRS may counteract a more generous anticipation. More exceptionally, the legislator breaks through the authoritative principle and prohibits the anticipation of future price changes in tax accounts (section 6 (1) no. 3a EStG). Therefore, in order to enable a widely unified balance sheet, the management might neglect future price changes in the commercial balance sheet referring to the principle of simplification or to cost-benefit considerations. However, time will tell how German managers will interpret the new advice.

From a national point of view the revised rules for provisions in HGB partly disharmonize with the principles of proper bookkeeping. The deletion of the provisions for accruals for internal obligations (e.g., provisions for deferred maintenance) was long overdue and is to be welcomed because it strengthens the consensus of the German accounting system. However, it does not go far enough because some of these provisions remain without any conceptual basis. Furthermore, discounting non-interest-bearing provisions contradicts the realization principle since unrealized interest income is recognized in profit or loss. Moreover, the anticipation of future price performance may be in line with the realization principle. But it is questionable whether the rule is consistent with the principle of objectification and whether the anticipation of expected price decreases fits the prudence principle.

4 Conclusion

1. The German legislator recognized the increasing influence of IFRS and that their accounting rules are different from HGB. With the German Accounting Law Modernization Act enacted in 2009 it aimed to modernize the German Commercial Code into a set of rules that is on a par with the international accounting standards.
2. A glance at the new accounting rules in detail shows the attempt to modernize HGB by bringing it closer to IFRS. However, this mission failed. The fundamental objectives of both accounting systems as well as their underlying principles still differ significantly. Therefore, implementing merely few rules borrowed from IFRS is only cosmetics. It does not lead to a new accounting system which is compatible with IFRS.

3. Furthermore, many of the new rules developed by the legislator in the German Accounting Law Modernization Act in 2009 do not fit into the improved German accounting system. Moreover, they violate the fundamental principles and weaken the consistency of the principles of proper bookkeeping.
4. The main reason for the unsatisfactory results seems to be obvious and lies in reforming the German accounting law by the legislator without considering the historical and current normative background of HGB and IFRS in a proper way.
5. Hence, the result of the reform would have been definitely more adequate if the German legislator had studied the contributions of *Jacques Richard*. He retires, but the recent development in Germany, and maybe also in France, shows that the accounting community cannot work well without his contributions. Today they are needed more than ever. Therefore, we are already looking forward for his forthcoming papers.

References

Alsheimer H (1974) Einhundert Jahre Prinzip der Maßgeblichkeit der Handelsbilanz für die Steuerbilanz. Zeitschrift für Betriebswirtschaft 44(12):841–848

Arbeitskreis 'Externe Unternehmensrechnung' der Schmalenbach-Gesellschaft für Betriebswirtschaft e.V. (2003) International Financial Reporting Standards im Einzel- und Konzernabschluss unter der Prämisse eines Einheitsabschlusses für unter Anderem steuerliche Zwecke. Der Betrieb 56(30):1585–1588

Ballwieser W (2008) § 252 HGB. In: Schmidt K (ed) Münchener Kommentar zum Handelsgesetzbuch, vol 4, 2nd edn. C.H. Beck/Vahlen, München, pp 157–185

Ballwieser W (2010) Chapter 3: Germany. In: Previts G, Walton P, Wolnizer P (eds) A global history of accounting, financial reporting and public policy: Europe. Emerald Group, Bingley, pp 59–88

Beisse H (1990) Rechtsfragen der Gewinnung von GoB. Betriebswirtschaftliche Forschung und Praxis 42(6):499–514

Bundestag-Rechtsausschuss (2009) Beschlussempfehlung und Bericht des Rechtsausschusses (6. Ausschuss) zu dem Gesetzesentwurf der Bundesregierung—Drucksache 16/10067. BT-Drucksache 16/12407

Clayton MR, Devlin D, Hinton JK (1979) Handbook on the EEC fourth directive. Price, Waterhouse & Co., Brussels

Ding Y, Richard J, Stolowy H (2008) Towards an understanding of the phases of goodwill accounting in four Western capitalist countries: from stakeholder model to shareholder model. Account Org Soc 33(7–8):718–755

Döllerer G (1971) Maßgeblichkeit der Handelsbilanz in Gefahr? Betriebs-Berater 26 (8):1333–1335

Eibelshäuser M (1987) Rückstellungsbildung nach neuem Handelsrecht: Ein Beitrag zur Auslegung von § 249 Abs. 1 Satz 1 HGB. Betriebs-Berater 42(13):860–866

Fourth Council Directive (78/660/EEC) of 25 July 1978 based on Article 54 (3) (g) of the Treaty on the annual accounts of certain types of companies, No L 222/11.

Haller A (2002) Financial accounting developments in the European Union: past events and future prospects. Eur Account Rev 11(1):153–190

Leuz C, Wüstemann J (2004) The role of accounting in the German financial system. In: Krahnen JP, Schmidt RH (eds) The German financial system. Oxford University Press, Oxford/New York, pp 450–477

Moxter A (1984a) Bilanzlehre: Vol. 1. Einführung in die Bilanztheorie, 3rd edn. Gabler, Wiesbaden
Moxter A (1984b) Das Realisationsprinzip—1884 und heute. Betriebs-Berater 39(28):1780–1786
Moxter A (1986) Bilanzlehre: Band II: Einführung in das neue Bilanzrecht, vol 2, 3rd edn. Gabler, Wiesbaden
Moxter A (1987) Zum Sinn und Zweck des handelsrechtlichen Jahresabschlusses nach neuem Recht. In: Havermann H (ed) Bilanz- und Konzernrecht—essays in honor of Reinhard Goerdeler. IDW, Düsseldorf, pp 361–374
Moxter A (2000) Missverständnisse um das Maßgeblichkeitsprinzip. Deutsche Steuer-Zeitung 88 (5):157–161
Moxter A (2003) Grundsätze ordnungsgemäßer Rechnungslegung. IDW, Düsseldorf
Moxter A (2007) Bilanzrechtsprechung, 6th edn. Mohr Siebeck, Tübingen
Pferdehirt H (2007) Die Leasingbilanzierung nach IFRS. Westdeutscher Verlag, Wiesbaden
RefE BilMoG (2007) Referentenentwurf eines Gesetzes zur Modernisierung des Bilanzrechts. http://www.der-betrieb.de/pdf/081107_BilMoG_RefE.pdf. Accessed 23 Apr 2014
RegE BilMoG (2008) Gesetzentwurf der Bundesregierung—Entwurf eines Gesetzes zur Modernisierung des Bilanzrechts. BT-Drucksache 16/10067.
Richard J (1995) General introduction. Eur Account Rev 4(1):81–86
Richard J (2004) The secret past of fair value: lessons from history applied to the French case. Account Eur 1(1):95–107
Richard J (2005) The concept of fair value in French and German accounting regulations from 1673 to 1914 and its consequences for the interpretation of the stages of development of capitalist accounting. Crit Perspect Account 16(6):825–850
Rost P (1991) Der internationale Harmonisierungsprozess der Rechnungslegung. Lang, Frankfurt am Main
Sachs M (2011) Art. 20 GG. In: Sachs M (ed) Grundgesetz: Kommentar. Beck, München, pp 787–848
Schmalenbach E (1962) In: Bauer R (ed) Dynamische Bilanz, 13th edn. Westdeutscher Verlag, Köln/Opladen
Schulte M (2010) Systemdenken im deutschen und französischen Handelsbilanzrecht. Gabler, Wiesbaden
Tipke K, Lang J (2002) Steuerrecht, 17th edn. Schmidt, Köln
Weber-Grellet H (1996) Steuerbilanzrecht. Beck, München
Wüstemann J, Wüstemann S (2010) Why consistency of accounting standards matters: a contribution to the rules-versus-principles debate in financial reporting. Abacus 46(1):1–27

Italy. The Transition to IFRS in Italy and Elsewhere, or from *Code Napoléon* to the Devolution of Sovereignty

Arnaldo Canziani

Abstract The approval and implementation of EU Directives started a process of clash between civil-law and common-law countries which, in creeping a way, is on move since then with pervasive effects on the accounting theory and practice and on the accounting profession as well. The story got underway by the unclear *true and fair* concept, implemented by each national state according to its previous legal and accounting tradition. To unravel the problem, the passage was suggested to IAS-International Accounting Standards, these ones being—on their turn—heavily country-minded.

As a result, a process was step by step implemented which led to the adoption of IFRS, the so-called *common global language* for accounting in Europe as well as in the world.

To be true, anyway, one should distinguish first between hotchpotch and harmonization as such (due to zillions of alternatives); secondly, between the grounding of standards in Anglo-Saxcon accounting and common law v. the implementation of the same ones within income-based theories of the firm and civil law as well.

1 Introduction, or the Clash Between Civil and Common Law

The harmonization processes proper to EEC (later EU) were often rooted in the clash among different languages, political traditions, social "visions of the world" as well as economic structures. This meant in many cases one or more compromises, under the swaying prevalence in time of one or another political approach, or even country.

In particular, those harmonization processes stemmed from the encounter of the two juridical families (David 1968; Larenz 1991) of *common law* v. *civil law*, i.e. between the two juxtaposed juridical systems of *consuetudo* v. Codes and

A. Canziani (✉)
Brescia University, Owensboro, KY, USA
e-mail: canziani@jus.unibs.it

D. Bensadon, N. Praquin (eds.), *IFRS in a Global World*,
DOI 10.1007/978-3-319-28225-1_21

statutes. The former ones rooted in the cases tradition and the role of precedents (*stare decisis*), the latter ones grounded on written norms (and *system* of norms). For common-law systems, in addition, it was a matter of identification of juridical premises, once the possibility was given to judges to refer their discretion not only to past cases, personal experience and subjective values but, further, to general welfare (Eisenberg 1988; Farber 2006; Schauer 1989, 2004, 2006).

That encounter took frequently place in the cooking of directives at the EU level, where Great Britain (and some other countries hosting a flexible legislation) faced European continental countries established on Codes after Code Napoléon, i.e. on whole juridical systems whose hierarchy was Constitution → Codes → laws → charters and bylaws.

These problems resulted of overwhelming an importance within EU 4th and 7th Directives, (i) as they radically modified in most cases previous accounting regulations, (ii) as they were at the very origin of such concepts—or even events—as <true and fair>, *fair value* in accounting as well as the institutionalization of IFRS as a conclusion.

2 The Anglicization of the 4th and 7th EU Directives and Its Consequences at European Level

2.1 The <True and Fair> Provision

The first drafts of the 4th EU Directive, of German nature were turned along years—due to the clever lobbyism of UK and other nations' representatives—to a final text of British imprint, especially as regards to the provision of *true and fair view*, modelled on the UK *Company's Act* of 1948. As long as that provision is regarded, one should anyway never forget the following juridical (and accounting) evidences:

1. the <true and fair> concept of 1948 was as new for companies as rare for English language in general, since it had not been utilized since John Donne's "*I swear/nowhere/lives a woman/true and fair*" (Canziani 1993: 165–168)[1]; in addition, the English word *true* recalls a subjective nor objective truth (Tooke remembers us its old form *trew*, coming from *throwed*, <reputed>) (Tooke 1806-7, vol. 2: 337–43);
2. <true and fair> is *adopted as* <general clause>, while these ones are *per se* general decision models like *bona fides* i.e. *good faith*, *reasons beyond one's control*, and so on (Grundmann and Mazeaud 2006; Teubner 1998);
3. this way, <true and fair> is not a premise rule of law or a *Grundnorm* (Larenz 1991: 266, 283), but only a general provision, to be cleared case by case in the

[1] The reference is to John Donne's work *Song, Go and Catch a Falling Star* (1600).

same Great Britain but today included—according to some authors and/or by some EU decrees (§ 2.3.)—into IFRS.

2.2 <True and Fair> Within National Adoptions of the Civil-Law Type

The abovementioned incertitude, widespread in Britain since 1948, was later on poured into the EU 4th Directive, here reinforced by its same wording, which asked for <a> (nor <the>) true and fair view; hence, into national adoptions.

Once compelled to host a common-law principle into Codes, most countries tried to translate its indefiniteness into wordings of the civil-law type (Hėritier 2001; Mastebroek 1995) as in these countries—either thanks to their systemic characteristics or due to them—the only way to be fair is to be true, as the only way to be true is to conform to law. <True and fair> this way (i) was reframed in general provisions (*image fidèle* in France, *veritiero e corretto* in Italy), such concepts being grounded generally on *bona fides* and specifically on the general principles of *completeness*, *exactness*, *clarity* further clarified in Codes, (ii) or merely concerned formats and notes (in Germany, via *Abkoppelungsthese*, Commercial Code, § 264.2.2.).

National implementations compelled firms to present high-quality information, as well as the regulations *prior* to the 4th Directive did, in some unexpected cases at least: e.g. the Italian annual accounts prepared according to Civil Code rules *before* its technical enrichment were fully comparable in disclosure and quality with other nations' ones obeying to the same 4th (Fee 1991).

2.3 Accounting Practice and IFRS to Implement <True and Fair>

Due to common law, in Great Britain the situation was a largely different one:

- "true and fair view is a technical term which is interpreted in several different ways" (Horrocks 1967);
- "A detailed prescriptive approach must inevitably be an authoritarian, and perhaps arbitrary, imposition of particular solutions, without adequately distinguishing the variety of circumstances." (Flint 1982).

In that country incertitude therefore arose as a substantial problem. As a consequence, the tendency was reinforced to apply codified uses both to establish rules to form annual accounts and to judge their truthiness and fairness in Courts. Those uses—simple *accounting practices* as underlined by different Authors from Great Britain to Italy to elsewhere (Mazza 1997)—were called <principles> and later on *common accounting principles*, then ennobled as *accounting standards* through a political process whose main characters were the accounting profession, the auditing firms, and international finance as well. Once the process was ended, the situation was e.g. described as such:

> Financial Reporting Standards are also based on IFRS and IAS issued by the IASB. The Financial Reporting Council collaborates with accounting standard-setters from other countries and the IASB in order to influence the development of international standards. Such standards have been adopted by the European Union in regulation 1606/2002/EC. Listed companies preparing consolidated accounts are under a duty to use these IAS and IFRS.
>
> Accounting standards may have indirect effect on the interpretation that the courts would give to true and fair view concepts. The court is likely to infer that, in general, compliance with accounting standards is necessary to meet the true and fair requirements. (Boyle and Birds 2014: 484, abridged).

The same position was later on sustained—tactfully in forms, but strongly and self-referentially in substance—within the IASB *Framework* (§ 46).

This process brought about some well-known advantages, with but two shortcomings. The obvious advantages consisted in (i) a well-defined frame of reference, in addition expressed in a set of very analytical technical prescriptions, (ii) the unification of criteria for listed companies to set annual accounts within the Anglo-Saxon world, so facilitating international information, communications, investments. The shortcomings—rarely discussed ones due to vested interests—are summarized in paragraphs 4 and 5.

3 The Coming in Power of IAS/IFRS: Technicalities, and Politics as Well

3.1 European Accounting Traditions Flooded by Anglo-Saxon Uses

IAS, later on IFRS, are so well-known to the reader as to make useless here any special narration concerning their origins, contents, technical functions at international level, and political meaning as well.

They stem from the abovementioned tradition and, in addition, from the globalization of financial flows, governed by Anglo-Saxons centres like London and New York, as well as by Anglo-Saxon actors like multinational companies, investments funds, pension funds, not to mention the *Big eights* merged later on. So, dating back from the 1970s, IAS gained practical and cultural space along years.[2] Once spread from the Anglo-Saxon world to Continental Europe, they were

[2] The International Accounting Standards Committee, promoted in 1973 by IFAC—International Federation of Accountants as its internal committee, became on April 1st, 2001 a private US Foundation whose issuing board, IASB (International Accounting Standard Board) is located in London.

formally introduced in EU by UE Regulations (July 19th, 2002, n. 1606, September 29th, 2003, n. 1725 as well as further ones implementing them[3]), to be today applied in some 120 countries all over the world.

Anyway, spite of its intrinsic reasons, the abovementioned process was not a spontaneous nor a neutral one, which is common after all for moral principles adopted to favour—or to cover—more practical interests (Goldthorpe 1984; Haas 1998; Knill and Lenschow 1998; Rayman 2006).

So, technical consequences apart, the extension of IAS/IFRS outside the Anglo-Saxon world meant from the legal point of view the addition—or even the substitution—(i) of a private jurisdiction to State laws, (ii) of common-law uses to Codes and statutes, (iii) of collective standards to civil and/or commercial norms.

3.2 *IAS/IFRS for Italian Companies*

While the obligations for Italian companies are now the standard European ones, some special regulations were put into force by the Italian legislators through Law under delegated power n. 366 (October 3rd, 2001), later on implemented by Legislative Decree January 17th, 2003, n. 6:

1. the <true and fair view> is overriding, this implying the refuse of IAS/IFRS once they contrast it;
2. companies not compelled to IAS/IFRS continue to apply (previous) norms derived from the adoption of the 4th EU Directive (Civil Code, articles 2423 to 2435b is for annual accounts, Legislative Decree 127/1991 for consolidated accounts);
3. tax laws established by the Decree of the President of the Republic 917/1986 regarding the Tax Consolidation Act are modified (articles 11–13), especially regards companies' income statement.

In addition, the above-mentioned delegated act and its actuation specified some further norms for annual accounts ending after September 30th, 2004:

(a) substance over form;
(b) *fair value* for intangibles;
(c) special technicalities to inscribe (1) deferred taxes; (2) leasing; (3) foreign exchange operations; (4) derivatives; (5) repurchase agreements, (6) the composition of equity (Ceriani 2006b).

All these principles, as other traditional ones, were anyway to be (re)framed within the new article 2423bis, section 1.1., Civil Code, which reaffirmed some

[3] Respectively: November 13th, 2004, n. 2236; December 29th, 2004, no.s 2236, 2237, 2238; February 4th, 2005, n. 211; July 7th, 2005, n. 1073; October 25th, 2005, n. 1751; November 15th, 2005, n. 1864; December 8th, 2005, n. 1910

basics characterizing national continental legislations since the nineteenth century: *continuity*, *pertinence* (costs and revenues belonging to the financial year, independently from either payment or collection), *caution* (*prudence* in France, *Vorsichtsprinzip* in Germany, a principle widespread all over the world, Commonwealth and IFRS apart).

The new text said among others:

> *Preparing the annual accounts . . . valuations criteria must obey to caution according to the going concern principle, taking into account-in addition-the economic function of both the active or passive element under examination*"; *Caution means to include in the P&L costs even if presumed and to exclude merely expected revenues, that's to say to include only realized profits, i.e. coming from operations or cycles already concluded within the financial year.*

Further dispositions—mainly the Legislative Decree n. 38/2005—defined the types of companies to which the adoption of IFRS was either imposed or permitted starting with annual accounts ending December 31st, 2005.[4]

As far as standards were concerned, Italian legislators cancelled the role of the long-dating O.I.C.—*Organismo Italiano di Contabilità* (Italian Accounting Foundation) established by the Italian accounting professions, to substitute its suggestions and/or codified rules by IFRS (Caratozzolo 2006). By this choice, the Parliament adopted the IFRS prescriptions in straight a way, obeying to well-known general principles just summarized as follows:

(a) A&L values can be classified with reference either to operations cycles (current v. non-current) or according to the liquidity-principle, in any case specifying the sums fallen due within 12 months (IAS n. 1, § 52);
(b) P&L values can be classified according either to their nature or scope (IAS n. 1, §§ 78 to 95); in any case, within the P&L or in notes, costs must be classified either by nature or scope (IAS n. 1, § 88);
(c) a flow-of-funds prospect is compulsory, as well as the one showing the increases/decreases of equity;
(d) the information requested by IAS must be presented within notes, as well as any further piece of information necessary to give consistency to the whole document.

In Italy as elsewhere, both positive and negative consequences emerged from the transition to IFRS (Potito 1973; Amodeo 1981; Bruni 1984; Onesti 1995; Mazza 1997; Capaldo 1998; Ceriani 2006a; Bruggemann 2013; Nobes 2013; Mohammadrezaei 2015). As for the advantages, one must account for (i) the extremely analytical accounting treatment of any business operation, (ii) the entrance of Italian accounts into world accounting habits.

[4] (i) Companies whose shares (or even bonds) were listed in EU Stock Exchanges; (ii) companies whose financial instruments were largely diffused; (iii) banks and financial institutions; (iv) insurance companies; (v) other companies not included in the above categories but anyway controlled, connected, or jointly ventured with companies belonging to numbers (i)–(v) above.

Anyway, these advantages resulted to be two-folded ones, as both the hyper-complexity of IFRS and their basic contrast with continental accounting theories give rise to a set of practical problems. The first among them was represented by the displacement of age-old, general principles in favour of Anglo-Saxon uses, privately coordinated, mutable along time, stemming from (temporary) majorities regarding accounting opinions, finally as international ones as they were diffused by powerful international interests. This meant the abandon of truth (either effective as measured by transactions or conventional as obeying to Codes' prescriptions) as well as of neutrality, consistency and caution in favour of a <true and fair> either ill-defined or rooted in <mark to market>. Some today debated problems stem in fact from the clash between the age-old principles of (i) the firm as a system, (ii) the unity of its values, (iii) the continuity of its life and the *financialization* approach of IAS/IFR.

One further, relevant problem lied in the dissonance between contemporary accounting systems of the income-type and the habits of English accounting. This as the basic imprint of IFRS was constituted by British accounting which, as a matter of fact (i) still lies on empirical generalizations, as well as on somehow unclear conceptions of the firm's economy, (ii) tends to evaluate assets first, in addition from the atomistic nor systemic point of view; (iii) never experimented the <income revolution> proper to continental accounting after 1900–1920 (§ 4.), (iv) this way resulting in sophisticated treatments of operations anyway conceived in old-fashioned ways (§ 5.1.).

4 Between Harmonization and Hotchpotch

4.1 European Self-Contained Theories of the Firm and Renewed Accounting Visions

Continental accounting—also thanks to the German *Fachhochschulen*, the French *Conservatoire des Arts et Métiers*, the Italian *Scuole Superiori di Commercio*—turned in late nineteenth century from mere technicalities to an accomplished science, this meaning—from the epistemic point of view—the creation of a new unified discipline, *Betriebswirtschaftslehre* in Germany, *Economia aziendale* in Italy, *Économie de l'entreprise* en France, encompassing in one accounting, management, strategy and finance (Canziani and Rondo Brovetto 1992; Canziani 2007), their pillars being the following ones among others (Canziani 2005):

1. the firm in its very nature isn't <a set of assets and liabilities>, nor <a nexus of contracts among the factors of production>, neither <a bilateral principal-agent relationship> (as proposed by Giuseppe Cerboni in 1886), but *a system of contracted prices turning themselves*—respectively—*into costs and revenues*;
2. the firm as a system is <the only economic unit able to produce income and to reproduce assets in systematic a way>, negotiating "in simultaneity and succession" prices and mobilizing fixed assets along time;

3. the operations of firms as “going economic concerns” are the object of measurement by accounting, which homogenises by direct measurement the multiple sub-systems of costs and revenues dispersed in nature, space-time, counterpart.

In parallel or slightly later, after 1914 a set of macroeconomic changes converted the attention of those schools to income and income flows. Dramatic inflation processes, industrial changes, and the crumbling away of the gold-standard system overturned in fact the global set of values and prices. As huge amounts of assets were now no longer in a position of producing profits, Accounting was taught that—from both logical and practical standpoint—the value of assets only depends from the amount of income they are able to generate (Schmalenbach 1913; Zappa 1929).

This further revolution regarding the interpretation of income and wealth enriched the abovementioned disciplines, which centred the value-attribution process upon *flow values* (income) instead of *stock* ones (capital). Accounting as a system to measure and assign values was now able to disregard old, earthbound habits now of no use from the accountability point of view:

- the physical nexus *inputs* → *outputs*,
- the chronological nexus *capital* → *income*.

Accounting took therefore the new role of measuring income *directly* (i.e. the costs and revenues the enterprise creates and destroys), income becoming in addition the very benchmark to assess the value of firm’s assets.

4.2 On the Basic Relevance of (i) Income, (ii) Income Statement, (iii) Costs and Revenues as <Primary Measures> in Accounting

As accounting established now its own procedures on the substantial nexus *income* → *capital*—looking at cost-prices and revenue-prices as primary measures—this made absolutely relevant (prevalent) the profit and loss account both for continental Europe and for the few Anglo-Saxon authors well aware of the problem.[5]

This new vision looked now at the income-statement as the very document by which: (i) to understand the amount and composition of income, (ii) to give proper evaluations to assets, i.e. to multi-annual costs to be transformed into revenues, as

[5] “Fifty years ago the principal interest of those concerned with . . . business enterprises centred on the periodic display of assets and liabilities (balance sheet). (. . .). . . at the present time the principal attention of investors, financial analysts, and the general public is focused on the statement setting forth the periodic net income or earnings of the business, with the balance sheet being viewed ‘. . .as the connecting link between successive income statements’.” (Hepworth, 1953); Report, 1971.

negotiated costs (revenues) express *directly* the value produced by inputs (outputs) in the firm's economy.

Basically, accounting was renewed according to the teachings of Schmalenbach, Zappa and others:

1. capital recalls income in any case, "the most important fact within firm life": due to this reason, accounting systems must represent *the formation* of income, which is related both to every administrative fact and the overall firm dynamics;
2. accounts are established on *exchange transactions as the 'critical event'*, and arranged in a system expressing every cost-revenue inter-dependence: monetary magnitudes stemming from transactions give origin to economic values *certain in nature*;
3. P&L prospects take a new form, following the very nature of firm's economic processes and operations (ended v. still going) as well as their proper representation.[6]

Every P&L mixes in fact—as the financial year puts them together—costs and revenues of certain v. uncertain a nature depending on their different proximity to transactions. They all are determined by the double entry system (labour costs, purchases, sales and so on) also thanks to statistical methods (depreciation, work in progress, stocks). The former values, as primary measures, are called *quantità economiche*; the latter ones are called *secondary measures* and distinguished between (i) *stime* (estimations), if they meet a proof in a short space of time (e.g. inventories, provisions for taxes or bad credits, (ii) *congetture* (conjectures) if they cannot meet any specific proof in a close time but only a judgement about their whole, systemic consistency (e.g. depreciation allowances) (VV.AA. 1982).

5 Technical Problems in the Applying the IFRS in Italy

5.1 The Shortcomings of IFRS Grounded in the Backwardness of British Accounting

Within the field of annual accounts, and accounting measurements in general, Great Britain didn't even perceive the controversy of income v. capital. Interpreting

[6] **Profit and Loss Account for the period (n)**

(−)	(+)
Initial work in progress (revenues for **n-1**)	Sales
Costs measured by money transactions	Final work in progress (costs for **n + 1**)
Amortisation, Depreciation, Provisions	Other revenues measured by monetary transactions
(*Profit*)	(*Losses*)

Accounting as training nor education, and holding fast to Marshall and J.M. Keynes as well, this country was as a consequence unable to analyze firms' economy according to the renewed scientific frameworks of continental Europe.

As a consequence, still building on medieval praxes and the first industrial revolution habits, Great Britain today so lays in the Nineteenth century mood as (i) to still describe the firm and its nature as <a set of assets and liabilities>, (ii) to magnify wealth looking directly to A&L to measure profitability, calling <balance sheet> that only format, (iii) to identify income as the increase between to subsequent wealth measurements (where profit is often considered to be gained only once the consignment is fulfilled). This means to mould firm's accounting on the physical and chronological development of productive processes, as if accounts should follow step by step raw materials → works in progress → products → credits → cash inflows, and so forth.

Once compared with continental traditions, it goes without saying that British Accounting is a horse of different colour, the shortcomings of IFRS and the problems of their application in Italy (and elsewhere) just coming from such differences as the following ones:

1. *recognition* based on substance nor on the juridical form, which is compulsory under civil law;
2. fiscal relevance of annual accounts based either on IAS/IFRS v. special tax-accounting rules (especially in Germany via *Steuerbilanz*);
3. inscription of R&D expenses within assets;
4. "fair" values and mark-to-market v. entry-values (so-called historical);
5. changes in accounting criteria chargeable to equity, which is prohibited in Italy (the same for further problems connected to creditors' protection);
6. disclosure of managerial accounting data, while in Italy annual accounts and cost accounting follow in most cases different tracks.

5.2 *From Caution Nor Conservatism to <Mark to Market>*

Only scholars not especially rooted in the field can still repeat so severe (blind?) critics to entry-values (so-called *historic* ones) as to say:

> i) "historic cost account is a source of irrelevant accounting data; its financial statements obscure real financial position and the results of operations of a firm and provide ample room for manipulation", ii) "movements in general price level are ignored in the historic cost accounting and deform its information"; iii) "it disregards also the effects of changes in the interest rates on the value of debt, so that the book value of liabilities does not represent their fair value", iv) "depreciation and amortization rarely reflect user cost, and the same is true for the process of determining the cost of manufactured inventory"; v) "fair value accounting in contrast measures and discloses the current value of assets and liabilities".

Some synthetic remarks are due here, easily referable ones to both <true and fair> and largely to IFRS:

1. within annual accounts, the income statement is the very specimen of a firm's economy, largely (totally?) based on current values, this being obvious for expenses on one side, but also for sales and depreciation allowances on the other (well-managed firms in fact depreciate with reference to current values, the same being for pricing, where raw materials stocks are valued at entry-cost, but production-costs—i.e. manufactured goods—are computed at LIFO, and in some cases at NIFO values);
2. as a result, <historic> costs represents the very values an enterprise underwrote, while possible differences can be explained either within the notes or the directors' relation;
3. P&L information cannot be manipulated inasmuch it obeys to *reliability*, *faithfulness*, *verifiability* nor to the so-called *relevance*, which favours in so many cases manipulations (from Enron to Parmalat) as (i) its values are not yet matched but merely supposed, subjective, and fancy ones in some cases, (ii) more generally, value-assignment must be referred to the firm as a system nor to single, specified objects, which loose their economic significance outside the whole operations of the firm;
4. the inclusion into P&L of realized gains only v. unrealized too, as well as unrealized losses, is a due <prudent exactness> (i) as unrealized gains could be mere hopes, while unrealized losses must be computed for in order to protect shareholders, (ii) to prevent any further manipulation by either directors willing to show brilliant annual profits (not to mention Fanny May and Freddy Mec as well as other bankrupted US banks) or managers willing to boost their own stock options and golden handshakes on third parties' money.

5.3 What About Overriding?

One further problem concerns overriding, a still opened one which can be substantially resumed as follows:

1. pure preachers of <true and fair> and British-minded scholars claim the general override of <true and fair> over (and in case against) every other provision, IFRS included (Flint 1982);
2. pure preachers of the absolute relevance of IFRS, IFRS-minded scholars, and the officials of both IASB and big auditing firm as well, they all claim the absolute overriding of IFRS over (and against) true and fair view;
3. regulations of the United States of America do not even mention <fair> (SFAS 162, FASB 2008) and exclude in addition—*§ A.12.*—any overriding at all.

National legislations are generally in favour of TFV, particularly in civil-law countries due to its introduction into Codes and laws hierarchy, IFRS being on the contrary mere private regulations. Generally speaking, this should mean a <true and fair> override, leaving anyway TFV, and its contrasts with IFRS, submitted to the appreciation of directors and auditors. In addition, in 2013, some relevant investors' associations[7] objected that:

4. IAS 39 (*Financial Instruments Recognition and Measurement*), and this way the system of IFRS, hosts *substantial legal flaws*;
5. as a consequence, IFRS contrasts with TFV as general provision;
6. further, all the annual accounts of banks are to be considered as faulty since 2005 or before, the same being for all the auditing reports and for dividends as well.

By now, the most authoritative opinion on the above conflict—especially as far as IAS 39 is concerned—is by barrister George Bompas QC (2013), while in October 2013 the FRC–*Financial Reporting Council* emitted a contrasting *opinion*, which in 82 paragraphs explained how and why the obedience to IFRS could give life—perfectly—to the TFV (Martin Moore, QC, *Opinion*).

6 Conclusions: From Continental Accounting Theories to IFRS, or the Devolution of Sovereignty

As Jacques Richard taught us, EU did not express a clear <European accounting model> through its Fourth and the Seventh Directives: the number of options, and in addition the summing of them, clearly showed that lack (Richard 2005).

A set of relevant, convergent international events took place immediately after, among them the set of US wars to bring democracy in the world, the enlarging of NATO treatise under US guidance and of WTO system under Anglo-Saxon influence. From the financial standpoint one must add-after the collapse of the dollar-standard system (1971)—(i) the *deregulation* after 1980,[8] i.e. the massive financialization of the world economy (*hot money* included) fuelling to 2007–2008 the most important financial centres of the world from New York to London, (ii) the US QE-*quantitative easing* to solve the 2007–2008 crisis.

These dynamics as a whole, and their systemic effects, can now easily explain the interest, the convenience, and so to say the need for the Anglo-Saxon world to get a (so to say) uniform accounting language of Anglo-Saxon an imprint around the world.

That end offered some relevant, further advantages to nations being—at the same time—users as well as monopolistic prompters of those practices. Nations being nevertheless the characters of the political processes intended to uniform accounting under the label of <international standards>.

---

[7] LAPFF—Local Authority Pension Forum; UK Shareholders Association; Universities Superannuation Scheme; Threadneedle Asset Management

[8] Especially due to (i) the *Depositary Institutions Deregulation and Monetary Control Act* (1980, PL 96-221); (ii) *Garn – St. Germain Depository Institutions Act* (1982, PL 97-320); *Gramm – Leach – Bliley Act* (1999, PL 106-102), repealing sections of the GLASS-STEAGALL Act (1933)

As a result, those nations (i) were able to impose their own language, uses, culture to accountancy in the whole world (or so); (ii) became the officiants, and the monopolists as well, of the new rites (or even religion) of IFRS; (iii) conformed to those conventions the international accounting thought all over the world, both forging new legislations and compelling others to abandon their own age-long and well-grounded traditions.

As far as EU is concerned, the goal was easily reached by dispositions (§ 3.1) which were acutely commented by professor Richard as follows:

> Even a minimal "European view" is over since the decision taken in 2003 by the Council ofMinisters to adopt the IASB rules in matter of consolidated accounts of quoted companies....; the European Union has then clearly renounced to have its own construction if not conception of accounting and has delegated this task to the IASB...
>
> But it must be said that the IASB claims to be a "neutral" organisation (...) There are certaindoubts to emit about the neutrality of the IASB: first, this organisation was composed at 50 % at its higher level of representatives of the USA and Great Britain; second, this organisation goes on with or follows, in matter of very important questions, the US change in accounting policy: no wonder that one could speak of the IASB as the "Trojan horse" of the US accounting legislator and of its indirect will to legitimate a "Texan model" of governance! (Richard 2005: 14).

From these dynamics some relevant consequences were derived, both technical and political ones. From the technical point of view one must underline (i) the introduction into companies' accounts of non-market or even invented data called <fair values>, as well as their massy mixture with true ones directly measured by monetary exchanges; (ii) the enclosure of un-realized revenues, in some cases wished-for ones; (iii) possible, unreasonable increases in the value of assets, (iv) distribution of fancy dividends in case. (The set of these inconsistencies raised recently basic doubts on those adoptions in the same Anglo-Saxon world, in parallel with the silence—or even the continuation of the story—from the whole EU and its technical organizations).

From the political point of view, this raises once more the sense of the European Union as such, and its goals, scope, functions, and future as well.

In the field of accountancy, in particular, the very chance was lost for Europe to reaffirm its traditional system of standard, well-grounded juridical and technical values. Further, the chance was lost to build—together with its own money, and laws—a true European system, while a very peculiar common-law system was adopted, a debate-defined one oriented by vested interests.

From the point of view of political science, such a dynamic can be defined *devolution of sovereignty*, which sadly happened without any substantial deepening and debate, while *it is inherent in the nature of sovereignty not to be amenable to the suit of an individual without his consent* (Hamilton, *The Federalist*, 1788).

This being from the point of view of public law, that dynamic seems to give life to long-lasting consequences—once remembered the shortcomings and defaults of IFRS—for both annual accounts and, at large, the accounting profession, the professional culture and the economic progress in general. In conclusion, and not as we are feasting him, we shall once more share Professor Richard's opinion:

> The IFRS are both obsolete and dangerous. The IFRS are obsolete because they remain stuck in a quaint conception that views financial capital and investors alone as the Alpha and Omega for managing accounting. The IFRS are dangerous because they embody a systematic and all-out assault on a fundamental principle underlying accounting—the principle of prudence, which forbids statements of potential profits and prescribes disclosures of potential losses. By even daring to herald a principle of "imprudence", the IFRS has contributed to the rise to power of the irresponsibility of financial capitalists and their executive agents.
>
> We will need to re-establish democracy within the national and international bodies governing accounting regulation to put an end to the domination of financial capital in accounting matters. (Richard, http://www.crefige.dauphine.fr/recherche/actualite/richard1.htm (abridged)).

Bibliography

Amodeo D (1981) Alcune considerazioni sugli standard contabili generalmente accettati, in VV. AA

Ardemani E (1984-90) L'impresa, 4 volumes. Giuffré, Milano

Biondi Y (2011) The pure logic of accounting: a critique of the fair value revolution. Convivium 1:1–46

Biondi Y, Zambon S (eds) (2013) Accounting and business economics. Insight from national traditions. Routledge, New York-London

Biondi Y, Canziani A, Kyrat T (eds) (2007) The firm as an entity and its economy. Routledge, London

Boyle & Birds (2014) Company law, 9th edn. Jordan Publishing, Bristol

Bruggemann U (2013) Intended and unintended consequences of mandatory IFRS adoption. Eur Account Rev: 1–37

Bruni G (1984) I principi contabili generalmente accettati. In: Ardemani E (ed) L'impresa, vol III

Canziani A (1993) Group accounting in Italy. In: Gray SJ, Coenenberg AG, Gordon PD (eds) Int Group Account. Routledge, London and New York, pp 152–169

Canziani A (2005) On the economic nature of the firm. In: Guidi M (ed) The changing firm. Contributions from the history of economic thought. Franco Angeli, Milano, pp 456–75

Canziani A (2007) Economia Aziendale and Betriebswirtschaftslehre as autonomous sciences of the firm. In: Biondi Y, Canziani A, Kyrat T (eds) The firm as an entity and its economy. Routledge, London, pp 107–130

Canziani A, Accounting and economia Aziendale in Italy, 1911 afterwards. In: Biondi Y, Zambon S (eds) Accounting and business economics. Insight from national traditions. Routledge, New York-London, pp 69–101

Canziani A, Rondo Brovetto P (1992) The emerging of the economics of firms in continental Europe during the 20's. In: Todd Lowry S (ed) Economia Aziendale and Betriebswirtschaftslehre as methodological revolutions, pp 168–191

Capaldo P (1998) Reddito, capitale e bilancio d'esercizio. Giuffré, Milano

Caratozzolo M (2006) Il Bilancio d'esercizio, 2nd edn. Giuffré, Milano

Ceriani G, Frazza B (2006a) L'implementazione dei principi contabili internazionali Nell'ordinamento giuridico italiano. Aracne, Roma

Ceriani G, Frazza B (2006b) Raccolta coordinata dei principi contabili internazionali IAS/IFRS e delle relative interpretazioni. Aracne, Roma

David R (1968) Major legal systems in the world today. Stevens & Sons, London

Eisenberg MA (1988) The nature of the common law. Harvard University Press, Cambridge

Farber DA (2006) The rule of law and the law of precedents. Minn Law Rev:1173–1203

FEE (1992) European survey of published accounts 1991. Fédération des Experts Comptables Européens, Bruxelles
Flint D (1982) A true and fair view in company accounts. Gee & Co. Ltd., London
Goldthorpe J (ed) (1984) Order and conflict in contemporary capitalism. Clarendon Press, Oxford
Gray SJ, Coenenberg AG, Gordon PD (1993) International group accounting. Routledge, London and New York
Green Cowles M, Caporaso J, Risse Th (eds) (2001) Transforming Europe. Cornell University Press, Ithaca
Grundmann S, Mazeaud D (eds) (2006) General clauses and standards in European Contract Law. Comparative law, EC law and contract law codification. Kluwer, The Netherlands
Guidi M (2005) (ed) The changing firm. Contributions from the history of economic thought. Franco Angeli, Milano
Haas PM (1998) Compliance with EU directives: insights from international relations and comparative politics. J Eur Public Policy:17–37
Héritier A (2001) Differential Europe: National Administrative responses to community policy. In: Green Cowles M, Caporaso J, Risse Th (eds) Transforming Europe. Cornell University Press, Ithaca, pp 44–59
Horrocks J (1967, October) Are published balance sheets untrue and unfair? Aust Account:567–576
Knill C, Lenschow A (1998) Coping with Europe: the impact of Britain and Germany administrations on the implementation of EU environmental policy. J Eur Public Policy 4:595–614
Larenz K (1991) Methodenlehre der Rechtswissenschaft, 6th edn. Springer, Berlin
Mastebroek E (1995) EU compliance: still a ‘black hole’. J Eur Public Policy 6:1103–1120
Mazza G (1997) Problemi di assiologia aziendale, 2nd edn. Giuffré, Milano
Mohammadrezaei F (2015, February) The effects of mandatory IFRS adoption: a review of evidence. Int J Disclosure Gov:29–77
Nicklisch H (1932) Die Betriebswirtschaft, 7th edn. Poeschel, Stuttgart
Nobes C (2013) The continued survival of international differences under IFRS. Account Bus Res 2:83–111
Onesti T (1995) Fattori ambientali e comportamenti contabili. Giappichelli, Torino
Potito L (1973) I principi contabili generalmente accettati. In: AA.VV. La certificazione professionale dei bilanci. Giannini, Napoli
Rayman A (2006) Accounting standards: true or false? Routledge, London
Report of the Committee on Foundations of Accounting Measurement (1971). The Account Rev (Supplement to vol. XLVI)
Richard J (2005) Fair value: towards a third stage of the French accounting capitalism? Université Paris Dauphine, Cahier de Recherche 2005-09, Cereg
Schauer F (1989, March) Is the common law law? California Law Rev:455–471
Schauer F (2004) The failure of the common law. Arizona State Law J:765–782
Schauer F (2006) Do cases make bad law? Univ Chicago Law Rev:883–918
Schmalenbach E (1913) Dynamische Bilanz, 4th edn. Gloechner, Leipzig
Teubner G (1998) Legal irritants: good faith in British law or how unifying laws ends up in new divergences. Mod Law Rev:11–32
Todd Lowry S (Ed) (1992) Perspectives in the history of economic thought, vol VII. Elgar for the History of Economics Society, London
Tooke JH (1806-7) ΕΠΕΑ ΠΤΕΡΟΕΝΤΑ, or the Diversions of Purley, 2 volumes. Wm. Duane, Philadelphia
VV.AA. (1982) Bilancio d’esercizio e amministrazione delle imprese. Studi in onore di Pietro Onida. Giuffré, Milano
Zappa G (1929) Il Reddito d’esercizio. Istituto Editoriale Italiano, Milano
Zappa G (1954-7) Le produzioni nell’economia delle imprese, 3 volumes. Giuffré, Milano

Japan. The Japanese "Dynamic-Conservative" Model to the Test of Global Convergence: From the Birth of Industrial Accounting to the Competition with the "Actuarial" Model

Clemence Garcia

Abstract In this paper, I used the classification of balance sheet theories by Richard (Comptabilités et pratiques comptables, Dalloz, 1996) in order to explain the main characteristics and the evolution of the Japanese accounting system since the Meiji Era. In this classification, Japanese accounting is dynamic for the purpose of cost calculation and profit measurement, and conservative in order to avoid dividend distribution and increase internal financing sources.

After the "lost decade", some actuarial rules based on fair value measurement were introduced for the purpose of global convergence of accounting standards. Yet, after the equivalence assessment of the EU (2005–2008), some accounting reforms were delayed because of the lack of consensus on comprehensive income and fair value, the conceptual groundings of the actuarial theory. Non-amortization of goodwill was also a major concern raised by companies and academics.

In the case of Japan, the "dynamic-conservative" model was indeed transformed through the harmonization process, but endorsement conducted by the ASBJ and the support of local preparers tend to secure its future on the domestic market.

1 Introduction

Since the Meiji Era (1868–1912), accounting regulation has been imported to Japan based on different Western models, including mainly the German Commercial Code in 1890[1] and the American Financial Instruments and Exchange Act (FIEA) in 1948. At the end of the 1990s, a third important set of reforms, the "accounting

[1] Revised in 1899.

C. Garcia (✉)
Faculty of International Social Sciences, Gakushuin University, Tokyo, Japan
e-mail: clemence.garcia@gakushuin.ac.jp

D. Bensadon, N. Praquin (eds.), *IFRS in a Global World*,
DOI 10.1007/978-3-319-28225-1_22

big bang", continued this tradition to converge towards western accounting standards (Kikuya 2001, p. 361).

In the 2000s, the global landscape of accounting changed dramatically. After the 2001 EU announcement of IFRS adoption and the 2002 "Norwalk agreement" between the IASB and the FASB, the Accounting Standards Board of Japan, followed the move in order to avoid being isolated from other developed countries and signed a convergence project with the IASB in 2004. The next stage of this process would have been mandatory adoption of IFRS, a possibility that was raised several times from the end of the 1990s (Kikuya 2001, p. 366).

The latest announcement of the Business Accounting Council[2] (BAC 2013, p. 1) officially excluded this possibility to the benefit of optional use of "endorsed" IFRS. This paradox may be seen as the result of a complex combination of economic and political circumstances, among which the decision of the American SEC not to adopt IFRS in 2012 is certainly a major factor (BAC 2013, p. 5). Yet, international relations fail to explain the opposition of the ASBJ against the "assets and liabilities view" and the particularities of Japanese accounting.

In this regard, it is worth considering some recent statements by the Keidanren (2013) and the BAC (2013). Both explain that accounting is not only a means of information for investors and creditors, but that it is also important for the purpose of internal management decisions (Keidanren 2013, p. 5; BAC 2013, p. 3). For this reason, they oppose convergence with standards that do not fit the needs of Japanese management.

Prior studies have already investigated accounting convergence issues in Japan (Kikuya 2001; Suzuki 2007a, b; Saito 2010, 2011; Tsunogaya and Chand 2012) focusing either on institutional changes (Kikuya 2001; Suzuki 2007a, b and Tsunogaya and Chand 2012) or on the conceptual differences between IFRS and Japanese standards (Saito 2010, 2011). In this paper, I adopt the theoretical framework of Richard (1996) in order to analyze how the traditional characteristics of Japanese accounting were transformed during the twentieth century until the convergence process with the IASB.

The remainder of this paper is organized as follows. Section 2 outlines the classification of accounting systems by Richard (1996). Sections 3–7 provides some details about the Japanese "dynamic-conservative" model and its transformation over time. The last section concludes by summarizing the reasons for which the "dynamic-conservative" Japanese model could survive despite the context of global convergence of accounting.

[2] The Business Accounting Council (BAC) is an advisory body of the Financial Services Agency (FSA) in charge of financial regulation in Japan.

2 Classification of Accounting Systems by Richard (1996)

Richard (1996) defines six different accounting models. The first one, cash accounting, measures "liquid capital" in the business and the global profit of operations by comparing cash receipts and expenses (Richard 1996, p. 18).

The second one is "static" accounting[3] developed by lawyers to prevent bankruptcy. In order to check if the sale of assets is enough to pay for all liabilities, static accounting relies on the "periodic liquidation fiction" assuming that the business is liquidated (Richard 1996, p. 33). In this model, consistently with the asset-liability view, the concept of net assets is fundamental, while net income is defined as the change in net assets during an accounting period (Richard 1996, p. 34). Measurement of assets is based on their market value, so that the concept of depreciation corresponds to the decrease in value of assets. Consistently with the liquidation fiction, static accounting is characterized by conservatism and involves a prudent assessment of nontransferable assets like intangibles.

The third model is "dynamic" accounting, aimed at measuring the profitability of own funds (Richard 1996, p. 51) and it spread with the industrial revolution in Europe and other industrial countries. Net income is defined as the difference of revenues and expenses for an accounting period according to the revenue-expense view (Richard 1996, p. 57) and its calculation relies on the correct allocation of costs to several periods following the realization of revenues. Unlike in the static model described supra, depreciation in the dynamic model does not reflect a loss in market value, but the cost of fixed assets consumed during the period (Richard 1996, p. 66). Conservatism is not an intrinsic characteristic of the dynamic model, yet the realization principle can be seen as one of its expressions since it tends to delay the recognition of revenues (Richard 1996, p. 64). One more characteristic of dynamic accounting is permanent inventory due to the importance given to cost calculation (Richard 1996, p. 67).

The fourth model, "actuarial" accounting, measures the global value of a business based on the net present value of future cash flows expected from the business (Richard 1996, pp. 72 and 78). Similarly with static accounting, actuarial accounting is based on the asset-liability view, in which performance is defined as the variation of net assets. Yet, the going concern principle adopted in this view implies replacing liquidation value with net present value for measurement purpose.

Richard (1996, p. 81) also defines two other models: tax accounting for the determination of taxable income and "macroeconomic" accounting for the purpose of national accounts, based on the economic concepts of production, intermediary consumption and added value.

In practice, some characteristics of these models can be found in domestic and international accounting standards, but there is no pure "static" or pure "dynamic"

[3] The "static" and "dynamic" models in Richard (1996) are defined after the work of Eugen Schmalenbach. This paper is based on their interpretation by Richard (1996).

accounting system: all accounting systems are hybrid compositions with some characteristics of different models. For example, French accounting is a combination of the static, dynamic, tax, and macroeconomic models (Richard 1996, pp. 109–121).

3 The Birth of the Japanese "Dynamic-Conservative" Model (1890–1945)

From the Meiji era (1868–1912) until World war II, economic development in Japan was driven by large and diversified industrial groups, the zaibatsu. After the Japanese defeat, the zaibatsu were abolished by Mc Arthur because of their participation in the war effort, but they were soon replaced with a more flexible structure, the keiretsu.

In terms of accounting regulation, the first requirements were introduced in the Code of Commerce in 1890, revised in 1899.[4] In this German-style reporting system, corporations were required to publish financial statements for the information of shareholders, and also to comply with dividend restrictions in order to protect creditors. In this regard, it is based on the asset-liability view with current value as the main measurement method (Saito 2011, pp. 3 and 4), which corresponds to the static model in Richard (1996) classification.

Concerning the financing sources of large companies, Miwa and Ramsyer (2002, p. 134) provide evidence that "for the bulk of their funds, they sold stock. Secondarily, they sold bonds and retained their earnings." This conclusion refutes the assumption that the prewar Japanese economy was dominated by the banking sector, so that economic circumstances appear to contrast with the philosophy of the Commercial Code about the protection of creditors.

On the other hand, in practice, the necessity to retain cash within the business in order to finance new activities may induce the same conservative accounting treatments as those required for the protection of creditors. For example, rapid expensing of some assets and the constitution of provisions tend to reduce distributable income, which is favorable both for creditors and companies to reduce dividends. Doing so, conservatism fits the interests of companies by helping the retention of cash for internal financing purpose, and those of creditors by improving corporate solvency.

At the very beginning of the twentieth century, most new businesses created as corporations were industrial companies, banks or insurance companies. By contrast, in the retailing sector, the old merchant houses turned into corporations only in the 1920s (Itabashi and Garcia 2011). As many industrial companies adopted Western style bookkeeping for the purpose of legal disclosure, industrial

[4] Before the introduction of Western accounting during the Meiji Era, Japanese merchant houses used single-entry bookkeeping for management purpose.

bookkeeping focused on cost calculation gradually spread in Japan. As a consequence, the static asset-liabilities view from the Commercial Code and the dynamic revenue-expense view were mixed in practice.[5]

In the academic world also, the influential work of E. Schmalenbach theorizing industrial dynamic practices spread gradually. Leading figures like K. Kurosawa and T. Ohta, who belonged to the dynamic school, played an important role in Japanese standard setting before and after World War II. The work of Schmalenbach was even influential among economists, like for example T. Nakanishi whose book *Theory of management expenses* (1936) is partly based on the dynamic theory.

During the imperialist period, the first accounting standard, the *Working Rules for Financial Statements* (1934) was issued by the Ministry of Commerce and Industry and a second one, *Draft Standards for Financial Statements for the Manufacturing Industry* (1941) was later issued by the Planning Bureau (Saito 2011). Even within the frame of a static German-style reporting system, it is interesting to underline that these two standards belong to the dynamic theory: for example, the latter one includes a model of balance sheet with some intangible assets (Kubota 2001).

One more important element of the Japanese accounting system is taxation. According to Itabashi and Garcia (2011), after income tax was introduced in 1917, the tax administration organized some conferences in order to teach western bookkeeping to companies and required their use in tax declarations. In the 1920s, tax rules were dynamic, but later diverged from pure dynamic theory for the purpose of state interventionism.

Because the Japanese reporting system was originally modelled after the German Commercial Code, the dynamic nature of Japanese accounting is often underestimated (for example, in Tsunogaya and Chand 2012, p. 120). In reality, the prewar Japanese accounting model was dynamic[6] for the needs of industrial capitalism with some static conservative practices in order to avoid excess distribution of dividends and to increase internal financing sources.

---

[5] Saito (2011, p. 5) explains that "there was a shift to valuation based on below-market value, and other schemes soon followed, with an acquisition cost-based valuation scheme gradually gaining ground.

[6] The case of goodwill is clear in this regard: in the 1920s, the tax administration recommended capitalizing and amortizing goodwill over a period of 10 years (dynamic model), contrasting with the tax treatment of goodwill in other developed countries at that time (Garcia 2011, p. 58).

4 From the FIEA to the "Accounting Big Bang" (1949–2003)

During and immediately after the American occupation (1945–1949), some structural reforms were passed in order to increase individual shareholding and to redistribute assets to the public. In this purpose, the FIEA (1948) and the Business Accounting Principles and Working Rules for Financial Statements (1949) provided a new framework for accounting disclosure and auditing (Saito 2011, p. 3). Although this reform was a major event in Japanese accounting history, the general philosophy of these new standards appears in fact very similar with the dynamic precursors issued in 1934 and 1941 (Saito 2011, p. 3).

One notable difference, though, was that the new American-style reporting system focused on the information of potential investors, while the Commercial Code gave more importance to the protection of creditors. Consistently, as investors are assumed to make investment decisions based on recurring earnings, the revenue-expense view was dominant in the new reporting system (Saito 2011, p. 3).

Between 1949 and 1974, several adjustments between the Commercial Code and the Business Accounting Principles were passed, but reconciliation issues ended up only in 2005 when the Corporate Law of 2005 stipulated that preparation of financial statements shall conform to generally accepted business accounting practices. Meanwhile, the tax system was also rebuilt in the postwar period after the Shoup report in 1949. These three sets of standards constitute what has been called the Japanese "triangular accounting system".

In the field of management accounting, the dynamic tradition was reinforced by further developments of the costing techniques in large industrial groups. The most famous example is the Toyota production system based on "kaizen costing" (Monden 1991). Just like for financial accounting, these changes reflect the development of prewar cost accounting. For example, advanced techniques of target costing and the determination of the optimal production level were already studied in Nakanishi (1936, pp. 60–109).

Besides, one of the major reforms in Commercial Law during the allied occupation was the ban of holding companies in order to abolish the zaibatsu. The result of this reform was that industrial groups turned from zaibatsu into "keiretsu" characterized with horizontal capital relationships between group companies. Cross-shareholding between allied companies was useful not only to control the shareholding structure, but also to reduce the distribution of dividends, since partners mutually agreed to retain internal financing sources. As a consequence, cross-shareholding reinforced the tradition of holding profits low through conservative accounting practices (Kikuya 2001, p. 365).

After 30 years of prosperity, the burst of the financial bubble (1986–1991) followed by a severe economic downturn in the 1990s lead to the necessity of reforming market infrastructures. The result was the accounting "Big Bang", including reinforcement and widening of the consolidation scope (implemented in 1999), introduction of the cash flow statement (1999), accounting for tax-effect

(1999), accounting for retirement benefits (2000), introduction of fair value accounting for financial instruments (2000 and 2001) and impairment of assets (2002). In 2003, a new standard for business combinations introduced the purchase method but the pooling-of-interests and amortization of goodwill remained.

In order to catch up with Anglo-Saxon accounting, many changes were based either on international standards or American ones (Saito 2011, pp. 6–8), resulting in some new standards being based on the asset-liability view. Taken separately, the new measurement standards belong to the "actuarial" theory (Richard 1996) since they are based on fair value measurement and not only on market value.

These reforms can be seen as a first test of the capacity of the "dynamic-conservative" model to converge with international standards. Unfortunately, as fair value measurement was introduced in the context of bear market and deteriorated economic circumstances, the reform was unfavorable and unpopular among listed companies. Consequently, proposals like widening the scope of fair value or replacing net income with comprehensive income drew constant opposition from preparers during the following decade.

5 Limits to the Reconciliation of Accounting Models (2004–2009)

In order to continue the harmonization process with more flexibility and resources,[7] the ASBJ was created as a private sector standard-setting body in 2001 to replace the BAC. Since many of the first members of the ASBJ also belonged to its predecessor, the work of the ASBJ was aligned with prior reforms of the BAC.

At that period, the move towards global convergence gathered momentum after the announcement of EU's adoption of IFRS in 2001, soon followed in 2002 by the "Norwalk Agreement" between the FASB and the IASB. As a response, the ASBJ launched two important projects: the "Conceptual Framework of Financial Accounting" completed in 2004, and the Convergence project with the IASB from 2004.

In 1998, during the accounting big bang, the Ministry of Finance considered preparing a conceptual framework, but the conclusion of preliminary work was that in the context of global convergence, Japan did not need a different framework from the American one (Garcia 2007). Six years later, the political context of global convergence had changed dramatically, so that the ASBJ decided to make its own framework for the purpose of international communication with the IASB and other standard-setters (Saito 2009).

The framework was issued in 2004 (revised in 2006) under the Anglo-saxon format: "objectives of financial reporting", "qualitative characteristics of

[7] The BAC stopped producing accounting standards, but it still issues some "opinions" about financial regulation.

accounting information", "elements of financial statements", and "recognition and measurement in financial statements". The main differences with its Western counterparts are listed by Ito (2005):

- The framework makes a synthesis of the traditional dichotomous views: the income statement approach and the balance sheet approach;
- it improves current accounting terminology and proposes more modern concepts: instead of "financial situation and management results", "investment position and results", instead of "realization principle", it uses "free of risks";
- it separates the definitions of "financial elements" and "recognition and measurement", it also proposes specific recognition rules.

In other words, the Japanese conceptual framework is a synthesis of several balance sheet theories. Assets, liabilities and net assets and comprehensive income are defined based on the asset-liability view, while revenue, expenses and net income are derived from the revenue-expense view. Similarly, in the recognition part, revenue recognition criteria include the realization principle ("free of risks") and are not based on the asset-liability view.

These characteristics reflect the long tradition of compromises in Japanese accounting: static from the Code of Commerce but dynamic in practice, later on sprinkled with actuarial rules based on fair value. In substance, the purpose of this framework was to reaffirm the importance of net income based on the realization principle without rejecting the asset-liability view that was dominant in the standards developed by the IASB from the end of 1990s. Using this framework, the ASBJ intended to support its "dynamic-conservative" model in the convergence process with the IASB.

After the end of the big bang, Japanese standards were still very different from IFRS and American standards. For example, they required goodwill amortization, allowed the pooling-of-interests, used a different definition of financial lease. . .all these differences were supposed to disappear until 2011.

A first stage of the process was achieved in 2006 with the reduction of minor differences with the IFRS. In a second stage (2007–2008), the ASBJ gave priority to the differences pointed out in the CESR[8] "equivalence assessment" in 2005. Since several "third countries" were assessed by the CESR in the same way as Japan, the ASBJ started cooperating with the standard setters of these countries (U.S., Korea and China).

Meanwhile, in August 2007, the IASB and the ASBJ signed the Tokyo Agreement to set a timeline for remaining issues in the convergence process. Consequently, the ASBJ released a concrete plan for convergence in December 2007 and went on suppressing differences with IFRS through 2008. In the negotiations with CESR, the primary party was the FSA, but the ASBJ provided some technical support for the discussions (Nishikawa 2011). In 2008, the CESR concluded that it was appropriate to consider Japanese accounting standards as equivalent with the

[8] Committee of European Securities Regulators.

IFRS. This ensured that Japanese accounting standards would continue to be accepted in the European markets after 2009.

6 The Japanese Model to the Test of Competition with IFRS (from 2010)

In 2009, the Business Accounting Council allowed the optional use of IFRS "as a basis for the consolidated financial statements by listed companies whose financial or operational activities are conducted internationally. In that case, such companies are required to be sufficiently prepared for IFRS reporting (BAC 2009, p. 3)." While authorizing optional use of IFRS, the BAC also mentioned that "the decision regarding the mandatory use of IFRS (was) aimed to be made around 2012 (BAC 2009, p. 4)."

With this decision, IFRS were given the same status as American standards on the Japanese stock exchanges from March 2010: optional use was allowed only for the consolidated statements of companies that (1) were listed,[9] (2) were able to prepare adequate financial statements, (3) published information based on IFRS for the purpose of foreign listing or other legal obligation, or owned a foreign subsidiary with capital equal to or exceeding two billion yen.

As a result, a handful of listed companies have decided to switch to IFRS from the beginning of the 2010s.

List of Japanese companies applying IFRS voluntarily in April, 2014

Company name	Category of industry	First reporting period
Nihon Dempa Kogyo	Electric appliances	March 31, 2010
Hoya Corporation	Precision Instruments	March 31, 2011
Sumitomo Corporation	Wholesale Trade	March 31, 2011
Nippon Sheet Glass	Glass & Ceramics Products	June 30, 2011
Japan Tobacco	Foods	March 31, 2012
DeNA	Services	June 30, 2012
Anritsu Corporation	Electric appliances	June 30, 2012
SBI Holdings	Securities	June 30, 2012
Tosei Corporation	Real Estate	February 28, 2013
Monex Group	Securities	March 31, 2013
Sojitz Corporation	Wholesale Trade	March 31, 2013
Marubeni Corporation	Wholesale Trade	March 31, 2013
Chugai Pharmaceutical	Pharmaceutical	March 31, 2013
Rakuten	Services	March 31, 2013

(continued)

[9] Large unlisted companies are required to publish financial statements under the same conditions as listed companies, but they were excluded from the scope of voluntary adoption of IFRS until 2014 (see infra).

Company name	Category of industry	First reporting period
Nexon	Information & Communication	March 31, 2013
Softbank Corporation	Information & Communication	June 30, 2013
Asahi Glass	Glass & Ceramics Products	December 31, 2013
Takeda Pharmaceutical	Pharmaceutical	March 31, 2014
Astellas Pharma	Pharmaceutical	March 31, 2014
Ono Pharmaceutical	Pharmaceutical	March 31, 2014
Sosei Group	Pharmaceutical	March 31, 2014
Daiichi Sankyo	Pharmaceutical	March 31, 2014
Ricoh	Electric appliances	March 31, 2014
Itochu Corporation	Wholesale Trade	March 31, 2014
Mitsui	Wholesale Trade	March 31, 2014
Mitsubishi Corporation	Wholesale Trade	March 31, 2014
Itochu Enex	Wholesale Trade	March 31, 2014

Source: Tokyo Stock Exchange (2014)

A first remark about voluntary adoption of IFRS in Japan is the concentration of companies in the pharmaceutical and the wholesale trade sectors. On the contrary, industrial groups, that adopted American standards in the past, did not switch to IFRS: large multinational companies like Toyota, Kubota or Panasonic are absent from this list.[10] This point illustrates how far the accounting policies of companies are coordinated within the same economic sector. For example, large trading companies all adopted IFRS at the same time, and many pharmaceutical companies too, while electric goods manufacturers and car manufacturers did not.

Several reasons are advocated by companies to explain these choices: international expansion, M&A strategy, the use of IFRS or American standards in other group entities. At this stage of the process, it is impossible to draw general conclusions on the opportunity or not to adopt IFRS for Japanese companies. Apart from the 27 companies presented above, 16 other ones are planning to adopt IFRS within the next 3 years (Tokyo Stock Exchange 2014). Compared with the total number of listed companies (3550 in 2013) and the number of companies eligible for the use of IFRS (621 in 2013), only a handful of companies made this choice (BAC 2013). In order to increase the optional use of IFRS, the BAC announced in 2013 that from 2014, all companies publishing financial statements under the FIEA[11] would become eligible to adopt "endorsed" IFRS. The counterpart of increasing the competition between Japanese standards and IFRS is that the ASBJ will be able to refuse some standards by the means of an endorsement process (Tsujiyama 2014, p. 36).

As a consequence, the FSA allows the use of four different standards for consolidated statements on the Japanese market: American standards and full

[10] One major exception is Ricoh that switched from U.S. GAAP to IFRS in 2014.

[11] Including listed companies (3550) and large unlisted companies (511) for a total of 4061 entities in 2013.

IFRS for restricted use, Japanese standards and "endorsed" IFRS for all reporting entities (Tsujiyama 2014, p. 38). The objective of this reform is to allow the competition of standards, which "would further promote convergence by bringing about a sort of "natural selection" based on market processes in the form of investor assessment and choice" (Saito 2011, p. 11).

One more incentive to increase the number of companies using IFRS in Japan is to keep a role in the development of new accounting standards with the IASB and the FASB (BAC 2013, p. 2). Besides, the endorsement process allowing the ASBJ to refuse some standards is also an important way to counterbalance the dominant position of the IASB in the convergence process.

7 The Endorsement Process as a Way to Secure the "Dynamic-Conservative" Model

In the 2000s, the convergence process forced the ASBJ to raise and discuss some new "actuarial" accounting treatments about which market constituents, along with academics could not reach a consensus easily. A typical example is accounting for lease transactions, a project that last 6 years due to some taxation issues until the final standard was eventually adopted in 2007 (Saito 2011, pp. 10–11).

Another long lasting debate of the ASBJ is accounting for business combinations. A first standard was issued in 2003, but it was not consistent with IFRS and American standards, since it allowed the pooling-of-interests method and required goodwill amortization. For the purpose of the CESR equivalence assessment, a second standard abolished the pooling-of-interests in 2008, despite the opposition of some market constituents that argued that the purchase method was inappropriate to account for mergers of equals (*Taitogappei*). Eventually, the issue of goodwill amortization still remained on the table since a consensus could not be found in the ASBJ.

Delaying or refusing some convergence decisions reflects "the standards setter's commitment on the importance of consensus building among market players (Saito 2011, p. 11)", which is a traditional characteristic of Japanese standard-setting. In other words, consensual views like goodwill amortization should not be sacrificed to the benefit of controversial ones for the sake of convergence. In practice, the equivalence assessment of the EU pushed the ASBJ to sacrifice part of this consensus (lease and business combinations).

At the same period, other convergence issues conflicted with the traditional dynamic view, like the revaluation model of tangible fixed assets, fair value measurement for biological assets and the nonrecycling of other comprehensive income. The Japanese conservative tradition was also in the way to development costs capitalization[12] and the reversal of impairment losses. Because of these

[12] The capitalization of "in-process" research and development costs acquired in a business combination was particularly criticized.

conflicts between the new "actuarial" model and the traditional "dynamic-conservative" model, the expectations of market constituents could not be satisfied. More reasons for discontent appeared as some international standards conflicted with tax and commercial law (lease, functional currency, revenue recognition, depreciation, impairment), and/or were expected to incur high implementation costs (development costs, impairment, revenue recognition).

This frustration tended to spread accounting lobbying outside of the standard-setting process with the support of business associations, political parties and related ministries. Political parties prove to be helpful for communication,[13] even if public statements about business accounting remain exceptional. Business associations like the Keidanren or JUAS[14] help coordinating the different actors by creating and managing ad hoc working groups in order to exchange different views on the accounting problems. Ministries often monitor these projects, provide subsidies to finance the working group activities and often publish their final output as official reports.

In this system, several channels of communication are offered to Japanese market constituents to express their views on accounting matters. Apart from the ad hoc working groups mentioned above, constituents are represented in the ASBJ indeed, but also in the BAC, and the third large organization involved is the business accounting chamber of the Ministry of Economy Trade and Industry. The Ministry of Justice, in charge of the Commercial Code, and the Ministry of Finance, in charge of taxation, may also be involved, but there is no permanent structure dedicated to accounting. Other divisions of ministries like for example the Small and Medium Enterprise Agency of the METI can also be take part in accounting regulation depending on the object of the reform.

As far as the convergence process in concerned, the result of the public coordination of lobbying was that several powerful actors like the Keidanren, the LPD and the METI issued some statements or reports to support the policy of the BAC to defend the traditional "dynamic-conservative" accounting model by the means of the endorsement process. According to Mandai (2014, p. 31) the endorsement process will allow the ASBJ to refuse some standards for three reasons: (1) the general philosophy of the standard, (2) its practical implementation difficulty and (3) incompatibility with other regulations. The "actuarial" problems like nonamortization of goodwill, nonrecycling of OCI and the scope of fair value may fall into the first category, so that Japanese companies would be dispensed of adopting these rules if the ASBJ decides not to endorse them.

[13] For example the Liberal Democratic Party issued an eight page statement in 2013 (only 3 weeks before the BAC opinion) about the reasons for which the convergence process with the IASB should not damage the interests of Japanese companies (Liberal Democratic Party 2013).

[14] Japan Users Association of Information Systems.

8 Conclusion

In this paper, I used the classification of accounting theories by Richard (1996) in order to explain the main characteristics and the evolution of the Japanese accounting model since the Meiji Era. Japanese accounting is dynamic for the purpose of cost calculation and profit measurement, and conservative in order to avoid dividend distribution and increase internal financing sources.

After the "lost decade", some actuarial rules based on fair value measurement were introduced for the purpose of global convergence. Yet, after the equivalence assessment of the EU (2005–2008), accounting reforms were delayed because of the lack of consensus on comprehensive income and fair value, the conceptual groundings of the actuarial theory. In the case of Japan, the "dynamic-conservative" model was indeed transformed through the harmonization process, but endorsement conducted by the ASBJ and the support of local preparers tend to secure its future on the domestic market.

References

Business Accounting Council (2009) Application of international financial reporting standards (IFRS) in Japan. http://www.fsa.go.jp/en/news/2009/20090612-3/01.pdf. Accessed 15 July 2014

Business Accounting Council (2013) The present policy on the application of international financial reporting standards (IFRS). http://www.fsa.go.jp/en/news/2013/20130621-1/01.pdf#search='The+Present+Policy+on+the+Application+of+International+Financial+Reporting+Standards+%28IFRS%29'. Accessed 15 July 2014

Garcia C (2007) Role and origins of the Japanese conceptual framework of financial accounting. Econ Res 139:29–37

Garcia C (2011) A brief history of accounting for goodwill in Japan and France: war, tax and accounting practice. Econ Res 48(1):45–64

Itabashi T, Garcia C (2011) About the westernization of Japanese bookkeeping (1865–1925). Presented at the IAAER accounting renaissance conference, 3–5 Nov 2011, Venice

Ito K (2005) Expectations and problems concerning the conceptual framework of financial accounting. Kigyo Kaikei 57(4):91–93

Keidanren (2013) Practical cases of IFRS voluntary adoption. http://www.keidanren.or.jp/policy/2013/057.pdf. Accessed 15 Jul 2014

Kikuya M (2001) International harmonization of Japanese accounting standards. Account Bus Financ Hist 11(3):349–368

Kubota H (2001) History of the establishment of Japanese accounting. Zeimukeirikyoukai, Tokyo

Liberal Democratic party (2013) Recommendations regarding the measures to deal with international accounting standards. https://www.jimin.jp/policy/policy_topics/pdf/pdf_111_1.pdf. Accessed 15 Jul 2014

Mandai K (2014) Decision-making regarding endorsed IFRS. Kigyo Kaikei 66(1):26–32

Miwa Y, Ramsyer M (2002) Banks and economic growth: implications from Japanese history. J Law Econ 45:127–164

Monden Y (1991) The Toyota production system: an integrated approach to just-in-time. Productivity Press, Cambridge, MA

Nakanishi T (1936) Theory of management expenses. Chikura, Tokyo

Nishikawa I (2011) A decade at the ASBJ, from the past to the future. Accounting Standards and Disclosure Quaterly. September 15. https://www.asbj.or.jp/asb/asb_e/asbj/message/voice/201109.pdf. Accessed 2014/07/15

Richard J (1996) Comptabilités et pratiques comptables. Dalloz, Paris

Saito S (2009) Significance of convergence and the role of IFRS in Japan. Meiji Gakuin University discussion paper series. http://www.meijigakuin.ac.jp/econ/academics/publications/pdf/200701.pdf. Accessed 2014/7/15

Saito S (2010) Research in accounting standards. Chuo-keizai, Tokyo

Saito S (2011) Accounting standard reforms in postwar Japan. In: Previts G (ed) Global accounting history: accounting, financial reporting and public policy. Bingley, Emerald

Suzuki T (2007a) Accountics: impacts of internationally standardized accounting on the Japanese socio-economy. Acc Organ Soc 32:263–301

Suzuki T (2007b) A history of Japanese accounting reforms as a microfoundation of the democratic socio-economy: accountics Part II. Acc Organ Soc 32:543–575

Tokyo Stock Exchange (2014) Voluntary application of IFRS (current and scheduled). http://www.tse.or.jp/listing/ifrs/list.html. Accessed 15 July 2014

Tsujiyama E (2014) Institutional issues surrounding the endorsement of IFRS. Kigyo Kaikei 66 (1):33–42

Tsunogaya N, Chand P (2012) The complex equilibrium paths towards international financial reporting standards (IFRS) and the Anglo-American model: the case of Japan. Jpn Account Rev 2:117–137

Norway. IAS 19 and Employee Benefits: Some Reflections on the Norwegian Experience

Jon Lundesgaard

Abstract The accounting law of employee benefit plans is complex, and it demands a lot of both prepares and users. It is an observation that this in itself is a problem. Benefit plans include such things as defined benefit pensions. On this, Norwegian companies report according to either the international standard, that is International Accounting Standard (IAS) 19 Employee Benefits, or the equivalent national standard. A fundamental question is what this does to financial statements, and whether it is an improvement. This has to do with more than just the problem of whether what is reported is distorted or even incorrect. A serious and possible result is that the company's situation is not understood in its essence, with all what this may lead to. Of course, this is something that concerns all parties involved. The effects of the accounting law of benefit plans are clarified on a more general basis, and by a case study. After a closer analysis of the problem of financial reporting, the conclusion is that the reporting of effects of benefit plans should be limited to notes, or otherwise.

1 The Norwegian Financial Reporting Context

Offering an overview of accounting regulation, Johnsen (1993) pointed to the interaction of formal legislation (statutory accounting law) and good accounting practice (practice codified in a less formal manner). In being less specific and detailed, formal accounting legislation is seen as constituting a legal framework including basic principles. In being more dynamic, the role of good accounting practice is to fill-in what is needed as result of changing economic conditions. This raises the question of how good accounting practice is formed and codified. In Norway, several non-governmental parties played important roles in this. In 1989, resources in working with good accounting practice were pooled under the umbrella of Norwegian Accounting Standards Board (NASB), formally established as a private foundation.

J. Lundesgaard (✉)
Hedmark University College, Elverum, Norway
e-mail: jon.lundesgaard@hihm.no

D. Bensadon, N. Praquin (eds.), *IFRS in a Global World*,
DOI 10.1007/978-3-319-28225-1_23

After exhaustive work of the Accounting Act Committee, the Norwegian Accounting Act of 1998 was adopted. In this, the author referred to (professor Atle Johnsen of Norwegian School of Economics/Bergen) played an important role. In accordance with what he saw as implicitly established, the law more clearly stated an income statement orientation. Matching of revenues earned with related expenses is fundamental, in addition to transaction historic cost (THC) based foundations. The legal authorization for the good practice part of regulation is found in Sects. 4–6 stating that "[t]he preparation of the annual accounts shall be in accordance with good accounting practice." The understanding is that good accounting practice is administered under the authority of NASB. Simply, as long as accepted by competent law making organs, NASB contributes in forming accounting regulation. As recently stated in connection with NASB (2014), this work has since 1989 been carried out in looking to international standard setting. In spite of not being a public administrative body, NASB brings about financial reporting guidelines with far reaching consequences. In Exhibit 1, the regulatory setting as formalized by the 1998 accounting law is illustrated.

Norway is not member of the EU, but since 1994 associated through the European Economic Area (EEA) agreement. The effect of this is that EU rulings are made effective in Norway. That is, EU accounting directives functioning as broader guidelines and EU regulations with the character of strict statutory law. In the field of accounting regulation, this comes with EU Regulation 1606/2002. That is EU (2002), which establishes the private foundation International Accounting Standards Board (IASB) as official supplier of important parts of financial accounting regulation in the EU. Companies which do not report according to IASB's international standards, report according to the national accounting regulation. In general, IASB's standards are referred to as International Financial Reporting Standard (IFRS) even though not all IASB standards are termed as such. In Norway, when it comes to financial reporting regulation, the situation does not differ that much from that of EU member states. As outlined in Exhibit 1, reporting according to the national accounting act is supplemented with national accounting standards (NRSs). Even if there is some mixing of regimes, financial reporting regulation in Norway is presently a double track system consisting of two separate and parallel regulatory regimes. Regimes are different in their foundations as IFRS is balance sheet oriented and open to "fair value accounting."

The double track system of accounting regulation is seen as a problem. Some simply see IFRS as superior due to balance sheet oriented foundations. Others conclude that capacities in forming standards anchored in a specific national approach to regulation are insufficient, and so the problem is seen as a practical

Exhibit 1 Accounting regulation in Norway around the turn of the century

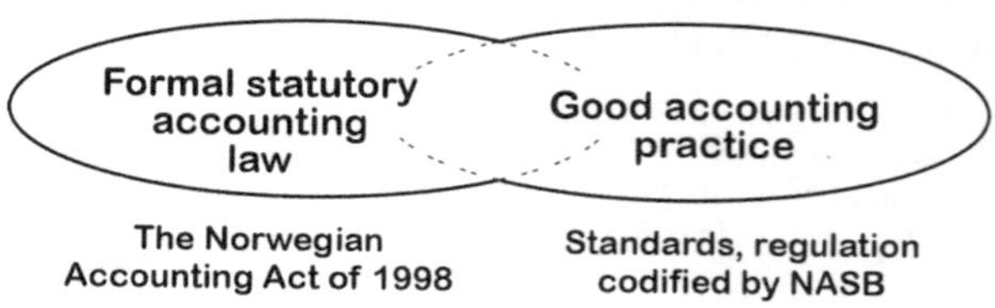

Exhibit 2 NASB's proposed comprehensive standard as part of a system of regulatory elements

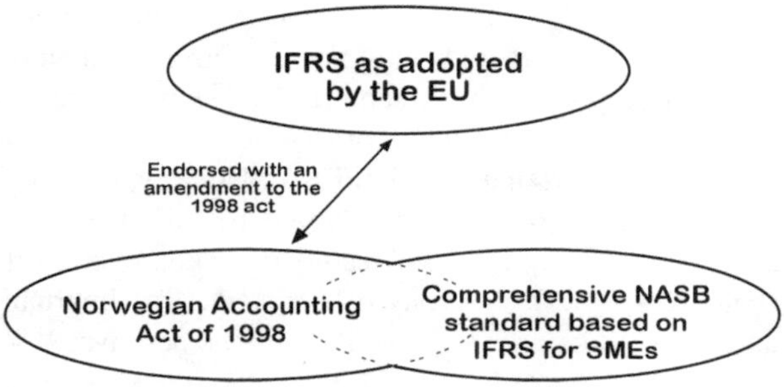

one. The coming of IASB (2009), that is IFRS for SMEs, has brought about progress in this. The idea is that this standard could replace national standards experienced hard to maintain. That is, all standards with the exception of two standards being the standard for smaller entities including simplified guidelines and a standard for NGO type of organizations. Of course, adverse foundations of the Norwegian Accounting Act of 1998 and of IFRS for SMEs are a challenge. In working with this, NASB has presented an adjusted Norwegian version of IFRS for SMEs. Adjustments are made where the standard is in conflict with 1998 accounting law. In April 2014, with NASB (2014) the resulting comprehensive standard is sent on hearing. This will lead to a picture of main regulatory elements as outlined in Exhibit 2.

In NASB (2014), adverse foundations referred to are played down and seen as a surmountable difficulty. This is less than obvious. With an adoption of NASB's comprehensive standard, the speculation is that the 1998 accounting act may come under pressure in direction of modifications in its orientation. Proactively, the Ministry of Finance on September 19 2014 asked a group of experts to look into this and other problems of accounting law. In a first report of June 26 2015, a new national accouning law based on the EU accounting directives is proposed. Due to this, the continued work with NASB (2014) has so far been stopped.

Since the beginning of the 1980s, the policy of international standard setting has been to require that effects of employee benefit plans are included in financial statements, and that details associated with this are reported in notes. Around the mid 1990s, in looking to international standard setting, NASB released (first as a preliminary standard) Norwegian accounting standard NRS 6 Pensjonskostnader (Pension Costs). This, and history as time passes, is an example of how IFRS more specifically has effects on national jurisdictional regulation. In adding some reflections, what is offered in the rest of this paper is an account of the Norwegian experience.

2 Financial Reporting on Employee Benefit Plans

Funded with plan assets or not, employee benefit plans often lead to future obligations believed to have the character of corporate liabilities. Plan assets held separate from the corporate sponsor raise the question of the funded status of the plan, and how the effects of this should be made visible in financial reports of the corporate sponsor. There are two alternatives. First, in including effects in the financial statement/report such as required by standard setters. Second, information on effects is limited to notes or otherwise.

With the introduction of IFRS in Norway, companies that report according to international standards are required to follow IAS 19 Employee Benefits. This standard is among the "old" standards taken over by the reorganized international standard setter. The acronym IAS stands for International Accounting Standard, and "new" standards are identified by the acronym IFRS. In the first half of 1980s, IAS 19 was adopted, and so SFAS 87 Employers' Accounting for Pensions issued by the American standard setter Financial Accounting Standards Board (FASB). Both standards require that effects of employee benefit plans are included in financial statements and NRS 6 is a follow-up of this. However, more was come.

- The inclusion of pension effects is not limited to reporting entities that report according to the 1998 law and thus NRS 6. Local governments have to do this too according to an adapted version of NRS 6. This is stated in Section 13 Regnskapsføring av pensjon (Pension Accounting) of regulations from the Ministry of Local Government and Modernisation (2000).
- The state accounting system is double track. First, a cash-based part in parallel to what is found in the state budget system administered by the Ministry of Finance. Second, in what more recently is stated in state accounting standards (SRSs) being an accrual-based system of preliminary character administered by a government agency, see Norwegian Government Agency for Financial Management (2011). SRS 25 Personal- og pensjonskostnader (Personal and Pension Costs) is concerned with what is found in NRS 6.
- The Norwegian Public Service Pension Fund is a state "pay as you go" (PAYG) arrangement. In spite of a state guarantee of what comes of employee benefits under the arrangement, institutions this applies for have to report according to the 1998 law and thus NRS 6. That is, to include pension effects based on a system with "fictive funds."
- The Contractual Early Retirement Scheme (Avtalefestet pensjon/AFP) is a special arrangement. We have an old and a new version of AFP and the new version raises accounting questions. The views of NASB (2010) and the Financial Supervisory Authority of Norway (2010) have been that pension effects should be included in accordance with NRS 6. Due to opposition against this, the Ministry of Finance (2011) came out with a report on the problem. In the autumn of 2013, the Ministry announced its intention not to require inclusion of accounting effects of the new AFP.

Internationally, pension accounting is discussed. Recently, this led to a new IAS 19 effective from January 1 2013. In this new standard, options are limited and effects come to the balance sheet via the income statement. Whether this will set an end to discussions is an interesting question. In Norway, considerable effort is spent in direction of bringing pension accounting in close to everywhere based on old versions of IAS 19. The new version will apply under NASB's proposed comprehensive standard, and this solves part of the problem in adjusting to IFRS.

In proceeding, the paper is organized so that the basics on pensions, and employee benefit plans in particular, are outlined in Sect. 3. The "mechanics" of pension accounting are complex, and we are not going all the way in this. Nevertheless, this has to be carried sufficiently far, and both Sects. 4 and 5 are needed for this. Section 6 is important in introducing the "two-process idea." In addition, effects of pension accounting are discussed. Section 7 includes a case study. In Sect. 8, the paper is concluded.

3 On Pension Plans

As to pensions of employees, employers are typically active in two ways. First, in contributing to funding plan assets of defined contribution plans. With the transfer of agreed on contributions obligations of the employer are settled. Second, in guaranteeing certain pensions as result of defined benefit plans. With this, obligations of the employer amount to more than just contributing to the plan. In Norway recently, a law on hybrid pensions is passed. However, fundamentally interesting accounting implications are the result of defined benefit plans. The guaranty of benefit plans lead to that this arrangement is less controllable by the employer, and eventually more costly depending on how good arrangements are for employees. With a contribution plan, employers know what pension expenses are. In a contribution plan, risk shifts so that risk associated with plan assets are borne by the employee/retiree. In Norway and internationally, the tendency has been in direction of contribution plans. Exhibit 3 contributes with a picture of the situation in the private sector.

The number of plans is increased due to mandatory aspects of law making. New plans are typically contribution plans. The number of benefit plans is reduced, to

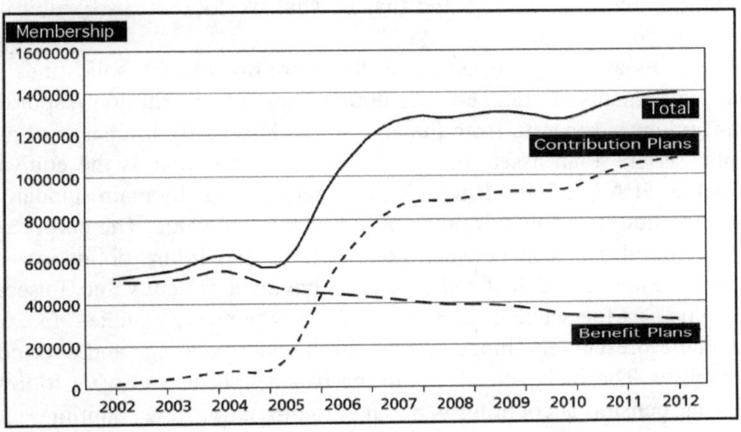

Exhibit 3 From Veland and Hippe based on FNO (Finans Norge) statistics

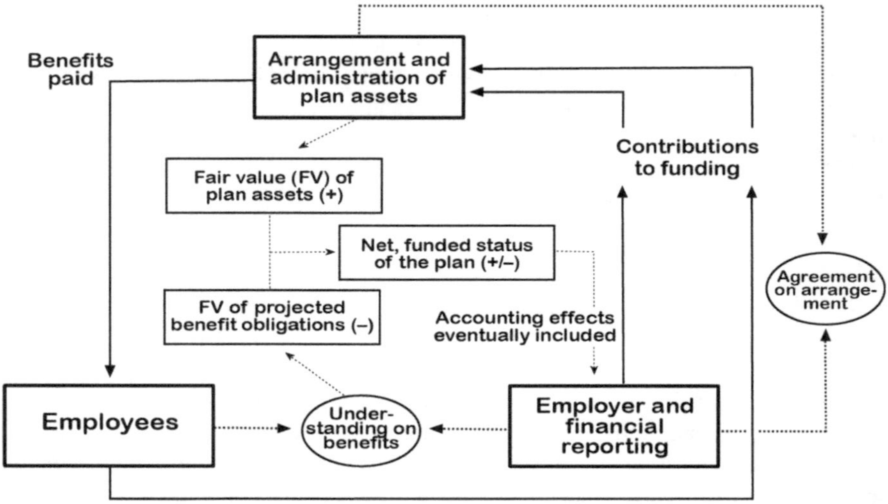

Exhibit 4 Some fundamentals of employee benefit plans

some extent as being a result of conversion from benefit to contribution plans. In business, defined benefit plans are less popular, and this may have something to do with accounting standards. In principle it is possible to make pension plans equivalent from an expected value point of view. However, in going from a benefit plan to a contribution plan employees are exposed to uncertainty. In assuming risk aversion, this is something that should be compensated for.

Defined benefit plans are funded or unfunded. Unfunded with no other provision arranged for, the benefits of future retirees are guaranteed by the employer's capacity to meet future obligations. This adds risks to unfunded plans. In many countries, lawmakers restrict the establishment of unfunded benefit plans. We may see funding as the normal case and that is what we look at. In Exhibit 4, some fundamentals are outlined.

Three parties are involved, and cash flows are drawn with solid lines. Understandings/agreements are marked with dotted lines. The institution responsible for the arrangement is separate from the sponsor and normally in charge of administering plan assets. Plan assets have a fair value understood as the equivalent to market value. SFAS 157 and IFRS 13 are understandings by main standard setters of what fair value is, being more than observed marked value. The purpose of plan assets is to build a bridge between contributions and future obligations. Future obligations are abstract, calculated constructs having a present value. In seeing this present value as a fair value, plan assets and obligations are matched. In matching, net outcome represents the funded status. Both under-coverage and over-coverage is a possibility. The inclusion of this in the balance sheet, and what follows with this, is what pension accounting is about. Traditionally, in accounting, adding to accounts financial information about transactions is essential. Obviously, in adding a net representing the funded status, something different is done.

4 The "Simple Mechanics" of Benefit Plan Accounting

The 1998 act defines what small companies are and they report according to a standard for smaller entities (NRS 8). Under conditions specified, pension accounting effects of defined benefit plans can be ignored. The employer's contribution to a benefit plan is the sole effect included (as an expense). That is, technically as for defined contribution plans. What are not small companies are other companies and they report according to NRS 6. Exhibit 4 may point in direction of that only the funded status of a defined benefit plan is included in financial statements, however, a specific pension expense effect and other items are included. These are summarized items being the result of primary, underlying elements.

In turning to what happens over a reporting period, some words about the dynamics of the funded status are offered. Stock and flow magnitudes are involved, and the funded status is a net stock magnitude with an opening and ending balance. The opening balance of the funded status is either a liability (under-coverage) or an asset (over-coverage). Consequently, the net of increments in plan assets and in projected benefit obligations may be an incremental liability/under-coverage, or an incremental asset/over-coverage. The combinations of this are outlined in Exhibit 5.

Case 1 and Case 4 end up with more of what is started out with. What the ending balance will be for Case 2 and Case 3 is less clear. In Case 2, the opening under-coverage is reduced, or eventually eliminated/more than eliminated (ending up with over-coverage). In Case 3, opening over-coverage is reduced, or eliminated/more than eliminated. Obviously, plan assets that "lag behind" (under-coverage) are

Opening balance - net funded status:	Over the period type of effect:	
	Under-coverage	**Over-coverage**
Under-coverage	Case 1	Case 2
Over-coverage	Case 3	Case 4

Exhibit 5 Combinations of opening balances and net increment effects

necessarily not always the case. How this all works together is related to more demanding questions about the built up and administration of plan assets, this on one hand. On the other hand we have everything of elements that contributes to the determination of projected benefit obligations.

Even if what is aimed at is keeping assets and obligations more strictly at par, it is less likely that this ends up at par from period to period due to uncertainty. A point of view forwarded is that this uncertainty is a minor problem due to that it will even out over time. This sounds fine. However, it is not unimportant whether disparities are smaller or bigger. In addition, we have the question of how long time it takes to even out. Moreover, the situation could be so that magnitudes swing back and forth, without coming to rest in evening out. Anyway, what reporting guidelines essentially are meant to bring about is that the status of benefit plans is included in the balance sheet. Under-coverage leads to a liability that reduces the owner's equity. Over-coverage brings in an added asset so that the owner's equity is increased. For first-time adopters of NRS 6 this is the effect and as such "simple mechanics." The "not that simple mechanics" include increments, and so primary, underlying elements play more explicitly a role.

5 The "Not That Simple Mechanics"

The "not that simple mechanics" of pension accounting is a practical reality for preparers and users of accounting information, and pension accounting is complex and difficult to understand. Intricacies being a consequence of both conceptual and legal complexities are not presented in full breath. In facing this, it is the intension to simplify in still being relevant. Pension expenses end up in the income statement and to begin with we are somewhat vague about what is included in pension expenses. In addition, we have an incremental item to start with referred to in "Eventual other elements." With this, in seeing the opening balance of the funded status as a liability at its absolute value (in Exhibit 6 below it is seen that the sign of this item is negative), we have the following.

OPENING BALANCE OF FUNDED STATUS
– EMPLOYER'S CONTRIBUTION
+ PENSION EXPENSE
+/– "EVENTUAL OTHER ELEMENTS"

= ENDING BALANCE OF FUNDED STATUS
==================================

The three incremental items above summarize to what in Exhibit 5 is referred to as "[o]ver the period type of effect." It is registered that this is more than the difference between pension expenses and the employer's contribution. Added are "Eventual other elements" (+/−). If this has to do with uncertainty and revised best accounting estimates, the guidelines for this apply (Sects. 4–2 of the 1998 act). Normally, the effect of revised accounting estimates end up in the income statement. However, openings are made for that effects of revised estimates can bypass the income statement and end up directly in the balance sheet. Alternatively, deferred recognition is accepted as a smoothing device. The inclusions of accounting estimates in financial statements bring about uncertainty associated with such estimates. In itself this is not of good, but has to be traded off with the informative value of estimates. Employee benefit pension accounting means accepting "a package" which includes accounting estimates. Under given circumstances, they contribute to major effects when revised and so the question of smoothing is raised. More fundamentally, this again leads to moral hazard type of problems such as in Norway investigated by Kinserdal (2006).

Now, we turn to the primary, underlying elements and how they are summarized. In including all necessary practical details, this is messy and a simplified version is presented. First, we are going exclude the effects of payroll tax. Second, any sort of effect that has to do with administrative costs is left un-discussed. Third, we see ending plan assets as fully known, and not as an estimate revised when fully known. That is, net earnings on investment are seen as fully known. Forth, details as to plan amendments are not dealt with. In Exhibit 6, a bird's view is offered. After that, the four summarized items in the illustration are briefly explained.

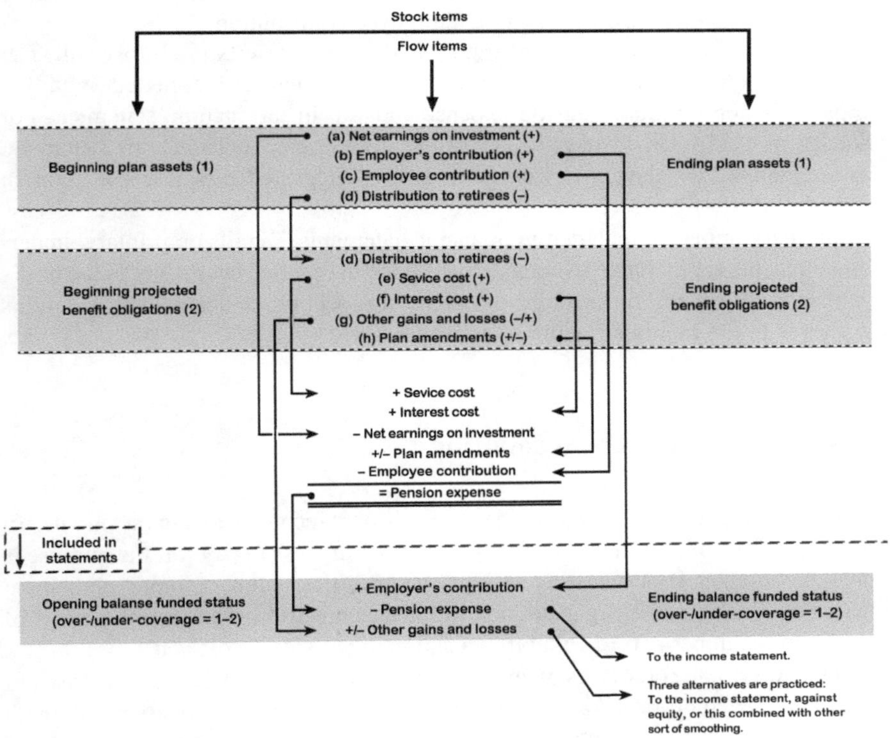

Exhibit 6 Included items and primary, underlying elements

Plan assets are means of the arrangement set aside separate from the sponsor (employer) under administration regulated by law. (d) Distribution to retirees contributes to a reduction in plan assets and leads at the same time to that projected benefit obligations are reduced.

Projected benefit obligations include (e) Service cost being the present value of retirement benefits earned by employees over a period. The calculation is based on a series of factors of actuarial and economic character. Projected benefit obligations are over the period, such as a year, is coming one period nearer in time and this leads to (f) Interest cost. Beginning projected benefit obligations is an estimate based on earlier set versions of the sort of factors that contribute to the determination of elements (e) and (f). These factors are of non-permanent character, and so, the beginning projected benefit obligations will have to be recalculated. This leads to actuarial gains and losses. Due to that we here omit effects of not fully known plan assets, else included on the way, the element is simply termed (g) Other gains and losses. A simple version of plan amendment is an increase in the promise from 66 to 70 % of salary earned. Plan amendments can also be made with effect backwards. The effects of all this are found in (h) Plan amendments.

Pension expense can be seen as an in-between calculation needed in the income statement. Flow items from updating projected benefit obligations, (e), (f) and (h) are included. In addition to this are elements associated with plan assets being (a) Net earnings on investment and (c) Employee contribution.

Funded status (over-/under-coverage) updating is now straightforward. The effects of Pension expense and Other gains and losses are netted with the Employer's contribution. Pension expense ends up in the income statement. For Other gains and losses, we have in addition to an ending up in the income statement, the alternatives as already discussed and now suggested down to the right in Exhibit 6.

Summary items are included in financial statements. Details on primary, underlying elements are included in notes. This is done in separate charts, not in the bird's eye manner of Exhibit 6. As addressed in the next section, the question is what this all does with the reported picture of a business.

6 Effects of Pension Accounting

Typically, organizing a business means non-spontaneously to bundle inputs. In directing effort to what there exist a sufficient willingness to pay for, the purpose is value creation. Infrastructures are input factors that adopt a more permanent character. This includes organizational infrastructure and organizing the effort of people. In the upper part of Exhibit 7, a summarized view is offered.

In the lower part, processes of employee benefit plans are included, being part of organizing the enterprise. As any activity of importance, processes associated with benefit plans are separate activities with effects of interest. However, it is apparent that benefit plans are different from business processes in not having an output with

Exhibit 7 Two processes, the business and employee benefit plan processes

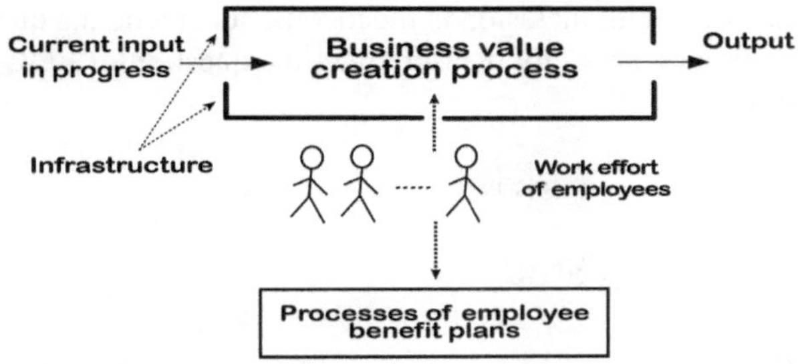

which explicit willingness to pay is associated. What is associated with a benefit plan are stock and flow items included in financial statements that reflect plan status. The purpose of this is to show what is the added effect.

Financial accounting is a long-established device in summarizing what goes on in a business. That is, to keep track of value creation processes and what the business idea gives. Traditionally, consolidation is part of this so that the entirety of the business is revealed. The idea behind pension accounting is to contribute to this in making the picture reported presumably more correct. However, the question is whether this is the case. In practicing pension accounting, the picture of what are core activities of a business is altered. In the following we take a look on this.

Volatility is the result of uncertainty and uncertainty is found everywhere. In financial reporting, this means that what has been reported does not necessarily repeat. The future contributes with surprises in form of "good news" or "bad news." If the future is seen as a likely path, what later is manifest typically deviates from this reference path. Uncertainty is at work and time-series characterized by this are volatile so that predictions are less than precise. With pension accounting, added uncertainty is brought into reported numbers. A contribution by Dichev (2008) documents that accounting numbers over time are more volatile. This may well be a result of else well-meant standard setting such as pension accounting. Obviously, for increased uncertainty to be traded off, increased relevance due to pension accounting is needed. For financial analysis information financially reported should be reliable and relevant. Relevance is two-sided in that we have both the accounting for stewardship point of view, and the question of usefulness as to the resource allocation problem of users. Analyses of financial statements play a role in this, and traditionally, solidity and profitability is something that is focused on.

Solidity is important in financing an enterprise and the distinction between equity and debt essential. Equity is what owners have paid in of capital, in addition to what is retained of earnings. Debts are liabilities, and ordinarily nominally fixed amounts (money items) with a given maturity and an agreed on payment of interest. Traditionally, as percent of what the balance sheet sums up to, equity is seen to signal solidity. The equity ratio says something about exposure to the burden of debt. With including effects of employee benefit plans this is upset.

Profitability is measured absolutely and relatively. Relatively, the return on equity (ROE) is important. Associated with the business value creation process, this is something that is of critical interest. Pension expense and other pension accounting flow items, are related to the business value creation process in a special manner. With inclusion in the income statement, the question of relevance is raised. With altered equity measurement the question of ROE measurement is even more critical.

7 A Case Study

Our case study is based on a social science institute with distinctive pension accounting effects in annual reports. The institution focused, Institute for Social Research (ISR), was established as an independent non-commercial foundation in 1950 and has played a prominent role in social science research in Norway. The case is first drafted as part of Lundesgaard (2014) in being one out of seven case studies. The employees of ISR have the state Norwegian Public Service Pension Fund as organizer of their pension arrangements being favorable defined benefit plans. From 2003 on, ISR includes pension effects in financial reporting based on NRS 6. Over the years focused, the activity level of ISR has been fairly stable so that effects are more easily seen. The activity of ISR is advanced and specialized social science research. A well-qualified core of research faculty has to be in place. In organizing, some farsightedness is needed and this all leads to fixed costs. Are means not correspondingly long-term, one is faced with a constant need to succeed with projects. That is the kind of situation ISR finds itself in, and it means that the "bottom line" is a result of income uncertainty. In facing uncertainty, independence is secured in owning important parts of the physical infrastructure such as buildings, in having "money in the bank," and in being close to debt-free. In the first annual report for 2002 studied, just that is what characterizes the picture. In Exhibit 8, a summary of the report for 2002 is included, and for this year, the equity ratio is impressing 73.98 %.

After years of pension accounting the equity ratio is down to 29.94 %, and ISR is seemingly in a very different situation. Based on income statements, balance sheets and notes reported, reworked statements including pension effects are presented in Exhibit 9.

Over the period, pension expense is a rather erratic figure. The zero pension expense in 2009 is special, and it is difficult to see how this comes about from what is reported. Volatility in pension expense leads to volatility in the operating result and in the "bottom line" (net profit or loss for the year). Calculating these items as percentages of revenue leads to relative measures of variation in figures over time (percentage operating result/percentage "bottom line").

2003	2004	2005	2006	2007	2008	2009	2010	2011	2012
7.50/ 9.19	0.47/ 1.18	0.50/ 1.32	−0.06/ 1.31	−2.34/ −0.63	−4.51/ −1.82	7.38/ 5.47	3.90/ 2.67	−5.13/ −4.38	0.21/ 2.29

Profitability jumps up and down all the way and it is of interest to see whether this in fact is so for the core activity. Revenues minus operating expenses, leads to a

Exhibit 8 The last financial statements of ISR not based on pension accounting (numbers are in kroner)

Income statement	2002
Revenue	34 968 889
Operating expenses*	-33 357 084
Pension expense**	**-1 527 996**
Operating result	83 809
Other profit/loss items	790 069
Net profit or loss for the year	873 878
Balance sheet	
Fixed assets	5 615 000
Current assets	16 637 486
Sum assets	22 252 486
Equity	16 462 304
Pension liabilities	----
Other liabilities	5 790 182
Sum equity and liabilities	22 252 486

* Exclusive pension expense.
** Equal to the employer's contribution.

simple measure of absolute operational contribution. Calculating this as percentage of revenue leads to time-series being less erratic.

2003	2004	2005	2006	2007	2008	2009	2010	2011	2012
6.92	8.78	6.20	4.30	8.50	6.97	7.38	4.64	−2.95	6.69

In concluding, pension accounting makes the "bottom lines" of the income statement less interesting from a practical point of view as an indicator of achievement.

For 2004, 2005 and 2006, pension liabilities are included with the same moderate amounts, and this is left uncommented in annual reports. ISR is practicing the "corridor approach" (smoothing) so what is pointed to may have something to do with this. Apart from these years, we find that pension liabilities are included with figures that really count. In any case, seen over the period, the balance sheet effects of pension accounting are important and for 2003 the effect is massive. For the period studied, equity ratios are found in what follows.

2003	2004	2005	2006	2007	2008	2009	2010	2011	2012
40.49	44.80	49.60	52.29	51.62	36.68	35.69	41.83	31.00	29.94

In 2002, the economic situation of ISR is good and over the period with pension accounting this has in reality been clearly so. Nevertheless, the picture reported looks rather desolate. In the balance sheets presented, ISR looks considerably less

Income statements	2003	2004	2005	2006	2007
Revenue	39 470 388	36 314 284	38 916 549	38 284 428	41 836 539
Operating expenses *	-36 738 021	-33 125 774	-36 502 750	-36 639 260	-38 281 801
Pension expense	**226 211**	**-3 017 421**	**-2 217 781**	**-1 668 238**	**-4 535 276**
Operating result	2 958 578	171 089	196 018	-23 070	-980 538
Other profit/loss items	669 970	256 810	319 310	523 445	716 883
Net profit or loss for the year	3 628 548	427 899	515 328	500 375	-263 655
Balance sheets					
Fixed assets	5 226 500	4 948 000	4 786 500	4 571 000	4 429 170
Current assets	18 830 177	17 749 563	22 277 672	22 055 163	22 035 116
Sum assets	24 056 677	22 697 563	27 064 172	26 626 163	26 464 286
Equity	9 740 053	10 167 952	13 423 585	13 923 960	13 660 306
Pension liabilities	**7 427 910**	**1 547 776**	**1 547 776**	**1 547 776**	**4 467 681**
Other liabilities	6 888 714	10 981 835	12 092 811	11 154 427	8 336 299
Sum equity and liabilities	24 056 677	22 697 563	27 064 172	26 626 163	26 464 286

Income statements	2008	2009	2010	2011	2012
Revenue	43 680 590	59 289 080	56 546 766	56 651 736	66 689 649
Operating expenses *	-40 637 007	-54 913 720	-53 923 091	-58 320 800	-62 227 878
Pension expense	**-5 013 827**	**0**	**-418 404**	**-1 238 371**	**-4 324 097**
Operating result	-1 970 244	4 375 360	2 205 271	-2 907 435	137 674
Other profit/loss items	1 173 962	-1 133 146	-696 056	426 174	1 387 703
Net profit or loss for the year	-796 282	3 242 214	1 509 215	-2 481 261	1 525 377
Balance sheets					
Fixed assets	4 240 000	21 437 000	20 992 000	21 600 400	21 301 033
Current assets	30 830 540	23 692 132	21 115 041	27 218 585	34 341 743
Sum assets	35 070 540	45 129 132	42 107 041	48 818 985	55 642 776
Equity	12 864 024	16 106 237	17 615 452	15 134 191	16 659 568
Pension liabilities	**9 751 316**	**10 240 771**	**12 946 144**	**13 041 035**	**15 465 936**
Other liabilities	12 455 200	18 782 123	11 545 445	20 643 759	23 517 271
Sum equity and liabilities	35 070 540	45 129 131	42 107 041	48 818 985	55 642 775

* Exclusive pension expense.

Exhibit 9 ISR's financial reporting 2003–2012 (numbers are in kroner) in practicing pension accounting

solid than what really is the case. The good economic situation, and the practicing of the "corridor approach," is what made it possible to escape ending up with negative equity. In Note 4 of the 2012 annual report, it is said that the total of pension liabilities, payroll tax included, is kr. 26,471,883. Due to the "corridor approach," what is in the balance sheet is kr. 15,465,936. This "backlog" set aside, an equity ratio around 10 % is what this leads to.

8 What Is More Meaningful, Reporting Limited to Notes?

Financial reporting has to do with information, and regulated are the structures of this in financial reports. In general, what is reported on is complex. In forming regulation, one is faced with a multitude of difficult trade-offs. What makes this still more difficult is a lack of consensus on fundamentals such as adverse approaches as the classical income statement approach and the balance sheet approach. How points of view are distributed is not a simple question to answer, even if Glover (2014), Macve (2014) and Zeff (2014) are of help in this.

The Norwegian Accounting Act of 1998 is based on the income statement approach, in addition to being THC based. IFRS is based on the balance sheet approach and so is FASB's approach to regulation. In addition, these two main standard setters have been widely open to including fair value accounting. Impairment is an example of why fair value, understood as a hypothetical market value, should play a role in accounting. Apart from this, regulation based on mixing type of approaches is likely to be a problem. FASB and IASB have been working hard in direction of the balance sheet orientation since the 1970s. Most eminently this is seen in conceptual frameworks such as the SFACs from FASB (SFAC (1984, 1985, 2010) are referred to) and IASB (1989, 2013). So far, this has led to very voluminous standards and to standards that are less than stable.

A seemingly obvious foundation for NASB's work with national standards is to base this on principles stated in the national accounting act. That is, on classical approaches to financial accounting. As pointed to in Sect. 1, less energy has been allocated to this due to the momentum of IFRS. NRS 6 on pension accounting is an example of how, at an earlier stage, elements of IFRS are brought into national regulation. As seen in the case study included in Sect. 7 effects of this can be massive.

The lack of consensus on fundamentals referred to, and positions taken, sometimes lead to heated exchange of points of view. Most likely, the explanation for this has to do with the complexity of the reporting problem. An answer to this could be to go to the users of financial reports. That is, such as to analysts having a professional interest in how financial reports are worked out. However, as Jiang and Penman (2013: 235) point to this is not that simple.

> Indeed, the accounting Boards [such as FASB og IASB] have been very keen to get the opinions of analysts. It appears, however, that this approach does not elicit clear recommendations. For example, the leadership of the CFA Institute [stands for Chartered Financial Analyst Institute being a worldwide organization of analysts with its seat in Charlottesville, Virginia (USA)] has come out strongly in favor of fair value accounting, while rank-and-file working analysts seem to have a different opinion. The Boards' recent insurance proposals have been controversial among analysts, some endorsement (largely in Europe) and some strong opposition (largely in the US). We suspect the reason is that analysts use accounting data in very different ways; there is no common platform for carrying out analysis.

This is rather depressing. However, as again pointed to by Jiang and Penman (2013) and as an alternative, residual income valuation (RIV) is an approach to analysis. The foundations of RIV are firmly anchored in fundamentals of financial accounting and economics of business. Stephen Penman has been important in doing work on this summarized in Penman (2011, 2013). In Lundesgaard (2012), this is taken advantage of. In RIV, it is easy to see how both the income statement and the balance sheet play a role. Taking this seriously, it leads astray to accentuate one before the other. Important is that RIV lends meaning to THC, and thus, to income statement matching. The balance sheet that is a result of this is important for RIV. In this, fair value accounting is a problem.

In the beginning of this section, two opposed positions on foundations of regulation were mentioned. RIV is pointed to as something else. In this, it is interesting that pension accounting has been argued for in taking advantage of each of the opposed positions mentioned. In Norway, Kvaal and Sellæg (2003) have argued in an extensive manner for this. Remarkably, points of departure do not matter. In any case, the effects of employee benefit plans should be included in financial statements. This may explain why pension accounting, after all, has been introduced in Norway without that much fuzz.

It is of good that foundations are discussed. In financial accounting, however, it is difficult to free oneself from the impression of some sort of impasse, or dead end. Pension accounting is something we now see in practice. Asking the question of what this all looks like in practice may bring us ahead. That is what is done in Sect. 7 with the ISR case. In spite of that this may well prompt accusations in direction of being anecdotal, effects are troublesome. To begin with in Sect. 2, it was stated that it is not necessarily so that the effects of employee benefit plans are to be made visible in including effects in financial statements. The problem with including effects is that the reported picture of the business process is garbled. Nevertheless, all what has to do with effects of employee benefit plans are still of interest. Thus, a solution to the problem is that relevant information is limited to notes or otherwise reported.

References

Dichev ID (2008) On the balance sheet-based model of financial reporting. Account Horiz 22 (4):453–470

EU (2002) Regulation (EC) No 1606/2002 of the European Parliament and of the Council of 19 July 2002 on the application of international accounting standards

Financial Supervisory Authority of Norway (2010) Regnskapsføring av ny AFP-ordning i privat sektor [Accounting for new AFP in the private sector]. Two letters (November 1 and December 1 2010) to the Ministry of Finance

Glover J (2014) Have academic accountants and financial standard setters traded places. J Account Econ Law Convivium 4(1):17–26

IAS 19 Employee benefits. EU Regulation no. 475/2012, including IAS 19 in the present version

IASB (1989) Framework for the preparation and presentation of financial statements. IASC/London, the predecessor institution of IASB

IASB (2009) IFRS for SMEs. International financial reporting standard for small and medium-sized entities. Approved July 2009. Later revised and re-issued in May 2015

IASB (2013) A review of the conceptual framework for financial reporting. Discussion Paper DP/2013/1, July 2013

IFRS 13 Fair value measurement. International Financial Reporting Standard from IASB, adopted May 2011 and made effective from January 1 2013

Institute for Social Research (ISR) Annual reports 2002–2012

Jiang G, Penman SH (2013) A fundamentalist perspective on accounting and implications for accounting research. China J Account Res 6:233–245

Johnsen A (1993) Accounting regulation in Norway. Eur Account Rev 2:617–626

Kinserdal F (2006) Accounting for and valuation of pensions in Norway. Earnings management and whether analysts detect it. PhD (dr. oecon.) Dissertation in Accounting. Norwegian School of Economics, Bergen

Kvaal E, Sellæg FE (2003) Regnskapsføring av pensjoner [Pension Accounting]. Praktisk økonomi & finans 2003(3):45–58

Lundesgaard J (2012) Residual income valuation and the normative problem in financial accounting. conference paper, 8. EUFIN (Praha) September 2012, a national conference and SASE (Milan) June 2013

Lundesgaard J (2014) Ytelsespensjoner og regnskap—Innarbeiding og konsekvenser [Employee benefit pensions and accounting. Inclusion and effects]. Oppdragsrapport nr. 8—2014, Hedmark University College

Macve R (2014) "Trading places". A UK (and IFRS) comment. J Account Econ Law Convivium 4 (1):27–40

Ministry of Finance (2011) Regnskapsføring av ny AFP [Accounting for new AFP]. Report from a working group dated October 7 2011

Ministry of Local Government and Modernisation (2000) Forskrift om årsregnskap og årsberetning (for kommuner og fylkeskommuner)—FOR 2000-12-15 nr. 1424 (Regulations of local government accounting)

NASB (2010) Regnskapsmessig behandling av overgang til ny AFP-ordning i privat sektor [Accounting for new AFP in the private sector]. October 2009, revised in 2009 and March 2010

NASB (2014) Norsk Regnskapsstandard [Norwegian accounting standard]. Draft of a comprehensive stand-alone standard for "other entities" based on IFRS for SMEs. On hearing as of April 2 2014

Norwegian Accounting Act of 1998. Unofficial translation by The Norwegian Institute of Public Accountants of Lov om årsregnskap m.v. (regnskapsloven)—Lov 1998-07-17 nr. 56

Norwegian Government Agency for Financial Management (2011) Anbefalte, men ikke obligatoriske, statlige regnskapsstandarder [Recommended, but not mandatory, state accounting standards], May 2011

NRS 6 Pensjonskostnader [Pension costs]. Norwegian Accounting Standard (NRS) from NASB April 1994, revised October 1995, and made definitive November 2000. After that revised several times

Penman SH (2011) Accounting for value. Columbia University Press, New York

Penman SH (2013) Financial statement analysis and security valuation, 5th edn. McGraw-Hill/Irwin, New York

SFAC (1984) Recognition and measurement in financial statement of business enterprises. Statement of financial accounting concepts No. 5 (December 1984), FASB

SFAC (1985) Elements of financial statements. Statement of financial accounting concepts No. 6 (December 1985). FASB, replaces SFAC # 3

SFAC (2010) Conceptual framework for financial reporting. Chapter 1, The objective of general purpose financial reporting, and Chapter 3, Qualitative characteristics of useful financial information. Statement of financial accounting concepts No. 8 (September 2010), FASB

SFAS No. 157 Fair value measurement. Statement of Financial Accounting Standards from FASB, adopted September 2006 and made effective from November 15 2007

SFAS No. 87 Employers' accounting for pensions. Statement of Financial Accounting Standards from FASB adopted December 1985

Zeff SA (2014) Some historical reflections on "have academics and the standard setters trading places". J Account Econ Law Convivium 4(1):41–48

Chile. Adopting the IFRS in Chile: Influences on Companies and the Capital Market

Digna Azúa and Verónica Pizarro

Abstract This study examines the initial impact of adopting the International Financial Reporting Standards (IFRS) in Chile, both on Chilean companies' financial statements and on their capital market. The aspects that we consider relevant are the following: (1) applying a fair value to the measurement of non-current assets and (2) variations in stock price, in the companies that started applying the Full-IFRS in 2009.

The results show that there are a significant number of companies that have experienced an increase in their book value equity (equal to or greater than 25 %). Nevertheless, the use of fair value in assets measurement is observed to be rare. With respect to market capitalization, this study shows that the publication of intermediate financial statements corresponding to the first quarter of 2009 may have generated a positive effect on stock prices on an average of 4.3 %.

1 Introduction

The adoption of the International Financial Reporting Standards (IFRS) is a common topic around the world, either because countries have accepted the option or because they have rejected it.

The IASB surveyed 138 countries all around the globe to determine their position as of 2014. They have used this information to create a profile for each country. One of the conclusions is that "only 8 jurisdictions neither require nor permit the use of IFRS by domestic companies".[1]

[1] http://www.ifrs.org/Alerts/Publication/Pages/Eight-new-jurisdiction-profiles-use-of-IFRS-around-world-September-2014.aspx

D. Azúa (✉)
Pontifical Catholic University of Valparaíso, Valparaíso, Chile
e-mail: digna.azua@ucv.cl

V. Pizarro
University of Chile, Santiago, Chile

D. Bensadon, N. Praquin (eds.), *IFRS in a Global World*,
DOI 10.1007/978-3-319-28225-1_24

This means that out of the 194 countries recognized by the United Nations (UN),[2] only a 67 % use the IFRS, either compulsorily or voluntarily, and apply them to some companies or, in the most extreme cases, to all companies.

In the opinion of the UN, this adoption process has been a long journey which started in 1973, as they declared during the Conference on Trade and Development of 2005: "The process of international convergence towards a global set of standards started in 1973 when 16 professional accountancy bodies from Australia, Canada, France, Germany, Japan, Mexico, the Netherlands, the United Kingdom and the United States agreed to form the International Accounting Standards Committee (IASC)".

The UN also considered during that Conference that "The process gained speed when the International Organization of Securities Commissions (IOSCO) endorsed the IASC standards for international listings in May 2000. It was further facilitated by the Regulation approved by the European Commission in 2002 requiring the preparation of the consolidated (group) accounts of listed companies in the European Union in accordance with IFRS".[3]

Just as the UN points it out, it is plausible to think that the convergence process towards a single set of norms started in 1973 when the IASC was created, although at that moment it was stated that the purpose of this body was to create good quality standards of accounting to be used by developing countries.

Nevertheless, the adoption of these standards in 2005 by the companies of the European Union in the presentation of the consolidated financial statements of domestic listed companies is one of the most significant milestones in this international standardization process.

Regarding Latin America, the adoption process of the IFRS has taken place, just as in the rest of the world, even when these countries share one characteristic: the companies listed make up a lower percentage than those which are not; however, the first are the ones that receive or could receive greater foreign investment.

The following table summarizes the dates of adoption of the IFRS in Latin American countries:

The years shown in the Table 1 indicate the start of the adoption of the IFRS. In most cases the adoption process was planned through stages, starting with domestic listed companies only.

However, unlike what happened in Europe, the adoption processes in many countries of Latin America is expected to be fully adopted by both listed and unlisted companies. As a result, local accounting standards should not be applied anymore, eventhough in many cases these standards developed favorably.

[2] UN (2014). "Concise Report on the World Population Situation in 2014", p. 1. http://www.un.org/en/development/desa/population/publications/pdf/trends/Concise%20Report%20on%20the%20World%20Population%20Situation%202014/en.pdf

[3] Trade and Development Board (2005). "Review Of Practical Implementation Issues Of International Financial Reporting Standards", United Nations Conference on Trade and Development. Geneva, 2005, p. 3. http://unctad.org/en/docs/c2isard28_en.pdf

Table 1 Adoption of IFRS in Latin American countries

Country	Adopts IFRS	Starts in
Argentina	YES	2012
Bolivia	YES	2015
Brazil	YES	2010
Chile	YES	2009
Colombia	YES	2015
Costa Rica	YES	2005
Ecuador	YES	2010
El Salvador	YES	2011
Guatemala	YES	2009
Honduras	YES	2012
Mexico	YES	2012
Panama	YES	2006
Paraguay	NO	Volunteer
Peru	YES	2012
Dominican Republic	YES	2014
Uruguay	YES	2012
Venezuela	YES	2008

Source: Jurisdiction Profiles, prepared by the IASB, 2014 (http://www.ifrs.org/Alerts/Publication/Pages/Eight-new-jurisdiction-profiles-use-of-IFRS-around-world-September-2014.aspx)

Due to this, Argentina, Chile, Brazil, Mexico, among others, have decided to postpone the application of the IFRS for unlisted companies and to wait for an appropriate standard to be generated for these organizations.

In the paricular case of Chile, this country had accounting standards set by the Institute of Accountants of Chile (Colegio de Contadores de Chile or CCCH).[4] According to Hermosilla (2010, p. 48) "The creation of accounting standards in Chile has always been influenced by foreign accounting standards. During the first period, between 1973 and 1994, the CCCH was inspired by the USA standards. In the second period, between 1995 and 1997, the CCCH followed the IASC work, and during the third period, between 1997 and 2007, in which they kept analyzing the work of the IASC/IASB and authorized the use of the international standard in the event of a regulatory gap on a particular subject".[5]

Similarly, according to Orellana (2014, p. 284) "the convergence towards the international standards started by the CCCH in 2008 constitutes a logical continuation in the history of standards creation in Chile, where international standards are seen as a model since 1995".[6]

[4] Colegio de Contadores de Chile, founded in 1958, according to Ley 13.011

[5] Free translation by the author.

[6] Free translation by the author.

Besides the pro-IFRS context in the Chilean accounting sphere, the free trade agreements signed by Chile with the United States and the European Economic Community increased the urgency to adopt the IFRS.

Also during the same period, Chile was ready to join the OECD, which took place on January 11th, 2010. The OECD is widely known for its promotion of the application of best corporate governance practices. As a result, this organization published in 2004 the "White Paper" for Corporate Governances in Latin America. This document states that an important element for developing corporate governance best practices is transparency, and to achieve this the IFRS must be applied.

This was a determinant factor for Chile to adopt the IFRS and to ask the CCCH[7] for guidance during the adoption process.

Thus, in 2004 the CCCH and the Inter-American Development Bank (IADB) signed the agreement for the adoption of the IFRS, which stipulated that the adoption had to start in 2009 for listed companies. The budged allocated by the IADB through the Multilateral Investment Fund (FOMIN) to carry out the project amounted to US$1.5 million.

The areas covered by the budged were:

- Convergence project
- Professional development and certification
- Training
- Dissemination

Another body that played an important role during this process was the Superintendence of Securities and Insurance (Superintendencia de Valores y Seguros or SVS), which regulates the activity of listed companies and the operation of the Chilean capital market. This body generated the agenda for the adoption of the IFRS that took place during the period 2009–2011 and that included all the companies regulated by the SVS.

The adoption process of the IFRS required the accounting professionals to be trained. In Chile this training programs are offered mainly by auditing firms, universities and the CCCH.

Regarding the conversion process for the financial statements, many mayor chilean companies hired international auditing firms operating in Chile, such as Pricewaterhouse, Delloite, Ernest & Young, KPMG, known as the big four.

From above mentioned, we can state that international auditing firms played a remarkable role in the adoption process of the IFRS in Chile, since they were actively involved in the professional training process, advising mayor companies during the financial statements conversion process and directing the Principles and Standards Commission of the CCCH, the body in charge of approving the IASB standards to be compulsorily applied in the country.

---

[7] According to Ley 13.011

The second phase of the adoption process of the IFRS included the approval of the IFRS standard for SMEs (small and medium-sized entities) by the CCCH, which have been applied since January 1st, 2013. Therefore, accounting professionals are currently undergoing constant training, both on new IASB standards and on IFRS for SMEs.[8]

2 Literature Review

The process of adopting the IFRS has excited considerably strong interest in the studying their impact on the financial statements of companies, capital market and the society.

Diverse literature supports this observation. Asbaugh and Pincus (2001) investigate the relationship between results-prediction errors and the differences between local regulations and the IFRS, concluding that this relationship is a positive one. Ding et al. (2007), work with data published by Nobes (2009) and complemente the studies of Ball et al. (2003) and Hope (2003), analyze the absence and divergence between local regulations and the IFRS in many countries. Their results suggest that the absence of accounting regulations is closely related to the development of a capital market and a high concentration of equity; conversely, divergence between local regulations and the IFRS is positively related to the economic development and the growth of the accounting profession. Kent and Stewart (2008) analyze the relationship between some aspects of corporate governance and the quantity of information disclosed in the IFRS adoption process, concluding that there is a positive relationship between the quantity of disclosed information and aspects associated with corporate governance.

Chile is a case in point in the adoption of IFRS, and the year 2009 offers ideal conditions for studying those effects because that year marks Chile's transition to the IFRS. As noted by several Chilean authors, we can expect important changes from the adoption of the IFRS. Relevant subjects include the application of fair value to assets (current and/or non-current; physical and/or intangible) along with the increase in the quantity and quality of information that to be disclosed in financial statements.

Some evidence has been gathered in studies conducted by Silva and Azúa (2006) on methods that may be used to apply the concept of fair value, as contained in the IFRS. These authors conclude that there are doubts regarding companies' capacity to adequately apply this concept.

[8] The CCCH established their applicability since January 1, 2013, by publishing "Boletín Técnico N° 82".

Pizarro (2006) analyzes the accounting categorization of intangibles by gathering the opinion of national experts who conclude that such categorizations should evolve towards the recommendations of the IFRS.

Jara (2007), who studied the effects of applying Impairment of Assets (IAS 36) in relation to companies' stock market/books, concludes, based on information current as of 2007, that companies showing signs of impairment in their assets do not necessarily recognize their impairment loss.

Zunino and Chandia (2007a, b) studied the effects of applying fair value to fixed and intangibles assets and the effects of applying IAS 41 (Biological Assets) on companies' statements. In their first study, they conclude that companies will be affected both by the adoption of new valuation criteria and by an increase in administrative costs. With respect to biological assets, they conclude that there is a difference in the effect on equity.

Silva and Azúa (2007) demonstrate that financial information disclosed in the notes of financial statements according to local PCGA do not satisfy the needs of external users, which suggests that adopting IFRS will result in a qualitative and quantitative change in information disclosure.

Subsequently, once the adoption process started, many studies were conducted by several academics to determine the impact of the adoption on the financial statements of Chilean companies. Table 2 shows some of these studies published in CAPICREVIEW, which specializes in accounting.

The studies in this Table are a sample of the topics analyze by Chilean academics before and during the adoption of IFRS.

As showed in the Table 2, 5 out of 10 studies were intended to analyze the impact of adopting IFRS on company equity. Among the main conclusions, we find that the revaluation of assets to determine a new attributed cost had a relevant effect, during the conversion of financial statements, according to IFRS 1 as an alternative method.

The relevance of the point above is considerable for our discussion, considering that Chilean accounting standards, specifically in the *Boletín Técnico N° 33* issued by the CCCH, does not allow any revaluating of assets, and historical cost must be used during their useful life.

Due to the relevancy of these topics for Chile, the following section shows the "Study on the impact of adopting the IFRS in Chile 2009", presented in the Permanent Academic Conference of Accounting Research (Conferencia Académica Permanente de Investigación Contable or CAPIC) of 2009. It analyzes the impact of applying the IFRS on the listed companies equity, in relation to the possibility of revaluating assets, specifically property, plant and equipment, biological and intangible assets, because of IFRS 1 (First-Time Adoption of IFRS) allows the revaluation of such assets only once, which is called deemed cost. The study also analyzes whether there was an impact on the stock price for those companies that adopted the IFRS in different stages of the process.

Table 2 studies pubilshed in CAPICREVIEW

Authors	Title	Conclusions
Riadi et al. (2009)	Impact on the Chilean stock market by the process of financial statement presentation under IFRS rules.	No changes were found in the value of the shares that can be related to the adoption of the IFRS.
Zuñiga et al. (2009)	Accounting convergence: deep accounting changes in Chile. Fixed Assets, a case to consider.	Analyzes the potential difficulties of revaluating assets in Chile.
Gómez (2009)	Valuation methods to fair value and audit.	Analyzes the risks of applying estimates to assets valuation.
Jara and Abarca (2009)	First application in Chile comprehensive income statement. An approach to its main components and characteristics.	Identifies the main changes observed when preparing comprehensive income statements.
Jara and Contreras (2010)	Adoption of IFRS by Chilean firms. Emphasizing quantitative effects on financial information.	The adoption of IFRS generated an increase in company equity. Also, it was determined that the main causes where the applications of IAS 16 and IAS 39.
Inostroza et al. (2011)	Initial impact of IFRS on financial statements: evidence for a simple of Chilean companies.	Adopting the IFRS generated an increase of 50 % in the equity of studied companies.
Hernández et al. (2011)	International financial reporting standards: impacts on property, plant and equipment in manufacturing companies.	The greatest impact was generated by the revaluation of assets, mainly land, in relation to IFRS 1.
Pizarro and Azúa (2011)	Biological resources: the impact of new international standards of financial information in agriculture.	There was an increase in the equity of an average 15 % and in the profits of 135 %, due to the application of fair value to the biological assets.
Peña and Torres (2012)	Critical analysis of the institution of the IFRS in Chile, a systemic approach.	Analyzes the drawbacks that unlisted companies may face towards the application of IFRS SME, which make up 99 % of Chilean companies.
Jara (2012)	Analysis of the observations made by the superintendent of securities and insurance of the first financial statements made under IFRS in Chile.	It was determined that the SVS made observations for 73 % of the 45 companies analyzed.

Source: Compiled by the author

3 Study on the Impact of Adopting the IFRS in Chile 2009

This study analyzes the changes in the equity and market capitalization during the IFRS adoption process in Chile.

Chilean companies presented a report about impact projections for the adopting IFRS, on their financial statements. These reports were published in September

2008 and February 2009 by companies that opted to start applying Full-IFRS in 2009.

The impact projections, reported by the 80 companies involved in the process, showed a variation in the equity of US$7.2 billion, and the cause of this variation is an interesting research subject.

As indicated by the IFRS 1, when converting financial statements from local GAAP to the IFRS, a series of adjustments must be carried out—some compulsory and some optional—that have an impact that should be seen in company equity.

Firstly, this study examines cases in which the impact in the equity valuation can be attributed to asset revaluation to establish whether applying these practices, which Chile did not previously use, was important to the adoption of the IFRS.

Secondly, this study analyzes the market-capitalization behavior of companies that were involved during the pre-adoption period and at the time that the first financial statements were issued under the IFRS.[9]

3.1 *Objectives of the Study*

According to the previous information, the objectives of the study are the following:

- Analyze the impact of the IFRS on companies' equity, primarily linked to the application of fair value to assets.
- Analyze the impact of the IFRS adoption on the capital market using the share prices of companies involved.

3.2 *Methodological Aspects*

3.2.1 Determine the Sample

According to the adoption calendar established by the SVS in 2007,[10] the listed companies registered in the SVS started to adopt the IFRS in the fiscal year 2009.

This study analyzes the situation of companies that opted for the Full-IFRS and began to disclose financial statements under the new regulations in the first quarter of 2009. Therefore, this study includes 80 listed companies.

---

[9] The dates analyzed are linked to the announcements made by the SVS about the IFRS adoption process and to company publications that announced the effects of the regulatory changes and presented their first financial statements under the IFRS.

[10] According to the outlines of Boletín Técnico N° 79 issued by the Colegio de Contadores de Chile.

3.2.2 Data Collection

The data used in this study was obtained from:

- Reports prepared by companies on impact projections, according to Circular 457 (July 20th, 2008) and published by the SVS, referring to functional currency, accounting policies and equity reconciliation.
- Financial statements prepared under the Full-IFRS for the first quarter of 2009.
- Announcements made by the SVS regarding the timeline and methodology of the adoption of the IFRS.
- Share prices of the sampled companies 10 days before and 10 days after the announcements considered as milestones.

Those documents were obtained from the SVS website and the Economática and the Santiago Stock Exchange databases.

3.2.3 Data Analysis Procedure

Impact on Equity, Measured at Book Value

To conduct the analysis of impact on equity, measured at book value, at the time of adoption of the IFRS, we used the following methodology:

Equity Variation Analysis The impact projections published in September 2008 were analyzed based on the report that contained indications of functional currency, accounting policies and equity reconciliation.

Applying Revaluation or Fair Value to Fixed Assets The notes to financial statements presented in the first quarter of 2009 were examined. This analysis allowed the identification of the companies that applied revaluation or fair value to the measurement of assets such as property, plants and equipment and biological and intangible assets, whether to determine their deemed costs at the time that financial statements were converted to the IFRS or for subsequent measurements.

Equity Variation and Asset Valuation Companies with significant variation in their book value equity were identified, and some cases were established in which these companies applied reevaluation or fair value at the time of conversion.

Impact on Equity, Measured at Market Value

Five high-impact milestones were selected in order to perform the analysis of the impact on the market capitalization of shares:

a) Disclosure of adoption calendar (August 28th, 2007);

b) Issuance of the list of companies obliged to adopt the IFRS (February 14th, 2008);
c) Date on which the first companies disclosed their reports on accounting criteria, accounting currency and reconciliation (September 30, 2009);
d) Date on which the second group of companies disclosed their reports on accounting criteria, accounting currency and reconciliation (February 28, 2009); and
e) Disclosure of the quarterly financial statements of the company (May 31st, 2009).

Subsequently, we extracted the share prices 10 days prior and 10 days after the above-referenced announcements and events from Economática and Santiago Stock Exchange databases.

Out of the 80 companies that were required to comply with the Full-IFRS in 2009, we selected those which had

- share prices available for all of the periods observed.

After the sample was subjected to these criteria, our sample was reduced to 48 companies only.

Using the share price data, we calculated the average for the period prior and subsequent to the announcement or milestone to detect an increase or decrease in market capitalization due to the effect of the announcement or milestone.

3.3 *Results*

3.3.1 Analysis of Preliminary Information

The analysis of the reports prepared by companies adopting the Full-IFRS, starting from the presentation from the first quarter of 2009 according to Circular 457 (June 20th, 2008), which refer to functional currency, accounting policies and equity reconciliation demonstrate, among other aspects, that:

- With respect to the accounting currency, 48 companies (60 %) specify the use of the Chilean peso, whereas 32 companies (40 %) specify using the US dollar.
- With respect to equity variations, 26 companies (32.5 %) show an increase or decrease in equity, equal to or greater than 25 %, caused by the conversion to IFRS.
- Among the 26 companies with a significant percentage of variation (equal to or greater than 25 %) in the book value of equity, 22 show a positive variation, i.e., an increase in the book value of equity.
- Among the 22 companies that experienced an increase in their book value of equity, 11 state they had applied fair value at the time of conversion to determine deemed cost to assets classified as property, plant and equipment, biological and/or intangible asset.

3.3.2 Impact on Equity, Measured at Book Value

The information disclosed in the notes of the financial statements, prepared under the Full-IFRS as of March 30th, 2009, provides prior factors regarding the way in which the concepts of reevaluation and fair value were applied according to the type of non-current assets:

Property, Plant and Equipment There are 47 companies that applied fair value at the time of conversion to determine deemed cost. However, only 16 companies declared that they would use revaluation model in subsequent measurements. Analyzing by sector, we observe that the use of the fair value to determine the deemed cost is most frequently applied in manufacturing (14 companies) and service (16 companies) sectors. Among the latter, 15 companies stated that they will continue to use revaluation model in subsequent measurements.

Nevertheless, the information disclosed in the financial statements does not allow us to determine with clarity the type of asset for which the fair value is most often used when determining deemed cost. Only 18 companies stated that the method would be used for a specific type of non-current assets, such as land (10), land and buildings (5) and machinery and facilities (3). In the other 29 cases, it is impossible to determine the item to which this method was applied: 10 companies provided no information and 19 companies provided only generic information only.

Biological Assets With respect to biological assets, there are 10 companies that applied fair value at the time of conversion to determine deemed cost and declared that they would use fair value less costs to sell in subsequent measurements. Analyzing by sector, we observe that the use of fair value to determine deemed cost is most frequently used in the sectors of agriculture, forestry and fishing (4 companies) and manufacturing (4 companies). In addition, 3 companies stated that they would use only fair value less costs to sell, in subsequent measurements.

Intangible Assets With respect to intangible assets, there are 17 companies that applied fair value at the time of conversion to determine attributed cost. However, there none of these companies declared the application of the fair value method in subsequent measurements. Analyzing by sector, we observe the most frequent use of the reevaluation method in determining deemed cost is concentrated in the service sector (11 companies).

3.3.3 Impact on Equity, Measured at Market Value

The results of this analysis are the following (Table 3):

The analysis shows that, *céteris paribus*, other events impacting the valuation of national companies, the first milestones associated with the adoption calendar issued by the SVS and the list of companies that were required to adopt the IFRS in 2009 have a positive effect on company market capitalization (0.96 %/1.49 %). Subsequently, reports issued by Chilean companies and disclosed to the SVS about

Table 3 Event variation

Event	Data	Variation (%)
IFRS Adoption Calendar	08-28-2007	0.96
Official Letter 438 List of Adopting Companies	02-14-2008	1.49
Reconciliation Disclosure 1	09-30-2008	−3.74
Reconciliation Disclosure 2	02-28-2009	−1.87
Quarterly Statement Disclosure	05-31-2009	4.35

the changes to accounting criteria, accounting currency and equity reconciliation (details of the equity variations due to the effect of the IFRS adoption) scheduled for September 2009 and February 2009 had a negative effect on companies' market capitalization (−3.74 % to −1.87 %). Finally, the most important event, in our opinion, in the definitive disclosure of quarterly financial statements under the IFRS, which companies delivered to the SVS in May 2009, had a positive effect greater than the earlier effects (4.35 %).

As for analysis by sector, we obtain the following results (Table 4):

The first milestones corresponding to the publishing of the adoption calendar had a positive effect concentrated in the financial sector (3.19 %). The opposite situation is true in the manufacturing sector, which experienced a negative effect (−0.07 %).

The second milestone had a positive effect primarily concentrated in the transport sector (3.66 %). The opposite situation is true in the manufacturing sector, which experienced a negative effect (−0.19 %).

The third and fourth milestones, associated with the disclosure of impact reports (accounting currency, accounting policies and equity reconciliation), had a negative

Table 4 Events variation by sector

	Variation by sector					Total var.
Events	Agriculture (%)	Finance (%)	Manufacturing (%)	Services (%)	Transport (%)	Sector Av. (%)
IFRS Adoption Calendar	0.46	3.19	−0.07	0.91	0.68	1.03
Official Letter 438 List of Adopting Companies	−0.67	1.44	−0.19	2.14	3.66	1.28
Reconciliation Disclosure 1	−2.69	−4.96	−4.83	−3.25	−3.22	−3.79
Reconciliation Disclosure 2	−0.38	−5.03	−1.69	−1.32	−1.87	−2.06
Quarterly Statement Disclosure	5.65	1.70	5.62	4.34	4.23	4.31

effect on all sectors, mainly affecting the finance and manufacturing sectors (−4.96 %/−5.03 % and −4.83 %).

The fifth event, which can be considered the most important event to date, and which corresponds to the disclosure of the quarterly financial statements under the Full-IFRS, generated in all sectors a positive impact on market capitalization, mostly affecting the agriculture (5.65 %) and manufacturing sectors (5.62 %).

4 Conclusions

This study provides the first data on the process of IFRS adoption in Chile, analyzing the impact of its adoption on equity measured at both book and market value.

Before the adoption of IFRS, Jara (2007), Zunino and Chandia (2007a, b), Silva and Azúa (2006, 2007) and Pizarro (2006), among others, conducted studies which allowed to assume that there will be significant impact, both in measurement and disclosure.

This study analyzed two aspects related to the adoption of IFRS. On the one hand, it examined the impact of applying fair value to the measurement of property, plant and equipment; biological and intangible assets, in company's equity. On the other hand, we examined the impact on the shares prices of the companies that began applying Full IFRS 2009.

The results show that, out of 80 listed companies that started to apply the Full-IFRS in the first quarter of 2009, 22 (27.5 %) experienced a positive impact on the book value of equity to a degree of 25 % or more of their initial value. Out of these companies, only 11 (13.7 % of the total number) indicated the use of fair value to determine the deemed cost of property, plant and equipment, biological assets and/or intangible assets.

This result is consistent both with the predictions of the authors previously mentioned and with the conclusions of the studies shown in Table 2, mainly with Jara and Contreras (2010), Inostroza and Yáñez (2011), Hernández et al. (2011), Pizarro and Azúa (2011), who confirmed the increases on the book value company equity, and related them with the application of fair value.

However, the use of the fair value should be observed carefully since in most cases it was only used to determine the deemed cost at the time of the conversion and on assets whose new value is less difficult to determine, such as land and buildings.

It is possible to suggest that the majority of these companies will not continue applying the fair value method because in many cases the methodologies to be applied are expensive, and if they are successful they will have a negative impact on the results of the company through the acknowledgement of a greater depreciation, which may affect the distribution of dividends.

In relation to disclosure, there was little information on the notes. In most cases they did not specify what assets were revaluated or what method was used. Thus, it is hard for an external user to venture an opinion on the decisions made by the management in relation to these subjects.

With respect to the market value of equity, we observe that in relation to the first and the second milestones, both announcements made by the SVS (i.e., scheduling a list of companies adopting the IFRS), the impact observed is positive, except for the manufacturing sector companies. In relation to the third and fourth milestone (impact projections presented by the companies), we observe negative behavior for all of the sampled companies. Finally, the fifth milestone (disclosure of financial statements prepared for the first quarter of 2009), we observe a positive effect. This situation shows that as users of financial statements become familiar with the application of the IFRS, their perceptions will improve, perhaps assisted by the fact that in the majority of cases, the IFRS generated an increase in the book value of company equities. Nevertheless, this variation made an average 4.2 %. This result is consistent with the idea of Riadi et al. (2009).

This study has allowed analyzing some of the impacts of adopting the IFRS in Chile. Today, 5 years after the application of these standards, we believe it is necessary to conduct further research and to confirm whether there have been any changes in the accounting policies the companies applied when adopting the IFRS. Such study would allow to determine how familiarized are these companies with the standards and whether the adoption of IFRS has been beneficial for financial statements users.

References

Asbaugh H, Pincus M (2001) Domestic accounting standards, international accounting standards, and the predictability of earnings. J Account Res 39(3):417–432

Ball R et al (2003) Incentives versus standards: properties of accounting income in four East Asian countries. J Account Econ 36:235–270

Ding Y et al (2007) Differences between domestic accounting standards and IAS: measurement, determinants and implications. J Account Public Policy 26:1–38

Gómez C (2009) Valuation methods to fair value and audit. Capic Rev 7:35–44

Hermosilla J (2010) Evaluation de la fiabilité de l'information comptable : une analyse théorique et appliquée au processus de production des normes comptables, le cas du Chili. Une approche par les logiques d'action et les conventions. Thèse de doctorat en sciences économiques et de gestion. Université Catholique de Louvain, p. 403

Hernández S, Vega M, Zúñiga W (2011) International financial reporting standards: impacts on property, plant and equipment in manufacturing companies. Capic Rev 9(1):21–31

Hope OR-K (2003) Disclosure practices, enforcement of accounting standards and analysts' forecast accuracy: an international study. J Account Res 41:235–272

Inostroza C, Pilar F, Yáñez V (2011) Initial impact of IFRS on financial statements: evidence for a simple of Chilean companies. Capic Rev 9(1):53–62

Jara L (2007) Stock exchange/book relation and its incidence in the application of the IAS 16. Revista Contabilidad Sistemas de la Universidad de Chile II(6):47–50

Jara L (2012) Analysis of the observations made by the superintendent of securities and insurance of the first financial statements made under IFRS in Chile. Capic Rev 10(1):9–23

Jara L, Abarca A (2009) First application in Chile comprehensive income statement. An approach to its main components and characteristics. Capic Rev 7:13–21

Jara L, Contreras H (2010) Adoption of IFRS by Chilean firms. Emphasizing quantitative effects on financial information. Capic Rev 8:13–24

Kent P, Stewart J (2008) Corporate governance and disclosures on the transition to international financial reporting standards. Account Finance 48:649–671

Nobes C (2009) Observations on measuring the differences between domestic accounting standards and IAS. J Account Public Policy 28:148–153

Orellana C (2014) L'évaluation comptable des réserves et ressources des entreprises de l'industrie extractive. Thèse de doctorat en sciences de gestion. Université Paris-Dauphine, p. 597

Peña A, Torres I (2012) Critical analysis of the institution of the IFRS in Chile, a systemic approach. Capic Rev 10(1):43–52

Pizarro V (2006) Intangibles in Chile: national accounting experts' opinion study on the normative treatment of intangibles in Chile. Capic Rev 4:21–32

Pizarro V, Azúa D (2011) Biological resources: the impact of new international standards of financial information in agriculture. Capic Rev 9(1):9–19

Riadi F, Beltramin V, Díaz J (2009) Impact on the Chilean stock market by the process of financial statement presentation under IFRS rules. Capic Rev 4:105–115

Silva B, Azúa D (2006) Notes on the concept of fair value. Capic Rev 4:63–74

Silva B, Azúa D (2007) Diagnosis for the first year of applying the Technical Bulletin 72. Capic Rev 5:33–40

Zuñiga F, Pacheco L, Díaz J (2009) Accounting convergence: deep accounting changes in Chile. Fixed assets, a case to consider. Capic Rev 7:75–82

Zunino M, Chandia K (2007a). From historical cost to fair value: effects on fixed and intangible assets. *Revista Estudios de Información and Control de Gestión, Universidad de Chile*. Primer semestre 2007

Zunino M, Chandia K (2007b) Biological assets: effects on results. Revista Contabilidad Sistemas de la Universidad de Chile 3(6):8–25

Estonia. Development of the Estonian Financial Reporting and Good Accounting Practice

Jaan Alver and Lehte Alver

Abstract Estonia has undergone enormous socio-economic changes during the last two decades. These changes, and the pressures for internationalization which have increased since Estonia's incorporation into the European Union in 2004, have had important consequences. Among them are changes in accounting legislation as well as in accounting practice.

The article deals with the development of financial reporting and Good Accounting Practice in Estonia. The main purpose of the article is to discuss the development of financial reporting in Estonia and the changes in Estonian accounting framework. The emphasis is on the changes in accounting and financial reporting which took place during 1990–1994, 1995–2002, 2003–2012 and in 2013.

The article is dedicated to professor Jacques Richard in honor of his seventieth birthday. Professor Richard with 48 other Frenchmen are among more than 900 individuals who have influenced accounting and finance, or have furthered the development of the field and have been included in the two-volume (1405 pages) *Encyclopedia of Accounting and Finance* composed by the authors of this article and published in 2011 in Estonia.

1 Introduction

Estonia is a small country in the Baltic Region of Northern Europe. It covers an area of 45,227 km^2. The population is about 1.28 million. Estonia is among the world's leaders in e-governance and features an impressively transparent system in which government decisions are almost instantly made available on the Internet. Estonia has a modern market-based economy since the end of 1990s and one of the highest per capita income levels in Eastern Europe. Estonia became a NATO member state on March 29, 2004 and a European Union member state on May 1, 2004. From January 1, 2011 euro is the official currency in Estonia.

J. Alver (✉) • L. Alver
Tallinn University of Technology, Tallinn, Estonia
e-mail: jaan.alver@ttu.ee

D. Bensadon, N. Praquin (eds.), *IFRS in a Global World*,
DOI 10.1007/978-3-319-28225-1_25

In the context of accounting, Estonia is one of the less-known states in Europe. Until the beginning of the twentieth century, there is very little information about accounting in Estonia. As Estonia was under foreign rulers for a long time (from 1220s to 1918), it is known that at different times in history accounting in Estonia was influenced correspondingly to the ruling power and all regulations for bookkeeping and accounting were developed and set up by (foreign) authorities—Denmark, Germany, Sweden and Russia.

On 30 June 1632, the King Gustav II Adolf of Sweden signed the Foundation Decree (founding charter) of *Academia Dorpatensis*, the predecessor of Tartu University. Unfortunately, little information on accounting and finance education in early periods is possible to find. The first accounting educators were mostly German mathematicians who taught cameral and commercial accounting. Estonian researchers Jaanus (1980), Piirimäe (1982) and Krinal (1999) have discussed these issues.

In 1802, the university was reopened in Tartu as *Kaiserliche Universität zu Dorpat* (in Russian Imperatorskij Derptskij Universitet). In 1803, the Chair (*Lehrstuhl* in German) of Cameralistics, Finance and Trade was established. In their research, the authors of the current paper discovered quite prominent persons involved in the teaching of bookkeeping and/or related subjects in Imperial University of Tartu. Among them, for example, are the architect of the main building of Tartu University professor Johann Krause; the economist and fiction writer, future rector of the University of Tartu Eberhard Rambach; the future rector of Kazan University Julius Mikszewicz; the eminent German economist and a distinguished leader of the historical school Adolph Wagner; Etienne Laspeyres, the founder of the index number formula method for determining price increases named after him.

The Estonian accounting regulation research has a short history compared to several other European countries. Few authors publishing about Estonian accounting issues include Alver et al. (1998), Alver et al. (2001), Alver and Alver (2005, 2008), Alver et al. (2013), Haldma (2001, 2003, 2006) and Tikk (2010). From the foreign authors Bailey (1995) should be marked. At the same time, Estonia is one of the first European countries, which allows International Financial Reporting Standards (IFRS) also in stand-alone financial statements for statutory purposes.

2 Accounting and Financial Reporting in 1918–1940

The Russian Revolution of 1917 gave Estonia the opportunity for freedom and the Republic of Estonia was proclaimed on February 24, 1918. The first period of independence lasted 22 years. Estonia underwent a number of economic, social, and political reforms necessary to come to terms with its new status as a sovereign state. On 1 December 1919 the university opened its doors as Tartu University of the Republic of Estonia with Estonian as the language of instruction. It is necessary to emphasize that in 1918–1940 the German educational influence could be noticed. The main idea of that approach was to classify bookkeeping (accounting) as a comprehensive branch of business economics education. Accounting was not yet determined as separate field of specialization. During this period only few subjects (bookkeeping, cameral bookkeeping, balance sheet analysis, commercial arithmetic and financial mathematics) were taught in Tartu University. In terms of the number of publications, the contribution of the small academic community to accounting related literature and research was relatively limited.

During the period of 1918–1940 accounting was primarily focused on trading companies, because these enterprises were the first, which recognized the need for recording business transactions. It is interesting that during the above-mentioned period the czarist Russian Commercial Code (CC) which was in force since 1836 regulated all areas of business activities in the independent Republic of Estonia, including accounting and taxation. The CC established the classification of enterprises, the books of accounting records, which each enterprise had to keep and the general accounting requirements. According to the Code, all enterprises were classified as big, medium, and small. The number of obligatory books were established and named by the CC. The CC also described how to document and record business transactions, how to make corrections, and retain the books. Correct keeping of accounting records (books) was very important. The main shortcomings of the Russian Commercial Code were as following:

- Due to its longevity, the CC was outdated;
- The bookkeeping requirements were set up for trading companies, but not for industrial enterprises;
- The requirement for physical inventory was missing;
- Many of the required accounting books mentioned in the CC were not used in the real life.

The most important law from this period (in force from January 1, 1926) was indisputable the Law of Golden Balances, which established the valuation principles for securities, inventories and tangible fixed assets. The importance of this law was to unify different currency units, because before enforcement of the Law of Golden Balances at the same time Russian gold and paper rubles as well as Estonian marks were used. Although the taxation system was originated from Russia, the Income Tax Law was one of the few taxation-related acts, which was put into the force during the independent Republic of Estonia.

Before the year 1935 all enterprises were allowed to keep their books in whatever language they wanted. Since the beginning of 1935, when the Law of Language for Accounting at Business Enterprises was put into force, all enterprises had to keep their books in Estonian only. The exception was given for enterprises where majority of ownership belonged to foreign owners.

The Bill of the Law on Accounting Act was prepared but, unfortunately, it was not enacted in the first Republic of Estonia.

3 Accounting and Financial Reporting in 1945–1990

After incorporation Estonia into the USSR in 1940, and in fact after the World War II, the Soviet system of bookkeeping was in use and accounting system in Estonia was part of the Soviet accounting system.

The Soviet accounting system was an integral part of the centralized administrative institutional structures for the direction and control of the command economic system.[1] Hence, from 1945 until 1990 the Soviet influence on accounting development (including accounting education development) was total.

The necessity of organizing a single accounting and statistical system and the leading role of the Council of Ministers of the USSR in the task, was established by the Soviet constitution. The government of the USSR had authorized the Soviet Ministry of Finance with direct supervision of accountancy in the country. The latter had a special department that effected overall methodological supervision over bookkeeping and accountancy of state, cooperative and public enterprises and organizations, approved standard documents and bookkeeping forms for enterprises and organizations, and instructions for their use (Kovalyov et al. 1991).

Accounting systems used in the West and in the USSR were quite different, being the products of different economic and social environments. Although accounting in the USSR, as in Western countries, fulfilled the role of stewardship, the difference in the nature of the economic system led to a difference in the determination of accounting priorities and accounting techniques. In the Soviet Union, the purpose of accounting had been declared the provision of control for the safeguarding of socialist property and control over the fulfillment of state plans.

The Soviet accounting system was designed to provide economic information, which is useful for central planning and for controlling the Soviet economy. This system was characterized by politicization of the theory and methodology as well as strict regulation and centralization of accounting. The basic accounting ideas were derived from papers of Marx and Lenin. Lenin's phrase "Socialism is first of all accounting" was always repeated.

The Soviet accounting was subdivided into simple bookkeeping, performed by the bookkeeping department and economic analysis, performed by the budgeting department. The main features of a system of unified socialist accounting implemented throughout the USSR were (Sokolov et al. 1998):

- A rigid hierarchical structure of the national economic system;
- A unified chart of accounts;
- The centralized regulation of accounting practice and authoritative prescription of accounting entries for typical transactions;
- The unification of primary documentation and uniform treatment of accounting data;

[1] An excellent description of Soviet accounting model is given by J. Richard (2003).

- Formats for authorized financial statements prescribed by the Ministry of Finance;
- The absence of independent audit and its substitution by strict intradepartmental control.

To give an opinion about the Soviet accounting, we agree with Richard (2003), who has noticed: “Many specialists consider that communist accounting practices were not real accounting. Of course, no one suggests that they did not use double-entry, but rather that it was more to do with keeping the books or counting rather than accounting.” We can only add that the predominance of the administrative methods for the management of the Soviet economy had adversely affected over many years the development of accounting.

4 Financial Reporting in 1990–1994

On March 30, 1990 Estonian newly elected Supreme Council declared Estonia to be an occupied country and proclaimed a period of transition to full independence. After declaring the restoration of the independence of the Republic of Estonia in 1990, it became possible to begin reform of accounting and join the system of accounting of developed market orientated countries. The first step on the way to change the situation was made in 1990, while Estonia remained, albeit reluctantly, a constituent republic of the USSR. On July 6, 1990, the Regulation of Accounting was adopted by the National Government, came into force on January 1, 1991 and was in force until the end of 1994. Although, legally, the measure was a regulation and not a statute (i.e. not approved by a legislative assembly but adopted by the executive action of the government) it was comparable to a fundamental, or basic, accounting law. The declared purpose of the Regulation was to bring about the organization of accounting in the conditions of a market economy. When examining the Regulation of Accounting, it should be borne in mind that it was framed when Estonia was still part of the USSR and the outcome of any transitional process for the Estonian economy was neither assured or certain. The major industrial enterprises were controlled from Moscow as, in the main, was the banking and monetary system. Estonia continued to be a part of the ruble zone and prices remained controlled.

The Regulation introduced a number of new accounting concepts and principles, new terms, and a new set of annual statements (including the balance sheet, the income statement and the statement of changes in financial position and notes).

In 1991, after the collapse of the USSR Estonia regained independence. The transition from command economy to market economy had a huge impact on a great number of aspects in business society, and on accounting as well. The old Soviet bookkeeping system with detailed rules serving the primary task of controlling that the national economic plans were fulfilled was replaced by a new accounting system. Nevertheless, it is necessary to emphasize that according to the

Regulation each enterprise was required to prepare a chart of accounts and the former Soviet standard chart of accounts was officially used in Estonia until the end of 1992. The emphasis, in the Regulation, upon the form rather than the content of the accounting record reflected the strength of the continuing influence of the Soviet accounting tradition. Primary attention was paid to the preparation of the accounting records: the proper and certified documentation of all transactions, the compilation of the accounting entries, the correction of errors, the retention of accounting records and the maintenance of accounting archives. Especial emphasis was placed upon the evidential nature of the accounting records (Bailey 1995). Real accounting continued to be perceived as properly subject to centralized prescription and its primary purpose the meeting of the needs of the central authorities of Estonia (Statistics Bureau, Tax Department) and not, as hitherto, those of the USSR (Alver and Alver 2008). Therefore, the main characteristic of that period is that it was mixed with the past (some elements of the former Soviet accounting system remained in force), present (real usage of new methods, principles and financial statements), and future (usage of many new terms of the market economy that really were not represented in the Estonian economy). The authors of current paper would like to emphasize the following changes:

- Each business entity had obligation to prepare own internal instructions on accounting as well as own chart of accounts;
- In revenue recognition the switch from cash basis to accrual basis was performed;
- Concept of commercial secret, which was not the issue before, was introduced;
- New accounting term, *goodwill*, was introduced. In the event of the purchase price being greater than the net book value of the assets and liabilities acquired the difference was to be treated as goodwill and amortized over 10 years. As Bailey (Bailey et al. 1995) has pointed out, this was the first occasion on which the existence of goodwill has been acknowledged in an accounting measure issued within the USSR;
- In accounting for depreciation, the depreciation was to be charged until fixed asset was fully depreciated. According to Soviet practice provided for the charging of depreciation for as long as the fixed asset remained in use;
- Accounting for bad debts, which was not known in the USSR, was introduced.

The Regulation was really an "accounting step" on the transition from command economy to market economy.

The Regulation aroused considerable interest elsewhere in the USSR. It was translated into the Russian language and published in a number of journals and influenced the drafting of accounting reform measures in other Soviet Republics. It is of special interest because the Regulation was the first measure adopted in any of the constituent republics of the USSR to mark a departure from the path of the Soviet accounting evolution. As pointed out by Bailey (Bailey et al. 1995), this event marked the beginning of the spread of accounting disharmony within the territories comprising the USSR.

In November 1990, leading accounting specialists from Baltic states met in Lithuania to consider the developing situation. The specialists recommended adherence to a singly approach to accounting reform through the adoption of a national chart of accounts and uniform accounting procedures, common to all three Baltic states (Bailey et al. 1995). Unfortunately, this approach was not adopted. The central authorities in each of the Baltic states lacked the willingness, and capacity to implement such a project.

5 Financial Reporting in 1995–2002

The second step started with introduction of the first Accounting Act (AA), which was passed by the Parliament on June 8, 1994 and came into force on January 1, 1995. It was supported by the introduction of the Estonian Commercial Code, which was passed by the Parliament on February 15, 1995 and came into force on September 1, 1995.

The purpose of the AA was to create the legal basis and establish the principles based on internationally accepted accounting principles, for accounting entities operating within the Republic of Estonia. At the same time the internationally accepted accounting principles were defined as the 4th EC Company Directive and the principles, standards and recommendations worked out by the International Accounting Standards Committee (IASC). The AA did not contain a detailed set of rules and can best be characterized as constituting a legal framework. The legal framework was general and applied to all legal entities and physical persons registered as businesses in Estonia (referred to as accounting entities in the Act). The AA was supplemented by a number of methodological recommendations (guidelines) on accounting matters issued by the National Accounting Board (NAB). These recommendations related to such accounting areas as accounting principles, preparation of financial statements, revenue recognition, business combinations and others. Altogether, there were 16 accounting guidelines (*Raamatupidamise Toimkonna juhend—RTJ*s). They set up a conceptual framework of generally accepted accounting principles, revenue recognition, business combinations, government grants, earnings per share and long-term contracts. The only problem was that these guidelines were not for obligatory use. They were only recommendations and in the case of contradictions with the AA, requirements of the AA have to be followed. Estonian Good Accounting Practice (Estonian GAP or EGAP) was introduced. It was declared to be based on internationally recognized accounting principles, which were established with the AA and RTJs. The objective of the annual statements was declared to give a true and fair view (TFV) of the accounting entity's assets, liabilities, owners' equity and profit/loss for the accounting period. The TFV override was declared.

The first AA was in force for 8 years (from 1995 to 2002) and was amended several times. Unfortunately, changes were mostly cosmetic. No attempt was made to enlist the support of the accounting community for changes in accounting practices. There were no publications of drafts of the Regulation on Accounting and the AA prior to their enactment. There have been no general discussions of the purpose or the proper understanding of the required accounting changes or the manner of their implementation.

6 Financial Reporting in 2003–2012

The third step started with the introduction of the new AA, which was passed by Parliament on November 20, 2002 and came into force on January 1, 2003. The purpose of the AA is declared to create the legal bases and establish general requirements for organizing accounting and financial reporting pursuant to internationally recognized principles. This AA, which is still in force, has been amended several times. The requirements of the Act were applicable to annual financial statements for reporting periods that began on January 1, 2003 or later. The new AA is applied to the Republic of Estonia as a legal entity in public law, local governments, all legal entities in private or public law registered in Estonia, sole proprietors, and branches of registered foreign companies that are accounting entities. A separate chapter "Specifications concerning organization of state accounting" was included in the AA. The old AA included 43 paragraphs but the new AA includes 62 paragraphs. The new AA also modified the status of the NAB, which became an independent commission.

The AA was supplemented by a number of guidelines of the NAB, which can be characterized as mini versions of IFRS. All accounting entities must choose one of the following two accounting frameworks:

- accounting principles generally accepted in Estonia (i.e. the EGAP);
- IFRS approved by the European Commission pursuant to the procedure provided for in Regulation No 1606/2002/EC of the European Parliament and of the Council on the application of international accounting standards.

It is necessary to emphasize that since 2003, IFRS are permitted for almost all companies instead of the local accounting guidelines. All listed companies as well as credit and financial institutions and insurance companies are required to apply IFRS in their consolidated and separate financial statements from January 1, 2005. For other companies it is optional to select the EGAP or IFRS for annual and consolidated financial statements. If IFRS have been selected than there is no need to prepare a second set of financial statements in accordance with local accounting guidelines.

The EGAP 2009 consisted of the NAB's guidelines and did not include all areas of accounting or included only in brief (17 EGAP guidelines made together about 400 pages). As the volume of the EGAP guidelines was considerably smaller than IFRS, some accounting areas were covered only very briefly or not at all. In areas, which were not covered by the regulations of the EGAP, the IFRS treatment was recommended, but was not mandatory. Each EGAP guideline contained a brief comparison with the respective IFRS/IAS standards. Nevertheless, there were no conceptual differences between the IFRS and the EGAP 2009. In some ways, the EGAP had less disclosure than the IFRS because it was allowed for SMEs. Therefore, large companies were expected to choose the Full IFRS option while other companies may use the set of Estonian accounting guidelines as their accounting framework. Again, the guidelines had only status of recommendations.

According to the AA the purpose of the annual financial statements (annual report) is declared to give a true and fair view of the financial position, economic performance and cash flows of the accounting entity. This was also an obligatory part of Management's declaration—according to the AA, there was a requirement that the written management's declaration submitted together with the annual financial statements shall be signed and dated by the entire management of the accounting entity declaring their liability for the preparation of the annual report and confirming that:

- the annual financial statements give a TFV of the financial position, economic performance and cash flows of the accounting entity; and
- the accounting entity is carrying on its activities as a going concern.

Unfortunately, the Management's declaration was repealed in 2009.

It is necessary to note that the true and fair view is not defined in the AA, guidelines or anywhere else. The TFV **override** was declared in the old AA, which was in force during 1995–2002, but this is not a case in the new AA. In RTJ 1, the position that the TFV on presenting the financial position, performance and changes in the financial position of an enterprise can still be followed by the management, despite the controversy of the requirements of the AA and the RTJs, is emphasized. The requirements of RTJs can be omitted if these procedures are recognized and explained in public in the notes to the annual accounts. Again, the problem can arise from the fact that the AA has a prevailing character and in case of contradiction between the AA and the guidelines the law will prevail. It should be mentioned that the importance of the TFV never has been an issue in the Estonian accounting theory as well as practice.

The length of a financial year is 12 months. At the end of each financial year, an accounting entity is required to prepare an annual report. It consists of the annual financial statements and the management report that should provide an overview of the activities of the accounting entity, circumstances that are material to the assessment of the financial position and business activities of the accounting entity, significant events that have occurred during the financial year and the likely future developments in the following financial year.

Instead of the former two basic statements (the balance sheet and the income statement), the annual report shall comprise the main statements (balance sheet, income statement, cash flow statement and statement of changes in owner's equity) and notes on the annual report. The auditor's report and, in the case of a company, the profit distribution proposal for the financial year should be annexed to the annual report.

Annual report should be filed at the Commercial Register during 6 months after the end of the financial year.

Unfortunately, there were some shortcomings in the Estonian accounting legislation, which are worth mentioning:

- The definitions of some basic terms differ materially from definitions included in IASB Framework;
- The TFV override is not emphasized in the AA. As the AA prevails over the RTJs, the true and fair recognition of the economic results cannot be guaranteed;
- Some standpoints of the Estonian accounting guidelines were not in line with IFRS.

7 Estonian Good Accounting Practice from 2013

Until 2013 the EGAP was based on the Full IFRS. EGAP included 17 guidelines what could be characterized as simplified versions of IFRS. Because the main users of Full IFRS are listed companies, financial institutions and other big companies but in Estonia about 99 % of undertakings are micro, small, or medium size companies, it is too complicate to use Full IFRS as a basis for the EGAP. That is why the NAB decided in 2011 to switch from Full IFRS to IFRS for SMEs.

Before changes in the EGAP, the AA was updated in accordance with changes in the business world. In 2009 the requirement for preparation of corporate governance report was included. According to the AA, the corporate governance report shall be prepared in such way, which provides a professional and interested person with the opportunity to obtain information concerning the activities of the accounting entity as regards the governance principles implemented in the company. In 2012, the annual report taxonomy was established by the Government of Estonia.

Pursuant to the AA, all entities are able to choose whether to prepare their financial statements in accordance with IFRS adopted by the European Commission or the EGAP. The EGAP 2013 shall be applied by such entities that do not need to prepare complete IFRS financial statements (for example, smaller and medium sized entities). From 2013 it is based on IFRS for SMEs but may in certain sectors permit or require methods different from IFRS for SMEs and set different requirements for disclosures in the notes. The guidelines of the NAB (Table 1) contain references to the specific paragraphs of IFRS for SMEs. For example, the reference to 13.4 of IFRS for SMEs refers to paragraph 4 of section 13 "Inventories" of IFRS for SMEs.

The guidelines of the NAB focus on the accounting areas that are relevant in Estonia. Therefore, the guidelines of the NAB do not cover all areas that are regulated by IFRS for SMEs, but only those that according to the NAB are relevant for a large number of entities in Estonia. In those areas in which the guidelines of the NAB do not specify a particular accounting policy but which are regulated by

Table 1 Guidelines (RTJ) issued by the National Accounting Board (2013)

No	Topic	IFRS for SMEs
RTJ 1	General Principles for Preparing the Financial Statements	RTJ 1 is based on IFRS for SMEs sections 2, 3, 8, 10, 22, 30, 32 and on concepts defined in section 2 "Concepts and Pervasive Principles".
RTJ 2	Requirements for Presentation in the Financial Statements	RTJ 2 is based on IFRS for SMEs sections 2, 3, 4, 5, 6, 7, 8, 33 and on concepts defined in section 2 "Concepts and Pervasive Principles".
RTJ 3	Financial Instruments	RTJ 3 is based on IFRS for SMEs sections 11, 12, 22 and on concepts defined in section 2 "Concepts and Pervasive Principles".
RTJ 4	Inventories	RTJ 4 is based on IFRS for SMEs sections 13, 25, 27 and on concepts defined in section 2 "Concepts and Pervasive Principles".
RTJ 5	Property, Plant and Equipment and Intangible Assets	RTJ 5 takes into consideration accounting policies prescribed in several sections of IFRS for SMEs, including 17, 18, 19, 25, 27 and concepts defined in section 2 "Concepts and Pervasive Principles" and "Glossary of Terms".
RTJ 6	Investment Property	RTJ 6 is based on IFRS for SMEs sections 16 and 11 and on concepts defined in section 2 "Concepts and Pervasive Principles".
RTJ 7	Biological Assets	RTJ 7 is based on IFRS for SMEs section 34 and on concepts defined in section 2 "Concepts and Pervasive Principles" and "Glossary of Terms".
RTJ 8	Provisions, Contingent Liabilities & Contingent Assets	RTJ 8 is based on IFRS for SMEs sections 21, 28 and 29 and concepts defined in "Glossary of Terms".
RTJ 9	Accounting for Leases	RTJ 9 is based on IFRS for SMEs section 20 and on concepts defined in section 2 "Concepts and Pervasive Principles" and "Glossary of Terms".
RTJ 10	Revenue Recognition	RTJ 10 is based on IFRS for SMEs section 23 and concepts defined in section 2 "Concepts and Pervasive Principles".
RTJ 11	Business Combinations and Accounting for Subsidiaries and Associates	RTJ 11 is based on IFRS for SMEs sections 9, 14, 15, 19, 22 and 30 and on concepts defined in section 2 "Concepts and Pervasive Principles" and the "Glossary of Terms".
RTJ 12	Government Assistance	RTJ 12 is based on IFRS for SMEs section 24 "Government Grants" and concepts defined in section 2 "Concepts and Pervasive Principles".
RTJ 13	Liquidation and closing reports	RTJ 13 is based on the general principles and policies of IFRS for SMEs and it takes into consideration international practice.
RTJ 14	Non-Profit Associations and Foundations	RTJ 14 is based on the general principles described in IFRS for SMEs, International Public Sector Accounting Standards (IPSAS), considering also international practice.
RTJ 15	Disclosures in the Notes	The requirements of the guideline ASBG 15 regarding information disclosure take into

(continued)

Table 1 (continued)

No	Topic	IFRS for SMEs
		consideration relevant requirements of IFRS for SMEs.
RTJ 17	Service Concession Arrangements	RTJ 17 is based on Section 34 of IFRS for SMEs and on concepts defined in sections 2 “Concepts and Pervasive Principles”.

Table 2 The main changes in the EGAP 2013

Accounting issue	EGAP 2009	EGAP 2013
Financial assets	Fair value through comprehensive income statement	Fair value through profit and loss
Investment property	Fair value or cost model	Cost model (Fair value model if cost-benefit approach is followed)
Accounting for associates	Equity method	Equity method, cost method and fair value method
Accounting for goodwill	Impairment of goodwill	Amortization
Accounting transactions with non-consolidating entities	Parent entity and business entity concepts were used	Through equity
PPE held for sale	Was classified	Is not classified
Development expenses	Capitalized	Expensed or capitalized
Borrowing costs	Expensed or capitalized	Expensed
Government grants	Net method is allowed	Recognition as income using the gross amount at the moment when obligations are fulfilled or using net method

IFRS for SMEs, it is recommended to use the accounting policy described in IFRS for SMEs as the basis. Table 2 compares the new and old EGAP.

The new changes in accounting legislation will take place soon. The Member States of the EU shall bring into force the laws, regulations and administrative provisions necessary to comply with the Accounting Directive 2013/34/EU by 20 July 2015.

8 Conclusion

The article dealt with the development of financial reporting in Estonia. After the fall of Soviet Union and declaration of independence, there were several accounting reforms.

The changes in accounting and financial reporting which took place during 1990–1994, 1995–2002, 2003–2012 and in 2013 were characterized. The analysis showed that the development of financial reporting and accounting has been based more on the Anglo-Saxon-IFRS standards than on the EU Directives.

References

Alver J, Alver L (2005) The development of accounting in the Republic of Estonia in 1918–1940. The 28th Annual Congress of the European Accounting Association. Göteborg, 18–20 May 2005. Programme and Collected Abstracts, p. 85

Alver J, Alver L (2008) Development of accounting and implementation of international financial reporting standards in Estonia. In: McGee RW (ed) Accounting reform in transition and developing economies. Springer, New York, pp 101–113

Alver J, Alver L, Mackevičius J, Paupa V, Bailey D (1998) Baltic States. In: Alexander D, Archer S (eds) European accounting guide, 3rd edn. Harcourt Brace & Company, San Diego, CA, pp 1464–1475

Alver J, Alver L, Mackevičius J, Paupa V (2001) Baltic states. In: Alexander D, Archer S (eds) European accounting guide, 4th edn. Aspen Law & Business, New York, pp 1481–1504

Alver L, Alver J, Talpas L (2013) Institutional pressures and the role of the state in designing the financial accounting and reporting model in Estonia. In: Albu CN, Mustaţă RV (eds) Accounting in Central and Eastern Europe. Research in accounting in emerging economics, vol 13. Emerald, Bingley, pp 91–120

Bailey D (1995) Accounting in transition in the transitional economy. Eur Account Rev 4(4): 595–623

Bailey D, Alver J, Mackevičius J, Paupa V (1995) Accounting law reform in the Baltic States: the initial steps. Eur Account Rev 4(4):685–711

Haldma T (2001) Accounting and Auditing in Estonia. In Audit & accounting. Managers School, Riga, pp 130–139

Haldma T (2003) Harmonization of Estonian accounting system with European framework. In Estonian economic policy on the way towards the European Union. Berliner Wissenschafts-Verlag GmbH, Tallinn, pp 503–512

Haldma T (2006) Factors affecting accounting development in the harmonization process with the international framework: the case of Estonia. In: Gregoriu GN, Gaber M (eds) International accounting: standards, regulation and financial reporting. Elsevier, Oxford, pp 457–482

Jaanus E (1980) About teaching of economic science in Tartu in by past centuries. Valgus, Tallinn

Kovalyov VV, Roshnov VS, Novodvorsky VD, Sokolov JV, Larionov AD (1991) Union of Soviet Socialist Republics. In: Alexander D, Archer S (eds) Comprehensive European accounting guide. Harcourt Brace Jovanovich, San Diego, CA, pp 991–1027

Krinal V (1999) About the past and the present of the Faculty of Economics of Tartu University. Tartu University Press, Tartu

Piirimäe H (1982) History of Tartu University I (1632–1798). Valgus, Tallinn

Richard J (2003) Accounting in Eastern Europe: from communism to capitalism. In: Walton P, Haller A, Raffournier B (eds) International accounting, 2nd edn. Thomson, London, pp 332–347

Sokolov YV, Kovalev VV, Bychkova SM, Smirnova IA (1998) Russian federation. In: Alexander D, Archer S (eds) European accounting guide, 3rd edn. Harcourt Brace & Company, San Diego, CA, pp 1612–1652

Tikk J (2010) The Internationalization of the Estonian accounting system. Ann Univ Petroşani Econ 10(2):341–352

Poland. Implementation of IFRS in Poland: Main Effects and Problems

Anna Szychta and Przemysław Kabalski

Abstract The chapter presents stages and problems in the reform of the Polish accounting regulation system since the early 1990s. It explains the effects of International Financial Reporting Standards (IFRS) application in 2005 by companies listed on the Warsaw Stock Exchange and highlights the main problems arising from the use of IFRS by companies in Poland, including the organizational, social and cultural dimensions. The changes that have been taking place since the early 1990s in financial accounting regulations and practice in Poland are connected with the reintroduction and development of a market-based economy and its adaptation to progressing globalization. The change process involves the gradual adjustment of financial accounting regulations to the requirements of the European Union and IFRS. Poland was at the forefront of European countries in terms of IFRS adoption. Nevertheless, mandatory use of IFRS is regarded in Poland as a milestone marking the beginning of a new epoch. The transition to IFRS resulted for many Polish listed companies in significant changes in their financial position and performance as presented in financial statements. Empirical research indicates that Polish accounting regulations are slightly more conservative than IFRS. The road to IFRS implementation and application is obstructed by a number of organizational, cultural and social barriers. The authors show that adaptation to IFRS in Poland has turned out to be a slow and difficult process.

1 Introduction

The adoption of International Financial Reporting Standards (IAS/IFRS) in Poland in 2005 is regarded as a milestone event. The mandatory application of these standards by listed companies (and optional by other entities) is an important process with multi-dimensional effects. However, it is important to note that prior to the adoption of European Union (EU) Regulation 1606/2002, the Polish

A. Szychta (✉) • P. Kabalski
Faculty of Management, Department of Accounting, University of Łódź, Łódź, Poland
e-mail: aszychta@uni.lodz.pl; pkabal@interia.pl

D. Bensadon, N. Praquin (eds.), *IFRS in a Global World*,
DOI 10.1007/978-3-319-28225-1_26

accounting regulation (PAR) system had selectively incorporated International Accounting Standards (IAS) since the mid-1990s.

The aim of this chapter is:

1. a synthetic presentation of stages in the reform of the Polish accounting system since the early 1990s, which aimed at its gradual adjustment to international solutions,
2. identification of the effects of IFRS application in 2005 by companies listed on the Warsaw Stock Exchange (WSE), and
3. highlighting the main problems arising from the use of these standards by companies in Poland, including the organizational, social and cultural dimensions.

This chapter is based on a literature review, analysis and interpretation PAR, the findings of research conducted by other authors, and their own studies investigating selected problems connected with IAS/IFRS application in Poland.

2 International Accounting Standards as an Element of the Accounting Reform in Poland After 1990

2.1 Stages in the Accounting Reform in Poland Since the Early 1990s

The transformation of accounting regulation and practice in the period of over 20 years of market economy development in Poland can be divided into four stages (see also Jaruga and Kabalski 2010):

1. preparatory stage of accounting reform (1991–1994),
2. creation of the Polish system of accountancy regulation conforming to the EU and IAS requirements (1995–2001),
3. modernization and adjustments of financial accounting regulations to the changing international and domestic regulatory context (since 2002),
4. implementation and application of IAS/IFRS by listed companies and other entities (since 2005).

In the years 1991–1994, accountancy in Poland was regulated by the Decree of the Finance Minister on the Principles of Accounting and the Commercial Code (in force from 1934 to 2000), applicable to business companies. Although this decree was the only implemented regulation to the 31.01.1989 Act on Financial Management of State Enterprises and the 19.12.1980 Act on Tax Liabilities, it was the first important step towards adjustment of Polish accounting to the market economy environment, because the principal rules of financial accounting, the measurement of balance-sheet items and income determination that it introduced were based on the Fourth EU Directive. Moreover, the provision that it contained, stating that "matters not regulated by the Decree should be guided by principles provided by accounting theory and applied in common practice" (Rozprządzenie 1991, para. 3.6), enabled the use of IAS rules despite there being no direct reference to these regulations. The impact of IAS on accounting practice was rather limited at that time, but the possibility to adopt the solutions that they prescribed provided the starting point for presenting international solutions to the Polish accounting community, mainly in a monthly journal *Rachunkowość* (e.g. Skowroński 1990; Mearns 1993; Skowroński and Jarugowa 1994; Gottlieb 1994).

The second stage of accountancy development in Poland began in early 1995, with the coming into operation of the Accounting Act (AA) of 29 September 1994 and the Act on Auditors and their Self-government of 13 October 1994.

The AA laid down rules for bookkeeping, stocktaking, balance-sheet items' valuation and income determination, and the preparation of financial statements (including the cash-flow statement) by business entities and capital groups. The rules of this Act apply to business entities including banks, insurers and public sector units. Through the enactment of this law the importance of accounting was recognised, and its principles were stated in a comprehensive way in one legal act of the highest order, not counting the Constitution.

The main objectives of this legal act were:

1. the adjustment of Polish accounting solutions to the principles adopted in EU countries and those prescribed in IAS, providing these are compatible with EU Directives;
2. definition, uniformization and stabilization of the requirements which should be fulfilled by accountancy and increasing the clarity of adopted solutions, so as to ensure the security of business operation for participants of the market economy and to promote the development of the capital market in Poland;
3. separation of the accounting system from unstable tax legislation, with the possibility to align tax and accounting regulations (through deferred income tax).

As a result of the enactment in 1994 of the AA, PAR were largely harmonised with the Fourth, Seventh and other EU Directives nearly 10 years before Poland's accession to the EU, which took place on 1.05.2004. Implementation in this Act of the accounting principles adopted by the EU in the form of Directives, as well as some of the IAS, meant that the accounting regulation system that developed in Poland in the 1990s combined a conservative continental tradition with the liberal Anglo-American approach. The adoption of IAS provisions required a transition to an investor-oriented approach, with its emphasis on measuring financial performance of enterprises for decision making purposes. It was a difficult and slow process, involving further changes in the accounting regulation system, education and attitudes of professional accountants.

The third stage of accountancy reform in Poland in the period of implementing modern market economy instruments began with the bringing into operation of the comprehensively revised version of the AA in 2000, effective from 1 January 2002. The amendment of the existing law was undertaken as a result of the need to eliminate the deficiencies of the AA and to ensure better adjustment of accounting solutions to the needs of capital market, as well as the participation of Poland in the global harmonization process through the introduction of regulations consistent with the solutions in IAS.

The main amendments to the AA included:

1. precise formulation of the basic principles of accounting and definition of fundamental concepts from the IASC's *Framework for the Preparation and Presentation of Financial Statements*;
2. new provisions addressing issues not regulated before in Poland by accounting law, such as: financial instruments, construction contracts, business combinations, leases, impairment, valuation in fair value;
3. modification or more precise articulation of terms and principles as a result of inclusion of new versions of IAS dealing with deferred income tax and consolidation of financial statements.

The amended version of the AA includes a direct reference to IAS (Ustawaz dnia 29.09.1994 r., art. 10, section 3), stating that "in matters not regulated by the provisions of the Act, entities may apply national accounting standards as issued by the Accounting Standards Committee in adopting their accounting policies. In the case of absence of a relevant national standard, entities may use International Accounting Standards." The optional character of this reference to IAS means that it was not binding and was only a guideline for business entities. Despite the ambiguity of this provision (lack of specification what the legislator meant by IAS), it played a positive role in shaping the perception of accountancy regulation through raising the awareness of the imminent existence in Poland of two parallel legislative systems based respectively on EU Directives and IAS (Dadacz and Gdański 2005, p. 3).

In Poland, as in other European countries with a legislative approach to accounting regulation, there was a need for systemic reorientation towards developing a parallel regulatory mechanism which would provide a counterbalance to strict legal rules with operation frequently delayed (Jaruga 1999, p. 9). Following the example of Anglo-American countries, a decision was taken to issue national accounting standards (NAS) to supplement legislative acts and implementing regulation by the Finance Minister, the reason being that provisions of the law regulate matters in general, and revision of the law requires time, which hampers quick and flexible reaction to the changing market economy environment. An important step in this direction had already been taken in the second phase of the reform, i.e. in 1997—it was the formation by the President of the Securities and Exchange Commission of the Accounting Standards Committee, headed by Professor Alicja Jaruga of the University of Łódź. It was replaced by the Accounting Standards Committee, established under the 2000 amendment to the AA. In the years 2003–2014, this Committee issued eight standards (expressly oriented towards IAS).

The inclusion in PAR of many of the provisions directly from IAS since 2002 meant considerable progress in the development of national accounting framework allowing much greater comparability with IAS. Nevertheless, there still were some differences between these two sets of regulation. The World Bank reported in 2002 that comparing PAR with IFRS across 164 requirements they found 50 % fully comparable, 15 % broadly comparable, and 35 % non comparable or nonexistent (based on Krzywda and Schroeder 2007, p. 81). It should be stressed that successive revisions of the AA were not aimed at the complete harmonization of PAR with IAS (Krzywda and Schroeder 2007, p. 81) but sought to ensure that financial statements of business entities provide information useful in making economic decisions by investors, management and other stakeholders, and to provide a basis for evaluating the competitiveness of companies and reducing investment and financial risk (see e.g. Lisiecka-Zając 1999).

The fourth stage of accounting development began in 2005, when Poland, as a member of the EU, was obliged to incorporate IFRS into the national accounting system under Regulation No. 1606/2002 of the European Parliament and the Council of 19 July 2002 on the Application of IAS. Incorporation of Regulation 1606/2002 in Poland was in the successive amendment to the AA of 27 August 2004. The Polish legislator extended the requirement to apply IFRS to all banks and permitted their use by some other entities. The revised Act allowed issuers admitted to trading on regulated markets, issuers seeking admission, parent companies and their subsidiaries and affiliates presenting consolidated financial statements under IFRS to present their single-entity statements in accordance with those standards. The obligatory and voluntary scope of IFRS application is shown in Fig. 1.

After 2005, PAR were revised repeatedly because of the need to make adjustments to changes in some of the IAS/IFRS (relating to e.g. consolidation and business combinations) and changes introduced in 2006 to EU Directives, and the need to incorporate revisions and specific solutions in commercial law (e.g. Commercial Code in force since 2001 or Act on Investment Funds). Currently,

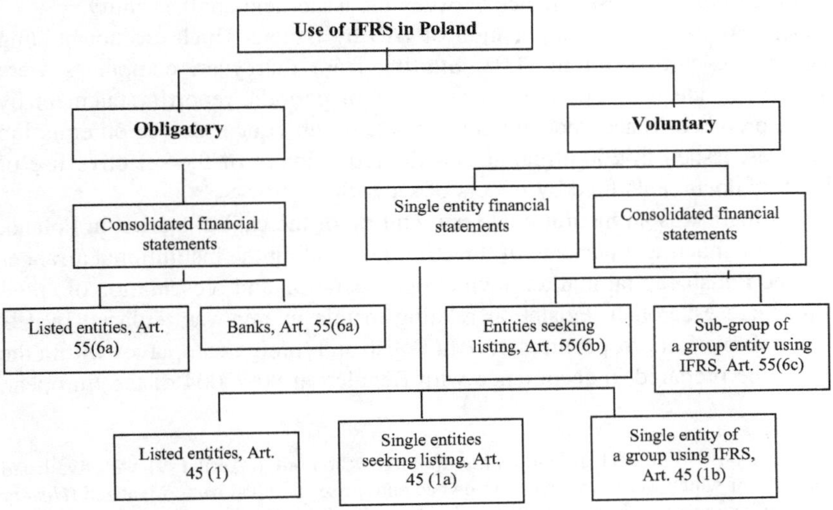

Fig. 1 Use of IFRS in Poland as required and permitted by the AA revised in 2004. Source: Krzywda and Schroeder (2007, p. 82), based on Helin (2006)

legislative work is in progress to prepare an amendment incorporating Directive 2013/34/UE of the European Parliament and the Council on financial reporting.

The changes in PAR and practice, oriented to the consolidation of a market economy in the country and adapting it to the challenges resulting from globalization processes, are progressing steadily, although not without certain problems and limitations, which will be discussed in parts 3 and 4 of this chapter.

2.2 IAS in Polish Capital Market Regulations

IAS were first incorporated into Polish capital market regulations in 1994.[1] Under the Decree on Emission Prospectuses and Periodic Reports, foreign issuers listed on the Warsaw Stock Exchange (WSE) or seeking listing could present a cash flow statement prepared in accordance with IAS 7, and in 1996 foreign issuers were permitted to prepare all their financial statements under IAS (Ignatowski 2009, pp. 372–373).

A relevant regulation of the Council of Ministers of 1998 introduced new rules concerning the contents of the emission prospectus and memorandum, thus enabling the preparation of financial statements, including consolidated statements, in accordance with IAS or US GAAP. Issuers were required to disclose the differences between adopted accounting principles and methods under IAS or US GAAP and domestic regulations in the form of notes (descriptive commentary) and quantitative explanation of the effect of using these regulations on the elements of financial statements. The latter requirement was limited in 2001 to disclosing at least the effect on equity, including the financial result. The use of IAS or US GAAP also applied to the business alliance between the issuer and another entity.

Further extension of the application of IAS by issuers which are not holding companies was introduced in 2003. Starting from that year, companies were required to include in the emission prospectus or periodic report a statement by segments, prepared in accordance with IAS 14. A subsequent decree on emission prospectuses, issued in 2004, maintained the requirement of the selective use of IAS/IFRS in documents filed by issuers of securities.

In 2005 there was an institutional restructuring of the capital market in Poland. As a result of enacting a package of three laws regulating the institutional arrangement of the Polish capital market, including preparation and presentation of emission prospectuses, Polish legislation relating to this matter was replaced by EU legislation. Emission prospectuses of both Polish and foreign companies within the EU should be prepared in accordance with Regulation 809/2004 of the European

[1] WSE was established in 1991. It held its first trading session on 16 April 1991 with five listed companies, all of which were formerly state-owned enterprises that had been privatized (*History* 2014). At the beginning of February 2014, 378 companies (335 domestic and 43 foreign) were listed on the WSE main market and 74 on the WSE parallel market (71 domestic and 3 foreign) (*Analizy* 2014).

Commission. This means that consolidated financial statements in emission prospectuses of Polish issuers—excluding special cases—and foreign issuers from the EU are to be prepared according to IFRS as adopted by the EU under Regulation 1606/2002.

3 The Main Effects of IFRS Adoption in Poland in 2005

Hoogendoorn (2006, p. 23) pointed out that adoption of IFRS in Europe in 2005 was the most revolutionary financial reporting development since Pacioli's doubly-entry bookkeeping, even more revolutionary than adoption of Fourth or Seventh EU Directive. This is because IFRS constitute a uniform accounting language in Europe, obligatory for about 7000 companies, but optionally used by a much larger number of business entities. In Poland, mandatory application of IFRS is regarded as an epoch-making development (Jaruga et al. 2007; Sobańska 2007), a new chapter in the development of PAR—appropriate to the new situation created by Poland's membership in the EU (Walińska 2012).

Implementation of IFRS in Poland has been the subject of numerous publications, mostly dealing with the impact of these standards on companies' financial reporting practices. The works published in 2005–2009 were primarily concerned with presenting the results of empirical research investigating the effect of IFRS on representing the financial position and the performance of public companies after first-time obligatory application of IFRS in 2005. They also analysed factors affecting the value of items in financial statements and criticized the differences between the formats and scope of information presentation used in financial statements and those prescribed in PAR, pointing out that it impairs fundamental analysis of companies (Ignatowski 2009, pp. 392–393). More recent publications analyse the results of adopted methods of measuring balance-sheet items, the format and contents of financial statements, disclosure and relevance of particular reported items, such as impairment and comprehensive income,[2] and organizational as well as behavioral problems arising from IFRS application (Kabalski et al., 2013; Kabalski 2012).

Below are presented the main objectives and conclusions from three comprehensive empirical research projects carried out in Poland just before and after IFRS adoption in 2005 (Table 1).

Analysis of financial statements for 2001 and 2003 conducted by Krzywda and Schroeder (2007, p. 83) has shown that the listed entities disclosed the main areas of differences between IFRS and PAR in the form of description only (qualitative differences). For 2004, companies were obliged to quantify the effect of the introduction of IFRS on their profit after tax and owners' equity (quantitative

[2] Publications in Polish are too numerous to be quoted here. Publications in English include e.g. Piosik and Poniatowska (2013) and Szychta and de la Rosa (2012).

Table 1 The main empirical research on effects of the implementation of IAS/IFRS in Poland

Authors	Sample period	Number and type of companies	Aims of research
Krzywda and Schroeder (2007)	2001, 2003 and 2004	Entities listed on the WSE: 73 in 2001 and 2003; 172 in 2004, including 101 to identify differences	– Analysis of the qualitative and quantitative data on the differences between PAR and IFRS – Identification of the type and frequency of occurrence of differences concerning equity and net income – Analysis of the Gray's index of conservatism for companies included in WIG, WIG20, TECHWIG and WIRR,[a] and by sectors of activity (branches)
Jaruga et al. (2007, 2008)	2004–2005	255 WSE listed companies, including 171 entities which prepared consolidated financial statements Effect of IFRS on the value of assets was examined in 79 companies, on equity and net income— in 103 companies	– Identification of the direction, level and causes of changes in the value of assets, equity and net income in consolitated financial statements prepared under IFRS in comparison with PAR
Ignatowski (2009)	2005	144 groups of companies listed on the WSH. Because of lack of complete data the analysis covered 120 groups	– Verification of hypotheses stating that: 1. the Polish accounting system is more conservative than IFRS, 2. IFRS have a stronger impact on large WIG20 companies than on smaller entities included in WIRR – Investigation of the scale of fair value application by WSE listed entities

Source: Own elaboration based on the above references

[a]The WIG20 represented the biggest 20 and most frequently traded companies, the WIG included the next 50 largest entities, the WIRR was a small company index and the TECHWIG consisted of companies in the information technology, media and telecommunication sectors (Krzywda and Schroeder 2007, p. 98)

differences). This research revealed that these items under PAR were materially understated in comparison with IFRS equivalents. The book value of equity in 2004 was understated by an average of between 6 % and 9 %, and post tax earnings were understated by an average of 35 %.

The quantitative differences were analysed by the frequency with which they were reported by financial statements preparers in 2004. Krzywda and Schroeder (2007, p. 97) identified (in 101 companies) 345 individual differences concerning the balance sheet. The four most frequently reported differences were:

1. revaluation of property, plant and equipment (PP&E) in accordance with IAS 16,
2. consequent adjustments to the estimate of deferred tax as result of the reported differences,
3. adjustments to goodwill on consolidation in accordance with IFRS 3,
4. discounting of long-term financial assets and liabilities in accordance with IFRS 37.

The authors have also analysed the Gray's index of conservatism (GIC).[3] In several of the 101 companies this index was 1, which means no impact of IFRS application on equity and net income. Insignificant changes in equity (between 0.5 % and 5 %) were noted in 60 % of the entities, and in net income—in 45 %. This result shows that in 2004 the effect of IFRS on these items was insignificant in every second company listed on the WSE. In the case of companies in which this effect was significant, the analysis has highlighted the more stubborn areas of difference which persisted over time in Poland: they relate mainly to the dominance of historical costs for fixed assets and are essentially fiscal driven (Krzywda and Schroeder 2007, p. 105).

The research carried out by Jaruga et al. (2007) examined the financial statements prepared at the end of accounting years 2004 and 2005. Of the 79 companies studied, the majority reported at the end of 2004 an increase in the value of assets (64.6 %), and the remaining companies reported either a decrease (31.6 %) or no change (3.8 %) in consolidated financial statements under IFRS in comparison with PAR. The greatest positive changes in assets occurred in 10 companies—between 14.14 % and 63.51 %. Value decreases were very small, mostly between 1 % and 0 %. The use of IFRS caused an increase in equity in the majority of companies (76.5 %), a decrease in 20.6 % and no change in 2.9 % of entities. The greatest positive changes were noted in 10 companies—from 39.45 % to 92.58 %. Equity decreases were relatively small, only in two cases they were −52 % and −62 %. The transition to IFRS resulted in an increase in the value of net income in 58.8 % of the entities. The greatest positive changes (from 66.47 % to 355.56 %) were reported by five companies. The decreases of net income were generally small; more than 50 % of the decreases were around 1 % (Jaruga et al. 2007, 2008).

The empirical research carried out by Jaruga et al. (2007) has confirmed the main causes of changes in the value of assets, equity and net income as identified by Krzywda and Schroeder (2007) on the basis of an analysis of financial statements prepared by public companies in Poland at the end of 2004. Jaruga et al. (2008) summed up their study by concluding that the transition to IFRS brought significant

[3] GIC is the ratio which shows the difference between a company's disclosed profit (determined in accordance with national regulations) and its adjusted profit as calculated in accordance with international method, e.g. IFRS. This ratio is calculated as: $1-[(R_A-R_D):|R_A|]$, where: R_A—adjusted profit, R_D—disclosed profit. Companies with a ratio of more than one would appear to employ accounting practice with outcomes which are relatively optimistic in relation to the yardstick, whereas companies with a ratio of less than one would appear to be relatively pessimistic or "conservative" (see Gray 1980, p. 67). GIC is also calculated for other items, e.g. owner's equity.

changes in the financial position and performance as reported by entities, and these changes show some economic potential of companies in Poland that was hidden under the AA, and bring net values of companies' assets closer to their market values. The results of this empirical research thus indicate that PAR are more conservative than IFRS regulations.

The most extensive research in Poland on the Gray's index of conservatism was carried out by Ignatowski (2009, pp. 402–421). The research was motivated by the ambiguity of the results of earlier studies. An analysis of the financial statements of 120 publicly listed companies in Poland led him to the conclusion that the hypothesis on greater conservatism of PAR compared with IFRS cannot be verified positively (although the mean value of the aggregate index for all the companies indicates a higher level of conservatism in PAR). Also, the hypothesis on the stronger impact of the IFRS system on large (WIG20) companies than on smaller (WIRR) companies seems to be questionable.

Ignatowski (2009, p. 439) emphasises in his study the traditionalism of Polish companies, which manifests itself in the approach to the presentation of financial statements and to making use of simplification at the time of the transition to IFRS. Traditionalism is also evident in the area of valuation. All studies conducted by different authors to examine Polish companies have revealed rare use of fair value (obviously, in areas where it is not obligatory). The reasons for such an attitude are not clear—it may be a dislike for new solutions (as Ignatowski is inclined to believe), domination of orientation to the future, or just pragmatism (because the use of fair value is more difficult and expensive for a company than valuation at cost).

4 Important Problems Concerning the Use of IAS/IFRS in Poland

4.1 Organizational Structures of Polish Enterprises in the Context of IFRS

The organizational structure is for many Polish companies a source of serious difficulties in effective implementation of the IFRS model. The traditional hierarchical structure is still a prevailing type in Poland. Its main drawback is that it hampers the flow of information between the different sections of an enterprise, which is a prerequisite for effective application of IFRS.

Findings of many research projects confirm the dominance in Polish enterprises of the traditional organizational structure, corresponding to the mechanistic conception of management (Gadomska-Lila and Lozano Platonoff 2011; KPMG 2009; Staniec and Zakrzewska-Bielawska 2010). The prevailing type is the hierarchical structure, composed of separate units (departments) with clearly assigned tasks and responsibilities. Free information flow is mainly within the organizational units,

Table 2 The characteristics of the mechanistic organization versus IFRS requirements

Characteristics necessary for effective IFRS implementation	Weaknesses of mechanistic organization type[a]
Cooperation between accountants and other functions	Strict organizational boundaries, weak coordination between departments
Interdisciplinary approach to solution of problems	Fragmentary approach to solution of problems, especially new ones
Support for accountants from other specialists	Passivity and indifference of staff to tasks not specified as their duties
Flexibility of solutions and the use of judgement	Very detailed specification of tasks, which favours thoughtlessness and blind obedience

Source: own elaboration
[a] Morgan (1997, Chap. 2)

whereas between the units it is rather weak. This results in emergence of organizational "silos", i.e. isolated sections of an enterprise with relatively large autonomy, but lacking effective cooperation and communication with other sections. They put their own goals before the goals of the enterprise as a whole. Matrix and network type, or process-based, structures are rather rare.

The mechanistic organizational structure dominant in Polish enterprises is evidently incompatible with IFRS requirements, which is shown in Table 2.

4.2 Organizational Culture of Polish Enterprises in the Context of IFRS

Another source of difficulties in the implementation and application of IFRS in Polish companies is their organizational culture. According to Kostera (1997, pp. 15–17), Polish enterprises generally exhibit features of counter-effective culture, such as distinction between "us" and "them" in various configurations (production staff versus design staff, staff versus management, blue collar versus white collar staff, etc.). Instead of a common culture there are separate subcultures which not only do not cooperate, but sometimes also engage in unreasonable competition. Interviews with accountants conducted by this author have revealed this to be one of the major difficulties in their work. It is a serious obstacle to the use of IFRS. Another feature of counter-effective culture is its being petrified and closed, in some cases so much so that sanation of the situation is not possible.

Kostera's opinion was formulated in 1997, so things may have changed over the 14 years that have passed since then. There must have been some changes for the better in this respect, but it would not be reasonable to expect a situation radically changed to the dominance of pro-effective culture. Gadomska-Lila wrote (2008, pp. 129 – 130) that organizational culture in Polish firms is changing slowly because of deeply-rooted negative models. Gradually, there is more team work, effective cooperation, flexibility and the ability to adapt to new conditions, but the situation is still far from ideal.

Heidtman and Wolfarth (2010) conducted a survey of 600 employees from 10 Polish enterprises (large and middle-sized). According to them, the results are so consistent that they can be regarded as reflecting the general situation. The authors found that Polish companies are dominated by "the culture of hierarchy and effective operation and the culture of the market, oriented to achievement". In the context of IFRS, domination of the culture of hierarchy poses a serious problem. It is one of the four main types of organizational culture; its characteristics correspond to bureaucracy. Its manifestations in the studied companies include, according to Heidtman and Wolfarth, unchangeability of roles, rigid arrangement of positions, subordination to procedures ("managing internal affairs through a number of formal rules and regulations", "procedures determine the pulse of life in the firm"), stability of the environment, attaching little importance to creativity and innovativeness (only higher-level management sees their importance), too little teamwork, openness and cooperation. These are conditions unfavourable to the application of IFRS.

Societal culture is among the factors that influence organizational culture. Polish societal culture in the context of business has been the subject of numerous studies, including international research. One of the most interesting and extensive studies was the GLOBE project, which was launched in the early 1990s under the scientific management of House (Spector et al. 2001, pp. 280–281). 170 researchers participated in this project. Information was collected from nearly 18,000 managers from 62 countries/cultures around the world. Discussion of the findings relating to Poland will be restricted here to those relevant to IFRS implementation.

In the GLOBE research, Poland holds 60th place in terms of orientation to the future. The low level of this orientation indicates, among others, problems with long-term planning (Zawadzka 2010, p. 56). It can be reasonably assumed that in relation to financial reporting it impairs understanding of the sense of future projections in recognition of transactions and events. Countries of Eastern Europe (including Poland) exhibit a high (though not highest) degree of power distance, and the lowest degree of institutional collectivism (together with countries of German and Latin Europe and Latin America). This means that people do not value collectivism and cooperation in an organization. At the same time, Eastern Europe is characterised by strong intragroup collectivism, which is mainly connected with family integrity (Zawadzka 2010, p. 60). The division of the world into a narrow circle of "us" (family, friends) and the alien rest of the people ("them"), called familism, which is typical of Poles, and influences social relations and attitudes at work (Nawojczyk 2006, p. 3067).

A more precise characterization of Polish societal culture in relation to the organization is provided by research carried out by Polish scientists. Features identified by Murdoch (1999, pp. 105–107) include formalization, attachment to hierarchy, inactivity, instilled helplessness and low ability to cooperate. According to Kożusznik (2002, pp. 236–245), Poles are characterised, as regards societal culture, by great power distance, a strong tendency to avoid uncertainty, and individualism. Polish societal culture characteristics influence the functioning in an organization and result in the following problems (Czubocha 2010, pp. 5–6):

1. narrow specialization and strictly defined roles and duties,
2. dominance of vertical communication,
3. absence of free communication between management and subordinates,
4. passivity of employees, who do show individual initiative but wait for orders from their superiors,
5. difficulties with teamwork,
6. conviction of employers and managers that employees should be under strict control.

To sum up, it has been found that Polish organizational culture is permeated (or even dominated) by characteristics that are not compatible with the IFRS model. The chief negative features are:

1. great power distance,
2. orientation to the past and problems with strategic thinking,
3. low level of institutional collectivism,
4. passivity of employees (waiting for orders from superiors),
5. preference for detailed and rigorous regulations.

4.3 The **Homo Sovieticus** *Personality of Employees in Poland Versus IFRS*

Another major problem is the mental suitability of Polish accountants to the "spirit" of IFRS. It seems worth considering whether certain personality traits, common in Poles, predispose them (or not) to IFRS-style accounting, especially in the context of the *homo sovieticus* (*HS*) syndrome.

The term *HS* was created by Zinovyev, a Russian writer and philosopher, to denote a personality type whose character, way of thinking and attitude were shaped by a totalitarian system (more specifically, communism). Characteristic features of the *HS* personality, according to Zinovyev, are enslavement (total submission to communist authorities), lack of intellectual independence, and lack of individuality and dignity. The term *HS* was popularised by Rev. Prof. J. Tischner, mainly in an essay "Solidarity Ethics and *Homo sovieticus*" published in 1992. It should be noted that for Tishner *HS* had a slightly different connotation than the original meaning—it was "closer to the Polish context in the PRL period" (Walter 2011).

What is Tischner's *HS*? Firstly, it is not any real person but an abstract being. Although it "never and nowhere materializes fully, its traces are present in society which have for decades been subjected to ideological indoctrination in a totalitarian system" (Walter 2011). Living in slavery, he was not responsible for his actions and did not take important decisions. He did not have to think because everything was simple. He was deprived of self-reliance by the authorities, which was the only body thinking correctly (Bożejewicz 2006, p. 142). Lack of ability to think independently is considered to be the main feature of *HS*. Walter (2011) claims that "*homo sovieticus* is not capable of critical analysis of the reality in which he participates". As he lacks self-reliance, he expects that the authorities will take care of everything, show the way, etc. Another characteristic feature of *HS* is subordination to a collective.

HS did not disappear with Poland's regaining independence after 1989. Many authors believe that its traits persist after the fall of communism (Walter 2011). Wnuk-Lipiński (2008) wrote that "*homo sovieticus* did not transform automatically into a citizen of a democratic country". He avoids subjectivity because it involves freedom of choice and personal responsibility for actions. He is used to inactivity and to the situation that decisions are taken for him, not by him" (Walter 2011).

Let us now confront the personality traits of *HS* with IFRS philosophy. First of all, IFRS solutions are flexible. Those who prepare financial statements are given freedom of choice in many instances, e.g. choice of the valuation model or method of recognition and presentation of a transaction, which is connected with the accounting policy. It should be stressed that the choice of accounting policy is often a strategic rather than a technical issue. The importance of such decisions makes the situation of *HS* even more difficult. Moreover, IFRS represent a principle-based approach, which means the need for making judgements. Accountants cannot "hide" behind rules and regulations neither in situations requiring a choice of accounting policy nor in cases of making personal judgements. They cannot feel safe that potential failure will be attributed to those to whom they are subordinated (strict regulations in this case). Responsibility for choice or judgement rests with them. For people with a *HS* personality this is not a comfortable situation. For them freedom is troublesome, not to say a burden.

As has already been noted, *HS* feels good only in situations when everything is simple. He likes to follow well-worn paths. But nothing is simple in IFRS. There is no uniform chart of accounts nor format of financial statements. The same event or element may be treated differently depending on the circumstances. In many instances there is no prescribed procedure.[4] The situation is all the more difficult because making an independent judgement requires critical analysis of the circumstances, whereas *HS* is not capable of such analysis. Table 3 presents characteristics required of accountants using IFRS in comparison with characteristics of *HS*.

As was mentioned above, IFRS require working in a team. In the process of preparing financial statements accountants must cooperate with other specialists. It might seem that *HS* should not have problems in this respect, as he has an instilled sense of collectivism. However, there is a great difference between teamworking ability and collectivism shaped by communism. The period of Soviet enslavement has contributed to the development of a dimorphic societal structure in Poland. Collective relationships are formed at low levels of social organization, such as

[4] Apart from a general guiding principle.

Table 3 Characteristics required of accountants using IFRS versus characteristics of *HS*

Accountant using IFRS	*Homo sovieticus* (HS)
Jaruga et al. (2006, pp. 77–78): "The application of these standards requires making your own judgements (. . .). Both preparers of financial statements and auditors must bear greater responsibility for their professional judgements"	P. Walter (2011): "(. . .) without responsibility for your own actions (. . .), without the need to make complicated choices in life", "reluctant to take any individual decisions", "avoiding responsibility", "avoiding subjectivity, used to passivity and to decisions being taken for him, not by him", "incapable of critical analysis of the reality", "thoughtless"

Source: own elaboration

family and friends. Such relationships have a primeval and spontaneous character. At the same time Poles do not identify strongly with their place of work. The level of their professional individualism is much higher than family individualism (Żakowska 2011). Although it does not seem justified to put all the blame for this situation on *HS*,[5] the period of Socialist enslavement has certainly strengthened Polish people's inability to form relationships in the public-institutional sphere. The functioning of *homo sovieticus* in teams is made even more difficult because of the instilled distrust and suspiciousness.

Do Poles in the twenty-first century still have features specific to the *HS* personality? Wnuk-Lipiński (2008) claims that although *HS* is in retreat, it is still present in Polish people. It does not depend on education, political views, age or place of residence. According to Szostak (2004), the socio-political changes that took place in Poland after 1989 have not changed social awareness sufficiently to get rid of the *HS* mentality. What is more, in some groups it seems to be even stronger.

To find out whether the *HS* personality still persists among Polish accountants, a questionnaire survey was conducted in 2011.[6] On the basis of 157 questionnaires returned by accountants from various firms and institutions (a broad spectrum of professions and positions connected with accounting) the following conclusions were formulated:

1. 24 % of those in the surveyed group display distinct (though to varying degrees) characteristics of the *HS* personality;
2. the enslaved attitude is less common in men than in women;
3. all people in this group, regardless of age, sex or length of work experience, can communicate effectively with their interlocutors, which is a positive feature in the context of IFRS;
4. those people who work in firms which apply IFRS have less intensive *HS* personality traits.

[5] According to some scholars, this type of mentality was shaped at the time of Partitions, or even dates back the beginning of Polish statehood (Żakowska 2011).

[6] For a more detailed description of this study see Kabalski et al. (2013).

In general, the *HS* personality type is quite often found (although it does not dominate) among accountants, which may be a serious barrier to the proper implementation and application of IFRS/IAS, since a comparison of *HS* style features and characteristics required in connection with IFRS shows clearly that these two elements are incompatible.

4.4 Problems with Translation of IFRS into Polish

The difficulties that occur in connection with the application of IFRS in Poland include the problem of translating them from English into Polish. These problems in part are objective, but also result from the wrong approach to the translation process.

Let us start with objective difficulties which are independent of the translator. The level of difficulty is determined, among other factors, by language distance (differences between the original and the target language) and cultural distance (cultural differences between the country of the original language and the country of the target language). In translating IFRS into Polish we have to deal with both these problems—in addition to cultural differences, which in the case of accounting are fundamental, linguistic divergence is significant, too. Another problem with translation is posed by the fact that IFRS are a specialist, highly technical text. Translators of specialised language are faced with many objective difficulties, which often result in the wrong rendering of the meaning. These include the lack of correspondence between available terminology and the reality to be described, linguistic ambiguity (polysemic, homonimic and synonimic), terms which do not have equivalents, and linguistic interference. Many specialist terms do not have equivalents in Polish. Some are practically impossible to translate (not only into Polish), such as *true and fair view*. All attempts at interpreting it have been more or less inadequate. This is also the case with many other terms, e.g. *comprehensive income*, *performance*. However, the Polish version of IFRS has a number of mistakes which are not due to objective difficulties, but to insufficient knowledge of the specialist terminology on the part of the translators, or a misunderstanding of some non-technical terms. An example is the word *systematic* with reference to intangible assets depreciation in IAS 38—the wrong translation resulted in prescribing a depreciation method that is contrary to both the letter and the spirit of the original text.

In addition to the problems mentioned above, the translation work was divided among several people, without proper coordination and supervision. As a result, in the Polish text there are sometimes several different words referring to one and the same original term. The poor quality of the Polish translation of IFRS is one of the obstacles to their successful application in Poland.

5 Final Remarks

The changes that have been taking place since the early 1990s in financial accounting regulation and practice in Poland are connected with the reintroduction and development of a market-based economy and its adaptation to progressing globalization. The change process involves the gradual adjustment of financial accounting regulations to the requirements of the EU and IFRS. It would not be an exaggeration to say that Poland was at the forefront of European countries in terms of IFRS adoption. Nevertheless, mandatory use of IFRS is regarded in Poland as a milestone marking the beginning of a new epoch. The transition to IFRS resulted for many WSE listed companies in significant changes in their financial position and performance as presented in financial statements. Empirical research indicates that PAR are slightly more conservative than IFRS. The road to IFRS implementation and application has been obstructed by a number of organizational, cultural and social barriers. Adaptation to IFRS has turned out to be a slow and difficult process.

References

Analizy i statystyki (2014) http://www.gpw.pl/analizy_i_statystyki. Accessed 4 Feb 2014

Bożejewicz W (2006) Tischner. Poglądy filozoficzno-antropologiczne. Oficyna Wydawnicza Łośgraf, Warszawa

Czubocha K (2010) Wpływ polskiej kultury narodowej i kultury organizacyjnej na funkcjonowanie polskich organizacji. Portal Innowacyjnego Transferu Wiedzy w Nauce. http://www.pitwin.edu.pl. Accessed 18 Jun 2010

Dadacz J, Gdański J (2005) MSR w polskim prawie bilansowym—szansa czy problem? Rachunkowość 4:3–6

Gadomska-Lila K (2008) Evolution of organisational culture of Polish companies in the context of their competitiveness—results of empirical research. Studia i Prace Wydziału Nauk Ekonomicznych i Zarządzania, vol 4. Wydawnictwo Naukowe Uniwersytetu Szczecińskiego, pp 119−134

Gadomska-Lila K, Lozano Platonoff A (2011) Relacje między kulturą organizacyjną a strukturą w świetle badań szczecińskich przedsiębiorstw. http://www.integracja.3is.pl/attachments/0000/0502/publikacje_naukowe_019.pdf. Accessed 4 Feb 2014.

Gottlieb MM (1994) Harmonizacja norm rachunkowości. Rachunkowość 6:253–257

Gray SJ (1980) The impact of international accounting differences from a security—analysis perspective: some european evidence. J Account Res 18(1):64–76. doi:10.2307/2490392

Heidtman J, Wolfarth A (2010) Współdziałanie zamiast rywalizacji. Harv Bus Rev Pol:18–20

Helin A (2006) Sprawozdania finansowe według MSSF: zasady sporządzania i prezentacji. BDO, C.H. Beck, Warszawa

History (2014) http://www.gpw.pl/historia_en. Accessed 4 Feb 2014

Hoogendoorn M (2006) International accounting regulation and IFRS implementation in Europe and Beyond—experiences with first-time adoption in Europe. Account Eur 3:23–26. doi:10.1080/09638180600920087

Ignatowski R (2009) Instytucjonalne uwarunkowania i otoczenia globalnych standardów rachunkowości. Wydawnictwo Uniwersytetu Łódzkiego, Łódź

Jaruga A (1999, June) Filling the gap in Polish GAAP. IASC Insight:19

Jaruga A, Kabalski P (2010) Poland. In: Previts G, Walton P, Wolnitzer P (eds) A global history of accounting, financial reporting and public policy. Europe. Bingley, Emerald, pp 139–162

Jaruga A, Szychta A (1997) The origin and evolution of charts of accounts in Poland. Eur Account Rev 6(3):509–526. doi:10.1080/713764733

Jaruga A, Frendzel M, Ignatowski R, Kabalski P (2006) Międzynarodowe Standardy Sprawozdawczości Finansowej. Kluczowe zagadnienia i rozwiązania praktyczne. SKwP, Warszawa

Jaruga A, Fijałkowska J, Jaruga-Baranowska M, Frendzel M (2007) The impact OF IAS/IFRS on Polish accounting regulation and their implementation in Poland. Account Eur 4(1–2):67–78. doi:10.1080/17449480701308675

Jaruga A, Fijałkowska J, Jaruga-Baranowska M (2008) Review of practical implementation issues relating to international financial reporting standardsCase study of Poland. Intergovernmental Working Group of Experts on International Standards of Accounting and Reporting. http://unctad.org/en/docs/c2isard46_en.pdf. Accessed 3 Feb 2014

Kabalski P (2012) Wybrane problemy stosowania Międzynarodowych Standardów Sprawozdawczości Finansowej w Polsce. Organizacja, kultura, osobowość, język. Wydawnictwo Uniwersytetu Łódzkiego, Łódź

Kabalski P, Tobór-Osadnik K, Wyganowska M (2013) International Financial Reporting Standards vs. homo sovieticus personality—the case of Poland. Int J Bus Social Res 3(6):17–35

Kostera M (1997) Zarządzanie personelem. PWE, Warszawa

Kożusznik B (2002) Zachowania człowieka w organizacji. PWE, Warszawa

KPMG (2009) Redukcja kosztów—doraźna potrzeba czy długofalowe działanie? Jak polskie przedsiębiorstwa podchodzą do optymalizacji kosztów. Raport KPMG Advisory. https://www.kpmg.com/PL/pl/IssuesAndInsights/ArticlesPublications/Documents/Raport-KPMG-redukcja-kosztow.pdf. Accessed 20 Feb 2014

Krzywda D, Schroeder M (2007) An analysis of the differences between IFRS and Polish accounting regulations: evidence from the financial statements of listed entities on the Warsaw Stock Exchange for the Calendar Years Ending 2001, 2003 and 2004. Account Eur 4 (1-2):79–107. doi:10.1080/17449480701343060

Lisiecka-Zając B (1999) Nowelizacja ustawy o rachunkowości (kierunki zmian). Rachunkowość 10:595–599

Mearns A (1993) Niektóre różnice między polskimi a międzynarodowymi normami rachunkowości. Rachunkowość 10:333–336

Morgan G (1997) Obrazy organizacji. Wydawnictwo Naukowe PWN, Warszawa

Murdoch A (1999) Współpraca z cudzoziemcami w firmie. Poltext, Warszawa

Nawojczyk M (2006) Universalism versus particularism through the European social survey lenses. Acta Phys Pol B 37(11):3059–3069

Piosik AK, Poniatowska L (2013) Determinants of upward revaluations of property, plant and equipment while adopting IFRS for the first time. Evidence from Poland. Zeszyty Teoretyczne Rachunkowości 70(126):105–128. doi:10.5604/16414381.1046266

Regulation (EC) No. 1606/2002 of the European Parliament and of the Council of 19 July 2002 on the Application of International Standards, OJ L 243, 11 September 2002. http://eur-lex.europa.eu/legal-content/EN/ALL/?uri=CELEX:32002R1606. Accessed 29 Jan 2014

Rozporządzenie Ministra Finansów z dnia 15.01.1991 r. w sprawie zasad prowadzenia rachunkowości, Dz. U. 1991, No. 10, poz. 35.

Skowroński J (1990) Polska rachunkowość otwiera się na świat. Rachunkowość 10:203–208

Skowroński J, Jarugowa A (1994) Rozwój polskiego prawa rachunkowości. Rachunkowość 1:7–15

Sobańska I (2007) Nowa orientacja systemu rachunkowości w praktyce polskiej w kontekście wdrażania MSR/MSSF. In: Rachunkowość, wczoraj, dziś, jutro. Stowarzyszenie Księgowych w Polsce, Warszawa, pp 277–300

Spector P, Cooper C, Sparks K (2001) An International study of psychometric properties of the Hofstede values survey module 1994: a comparison of individual and country/province level results. Appl Psychol Int Rev 50(2):269–281. doi:10.1111/1464-0597.00058

Staniec I, Zakrzewska-Bielawska A (2010) Organizational structure in the view of single business concentration and diversification strategies—empirical study results. In: Recent advances in management, marketing, finances. WSEAS Press, Penang, Malaysia, pp 87–92

Szostak W (2004) Świadomość homo sovieticus w III Rzeczypospolitej. In: Kornaś J (ed) Kryzys Rzeczypospolitej? Studia z zakresu funkcjonowania systemu politycznego. Weisa, Kielce, pp 13–26

Szychta A, de la Rosa D (2012) Comprehensive income presentation under IAS 1: the reporting practices of the largest companies listed on the Warsaw Stock Exchange. Zeszyty Teoretyczne Rachunkowości 68(124):121–145

Tischner J (1992) Etyka Solidarności oraz Homo sovieticus. Społeczny Instytut Wydawniczy Znak, Kraków

Ustawa z dnia 29.09.1994 r. o rachunkowości, Dz. U. 1994, No. 121, poz. 591, z póź. zm. http://isap.sejm.gov.pl/DetailsServlet?id=WDU19941210591. Accessed 29 Jan 2014

Walińska E (2012) „Kroki milowe" w rozwoju polskiej regulacji rachunkowości w warunkach gospodarki rynkowej. In: Sobańska I, Kabalski P (eds) Współczesne nurty badawcze w rachunkowości. Wydawnictwo Uniwersytetu Łódzkiego, Łódź, pp 223–243

Walter P (2011) Homo sovieticus—spór o człowieka. *Racjonalista*. http://www.racjonalista.pl/kk.php/s,6908. Accessed 20 Feb 2014

Wnuk-Lipiński E (2008) Długie pożegnanie. Homo sovieticus dzisiaj. Tygodnik Powszechny. http://tygodnik2003-2007.onet.pl/1548,1462351,1,559916,dzial.html. Accessed 10 Feb 2014

Żakowska M (2011) Polskie dylematy aspołecznego kolektywisty. Racjonalista. http://www.racjonalista.pl/kk.php/s,4615. Accessed 5 Feb 2014

Zawadzka AM (ed) (2010) Psychologia zarządzania w organizacji. Wydawnictwo Naukowe PWN, Warszawa

Romania. Shifting to IFRS: The Case of Romania

Liliana Feleagă and Niculae Feleagă

Abstract This paper aims to study the implementation process of the International Financial Reporting Standards (IFRS) in one of ex-communist countries, Romania. This country provides a particular interest for the study because, by its recent history, the national institutional orientation differs to the origins of IFRS. To highlight how Romania has moved to implement the requirement for group and individual listed companies to prepare IFRS accounts, we have organized this as it follows. We begin with an analysis of the relevant literature on the issues that might arise and on the factors which can affect the appropriateness and effectiveness of the implementation of IFRS. Than we analyze the legislation and regulations in Romanian accounting before and after the IFRS adoption. The analysis of the legislative and institutional approach is supported by interviews with Romanian regulators, accountants, auditors and academics.

1 Introduction

The financial reporting development from last decades was closely linked to the globalization of capital markets and to the demand for international comparability. In accounting literature, the issue of comparability was often presented as attainable through the wide adoption of IFRS. Besides, the IFRS development was based on the idea that a single set of high-quality global accounting standards is the fittest way to increase the comparability of financial statements and reduce the cost of their preparation. Studies have shown, however, that to be effective, accounting and reporting systems must reflect the context in which they operate (Burchell et al. 1980). In other words, the effects of IFRS adoption is influenced by factors that are specific to the country and to individual firms (Ding et al. 2007), which means that it is possible that the adoption of international referential does not automatically lead to an increased comparability in financial reporting. However, many developed countries have already adopted IFRS and others plan to adopt

L. Feleagă (✉) • N. Feleagă
Bucharest University of Economic Studies, Bucharest, Romania
e-mail: liliana.feleaga@cig.ase.ro; nfeleaga@yahoo.com

D. Bensadon, N. Praquin (eds.), *IFRS in a Global World*,
DOI 10.1007/978-3-319-28225-1_27

them. Simultaneously, the developing countries engaged in this adoption process, although their socially, politically, economically and culturally environment differs from that of developed countries, fact which has led to a real revolution in financial reporting. The objective of this paper is to analyze the implementation process of IFRS in Romania, which can be characterized as an emerging transitional country, splitting from Eastern Bloc domination in the 1990s and subsequently becoming a member of the European Union. Like other emerging countries, it has experienced rapid changes in accounting practice and regulation, managing to shift from a communist system to the IFRS adoption. In these circumstances, this country presents a particular interest to study, because, by its history, the national institutional orientation differs from the origins of IFRS.

The paper is organized as follows: after reviewing the relevant literature on how appropriate IFRS might be for transitional economies, we analyzed the legislation and regulations in Romanian accounting before and after the IFRS adoption. The analysis of the legislative and institutional approach is supported by the interviews conducted with Romanian regulators, accountants, auditors and academics. We discuss the implications of these results in the conclusion and suggest further research questions.

2 Literature Review

Today, over 120 countries require or authorize their financial markets listed companies to use IFRS in order to improve the quantity and the quality of information published in the financial statements (Ball 2006; De Franco et al. 2010) and to increase the transparency and comparability of such information (Jermakowicz 2004; Ding et al. 2007). Wanting to participate in the wealth and financial opportunities promised by globalization, emerging countries took the way to the adoption of IFRS. Previous studies have shown *inter alia* that the adoption of IFRS is associated with: increasing the efficiency of resource allocation, increasing capital mobility, decreasing the cost of capital and reducing information asymmetry (Hail and Leuz 2006; Barth et al. 2008; Daske et al. 2008). In addition, IFRS adoption saves time and effort compared with developing own national standards (Frey and Chandler 2007), replaces the lack of expertise of the national regulators (Irvine and Lucas 2006) and can be rationalised more easily from a political point of view, because it is not the product of a single country (Saudagaran and Diga 1997).

Cooke and Wallace (1990) showed, however, that for developing countries, it is more likely than in developed countries that the level of corporate financial disclosure regulation to be determined by external factors. Therefore, we must bear in mind that in developing countries, the adoption of IFRS was made sometimes at the pressure of external organizations such as the World Bank and International Monetary Fund, which have conditioned the assistance offered by applying the international accounting referential (Sucher and Alexander 2004; Mir and Rahaman 2005; Le and Barbu 2010; Albu et al. 2011). In addition, international accounting and auditing firms have driven the adoption of IFRS (Cooper et al. 1998; Chand 2005) in developing countries. These companies, who possess knowledge and expertise on the IFRS, have acquired the necessary power to influence the organizations' options related to their reporting process, because the World Bank required the financed projects to be audited by "internationally reputable firms of accountants" (Annisette 2004).

IFRS implementation is not simple, if we want it to represent a regulated reality and not just an image. It is not enough to share rules to create a common business language. Management incentives and national institutional factors play an important role in shaping the characteristics of financial reporting (Jeanjean and Stolowy 2008). In these circumstances, it appears legitimate the question whether IFRS is relevant to developing countries?

Literature on developing economies already deals with this issue. The results of various studies, however, are far from being convergent. Thus, while some studies argue that IFRS adoption leads to increasing the quality of accounting in developing countries (Turner 1983), others warn that this referential can fail to cover all the accounting needs of the concerned countries (Tyrrall et al. 2007). The complicated nature of some of the IFRS standards and the lack of guidance for the application of the new standards represent possible obstacles to the transition to IFRS (Larson and Street 2004). For this reason, many European companies did not apply IFRS if there were not required by law (Jermankowicz and Gornik-Tomaszewski 2006). The problem is even more delicate for developing countries, where the profession is not sufficiently advanced to be able to interpret and apply the professional judgment aspects of IFRS (Nobes 1998). In these circumstances, before moving to IFRS, the implementation requires a strong process on education and training line in relation to these standards (Sucher and Alexander 2004). In addition, even if in national regulations have emerged a number of changes, such as recognition of the principle substance over form, the large differences between local practices of financial reporting, oriented on taxation, and IFRS reporting, oriented on investors, may affect the degree of compliance with IFRS (Sucher and Bychkova 2001), leading to *de jure* of accounting changes to be very different from de facto situation. To these may be added structural difficulties such as lack of active markets and corruption (Sucher and Bychkova 2001), cultural impediments (Ampofo and Sellani 2005) or language impediments (Evans 2004). Thus, different countries may face problems related to the efficiency and quality of IFRS translation (Tokar 2005) or problems with the understanding and interpretation of the standards. In addition, the standards evolve continuously, making the transition to the status of full compliance under IFRS to be more difficult (Joshi et al. 2008).

It is worth mentioning that the generalization is not possible because the group of developing countries is not homogeneous (Chamisa 2000). Each country has a different historical background, is in a different stage of development and is facing different pressures. Therefore the implementation manner and the effects of implementing IFRS differs from one country to another. Thus, in some countries a gradual adoption of IFRS was undertaken while in others the standards have been adopted in a single step. In some countries the implementation of IFRS was a success (a high level of compliance), while others failed (a high level of non-compliance) in this aspect. And even if a generalization is not possible, the experience of various countries is useful for understanding the implementation of IFRS and its implications.

3 The Waves of Romanian Accounting Reform

Until 1990, for four decades, Romania has operated under a centralized and planned economy. The accounting system was one tier (Richard 1988), which did not make the distinction between financial accounting and management accounting. Monism was possible because the external accounting functions were performed only in connection with the "centralizing data" and "control" of them by the superior authority, by the financial administration and by banking system. The accounting information was not transparent and the company's secret prohibited its dissemination. The trading partners did not have access to financial statements and in the same manner, there were no investors, nor competitors. Except the external features (centralization and control) the accounting information products were for the management, to the extent that they had a real decision power. The accounting cycle of data processing targets the tracking of production, distribution, circulation and consumption processes, which makes the system of accounts used to record the alleged operations of these processes to be in the spotlight. The role of the financial statements was relatively marginalized, because the economic and financial analyzes developed based on them, remained in the theory field, the margin of the intervention of leaders being limited. After the fall of communism, Romania's transition to a market economy required a reform of the accounting system in all its resorts: objectives, functions, methods, tools, organization, normalization features, status accounting profession etc.

Own practice could not represent a reference for the development of rules (Colasse 1992), because Romania had lost the accounting tradition. Therefore, it was searched inspiration abroad.

The first "wave" of accounting reform (1991–1998) was conducted under French guidance. Choosing the French accounting system as a model of inspiration was made subjectively prevailing the tradition, the preferential scientific relations and the cultural line between the two nations (King et al. 2001), the economic exchanges (Richard 1995), the Latin country (Feleagă and Feleagă 2009) and that referential compliance with European Directives (ED) (Barbu et al. 2012). Further analysis demonstrated, based on economic, financial, fiscal, social, legal and cultural variables, that the choice was a correct one, the French accounting system was at that time the only system easily adaptable to Romanian imperatives, conditions and traditions (Feleagă 1992; Feleagă and Ionaşcu 1993). Although the "technical" arguments can be criticized (Richard 1995), in the Romanian practice, the French model has never been perceived as a "cultural invasion".

The French counselors' support (Duţia 1995) and the training in the spirit of the "Entity Accounting System" (Delesalle and Gelard 1991) led to the implementation of a dualist accounting system (Feleagă et al. 1993) which resulted in the French financial roots of the accounting system, with macroeconomic and fiscal objectives (Richard 2003). However, a number of institutional elements and remaining mentalities from the old regime have affected the quality of accounting reform. The standardization body, represented by the public power, was more concerned about the components of the chart of accounts, the financial statements being not proper used. The evaluation rules were stationed at some considerations on historical costs. Although the Romanian economy was hit by hyperinflation, the financial statements have not been restated accordingly, which favored the manifestation of the disinvestment phenomenon. When, finally, they have resorted to reprocessing, it was done on a tax basis. Moreover, taxation was heavily involved in all accounting structures. The management accounting limited to cost calculation and methods used in this context were often outdated.

The second "wave" of reform (1999–2005) was carried out under the Scottish counseling. The decision regarding the counseling was a political one, based on an agreement between the Ministry of Foreign Affairs of Romania and the British Government. Through this decision, the Know How Fund established a team of Scottish experts which was entitled to advise the Ministry of Public Finance on the issue of the Romanian accounting system reform (King et al. 2001). The objective of this stage was the implementation of the International Accounting Standards (IAS) for listed and unlisted major companies, to give a signal that Romania is a well regulated business environment favorable to foreign investment. In 1999 were issued the accounting regulations harmonized with the 4th ED and with the IASs (Order no. 403) that have been applied experimentally in a number of 12 non-financial companies. Following the conclusions of the action of experimentation, the accounting rules have been improved, being drafted the Order no. 94/2001. Under the new order entered about 1500–1700 entities, which were either traded on the market, or were in the process of privatization and had an interest on attracting international capital investment. The intention to harmonize the accounting rules both with the ED and with the IASs has led to difficulties in implementing, being known the existing conflict between the continental accounting model, specific to our country, and the Anglo-Saxon accounting model, specific to international referential (Nobes 1983). In addition, the harmonization with IAS led to the appearance of new elements such as: the call for appraisal and professional judgment for grounding of accounting solutions, the adoption of some concepts from international standards other than the ones from national practice (e.g., deferred taxes); the introduction of new accounting principles (the principle of substance over form and the materiality principle); the foreknowledgement for some deviations from the principle of intangibility of the balance sheet, a principle with tradition in Romanian accounting, and the use of new valuation bases (e.g., the fair value and the present value).

Therefore, it was necessary "to think carefully about preserving useful aspects of previous experience, particularly the Chart of Accounts, to be aware of the complexities of interaction between tax law and accounting law; to have regard for the need to develop the concept of auditing while remaining aware of the tensions arising as a new profession develops; to consider the needs of an emerging capital market; to place strong emphasis on having adequate training available; to be aware of how external influences have shaped developments, and to weigh the benefits of IAS harmonization with the pressure for compliance with EU directives" (King et al. 2001).

Although the IAS have been translated into Romanian (2000) and Ministry of Public Finance has published a practical guide for the implementation of IASs (2001), this wave of reform had only a limited effect on the transparency of financial information, on the exercise of the professional judgment and on the quality of financial information. Among the causes identified can be mentioned: the maintenance of significant differences between the Order no. 94 and IASs (World Bank 2003), the lack of necessary resources to implement a reporting system based on IASs and the managers' low awareness of the importance of such a system (Feleagă and Feleagă 2009); the difficulty of assimilating IASs by accountants, who are accustomed rather to make fiscal judgments than economic judgments (Larson and Street 2004); the low disconnection of accounting from taxation (Filip and Raffournier 2010), and the lack of pressure for providing quality information in terms of underdeveloped capital markets (World Bank 2003).

The third "wave" of reform has its origins in 2005, when the accounting system was oriented in two directions. A large majority of entities have begun to apply the rules of the Order no. 1752/2005, which is calling for full compliance with ED. In fact, these regulations preserved the elements of all previous stages of reform: some of the axes of the French General Accounting Plan (Richard 1995), measures, models of financial statements and valuation rules derived from steps taken on Europeanization line of the accounting system practiced in Romania, as a consequence of the processes of harmonization with the ED, the presence in regulations of some accounting policies derived from IASs. However, "the absence of many elements of the necessary supporting infrastructure, combined with Romania's rule-based accounting traditions, present challenges in ensuring that the principles contained in European Union legislation are applied in a manner that leads to high quality financial reporting" (World Bank 2008).

The second direction of the accounting development aimed the mandatory application of IFRS starting from 1st January 2007, for the consolidated financial statements of listed companies and those of the financial and banking institutions. In addition, it was suggested that the other public interested entities may apply IFRS in individual or consolidated financial statements, for their own information needs. However, in relation to the state, all entities, including those applying IFRS, were obliged to prepare annual financial statements in accordance with ED. The obligation to apply IFRS has been extended on the recommendation of the World Bank (ROSC 2008) through the publication of the Order no. 881/2012. Under this order, starting with the financial year 2012, companies whose securities are admitted to trading on a regulated market are required to apply IFRS in individual annual financial statements. In this way, "Romania wanted to assure itself that its accounting system was current and relevant, and that it corresponded to the system used by other developed countries" (Barbu et al. 2012).

4 Investigating the Perceptions Concerning the Adoption of IFRS in Romania

To give a more complex picture of what the adoption of IFRS ment in Romania, we consider more relevant that, in addition to legislative analysis, to identify how these accounting changes were perceived by regulators, accountants, auditors and academics. The primary source of data were the interviews. Thus, a total number of eight interviews were conducted, over a period of 5 weeks, from June to July 2013 on the topic of the adoption of IFRS in Romania. The sample selection was based on the variety of respondents rather than on the number of respondents, so that the subject considered to be analyzed from different perspectives. Therefore, the final sample consisted of: two accountants, two auditors, two officials from the Ministry of Public Finance and two academics. All respondents had experience in applying IFRS and Romanian accounting regulations. In addition, some respondents hold or have held important professional positions, being experienced enough to make authorized comments about the regulation of accounting in Romania. The interviews were unstructured and open ended to allow respondents to freely express their views.

4.1 The Justification of IAS/IFRS Adoption

As stated above, in Romania, the adoption of international standards started in 1999, even if it was only about a partial application. "The acceleration of the privatization process, the development of the capital market and the free market economy, as well as strengthening relations with the European Union for the accession process, required the continued development of the Romanian accounting system, aiming at a better harmonization with the ED and IASs." (Regulator 1)

And even if we had the necessary resources, "it was not appropriate for Romania to develop its own accounting standards when it was already obvious that sooner or later all countries will go on the road to IFRS. The government's decision to adopt IFRS was a correct one." (Regulator 2)

"For a developing country like Romania, elaborating their own standards would involve an expense that would not have been able to afford it. . . . In addition, the adoption of IFRS represented already a sign of the alignment to the accounting practices and to the accounting transformation at global level." (Academic 1)

The respondents' general perception was that the adoption of the international accounting referential was made due to the pressure of some external organizations.

"The adoption of IFRS has been started under the pressure of international bodies. It was a political decision!"(Academic 2)

"Behind the adoption of IFRS is money received by the Romanian Government." (Accountant 1)

"The fact that Romania received a strong support from the Know How Fund increased the speed of the process of IFRS adoption in Romania." (Regulator 2)

After the adoption of the international standards it was necessary to pursue the compliance with these standards, establishing the audit obligativity of the financial statements. Therefore, "the imposed reform of the accounting profession organization system lead to the establishment of the financial auditor profession, as a guardian of the compliance and satisfaction of public interest regarding to the financial reporting and disclosure. Obviously, the interest was to facilitate the establishment of companies in Romania at that time called Big Five. It is known that international audit firms have taken the policy decision to promote IFRS and have devoted considerable resources to do so." (Academic 2)

4.2 The Benefits of Adopting IFRS

All categories of respondents recognized, however, that there are benefits from the adoption of international accounting referential:

Regulator 1: "Adopting IFRS in Romania had as main objective the creation of an attractive business environment for investors."

Academic 1: "Applying IFRS ensures a higher level of trust and leads to increasing the access to capital markets. It also allows multinational groups to apply accounting principles common to all branches, which can optimize the internal communication, and also the quality of reporting to management."

Auditor 1: "In markets with a growing competitive level, the application of IFRS allows companies to report to other similar companies from a global level and allows investors and other interested users to compare the performance of the company with global competitors."

Accountant 1: "Applying IFRS may facilitate the purchases and sales processes by providing a higher level of trust, relevance and consistency of accounting interpretation."

Accountant 2: "By applying IFRS the reliability of the company increases and the capital costs are lower...."

4.3 Critical Issues Associated with the Adoption of IFRS

The respondents identified major problems generated by the adoption of IFRS. The first such problem concerns the relationship between accounting and taxation:

Accountant 1: "Given that, nowadays, companies whose securities are admitted to trading on a regulated market are required to apply IFRS for individual annual financial statements, many professionals are concerned about how this foreknowledgement will affect the income tax calculation."

Academic 2: "Probably the result according to IFRS will be bigger and more subjective. I wonder how the fiscal authorities will handle this situation?"

Auditor 1: "In Romania, the fiscal authority is very strong and can affect the de facto implementation of IFRS. The compliance with tax legislation will always prevail over accounting legislation."

Auditor 2: "The problem concerns the mentality ... what sometimes happens in practice is significantly different from the legislative requirements, because the fiscal purposes sometimes prevail in preparation of the financial statements."

Another major problem reported in the context of the interviews is the complexity of IFRS:

Academic 1: "It is likely that standards such as those related to the treatment of financial instruments (IAS 39), provisions (IAS 37) and depreciation (IAS 36) to cause problems, due to their complexity, for a part of Romanian accountants. If to these are added the fair value measurement, the use of estimates and the preparation of group accounts, things become more complicated."

Accountant 2: "In Romania, there is not an active market for more tangible assets. Therefore, the use of fair value can be an excuse to manipulate the financial statements."

Auditor 2: "In some companies, the implementation of certain standards depends on the attitude of auditors. For example, if auditors not require the recognition of depreciation, companies do not volunteer do it."

Regulator 1: "The Romanian accountants are accustomed to receive detailed solutions from the Ministry of Public Finance. It is difficult to understand that they must change their mentality. It is expected that in cases where IFRS do not provide clear instructions or alternative treatments are available, the Romanian accountants to adopt the solution that involves a minimal use of professional judgment and a minimal information disclosure."

Regulator 2: "International standards are changing frequently, which causes problems not only for preparers of financial statements but also for national regulator. Beyond the technical accounting issues, significant difficulties related to translation might appear. Such problems have been identified at the implementation level by companies and by auditors, but also at the legislation level."

Auditor 1: "Beyond the complexity of the rules, their translation can create problems. There are English terms that do not easily finds a counterpart in Romanian: swaption (IAS 39), roll back (IFRS 1), roll forward (IFRS 1), clin-up call (IAS 39), etc. Therefore, the accountant can not understand the text if he is not going to the English source."

5 Conclusions

In a world increasingly globalized, the developing countries and the emerging economies have quickly adopted IFRS in order to gain legitimacy in the capital markets. IFRS implementation process, however, is not simple. The literature review revealed that contextual factors, such as the state's role in the accounting normalization process, the pressure of the users of financial statements or the relationship between the financial reporting and taxation, can affect the appropriateness and effectiveness of the IFRS 's implementation in emerging economies. In addition to this, there are specific factors such as the differences between the local accounting standards and IFRS, the certain particular problems relating to individual standards, the availability of market data to use fair value or the extents of education and training in international accounting. Therefore, developing countries and emerging economies represent a wide source of research opportunities.

The objective of this study was to examine the process of implementation of IFRS in Romania and to observe the perceptions of the regulators, accountants, auditors and academics about the transition to these rules. Romania is an interesting country to study in terms of accounting classifications. Thus, if we use the classification model developed by Nobes (1998), Romania could be seen as a country where corporate finance is provided more via loans than equity, in which the accounting rules are dominated by fiscal considerations and in which the legal systems are combined in codes of detailed rules, in various areas, including accounting. However, Romania adopted IFRS, which is a diametrically opposed accounting system.

Based on a review of the law and on the interviews conducted with accounts prepares, auditors, academics and accounting standard setters, paper highlights the key issues that emerged during the circumstance of the transition of the Romanian listed companies to IFRS. This experience may be relevant for other emerging countries which will take the road to IFRS.

Although the adoption of IFRS is considered a response to the pressure of foreign financial institutions and international audit firms, all respondents agreed that this process leads to greater comparability of accounting information and improve the financial reporting. Such advantages are sometimes overshadowed by the fact that although some companies apply IFRS, in reality, their practices bear the imprint of routines established in the pre-IFRS period.

This study has several limitations. Thus, although we tried to surprise, during interviews, details of the implementation process, it was not possible to identify all the implications, because the application of full IFRS for individual accounts is in its infancy in Romania. In addition to this, the sample was too small, even if through the selection we tried to ensure that it encompasses various interest groups and that the persons involved are experts in their field. However, this work provides a pointer to research areas that could be developed more deeply and are likely to impact other developing countries or emerging economies that apply IFRS.

References

Albu N, Albu CN, Bunea S, Calu DA, Gîrbina MM (2011) A story about IAS/IFRS implementation in Romania. J Account Emerg Econ 1(1):76–100

Ampofo AA, Sellani RJ (2005) Examining the differences between United States Generally Accepted Accounting Principles (U.S. GAAP) and International Accounting Standards (IAS): implications for the harmonization of accounting standards. Account Forum 29 (2):219–231

Annisette M (2004) The true nature of the World Bank. Crit Perspect Account 15:303–323

Ball R (2006) International Financial Reporting Standards (IFRS): pros and cons for investors. Account Bus Res (1):5–27

Barbu E, Farcane N, Popa A (2012) Critical analysis of developments in Romanian accounting during the 20th century: a Neo-institutional approach. Int J Crit Account 4(2):175–193

Barth ME, Landsman WR, Lang MH (2008) International accounting standards and accounting quality. J Account Res 46(3):467–498

Burchell S, Clubb C, Hopwood A, Hughes J, Nahapiet J (1980) The role of accounting in organizations and society. Acc Organ Soc 5(1):5–27

Chamisa EE (2000) The relevance and observance of the IASC standards in developing countries and the particular case of Zimbabwe. Int J Account 35(2):267–286

Chand P (2005) Impetus to the success of harmonization: the case of South Pacific Island nations. Crit Perspect Account 16(3):209–226

Colasse B (1992) A l'Est, quoi de nouveau? Compte-rendu d'une rencontre-débat. *Revue Française de Comptabilité* (233):54–56

Cooke TE, Wallace RSO (1990) Financial disclosure regulation and its environment: a review and further analysis. J Account Public Policy 9:79–110

Cooper DJ, Greenwood R, Hinings B, Brown JL (1998) Globalization and nationalism in a multinational accounting firm: the case of opening new markets in Eastern Europe. Acc Organ Soc 23(5/6):531–548

Daske H, Hail L, Leuz C, Verdi RS (2008) Mandatory IFRS reporting around the world: early evidence on the economic consequences. J Account Res 46(5):1085–1142

De Franco G, Kothari SP, Verdi RS (2010) The benefits of financial statement comparability. Working paper. MIT Sloan School of Management

Delesalle E, Gelard G (1991) Exporter la comptabilité: le système comptable d'entreprise. Revue Française de Comptabilité (223):75–91

Ding Y, Hope OK, Jeanjean T, Stolowy H (2007) Differences between domestic accounting standards and IAS: measurement, determinants and implications. J Account Public Policy 26 (1):1–38

Duţia T (1995) The restructuring of the system of accounting in Romania during the period of transition to the market economy. Eur Account Rev 4(4):739–748

Evans L (2004) Language, translation and the problem of international accounting communication. Account Audit Account J 17(2):210–248

Feleagă N (1992) A l'Est, quoi de nouveau? Compte-rendu d'une rencontre-débat. Revue Française de Comptabilité (233):54–56

Feleagă N, Ionaşcu I (1993) Contabilitate financiară, vol 1. Editura Economică, Bucharest

Feleagă N, Feleagă L (2009) Reform after reform: a critical analysis of the Romanian accounting evolution. Int J Bus Res 9(1):87–89

Feleaga N, Florescu V, Rigal JJ (1993) Audit du système comptable dans le contexte de l'insertion internationale des entreprises roumaines. Actes du Congres 1993 de I'Association Française de Comptabilité, pp 643–657

Filip A, Raffournier B (2010) The value relevance of earnings in a transition economy: the case of Romania. Int J Account 45:77–103

Frey N, Chandler R (2007) Acceptance of International Accounting Standard-setting: emerging economies versus developed countries. Res Account Emerg Econ 7:147–162

Hail L, Leuz C (2006) International differences in the cost of equity capital: do legal institutions and securities regulation matter? J Account Res 44(3):485–531

Irvine HJ, Lucas N (2006) The rationale and impact of the adoption of International Financial Reporting Standards: the case of the United Arab Emirates. Working paper. University of Wollongong, Wollongong

Jeanjean T, Stolowy H (2008) Do accounting standards matter? An exploratory analysis of earnings management before and after IFRS adoption. J Account Public Policy 27(6):480–494

Jermakowicz EK (2004) Effects of adoption of international financial reporting standards in Belgium: the evidence from BEL-20 companies. Account Eur 1(1):51–70

Jermankowicz EK, Gornik-Tomaszewski S (2006) Implementing IFRS from the perspective of EU publicly traded companies. J Int Account Audit Tax 15(2):170–196

Joshi PL, Bremser WG, Al-Ajmi J (2008) Perceptions of accounting professionals in the adoption and implementation of a single set of global accounting standards: evidence from Bahrain. Adv Account 24(1):41–48

King N, Beattie A, Cristescu AM, Weetman P (2001) Developing accounting and audit in a transition economy: the Romanian experience. Eur Account Rev 10(1):149–171

Larson RK, Street DL (2004) Convergence with IFRS in an expanding Europe: progress and obstacles identified by large accounting firms' survey. J Account Audit Tax 13:89–119

Le T, Barbu E (2010) Accounting as catalyst of economic transition: an overview of the twenty-year progression from a communist to a capitalist accounting system. Document de recherche du CERAG. n° 2010-02 E2

Mir MZ, Rahaman AS (2005) The adoption of International Accounting Standards in Bangladesh. an exploration of rationale and process. Account Audit Account J 18(6):816–841

Nobes C (1983) A judgmental international classification of financial reporting practices. J Bus Finance Account 10:1–19

Nobes C (1998) Accounting in Developing Economies. ACCA, London

Richard J (1988) Pour un plan comptable moniste français. Actes du Congrès 1988 de l'Association Française de Comptabilité. Nisa, pp 307–357

Richard J (1995) The evolution of the Romanian and Russian accounting charts after the collapse of the communist system. Eur Account Rev 4(2):305–322

Richard J (2003) Accounting in Eastern Europe: from Communism to Capitalism. In Walton P, Haller A, Raffournier B (eds) International accounting, 2nd edn. Thomson Learning London, pp 332–347

Saudagaran SM, Diga JG (1997) The impact of capital market developments on accounting regulatory policy in emerging markets: A Study of ASEAN. Res Account Regul (suppl 1):3–48

Sucher P, Alexander D (2004) The preparation of IAS financial statements: a case study in a transitional economy. Res Account Emerg Econ 2:117–148

Sucher P, Bychkova S (2001) Auditor independence in economies in transition: a Study of Russia. Eur Account Rev 10(4):817–841

Tokar M (2005) Convergence and the implementation of a single set of global standards: the real-life challenge. Account Eur 2(1):47–68

Turner JN (1983) International harmonization: a professional goal. J Account: 58–59.

Tyrrall D, Woodward D, Rakhimbekova A (2007) The relevance of International Financial Reporting Standards to a developing country: evidence from Kazakhstan. Int J Account 42 (1):82–110

World Bank (2003) Romania: Report on the Observance of Standards and Codes (ROSC). Washington, DC. Available at www.worldbank.org/ifa/rosc_aa_rom.pdf. Accessed 30 Sept 2013

World Bank (2008) Romania: Report on the Observance of Standards and Codes (ROSC). Washington, DC. Available at: http://siteresources.worldbank.org/ROMANIAEXTN/Resources/Romania_Final_A&A_ROSC.pdf. Accessed 30 Sept 2013

Tunisia. IFRS for SMEs and Tunisian Accounting

Salma Damak-Ayadi

Abstract The International Accounting Standard Board (IASB) continues to work with regulators in some countries toward the adoption of full IFRS. This study reports on an exploratory review of Tunisian's Certified Public Accountants (CPA) perceptions about important issues relevant to developing and implementing the IFRS for SMEs. All Tunisian companies are required to prepare their financial statements according to the Tunisian Accounting System (SCT) since 1997. The paper provides insight into the perception of CPA on IFRS for SMEs based on a questionnaire. The 87 responses received indicate that (1) the CPA consider that the SCT as pretty consistent with international standards. (2) It is also preferable to adopt the international standard specific to SMEs in order to improve the quality of information supplied by the Tunisian SMEs and to better comparability and transparency. (3) The costs of implementation and adaptation are the main obstacles to the success of this adoption. This study has an impact on various involved parties (Tunisian companies, accountants, accounting standard-setter and public authorities). The topic is judicious because the prominence of IFRS for SMEs is growing in emerging countries. In addition to mandatory reporting, voluntary reporting under IFRS for SMEs is expected to increase significantly for companies seeking to raise capital in international markets.

1 Introduction

The IAS/IFRS are currently used in over one hundred countries currently. This application is mainly specific to listed companies and large sized ones.[1] Thus, the same country may adopt international and national accounting standards. This cohabitation could create some problems of convergence and comparability of accounting practices in this country. It may lead to a significant disparity from

[1] For more details: www.iasplus.com.

S. Damak-Ayadi (✉)
IHEC Carthage, LIGUE, Tunis, Tunisia
e-mail: salmadamak@yahoo.fr

D. Bensadon, N. Praquin (eds.), *IFRS in a Global World*,
DOI 10.1007/978-3-319-28225-1_28

one country to another generally accepted accounting principles applicable to financial statements individual corporations, which adversely affect the comparability and constitute an obstacle to a transition to the full IFRS where an entity decides to go to the capital markets.

Besides, full IFRS were designed to meet the needs of equity investors in companies in public capital markets; they cover a wide range of issues, contain a sizeable amount of implementation guidance and include disclosures appropriate for public companies. Users of the financial statements of SMEs do not have those needs. They are more focused on assessing shorter-term cash flows, liquidity and solvency. According to the IASB, full IFRS impose on SMEs a burden that has been growing as full IFRS have become more detailed and as more countries have begun to use them. Thus, in developing the proposed IFRS for SMEs, IASB's twin goals were to meet user needs while balancing costs and benefits.

Many national accounting standard setters have supported the initiative of the IASB to develop financial reporting standards adapted to SMEs. Therefore, in 2003, the IASB initiated a reflection on the development of a set of accounting standards adapted to these entities.

The IASB issued on June 24, 2004, a document for discussion entitled "Preliminary views on Accounting standards for small and medium-sized entities" aiming at developing accounting standards adapted for SMEs.

This document highlighted a number of issues to which the IASB proposed a first approach. The main treated problems, as well as the approach developed by the IASB are the importance of a financial reporting standards adapted for SMEs, the objectives and the field of application of this standard, the basis of concepts and principles adopted compared to the full IFRS and the presenting format of the financial reporting standards for SMEs.

As a result of this first stage of consultation to validate its approach, the Board has decided to continue its project to develop an exposure draft. In 2005, the IASB conducted a questionnaire on the amendments to the principles of accounting and evaluation under full IFRS, to adapt them to the needs of SMEs. This questionnaire has been prepared to enable the identification of the key issues to be discussed during public meetings.

The IASB addresses separately the problems related to the presentation and information to be provided, while recognizing that these themes derive in part from those relating to accounting and evaluation.

The IASB has published online on its website, on November 9, 2006, an exposure project of IFRS for SMEs prepared by its staff. Two documents have been published on that occasion. The first includes the project of IFRS as well as an invitation to guest project. The second corresponds to a draft implementation guide presented in the form of financial statements illustrated, to which is attached a list of control of disclosures.

The decision related to the adoption or not of the IFRS for SMEs would be taken at the level of each country. For example, the European Union requires listed companies to apply full IFRS for their consolidated accounts, but each Member State could decide what accounting standards SMEs need to apply.

On July 9, 2009, the IASB issued the final version of its standard. It included 35 sections representing the themes that were of interest to SMEs and constituted a stand-alone document compared to the full IFRS which greatly facilitated its application. This implementation was characterized by the possibility for each jurisdiction to incorporate the standard dedicated to SMEs without having to apply full IFRS in their sets.

Actually, 62 jurisdictions require or permit the IFRS for SMEs[2]:

- "Eight jurisdictions require the IFRS for SMEs for all SMEs that are not required to use full IFRS;
- Thirty-seven jurisdictions give an SME a choice to use full IFRS instead of the IFRS for SMEs
- Sixteen jurisdictions give an SME a choice to use either full IFRS or local GAAP instead of the IFRS for SMEs; and
- One jurisdiction requires an SME to use local GAAP if it does not choose the IFRS for SMEs".

Although Tunisia has openly announced its option to international standards as well as several other countries that are paving the way to modernization, application of IFRS for SMEs remains a challenge to address. The objective of this paper is to analyze the possible adoption of this international standard in Tunisia.

2 Accounting Standardization Strategy in Tunisia

The history of accounting standardization in Tunisia has gone through several stages that we will outline in this section.

Damak-Ayadi (2009) presented different standardization strategies based on two criteria; the state and professional bodies' intervention in the production of standards in any country and the use of full IFRS. Based on the role played by the IASB, this typology allows observing the position of different countries to the process of harmonization. We distinguished 4 strategies; delegation of standardization to the IASB, convergence to full IFRS, delegation of standardization to other international bodies and self-normalizing strategy.

[2] List from www.iasplus.com: Anguilla, Antigua and Barbuda, Argentina, Azerbaijan, Bahamas, Bahrain, Bangladesh, Barbados, Bhutan, Bosnia and Herzegovina, Botswana, Brazil, Cambodia, Chile, Colombia, Costa Rica, Dominica, Dominican Republic, Ecuador, El Salvador, Fiji, Georgia, Ghana, Grenada, Guatemala, Honduras, Hong Kong, Iraq, Ireland, Israel, Jamaica, Jordan, Kenya, Lesotho, Macedonia, Maldives, Mauritius, Montserrat, Myanmar, Nicaragua, Panama, Nigeria, Rwanda, Saint Lucia, Saudi Arabia, Sierra Leone, Singapore, South Africa, Sri Lanka, St Kitts and Nevis, St Vincent and the Grenadines, Swaziland, Switzerland, Tanzania, Trinidad and Tobago, Turkey, Uganda, United Arab Emirates, United Kingdom, Venezuela, Zambia, and Zimbabwe.

Based on this typology, we tried to study the different strategies which are adopted in Tunisia.

Tunisian accounting framework and the standards applied since 1997 are highly inspired by the international standards.

However, 15 years later, the SCT was not reinforced by constant updates to reflect changes in international practice that is the foundation of this regulation. The inadequacy of this Tunisian accounting system to the specific needs of SMEs has resulted in the inability of Tunisian accounting regulations to set up a financial information quality.

Delegation Strategy

Accounting rules were first introduced in the Commercial Code enacted in 1850 which draw the French Commercial Code. In May 1881, the French protectorate was decreed which resulted in the application of the French legislation. The first was established by the decree of 22 February 1942. Subsequently, the PCG was approved by the Ministerial Decree of 18 September 1947. The latter plan was revised in 1957.

Since its independence in 1956, Tunisia has initiated studies and researches in order to replace its accounting system thus reinforcing its sovereignty and breaking the ties with the former French colonialism. Most importantly the Tunisian state had to deal with the inability of the financial statements in order to play its economic role given the shortcomings that it had regarding to the adaptation of national accounting needed by enterprises.

Convergence Strategy to the French Standards

Since 1963, the need for a number of fundamental changes to the accounting system was made more apparent. The changes were designed to overcome the shortcomings in the application of the accounting plan 1947 (revised in 1957), on the one hand and adjust business accounting needs of national accounts on the other hand. Considered as a symbol of sovereignty of the Tunisian government in an independent country, the PCG 1968 was promulgated.

The main innovation of this plan lays in determining the outcome through successive and significant steps, using the language of national accounting. Thus, these results are divided into four different accounts that correspond precisely to those of the national accounting. The PCG 1968 was among the first to introduce the concept of intermediate balances and especially the concept of added value. Moreover, the reform commission has developed a special plan with a simplified accounting scheme to make it easier for small and medium enterprises that cannot provide adequate human resources for the implementation of the PCG 1968. Finally, the reform commission has also developed an accounting system adapted to the specificities of cooperative enterprises.

In 1982, The Institute of Chartered Accountants of Tunisia (Ordre des Experts Comptables Tunisien OECT) was created as a professional organization with legal personality grouping professionals authorized to practice as an accountant. It was placed under the Ministry of Finance. The OECT is responsible for ensuring the normal functioning of the accounting profession, for ensuring that members respect all relevant rules and obligations and for defending the honor and independence of the profession.

The OECT has decided since its creation the establishment of an internal organ of the normalization "Accounting Standards Committee" whose contribution was crucial in the early years. But their recommendations did not have the force of law for companies. This committee has substantially reduced its field of intervention for development of the National Council of accounting (Conseil National de Comptabilité CNC) since 1995.

We would notice that the directions of both the PCG 1947 and the PCG 1968 were characterized by the dominance of the State as the main user information from the financial statements. Indeed, the Tunisian State, through its policies, has always sought to essentially adapt its accounting system from its national strategic needs by neglecting the usefulness of accounting information for the other economic actors.

In 1990, The Tunisian State turned to a policy of market economy, with the globalization of international markets and the massive influx of foreign investors.

Convergence Strategy to the International Standards

The French accounting model, in force since 1968, did not facilitate the projection of an accurate picture of economic entities. The accounting model of Anglo-Saxon inspiration is considered as more suitable for the managerial, economic and financial decision-making. It permits to produce understandable accounting and financial information, legible and credible for the users both at the national and international levels.

Thus, Act 96-112 has promulgated in 1996, the SCT including the aims which were oriented towards upgrading financial information. The latter has to be equipped with certain qualitative characteristics so that it can meet the needs of the various operators, the staffing of the entities to support accountability for improved transparency and to upgrade accountant Tunisian language compared to international practices.

Although recent changes in the Tunisian accounting standards have contributed to enhancing transparency, some weaknesses still hamper the reliability and comparability of financial information.

The stakes are, in Tunisia, financial reporting standards as a major concern of the accounting profession and the authorities concerned seeking to find the adequate framework to the recognition of full IFRS as an accounting reference language and the implementation of a convergence of the accounting system business program.

The OECT saw it necessary to focus reflection on the appropriateness of applying IFRS for SMEs taking into account the qualitative requirements of the financial information.

Tunisia has contributed to the strengthening of transparency of financial information through the promulgation of a law on the SCT which came into force in January 1997, but this does not prevent that weaknesses still hamper the reliability and comparability of information.

Indeed the principles of accounting, evaluation and presentation provided by Tunisian standards are largely inspired by the earlier version of the full IFRS.

However, in some cases, these standards provide more simplified methods and require less publication requirements than the full IFRS, these simplifications are generally adequate to meet the identified needs of users of the financial statements of SMEs.

Tunisia consists of 95 % of SMEs, thus requiring a program of monitoring of remediation to prepare them for the new global context and to advance the new standard IFRS for SMEs.

3 Literature Review

The definition of SMEs according to the European Commission recommendation is based on the number of employees which is as follows (OECD 2004: 11): Micro enterprises/entities (less than ten employees); Small enterprises (less than 50 employees); and Medium enterprises (less than 250 employees).

There is no universally accepted definition of SMEs in Africa (Beyene 2002). According to the Financial Market Council in Tunisia, "are considered as SMEs, the companies that the fixed assets don't exceed four million dinars and that the number of employees don't exceed 300" (CMF 2006). Thus, 95 % of Tunisian companies can be regarded as SMEs.

According to IASB, "SMEs are entities that publish general purpose financial statements for external users and do not have public accountability. An entity has public accountability under the IASB's definition if it files, or is in the process of filing, its financial statements with a securities commission or other regulatory organization for the purpose of issuing any class of instruments in a public market; or it holds assets in a fiduciary capacity for a broad group of outsiders. Examples of entities that hold assets in a fiduciary capacity include banks, insurance companies, brokers and dealers in securities, pension funds and mutual funds. It is not the IASB's intention to exclude entities that hold assets in a fiduciary capacity for reasons incidental to their primary business (for example, travel agents, schools and utilities) from utilizing IFRS for SMEs".

IFRS for SMEs is viewed as an accounting framework for entities that are not of the size nor have the resources to use full IFRS.

In previous literature, we defined many factors which affected the adoption of full IFRS by countries.

First, we will consider the economic development. It has been demonstrated by several studies to play a very important role in the evolution of accounting systems (Stulz and Williamson 2003; Beck and Levine 2004; Zeghal and Mhedhbi 2006) using different economic ratios.

The relationship between financial markets and accounting practices has been established by various studies. A large financial market with various shareholder groups seeking better production of information can be influenced by total market capitalization and the requirements of the stock exchange. Many previous studies have recognized the role of financial markets in determining the elements of accounting systems and their developments (Meek and Gray 1989; Salter and Niswander 1995; Lau and Ma 1997; Archambault and Archambault 2003; Hassabelnaby et al. 2003; Barbu 2005; Zeghal and Mhedhbi 2006).

Second, the accounting profession is at the heart of the accounting environment and with it the accounting systems are in constant development. The accounting profession is a vector of development of any accounting system in the world. Previous researches have studied the development of the accounting profession and its impact on accounting and in particular the choice of international standards and have established the existence of some influence (Salter and Niswander 1995; Chamisa 2000; Hassabelnaby et al. 2003; Ashraf and Ghani 2005; Lopes and Rodrigues 2007). The audit plays a key role in the development of accounting. Some authors have measured the development of accounting systems through the number of audit firms in a country (Hassabelnaby et al. 2003). In other studies of companies, some authors have considered that if a company is audited by a Big 4 so it provides a high quality of financial statements (Archambault and Archambault 2003; Lopes and Rodrigues 2007). Joshi and Ramadhan (2002) found that the influences of external auditors were one of the reasons that pushed small businesses in Bahrain to voluntarily adopt the international standards.

Third, some researchers have concluded that culture influences accounting systems adopted in countries.

The language has been used as a cultural factor by some authors (Nair and Frank 1980; Stulz and Williamson 2003; Nabar and Boonlert-U-Thai 2007). For Nobes (1998), similarities of language can contribute to the strength of the dominant culture and language differences can slow the transfer of accounting technology. It is therefore essential in the business world since it allows to trade between countries and implicitly determines the level of relations between them. Some languages have emerged in some countries through many factors, including colonization, and conquests. The English has been considered by most studies as a major factor pushing countries to adopt or converge with international standards (Lau and Ma 1997; Walton and Haller 2003; Zeghal and Mhedhbi 2006) which are established in English.

Colonization factor has been studied by some researchers (Briston 1978; Hove 1986; Parker 1989; Baydoun and Wilett 1995; Lau and Ma 1997; Nobes 1998; Chamisa 2000; Ashraf and Ghani 2005). It was accepted that it is an important factor in determining the choice of the accounting systems. Some countries have been affected by large external cultural influences.

External variables are factors that push the accounting regulators in a country to neglect internal factors, such as colonial ties which may explain certain transplantation of accounting systems. Indeed, the great colonial powers export several characteristics of their administrative, legal, economic and educational systems of their colonies. Consequently, after independence, former colonies have inherited some of their characteristics on which they based their political, economic, legal, and educational systems. Briston (1978) noted that the colonial inheritance is probably the major factor behind the general system of financial reporting in several countries outside of Europe. Thus, it was observed that in a number of countries, the British influence was very strong and in almost all colonial territories in which industrial development has taken place under British rule. Parker (1989) found that succession was extended to colonial legal systems and other contextual and cultural factors.

Baydoun and Wilett (1995) emphasized that the accounting systems in Arab countries are influenced by accounting practices across Western colonialism past. Chamisa (2000) argued that during the many decades of colonial domination, the imperial countries imposed their economic systems, political systems, educational systems, legal systems, accounting systems, professional associations, language, religion, customs cultures in their respective colonies.

Walton and Haller (2003) also argued that the colonies of Western countries have seen no virtue in trying to reinvent accounts but they were able to use IAS as an alternative to continue to follow their direct historical links. In studies that have linked to colonization using international standards, the Anglo-Saxon settlement has been considered as a determining factor in choosing these standards (Taplin et al. 2002; Walton and Haller 2003; Zeghal and Mhedhbi 2006). Thus, it was assumed that if a country was colonized by the Anglo-Saxon, it would tend to apply international standards.

According to Nobes (1998), religion and culture can be closely linked. Maali et al. (2006) conducted a study of 29 Islamic banks located in 16 countries to compare the level of social disclosure made by these banks operating under Islamic principles. Indeed, for Islamic firms, the primary objective of financial reporting is to demonstrate compliance with Islamic Sharia. The reason is that for pious Muslims Sharia is a priority. In this respect, Baydoun and Wilett (1995) noted that "accounting is an opportunity to demonstrate compliance with religious requirements."

According to Archambault and Archambault (2003), religious beliefs have great influence on the cultural tissue of a country. These authors, by selecting the religion to measure culture of 33 countries, found that religion has a significant impact on disclosure.

For Askary et al. (2008), religion may be a cultural factor affecting the accounting system in the world. Unfortunately, religion has not been empirically treated in an abundant manner as other factors, yet some studies do acknowledge the existence of a relationship between this factor and accounting (Lau and Ma 1997; Nobes 1998; Haniffa and Cooke 2002; Maali et al. 2006; Askary et al. 2008), particularly regarding financial disclosure (Archambault and Archambault 2003) and investor protection (Nabar and Boonlert-U-Thai 2007).

In Bahrain, Joshi and Ramadhan (2002) argued that among the reasons which have led small businesses and low-share companies to voluntarily adopt IAS rather than U.S. or British standards, the existence of an accountant staff with the ability to implement IAS and to observe the international standardization process without any problems.

Previous literature related to the IFRS for SMEs is less abundant. It have studied financial reporting needs of SMEs (Paoloni and Demartini 1997), costs and benefits of financial reporting for SMEs (Carsberg et al. 1985; Collis and Jarvis 2000; Collis et al. 2001) and the usefulness of the IFRS for these companies (Mandler 2003).

Our study can be classified as the third category of studies. In the German context, Mandler (2003) surveyed SMEs in order to assess the usefulness of the IFRS-System for these companies. He concluded that among the larger SMEs 14 % has already made use of the IFRS. The main reason for this was a better comparison with other companies at an international level. However, the study also revealed that high implementation costs were perceived to be the most severe disadvantage of the IFRS for SMEs. According to Schutte and Buys (2011), research revealed that inconsistent accounting practices were often attributable to environmental factors of which cultural differences appear to be the most significant. Prior research considered cultural dimensions in classifying and evaluating cultural differences, which have also been extended into accounting values. Their study tried to identify the relevant accounting values when a global set of accounting standards is implemented by the SME sector. Based on a sample consisting of final-year accounting students from two different universities one in South Africa and the other in the UK, our results suggest that contrasting accounting values are considered necessary when adopting a global set of accounting standards by the SME sector.

In this paper, we report on an exploratory study of Tunisian's CPA perceptions about important issues relevant to developing and implementing the IFRS for SMEs.

4 Methodology

In Tunisia, all companies must apply the SCT since 1997. Following the publication of IFRS for SMEs in 2009 and its application in many emerging countries, we have conducted a study about the possibility of adopting IFRS for SMEs in Tunisia. We tried to reach our goal by analyzing the answers of our questionnaire conducted in 2014. As most of the cited literature on SME financial reporting is based on surveys this method was considered to be appropriate for the present analysis too.

This survey attempts to identify the perception of Tunisian certified public accountants on the possibility of applying the IFRS to SMEs in Tunisia.

We selected six questions which are defined in the following table. They are related to the opinion of the accountants about the adoption of the IFRS for SMEs in Tunisia and the main advantages and disadvantages of its application by Tunisian firms.

Questionnaire
Question 1-Could you describe the SCT1997 compared to the full IFRS?

- The SCT 1997 is completely different from the full IFRS
- There are few differences between the SCT1997 and the full IFRS
- The SCT1997 is consistent with the full IFRS

Question 2-Are the full IFRS intended to be applied to companies regardless of industry and of their size?

- Yes
- No

Question 3-Do you think that it's better to have a specific accounting standard for SMEs?

- Yes
- No

Question 4-Do you think that it is appropriate to apply the IFRS to SMEs in Tunisia?

- Yes
- No

Question 5-What is the main advantage of the IFRS for SMEs?

- Better quality information
- Greater transparency
- Other

Question 6-What is the main disadvantage of the IFRS for SMEs?

- The complexity (fair value ...)
- The cost
- Other

Sample Selection
Our questionnaire is sent to a sample of Tunisian Certified Public Accountants (CPA). We used the mailing list published in the web site of "Ordre des Experts Comptables de Tunisie" (OECT).

The total number of CPA enrolled in the OECT is 888.

In our sample, we have eliminated all cases described as follow:

- CPA who are not practicing (deceased, suspended, strike off the OECT)
- CPA whose emails are not available on the site
- CPA whose emails are not active
- CPA whose answers are not complete

Two months after the mailing of the questionnaire, we have collected 87 usable responses.

In our research, we have considered CPA who may influence accounting practice and regulations in Tunisia. The aim of our study is to demonstrate that in their views on IFRS for SMEs, these professionals are influenced by the accounting culture in which they operate. Thus, it is essential to mention advantages and disadvantages of the IFRS for SMEs, because we believe that at least for companies which want to be listed, this accounting standard will present further interest.

The following section outlines our results.

5 Results Presentation

Our results are summarized in the table (Table 1).

SCT and Full IFRS
100% of respondents agree that SCT is not completely different from international standards.

However, the majority of CPA consider that the harmonization degree between the two systems is high.

In fact, 78 % of CPA find that they are in harmony except lack of update and 22 % think that there are quite significant differences between the SCT and the international standards.

The Need for a Specific Standard for SMSs in Tunisia: IFRS for SMSs
80 % of respondents believe that the accounting standards should not be applied without taking into account the company specificities such as its size and industry. So, a specific standard for SMEs is appreciated. Only 20 % think that it's not necessary.

For the Tunisian context, 61 % of CPA think that it's appropriate to apply the IFRS for SMEs for Tunisian companies. The rest have an opposing position.

Main Advantages of IFRS for SMEs Adoption
The majority (52 %) of CPA consulted believe that the major advantage of the IFRS for SMEs is that it provides better information, 26 % think it brings a greater transparency and 22 % choose other benefits.

In fact, international standards provide comparability with international markets. It let managers locate the level of performance of Tunisian SMEs compared to other SMSs in other countries. So, it could minimize the cost of capital for Tunisian SMEs to raise funds on the international market.

Some CPA advanced that international standards make assistance to the development of SMEs through better visibility to foreign investors. These still looking for better level of profitability and performance may using the tools of reporting having visibility clear and structured development of Tunisian SMEs capacities. A high financial information quality may lead to the development of the financial

Table 1 Results of the survey

Question 1	Completely different	Few differences	Consistent	Total
Could you describe the SCT1997 compared to the full IFRS?	0 %	22 %	78 %	100 %
Question 2	**Yes**	**No**		
Are the full IFRS intended to be applied to companies regardless of industry and especially their size?	25 %	75 %		100 %
Question 3	**Yes**	**No**		
Do you think that it's better to have a specific accounting standard for SMEs?	80 %	20 %		100 %
Question 4	**Yes**	**No**		
Do you think that it is appropriate to apply the IFRS for SMEs in Tunisia?	61 %	39 %		100 %
Question 5	**Better quality information**	**Greater transparency**	**Other**	
What is the main advantage of the IFRS for SMEs?	26 %	52 %	22 %	100 %
Question 6	**The complexity**	**The cost**	**Other**	
What is the main disadvantage of the IFRS for SMEs?	17 %	72 %	11 %	100 %

markets by ensuring quality having been adopted after a process information high-performance.

Main Disadvantages of IFRS for SMEs Adoption

72 % of CPA believe that the major disadvantage of IFRS for SMEs is the high costs of implementation. 17 % find that they are too complex to be applied in Tunisia.

The other participants suggested that Tunisian accounting organism for the standardization would lose its authority and its decision-making power on standardization, at least to a large extent. More responsibility for the maintenance of the standards should be for the IASB. In fact, The Tunisian participation would be limited to review and comment on the proposed amendments as appropriate.

Besides, the IASB preconises the modification of the provisions of the standard IFRS for SMEs at three-year intervals unless changes deemed important by the IAS/IFRS standards require the shortening of deadlines. The frequency of these changes and the deadlines for their translations (original document in English) and their adoptions could be harmful for the SMEs since they will have to readapt compared these changes with all the accounting, organizational and fiscal consequences that this entails.

We noted that the IFRS for SMEs was not necessarily adapted to the Tunisian context in certain cases.

There are, in some cases, differences between legal provisions and national regulatory and international standard. Strict adherence to standard IFRS for SMEs would pose legal issues and may break Tunisian taxation-accounting connectivity and the obligations of SMEs increased sentencing of tax payable.

Due to the use of measurement methods, IFRS for SMEs could increase in the volatility of results of the Tunisian SMEs. This standard requires to recourse to the principle of fair value (financial instruments, agriculture, advantage to the staff. . .), even though she has tempered the use of this principle to the full IFRS. This remedy would risk certainly increase the volatility of results of these entities especially where markets would be unstable and not efficient.

Many Tunisian SMEs should likely modernize or barely improve their information systems to comply with the IFRS for SMEs. More training costs of staff necessitated by this passage would be very important especially if we consider that Tunisian SMEs do not generally have adequate skills and material and financial resources necessary to support such a change.

6 Conclusion

A large number of the CPA, participating in our survey, was aware of the differences between the SCT and IFRS standards. They think that it is a good opportunity for companies to opt for the international standard that takes into consideration the size of the company while providing better information and greater transparency.

The costs of implementation and the necessary adaptations are the main obstacles for such process for companies with limited financial and human resources.

References

Archambault JJ, Archambault ME (2003) A multinational test of determinations of corporate disclosure. Int J Account 38:173–194

Ashraf J, Ghani WI (2005) Accounting development in Pakistan. Int J Account 40:175–201

Askary S, Yazdifar H, Askarany D (2008) Culture and accounting practices in Turkey. Int J Account Audit Perform Eval 5(1):66–88

Barbu E (2005) Une meilleure connaissance de l'environnement comptable : condition sine qua non d'une meilleure compréhension de l'harmonisation comptable internationale. Association francophone de la comptabilité. Comptabilité et connaissance, Lille

Baydoun N, Wilett R (1995) Cultural relevance of Western accounting systems to developing countries. Abacus 31(1):71–90

Beck T, Levine R (2004) Stock markets, banks, and growth: panel evidence. J Bank Finance 28(3): 423–42

Beyene A (2002) Enhancing the competitiveness and productivity of small and medium scale enterprises (SMEs) in Africa: an analysis of differential roles of national governments through improved support services. Council Develop Social Sci Res Afr 27:130–156

Briston R (1978) The evolution of accounting in developing countries. Int J Account Educ Res 16: 12–26
Carsberg BV et al (1985) Small company financial reporting. Prentice Hall, Englewood Cliffs
Chamisa E (2000) The relevance and observance of the IASC standards in developing countries and the particular case of Zimbabwe. Int J Account 35(2):267–286
CMF (2006) Financial Market Council in Tunisia, Bulletin du CMF 2588 du Mercredi 03 Mai 2006
Collis J, Jarvis R (2000) How owner-managers use accounts, research monograph. ICAEW, London
Collis J, Dugdale D, Jarvis R (2001) Deregulation of small company financial reporting. In: McLeay S, Riccaboni A (eds) Contemporary issues in accounting regulation. Kluwer Academic Publishers, Boston, pp 167–185
Damak-Ayadi S (2009) De l'efficacité des mesures de convergence pour préparer le passage aux IAS/IFRS en France. La Revue des Sciences de Gestion 236:73–84
Haniffa RM, Cooke TE (2002) Culture, corporate governance and disclosure in Malaysian corporations. Abacus 38(3):317–349
HassabElnaby HR, Epps RW, Said AA (2003) The impact of environmental factors on accounting development: an Egyptian longitudinal study. Crit Perspect Account 14:273–292
Hove M (1986) The Anglo-American influence on international accounting standards: The case of the disclosure standards of the international accounting standards committee. In: Wallace RSO, Samuels JM, Briston RJ (eds) Research in third world accounting, vol 1. JAI Press, London, pp 55–66
Joshi PL, Ramadhan S (2002) The adoption of international accounting standards by small and closely held companies: evidence from Bahrain. Int J Account 37:429–440
Lau A, Ma R (1997) A broad perspective on Financial Reporting in the Pacific Asia. In: Ma R (ed) Financial reporting in the Pacific Asia region world scientific: accounting and business in Asia. World Scientific Publishing, Singapore, pp 55–92
Lopes PT, Rodrigues LL (2007) Accounting for financial instruments: an analysis of the determinants of disclosure in the Portuguese stock exchange. Int J Account 42:25–56
Maali B, Casson P, Napier C (2006) Social reporting by Islamic Banks. Abacus 42(2):266–289
Mandler U (2003) IAS/IFRS für mittelständische Unternehmen: Ergebnisse einer Unternehmensbefragung. Kap Rechn 3:143–149
Meek GK, Gray SJ (1989) Globalization of stock markets and foreign listing requirements: voluntary disclosure by continental European companies listed on the London Stock exchange. J Int Bus Stud 20:315–336
Nabar S, Boonlert-U-Thai KK (2007) Earnings management, investor protection and national culture. J Int Account Res 6(2):35–54
Nair RD, Frank WG (1980) The impact of disclosure and measurement practices in international accounting classifications. Account Rev 3:426–450
Nobes C (1998) Towards a general model of the reasons for international differences in financial reporting. Abacus 34(2):162–185
OECD (2004) 2nd Conference of ministers responsible for small and medium-sized enterprises (SMEs), Promoting entrepreneurship and innovative SMEs in a global economy: towards a more responsible and inclusive globalisation, Istanbul, Turkey, 2004
Paoloni M, Demartini P (1997) Small company financial reporting: users and information needs. Paper presented at the annual congress of the EAA, Graz
Parker RH (1989) Importing and exporting accounting: the British experience. In: Hopwood AG (ed) International pressures for accounting change. Prentice Hall, Hemel Hempstead
Salter SB, Niswander F (1995) Cultural influence on the development of accounting systems internationally: a test of Gray's (1988) theory. J Int Bus Stud 26:379–397
Schutte D, Buys P (2011) Cultural considerations and the implementation of IFRS: a focus on small and medium entities. J Soc Sci 26(1):19–27
Stulz RM, Williamson R (2003) Culture, openness, and finance. J Financ Econ 70(3):313–349

Taplin R, Tower G, Hancock P, Street S (2002) Disclosure (Discernibility) and compliance of accounting policies: Asia-Pacific evidence. Account Forum 26:172–190

Walton P, Haller A (2003) Country differences and harmonization. In: Walton P, Haller A, Rafournier B (eds) International accounting, 2nd edn. Thomson Business Press, London

Zeghal D, Mhedhbi M (2006) An analysis of the factors affecting the adoption of international accounting standards by developing countries. Int J Account 41:373–386

Vietnam. Institutional Theory and Accounting Change: An Analyze of Accounting Regulations in Vietnam

Nguyen Cong Phuong

Abstract This paper's aim is to explore how institutional pressure exerted on regulators influenced the their decision to adapting a capitalist accounting system in the national accounting during Vietnam's reforms and integration process into the global economy. Based on the institutional theory, the paper shows that in the first phase Vietnam adapted the former socialist accounting system, moving towards a private capitalist accounting model but preserving many fundamental peculiarities of the accounting system under a centrally planned economy. In the second phase, facing situations where there are uncertainties about the proper approach to set accounting standards, regulators have sought standards of the IASB that are viewed as being more legitimate and "mimic", regardless of their actual usefulness in Vietnam's context. As a result, besides potential benefits, the Vietnamese accounting standards are less efficient for the domestic enterprises. Instead of applying the accounting standards, the domestic enterprises prefer to continue to use the Uniform Accounting System to prepare the financial statements. Those problems suggest that accounting regulators in transitional and developing countries may face issues similar to those in Vietnam.

1 Introduction

Much of the existing research treating the financial accounting regulations argues that the evolution of accounting regulations in a particular country results from changes in the economic and political environment (e.g. Gilling 1976; Hopwood 1983; Mueller 1967; Nobes 1998; Richard 1977, 1980a). Thus, interpreting the accounting regulations requires an exploration of the complexity of the social, political and economic context wherein these regulations merge and change (Hopwood 1987; Laughlin 1987).

The aim of this research is to explore the accounting regulations during Vietnam's reforms and integration process into the global economy in the light of

N.C. Phuong (✉)
College of Economics, University of Danang, Danang, Vietnam
e-mail: Phuong.nc@due.edu.vn

D. Bensadon, N. Praquin (eds.), *IFRS in a Global World*,
DOI 10.1007/978-3-319-28225-1_29

the institutional theory. It draws on the isomorphism processes of the institutional theory in order to explore how institutional pressure exerted on regulators, mainly the Ministry of Finance, influenced the decision of these regulators to incorporate international accounting standards into national accounting in Vietnam. This harmonization process was heavy influenced by the Vietnamese state's desire to integrate its economy into the global economy and attract foreign investments. The analysis also shows that accounting regulations in a harmony with international standards have resulted in potential benefits and some difficulties, especially Vietnamese accounting standards are less efficient because of differences in the economic system and accounting tradition which are previously discussed in the literature. Indeed, international harmonization of the accounting system in Vietnam faced issues due to a "socialist market economy" characterized by a mixed economy with a combination of both private and public ownership of production means, the leading role of state owned enterprises (SOE's) and strong control of the state-party over the socio-economy. Faced with these issues, regulators have been careful in their approach to develop and find ways to combine or adapt when pushing for accounting development which has resulted in the co-existence of Vietnamese accounting standards in a harmony with international accounting standards and a Uniform Accounting System that has preserved the control function of accounting.

This paper try to deeply explore the accounting regulations in Vietnam. Several studies have been devoted to the analysis of Vietnamese accounting under the economic transition (Nguyen and Eddie 1995; Yang and Anh 2003) and in international dimension (Anh Tuan and Guangming 2014; Huong 2013). This paper is placed at a different level of analysis, that of accounting regulations in light of the institutional theory in the spirit of the work of Chu Thanh (2004), Phuong and Richard (2011), Phuong and Nguyen (2012). It also provides insight into problems encountered by regulators who are setting accounting standards in a harmony with international accounting standards. These problems suggest that accounting regulators in transitional and developing countries may face issues similar to those in Vietnam.

2 Institutional Theory

This section aims to discuss a number of key dimensions of the institutional theory to understand Vietnamese accounting regulations in a harmony with international accounting standards. Institutional theory assumes that organizations respond to pressure from their institutional environment through adopting structures and management practices that are socially accepted as being the appropriate organizational choice, even though those practices might be inefficient (DiMaggio and Powell 1983; Meyer and Rowan 1977). The basic premise of institutional theory suggests that an organization's tendency toward conformity with predominant norms, traditions and social influences in their internal and external environment will lead to homogeneity among organizations in their structures and practices.

Thus, the institutional theory is usually regarded as an explanation of convergence (isomorphism).

Two of the most important components of the institutional theory are the institutionalization process and the isomorphism process. Tolbert and Zucker (1983) define "institutionalization" as the process through which components of formal structure become widely accepted, as both appropriate and necessary, and serve to legitimate organizations. They argue that the initial decision to adopt an innovation in a formal structure depends, to a large degree, on how the adoption will improve its internal process. Another key aspect of institutional theory is the argument that organizations are structured by phenomena in their institutional environment and gradually become isomorphic with them (Meyer and Rowan 1977). The institutional theory uses isomorphism processes to explain the processes behind obtaining social legitimacy. Isomorphism processes are drivers that how and why organizations, over time, have a tendency to move from diversity to similarity. The institutional theorists argue that obtaining social legitimacy is an underlying reason behind organizations' conformity with the institutional environment. The institutional isomorphism, a type of isomorphism along with competitive isomorphism, is concerned with social forces that impose certain pressures to develop particular practices that are socially accepted.

Various studies use institutional theory to explore the complexity of the social context in which accounting systems operate while illuminating the role of accounting systems during social transformation (Burchell et al. 1980; Burchell et al. 1985; Hopwood 1987; Richard 1977, 1980b).

3 Institutional Changes and Evolution of Vietnamese Accounting Regulations

The accounting regulation covers the setting, implementation and control of the application of accounting standards. It unfolds in a given geopolitical space, which may be national or international. In this space, the accounting regulation focuses on standards and relies on a device generally including the following elements: a (or more) standards-setting body; an entity federating accounting profession, which has to be implement the standards; and another governing the auditor, who will verify the application of standards.

This section focus on the evolution of Vietnam accounting regulations in response to institutional changes. This evolution is divided into two phases following the progress of institutional changes. The analyse shows in the first phase Vietnam adapted the former socialist accounting system, moving towards a private capitalist accounting model but preserving many fundamental peculiarities of the old system. In the second phase, the development of accounting aims to implement Vietnam's commitments to harmonize its accounting system with the world.

3.1 *Economic Reforms and the Accounting Reform*

3.1.1 Economic Reforms

The Vietnamese economic reform launched in the Sixth Congress of the Communist Party in 1986, resulted in a shift of Vietnamese economy from a central planning economy to a "socialist market economy". Macro-economic stabilization, the restructuring of the economic system and opening of "doors" to the rest of the world, contributed towards remarkable changes in the socio-economic environment (Cuong et al. 1998; Leung and Riedel 2001, p. 3) in which accounting took place. Since 1987, many reforms have been implemented and this process has been accelerated since 1989 (Cuong et al. 1998, p. 37–48; Riedel and Turley 1999; Vu 1998). The changes could be seen via the price liberalization to eliminate the two price system that prevailed under the centrally planned economy; the removal of barriers to internal trade; and steps to create a modern banking system by splitting off the commercial banking functions of the State Bank and facilitating the establishment of new foreign and domestically owned banks. The changes could also be found in the partial liberalization of foreign investment and international trade; efforts to formalize entry into the multilateral and regional trading system and to regularize bilateral trading and investment relations; and the creation of foreign exchange market reforms and shifting to a more market determined exchange rate system.

Like China, Vietnam has adopted a different approach of gradual economic reform while the single party has stayed in power (Guo 2004, p. 393). This progressive approach has been conducive to the continuation of strong governmental control and of a leading role in economic development for SOEs. The policy, so called "*Đổi mới*"[1] that started in 1986 has caused the Vietnamese economy to become a type of mixed economy with a combination of private and public ownership of production means. Vietnam is only partly market driven, retaining non-market capitalist forms of production and ideology. The leading role of SOEs and strong control of the state-party in the socio-economy make the Vietnamese economy different from a traditional mixed economy such as that in France in the 1960s (Nguyen Cong Phuong and Richard 2011, p. 708). The Vietnamese economy is officially a "market-oriented socialist economy under state control" (Communist Party of Vietnam 1991).

3.1.2 A New Accounting System Moving Towards a Private Capitalist Accounting Model

Transitional reforms have been carried out in Vietnam since 1986. The institutional and economic reforms, in particular restructuring and opening the economic

[1] "Renovation" in English.

system, have constituted remarkable changes in the social environment of accounting. These changes relate to social players (such as entrepreneurs, foreign investors and bankers), administrative functions, ownership structure. As a result, the traditional accounting system of Vietnam, based originally on a Soviet-style planned and centralized economy which existed for national economic planning and control rather than for micro-economic decision-making, was no longer suited (Dang Van Thanh 1995, p. 2). Taking into account this new environment, accounting information in Vietnam plays a more and more important role not only for the macroeconomic regulation, but for business management and stakeholders also.

To respond to pressures from the institutional environment, Vietnamese government launched accounting reform in 1991, 5 years after the launching of the policy "*Renovation*". As a result, a new accounting system, called the Uniform Accounting System (henceforth, UAS), was promulgated in 1995 by the Vietnamese Ministry of Finance.[2] The UAS is intended to be used by all enterprises in Viet Nam.[3] But the main reporting focus of UAS is directed at government enterprises and related agencies. The UAS is a system of accounting, not a set of standards, and its main purpose is to outline in detail the following accounting guidelines and functions. It consists of a chart of accounts, uniform book keeping and rigid formats of financial statements. It also explains how accounts are applied to typical economic transactions and how financial statements are prepared rather than set out the accounting principles to organize transactions to preparer financial statements giving a true and fair view.

Under UAS, the main accounting changes concern the modification of accounting objectives to take into account the information needs of new users; the emergence of a new concept of capital and new definitions of assets, revenue and expense, income; the modification of valuation principles; and the reshaping of financial statements. This changes are aligned with capitalist accounting concepts and principles (For more detail, see Nguyen Cong Phuong and Richard 2011, pp. 710–715).

In this phase, Vietnam adapted the former socialist accounting system relatively "quietly", moving towards a private capitalist accounting model but preserving many fundamental peculiarities of the old system which can be explained by the continuity of the political, economic and social environment. Although economy has moved to a "market-oriented economy", the state bureaucracy still play a dominant role in the economy (Riedel and Turley 1999). Accounting regulation, together with other management instruments, plays a central role for the government's macroeconomic regulation. Indeed, the UAS allows the state to continue to meet the requirement of political and macro-economic control. The latter stipulates political and macro-economic control of the accounting system:

---

[2] Decision 1141/TC/QD/CDKT issued by the Ministry of Finance on November 1, 1995 entitled Promulgating the New Vietnamese Accounting System (NVAS) effective January 1, 1996.

[3] The Ministry of Finance promulgated the Circular 60/TC-CDKT, September 1, 1997, providing accounting guidelines for foreign invested companies in Vietnam.

> *Accounting is an important part of the State's economic and financial management instruments. Accounting information must meet the requirements of the State administration so that the state prepares the economic plans and controls the economy* (Ministry of Finance 1995, p. 5; 2006, p. 7).

Mr. Dang Van Thanh, a former director of the Department of the Accounting Policies (within the Ministry of Finance), whose mandate ran from 1994 to 1998, point out that:

> *Since accounting is a crucial factor in the system of governmental administration, its instruments play an important role in the management, direction and control of economic activities.... Accounting should provide useful information to enable users to make economic decisions. Therefore, the role of accounting is important not only for the state, but also for enterprises and others* (Dang Van Thanh 1995, p. 1).

Accounting is seen as "*the State's economic and financial management instruments*". Thus, the state management aspect is always present in the accounting system in that its main financial reporting focus is government and related agencies and its purpose is to set the standard forms and other disclosures for easy compilations and comparatives by the authorities (Yang and Anh 2003, p. 177).

However, the economic transition has led to the emergence of accounting interest groups alongside the state, such as entrepreneurs, foreign investors and bankers. This situation required regulators to change accounting objectives. The accounting information must play a important role not only for the macroeconomic regulation, but for business management and stakeholders also. Thus, the financial statements (including balance sheet, income statement, notes to financial statements and optional cash flows) prepared following the UAS should:

> *Provide useful economic and financial information for evaluation and predicting the financial performance and position of enterprise. Financial information is also useful to owners, managers investors, and creditors in decision-making* (Ministry of Finance 1995, p. 2).

Together with moving towards a capitalist accounting model, the Vietnamese accounting preserves the "philosophy of macro control". Furthermore, the fact that UAS provides detailed guidelines for recognition (list in detail line-by-line accounting entries for typical economic transactions) rather than set out the accounting principles to organize transactions to preparer financial statements giving a true and fair view reflect the "philosophy of micro control". The micro-management tendencies of UAS could be seen in part as an attempt to reduce mistakes that may be made by inexperienced accountants and bookkeepers at the time.

The above analysis shows that the introduction of a new accounting system was a result of remarkable changes in the socio-economic environment. The accounting, as a institutional steering mechanism, was rooted in the system of governmental administration. Although Vietnamese accounting has moved towards a capitalist accounting model, the accounting system is regulative mechanism that directs organizations and accountants in line with changes in institutional environment. The following section analyses the regulative tendency of the accounting during Vietnam's deeper integration into the world economy.

3.2 Deeper Integration into the World Economy and the Accounting Development in Harmony with IAS/IFRS

3.2.1 Deeper Integration into the World Economy

In parallel with domestic reforms, Vietnam has undergone a process of largely integrating its economy into the regional and the global economy. Vietnam has made important commitments to trade liberalization under various bilateral and multilateral agreements. It became a member of ASEAN, and the ASEAN Free Trade Area (AFTA) in 1995, and the Asia-Pacific Economic Cooperation (APEC) in 1998. Vietnam also signed a bilateral trade agreement (BTA) with the United States in 2000, marking a major step toward fully normalizing U.S.-Vietnam commercial relations. Vietnam also became a member of the WTO in late 2006. In line with commitments made under these international agreements, significant progress has been made in liberalizing foreign trade and promoting foreign direct investment (FDI). As a result, the dollar value of exports has increased from nearly US$0.9 billion in 1986 to US$36.5 billion in 2005, marking an annual compound growth rate of 21.6 %. Foreign investors have been attracted in increasing numbers and FDI commitments and disbursements have seen a steep rise.

Aspiring to further integrate into the global economy, Vietnam is confronted with tremendous political, economic and institutional challenges. Issues to be addressed include technical questions such as the gradual giving up of the foreign trade monopoly, tariff reductions, abolishing quota restrictions, and the investment regime.

In January 1998 the revised Commercial Law came into force without substantially reforming licensing procedures. A full decentralization of trading rights was postponed. Under the impression of the Asian Economic Crisis and for the sake of "national interest" Vietnam codified the trade monopoly for a number of "strategic products" (for example, export of crude oil and of rice). In September 1998 relief was given by Decree No. 57/1998/ND-CP which abolished—in principle—the general export licensing requirement. Domestic enterprises, irrespective of ownership structure (state or private), business scope (production or trade) and size of capital (no minimum working capital requirements) were allowed to trade directly and freely with foreign clients.

The new "Law on Export & Import Duties on Commercial Goods" of December 1987 was based on a simple tariff scheme that followed the Brussels Tariff Nomenclature. The legal basis of the tariff regime was modified in 1991, 1993 and 1998. Subordinate regulations, however, made cross-border transactions increasingly complex and time-consuming (Schmidt 2004, p. 65). In order to improve transparency of its trade regime, recently Vietnam has aimed at applying a uniform and consistent import tariff regime. Since 1 January 2000 tariff rates comply with the Harmonized System Convention.

In brief, gradual world market integration and the intensification of international trade relations have become a central pillar of Vietnam's economic policy. The accession to WTO, implementing ASEAN/AFTA as well as US BTA liberalization commitments and the emerging obligations from APEC or ACFTA determined the timing and sequencing of the country's reforms. Vietnam must be prepared to enter into binding commitments beyond obligatory WTO provisions, e.g. about privatizing state-owned enterprises, transparent and non-discriminatory tender procedures for procurement of government entities. Hence economic integration turns out to be a severe test for Vietnam's administrative and governance capacity. The need to bring national legislation into conformity with international rules, negotiating and implementing concessions on market access for trade in goods and in services, notification requirements, emerging new trade issues and the necessity to consult and consider viewpoints of all relevant national stakeholders places heavy burdens on each applicant that not infrequently exceed its institutional capacity for formulating policy options (Schmidt 2004, p. 82).

The following section will discuss Vietnamese accounting regulations in a harmony with the international accounting standards in context of Vietnam's deeper integration into the global economy.

3.2.2 Institutional Isomorphic Pressures for Accounting Regulations in a Harmony with IAS

The effect of becoming membership in various international organizations is the creation of a constant force for continuing harmonization with world business practices. The resultant tendency towards harmonization should also infiltrate accounting practices. As a result of integration in the global economy, the accounting reform in Vietnam entered into a second phase, starting in 1996 with the technical and financial assistance of the Euro-TapViet project,[4] the World Bank and the Asian Development Bank. Having become a member of International Federation of Accountants Committee, Vietnam has committed itself to ensuring that Vietnamese accounting standards are in conformity with IAS. The objective of this phase is to establish *the accounting standards in a harmony with IAS/IFRS and in accordance with market economy under socialist orientation* (Dang Van Thanh 2001; Narayan and Godden 2000). As a result, Vietnam promulgated the first four accounting standards on December 31, 2001. From 2001 to 2006, 26 accounting standards (henceforth, VAS) were promulgated[5] while preserving UAS for retaining governmental control.

---

[4] Euro-TapViet, a Vietnam-EU economic cooperation program, extended effective technical assistance to Vietnam to boost its capacity for supervising insurance market, drafting Insurance Business Law, improving staff capacity, and developing the Vietnamese accounting system towards international standards.

[5] The commitment of the Minister of Finance to complete a full set of accounting standards by 2005 is part of the effort for the targets proposed by World Bank (2002).

Vietnam's concerns about transparent information and international harmonization of accounting for the purposes of further integrating its economy into the global economy and attracting foreign investments lead to the development of accounting systems in harmony with the IAS/IFRS. Vietnam aims to implement its commitment to harmonize its accounting system with the world, as stated by Mr Bui Van Mai, director of the Accounting Department, Ministry of Finance at that time, "*Vietnamese accounting should be harmonized 90% with IAS/IFRS*".[6]

Several studies examining the harmony of VAS with IAS/IFRS shows that overall, the VAS are aligned almost entirely with the 2005 version of standards of the IASB (Adams and Linh 2003; Anh Tuan and Guangming 2014; Nguyen Anh Tuan and Gong 2012; Pham Hoai Huong 2013). For example, Pham Hoai Huong's study (2013) shows that the percentage of overall *de-jure* convergence between VAS and the 2005 version of IAS/IFRS for key standards is 84 %. This is broken down into its two components: the measurement of *de-jure* convergence is 88 %, whereas the disclosure of *de-jure* convergence is 81 %. However, instead of embracing the independent accounting philosophy inherent within IAS, the restrictive accounting philosophy has been preserved so that the accounting system allows little scope for judgments. There is also limited disclosure, resulting in limited value to users.

This convergence of VAS with IAS/IFRS may be explained by the external pressures from Vietnam's integration into the world economy. The basic premise of institutional theory suggests that an organization's tendency toward conformity with predominant norms, traditions and social influences in their internal and external environment will lead to homogeneity among organizations in their structures and practices. The Vietnamese government, which is partly self-motivated (its commitment to harmonize its accounting system with the world) and partly under external pressure (Vietnamese accounting development initiated by the World Bank, IMF and ADB), has been promoting accounting standards in a harmony with IAS/IFRS. In addition, it was impossible for Vietnam to refuse this alignment due to the heavy pressure exerted by its main commercial partners for the country to be accepted as a member of the WTO. On the other hand, one of the reasons why the U.S. and Europe imposed dumping duty sanctions on Vietnamese enterprises is that their accounting system does not conform to international standards (Vo Thanh Thu 2009). The appearance of foreign investors also has posed an urgent question about building an accounting system to meet demands of international investors and achieve harmony with international practices. Many foreign investors complained that the uniform accounting system did not meet their needs. For example, Richard Martin, Chairman of the ANZ Bank branch in Hanoi said, "We hope to better understand local creditworthiness. Right now, local accounting and audit practices do not give us the level of comfort we need. But it's clear they'll change soon" (Murphy 1993, p. 30).[7] A report by the World Bank concludes that the UAS is not

[6] An interview by VnExpress was released on March 27, 2003.

[7] Cited by Nguyen and Eddie (1995).

yet fully consistent with international standards (World Bank 2001, p. 21). Thus, Vietnamese government responds to these pressures from their external environment through adopting accounting standards that are globally accepted as being the appropriate choice, even though those standards are less efficient for domestic enterprises (see below).

Besides, according to the mimetic isomorphism mechanism of the institutional theory, when Vietnam has faced situations where there are uncertainties about the proper approach to set accounting standards, it has sought standards of IABS that are viewed as being more legitimate and "mimic", regardless of these norms' actual efficiency in Vietnam. In fact, it is difficult to develop accounting standards in Vietnam because the accounting profession is powerless, and the regulators have little experience in setting accounting standards. They did not thoroughly comprehend international standards (Chu Thanh 2004, p. 297, 302). Thus, the regulators, mainly the Ministry of Finance, have preferred the adoption of international accounting practices instead of developing domestic accounting regulations. Vietnam must inherit its standards largely from international accounting standards which are suitable in developed capitalist economies, but might be less consistent with the needs and economic structure of developing countries, especially the "socialist market economy" in Vietnam (Phuong and Nguyen 2012, p. 443). The regulators cannot resolve issues due to adapting the contents of international accounting standards to Vietnamese accounting mechanism so that they are congruent with the Vietnamese environment, especially with government regulations and level of expertise and knowledge of Vietnamese accountants. However, Vietnamese government's mimetic behaviour has considerable economic benefit because it reduces the cost of finding a viable solution when Vietnam has faced process of moving toward the the regional and global economy.

3.2.3 Potential Benefits and Issues of the Regulations Aligned with IAS/IFRS

As stressed above, faced with uncertain situations about the approach to set accounting standards, Vietnamese government has been careful in its approach to set accounting standards through adopting accounting standards of the IASB regardless of these standards' actual efficiency in Vietnam. These Vietnamese accounting standards (VAS), aligned almost entirely with the international accounting standards, when used in a mixed economy known as "a market economy under socialist orientation" can result in some consequences.

The potential benefits of the regulations aligned with IAS/IFRS are the ones stressed in the literature. Firstly, as a result, the harmonization process has reflected Vietnamese government's voluntary/mandatory convergence into the international accounting community with the aim at creating a transparent business environment for foreign investors (Phuong and Nguyen 2012, p. 435). The capital flows moving from developed countries to Vietnam are increasing. Vietnam has attracted more foreign investments. The existence of multinational enterprises, joint-ventures and associates is a "product" in the process of integration into the global economy including the convergence of accounting system with IAS/IFRS. Secondly, the national accounting regulations in a harmony with IAS/IFRS reduce the gaps between Vietnamese accounting and international standards. In regards to multinational enterprises operating in Vietnam, the greatest benefit from harmonization is the comparability of international financial information. According to Nguyen Cong Phuonng and Renault (2006) and Nguyen Cong Phuong (2012), the adoption of IAS/IFRS has improved the quality of financial information, especially with regard to clarity of content and comparability. Such comparability eliminates current misgivings about the reliability of financial reporting and removes one of the most important impediments to the flow of international investment. Concerning domestic enterprises, harmonization provides evidence of fair presentation as domestic firms have globally engaged in business transactions, avoiding such disputes as price dumping. Thus, some domestic firms have indirectly benefited from the process of harmonization.

However, the VAS aligned with IAS/IFRS is not efficiently applied in Vietnam's socio-economic context where the objectives of Vietnamese accounting are characterized by the requirements of political and macro-economic control (see Ministry of Finance 1995, p. 5; 2006, p. 7). In other words, IASs are in conflict with Vietnamese socio-economic reality. Indeed, IAS/IFRS focuses on the needs of investors in equity while Vietnamese government emphasizes the macroeconomic accounting information (Nguyen Cong Phuong and Richard 2011). Harmonization with IAS/IFRS means that the needs of the state and enterprises play a role subordinate to the needs of the investors in equity. The VAS is not perceived to be more successful for most domestic enterprises since Vietnam lacks competent personnel and strong professional accountancy bodies to implement the accounting standards. As the VAS contain concepts and principles in line with IASB standards which do not reflect the socio-economic reality of Vietnam, enterprises often use the Uniform Accounting System to record, recognize and measure transactions and to prepare financial statements. In fact, the VAS contain concepts and principles to guide the professional application of accounting methods based on conventions raised in the context of capitalist and developed countries, whereas the UAS, consisting of a chart of accounts and rigid formats of financial statements, is an explanation of how accounts are applied to typical economic transactions and how financial statements are prepared. The UAS focuses on recording, recognition and measurement of transactions whereas the VAS focuses on recognition, measurement and disclosure. The implementation of VAS arguably requires a high degree of professional judgment, but the scope of professional judgment is restricted. According to Dang Van Thanh,[8] this is what macro management and accounting practice have been accustomed to doing for a long time in order to comply with

[8] Interview of *Stocks Investment*, 12 April 2009. Mr. Dang Van Thanh was former director of the Department of Accounting Policies, Ministry of Finance and is president of Vietnam Association of Accountants and Auditors.

accounting rules, which explains how the accounts are applied to typical economic transactions and how the financial statements are prepared. Furthermore, according to Bui Van Mai,[9] while accounting standards are concepts and principles designed to guide the professional application of accounting methods, Vietnamese accountants have long been accustomed to the rigid rules and the majority of them do not have the competence and experience in making professional judgments concerning choices of accounting policies. According to these arguments, Nguyen Cong Phuong's study (2012) showed that 6 % of 191 respondents have applied the accounting standards to prepare the financial statements. Those respondents said that accounting standards are less used due to: i) too abstract (26 %), ii) No explanations of how accounts are applied to typical economic transactions and how financial statements are prepared (27 %); iii) accountants' lack of the competence and experience in making professional judgments concerning choices of accounting policies (41 %). This testifies the obstacles in the accounting harmonization process evidenced in the literature.

4 Conclusion

The Vietnamese government's decision to develop a accounting system in a harmony with the IAS/IFRS is being viewed as the appropriate choice. However, international harmonization which preserves national particularities of an accounting system is a not easy task. It will take time, but progressively. Vietnamese accounting regulators gain this experience and learn how to solve problems. Vietnamese government, which is partly self-motivated and partly under external pressure, has developed domestic accounting standards similar to IAS/IFRS which are suitable in developed capitalist economies, but are less consistent with the needs and economic structure of the country. Faced with those issues, regulators have been careful in their approach to develop accounting: they continue to preserve the UAS alongside the appearance of VAS. However, the problems related to international harmonisation could become major ones if the VASs were to be aligned further with the standards of the IASB, especially the principle of fair value,[10] and accounting professionals will become highly qualified. The adoption of this principle would result in major consequences for management goals because potential profits will be recognized and the accounting value of firm will be brought near to the market value.

[9] Interview of *Stocks Investment*, dated 10 August 2008. Mr. Bui Van Mai was former director of the Department of Accounting Policies and is vice-president of Association of Accountants and Auditors.

[10] The Vietnamese Ministry of Finance published a draft of eight existent standards and calls for a review of those standards on October 10, 2013. Among important changes, the revaluation of PP&E at fair value will be allowed and goodwill will no longer be amortized, but kept unchanged on balance sheet unless cataclysm. In addition, IAS 39 is allowed to apply in Vietnam since 2012.

References

Adams HA, Linh TD (2003) Vietnamese accounting standards: intent and purpose contrasted to international accounting standards. ACW, Hanoi, Vietnam

Anh Tuan N, Guangming G (2014) Measurement of formal convergence of Vietnamese accounting standards with IFRS. Aust Account Rev 24(2):16

Burchell S, Clubb C, Hopwood A, Hughes J, Nahapiet J (1980) The roles of accounting in organizations and society. Account Organ Soc 5(1):5–27

Burchell S, Clubb C, Hopwood AG (1985) Accounting in its social context: towards a history of value added in the United Kingdom. Account Organ Soc 10(4):381–413

Communist Party of Vietnam (1991) Seventh Congress of the Communist Party of Vietnam. Hanoi

Cuong LV, Hac TH, Dao TTA (eds) (1998) L'économie vietnamienne de 1976 à 1994. L'Harmattan

DiMaggio PJ, Powell WW (1983) The iron cage revisisted: institutional isomorphism and collective reationality in organizational field. Am J Sociol 48:14

Gilling DM (1976) Accounting and social change. Int J Account Spring:59–71

Guo S (2004) Economic transition in China and Vietnam: a comparative perspective. Asian Profile 32(5):393–410

Hopwood AG (1983) On trying to study accounting in the contexts in which it operates. Account Organ Soc 8(2–3):287

Hopwood AG (1987) The archeology of accounting systems. Account Organ Soc 12(3):207–234

Huong PH (2013) De jure convergence between Vietnamese and international accounting standards. Working paper. College of Economics, University of Danang, Vietnam

Laughlin RC (1987) Accounting systems in organisational contexts: a case for critical theory. Account Organ Soc 12(5):479–502

Leung S, Riedel J (2001) The role of the state in Vietnam's economic transition. Working paper. Asia Pacific School of Economics and Government, The Australian National University

Meyer J, Rowan B (1977) Institutionalised organizations: formal structure as myth as ceremony. Am J Sociol 83:24

Ministry of Finance (1995) Enterprise accounting system. Ministry of Finance, Hanoi, Vietnam

Ministry of Finance (2006) Enterprise accounting system. Ministry of Finance, Hanoi

Mueller GG (1967) International accounting. Macmillan, New York, NY

Murphy K (1993) ANZ steals a march in bustling Hanoi. Bus Rev Wkly 11(1):30

Narayan FB, Godden T (2000) Financial management and governance issues in Viet Nam. Asian Development Bank, Manila

Nguyen DT, Eddie IA (1995) Reform of the accounting system in Vietnam. Int J Bus Stud 2:1–15

Nobes CW (1998) Towards a general model of the reasons for international differences in financial reporting. Abacus 34(2):162–187

Phuong NC (2012) Global economic Integration and developing Vietnamese accounting from 1995: reality, challenges and prospects. Working paper. College of economics, University of Danang

Phuong NC, Nguyen TDK (2012) International harmonization and national particularities of accounting: recent accounting development in Vietnam. J Account Organ Change 3(8):21

Phuong NC, Richard J (2011) Economic transition and accounting system reform in Vietnam [Working paper]. Eur Account Rev 20(4):693–725

Phuonng NC, Renault M (2006) The new system of business accounting in Vietnam: an empirical assessment. Paper presented at the EAA Annual Congress of the European Accounting Review, Dublin, Ireland

Richard J (1977) Etude comparative des methodes d'analyse de la gestion des entreprises industrielles dans quatre pays appartenant a des systemes economiques et politiques differents: Etats-Unis, France, RDA et URSS. Ph.D. Dissertation, Universite de Paris Sorbonne

Richard J (1980a) Comptabilite et systemes economiques. Ph.D. Dissertation, Universitee de Paris Sorbonne

Richard J (1980b) Comptabilité et systèmes économiques. Thèse d'État, Université de Paris I Panthéon – Sorbonne, Paris
Riedel J, Turley WS (1999) The politics and economics of transition to an open market economy in Vietnam. Working paper. OECD
Schmidt U (2004) Vietnam's integration into the global economy: achievements and challenges. Asia Eur J 2:21
Thanh DV (1995) The initial steps of accounting reform in Vietnam. J Financ 12:1–2 (in Vietnamese)
Thanh C (2004) Accounting changes in a transition economy: the case of Vietnam. University of Wollongong, Wollongong
Thu VT (2009) Vietnamese enterprises meet obstacles as accounting standards disharmonizing with the international accounting standards. Interviewed by Hong Van ngày, Saigon Times, 14 August 2009. Retrieved from http://www.thesaigontimes.vn/Home/kinhdoanh/xuatnhapkhau/22251/
Tolbert PS, Zucker LG (1983) Institutional sources of change in the formal structure of organizations: the diffusion of civil service reform, 1880–1935. Adm Sci Q 28(1):18
Tuan NA, Gong G (2012) Vietnamese accounting reform and international convergence of Vietnamese accounting standards. Int J Bus Manage 7(10):11
Van Thanh D (2001) Accounting Vietnam in the reform process and international integration. Account Rev 28:2 (in Vietnamese)
Vu QV (1998) Le développement de l'économie vietnamienne de 1985 à 1995: une analyse institutionnelle. In: Cuong LV, Mazier J (eds) L'économie vietnamienne en transition: les facteurs de la réussite. Editions L'Harmanttan, Paris, pp 129–157
World Bank (2001) Vietnam: country financial accountability assessment
World Bank (2002) Vietnam: country financial accountability assessment
Yang DC, Anh NT (2003) The enterprise accounting system of Vietnam and United States generally accepted accounting principles: a comparison. Adv Int Account 16:175–204

FSC
www.fsc.org
MIX
Papier | Fördert
gute Waldnutzung
FSC® C083411

Kolibri 360 GmbH
Ferdinand-Jühlke-Straße 7
99095 Erfurt, Deutschland
produktsicherheit@kolibri360.de